Ireland, slavery and the Caribbean

Manchester University Press

STUDIES IN IMPERIALISM

General editors: Andrew S. Thompson and Alan Lester
Founding editor: John M. MacKenzie

When the 'Studies in Imperialism' series was founded by Professor John M. MacKenzie more than thirty years ago, emphasis was laid upon the conviction that 'imperialism as a cultural phenomenon had as significant an effect on the dominant as on the subordinate societies'. With well over a hundred titles now published, this remains the prime concern of the series. Cross-disciplinary work has indeed appeared covering the full spectrum of cultural phenomena, as well as examining aspects of gender and sex, frontiers and law, science and the environment, language and literature, migration and patriotic societies, and much else. Moreover, the series has always wished to present comparative work on European and American imperialism, and particularly welcomes the submission of books in these areas. The fascination with imperialism, in all its aspects, shows no sign of abating, and this series will continue to lead the way in encouraging the widest possible range of studies in the field. 'Studies in Imperialism' is fully organic in its development, always seeking to be at the cutting edge, responding to the latest interests of scholars and the needs of this ever-expanding area of scholarship.

To buy or to find out more about the books currently available in this series, please go to: https://manchesteruniversitypress.co.uk/series/studies-in-imperialism/.

Ireland, slavery and the Caribbean

Interdisciplinary perspectives

Edited by

Finola O'Kane and Ciaran O'Neill

MANCHESTER UNIVERSITY PRESS

Copyright © Manchester University Press 2023

While copyright in the volume as a whole is vested in Manchester University Press, copyright in individual chapters belongs to their respective authors, and no chapter may be reproduced wholly or in part without the express permission in writing of both author and publisher.

Published by Manchester University Press
Oxford Road, Manchester M13 9PL

www.manchesteruniversitypress.co.uk

British Library Cataloguing-in-Publication Data
A catalogue record for this book is available from the British Library

ISBN 978 1 5261 5099 8 hardback
ISBN 978 1 5261 8229 6 paperback

First published 2023

The publisher has no responsibility for the persistence or accuracy of URLs for any external or third-party internet websites referred to in this book, and does not guarantee that any content on such websites is, or will remain, accurate or appropriate.

Typeset by Newgen Publishing UK

To David Dickson, teacher, colleague and friend.

Contents

List of figures	ix
Notes on contributors	xiv
Foreword: Irishness is back – From West Britain to West Indies – Sir Hilary Beckles	xviii
Acknowledgements	xxii
Introduction – Finola O'Kane and Ciaran O'Neill	1

Part I: Setting out the terrain

1 Setting out the terrain: Ireland and the Caribbean in the eighteenth century – David Dickson	21
2 From perfidious papists to prosperous planters: Making Irish elites in the early modern English Caribbean – Jenny Shaw	40
3 Free, and unfree: Ireland and Barbados, 1620–1660 – David Brown	54
4 Trade, plunder and Irishmen in early English Jamaica – Nuala Zahedieh	74
5 Doing business in the wartime Caribbean: John Byrn, Irish merchant of Kingston, Jamaica (September–October 1756) – Thomas M. Truxes	87

Part II: Consolidating territories

6 Ireland and British colonial slave-ownership, 1763–1833 – Nicholas Draper	103
7 Soldiers, settlers, slavers: Irish lives on the Spanish borderlands of North America and the Caribbean in the revolutionary 1790s – José Brownrigg-Gleeson	125
8 Searching for sovereignties: The formation of the penal laws and slave codes in Ireland and the British Caribbean, c. 1680–c. 1720 – Aaron Graham	142

9   Comparing imperial design strategies: The Franco-Irish
    plantations of Saint-Domingue – Finola O'Kane   156
10 Sir Eyre Coote and the governorship of Jamaica, 1805–1808
    – David A. Fleming   179
11 In search of excess: Lambert Blair and his appetites
    – Ciaran O'Neill   193

Part III: Comparative perspectives

12 Two islands, many forts: Ireland and Bermuda in 1624
    – Emily Mann   215
13 Imperial barrack-building in eighteenth-century Ireland
    and Jamaica – Charles Ivar McGrath   240
14 Architectures of empire in Jamaica: The Irish connection
    – Louis P. Nelson   256
15 Designed in parallel or in translation? The linked Jamaican
    and Irish landscapes of the Browne family, marquesses of Sligo
    – Finola O'Kane   282
16 Formations and deformations of empire: Maria Edgeworth
    and the West Indies – Claire Connolly   302
17 How the Irish became black – Natalie A. Zacek   321
18 'Where are you actually from?': Racial issues in the Irish
    context – Sandrine Uwase Ndahiro   337

Index   352

Figures

0.1 Hollar Parsons, map of Inishowen, 1661 (1609 survey), the Long Room, Trinity College Dublin. Courtesy of the Library of Trinity College Dublin.   3

0.2 Honoré Daumier, *Irlande et Jamaïque – Patience! ...*, *Charivari*, 11 April 1866, in Loys Delteil, *Honoré Daumier (IX)*, in *Le peintre graveur illustré*, Vols XX–XXIX (Paris, 1925–30), Vol. XXVIII (1926), no. 3494.   12

5.1 Michael Hay, map of Kingston, 1745, Library of Congress, Geography and Map Division, G4964.K5G46. 1745.H3.   88

7.1 *Dn. Cornelio McCurtin, y marca de su caballo*, 1796. Ministerio de Cultura y Deporte, Archivo General de Indias (Seville), MP-Estampas, 32.   126

7.2 *Carta geográfica de todas las islas Antiles y las costas del continente de la América, desde el río Orinoco, Norte y Oeste, incluyendo el Seno Mexicano, y canal de la Bahama Viejo, el Pasaje de Barlovento, y las sondas, bajos y bancos que en aquellos mares hasta al presente se han encontrado*, ca. 1788. Ministerio de Cultura y Deporte, Archivo Histórico Nacional (Madrid), Estado, MPD. 769.   127

7.3 Richard Bateman Lloyd, *Aruba 1815*, Coleccion Arubiana-Caribiana, Biblioteca Nacional Aruba.   135

9.1 Detail of the Laborde plantation, Haut du Cap, Saint-Domingue, *Plan de différentes possessions à St. Domingue [sur la Rivière du Haut du Cap, près de la ville du Cap-Français], concernant Ferrary, Beaujouan, Sicard, etc.*, 1780, Bibliothèque nationale de France, département Cartes et plans, GD SH 18 PF 152 DIV 3 P 1. Source: gallica.bnf.fr/BNF.   159

9.2 *Plan de la ville du Cap et de ses environs depuis Limonade jusques et compris la baye de l'Acul pour servir à faire voir les ouvrages projetés pour sa déffense/dressé par ordre* de Monsieur de Bellecombe, ... gouverneur général de St. Domingue, 1760, Bibliothèque nationale de France, département Cartes et plans, GE SH 18 PF 149 DIV 1 P 4. Source: gallica.bnf.fr/BNF. 160

9.3 The Franco-Irish plantations discussed in this chapter, marked on Godino de Villaire and Jean-Baptiste Philibert, *Carte indiquant les parties levées de l'Ile de Saint-Domingue et celles qui ne le sont pas, 3 février 1789*, Archives nationales d'outre-mer, France, FR ANOM 15DFC0218A. 161

9.4 *Plan de la plaine de Léogane indiquant la distribution des eaux de la Grande Rivière dans cette plaine. 15 février 1735, Orientation fleurdelysée. Echelle de 1*, Archives nationales d'outre-mer, France, FR ANOM 15DFC0685C. 162

9.5 Location of Walsh, Butler and MacNemara plantations underlined on René Philipeau, *Plan de la plaine du Cap François en l'Isle St. Domingue* (Paris, 1786), Library of Congress, G4944.C3G46 1786.P5. Courtesy of the Library of Congress. 164

9.6 Detail showing the Walsh and Butler plantations on the River Fossé and the Grande Rivière from René Philipeau, *Plan de la plaine du Cap François en l'Isle St. Domingue* (Paris, 1786), Library of Congress, G4944.C3G46 1786.P5. Courtesy of the Library of Congress. 167

9.7 Philippe Becoulet, photograph of an underground water-holding chamber on the Butler Bois de Lance plantation, *c*. 2000. 168

9.8 Philippe Becoulet, photograph of a collapsing brick-and-masonry wall structure on the modern-day course of the River Fossé on the Butler Bois de Lance plantation, *c*. 2000. 168

9.9 Detail showing the Walsh plantation, from *Plan de la ville du Cap et de ses environs depuis Limonade jusques et compris la baye de l'Acul pour servir à faire voir les ouvrages projetés pour sa déffense/dressé par ordre de Monsieur de Bellecombe, ... gouverneur général de St. Domingue*, 1760, Bibliothèque nationale de France, 1760, GE SH 18 PF 149 DIV 1 P 4. Source: gallica.bnf.fr/BNF. 169

9.10 Walsh Sugar mill. Moulut, *Plans et profils d'une redoute construite sur le moulin à sucre de l'habitation Walch à 200 mètres au nord est du redan cotté 8 sur la carte générale des défense du Cap. Echelle de 10 mètres des profils et de 20 mètres pour les plans, 1er pluviose an 11 (1er février 1803)*, Archives d'outre-mer, France, FR ANOM 15DFC0411bisB. 170

9.11	Detail showing the Walsh and O'Rourke plantations, from René Philipeau, *Plan de la plaine du fond de l'Isle de vache de l'Isle St Domingue avec les divers cannaux d'arrosage*, *c.* 1787[?], Bibliotheque nationale de France, département Cartes et plans, GE B-6932 (RES). Source: gallica.bnf.fr/BNF.	171
11.1	James Leakey, *Portrait of Mr James Blair (1789–1841)*. Image Courtesy of Bonhams.	193
11.2	James Leakey (attributed), miniature portrait of Lambert Blair. Courtesy of Bearnes, Hampton & Littlewood.	199
11.3	P. F. Martin, map of St Eustatia, 1781. Image courtesy of Statia Government.	202
11.4	*The Late Auction at St Eustatia* (London: E. Hedges, 11 June 1781). Courtesy of the Library of Congress.	202
12.1	'The River of Waterford', in Nicholas Pynnar, *The State of the Fortes of Ireland as they weare in the yeare 1624*, British Library, Add. MS 24200, fos 2v–3r.	215
12.2	'The forte of Duncannon in ye harbor of Waterford', in Nicholas Pynnar, *The State of the Fortes of Ireland as they weare in the yeare 1624*, British Library, Add. MS 24200, fos 5v–6r.	216
12.3	'The Fort of Castle Parke', in Nicholas Pynnar, *The State of the Fortes of Ireland as they weare in the yeare 1624*, British Library, Add. MS 24200, fos 20v–21r.	216
12.4	Chart by Juan Vespucio, 1520, Seville, Archivo General de Indias, MP-Europa_Africa, 125.	220
12.5	'A Mappe of the Somer Isles and Fortresses', in John Smith, *The Generall Historie of Virginia, New-England, and the Summer Isles* (London, 1624).	226
12.6	'A Mapp of the Sommer Ilands', engraved by Abraham Goos for George Humble, 1626, and published in John Speed, *Prospect of the Most Famous Parts of the World* (London, 1627).	227
12.7	'Mr Griffin', *A True Description of the North Part of Ireland*, *c.* 1601, Trinity College Dublin, MS 1209/14. Reproduced courtesy of Trinity College Dublin.	229
14.1	Colbeck Castle, St Catherine Parish, Jamaica, *c.* 1775, photo by the author.	256
14.2	Lulworth Castle, Dorset, England, *c.* 1607, photo by the author.	257
14.3	Tattershall Castle, Lincolnshire, England, 1434–46, photo by the author.	259

14.4	Hardwick Hall, Derbyshire, England, 1590–7, photo by the author.	260
14.5	John Vanbrugh, Blenheim Palace, Oxfordshire, England, 1705–24, photo by the author.	261
14.6	Map locating tower houses in the British Isles, reproduced from Michael W. Thompson, *Decline of the Castle*, map, p. 22.	262
14.7	Rathfarnham Castle, Dublin, Ireland, *c*. 1585, photo by the author.	263
14.8	Monkstown Castle, Co. Cork, Ireland, *c*. 1636, photo by the author.	264
14.9	Kanturk Castle, Co. Cork, Ireland, *c*. 1609, photo by the author.	265
14.10	Stewart's Castle ruins, Trelawney Parish, Jamaica, begun 1760s, photo by the author.	266
14.11	Plan of Stewart's Castle, drawn by students of Falmouth Field School, University of Virginia, 2008.	267
14.12	Claypotts Castle, near Dundee, Scotland, 1569–88, photo by the author.	269
14.13	Kew Park, Westmoreland Parish, Jamaica, late eighteenth century, photo by the author.	272
14.14	Plan of Edinburgh Castle, St Ann Parish, Jamaica, measured by the author, drawn by Jason Truesdale.	272
14.15	Edinburgh Castle, St Ann Parish, Jamaica, photo by the author.	273
14.16	Monea Castle, Co. Fermanagh, Ireland, *c*. 1616, photo by the author.	274
15.1	James Arthur O'Connor, *View of Westport from the Northeast*, 1818, Victoria and Albert Museum, London. © Victoria and Albert Museum.	283
15.2	Patrick Browne, *A new map of Jamaica; in which the several towns, forts, and settlements, are accurately laid down as well as ye situations & depts. of ye most noted harbours & anchoring places* (London, 1755), Library of Congress. Courtesy of the Library of Congress.	283
15.3	Detail of James Craskell, *Map of Middlesex*, Jamaica, 1756, Library of Congress. Courtesy of the Library of Congress.	285
15.4	Cover of George W. Hildebrand, *Marquess of Sligo*, survey book of Westport, Co. Mayo and Kelly's Pen plantation, Jamaica, 1817, private collection.	288

15.5	George W. Hildebrand, *Marquess of Sligo*, survey book of Westport, Co. Mayo and Kelly's Pen plantation, Jamaica, 1817, p. 3, private collection.	289
15.6	Amalgamated collage by Neil Crimmins of the forty-six Westport, Co. Mayo pages of the complete survey by George W. Hildebrand, *Marquess of Sligo*, survey book of Westport, Co. Mayo, and Kelly's Pen plantation, Jamaica, 1817, pp. 1–46, private collection.	289
15.7	George W. Hildebrand, *Marquess of Sligo*, survey book of Westport, Co. Mayo and Kelly's Pen plantation, Jamaica, 1817, p. 1, private collection.	290
15.8	George W. Hildebrand, *Marquess of Sligo*, survey book of Westport, Co. Mayo and Kelly's Pen plantation, Jamaica, 1817, p. 7, private collection.	291
15.9	Amalgamated collage by Neil Crimmins of the ten Kelly's Pen, Jamaica pages of the complete survey by George W. Hildebrand, *Marquess of Sligo* survey book of Westport, Co. Mayo and Kelly's Pen plantation, Jamaica, 1817, pp. 48–58, private collection.	292
15.10	James Arthur O'Connor, *A View of Fin Lough and Delphi Lodge*, 1819, private collection.	294
15.11	Isaac Mendes Belisario, *Kelly's Walk Plantation, The Great House, Jamaica*, c. 1836–42. Courtesy of the National Gallery of Jamaica.	296
15.12	Isaac Mendes Belisario, *Kelly's Walk Plantation, the Sugar Works*, Jamaica, c. 1840. Courtesy of the National Gallery of Jamaica.	296
15.13	Isaac Mendes Belisario, *View of Cocoa Walk Plantation*, Jamaica, c. 1840. Courtesy of the National Gallery of Jamaica.	297
15.14	Isaac Mendes Belisario, *View of Cocoa Walks District*, Jamaica, c. 1840. Courtesy of the National Gallery of Jamaica.	297
18.1	Presence of black population in Ireland between 2006 and 2016. Source: CSO Statbank Tables E7016, E7057, CO507, CO501 and B1201.	342
18.2	A Twitter handle arguing against the constant need to bring up Irish colonial history. Reproduced with permission.	345

Notes on contributors

Sir Hilary Beckles is the eighth Vice-Chancellor of the University of the West Indies. Under his leadership the institution has spearheaded an aggressive global reputation, building strategy that has resulted in ten global centres in partnership with universities in North America, Latin America, Asia, Africa and Europe. He has lectured extensively in Europe, the Americas, Africa and Asia, and has published over 100 peer-reviewed essays in scholarly journals, and over twenty books on a range of subjects including Atlantic and Caribbean history, gender relations in the Caribbean, sport development and popular culture.

David Brown is Archival Discovery Lead for Beyond 2022: Virtual Record Treasury of Ireland. Prior to this, he has worked on the Irish Research Counci-funded Down Survey of Ireland project and a multivolume critical edition of the Books of Survey and Distribution for the Irish Manuscripts Commission. His monograph *Empire and Enterprise: Money, Power and the Adventurers for Irish Land during the British Civil Wars* was published by Manchester University Press in 2022.

José Brownrigg-Gleeson is a Maria Zambrano research fellow at the Universidad de Salamanca in Spain, where he is a member of the research group GIR-Indusal. Formerly an Irish Research Council postdoctoral fellow at the National University of Ireland, Galway, and a National Endowment for the Humanities fellow at the University of Notre Dame, his research centres on the interactions between Ireland, the Irish diaspora and the Hispanic world during the Age of Revolutions. His most recent article is 'Fighting an empire for the good of the empire? Transnational Ireland and the struggle for independence in Spanish America', *Radical History Review* 143 (May 2022).

Claire Connolly is Professor of Modern English at University College Cork and has published extensively on eighteenth- and nineteenth-century Irish literature. With Marjorie Howes (Boston College), she was General Editor of a new six-volume series, *Irish Literature in Transition, 1700–2015* (2020); and she is also the editor for Volume II of the series, *Irish Literature in Transition, 1780–1830*.

David Dickson is Professor Emeritus of Modern History at Trinity College Dublin. He has had a longstanding interest in Ireland's place in transatlantic empires, a theme explored in his *Old World Colony: Cork and South Munster 1630–1830* (2005), and in *The First Irish Cities: An Eighteenth-Century Transformation* (2021).

Nicholas Draper was the founding director of the Centre for the Study of the Legacies of British Slavery at University College London (UCL) until his retirement in August 2019; co-director of the *Structure and Significance of British Caribbean Slave-Ownership 1763–1833* project at UCL between 2013 and 2015; and a founder member of its precursor, the *Legacies of British Slave-Ownership* project, between 2009 and 2012. His book *Legacies of British Slave-Ownership: Colonial Slavery and the Formation of Victorian Britain* (with C. Hall and others) was published in 2014. His *The Price of Emancipation: Slave-Ownership, Compensation and British Society at the End of Slavery* (2010) was awarded the Royal Historical Society's Whitfield Prize and shortlisted for the Frederick Douglass Prize.

David A. Fleming is a historian of eighteenth-century Ireland. On completing his undergraduate studies at the University of Limerick, he was awarded, in 2006, a D.Phil. from the University of Oxford, where he had been a senior scholar at Hertford College and an Arts and Humanities Research Council postgraduate awardee. His research concentrates on the social and political development of eighteenth-century Ireland, and he has published on topics including provincial politics, poverty, religious conversion, associational behaviour and prostitution. Dr Fleming was commissioned, in 2012, to write the official history of the University of Limerick.

Aaron Graham is a lecturer in early modern British economic history in the Department of History at University College London. He is currently finishing a study of state formation and slavery in Jamaica during the Age of Revolutions, entitled *Tropical Leviathan: Slavery, Society and Security in Jamaica, 1770–1840*.

Emily Mann is Associate Professor of Architectural History, Race and Spatial Justice at the Bartlett School of Architecture, University College London, having previously taught and studied at the Courtauld Institute of Art in London. She is the incoming editor (from 2023) of the journal *Architectural History*.

Charles Ivar McGrath lectures in history at University College Dublin. His publications include *The Making of the Eighteenth-Century Irish Constitution: Government, Parliament and the Revenue, 1692–1714* (2000); *Ireland and Empire, 1692–1770* (2012); and *Lansdowne FC: A History* (2022). He has co-edited three essay collections, published articles in *Irish Historical Studies*, *Parliamentary History*, *Eighteenth-Century Ireland*, *English Historical Review* and *History of European Ideas*, and has provided chapters and entries in a range of edited collections and biographical dictionaries. He is co-principal investigator, with Dr Suzanne Forbes, of the Open University, on a Government of Ireland/HEA Shared Ireland North–South Research Programme project entitled *Our Shared Built Military Heritage: The Online Mapping, Inventorying and Recording of the Army Barracks of Ireland, 1690–1921*.

Sandrine Uwase Ndahiro is a third-year English Ph.D. student at the University of Limerick. Sandrine's research employs theoretical frameworks associated with the field of postcolonial studies to read the environmental crisis unfolding in Africa from an Africanist cultural perspective. She has published various works on race, identity and the Anthropocene.

Louis P. Nelson is Professor of Architectural History and the Vice-Provost for Academic Outreach at the University of Virginia. He is a specialist in the built environments of the early modern Atlantic world, with published work on the American South, the Caribbean, and West Africa, including two book-length monographs, three edited collections of essays and numerous articles. *The Beauty of Holiness: Anglicanism and Architecture in Colonial South Carolina* (2009) was widely celebrated and *Architecture and Empire in Jamaica* (2016) won three major book awards.

Finola O'Kane is a landscape historian, architect and conservation specialist. A professor at the School of Architecture, Planning and Environmental Policy, University College Dublin, she has published widely on eighteenth-century Irish and Caribbean landscapes, and on Irish urban and suburban history. Her books include *Landscape Design in Eighteenth-Century Ireland: Mixing Foreign Trees with the Natives* (2004), *Ireland and the Picturesque: Design, Landscape Painting and Tourism in Ireland 1700–1830* (2013) and the forthcoming *Landscape Design and Revolution in Ireland and the United States, 1688–1815*.

Ciaran O'Neill is Ussher Associate Professor in Nineteenth-Century History at Trinity College Dublin. His books include *Catholics of Consequence: Transnational Education, Social Mobility and the Irish Catholic Elite, 1850–1900* (2014), which was awarded the James S. Donnelly Sr Prize for History and the Social Sciences in 2015. He is co-director of the *Trinity Colonial Legacies* project and is preparing a monograph entitled *Life in a Palliative State: Power and Powerlessness in Union Ireland* (forthcoming in 2023).

Jenny Shaw is Associate Professor of History at the University of Alabama, where she teaches classes on race and slavery in the Atlantic world. Her first book, *Everyday Life in the Early English Caribbean: Irish, Africans, and the Construction of Difference*, was published in 2013. She is currently finishing her second book, provisionally entitled *The Women of Rendezvous: A Transatlantic Story of Family and Slavery*.

Thomas M. Truxes is a Clinical Professor of Irish Studies and History at New York University. He has written extensively on the commercial economy of the early modern Atlantic, particularly Ireland's trade with British America and the transnational Caribbean in the era before the American Revolution. His most recent book, *The Overseas Trade of British America: A Narrative History*, was published in 2021.

Natalie A. Zacek is Senior Lecturer in American Studies at the University of Manchester. Her first book, *Settler Society in the English Leeward Islands, 1670–1776* (2010), won the Royal Historical Society's Gladstone Prize. She is currently completing a book about horse-racing in the nineteenth-century United States, and is beginning a study of the impact of West Indian absentee planters on later Georgian London.

Nuala Zahedieh is a Research Associate at the Centre for History and Economics, University of Cambridge and a Research Fellow at the Wilberforce Institute for Slavery and Emancipation, University of Hull. She is formerly Professor of Economic and Social History at the University of Edinburgh where she taught from 1989–2021. Her research focuses on the British Atlantic economy in the age of slavery and publications include *The Capital and the Colonies: London and the Atlantic Economy, 1660–1700* (2010).

Foreword: Irishness is back – From West Britain to West Indies

Sir Hilary Beckles

Periodically, spots of grey appeared in the constructed 'Black Atlantic' that were as prominent as they were problematic. The oppressed, ganged and enchained labour force that gave rise to England's plantation America was initially brown and white before emerging hegemonically as black.

In the colour coalition the Irish, especially in the West Indies, were considered an intriguing lot. They were located between the pillars of a colour-coded racial paradigm that upheld white supremacy as the superlative. In general, they were considered by their English overlords neither 'slave nor free', neither 'white nor black'. The legacy of this history is felt as ontological fragments of postmodernity creating volatility in the otherwise relatively uniformed cultural identity of the Irish.

In the early twenty-first century, with the Black Lives Matter movement, Irishness is back with a bang. Seeking to define themselves against the background of a brutal British colonialism, and the arrival of large numbers of people of colour in Ireland the island, for the Irish, reflection time is now at a prime. In the West Indies the English derided them as 'Irish blacks'; today, many of them are ideologically bent out of shape in an effort to accept and accommodate within Irish national identity those who defined themselves as 'Black Irish'.

As a student of British imperialism, living in England in the 1970s, I experienced the first shock waves of the explosion in interest in Irish colonial studies. It propelled and defined my academic interest beyond the boundaries of my Black West Indian identity. There was a faint feeling of affinity and sympathy with the Irish within the West Indian community as if, somehow, we were distant cousins and fellow sufferers.

I had no way of knowing if this was a reciprocated sensation, though it was widely believed that our pubs were spared as a signal of an imagined solidarity. At the time it was the most watery way of looking at history and thinking about the politics of identity. It was an easy matter to dismiss such thin thoughts and to get on with the real political business of seeing all white people as racial oppressors. I was as disturbed by this compulsion as

I was by reports of Irish skinheads taunting black teenagers on the streets of Birmingham. The age of the deep intellectual probe was yet to surface. Everyone, it seemed, was keen on keeping the narrative simple.

Within a decade the time had come, and when it did the research productivity was palpable. The brilliant chapters gathered in this collection constitute and delineate the fragments found since then, shards of a broken mirror in which whole images are taking shape in a way unimaginable before. The black 'windrushed' migrants from the West Indies came face to face, once again, this time in Britain, after two centuries, with the Irish poor. This was a historical moment with special sociological and epistemic significance.

As England's first colonials the Irish were an experiment in racial and cultural categorisation. This took place shortly before the notion of white-the-colour became an ethnic descriptor for European. Used initially by the Africans to define the enslaving 'Christians', and subsequently embraced by the English themselves, the Irish were excluded on the basis of their bondage amongst the blacks.

Many of my contemporaries considered it weird when I declared an intention to examine the subject at graduate level. Irish indentured and 'free' workers outnumbered Africans on the first seventeenth-century English sugar plantations in the West Indies. Within the white community it was considered a racially divisive experience to observe them 'slaving' alongside chattelised Africans. It produced a rich literature that gave deep insights into the intersections of race and poverty on the plantations. In this way the Irish poor, Catholic and ethnically conscious, described by the English as a 'riotous and unruly lot', were the subject of the first plantation polemic on being black-poor while white.

In the postcolonial Caribbean there remains a fast dying legacy of the Irish as the 'white niggers' of the English. Rushed to England in the 'Windrush' after the Second World War, it was however of academic concern that the world of the White Irish in the black Caribbean had more or less gone with the wind. The arrival signs in English cities bolted on the doors of craved accommodation – 'no Niggers no Irish' – constituted a fascination for blacks that called them to engage in creative constructions.

The Irish were ravaged and plundered by English conquistadors at home and abroad in the formative stages of the New World colonisation. As a conquered people their labour power was made ruthlessly available in the tens of thousands by Oliver Cromwell, the English Protector, who was prepared to bankroll the emerging sugar baron. In the West Indies, as prisoners of war, defenceless poor, convicts, they served ten-year contracts of indenture. They were shipped out, many in chains, on one-way tickets, and on pain of death if they returned.

Rounded up and deported they constituted the spine of the slavery system the English built on to which the bodies of enchained Africans were bolted for life over a period in excess of 200 years. The initial sugar gangs of Barbados, St Kitts and Jamaica especially were multiracial constructs in which all were branded with the word 'slave', despite laws that attributed that status exclusively to Africans.

Loosely linked as 'white slaves', some conspired to assist the enslaved blacks in their freedom rebellions. The majority however, capitalised on the 'whiteness' principle and sought to carve a colonial life of relative privilege in the slave society, serving as military enforcers and social oppressors of Africans. Socially rejected by the English as culturally and racially inferior, yet sharing the racist attitudes against the Africans, they came to occupy 'Irish Towns' indicative of their segregation.

The rise of the global Black Lives Matter movement finds the Irish poor in occupation of these partitions within race-based paradigms. Vague memories speak of their support for black rebellion. Stronger symbolisms depict their representation in multiple ways of the white-supremacy culture of western colonialism.

Ireland today is a long way from the sugar plantations of the seventeenth-century Caribbean. The 'Irish Town' in the hills of Jamaica is fully occupied by blacks; Montserrat, the island England assigned to Irish Catholics, where they were effectively quarantined during Anglo-French conflicts, is only linguistically associated with their earlier occupancy. In general, they threw in their lot in the colonies with the English, who assigned to them the lowest rank on the whiteness roster.

The chapters of this book deal with contemporary perspectives in Irish studies and social living beyond the moment of English military conquest and colonisation of the island. Time heals and hurts; it conceals and reveals. Ireland is now a prime site for the re-examination of the complexity of racism and the hatred it houses. Many blacks escaped the Irish bombs planted in the English inner cities, and even more who served in the English army in Belfast and beyond cared little about the role of the Irish in facilitating black rebellion against the English in the West Indies. The stories presented here serve to elevate Irish colonial studies and racial politics to the new heartland of the Black Atlantic.

For the experts there are no surprises here – only that it has taken too long to excavate this past and critically examine the present, particularly through the lens and living of Afro-Irish communities, celebrities and the common folk. These everyday people beat the pavement seeking jobs and justice, peace and prosperity, with their complex identities of blackness and whiteness on the island.

Irishness, then, is back on the blackboards. There is no better barometer than this book to measure the parameters of recent research and erupting discourses. From the inner cities of Ireland to colonial outposts, conversations are presented here as academic content inviting critical review. There is uniqueness in the uniformity of the chapters, which traverse interdisciplinarity at its finest. The past and the present collide in narratives of inter- and trans-identity, shaping for the Atlantic the grey space occupied by the Irish. There is much here to digest. Critically, it is a new beginning in blackness studies as well.

Acknowledgements

The authors would like to acknowledge the heroic patience shown by our contributors, whose work was first aired in 2017 and 2018, in two separate conferences held at TCD and at UCD respectively. It has taken a longer period of time than we could ever have envisaged to bring their important work to publication and they have shown extraordinary patience and fortitude along the way.

We would like to acknowledge the help and guidance of several people, but most especially that given to both of us by David Dickson, whose sound advice and kindness have helped us both over recent years. We are indebted to Holly Ritchie, whose work on the first round of edits greatly helped both of us to bring quite a large manuscript into some sort of order. At Manchester we were ably guided through the publication cycle by Emma Brennan, Meredith Carroll, Paul Clarke, Robert Whitlock and Helen Flitton, and we thank Alan Lester for his work in the background as a series editor.

Our colleagues and students at UCD and TCD have supported this project with enthusiasm and no little forbearance. We thank Anne Fuchs at the UCD Humanities Institute and the team at Trinity Long Room Hub for hosting the events that inspired the book. We owe a debt to the wider community of scholars from whose work we have learned so much. Ciaran would like to thank his family, Maija, Orla and Alva. Finola thanks Neil, Aoibh, Ruth, Toby, Ivan and Philip.

Introduction

Finola O'Kane and Ciaran O'Neill

Why compare Ireland and the Caribbean? Ireland is an island after all, not a vast geographical region, only forming part of a much smaller archipelago on the edge of western Europe. In this book we do not explore the relationship of Ireland with the entirety of the Greater Caribbean, though we do include essays that take account of Irish presence in Guyana, Louisiana and Florida. Mostly we are comparing island experiences – because islands have similar infrastructural histories and share some of the same issues relating to trade and communication. We include essays that consider the Irish relationship to Montserrat, Barbados, Trinidad, St Eustatius, Saint Domingue and of course Jamaica: in this period arguably Great Britain's most important island after Ireland. It looms large in this volume, as it has in all previous scholarship linking Ireland with the region. Jamaica and Ireland's spatial comparison is a logical one, as both islands were organised and laid out quickly in the aftermath of Cromwellian upheavals. Ireland, although much closer to the global centres of political power than any Caribbean island, was also profoundly affected by an intervening area of sea. This maritime space acted on trade and communication to produce distinct cultural effects, and the distance and time from London and Paris or Charleston and Boston by sea affected decision-making in Ireland and all the islands of the Caribbean. Dublin, despite its size and significance in the eighteenth century, still had to await the final passing of its parliamentary bills in London, where legislation was eventually passed into law and where the final courts of appeal were also situated. This delaying interval, and the absenteeism that it engendered and encouraged, gave Ireland and the Caribbean a similar governance problem – how to manage countries at a distance by controlling the consequences of this time interval across an interstitial maritime space. Our cover image of Kelly's Pen, St Dorothy's Parish, Jamaica – a painting of *c.* 1840 by Isaac Belisario – captures the collapse of time and space between the islands of Jamaica and Ireland. A calm depiction of an industrious Irish plantation in Jamaica, Belisario's idyllic rendering of a slave plantation owned by a family from the west of Ireland raises questions that the artist may not have himself intended.

The Caribbean was the crucible of Atlantic slavery and the plantation system that sustained it. The impact of Irish people on the evolution of the Caribbean archipelago is not well understood, nor is the reverse impact of the Caribbean on Irish mentalities, networks, towns and landscapes. Researching Ireland's role in slavery's transatlantic web of commerce, improvement and monoculture agriculture is complicated by the overwhelming watershed of the Irish famine of 1845–9,[1] which continues to distort the interpretation of earlier events, and the popular correlation of Cromwellian indentured servitude with inherited matrilineal chattel slavery. Irish identity in the Caribbean ranged from indentured servants to great planters. Irish people could also be subversive players in British imperial contexts. As their Catholic identity was thought to negate any loyalty to Britain, they were employed as key diplomats and colonisers in the French, Spanish and Portuguese empires.[2] In the USA's antebellum period pro-slavery arguments favourably contrasted the material conditions of enslaved people with those of the Irish peasantry. This lends the Irish relationship with the Caribbean a particular complexity, in that the European home ground was often a poorer environment. Both had to contend with plantation and both with the sustained impact of absenteeism. Both also had to contend with the sustained impact of poverty, drawing ever more comparative comment from both the pro and anti-slavery lobbies while the legacy of Ireland's devastating famine in 1845–9 has tended to mask Ireland's own involvement in creating tragic histories in other countries and on other islands.

What Ireland does share with the Caribbean is a history of colonisation. Ireland was England's first island colony, and the plantation(s) of Ireland shared many of the features of parallel and future colonial activity in the Caribbean. Terms such as 'planter' and 'plantation' first appeared in elite circles in the late sixteenth century in relation to Ireland, and were immediately applied elsewhere in the American colonies and the West Indies.[3] Ireland was an 'old world colony', as well as a laboratory for empire, and many of the elite families involved in the exploitation of this first colony applied these lessons elsewhere. Union with Scotland and the religious wars of the seventeenth century saw the English empire evolve into a British empire, resulting in a further diminution of the Catholic Irish as a power at home or abroad and facilitating their refraction across the colonising infrastructures of other European empires. This had many outcomes. A descendant of Rory O'Moore, the Catholic rebel leader of the 1641 rebellion, became the first governor of the Carolinas in 1703, via Barbados.[4] Others of the Catholic 'wild geese' elite families could be found in Nantes and Bordeaux among the planter-merchant elite of the French West Indies in the same period. But their Catholicism did not prevent the Catholic Irish from profiting from the British West Indies, whether directly as planters in the case of many Catholic dynasties in the west of Ireland or as provisioning merchants in the south near the port city of Cork.

The sense of Ireland as an island defined by early modern plantation means that we can draw much deeper parallels on both sides of the Atlantic during the seventeenth century.[5] There are many cases of either literal transportation of plantation technologies, or urban planning – of ideologies, as well as several interesting cases of intellectual projections – all of which show how Ireland was an important node in the neural network of the colonial project. An early example of the former is Sir Arthur Chichester's plantation of Inishowen in 1609, which created an identifiable colonial template of land organisation that can be traced elsewhere in the empire, and one defined by working inland from the seashore (Figure 0.1).[6] At around the same time the connections between the city of Derry/Londonderry (founded 1613) and several colonial cities modelled on it have received some attention, particularly those in Georgia. The figure of Bishop George Berkeley shows how closely connected the real and imagined colonial project could be. Berkeley's transformation from a brilliant early-eighteenth-century metaphysician and critic of Descartes and Locke to an apologist

Figure 0.1 Hollar Parsons, map of Inishowen, 1661 (1609 survey), the Long Room, Trinity College Dublin.

for enslavement in general and a literal enslaver in his own right highlights the trajectory many less prominent Irish people would take in the centuries either side of his own. Berkeley conceived of a utopian colony in Bermuda, and later in Georgia, based partly on his own intellectual project, but also on his practical knowledge of how Derry/Londonderry was planted.[7] He gave sermons that sought to legitimate the idea that enslaved people could be baptised Christian but remain enslaved regardless. Berkeley's utopian visions of a college in Bermuda, staffed by Trinity fellows, may have been colonial fantasies, but they were fantasies forged in Ireland.[8]

Triangulation is a surveying term used to describe 'the tracing and measurement of a series or network of triangles in order to determine the distances and relative positions of points spread over an area, especially by measuring the length of one side of each triangle and deducing its angles and the length of the other two sides by observation from this baseline'.[9] It is very important for ensuring accurate measurements and for providing an overall corrective 'checking' geometry to an entire survey. In psychology it is also used to describe problematic and manipulative triangular relationships that seem useful analogies to the consequences of absenteeism and, at a State level, colonialism.[10] A few of the chapters triangulate between Ireland, Great Britain, and Jamaica, though most chapters compare only two countries and the relationship described becomes arguably less complicated. But mostly it is not. The Caribbean, crucible of modern capitalism, is the transimperial archipelago of the modern world. The complexity of the historical relationships between the Caribbean islands and the European countries that 'owned' them defies any straightforward analysis. Thus we opt not to collapse Irish presence in the region even further by using the terminology of the Green Atlantic, especially as the colour green implies, when applied to the Irish *by* the Irish, a very clear sense of patriotic or nationalist separation from the British. Green is a political colour in Ireland and one that denotes a righteous cause of self-determination, perhaps even de-colonial impulses. The greenness of the Irish is occasionally evident in the Irish in the Greater Caribbean, but is not in any way applicable to a majority of them and seems a deeply anachronistic identity when applied to individuals who acted brutally against those further down the social hierarchy and in their own interest.

Previous attempts to link the Black Atlantic with the so-called Green Atlantic have stressed the similarities between the Irish and Caribbean experience of colonialism, and their shared trajectories in the de-colonial process beginning in the twentieth century. For this reason most of the comparative or interdisciplinary research to date has focused predominantly on modern literature rather than history. Our volume does not attempt to negate or undermine such comparisons, but it certainly does seek to reveal the extent to which the Green Atlantic partook, enthusiastically, in the colonisation of the Black Atlantic, and to show that the role Irish people played in this process is more spatially and politically variegated than the literature at present suggests. One of the key contributions this volume seeks to make is to reveal the extent to which Irish people were present at nearly every level of Caribbean society, from planter and governor down to trader, to small retailer, to indentured labourer. We will also argue that Irish people served many imperial masters and often to their own advantage. Irish enslavers and merchants exploited the Caribbean under the protection of French, British, Danish, Dutch and Spanish regimes. The relative ease with which they did so marks the Irish as outliers in the region, enabled by their apparent disloyalty to their own Government as well as their religious plurality. The Caribbean may have been a place for 'renagadoes of all nations', but few could move between European powers with the relative ease of the Irish.[11] For this reason we argue that the direct comparison of the Black and Green Atlantics is a flawed one and necessarily involves privileging the cultural over the political, itself one of the most common critiques of the conceptual framework in Paul Gilroy's seminal 1993 work *The Black Atlantic*.[12] This is useful to those working in disciplines such as cultural geography and comparative literature, both fields in which the terms have been utilised to good effect.[13] It is less useful, we argue, for historians, and particularly historians interested in Ireland's relationship with empire.

The full spatial impact of slavery is not well researched. Many continue to reduce colonial landscape design to a world of small, simple, walled and productive gardens, for a variety of disciplinary and ideological reasons.[14] The search for 'the dark side of the landscape' began in the interdisciplinary work of John Barrell, Denis Cosgrove, Stephen Daniels, Stephen Copley and Peter Garside,[15] and was then expanded into the field of art history and empire by the research of Malcolm Andrews, Jill Casid, Kay Dian Kriz, John Bonehill, Tim Barringer and Geoff Quilley, among others.[16] Architectural history frequently ignores the wider landscape setting but exceptions to this rule in American architectural history can be found in the work of Dell Upton, John Michael Vlach and Peter Martin.[17] Little attention, in either art- or architectural history, has been devoted to Ireland's role in defining and undermining plantation, with a notable exception in the field of historical geography.[18] Yet American landscape history has frequently identified Ireland as the point of origin for British plantation design.[19] Caribbean geographers have also looked to Ireland for the roots of early plantation geography and structure.[20] Ireland continues to play an important role in the postcolonial space of many disciplines, notably that of literature.[21]

Slavery, and its many impacts, is an expanding study area, but the separate disciplinary advances have not been fully amalgamated. Comparative work in history is inspiring but rarely analyses the physical environment or ways of representing it.[22] Architectural and art historians, although alive to the necessity of examining some written documents, rarely read personal letters closely, where design motive can often be most easily identified and revealed. Specific disciplinary emphases vary from archaeology's focus on the material culture of slavery to the recent comparative transatlantic analysis of British historical geographers.[23] B. W. Higman's groundbreaking work on Jamaica's plantation maps has revealed a fascinating and detailed history of Jamaican plantation design.[24] The weaker position of historical geography in the United States means that 'the study of estate landscapes has been surprisingly uncommon in plantation archaeology in the New World, despite the central importance of agricultural estates and plantation slavery to the 17th-, 18th- and 19th-century histories of the much-excavated regions of the island Caribbean or the Chesapeake'.[25] The more marginalised position of 'Atlantic history' in French historiography means that less work may have been done on French plantations,[26] yet the difficulty probably lies in monolingualism, particularly when researching a region that was profoundly multilingual.[27] Past and recent scholarship has revealed that Irish precedents in designed plantation practice set the course for much of the British empire.[28] Vincent Brown's innovative History Design Studio at Harvard has brought more spatial and visual analysis to history.[29] University College London's (UCL) influential *Legacies of British Slave-Ownership* project has digitised the compensation records, but despite acknowledging that Irish estates 'were part of the numerator and denominator' of the project's calculations and published figures, it avoided any Irish analysis.[30] Nicholas Draper's introduction to the book *Slavery and the English Country House* writes of the project's unfulfilled intention 'to complete its work on the Irish slave owners' while acknowledging that they had to be 'realistic about its ability to trace their impact on the development of modern Ireland in the same way' as 'the formation of modern Britain'.[31] Irish scholars interested in tracing the various Atlantic legacies in Irish landed estates are generally met with significant obstacles. The post-famine Encumbered Estates Act meant that many of the bigger estates were broken up into smaller ones in a subdivision that was accelerated by the various land Acts and commissions operating into the 1920s and 1930s.[32] The abandonment – often enforced by arson – of many historic houses in the same period means that the built environment of Irish estates is equally uneven. Nevertheless we contend that careful attention to the Irish estate and plantation landscape, informed by a transnational, comparative and interdisciplinary approach, can pay dividends. It is clear from the fragments that remain in our archives and in the ruins scattered across the countryside that Irish families were deeply embedded in the exploitation of the Atlantic economy, responsible for the enslavement of vast numbers of African people, and that they benefited directly from doing so.

This book aims to bring together the work of scholars concerned to write a wider interdisciplinary history of Ireland, slavery and the Caribbean drawn from many viewpoints. It is particularly concerned to document Ireland's involvement in slavery and the Caribbean during the long eighteenth century, arguably a period when Ireland itself was not fully amalgamated into Great Britain. This is also the period when Ireland's involvement in the Caribbean may have peaked, leading many of the most successful Irishmen to return to Ireland with their profits, where they were overlaid with other investments or diverted into dowries and other means of inheritance. As the *Legacies of British Slave-Ownership* project has shown, such eighteenth-century income streams have often been lost through their smooth confluence into the general economy, with the helpful connivance of the benefiting families who often took care to diversify their assets as quickly as they could.[33] Ireland's famine-stricken nineteenth-century history should not conceal the extent to which Irish cities and towns saw their villa belts and genteel suburbs improved by such returning wealth. The nineteenth century also brings the British abolition of the slave trade and then slavery, Catholic Emancipation, Jamaican Emancipation, the American Civil War and other complex issues into the frame of reference, and these we have not fully explored. Nor have we made a comparative imperial history that interrogates how the British, French and Spanish empires differed in their approaches to colonial governance, political and military systems, and urban landscape and plantation design. The impact and legacy of the Haitian Revolution and the extraordinary foundation of an independent black republic is not fully understood, and its comparative relevance to Ireland remains untested.[34] Many ideas that were subsequently espoused in the American south were planned and developed in the Caribbean, and the specific trajectories and influences of Irishmen who arrived in the United States via the Caribbean are not explored in detail. This book cannot cover all the relationships that developed among the merchants, planters, clerics, diplomats, enslaved people, soldiers, servants, men, women and children of Ireland and the Caribbean. Nor can it comprehensively frame the larger evolving and historic relationships between Ireland and France, Spain, the United States or the remainder of Great Britain. But it can make a start.

Ireland's role in the transatlantic triangular trade of provisions, enslaved people and sugar has not been broadly researched, the notable exception being Nini Rodgers's 2007 *Ireland, Slavery and Anti-Slavery: 1612–1865*.[35] A heavy historiographical bias towards early modern connections between Britain and Ireland and the Caribbean exists, a trend that became entrenched after the important and groundbreaking doctoral work of Hilary Beckles on white labour in Barbados.[36] Many key articles that touch on the issue of Irish participation in the slave trade are focused on three main islands, and are based firmly in the seventeenth and eighteenth centuries.[37] These three islands are Barbados, Montserrat and Jamaica, all of which dominate our understanding of Irish presence and connection to the region since the foundational work of Aubrey Gwynn on Irish migration to the region, the bulk of which appeared in the late 1920s.[38] Scholarship of the past two decades has remained firmly focused on these islands.[39] This is also true of problematic and popular history titles such as Sean O'Callaghan's *To Hell or Barbados* (2000) or Kate McCafferty's 2002 novel *Testimony of an Irish Slave Girl*. Recent collections on the relationship between Ireland and the Caribbean have invariably focused on twentieth-century comparative literature, with historical links backgrounded in those recent special issues and collected essays that have appeared in the past five years.[40] Monographs and journal articles by Maria McGarrity and others speak to an ongoing interest in comparing the work of writers such as Derek Walcott and Seamus Heaney, and McGarrity in particular has done much to historicise that relationship.[41] Some work has appeared on religious missions to the region, particularly those of the seventeenth century, and with an even more recent emphasis on the presence of Catholics in the region.[42]

It is becoming increasingly necessary, for ethical reasons, to write from a defined and exact position and not to adopt the perspective of distant groups or individuals, with all the difficulties of representation and interpretation that this entails. All the chapters in this volume focus on instances of Irish action and inaction, where an exposition of the Irish protagonist's viewpoint may serve to distinguish and differentiate that viewpoint from that of the enslaved. We have also to reiterate regularly that the bedrock of the Caribbean's extraordinary and rapid development from 1620 to 1830, with all of the intrinsic racial violence; severe inequity; and constant environmental, ecological and human destruction that this entailed, was matrilineal chattel slavery. Nor do we have enough perspectives drawn from the point of view of the enslaved population, a problem for historians of the topic in general. We have tried to be careful with language and not to include unnecessary salacious detail of subjugation and disempowerment, as many authors now argue that such detail demeans the enslaved. We have attempted on occasion to balance the implied power differential of such words as 'slave-owner' and 'slave' but think a rigorously inflexible approach unhelpful for their historical, situational or implied meanings. Nor do we wish to date the book and its language too precisely. Many chapters work closely with documentary sources that have not been substantially mined for such perspectives before, leading hopefully to a more nuanced general history in time. We unfortunately do not have any representative essay from archaeology, where the close study of material culture has often brought the reality of enslavement to life. The volume inserts the legacy of slave-ownership into Irish history – which has blithely considered itself post-colonial rather than colonial for far too long. In documenting the legacy of Irish slave-ownership we also hope to make an unsettling contribution to mainstream histories of Ireland by looking at the translated legacy of Caribbean design back to the 'homeland'.

The study of Ireland's role in the transatlantic slave trade and its connected processes is but a 'nascent study' area. It is therefore difficult to frame this collection thematically, as much of the groundwork has been completed in both the UK and the USA, and not in Ireland. We do not have the secondary source material and detailed case-studies that would make a single unified overarching theme or question possible for this volume. Relatively little has been written on the deep Irish connections to both the francophone Caribbean and the Hispanic Caribbean.[43] Orla Power has conducted systematic work on the Irish in the Danish empire; almost nothing has been done on the Irish in the Dutch empire.[44] Historians such as Silvia Marzagalli warn us in any case to be wary of 'essentialising' any merchant as 'Dutch', 'English' or 'French' when it is so obvious that they 'played with multiple identities and affiliations, depending on the nature of the economic transactions in which they were involved, and on the equally blurred identities of the partners with whom they were dealing'.[45]

The volume is interdisciplinary, and the advances that have been made in one discipline (material culture theory for example) are not yet equally translated into others. The selection of one question or theme may have particular relevance in one discipline but not in another. It may also give preference to a particular geographical or political area over another (racial theory in the USA for example). The volume is also conscious of the pressing question (In what way were the forms of involvement different between the French and British empires?) that all scholars of the long eighteenth century would dearly love to answer, but has not yet been attempted because of its essential difficulty. The ambition of this book is to begin that work of comparative history, which is but rarely attempted and only where detailed case-studies and exceptional sources exist.[46]

So, what are we comparing and why? Ireland is an 'old world colony', where many of the British empire's designs were initially tested and then transported to be replicated elsewhere, particularly those connected to political and military governance and the appropriation and division of land. It is useful for Emily Mann to compare the forts of Africa with those of Ireland and the Caribbean, and for Louis P. Nelson to compare Jamaican houses with those of the north of Ireland and of Scotland, as all essentially stemmed from a similar motive: to occupy and control areas of land and sea efficiently, where little other infrastructure existed. Ivar McGrath and Louis P. Nelson discuss the design descent of those key pieces of imperial infrastructure – the great house and the barracks – while David A. Fleming compares aspects of the evolution of political structures in the two islands of Ireland and Jamaica. Chapters that are particularly concerned with maritime identity and its consequences include those of Tom Truxes, David Dickson and David Brown. The unusual number of Irish-Caribbean Governors and Lord Justices of Jamaica (from Dennis Kelly to Eyre Coote, the Third Marquess of Sligo, Sir George Nugent and the Earl of Belmore) suggests that the Anglo-Irish may have appeared particularly suited for leadership roles in the Caribbean. Ireland's sectarian and revolutionary histories also coloured the behaviour of some Irish people abroad, whether through the easy assimilation of some Irishmen into the ruling structures of Catholic empires, or their calculated manipulation of identity for their own various advantages. Jenny Shaw, Nuala Zahedieh, José Brownrigg-Gleeson and Ciaran O'Neill explore the mutable and fluid identities that Irish people adopted in the Caribbean and why they did so. Irish–Caribbean and Caribbean–Irish translations are arguably more direct and simple than those of more settled landscapes and traditions (for example, the English village common was not translated for many reasons – political, ideological and practical). This character of 'country as test site' also probably made it logical and easier for Caribbean designs to be reciprocally transported into Irish ground, particularly where family ties existed, or where patterns of absenteeism made the imitation of Caribbean patterns less outlandish than in the home counties. Chapters that touch on issues of cultural transfer include those of Finola O'Kane, Claire Connolly and Natalie A. Zacek. Nicholas Draper places Ireland within the framework of UCL's *Legacies of British Slave-Ownership* project and sets a course for further research. The importance of a more nuanced understanding of Ireland's place in the slave economy is underlined in the last contribution by Sandrine Uwase Ndahiro. Writing from the unique perspective afforded to her by her 'liminal' identity as both Rwandan and Irish, her commentary on racial contexts in contemporary Ireland shows that Ireland's own domestic experience of colonialism is sometimes contorted in contemporary debates around race and identity in Ireland. The invocation of shared victimhood in debates around racial discrimination in Ireland can have the effect of minimising or equivocating the negative experiences of people who are both black *and* Irish. Ireland's relatively small resident black population (about 65,000 people) often face a level of discrimination that remains underacknowledged in public discourse and demonstrates a critical gap in the public understanding of Irish connections to, in particular, the Caribbean.[47]

Contributors have been asked to develop, where possible, design comparisons between Ireland and the Caribbean, where a known pattern of transfer has occurred (Irish/Jamaican architecture, Irish/Caribbean barracks, Irish/Jamaican plantation layout and design). Provocative comparison between Ireland and the Caribbean, such as when Irish social problems were compared with the Caribbean, particularly in the period 1620–1860, has also been encouraged. The Irish historiography on slavery is also usefully compared with that of the other countries of the British Isles and America, or with that of other empires. Ideological comparison of the legal definition and construction of power relations and connected governance structures is of general interest, particularly with the revolutionary ideologies of the 1776–98 period. The book is divided into three sections in approximate chronological order, while also roughly corralling connected disciplinary perspectives. The book's first part, 'Setting out the terrain', explores the early formation of the Irish Caribbean's economic, political and trading environment. The book's second part, 'Consolidating territories', examines the second stage of colonisation, when infrastructures together with their accompanying political and legal systems took shape. The third part, 'Comparative perspectives', places scholarship on the Irish Caribbean within broader analytical frameworks. It assesses the complex spatial and artistic legacy of Caribbean plantation while also suggesting some comparative interdisciplinary nuances.

Visual images often have a pronounced ability both to condense and to complicate an argument. In 1866 the French satiric artist Honoré Daumier represented the Anglo-Irish–Jamaican relationship in a satirical print. His caricatures of the Anglo-Irish relationship touched principally on Ireland's poverty and its legal system, already familiar subjects in his caricatures of French society.[48] In the 1866 lithograph *Irlande et Jamaique – Patience!*, Daumier crossed the Atlantic to bring Britain's Caribbean colony of Jamaica into the frame. In the lithograph, a fat and sturdy John Bull, brandishing a long stick, glares at an enslaved Jamaican whispering into an Irish peasant's ear (Figure 0.2). Both of the tall, thin men are miserably attired in ragged and ill-fitting clothes, while the Jamaican's stripy culottes and the Irishman's clenched fists suggest the hatching of a potentially violent plot. Depicting the pair standing barefoot together, the pen-and-wash drawing employs shadow very effectively by managing to blur any easy visual distinction between white and black skin. The Irish peasant's trousers could be black, his face a mixture of the two, and the Jamaican torso could be shadowed to match the Irishman's hands. Yet the drawing is sufficiently detailed to cast one figure as Jamaican and the other Irish, particularly for those familiar with Daumier's subversive pages in *Actualités*. Spatially, the three men mark out a triangle with their feet: one where Ireland has crossed the Atlantic to stand furiously with Jamaica, while John Bull remains at the far shore of the horizon line. The triangle that their feet describe is clearly not an equilateral one – Jamaica and Ireland are positioned together, and separated from John Bull by obtuse and acute angles. Ireland, as this lithograph implies, was in

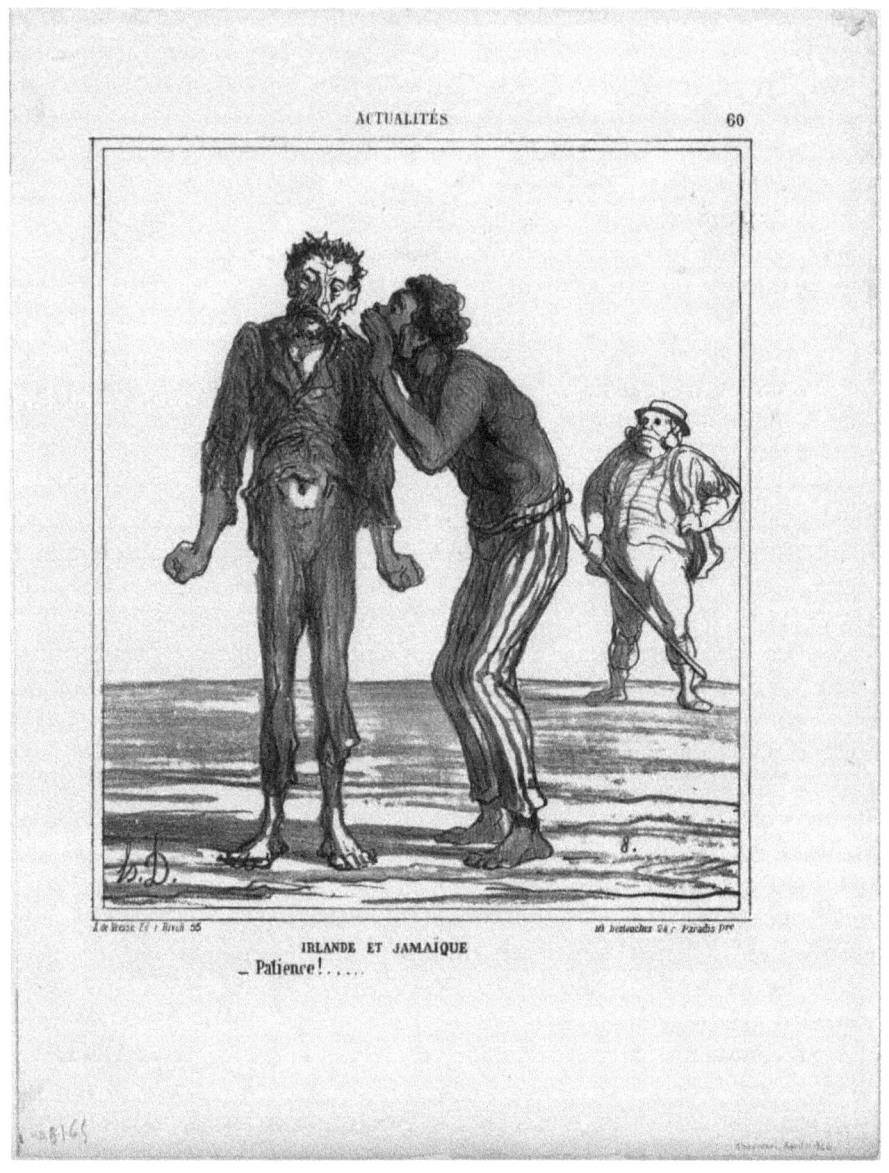

Figure 0.2 Honoré Daumier, *Irlande et Jamaïque – Patience! ...*, *Charivari*, 11 April 1866, in Loys Delteil, *Honoré Daumier (IX)*, in *Le peintre graveur illustré*, Vols XX–XXIX (Paris, 1925–30), Vol. XXVIII (1926), no. 3494.

a strangely mutable and movable position for a western European nation by 1866. The country could be cast as colonial or imperial, rich or poor, slavery-ridden or famine-ridden. While Daumier, as a Frenchman, aligns Ireland with the enslaved peoples' cause, he also erroneously simplifies it – many Irishmen took the part of John Bull once outside Ireland and benefited greatly from the empire's expansion. But it is clear from his drawing that a Frenchman of the 1860s found comparing Ireland and Jamaica usefully provocative. Although this probably reveals more about the Franco-English relationship in 1866 than any transatlantic triangle, Daumier's caricature nevertheless exposes some essential similarity between the two island outposts of Great Britain by strongly implying that the poor and barefoot of both contexts bore the brunt of colonial exploitation; that the experience of being empoverished and underfoot was similar in both places (in the aftermath of the emancipation of enslaved Jamaicans in 1834); and that the power of John Bull was very much greater, and more dangerously infuriating, than any difference that might exist between them. Daumier, as a Frenchman, seems to suggest that the ideals of liberty and equality would logically see Irishmen look to the Caribbean for fraternity, and that such an alliance would lead to something interesting. This is what we, with our contributors, but without the necessity for secrecy, and as a collegial, transatlantic community, have tried to do in this book.

Notes

1 See David Dickson, *Old World Colony: Cork and South Munster, 1630–1830* (Cork: Cork University Press, 2005); and Kristen Block and Jenny Shaw, 'Subjects without an empire: The Irish in the early modern Caribbean', *Past and Present* 210:1 (February 2011), 33–60.
2 For example see Igor Pérez Tostado, *Irish Influence in the Court of Spain in the Seventeenth Century* (Dublin: Four Courts Press, 2008); and Block and Shaw, 'Subjects without an empire'.
3 For an early usage see Thomas Blennerhasset, *A Direction for the Plantation in Ulster* (London, 1610). Linde Lunney, 'Blenerhasset (Hasset, Blennerhassett), Thomas', *Dictionary of Irish Biography* (2009), www.dib.ie/biography/blenerhasset-hasset-blennerhassett-thomas-a0738 (accessed 8 August 2022).
4 Kinloch Bull, 'Barbadian settlers in early Carolina: Historiographical notes', *South Carolina Historical Magazine* 96:4 (1995), 329–39; Mabel L. Webber, 'The first Governor Moore and his children', *South Carolina Historical and Genealogical Magazine* 37:1 (1936), 1–23.
5 Philip D. Curtin, *The Rise and Fall of the Plantation Complex* (Cambridge: Cambridge University Press, 1998), p. 77; and Audrey Horning, *Ireland in the Virginian Sea: Colonialism in the British Atlantic* (Chapel Hill: University of North Carolina Press, 2013), pp. 19, 181.
6 P. Roebuck, 'The making of an Ulster great estate: The Chichesters, barons of Belfast and viscounts of Carrickfergus, 1599–1648', *Proceedings of the Royal Irish Academy* 79C (1979), 11–12.
7 This episode is covered in depth by Tom Jones, *George Berkeley: A Philosophical Life* (Princeton: Princeton University Press, 2021), pp. 347–8; and in Deirdre Ní Chuanacháin, *Utopianism in Eighteenth Century Ireland* (Cork: Cork University Press, 2016), Chapter 4.

8 A. A. Luce, 'More unpublished Berkeley Letters and New Berkeleiana—including the petition of George Berkeley and others for the founding of St. Paul's College, in Bermuda, with the report of the Attorney and Solicitor General thereupon', *Hermathena* 23:48 (1933), 25–53.
9 www.lexico.com/en/definition/triangulation (accessed 22 August 2019).
10 It is also used in politics: 'The action or process of positioning oneself politically between traditional left-wing and right-wing standpoints'; *Oxford English Dictionary*, s.v. *triangulation* (n.), www-oed-com.ucd.idm.oclc.org/view/Entry/205691 (accessed 22 August 2019).
11 The phrase belongs to James Marriott; Sir James Marriott and Sir George Hay, eds, *Decisions in the High Court of Admiralty: During the Time of Sir George Hay, and of Sir James Marriott, Late Judges of That Court* (London: R. Bickerstaff, 1801), p. 261.
12 Paul Gilroy, *The Black Atlantic: Modernity and Double Consciousness* (London: Verso, 1993). For an excellent overview of this wider debate see Lucy Evans, 'The Black Atlantic: Exploring Gilroy's legacy', *Atlantic Studies* 6:2 (2009), 255–68; Laura Chrisman, *Postcolonial Contraventions: Cultural Readings of Race, Imperialism and Transnationalism* (Manchester: Manchester University Press, 2003), pp. 73–88.
13 The term was popularised by Kevin Whelan, 'The Green Atlantic: Radical reciprocities between Ireland and America in the long eighteenth century', in Kathleen Wilson, ed., *A New Imperial History: Culture, Identity, and Modernity in Britain and the Empire, 1660–1840* (Cambridge: Cambridge University Press, 2004), pp. 216–38.
14 This argument is perhaps most forcibly made in Barbara Wells Sarudy, *Gardens and Gardening in the Chesapeake 1700–1805* (Baltimore: Johns Hopkins University Press, 1998), preface. See also Therese O'Malley, 'Landscape gardening in the early national period', in Edward J. Nygren, ed., *View and Visions: American Landscape before 1830* (Washington, DC: Corcoran Gallery of Art, 1986), pp. 133–59.
15 John Barrell, *The Dark Side of the Landscape: The Rural Poor in English Painting, 1730–1840* (Cambridge: Cambridge University Press, 1980); Denis Cosgrove and Stephen Daniels, eds, *The Iconography of the Landscape* (Cambridge: Cambridge University Press, 1995); Stephen Copley and Peter Garside, eds, *The Politics of the Picturesque: Literature, Landscape and Aesthetics since 1770* (Cambridge: Cambridge University Press, 1994).
16 Malcolm Andrews, *The Search for the Picturesque: Landscape Aesthetics and Tourism in Britain, 1760–1800* (Aldershot: Scolar Press, 1989); Jill H. Casid, *Sowing Empire: Landscape and Colonization* (Minneapolis: University of Minnesota Press, 2005); Kay Dian Kriz, *Slavery, Sugar and the Culture of Refinement* (New Haven: Yale University Press, 2008); Geoff Quilley and Kay Dian Kriz, eds, *An Economy of Colour: Visual Culture and the North Atlantic World, 1660–1830* (Manchester: Manchester University Press, 2003); John Bonehill and Geoff Quilley, *Conflicting Visions: War and Visual Culture in Britain and France c. 1700–1830* (London: Routledge, 2005); Tim Barringer, Gillian Forrester and Barbaro Martinez-Ruiz, eds, *Art and Emancipation in*

Jamaica: Isaac Mendes Belisario and His Worlds (New Haven: Yale University Press), 2007.
17 Dell Upton, 'Landscape history or architectural history?', *Journal of Architectural Education* 44:4 (1991), 195–9; Peter Martin, *The Pleasure Gardens of Virginia: From Jamestown to Jefferson* (Princeton: Princeton University Press, 1991); John Michael Vlach, *Back of the Big House: The Architecture of Plantation Slavery* (Chapel Hill: University of North Carolina Press, 1993); John Michael Vlach, *The Planter's Prospect: Privilege and Slavery in Plantation Art* (Chapel Hill: University of North Carolina Press, 2002).
18 See William Smyth, 'A global context. Ireland and America: England's first frontiers', in *Map-Making, Landscapes and Memory: A Geography of Colonial and Early Modern Ireland, c. 1530–1750* (Cork: Cork University Press, 2006), Chapter 12.
19 See Vlach, *Back of the Big House*, p. 2; and Louis P. Nelson, *Architecture and Empire in Jamaica* (New Haven: Yale University Press, 2016), pp. 54–64.
20 B. W. Higman, *Jamaica Surveyed: Plantation Maps and Plans of the Eighteenth and Nineteenth Centuries* (Kingston: University of the West Indies Press, 2001), p. 56. See also J. H. Andrews, *Plantation Acres: An Historical Study of the Irish Land Surveyor* (Omagh: Ulster Historical Foundation, 1985); and J. H. Andrews, *A Paper Landscape: The Ordnance Survey in Nineteenth-Century Ireland* (Dublin: Four Courts Press, 2002), pp. 9–10.
21 Edward Said, *Culture and Imperialism* (New York: Vintage, 1994); and Declan Kiberd, 'Introduction', in James Joyce, *Ulysses* (Harmondsworth: Penguin, 2000).
22 Peter Kolchin, *Unfree Labor: American Slavery and Russian Serfdom* (Cambridge, MA: Belknap Press, 1987); Richard S. Dunn, *A Tale of Two Plantations: Slave Life and Labor in Jamaica and Virginia* (Cambridge, MA: Harvard University Press, 2014).
23 For an archaeological approach see Paul A. Shackel and Barbara Little, eds, *Historical Archaeology of the Chesapeake* (Washington, DC: Smithsonian Institution Press, 1994). For a comparative historical geography approach see Susanne Seymour, Stephen Daniels and Charles Watkins, 'Estate and empire: Sir George Cornwall's management of Moccas, Herefordshire and La Taste, Grenada, 1771–1819', *Journal of Historical Geography* 24:3 (1998), 313–51.
24 Higman, *Jamaica Surveyed*; and B. W. Higman, *Plantation Jamaica, 1750–1850: Capital and Control in a Colonial Economy* (Kingston: University of the West Indies Press, 2008).
25 Dan Hicks, ' "Material improvements": The archaeology of estate landscapes in the British Leeward Islands, 1713–1838', in K. Giles and J. Finch, eds, *Estate Landscapes: Design, Improvement and Power in the Post-Medieval Landscape* (Woodbridge: Boydell and Brewer, 2007), pp. 205–27.
26 Cécile Vidal, 'The reluctance of French historians to address Atlantic history', *Southern Quarterly* 43 (2006), 153–89; but for a case-study of a great French planter in Saint-Domingue see François d'Ormesson and Jean-Pierre

Thomas, *Jean-Joseph de Laborde: Banquier de Louis XV, mécène des lumières* (Paris: Perrin, 2002).
27 See in particular Gabriel Debien, *Les esclaves aux Antilles Françaises (XVIIe–XVIIIe siècles)* (Fort-de-France: Société d'Histoire de la Martinique, 1974); Jacques de Cauna and Cécile Révauger, *La Société des plantations esclavagistes: Caribes francophone, anglophone, hispanophone; regards croisés* (Paris: Indes Savantes, 2013); Jean-Louis Donnadieu, *Un grand seigneur et ses esclaves: Le comte de Noé entre Antilles et Gascogne, 1728–1816* (Toulouse: Presse Universitaires du Mirail, 2009).
28 Louis P. Nelson, *Architecture and Empire in Jamaica* (New Haven: Yale University Press, 2016), pp. 54–64; Higman, *Jamaica Surveyed*, 56.
29 https://historydesignstudio.com (accessed 30 August 2022).
30 Centre for the Study of the Legacies of British Slavery, www.ucl.ac.uk/lbs/ (accessed 8 August 2022). See also Nicholas Draper, ' "Dependent on precarious subsistences": Ireland's slave-owners at the time of Emancipation', *Britain and the World* 6:2 (2013), 220–42.
31 Nicholas Draper, 'Slave ownership and the British country house: The records of the slave compensation committee as evidence', in Madge Dresser and Andrew Hann, eds, *Slavery and the British Country House* (Swindon: English Heritage, 2013), pp. 17–28.
32 Terence Dooley, *The Land for the People: The Land Question in Independent Ireland* (Dublin: University College Dublin Press, 2004), remains the best account of this.
33 For an example of the Irish La Touche family's abilities in this regard see Finola O'Kane, 'What's in a name? The connected histories of Belfield, Co. Dublin and Belfield, St. Mary's, Jamaica', in Finola O'Kane and Ellen Rowley, eds, *Making Belfield: Space and Place at UCD* (Dublin: Universitiy College Dublin Press, 2020), 150–64.
34 For an interesting approach see Julius S. Scott, *The Common Wind: Afro-American Currents in the Age of the Haitian Revolution* (London: Verso, 2018).
35 Nini Rodgers, *Ireland, Slavery and Anti-Slavery: 1612–1865* (Basingstoke: Palgrave Macmillan, 2007).
36 Hilary Beckles, 'White labour in black slave plantation society and economy: A case study of indentured labour in seventeenth century Barbados', Ph.D. thesis (University of Hull, 1980).
37 Hilary McD. Beckles, 'A "riotous and unruly lot": Irish indentured servants and freemen in the English West Indies, 1644–1713', *William and Mary Quarterly* 47 (1990), 503–22; Hilary McD. Beckles, *White Servitude and Black Slavery: White Indentured Servitude in the Caribbean, 1627–1715* (Knoxville: Tennessee University Press, 1989).
38 Aubrey Gwynn, 'Early Irish emigration to the West Indies (1612–1643)', *Studies: An Irish Quarterly Review* 18:71 (September 1929), 377–93; Aubrey Gwynn, 'Indentured servants and Negro slaves in Barbados 1612–1650', *Studies: An Irish Quarterly Review* (1930), 279–94; Aubrey Gwynn, 'Documents relating to the Irish in the West Indies', *Analecta hibernica* (1932), 139–286.

39 Jenny Shaw, *Everyday Life in the Early English Caribbean: Irish, Africans, and the Construction of Difference* (Athens: University of Georgia Press, 2013); Karst de Jong, 'The Irish in Jamaica during the long eighteenth century (1698–1836)', Ph.D. thesis (Queen's University Belfast, 2017); Donald Harmon Akenson, *If the Irish Ran the World: Montserrat, 1630–1730* (Montreal: McGill-Queen's University Press, 1997); John C. Messenger, 'The influence of the Irish in Montserrat', *Caribbean Quarterly* 13:2 (1967), 3–26.

40 There are just five historical essays out of the seventeen collected in Alison Donnell, Maria McGarrity and Evelyn O'Callaghan, eds, *Caribbean Irish Connections: Interdisciplinary Perspectives* (Kingston: University of West Indies Press, 2015). The same bias towards comparative literature is clear in the only other recent collection, David Lloyd and Peter O'Neill, eds, *The Black and Green Atlantic: Cross-Currents of the Irish and African Diasporas* (Basingstoke: Palgrave, 2009). A recent special issue of the *Caribbean Quarterly* features three historical essays.

41 Maria McGarrity, *Washed by the Gulf Stream: The Historic and Geographic Relation of Irish and Caribbean Literature* (Newark, NJ: Associated University Presses, 2008); Abigail L. Palko, *Imagining Motherhood in Contemporary Irish and Caribbean Literature* (Basingstoke: Palgrave Macmillan, 2016); Eve Walsh Stoddard, *Positioning Gender and Race in (Post) Colonial Plantation Space: Connecting Ireland and the Caribbean* (Basingstoke: Palgrave, 2012). Michael G. Malouf, *Transatlantic Solidarities: Irish Nationalism and Caribbean Poetics* (Charlottesville: University of Virginia Press, 2009); Mary Gallagher, ed., *'Ici-là': Place and Displacement in Caribbean Writing in French* (Amsterdam: Rodopi, 2003).

42 Crawford Gribben and Scott Spurlock, eds, *Puritans and Catholics in the Trans-Atlantic World 1600–1800* (Basingstoke: Palgrave, 2016); Shona Helen Johnston, 'Papists in a Protestant world: The Catholic Anglo-Atlantic in the seventeenth century', Ph.D. thesis (Georgetown University, 2011); Block and Shaw, 'Subjects without an empire'; Robert Emmett Curran, *Papist Devils: Catholics in British America, 1574–1783* (Washington, DC: Catholic University of America Press, 2014); S. Karly Kehoe, 'Colonial collaborators: Britain and the Catholic Church in Trinidad, *c*. 1820–*c*. 1840', *Slavery & Abolition* 40:1 (2019), 130–46.

43 For the latter see José Brownrigg-Gleeson's chapter in this volume; Oscar Recio Morales, *Ireland and the Spanish Empire 1600–1825* (Dublin: Four Courts Press, 2010); and Margaret Brehony, 'Irish migration to Cuba, 1835–1845: Empire, ethnicity, slavery and "free" labour', Ph.D. thesis (National University of Ireland, Galway, 2012). For the former see Finola O'Kane's chapter in this volume; an interesting account of shadow French traders who were really Irish in Silvia Marzagalli, 'Establishing transatlantic trade networks in time of war: Bordeaux and the United States, 1793–1815', *Business History Review* 79:4 (Winter 2005), 811–44; and Silvia Marzagalli, 'The French Atlantic world in the seventeenth and eighteenth centuries', in Nicholas Canny and Philip Morgan, eds, *The Oxford Handbook of the Atlantic World* (Oxford: Oxford University Press, 2011), pp. 235–51.

44 Orla Power, 'Irish planters, Atlantic merchants: The development of St. Croix, Danish West Indies, 1750–1766', Ph.D. thesis (National University of Ireland, Galway, 2011). For the Irish in the Dutch empire see Ciaran O'Neill's chapter in this volume; and Thomas Truxes, 'Dutch–Irish cooperation in the mid-eighteenth-century wartime Atlantic', *Early American Studies* (2012): 302–34.
45 Silvia Marzagalli, 'The French Atlantic and the Dutch, late seventeenth–late eighteenth century', in Gert Oostindie and Jessica V. Roitman, eds, *Dutch Atlantic Connections, 1680–1800* (Leiden: Brill, 2014), pp. 101–18 (p. 104).
46 See Peter Burke, *Venice and Amsterdam: A Study of Seventeenth Century Elites* (London: Temple Smith, 1974), introduction; and Kolchin, *Unfree Labor*.
47 Black British citizens make up about 3 per cent of the total population of the UK, but the figure in Ireland is much smaller for historic reasons, amounting to less than half of the UK figure (1.4 per cent) in proportionate terms; Frances McGinnity, Matthew Creighton and Eamon Fahey, *Hidden versus Revealed Attitudes: A List Experiment on Support for Minorities in Ireland* (Luxembourg: Publications Office of the European Union, 2020), p. 3. For more on the historic fluctuation in the category of the Irish race see Ciaran O'Neill, '"Harvard scientist seeks typical Irishman": measuring the Irish Race, 1888–1936', *Radical History Review* 143 (2022), 89–108.
48 See Claude Julien Rawson, *God, Gulliver, and Genocide: Barbarism and the European Imagination, 1492–1945* (Oxford: Oxford University Press, 2007), p. 360; N.-A. Hazard and Loys Delteil, *Catalogue raisonné de l'oeuvre lithographique de Honoré Daumier* (Paris, 1904), p. 655, no. 3165. It is one of several satires by Daumier on the British in Ireland and elsewhere during this period; see also nos 3616; 3657; and, in Vol. 29 (*Daumier X*), 3818 and 3835–7 (all dating from 1867–71).

Part I

Setting out the terrain

1

Setting out the terrain: Ireland and the Caribbean in the eighteenth century*

David Dickson

In October 1780 a hurricane of unprecedented severity ravaged the islands of the eastern Caribbean. It arrived in Barbados just days after another hurricane had wreaked havoc in Jamaica – more than a thousand miles away. The conventional estimate is that the 'Great Hurricane', with winds of up to 200 m.p.h., cost over 22,000 lives, African and European, on land and at sea. Certainly there were far more casualties than were caused by the Anglo-French war then convulsing the region. It was the worst natural disaster since Europeans had begun their own ravaging of the Greater Caribbean two and a half centuries earlier, and fatalities caused by a natural disaster have only been surpassed once since then, with the Martinique volcanic eruption of 1902. News of the Great Hurricane reached Europe in December, and from early January newspapers were filled with the apocalyptic accounts of eyewitnesses. Coming in the midst of war the naval losses caused shock waves in London, but relief measures in response to the civilian losses were very slow to be finalised (although the huge sum of £120,000 was eventually allocated by Westminster). For many months the islands had to make do. Yet in Ireland's largest cities, public subscriptions were raised during January and February 1781 to fund relief shipments to Barbados and Jamaica. Around £1,000 was raised in Cork, several hundred in Waterford, and over £9,000 in Dublin; the latter came from more than 500 individual donations, with the established Church of Ireland organising collections to swell the fund. The first relief ship left Dublin at the beginning of March; destined for Barbados, it was loaded with 'flour, beans, herring and manufactures'.[1]

No other natural disaster attracted such attention in eighteenth-century Ireland, not even the far more deadly Portuguese earthquake of 1755. The striking local response to the Great Hurricane suggests a high level of intimacy between Ireland and the Caribbean. Yet on the face of it this was not so. Compared with London or Bristol, there were few people of African ancestry to be seen in eighteenth-century Irish cities, and knowledge of the Caribbean was almost entirely through the printed page or printed image.[2]

Irish involvement in the seventeenth-century development of the 'English' Caribbean had indeed been substantial and very visible, in terms of both migration and trade. From the 1620s the movement across the Atlantic had been part voluntary, part coerced. It had involved all shades of Irish people – restless New English settlers, displaced Old English Catholics (especially from the port towns of the south and west), and of course victims of the Cromwellian *nakba* in the 1650s (principally Gaelic Irish, and from the province of Munster).[3] As far as direct trade is concerned, the early 1680s were probably the high point for Irish visibility in Caribbean trade – with small vessels criss-crossing the Leewards and sailing down to Barbados – by which time roughly a third of all vessels arriving at Bridgetown (then epicentre of English sugar production) were Irish.[4]

Now, 100 years later in the era of the Great Hurricane, Irish involvement in the English Caribbean was very different: Irish-based traders had since the 1680s been marginalised by the English Navigation Acts and had not been allowed to import sugar directly from the English islands into Irish ports. And more than a century had passed since Irish merchants had been excluded from West Africa, specifically from trading in human cargoes; initially that was a London corporate monopoly, which was relaxed to include all English merchants in 1698, then all Scots too in 1707. Therefore what possible interest could the citizens of Dublin and Cork in 1780 have had in taking the lead in rebuilding shattered lives in the distant Caribbean, compared to the citizens of Bristol, Liverpool, or Glasgow, where the Caribbean slave economy was crucial in their commercial ascendancy, or of London, the financial engine-room of the British Atlantic?

One answer may lie in the near coincidence of the hurricane and the repeal in Westminster of those parts of the Navigation Acts that for a century had prevented the direct entry of high-value colonial goods into Ireland – creating 'free trade' (as it was characterised in Ireland). These concessions, won under duress at the end of 1779, generated a heady optimism that Ireland was now poised to enjoy the full fruits of empire, its leading ports to become international entrepôts in the sale of sugar and tobacco. Free trade also opened the English-controlled trading posts along the West African coast to Irish traders, an opportunity to participate in the English slave trade for the first time. A fierce political campaign, led by Dublin merchants and sugar bakers, ensued during 1780, the aim being heightened tariff protection for the 'free-trade' sugar that could now be refined in Ireland. Sugar was thrust into the forefront of public controversy and accorded an exaggerated role in debates on Irish economic recovery. The tariff battle ended in a draw.[5]

Such concerns will have influenced the campaign for Caribbean aid. War may also have been a factor. The Great Hurricane occurred four years into a disastrous war for Britain, with loss of the American colonies threatened and Britain's Caribbean islands in grave danger as well. The sensational events on Dominica a year previously had a particular Irish resonance: a French force (including men from Dillon's regiment of the Irish Brigade) had recaptured the island, and its Antrim-born Governor Earl Macartney and his Galway-born (and Catholic) Attorney-General George Staunton were among several officials taken prisoner (to be released from France some months later). Within Ireland, or at least within the Protestant parliamentary world, there was now a sharpened sense of identification with an Atlantic empire in existential danger. The flush of generosity towards the sugar islands may have reflected this passing mood.[6]

However, direct Irish commercial involvement in Caribbean waters before 1779, while modest, had never been entirely absent. Westward transatlantic trade in Irish commodities had been largely unrestricted and, by whatever legal ploy, a few Irish-based vessels had taken part in slaving voyages out of West Africa: two in the 1710s, six between 1747 and 1756, two in the early 1770s; seven of these ten voyages had originated in the port of Cork.[7] As for direct trade eastwards into Ireland, banned in 1696, this was permitted from 1731 for colonial goods *other than* sugar, tobacco, logwood or indigo. But ventures to the Caribbean on Irish merchants' account remained fairly modest and the vessels involved small. The overriding problem for prospective Irish shippers was the very restricted choice of return cargoes: the only viable Caribbean product that (from 1731) could be directly imported was rum. As a result, most Irish vessels trading to the Caribbean backtracked to the mainland colonies of North America in order to make up their return freight. There was, however, a distinct jump in the number of small Irish vessels, mainly from Cork and Belfast, entering the Caribbean in the 1770s, reflecting the sharp reduction in import duties on rum; around seventy-five vessels registered in Cork dropped anchor in the English islands in 1776, with Antigua (the leading producer of rum for the Irish market) the most prominent, followed by Jamaica, and at that time there were at least ten Belfast vessels engaged primarily in Caribbean trade. Possibly some of these dabbled in the inter-island slave trade as well.[8]

But this is of course only a small part of the story: Irish ships may have been outnumbered on the quays at Kingston and Bridgetown in the eighteenth century, but Ireland remained the dominant supplier of salted beef and butter, pork and herring, candles and soap, leather and shoes, for all the English islands. This composite trade had begun in the 1620s and had grown dramatically from the 1650s, despite the dislocating effects of the first Navigation Acts. Ireland's transatlantic 'provisions trade' flourished for a century – up to the American Revolution – and it enjoyed several bursts of growth during that time. The accepted estimate, based on Irish Customs data, is that over 85 per cent of beef and 80 per cent of butter exported from

Ireland to the British American colonies 'in the late colonial period' was destined for the Caribbean islands.[9] Up to eight Irish ports were involved to begin with, but war at sea and economies of scale ended the participation of secondary trading centres, and there was a diminished role for every Irish port bar one: Cork city. From the 1690s it became the great supply point for the Atlantic provisions trade. In the case of Jamaica, the largest individual market, virtually all beef and butter imports by mid-century were coming from Cork. Yet of the fifty-three ships arriving there with cargoes from the city in 1752/3, only four had *begun* their journey in the Irish port. Cork was no longer an independent hub for Caribbean trade; rather it was the merchants of Bristol, Liverpool and London who provided the capital and the shipping and who marshalled the heterogeneous supplies required by the plantation economy, with Cork merchants fulfilling bespoke orders for 'wet provisions', while competing with each other on price, product quality, speed of delivery and the length of credit on offer. But the modest number of Cork-owned vessels appearing in the Caribbean after the 1720s was not so much an indicator of the port's commercial backwardness as of the working out of economies of scale and lines of specialisation within the British Atlantic trading system, reflecting in this case the near-absence within the Caribbean of legal and attractive return cargoes to Ireland.[10]

There were by then very few Cork-born merchants to be seen in the islands, even by Irish standards. The fortunes made by the city's big merchant houses stayed in Ireland, much of that wealth going into property development in town and country. And if the younger sons in such families chose to take a mercantile apprenticeship elsewhere in the English-speaking world, it was more likely to be Dublin, Bristol, Bordeaux or London rather than any Caribbean (or American) destination.[11]

From the 1650s white settlers, slave-owners, factors and other operatives on the English-controlled Caribbean islands put a premium on familiar European foodstuffs to supplement what was locally available, and as sugar cultivation was ruthlessly pursued on the rich volcanic soils of the Lesser Antilles, food production was marginalised and dependence on Irish, continental and American supplies intensified. In response Irish merchants, using Portuguese and French salt and applying Dutch techniques, had perfected the production of 'long-life' beef and butter that would endure tropical temperatures and still be appetising. White indentured servants, so important in the sugar islands in the early days, ate their full share of the salt beef and butter, but by the mid-eighteenth century the foremost Caribbean consumers of Irish provisions (and Irish candles, soap, shoes and linens) were the self-employed, middle-status white households, based in town and countryside, who were enjoying a long-term rise in living standards and an exceptionally rich diet. This heterogeneous group was certainly the single most important market for Cork's vast trade in salted beef.[12] The enslaved populations of the English islands got their protein not, it seems, in this way, but rather from garden-reared chicken, plantain and yams, and from imported supplies of maize, beans, dried cod and salted herring.[13]

From the 1760s the fundamentals were changing. It was a time of unprecedented growth in sugar production both on the British and the French islands, accompanied by a relative, then an absolute, decline of the white population, and by a huge increase of those of African ancestry, enslaved and free. In narrow trading terms this meant a softening in demand for high-quality salted beef and butter in the islands, a growth in the importance of salted pork, and a surge in demand for salted herring and coarse linen – to a large extent, food and clothing for freed and enslaved African consumers. Most of the thousands of barrels of 'Irish' herring entering the Caribbean were imported from Sweden or from the west of Scotland and rebarrelled in Cork, but they were supplemented by Irish-sourced fish. Local herring was never in more plentiful supply than in the 1770s, when direct exports from the west of Ireland to the Caribbean, particularly from Donegal, soared; but then in the mid-1780s, with the sudden departure of herring shoals, exports were halted. Overall, Irish provisions exports to the Caribbean fell back after the American Revolution, north American supplies replacing Irish, and Irish food exports being increasingly directed towards the burgeoning British market next door.[14] However, linen and other textile exports to the islands held up, and that was important as we shall see.

Irish exports to the slave islands of other European empires were managed rather differently. Most were sent indirectly (via European entrepôts), or delivered covertly. The French possessions in the Caribbean had been slower to develop as sites of sugar production, but from the 1660s French merchants purchased Irish salted beef to supply both European settlers and their enslaved workers. In the 1670s the French government sponsored attempts to find substitutes for Irish beef, but their dependence on Irish supplies was already well established. Half a century later the remarkable expansion of sugar and coffee production on their Saint-Domingue colony – between the 1720s and 1740s – had a striking knock-on effect on the export levels of Cork beef to Nantes and Bordeaux. Indeed such was the pressure to secure Irish provisions that for a dozen years official regulations were relaxed in the 1730s allowing French vessels to sail directly from certain Irish ports to the French islands.[15]

So-called 'French beef' had its own price range in Cork: this category referred to the lowest-quality meat sold by commercial butchers – cuts from the carcasses of scrawny old cows – which provided a bountiful supply of discount protein for enslaved consumers. For most of the eighteenth century, Cork city handled around three-quarters of Irish beef exports to

France and the French islands – an even greater share than its proportion of shipments to the English islands (although both volume and unit value of the latter were generally higher), and Cork beef was rightly seen as a strategic commodity in wartime by the navies of both France and Britain. Thus when Richard Bradshaw, former mayor of Cork and perhaps the city's wealthiest merchant, was implicated during a time of war in 1744 in trading provisions with the French island of Martinique, the issue exercised even Crown ministers in London. Bradshaw only escaped retribution because of powerful political connections at home.[16]

The dynamism of Ireland's beef trade to France slackened after the 1750s. This suggests that, despite the huge expansion of numbers of enslaved workers across the French Caribbean, indigenous food production was becoming more important and enslaved households were sourcing a greater diversity of local foods (although wartime interruptions to food imports later in the century could still cause intense hardship on the French islands).[17]

Another difference in Irish trade with the French islands compared to the English was in the degree of local agency, and again this is most evident in Cork. Few of the leading Bristol or London principals who ordered provisions in Cork appear to have had any family connection with the city.[18] By contrast, many of those merchants in the mainland ports of western France who bought foodstuffs in Ireland for forwarding to French colonial markets were themselves Irish-born or of Irish ancestry, and much of Cork's trade with western France was on Irish vessels. French-based merchants of specifically Cork origin were fewer in number than those with a Galway or Waterford background (reflecting seventeenth-century upheavals more than eighteenth-century opportunities), but expatriate families from all of the old Irish trading towns mixed and collaborated, and this constellation of Irish traders helped shape the character of France's transatlantic connections. Irish merchants always had a covert advantage during the periods of Anglo-French war, being experienced in the dark arts of delivering Irish provisions to the 'French' islands (and the French navy), a process that involved the use of neutral island entrepôts, false papers and trusted supply lines. However, the vessels involved ran the risk of capture by English privateers, not helped by the ambiguous status of their owners – 'ambiguous' in the sense that many of these interlopers, particularly those with strong Cork connections, were Catholic in religion and, up to the 1740s at least, harbouring vestigial loyalties to the Jacobite cause.[19]

A few of these Irish merchant firms based in the French ports, specifically in Nantes, became heavily involved in the African slave trade, including several of Cork origin, notably the Riordans, who purchased and traded some 3,000 enslaved people spanning eleven voyages between 1734 and 1749. But the most notorious clan were the Sheils and Walshes, second-generation émigrés from Dublin and Waterford: Antoine Walsh secured an unprecedented dominance in the organisation of slave-trading voyages out of Nantes, an ascendancy that spanned two decades, and he tried to extend French commercial activity in Africa southwards along the Angolan coast. But 'Milord Walsh' chose to spend his final years in Saint-Domingue, dying at Cap Français in 1766, one of the richest Irish traders in the Caribbean with plantations in two parts of the island. Indeed, a number of the Hiberno-French families that prospered in servicing the slave economy, whether based in France or on the islands, were gradually drawn into plantation investment, with some of them being accepted into the creole elite in Saint-Domingue and Martinique: as Kate Hodgson has noted, their success was reflected in the remarkable fact that of the twelve Saint-Domingue representatives coming to the French National Assembly in 1789, three were of Irish descent or connected to such families, and this from a colony with no fewer than 8,000 *habitations*, i.e. plantations.[20]

But what of the broader human movement, westwards and eastwards? How prominent were people of Irish extraction in the wider world of sugar and slavery, and can we track the profits of slavery and sugar production flowing back to Ireland? Recent work in Scotland on the role of the slave trade and of Caribbean-generated capital has led to a complete reassessment of all this in Scotland's great leap forward.[21] Was there anything similar happening in Ireland? With the large-scale loss of eighteenth-century Irish testamentary records it is hard to track the transfer of wealth, but there are some clues.

Sir William Stapleton (dying in 1686) had been the Governor of the English Leeward Islands for fifteen years and, although a Catholic, had during that time built up properties on four of the islands; in his will he directed that 'all my monies [are] to be invested in land in Ireland'. But that was before the Williamite victory in 1691. From that time we can be confident that no expatriate Catholic would have even tried to invest in Irish land. And although bequests for religious or charitable purposes back home were not uncommon among Catholic traders in the Caribbean, the bequest of substantial overseas real estate or liquid assets to family members in Ireland was, it seems, only done covertly, if at all. Thus the small group of Catholic Irish merchants who amassed great wealth in St Croix under the Danish flag in the 1750s and 1760s, when they retired, went not to Ireland but to Copenhagen or London. And Hiberno-French plantation-owners who returned to Europe seem to have settled in the hinterlands of the French Atlantic ports, none more spectacularly than Antoine Walsh's elder son at Château Serraint on the Loire. However, a group of Catholic merchants in Limerick (Creaghs, Roches, Stacpooles and Kellys) had multiple family links to property and slave-trading in Barbados, Jamaica and

Saint-Domingue, and they may have been an exception here: some of the profits from long-distance trading and privateering stayed local and were channelled into Limerick property development later in the eighteenth century. For Protestant émigrés in the islands, some movement of assets through family inheritance did bring wealth home, but the likelihood is that this also only became a significant trend late in the eighteenth century. Typical of earlier times was John Perrie, an Anglican who had served his time as a merchant apprentice in Cork in the 1680s and became a highly successful trader in Antigua, diversifying into sugar production and using enslaved labour; he died back in Co. Cork in 1713 and, in leaving most of his wealth to his five daughters, he scattered his fortune among Ireland, Carolina and Antigua, plus a sum of £700 (about 5 per cent of his assets) to purchase property to fund poor relief in parishes in Cork and Antigua. But insofar as a general pattern is discernible, those of Irish Protestant background repatriating wealth from the English islands gravitated towards London, not homewards – like the Scots. One of the most striking and well-documented exceptions followed the marriage between two Protestant families, each of which had strong Catholic affiliations: the Galway Kellys and the Mayo Brownes. Elizabeth Kelly, sole legitimate heiress of her father's modest Galway and vast Jamaican properties, was betrothed to Peter Browne in 1752, future second Marquess of Sligo and later the first developer of Westport, Co. Mayo. The wealth of Elizabeth's father, Dennis, reflected his professional success as a chameleon lawyer, a leading Jamaican politician and a judge. The outcome of the match was the long-term flow of rentier income back to Ireland, not a capital transfer, or not at least until the slave compensation scheme of the 1830s.[22]

Dennis Kelly's story was unusual but not unique. Among the teeming numbers of young merchants, planters' agents, brokers and attorneys in the Caribbean port cities during the eighteenth century, those of Irish ancestry were never hard to find – scarcest perhaps in Barbados, more obvious in Jamaica, and from the 1760s increasingly visible in the Windward Islands. But the seventeenth-century diaspora of Munster and Galway families to the Leewards, most evident in the tiny Irish seed-bed of Montserrat, still registered a century later, both there and on neighbouring islands. Among Montserrat's natives who featured elsewhere were Nicholas Tuite, the 'great master of trade', who transformed St Croix in the 1750s, and Richard Farrell, who built a Cuban fortune and founded a remarkably successful dynasty based originally on Anglo-Spanish slave-trading.[23] And wherever early Irish settlers gained a foothold in landed property, the descendants of such families remained visible in the historical record and, to a lesser extent, on the ground. But what is harder to track are the movements of the descendants of the seventeenth-century landless labourers in Barbados or the micro-farmers of Montserrat and, later, the trajectory of the craftspeople, mariners, soldiers, book-keepers and store-men who drifted out from Ireland to try their fortune in the islands. This migration probably peaked between the 1680s and the 1720s, an era of marked instability at home (political, then economic), and it continued despite repeated attempts to block the inflow of Catholic indentured servants onto several islands. When the Governor of Jamaica in 1731 complained that 'low' Catholic Irish had been 'pouring in upon us in such shoals' in recent years, it was a plausible if exaggerated claim; it came just after the indentured migration from Ireland to the continental colonies had reached its first peak.[24]

By mid-century, migration from Ireland to the Caribbean of those without assets or 'connections' was in slow decline. As European numbers stabilised or contracted in almost every island, Irish newcomers required particular skills to survive and thrive: men such as Curtis Brett (1724–84), youngest son of a Dublin clothier and trained to the printing press (first in Dublin, then in London), who was hired to act as a store-keeper in Kingston in 1748. But shortly after his arrival he turned his hand to printing and launched the *St Jago Intelligencer* in 1756: thus began a highly profitable fourteen-year career as printer/publisher and merchant before he relocated to England (but retaining Dublin links).[25] His contemporary Patrick Browne (1720–90), the Mayo-born and continentally educated physician, was also based in Kingston for much of the 1750s, but the works for which he became famous, *The Civil and Natural History of Jamaica* (1756) and his separately published map of the island, were too ambitious for Brett's modest press, being published (and republished) in London. Brett, as far as we know, had no family links with the Caribbean, whereas Browne had spent his teenage years in Antigua with a relative before beginning his medical training. These two Irish migrants were only unusual in their highly successful sojourns in the islands, but like thousands of other Irish sojourners they did not put down roots, did not marry into the creole elite, and did not invest in land: they moved on, having drawn ample benefit from the patronage of the plantocracy.[26]

And then there were the comet-like Irish careers within that plantocracy spanning a single generation. Several of these have been closely studied of late (the Kellys and Arcedecknes in Jamaica, Nicholas Tuite in St Croix, John Black in Trinidad, and the Blair brothers in Berbice and Demerara), men who left a huge mark within their field of operations but did not establish local dynasties. Hidden behind them were platoons of other Irish, relatives and dependants, clergy, and book-keepers, who bobbed along in their wake. All, we can assume, were involved in slavery and treated enslaved families in no way differently from English or Scottish settlers, who (Montserrat excepted) were far more numerous. And as with the late-coming Scots, the origin of most Irish plantation-owners active in the eighteenth century was in the island ports, transitioning from being merchants, attorneys or factors into a close involvement or part ownership of pens and plantations, a move often precipitated by planter indebtedness or local marriage alliances rather than a planned investment strategy (but more case studies are needed to tease this out).[27]

Many of the subscribers to the Dublin Hurricane Fund in 1781 reappear two years later among the first investors in the Bank of Ireland, Ireland's first public bank. The bank was in large measure the creation of one family, the private banking firm of La Touche, by then in its third generation of existence with its business serving upper-class Ireland and the State itself. Their conspicuous wealth and financial influence were by then self-evident, and it is not entirely surprising that the contribution of £1,000 by 'Mess. Latouche and sons' to the Hurricane Fund was by far the largest gift. The La Touche family were also present on the ground in the Caribbean, with John James Digges La Touche (?1750–96), a younger son of a younger son of the bank's founder, living out his adult life in Jamaica, possibly a port merchant to begin with, but marrying a propertied widow in St Mary's Parish. With a brother who had done well in the employ of the East India Company, this distaff branch of the family prospered from empire in their own way. Unlike his cousins and (to a much lesser extent) his two brothers, John James did not invest in the new bank back home; he died childless in Kingston and was almost written out of the family's illustrious history (although his Jamaican property in land and enslaved persons passed back to his brothers and nephews in Ireland). On balance, it seems unlikely that the generosity of the Dublin bankers in 1781 was directly linked to their cousin's plight in Jamaica (the plantation was not in the area most affected by either hurricane).[28]

There were only a few business names among the hundreds of gentry subscribers to the Hurricane Fund; these were Dublin sugar refiners, importers of cotton wool, and a handful of other merchants – Anthony McDermott, Randall McDonnell and Leland Crosthwaite, all active traders to the Caribbean, and Mathew Cardiff, a ship-owner who had recently built the 300-ton *Hibernia* for the 'new' Caribbean trade – 'the largest vessel ever built in this port'. But strangely, the city's wealthiest sugar and rum importer, Edward Byrne, was missing from the list, as were his occasional partners the O'Connor brothers; they were Catholic traders in what was still a Protestant-dominated city, and well practised in keeping their powder dry. The O'Connors remained the largest Dublin firm trading directly with the islands over the next thirty years; and as mortgagees they took control of the Mount William plantation in Antigua at the turn of the century.[29]

Such direct involvement by Dublin or Cork merchants in the islands was certainly unusual, then or thereafter. Despite the iconography displayed on Dublin's palatial new Custom House in the 1780s, with allegorical references to Neptune, Africa and America, the 'free trade' of 1780 was not the transformative event its proponents expected.[30] In the case of Cork the number of locally based ships venturing into the Caribbean reached a peak in the early 1780s, followed by a marked decline. By contrast, Belfast voyages increased, principally to Jamaica. Overall, the value of direct Irish imports from the Caribbean almost doubled between the prewar levels in 1773/7 and those in 1783/97, but now it was an industrial raw material – cotton wool, not sugar or rum – driving this trend.[31]

Talk of exploiting 'free trade' in West Africa came to nothing: in Limerick there was one attempt in 1784 to raise funds for a slaving vessel to test the middle passage, but the initiative stalled, as did a similar one in Belfast in the same year. Indeed, the controversy over slaving went public in the North. Thomas McCabe, watchmaker, is traditionally credited with halting the ambitions of one of the wealthiest Belfast merchants, Waddell Cunningham. Formerly a New York merchant, Cunningham had unrivalled knowledge of Caribbean trade, licit and illicit, and in 1763, with his long-time business partner Thomas Greg, he had purchased a plantation in Dominica as it passed from French to English control. This seems to have nudged other Belfast merchants to invest in the Windwards. McCabe by contrast was a Belfast artisan made good, who was later proud to bear the moniker 'the Irish slave'.[32]

Belfast's commercial activity in the islands was of very long standing, although the impact of the Navigation Acts on the town's ambitions seems to have been severe.[33] But two factors revived Belfast's links with the English Caribbean in the late eighteenth century. First, there was the growing importance of merchants of Ulster origin within the trading communities of Charleston, Baltimore, Philadelphia, New York and even Boston; many of these traders became heavily involved in servicing all of the Caribbean islands, supplying fish, dry goods and timber, and in so doing they did not lose their links with home. Second, there was the demand for linen cloth in the islands, both cheap and fine, which increased greatly after mid-century. Linen sourced from within Ulster proved the strongest calling card for traders in Belfast (and Newry, Derry and Donegal) seeking to build up direct Caribbean links. Printed linens and cottons were by then finding cross-cultural markets, with free non-white men and women active consumers. Some of the wealth generated by this late bloom of Ulster commerce in the Caribbean may have brought wealth home and contributed to the beginnings of Belfast's industrialisation, although that remains quite speculative.[34]

Opponents of Cunningham's slaving venture in 1784 seem to have been the generally younger radical voices, men and women heavily influenced by the American Revolution but grounded in New Light Presbyterian theology. Indeed, the first Enlightenment critic of slavery was Francis Hutcheson,

Ulster-reared and Dublin-matured, before he went to Glasgow and gained an international reputation. But it is perhaps a sign of the limited direct contacts between Belfast and the Caribbean that until late in the century Hutcheson's views on slavery had little local purchase. However, that was changing in the 1780s, and after Olaudah Equiano made his famous visit to Ireland in 1791, travelling from Dublin first southwards, then to the North, he recalled that it was in Belfast that he received the warmest hospitality.[35]

Judging by the subscription list to the Irish edition of his *Narrative of the Life of Olaudah Equiano* (1789), Equiano's Cork and Dublin hosts were Quaker merchant families. The social philosophy of Irish Quakers was very similar to that of their English co-religionists; several Dublin Quakers had personal links with early London abolitionists, and they particularly valued their connections with Edmund Burke. He was an alumnus of the most successful Quaker academy in Ireland, the Shackletons' school at Ballitore. Burke's towering importance in British public life, and his skills in Parliament and on the page, have ensured that his views on slavery and its place in the growth of the British empire have attracted great interest, not least because they were ambiguous and inconsistent. Those who have studied Burke's ideas and influence on the politics of his home country, specifically in relation to the anti-Catholic penal laws, have noted the distance between Burke's private views and his public positions, and it is at least plausible that his private views on slavery may have been more radical than his public friendship with West India merchants in London and Bristol might suggest. Through family involvements in Jamaica (some of them dubious) he had a particular knowledge of the island and, despite his few parliamentary speeches on the West Indies (compared with the many on India), he appeared remarkably well informed. He managed to project a public disdain for slavery while remaining a close ally of the powerful West India lobby; indeed, for most of his life he was convinced that Britain's weight in the world rested in large part on the prosperity flowing from the Caribbean. However, Burke's importance in the tortured history of emancipation lies not, it seems, in his being a covert abolitionist, but in his development (specifically in the unpublished *Sketch of a Negro Code* [1780]) of a politically astute programme of structural amelioration, and for his contention that those traded into slavery necessarily became subjects of the British Crown and thereby acquired certain inalienable rights. This led to his full conversion to the abolitionist cause in 1788 (perhaps helped by his ongoing friendship with the Shackletons), but it was only for a few short years until his all-consuming fear of Pandora's revolutionary box distanced him from the abolitionist cause.[36]

Burke may have been one of the first to articulate an exit strategy for Britain out of its economic dependence on slavery, but there are several others with strong Irish links who also saw themselves as 'ameliorists': Samuel Martin, the Antigua-based and widely read advocate for 'enlightened' management of an enslaved labour force; Joshua Steele, coming to his Barbados plantations in old age in the 1780s, who tried to implement a liberal policy on his property that echoed some of Burke's ideas; William Preston, the Dublin barrister who published the only extended and closely argued critique of Bryan Edwards's apologia for Jamaica slavery in 1792; and Sir Jeremiah Fitzpatrick, Dublin physician turned social reformer.[37]

One of Burke's many Cork cousins, Nano Nagle, the philanthropist and founder of the Presentation Order, had a singular approach to amelioration: in 1770 she was planning to send a large cohort of children educated in her city free schools to a Caribbean island to provide a programme of religious instruction to 'the little blacks', believing that 'it lies in the power of the poor to be of [more] service that way than the rich'.[38] The site of Nagle's experiment is unknown, as is the outcome. But civil society in Cork had begun to focus on the slave trade by this time as evidenced by motions in the local debating salons, and opinions there seem to have lain on the side of abolition. Plantation employment remained an attractive career choice, however: one young Corkman sailed to Antigua in 1774 to become 'attorney', i.e. a plantation manager, for Chief Justice Stephen Blizard; he spent eight years there, a time of unprecedented drought and commercial dislocation.[39] Back home by 1789, he published (anonymously) a rebuttal of the horror stories then circulating about life in the sugar plantations; he claimed to provide granular detail of everyday life in Antigua, on diet and dress, work patterns, maternity and medical provision, punishment, and recreational culture. He attacked the excesses of tyrannical managers, incompetent medics and disengaged plantation-owners, and he took as axiomatic 'the common ties of humanity' between white and black. But such special pleading was already familiar in England; his mild apologia for contemporary slavery, careful not to offend and profoundly racist, was well tailored for a local readership.[40]

This defensive memoir was a response to moves within Cork's powerful Committee of Merchants (led by Quakers and ex-Quakers) to organise a petition in 1788 against the slave trade, an initiative that failed to gain traction (whereas in Dublin, the equivalent Chamber of Commerce passed a resolution condemning the 'odious traffic'). Then, in Cork in the 1790s, the somewhat quixotic Denis Driscol championed 'the persecuted sons of Africa' and the Haitian Revolution in the pages of his radical if erratic *Cork Gazette*, while Cork-born army veteran turned Jacobin Thomas Russell became a visceral opponent of slavery (although his radical friends did not follow him in refusing to consume beverages containing sugar).[41] And even though Belfast's *Northern Star*, much the most successful Irish radical newspaper, gave extensive coverage to the case for abolition of the slave trade, it still allowed advertisements for sugar and rum. Indeed, the dominant view among all United Irish activists, certainly outside the North, was that 'emancipation' was then a local Irish issue – for, as Wolfe Tone put it in 1791, had not Irish Catholics been 'above a century in slavery'?[42] This all-powerful trope was a reworking of the conventional characterisation of *Ireland* as 'an isle of slaves', occasioned by Westminster's assertion of primacy over the Irish Parliament, and this refashioned usage – of *Catholic* slavery and longed-for emancipation – perhaps distracted radicals from a closer interest in the Caribbean.[43] Only once in the 1790s did the evils of African slavery become a central element in political protest: facing the prospect of transshipment to the disease-torn Caribbean in 1795, where thousands of raw Irish recruits were on active service, disaffected elements within two army regiments camped in Cork mounted a full-scale mutiny and took over the city's Grand Parade. They appealed for public support and made a rhetorical call: 'you unfortunate and enslaved natives of Africa, are you to feel our steel? Are we to be made to shed your innocent blood with our murderous arms?'. But army cannon directed at the mutineers ended the matter without bloodshed.[44]

The destination for these protesters was probably Saint-Domingue, previously one of those hotspots of émigré Irish settlement. Now, in the mid-1790s, British intervention and a failed conquest were magnifying the chaos of a colony in flames. It was a full generation later before Daniel O'Connell (without, it seems, any family baggage from the Caribbean) managed to weave two very different concepts of emancipation, Irish and African, into a single message and a much strengthened international cause.

Notes

* A version of this chapter was given at the annual conference of the Economic and Social History Society of Ireland, Galway, December 2021; I am very grateful for comments and suggestions made on that occasion.
1 *Freeman's Journal*, 6–9, 9–11, 11–13 January 1781; *Finn's Leinster Journal*, 6–10, 13–17 January 1781; *Saunders's News-Letter (SNL)*, 15, 19, 22, 27 January; 2, 3, 8, 12, 22, 24 February; 1, 3, 12 March; 7 June 1781; *Walker's Hibernian Magazine* (1781), 46–52, 447–8; *Caledonian Mercury*, 22 January 1781; *Cork Evening Post*, 5 February 1781; *Royal Gazette of Jamaica*, 14 April 1781; Richard Harrison, *Merchants, Mystics and Philanthropists: 150 Years of Cork Quakers* (Cork: Society of Friends, 2006), pp. 71, 214n; Wayne Neely, *The Great Hurricane of 1780: The Story of the Greatest and Deadliest Hurricane of the Caribbean and the Americas* (Bloomington: Indiana University Press, 2012), pp. 217–19, 228–9, 233.

2 W. A. Hart, 'Africans in eighteenth-century Ireland', *Irish Historical Studies* 33 (2002–3), 19–26.
3 Kirsten Block and Jenny Shaw, 'Subjects without an empire: The Irish in the early modern Caribbean', *Past and Present* 210:1 (February 2011), 33–60.
4 Thomas M. Truxes, *Irish–American Trade 1660–1783* (Cambridge: Cambridge University Press, 1988), pp. 94–5; Jean Agnew, *Belfast Merchant Families in the Seventeenth Century* (Dublin: Four Courts Press, 1996), pp. 105–6; David Dickson, *Old World Colony: Cork and South Munster 1630–1830* (Cork: Cork University Press, 2005), pp. 116–17.
5 Nini Rodgers, *Ireland, Slavery and Anti-Slavery: 1612–1865* (Basingstoke: Palgrave Macmillan, 2007), pp. 161, 173–5; Truxes, *Irish–American Trade*, p. 17.
6 *Dictionary of Irish Biography* (*DIB*), 'Sir George Staunton'; Jennifer A. McLaren, 'Irish lives in the British Caribbean: Engaging with empire in the revolutionary era', Ph.D. thesis (Macquarie University, 2018), pp. 180–200, 231–2.
7 Trans-Atlantic Slave Trade Database, www.slavevoyages.org (accessed 10 September 2021).
8 *Lloyd's Register of British and Foreign Shipping* (1775); Norman E. Gamble, 'The business community and trade of Belfast 1767–1800', Ph.D. thesis (University of Dublin, 1978), p. 292; Truxes, *Irish–American Trade*, pp. 29–30, 92–3, 215–17; R. C. Nash, 'Irish Atlantic trade in the seventeenth and eighteenth centuries', *William and Mary Quarterly* 42 (1985), 329–56 (pp. 345n, 355–6); L. M. Cullen, *Economy, Trade and Irish Merchants at Home and Abroad 1600–1988* (Dublin: Four Courts Press, 2012), pp. 107–9.
9 Nash, 'Irish Atlantic trade', pp. 330–1, 352; Truxes, *Irish–American Trade*, pp. 89, 167–8; Joseph T. Leydon, 'The Irish provisions trade to the Caribbean, c. 1650–1780: An historical geography', Ph.D. thesis (University of Toronto, 1995), p. 105; Dickson, *Old World Colony*, pp. 135–53; Rodgers, *Ireland, Slavery*, pp. 127–30.
10 Nash, 'Irish Atlantic trade', pp. 344–6; Truxes, *Irish–American Trade*, pp. 90–1, 337n; Dickson, *Old World Colony*, pp. 149–50; Jack P. Greene, *Settler Jamaica in the 1750s: A Social Portrait* (Charlottesville: University of Virginia Press, 2016), pp. 18–19.
11 Truxes, *Irish–American Trade*, pp. 92, 99; Leydon, 'The Irish provisions trade', p. 209; Natalie Zacek, *Settler Society in the English Leeward Islands 1670–1776* (Cambridge: Cambridge University Press, 2010), p. 92.
12 Nash, 'Irish Atlantic trade', pp. 334–7, 354; Greene, *Settler Jamaica*, pp. 196, 206–7.
13 'S. K.', *A Short but Particular Impartial Account of the Treatment of Slaves in the Island of Antigua* ... (Cork, 1789), pp. 15–20; Truxes, *Irish–American trade*, p. 91; Barry W. Higman, *Slave Population and Economy in Jamaica, 1807–1834* (Cambridge: Cambridge University Press, 1976), pp. 30, 136–7; Nash, 'Irish Atlantic trade', 335; Rodgers, *Ireland, Slavery*, pp. 179–81.
14 Arthur Young, *A Tour of Ireland ... in ... 1776, 1777 and 1778* (Dublin: printed by G. Bonham for Messrs Whitestone *et al.*, 1780), Vol. I, pp. 226–36; *Hibernian*

Journal, 4 October 1784; Gamble, 'The business community', pp. 271, 279–81, 294; Nash, 'Irish Atlantic trade', 331, 335, 340; Truxes, *Irish–American trade*, pp. 89, 96–7, 164–5, 187–8; Agnew, *Belfast Merchant Families*, p. 106; Rodgers, *Ireland, Slavery*, pp. 150–1, 180; Nicholas Crawford, '"In the wreck of a master's fortune": Slave provisioning and planter debt in the British Caribbean', *Slavery and Abolition* 37:2 (2016), 353–74.

15 Bertie Mandelblatt, 'A transatlantic commodity: Irish salt beef in the French Atlantic world', *History Workshop Journal* 63 (2007), 18–47.

16 John Yeamans, [London], to the Duke of Bedford, 30 May 1745, Shannon papers, Public Record Office of Northern Ireland (PRONI), D2707/A/1/9/6; Nash, 'Irish Atlantic trade', 335 341–4; Leydon, 'The Irish provisions trade', p. 118; Dickson, *Old World Colony*, pp. 136–7, 143, 149–50, 152–3.

17 Nash, 'Irish Atlantic trade', 335–6; K. G. Kelly and Diane Wallman, 'Foodways of enslaved laborers on French West Indian plantations (18th–19th century)', *Afriques: Débats, méthodes, et terrains d'histoire* 5 (2014), 28–30; Trevor Burnard and John Garrigus, *The Plantation Machine: Atlantic Capitalism in French Saint-Domingue and British Jamaica* (Philadelphia: University of Pennsylvania Press, 2016), pp. 112–15.

18 Rodgers, *Ireland, Slavery*, pp. 98–9, 128. On London see David Dickson, Jan Parmentier and Jane Ohlmeyer, eds, *Irish and Scottish Mercantile Networks in Europe and Overseas in the Seventeenth and Eighteenth Centuries* (Ghent: Academia Press, 2007), Chapters 10–12, by Craig Bailey, L. M. Cullen and Thomas M. Truxes.

19 Nash, 'Irish Atlantic trade', pp. 348–9; Truxes, *Irish–American Trade*, pp. 150, 238–41; L. M. Cullen, John Shovlin and T. M. Truxes, eds, *The Bordeaux–Dublin Letters, 1757: Correspondence of an Irish Community Abroad* (Oxford: Oxford University Press, 2013), pp. 22–3, 42–3.

20 L. M. Cullen, 'The Irish merchant communities of Bordeaux, La Rochelle and Cognac in the eighteenth century', in L. M. Cullen and P. Butel, eds, *Négoce et industrie en France et en Irlande aux XVIIIe et XIXe siècles* (Paris: CNRS, 1980), pp. 52, 55–7; Dickson, *Old World Colony*, pp. 159–63; Rodgers, *Ireland, Slavery*, pp. 106–12, 132–3; Cullen, *Economy, Trade and Irish Merchants*, pp. 191–3; Guy Saupin, 'Les réseaux commerciaux des Irlandais de Nantes sous le règne de Louis XIV', in Dickson *et al.*, *Irish and Scottish Mercantile Networks*, pp 115–46 (pp. 136–40); Kate Hodgson, 'Franco-Irish Saint-Domingue', *Caribbean Quarterly* 64 (2018), 434–51.

21 T. M. Devine, 'Did slavery make Scotia great?', *Britain and the World* 4:1 (2011), 60–2; T. M. Devine, ed., *Recovering Scotland's Slavery Past: The Caribbean Connection* (Edinburgh: University of Edinburgh Press, 2015).

22 *SNL*, 23 October 1784; V. L. Oliver, *The History of the Island of Antigua: One of the Leeward Caribbees in the West Indies, from the First Settlement in 1635 to the Present Time* (London: Mitchell and Hughes, 1894), Vol. I, pp. 52, 84; Vol. II, pp. 57–8, 67, 301–4; Vol. III, pp. 3, 21, 100–1, 223, 436; L. M. Cullen, 'Merchant communities overseas, the Navigation Acts and Irish and Scottish responses', in Cullen and T. C. Smout, eds, *Comparative Aspects of Scottish and Irish Economic and Social History 1600–1900* (Edinburgh: John Donald, 1977), pp. 170–1; Zacek, *Settler Society*, pp. 85–7; Orla Power, 'Irish planters,

Atlantic merchants: The development of St. Croix, Danish West Indies, 1750–1766', Ph.D. thesis (National University of Ireland, Galway, 2011), pp. 185–90; D. H. Akenson, *If the Irish Ran the World: Montserrat 1630–1730* (Liverpool: Liverpool University Press, 1997), pp. 95–100; Rodgers, *Ireland, Slavery*, pp. 62–5, 113, 133–7, 164; 'Dennis Kelly', *Legacies of British Slave-Ownership*, www.ucl.ac.uk/lbs/ (accessed 8 August 2022); David Dickson, *The First Irish Cities: An Eighteenth-Century Transformation* (New Haven: Yale University Press, 2021), p. 65.

23 Sir Henry Blackhall, 'The Galweys of Munster', *Journal of the Cork Historical and Archaeological Society* 74 (1969), 80–2; Akenson, *If*, pp. 148–52; Rodgers, *Ireland, Slavery*, p. 56; Oscar Recio Morales, *Ireland and the Spanish Empire 1600–1825* (Dublin: Four Courts Press, 2010), pp. 243–5; Power, 'Irish planters', pp. 37–8, 41.

24 Truxes, *Irish–American Trade*, pp. 143–4; Rodgers, *Ireland, Slavery*, p. 45; Block and Shaw, 'Subjects without an empire', 58–9; Zacek, *Settler Society*, pp. 93, 98.

25 Brett letters (in private possession); Roderick Cave, 'Printing in eighteenth-century Jamaica', *The Library* 33 (1978), 191–2.

26 Hilary McD. Beckles, 'A "riotous and unruly lot": Irish indentured servants and freemen in the English West Indies, 1644–1713', *William and Mary Quarterly* 47 (1990), 503–22 (522); Greene, *Settler Jamaica*, pp. 8–9, 17–23; Marc Caball, 'Transforming tradition in the British Atlantic: Patrick Browne (*c.* 1720–1790), an Irish botanist and physician in the West Indies', in John Cunningham, ed., *Early Modern Ireland and the World of Medicine: Practitioners, Collectors and Contexts* (Manchester: Manchester University Press, 2019), pp. 211–31.

27 Akenson, *If*, pp. 174–5; Rodgers, *Ireland, Slavery*, p. 94; Power, 'Irish planters', *passim*; Barry W. Higman, *Plantation Jamaica 1750–1850: Capital and Control in a Colonial Economy* (Kingston: University of the West Indies Press, 2008), pp. 147–51, 166–226; Karst de Jong, 'The Irish in Jamaica during the long eighteenth century (1698–1836)', Ph.D. thesis (Queen's University Belfast, 2017), pp 105–7, 114–16; J. J. Wright, *An Ulster Slave-Owner in the Revolutionary Atlantic: The Life and Letters of John Black* (Dublin: Four Courts Press, 2019); 'James Blair', *Legacies of British Slave-Ownership*.

28 F. G. Hall, *The Bank of Ireland 1783–1946* (Dublin: Hodges Figgis, 1948), pp. 475–7, 496–8, 508–10; Michael McGinley, *The La Touche Family in Ireland* (Greystones: La Touche Legacy Committee, 2004), pp. 52–5, 112; 'Peter Digges La Touche', 'William Digges La Touche', *Legacies of British Slave-Ownership*.

29 *Lloyd's Register of British and Foreign Shipping* (1775, 1781); *SNL*, 20 December 1780, 11 January, 22 February 1781; 23 March, 19 November 1785; 26 June 1786; 5 January 1787; *Hibernian Journal*, 23 May 1783; 'Sweetman family papers', National Library of Ireland Collection List 156, pp. 19–23; *DIB*, 'Edward Byrne', 'Valentine O'Connor'.

30 Edward McParland, *James Gandon: Vitruvius hibernicus* (London: Zwemmer, 1985), p. 68.

31 In the Lloyd's registers, Irish and principally Cork departures to the Caribbean fell back during the 1780s (with only Jamaica holding up), and arrivals declined even more so: *Lloyd's Register of Shipping* (1781, 1786, 1792); Gamble,

'The business community', pp. 279–81, 288; David Dickson, 'Aspects of the rise and decline of the Irish cotton industry', in Cullen and Smout, *Comparative Aspects*, pp. 104–5; Nash, 'Irish Atlantic trade', 339, Table IV; Leydon, 'The Irish provisions trade', pp. 280, 314.

32 Rodgers, *Ireland, Slavery*, pp. 146–51, 156–8. Cf. Gamble, 'The business community', pp. 270, 273, 290–1.

33 Agnew, *Belfast Merchant Families*, pp. 105, 118–24.

34 *DIB*, 'Oliver Pollock'; Gamble, 'The business community', pp. 267–88; Truxes, *Irish–American Trade*, pp. 91–2, 95; Rodgers, *Ireland, Slavery*, pp. 83–90, 146–9; McLaren, 'Irish lives', pp. 158–61.

35 Nini Rodgers, *Equiano and Anti-Slavery in Eighteenth-Century Belfast* (Belfast: Belfast Society, 2000), pp. 4–7; Martyn J. Powell, *The Politics of Consumption in Eighteenth-Century Ireland* (Basingstoke: Palgrave Macmillan, 2005), p. 224.

36 Rodgers, *Ireland, Slavery*, pp. 184–7; P. J. Marshall, *Edmund Burke and the British Empire in the West Indies: Wealth, Power, and Slavery* (Oxford: Oxford University Press, 2019), pp. 21–2, 103, 177–222; Gregory M. Collins, 'Edmund Burke on slavery and the slave trade', *Slavery and Abolition* 40:3 (2019), 494–521; Daniel I. O'Neill, 'Edmund Burke on slavery and the slave trade: A response', *Slavery and Abolition* 41:4 (2020), 816–27.

37 Samuel Martin, Antigua, to [James, Viscount Limerick], 6 February 1754, Roden papers, PRONI, MIC 147/9; William Preston, *A Letter to Bryan Edwards, Esquire, Containing Observations on Some Passages of His 'History of the West Indies'* (London, 1795); Oliver MacDonagh, *The Inspector General: Sir Jeremiah Fitzpatrick and the Politics of Social Reform, 1783–1802* (London: Croom Helm, 1981), pp. 284–91; David Lambert, *White Creole Culture: Politics and Identity during the Age of Abolition* (Cambridge: Cambridge University Press, 2010), pp. 41–72; *DIB*, 'Joshua Steele'; Rodgers, *Ireland, Slavery*, p. 75; Devin Leigh, 'A disagreeable text: The uncovered first draft of Bryan Edwards's Preface to *The History of the British West Indies*, c. 1792', *New West Indian Guide* 94:1 (2020), 39–74.

38 Nano Nagle letters, www.digital.ucd.ie/view-media/ucdlib:153350/canvas/ucdlib:153370 (accessed 1 March 2020).

39 A. J. Berland and G. D. Endfield, 'Drought and disaster in a revolutionary age: Colonial Antigua during the American Independence War', *Environment and History* 24:2 (2018), 209–35.

40 'S. K.', *A short but Particular Impartial Account*, passim. The Blizard plantation was located at New North Sound, but 'S. K.' has not been identified.

41 Mary McNeill, *The Life and Times of Mary Ann McCracken, 1770–1866* (Dublin: Allen Figges, 1960), p. 293; Mary Helen Thuente, *The Harp Re-Strung: The United Irishmen and the Rise of Irish Literary Nationalism* (Syracuse, NY: Syracuse University Press, 1994), pp. 20, 44, 92; Michael Durey, *Transatlantic Radicals and the Early American Republic* (Lawrence: Kansas University Press, 1997), p. 285; Powell, *The Politics of Consumption*, pp. 224–5.

42 [T. W. Tone], *An Argument on Behalf of the Catholics of Ireland*, 2nd edn (Belfast: Belfast Society of United Irishmen, 1791), pp. 17, 28; Durey, *Transatlantic Radicals*, pp. 268, 282–8; Dickson, *Old World Colony*, pp. 459–60.
43 Burke was perhaps the first public figure to characterise Irish Catholics as an enslaved people: Marshall, *Edmund Burke and the British Empire*, p. 21.
44 K. P. Ferguson, 'The army in Ireland from the Restoration to the Act of Union', Ph.D. thesis (University of Dublin, 1981), pp. 96, 171–3; R. N. Buckley, *The British Army in the West Indies: Society and the Military in the Revolutionary Age* (Gainesville: University Press of Florida, 1998), pp. 106–8; Powell, *The Politics of Consumption*, p. 70; McLaren, 'Irish lives', pp 90n, 99–104; Hodgson, 'Franco-Irish Saint-Domingue', 443–6.

2

From perfidious papists to prosperous planters: Making Irish elites in the early modern English Caribbean

Jenny Shaw

Irish labourer Cornelius Bryan began his Caribbean sojourn in the 1650s as the archetypical perfidious papist. Hauled in front of the Barbados Council and accused of slandering English colonists by threatening to drink their blood, he was ordered to receive twenty-one lashes on the 'bare-back' at the public square in the island's capital, Bridgetown. Bryan, who was also accused of 'raising a mutiny', was ordered by English officials to leave the island within the month.[1] Thirty years later Bryan died in the colony having never departed its tropical shores. Shortly following the demand that he leave Barbados he petitioned the Council to remain and was granted his request 'provided he give security for [his] good behaviour'.[2] More surprising than the English change of heart was the reversal in fortunes that Bryan himself experienced over the course of the next three decades. Barbados deeds and the 1680 census chart his rise to island planter and his acquisition of two servants and nine enslaved Africans to work his small estate in St James's Parish.[3] His will, proved seven years later, noted that Bryan left behind a wife and six children, to whom he bequeathed his worldly goods. His property included a feather bed; a cedar chest; 22 acres of land; a black horse; and thirteen enslaved Africans, all of whom were carefully parcelled out among his progeny and his spouse.[4] Despite his precarious beginnings and lowly status as an Irish Catholic in an English colony, Cornelius Bryan ended his life resembling the very English elites he had maligned thirty years earlier: he was now a planter, albeit an Irish one.

To comprehend Cornelius Bryan's shift in status, it is first necessary to understand the uneasy space that Irish Catholics occupied in England's colonial hierarchy. Not only did their Catholicism make Protestant English authorities suspect most Irish capable of acting against the empire from within, but English exposure to Irish social and cultural practices in Ireland resulted in the characterisation of the Irish as barbarous and uncivilised. According to English colonisers, the Irish did not use resources productively, did not wear the right clothing, did not engage in legitimate marriages and did not worship the right God.[5] These beliefs were underscored by the Irish Rebellion of 1641, during which hundreds of Protestant English settlers in the northeast of the island were killed by Catholics.[6] The pamphlet war following this incident reinforced the English conception that Irish Catholics were savage and beyond the scope of civilised society; it was in this atmosphere that around 10,000 Irish were shipped to the Caribbean as part of Oliver Cromwell's policy of transportation, Cornelius Bryan probably among them.[7] Upon arrival these Irish transportees laboured in the island's sugar fields while anxious English officials feared they would ally with enslaved Africans or Catholic European competitors to challenge English authority.[8] Placing Bryan's outburst against English settlers in this context, we can understand both how his antipathy was read by authorities, and why those authorities responded as they did.

But not all Irish in the Caribbean were representative of this outcast demographic. Some Irish subjects played key roles in England's imperial project not as labourers who provided crucial work in sugar fields but as wealthy plantation-owners and enslavers themselves.[9] For the 1650s was not just a decade of Irish immigration into the Caribbean, it was also the period that saw the so-called sugar boom drive the mass importation of enslaved Africans to the region and led to the rise of the first fully fledged slave society in the Americas. By the closing decades of the seventeenth century Barbados had transformed from a small and insignificant island on the eastern edge of the Caribbean Sea to England's most prosperous imperial possession.[10] Significantly, some Irish took advantage of the changes wrought by this moment of demographic and social upheaval to become planters who worked to uphold the system rather than subvert it, shifting English conceptions regarding their suitability for civilisation. Other Irish arrived in the Caribbean with sufficient capital to purchase land and enslaved people, immediately laying claim to a place among the planter elite.[11] Some even reached the upper echelons of power on the islands, their Irish backgrounds not automatically prohibiting their place within colonial administrations.

So how did Cornelius Bryan and others like him make the shift from untrustworthy outsider to seemingly loyal cog in England's imperial machine? And what does his transformation reveal about the strategies that Irish Catholics employed to temper accusations of treachery in the English Caribbean? Answering these questions requires not focusing on Bryan's trajectory alone, but examining his fortunes alongside two other Irish Catholics, John Blake and William Stapleton. These men first acquired property in land and enslaved Africans, joining the planter class alongside the English. They then began emulating English social and cultural norms as a way to distance themselves from their lower-order compatriots and participate in the emerging racial hierarchy. Finally, these Irish reduced the threat posed by their faith, rendering their Catholicism less visible by avoiding direct references to religious practices and quieting demands for priests. These examples demonstrate not only the ways that some Irish Catholics survived and thrived in the English Caribbean, but also how English concerns about their perceived barbarism and savagery were laid to rest. As invested in upholding hierarchies of race and class as their English counterparts, the Irish navigated colonial Caribbean systems in order to find economic and political success at the heart of the English Empire.

Property and prosperity

One way that Irish Catholics cemented their status in the English Caribbean was by acquiring property first in land, and then in enslaved Africans. Although the sugar boom in Barbados spurred the large-scale acquisition of land by some of the island's wealthiest elites, it is important to note that the majority of planters worked relatively small plots of land: the mean size of a plantation in 1680 was only 29 acres, while the median size was smaller still, a mere 10 acres.[12] According to the 1680 census, sent to the Lords of Trade and Plantations by Barbados Governor Jonathan Atkins, many planters who occupied these lands were Irish. Bryan is listed twice in the census: once as a landowner and an enslaver in St James's Parish, and again as a member of the 'troop of Horse' providing for the defence of the island.[13] He had been busy since his 1656 encounter with the English law. By 1659 he had amassed 'a valuable summe of muscovado sugar' sufficient to purchase 7 acres of land in St Michael's Parish in the southwest of the island.[14] In 1675 Cornelius and his wife, Margaret Bryan, sold 'ten acres of land be it more or less with the houses, edifices and buildings thereon … situate and lying in the said parish of Christ Church'. The Bryans got 10,000 lb of sugar and £50 in 'lawfull money of England' for their property.[15] Although we do not know when they moved from Christchurch the Bryans were in St James's Parish by 1680 when the census was recorded.[16] Two years later, Cornelius increased his landholdings to 22 acres, buying the excess from property formerly possessed by John Page Clerke and his wife, Sarah.[17]

Cornelius Bryan was not the only Irish man in Barbados to hold a small plot of land or to enslave Africans. Teague Murfee's name appears in the census entry for St Peter's Parish, in the northern part of the colony. He was listed as a property-owner with 5 acres of land and five 'negroes' in his household.[18] Other Irish enslavers in Barbados included Dermon Mollony in St Philip, Dermon Conniers in St Joseph, Dennis Murfee in St Lucy, and

Daniell Maccoline in St John. In St Peter, Thomas Clarke held 3 acres and four enslaved people, and in St Michael, Bryan Murphey had 5 acres, four enslaved people, and one hired servant. Christchurch, one of the island's most fertile parishes, boasted numerous Irish landowners who claimed between 6 and 20 acres and between one and nine enslaved Africans: Teague Conoghlan, Bryan Connor, Daniel Cockron, Morris Fitzgerland, Dennis Kelly, Daniel MacGranah and Bryan MacBready were just some of the Irish men in this parish who had achieved the status of landed proprietor.[19] These men used their property to support their wives and children, and to provide for future generations.

Similar trends are visible in Montserrat where Irish settlers accounted for 70 per cent of the European population.[20] The colony's 1678 census reveals that almost three-fifths of the male Irish population of Montserrat owned land in male-partnered households.[21] Patrick and Mathew Darcy, brothers who shared land in Colonel Cormack's Division, were just two of them. Their census entry does not indicate whether there were women, children, servants or enslaved Africans in their household, although there probably were – at the end of the census the numbers in each group were listed in bulk, counted, but not attributed to any particular property.[22] Irish men in Montserrat may have pooled their resources in order to achieve a stake in colonial property, but like their Barbados compatriots they were now marked as belonging to the most important category on the island – landowners – and as such were asserting a status recognised by English elites.[23]

Although the vast majority of Irish property-owners held small plantations in Barbados and the Leeward Islands, making the transition from servant or labourer to planter, some Irish Catholics arrived in the colonies with the financial means to enter the planter class. The so-called 'fourteen tribes' of Galway, a prominent group of Catholics with Old English ancestry (who had been substantial landowners in Ireland until the Cromwellian era, when those lands were confiscated by the Protectorate), were particularly well represented in this endeavour.[24] The Blakes, the Lynches, and the Frenches arrived in the West Indies with the goal of making profits sufficient to buy back their Irish estates.[25] In the Caribbean, as in Ireland, they continued to operate within networks that drew on older associations, trading and intermarrying with other Irish families, making these Irish settlers similar to English planters who also drew on transatlantic familial connections in their business relations.[26]

Brothers Henry and John Blake travelled to the Caribbean in the 1660s to take advantage of the recent availability of land produced by confiscations following England's recent war with France, during which many Montserrat inhabitants sided with their co-religionists. The brothers set up joint ownership of one of the largest plantations on Montserrat, where Henry initially took up residence and began producing first tobacco and indigo, and then, by the mid-1670s, sugar.[27] John became a merchant in Bridgetown, Barbados, where he made deals with his brother-in-law Robert French to sell goods back to Galway.[28] Other prominent Irish planters in the Caribbean included Nicholas Rice and his nephew George Rice, both from Limerick. Each owned a large plantation in St Philip's Parish on Barbados, totalling 301 acres in the 1670s. William Stapleton, who rose to prominence as Governor in the Leeward Islands, had a Montserrat plantation encompassing 525 acres in 1668. By the time of his death two decades later he held similarly large estates on Antigua, Nevis and St Christopher.[29]

As members of the elite, these men were not only creating the circumstances under which they might build personal fortunes; they were also specifically concerned with the success of England's imperial ventures. This meant that these wealthier Irish Catholics, just as much as their English counterparts, sought to avoid the damaging effects of wars with foreign powers or internal uprisings by servants or enslaved Africans. It also meant that they were invested in the developing racial hierarchy on the islands. Irish Catholic enslavers distinguished themselves from poorer Irish servants and the inferior racial and gendered stereotypes that English observers associated with those groups.[30] Separating themselves from the Irish settler underclass further cemented the place of landowning Irish among the Caribbean elite.

Embracing English attitudes

John and Henry Blake emulated precisely the sort of derogatory attitudes that English elites held towards subordinates in correspondence from 1675. The letters, which concerned the women in John's Bridgetown household – his wife, an Irish servant and an enslaved African – reveal much about the brothers' ideas about hierarchy and its connection to mastery of the home. In 1668 Henry and John arrived in the Caribbean alone – their wives and children remained in Ireland. But in the mid-1670s, John decided to send for his wife, perhaps realising that his stay in the West Indies would be permanent. She was accompanied on her journey to Barbados by an unnamed Irish servant woman who appears to have caused a great deal of consternation among the male members of the Blake family.[31] In two extant letters, this servant woman, and the enslaved woman who was to replace her, became the means through which the brothers articulated their standing among island elites.

Henry was the first to mention the servant woman, expressing concern about her moral standing in a letter dated 29 May 1675, in which he described her as a 'whore' and suggested that 'she may be the occasion of

[John's] confusion by her seducement'. He noted that both their younger brother Nicholas, and their brother-in-law Robert French, had expressed similar concerns to John about the servant woman's character. In his reply in November of the same year, John asserted that while he understood his male relations' trepidation, the servant woman, whom he described as a 'wench', exhibited none of the undesirable traits ascribed to her, and that he had her under his control.[32] John clearly wanted to persuade his brothers that it was more prudent to keep a woman whose alleged vicissitudes he understood than to risk bringing an unknown entity into his home, arguing that any replacement 'may prove ten times worse than her'.[33] He claimed that the servant's labour was indispensable because his wife was too weak to manage household tasks herself, and finished the letter by suggesting that he had recently purchased 'a neger wench', but that until she was trained in how to run his household he could not afford to give up his Irish maid.[34]

Henry and John employed the terms 'whore' and 'wench' to underscore their superior status over the women who worked in John's household. Moreover, John understood that by removing his wife discursively from the discussion of everyday domestic labour within the household and by calling the character of a female servant into question he was conferring higher status upon himself and reinforcing the distance between the women in both social and economic terms. His wife may well have been incapable of taking on the kinds of tasks performed by the servant herself, but even had she been healthy it is unlikely that John would have wished her to perform such menial labour, as it would have marked her (and by association him) as being of lower status.[35]

John's letter revealed one more key component of the Irish Catholic transition to elite status: an investment in the emerging racial hierarchy on the islands. The one sort of labourer John could effortlessly substitute for his Irish servant was an enslaved woman, the 'neger wench' whom he suggested was being 'brought to knowledge' in his home.[36] Enslaved women who worked in households were an increasingly common feature of Barbados society by the 1670s.[37] John knew that there would be additional status attached to his ability to staff his home with an enslaved woman rather than an Irish servant. And the matter-of-fact way he stated the issue underscores his belief that his brothers would understand this concept and not object. Indeed, the Barbados census of 1680 showed that almost without exception every elite Bridgetown merchant had an enslaved person in their home. John was now among their number.

Cornelius Bryan's references to enslaved women in his will also demonstrate his absorption of elite ideals about racial hierarchies on the islands. In the manner of enslavers across the colonies, Bryan bequeathed to his wife, Margaret, 'one Negroe woman by name Grace' to be 'at her disposal forever'.[38] Bryan left another enslaved woman, Betty, to his eldest daughter, Alice. Like John Blake, Bryan recognised the importance of having an enslaved woman work within the home in his bequests to his wife and daughter. But there was an additional understanding of the specific value of enslaved women contained within his gesture. By leaving enslaved women to his wife and eldest daughter, he was also bequeathing their reproductive potential, increasing the chances of growing their family's wealth in the future.[39] Such attitudes about the reproductive value of enslaved women were widely held by English enslavers. That Bryan had so fully absorbed them indicates his acceptance of their ideas governing race, reproduction and slavery.

Bryan was not the only Irish planter to parcel out his property in this way. In 1673, Dennis Brien of St Andrew's Parish left an enslaved girl 'and her increase' to his son.[40] Cornelius Clancy acted similarly in Christchurch Parish in 1681 when he left two enslaved women 'and their increase' to be divided among his daughters Katherine, Wynefrid and Honor.[41] Teague Curreen from St Joseph left 'the negro Girl Pegg and her pickanniny' to his daughter Susannah in 1690, while Dennis Murphey in St Andrew's left an enslaved woman, Nanny, to his wife but 'her increase' to his sons when he wrote his last will and testament in 1696.[42] All of these men, and the scores of others like them, demonstrated their engagement with, and acceptance of, the system of racial slavery developing within the English Caribbean.

By employing the practices and discourses of English elites and embracing the hierarchies of colonial Caribbean society, Irish Catholic men forced English officials to reckon with their presence in the colonies in new ways. Protestant English colonials saw in propertied Irish Catholics men whose familial ties and relationships with inferiors very much resembled their own. The one distinction that remained was that of religion. As the spectre of Irish perfidy lingered, some Irish Catholics found yet another way to demonstrate their loyalty to England's imperial enterprise by rendering their religious practices unthreatening altogether.

Reducing religious threats

In the late 1660s, William Stapleton was appointed Governor of Montserrat; by the early 1670s he ascended the political ladder to become Governor of all the Leeward Islands.[43] Stapleton's rise was predicated on his loyalty to the English Crown during war with France in the late 1660s and his ability to reduce the threat posed by his Catholic faith by successfully steering the Leeward Islands through a period of relative peace in the decades that followed. Issues of revolt, rebellion and unruly Irish subjects did not arise during Stapleton's time in charge, or if they did, Stapleton did not allow that information to bleed into his correspondence with London. Moreover, Stapleton never referenced his own faith in his reports to the metropole, and he thought better of mentioning whatever religious demands arose among the Irish under his charge, despite their position as the majority population on the island.[44]

The only Montserrat Act that touched on the subject of religion was passed shortly after Stapleton became Governor in 1668. 'An Act for the raising a Maintenance for a preaching Minister' noted that as a result of the recent war with France the colony had been 'much destitute of a preaching Minister', causing 'Breaches of the Sabbath, and a general Neglect of publick Worship'. Stapleton's remedy was to request that 'an able preaching Orthodox Minister be procured' who would perform church services and administer the sacraments 'according to the Canons of the Church of *England*, and the known Laws of the said Realm'.[45] Reading this law, it seems that Stapleton actively encouraged Protestant worship in Montserrat. But a closer look indicates that what he was actually doing was assuaging London's anxieties about the large population of Irish Catholics on the island. One minister, while a start, would not be sufficient for the whole population of the island, and although Church of England preachers seemed always to be in short supply in the English Caribbean, the fact that not a single Protestant minister could be found on Montserrat suggests that the majority Catholic population were satisfying their religious needs elsewhere.[46]

Stapleton continued this kind of measured response when he was appointed Governor of all the Leeward Islands. In 1676, he made his most explicit statement about religion when he was specifically asked by the Lords of Trade and Plantations about the beliefs of the populations of each Leeward Island. Although he indicated that 'in Mountserrat there the most part are Roman Catholiques', he went on to stress that 'they give noe scandal to the Protestant Church which is the prevalent perswasion, for the minister when any comes preaches as in any other Island, every Licence of marriage, Probatt of wills, and all other Ecclesiasticall Acts are done according to the Cannons of the Church of England'.[47] Though 'the Romish in Montserratt is six to one Protestant', official religious ceremonies occurred under the auspices of the Church of England, at least on paper if not in practice. Stapleton's strategy facilitated a reading in London in which Catholics on the island were willing to accept the Church of England as a valid entity when it came to baptising their children, marrying and proving wills. By emphasising his engagement with Protestant norms, Stapleton subordinated his own Catholicism and that of the majority Irish population.[48]

Evidence suggests that despite his endorsement of Protestant ministers, Stapleton permitted Catholic practices to continue on Montserrat. During

James II's reign, Irish Catholics on the island petitioned the King for the right to support 'the Clergy [Catholic priests] under whose care wee were', rather than pay tithes to Protestant churches.[49] Although Stapleton died shortly before this petition was written, it is clear from the petitioners' plea that Catholic clergy had been active in Montserrat for decades and that they were part of the island's infrastructure when Stapleton was Governor. By avoiding discussions about religion on the islands as much as possible, Stapleton encouraged the impression of Irish Catholics as willing participants in England's colonial project. His strategy seemed to succeed in reducing English anxiety about Irish Catholics as a fifth column in their midst, as the volume of correspondence from London on this subject dropped off precipitously during his time in charge.[50]

Stapleton's success at softening the rebellious aspects of Irish Catholicism helped him promote a lifestyle that landowning Irish men could emulate. Similar attempts to downplay faith can be found in the actions of other Irish Catholics. Like half the Irish Catholic men who commissioned wills in Barbados, Cornelius Bryan asked to be buried in his garden at the discretion of his executors, who included his wife, Margaret.[51] Requesting burial on his land removed any questions about the appropriate place to lay his body, as churchyards in Barbados at this time were all Church of England. In Ireland women were in charge of burial rituals, so asking to be laid to rest in such a manner may have been Bryan's way of reconciling his Catholic faith with his status as planter.[52] Other planters like Teague Curreen and Patrick Collins made similar requests.[53] The Blakes said even less about their religious practices. John and Henry both asked to be remembered 'to Father Daniell', the family priest in Galway, but nothing else about how they practised their religion has made it into the record.[54] It seems probable that they simply kept their faith to themselves in Barbados and worshipped quietly in Montserrat under Stapleton's rule.[55] Little wonder that elite English men could look at their Irish counterparts and see an image that closely reflected their own.

Conclusion

By the start of the eighteenth century some Irish Catholics were accepted as members of the elite in English Caribbean colonies. Cornelius Bryan, Henry and John Blake, William Stapleton, and other small Irish landowners on both Barbados and Montserrat increasingly participated in the most American of institutions, the buying and selling of African women and men whose labour would be used to produce wealth in the form of sugar. It was not simply their roles as enslavers, however, that allowed Irish property-holders to join the ranks of the elite. These men had to adopt the kinds of attitudes towards inferiors, especially servants and enslaved Africans, that demonstrated their suitability for the upper strata of island society. And tempering fears about their Catholicism was the final step in their journey to more closely resembling English elites. By working within the hierarchies of the colonial Caribbean instead of trying to subvert them, these men encouraged English officials to rethink their former hostility towards anyone hailing from Ireland. Distinctions between English and Irish blurred as Irish Catholics such as Bryan, the Blakes, and Stapleton found ways to make themselves indispensable to England's imperial ambitions. Even the smallest acreage allowed former servants and labourers to turn a profit, find security, purchase an enslaved person, and so have an investment in the colonial system.

Cornelius Bryan began his Caribbean life on the margins of English colonial society – resentful of island authorities, his body bearing the scars that proved his antipathy towards English colonists. He died a planter, his life symptomatic of a larger trend in the experiences of Irish Catholics who navigated life in a Protestant English setting. In far-flung colonial settings, differences that were initially of central importance – like Bryan's Catholicism – began to recede as other categories, such as race, became the key markers of difference in society. It is hard to imagine someone like Bryan making similar threats in Ireland in the 1650s and being able to alter his life so dramatically. But in Barbados, where being white increasingly trumped other differences, routes to success were possible. Bryan may have harboured ill feelings towards English colonials, or he may never have felt any contradiction between his embrace of English imperialism on the one hand and his Irish background on the other. Regardless, he positioned himself such that enslaved Africans and poorer Irish servants were firmly below him in the complex colonial hierarchy, allowing himself to be accepted into white society in the process. The landowning enslaver and father of six who died on the island in 1686 bears little resemblance to his younger, more rebellious self. Twenty-two acres and thirteen enslaved Africans may not have constituted a large amount of property in late-seventeenth-century Barbados, but it was more than sufficient to turn a once perfidious papist into a planter who could prosper in the heart of England's Protestant empire. And Bryan was not alone.

Notes

1 Bridgetown Public Library (BPL), Lucas MSS 1.179, 15 January 1656.
2 The National Archives, London (TNA), CO 31/17/43, fo. 127, Barbados Council Minutes, 6 February 1656.
3 Barbados Department of Archives (BDA), RB 3/5, fo. 720, 16 March 1659; BDA, RB 3/9, fo. 89, 21 May 1675; BDA, RB 3/11, fo. 573, 20 October 1682; TNA, CO 1/44, no. 47 ii; TNA, CO 1/44, no. 47 xxxiv M.

4 BDA, RB 6/40, fo. 398, 21 May 1687.
5 Jane H. Ohlmeyer, *Making Ireland English: The Irish Aristocracy in the Seventeenth Century* (New Haven: Yale University Press, 2011); Nicholas P. Canny, *Making Ireland British* (New York: Oxford University Press, 2001); Kathleen M. Noonan, '"The cruel pressure of an enraged, barbarous people": Irish and English identity in seventeenth-century policy and propaganda, *Historical Journal* 41 (1998), 151–77; Anne Laurence, 'The cradle to the grave: English observations of Irish social customs in the seventeenth century', *Seventeenth Century* 3 (1988), 65–78; Ann Rosalind Jones and Peter Stallybrass, '"Rugges of London and the deuills band": Irish mantles and yellow starch as hybrid London fashions', in Lena Cowen Orlin, ed., *Material London, ca. 1600* (Philadelphia: University of Pennsylvania Press, 2000), pp. 128–35; Ann Rosalind Jones and Peter Stallybrass, 'Dismantling Irena: The sexualising of Ireland in early modern England', in Andrew Parker, Mary Russo, Doris Sommer, and Patricia Yaeger, eds, *Nationalisms and Sexualities* (New York: Routledge, 1992), pp. 151–71; Kathleen M. Brown, *Good Wives, Nasty Wenches, Anxious Patriarchs: Gender, Race, and Power in Colonial Virginia* (Chapel Hill: University of North Carolina Press, 1996), pp. 35–6.
6 Robert Armstrong, *Protestant War: The 'British' of Ireland and the Wars of the Three Kingdoms* (Manchester: Manchester University Press, 2005), Chapters 1 and 2. On the pamphlets produced and disseminated by English Protestants across the Three Kingdoms see Micheál Ó Siochrú, 'Atrocity, codes of conduct, and the Irish in the British civil wars, 1641–1653', *Past and Present* 195 (2007), 55–86; and Vincent Carey, 'Icons of atrocity: John Derricke's *Image of Irelande* (1581)', in Allison B. Kavey, ed., *World-Building and the Early Modern Imagination* (New York: Palgrave Macmillan, 2010), pp. 233–54.
7 Estimates of the numbers of Irish shipped to the Caribbean vary widely, but a range from 10,000 to 25,000 is probably most accurate. For the lower figure see Donald Harman Akenson, *If the Irish Ran the World: Montserrat, 1630–1730* (Montreal: McGill-Queen's University Press, 1997), p. 19. For the higher estimate (which includes Virginia) see William J. Smyth, *Map-Making, Landscapes and Memory: A Geography of Colonial and Early Modern Ireland, c. 1530–1750* (Cork: Cork University Press, 2006), pp. 161–2.
8 Hilary McD. Beckles, '"A riotous and unruly lot": Irish indentured servants and freemen in the English West Indies, 1644–1713', *William and Mary Quarterly* 47 (1990), 503–22. For work that briefly discusses the Irish see Russell R. Menard, *Sweet Negotiations: Sugar, Slavery, and Plantation Agriculture in Early Barbados* (Charlottesville: University of Virginia Press, 2006), p. 44; Richard S. Dunn, *Sugar and Slaves: The Rise of the Planter Class in the West-Indies, 1624–1713* (Chapel Hill: University of North Carolina Press, 1972), p. 69; and Carl Bridenbaugh and Roberta Bridenbaugh, *No Peace beyond the Line: The English in the Caribbean, 1624–1690* (Oxford: Oxford University Press, 1972), p. 112.
9 Akenson, *If*; Natalie A. Zacek, *Settler Society in the English Leeward Islands, 1670–1776* (Cambridge: Cambridge University Press, 2010), pp. 46–120;

Riva Berleant-Schiller, 'Free labor and the economy in seventeenth-century Montserrat', *William and Mary Quarterly* 46 (1989), 539–64; Lydia Pulsipher, 'The cultural landscape of Montserrat, West Indies, in the seventeenth century: Early environmental consequences of British colonial development', Ph.D. thesis (Southern Illinois University at Carbondale, 1977). On later associations between Irish Catholics and African slavery see Nini Rodgers, *Ireland, Slavery and Anti-Slavery: 1612–1865* (London: Palgrave Macmillan, 2007); and Peter D. O'Neill and David Lloyd, eds, *The Black and the Green Atlantic: Cross-Currents of the African and Irish Diasporas* (London: Palgrave Macmillan, 2009).
10 Dunn, *Sugar and Slaves*, pp. 59–67; Menard, *Sweet Negotiations*, pp. 39–41; Susan Dwyer Amussen, *Caribbean Exchanges: Slavery and the Transformation of English Society* (Chapel Hill: University of North Carolina Press, 2007), pp. 125–9.
11 Akenson, *If*; Jenny Shaw, *Everyday Life in the Early English Caribbean: Irish, Africans, and the Construction of Difference* (Athens: University of Georgia Press, 2013), esp. Chapter 6.
12 Dunn, *Sugar and Slaves*, pp. 67, 88–9, 91; Bridenbaugh and Bridenbaugh, *No Peace*, pp. 14, 111–13.
13 TNA, CO 1/44, no. 47 ii; TNA, CO 1/44, no. 47 xxxiv M.
14 BDA, RB 3/5, fo. 720, 16 March 1659.
15 BDA, RB 2/9 fo. 89, 21 May 1675.
16 TNA, CO 1/44, no. 47 ii.
17 BDA, RB 3/11, fo. 573, 20 October 1682.
18 TNA, CO 1/44, no. 47 XXI.
19 TNA, CO 1/44, no. 47 X, XII, XV, XVI, XVII, XXI.
20 TNA, CO 1/42, fos 45–59; Akenson, *If*, pp. 105–16; Zacek, *Settler Society*, pp. 46–65; Shaw, *Everyday Life*, Chapter 2.
21 Pulsipher, 'The cultural landscape', p. 64; Berleant-Schiller, 'Free labor'. Despite this demographic imbalance, Akenson suggests that Irish men in Montserrat were more likely to be married than their English counterparts; *If*, p. 115.
22 TNA, CO 1/42, fos 46–7.
23 For the Chesapeake comparison see Lois Green Carr and Russell R. Menard, 'Immigration and opportunity: The freedman in early colonial Maryland', in Thad W. Tate and David L. Ammerman, eds, *The Chesapeake in the Seventeenth Century: Essays on Anglo-American Society and Politics* (Chapel Hill: University of North Carolina Press, 1979), pp. 206–42.
24 See Canny, *Making Ireland British*, pp. 412–14, 456, 553; Brendan Bradshaw and Dáire Keogh, eds, *Christianity in Ireland: Revisiting the Story* (Dublin: Columba Press, 2002), p. 81; Louis B. Cullen, 'Galway merchants in the outside world, 1650–1800', in Diarmuid O'Cearbhaill, ed., *Galway Town and Gown, 1484–1984* (Dublin: Giull and Macmillan, 1984), pp. 69–70; Akenson, *If*, p. 69.
25 See, for example, letter from Henry Blake to John Blake, Montserrat, 23 May 1676, reprinted in Vere Langford Oliver, *Caribbeana: Being miscellaneous*

papers relating to the history, genealogy, topography, and antiquities of the British West Indies, 6 vols (London: Mitchell, Hughes and Clarke, 1910–19), Vol. I, p. 56.

26 Family tree, in *ibid.*, Vol. I, pp. 53–4. For more on elite Irish marriage alliances see Mary O'Dowd, *A History of Women in Ireland, 1500–1800* (London: Longman, 2004), pp. 14–15.

27 Letter from Henry Blake to John Blake, Montserrat, 22 July 1673, in Oliver, *Caribbeana*, Vol. 1, pp. 51–2.

28 Montserrat, 11 May 1676, in *ibid.*, Vol. I, p. 56.

29 Manchester, John Rylands Library, Stapleton MSS, Box 2, no. 1, fo. 4, no. 4.

30 Shaw, *Everyday Life*, pp. 163–7; Jennifer L. Morgan, *Laboring Women: Reproduction and Gender in New World Slavery* (Philadelphia: University of Pennsylvania Press, 2004), p. 148; Hilary McD. Beckles, *White Servitude and Black Slavery, 1627–1715* (Knoxville: University of Tennessee Press, 1989), p. 139; Dunn, *Sugar and Slaves*, p. 108.

31 On Irish women managing households in the absence of husbands who had journeyed overseas see O'Dowd, *A History*, pp. 92–3. For Irish women travelling to the Caribbean see Jerrold Casway, 'Irish women overseas, 1500–1800', in Margaret MacCurtain and Mary O'Dowd, eds, *Women in Early Modern Ireland* (Edinburgh: Edinburgh University Press, 1991), pp. 112–32 (pp. 125–7); Cecily Forde-Jones, 'Mapping racial boundaries: Gender, race, and poor relief in Barbados plantation society', *Journal of Women's History* 10 (1998), 9–31 (p. 13); and Amussen, *Caribbean Exchanges*, p. 228.

32 Montserrat, 29 May 1675, in Oliver, *Caribbeana*, Vol. I, p. 55. John claimed that he used 'the most severe correction' to keep the servant woman in line. Punishments for servants in the Caribbean exceeded those meted out in England in the 1650s; Dunn, *Sugar and Slaves*, p. 72.

33 The presence of the servant 'wench' allowed a hierarchy of labour to develop in the households of the elite; Brown, *Good Wives*, p. 101.

34 Bridgetown, Barbados, 5 November 1675, in Oliver, *Caribbeana*, Vol. I, pp. 55–6.

35 Morgan, *Laboring Women*, p. 225; Mary Beth Norton, *Founding Mothers and Fathers: Gendered Power and the Forming of American Society* (New York: Alfred A. Knopf, 1996), pp. 10, 29–30, 57, 77.

36 Bridgetown, Barbados, 5 November 1675, in Oliver, *Caribbeana*, Vol. I, pp. 55–6.

37 Morgan, *Laboring Women*, p. 148; Amussen, *Caribbean Exchanges*, pp. 88–9; Hilary McD. Beckles, *Natural Rebels: A Social History of Enslaved Black Women in Barbados* (New Brunswick: Rutgers University Press, 1989), pp. 57–8.

38 BDA, RB 6/40, no. 398.

39 Morgan, *Laboring Women*, pp. 82–3.

40 BDA, RB 6/6, fo. 141, 12 December 1673.

41 BDA, RB 6/14, fo. 278, 16 September 1681.

42 BDA, RB 6/41, fo. 359, 23 September 1690; RB 6/11, fo. 432, 12 January 1696.

43 For more on Stapleton's role see Akenson, *If*; Zacek, *Settler Society*; and Shaw, *Everyday Life*, esp. Chapters 2 and 6.
44 TNA, CO 153/3, fo. 119, Stapleton to the Lords of Trade and Plantations, Nevis, 29 March 1684; TNA, CO 1/29, no. 15, 'An Account of the Leeward Islands', transmitted 17 July 1672.
45 TNA, CO 176/1, 'The Laws of Montserrat' (my emphasis).
46 On the lack of Church of England ministers see Larry Dale Gragg, *Englishmen Transplanted: The English Colonization of Barbados, 1624–1660* (Oxford: Oxford University Press, 2003). On Irish religious practices in the Americas in the seventeenth century see Akenson, *If*; Zacek, *Settler Society*; and Shona Helen Johnston, 'Papists in a Protestant world: the Catholic anglo-Atlantic in the seventeenth century', Ph.D. thesis (Georgetown University, 2011).
47 TNA, CO 153/2, fo. 187, Stapleton to the Lords of Trade and Plantations, 19 August 1676, answer to question 20.
48 Zacek, *Settler Society*, pp. 83–4; Akenson, *If*, p. 102. See also Shaw, *Everyday Life*, Chapter 6.
49 TNA, CO 1/63, no. 70, 'Petition of Roman Catholicks', Montserrat, 23 November 1687.
50 For the tenor of discussion before and after Stapleton's tenure see BPL, Lucas MSS, reel 1, fo. 368, 22 September 1657; TNA, CO 152/37, no. 10, 10 June 1689; TNA, CO 28/37, no. 21, 2 September 1689; TNA, CO 31/4, fo. 339, 20 April 1693. See also Johnston, 'Papists in a Protestant World', p. 247.
51 BDA, RB 6/40, no. 398.
52 Laurence, 'The cradle to the grave', pp. 76–8; Susan Leigh Fry, *Burial in Medieval Ireland, 900–1500: A Review of Written Sources* (Dublin: Four Courts Press, 1999), pp. 124–6; Clodagh Tait, *Death, Burial, and Commemoration in Ireland, 1550–1650* (London: Palgrave, 2002).
53 BDA, RL 1/1, p. 371, 3 April 1668; BDA, RL 1/17, p. 111, 24 November 1678.
54 Montserrat, 29 May 1675, and Bridgetown, Barbados, 5 November 1675, in Oliver, *Caribbeana*, Vol. I, pp. 55 and 55–6 respectively.
55 For more on Irish Catholic practices in the Caribbean see Shaw, *Everyday Life*, Chapters 4 and 5.

3

Free, and unfree: Ireland and Barbados, 1620–1660

David Brown

In August 1649, the greater part of Oliver Cromwell's army for the conquest of Ireland arrived at Ringsend, near Dublin. The crossing of this invasion force was assisted by the English Parliament's Admiral for the Irish Seas, George Ayscue. Ayscue commanded a smaller force with a similar mission to Barbados and the Antilles in the autumn of 1651.[1] The primary aim of both expeditions, to Ireland and Barbados, was to secure parliamentary rule in each and to prevent either from becoming a source of support for Charles II. Until Charles's Restoration in 1660, a small group of English naval and military commanders, civil officials and private merchants designed and resourced England's nascent empire. The extreme violence of Ireland's conquest contrasts with the relative peacefulness of Barbados's capitulation to Parliament, and while Barbados experienced its first sugar boom in the 1650s, Ireland suffered a long decade of military rule and local insurgencies. Under the Cromwellian Protectorate, 1653–8, the role of African enslavement in Barbados's system of plantation agriculture shifted from importance to ubiquity. Ireland's role in this terrible transformation was as the labour supply of last resort, when supplies from Africa were interrupted or unavailable. During the 1650s, Irish people were sent involuntarily to labour in Barbados in conditions that were similar to, but not identical with, slavery. This chapter examines Irish sources that have newly come to light, in concordance with primary sources in Barbados and elsewhere, to create a chronology and contextualise the circumstances under which transportations of people took place from Ireland, and the outcomes.[2]

The historiographies of Cromwellian rule for Ireland and Barbados have evolved separately, as both countries exited from colonial rule in different ways. Ireland fought a war of independence from 1919 to 1922 before suffering a phased and divisive partial sovereignty, while Barbados achieved full independence through a negotiated settlement almost a half century later.[3] From the Irish perspective, apart from a brief mention by John Prendergast at the end of the nineteenth century, the first, and essentially last, detailed study from primary sources of the Irish in Barbados was by Aubrey Gwynn in the 1930s.[4] Working after the destruction of the Public Record Office of Ireland in 1922, Gwynn found his sources limited to published calendars of English State papers; a small number of printed extracts from the records of the Commonwealth and Protectorate Governments in Ireland, copied before the original records were destroyed; and Ligon's *History*, written in 1657.[5] Gwynn did not have access to a full set of original State papers, or to archival sources in Barbados. Nonetheless, Gwynn's remains the standard text, drawn on by subsequent scholars in Ireland together with the same published accounts that Gwynn used as his own sources.

The equivalent to Gwynn's scholarship from the Barbados perspective draws from the pioneering research by Sir Hilary McD. Beckles, who has published extensively on this topic since 1981.[6] Beckles can be credited with the scrupulous separation of 'servant', an unfree labourer whose service would eventually terminate, and 'slave', whose unfree status was permanent and hereditary. In this system, servants were invariably white, and European, enslaved people mostly black and African, while some Amerindians also continued to be exploited by the planters. Beckles was careful to point out that little is revealed about the Irish in Barbadian primary sources during the period of the Protectorate.[7] This cautionary note, however, has gone unheeded during an avalanche of recent interest in the topic that has produced much commentary but little by way of detailed further archival research. An ideological history has instead emerged, reflecting modern trends towards simplification and polarisation. Jerome Handler and Matthew Reilly tie this limited debate to the campaign for financial compensation for historical enslavement and argue that the mere acknowledgement of Irish enslavement 'has been used to undermine arguments in favour of reparations for the injustices of slavery'.[8] This is true, but this approach, taken without re-examining the sources, veers towards a form of self-censorship that academic historians cannot accept. From an Irish perspective, the foregrounding of Irish suffering serves to underscore the traditional narrative of Catholic Ireland as an imperial conquest, subjugated by an aggressive and mighty neighbour. The revisionist reality is far more nuanced, and historians now preserve the contemporary categorisations of the early modern inhabitants of Ireland into New English, Old English and native Irish divisions. New English refers to immigrants from Britain who settled in Ireland during the course of a wave of plantations from the late sixteenth to the early seventeenth century, while native Irish are the original, indigenous and almost invariably Catholic population. The Old English are the vaguest of the three groups, defined by Aidan Clarke in 1966 as 'neither Irish nor Protestant but characterised by a set of common interests and attitudes'.[9] Originally descended from the Anglo-Norman colonisation of the late Middle Ages, this group also incorporated families of native

Irish stock who had adopted their customs or were welcomed into their pre-Reformation ascendancy for other reasons. Many came from the merchant classes, and these Old English merchants continued to dominate all seaports in Ireland outside Ulster well into the plantation period. Colonists from Ireland during the seventeenth century brought these cultural and ethnic differences with them to the new plantations in the Caribbean. Given the commercial dominance of Old English merchants in Irish ports, it is unsurprising that these merchants featured strongly in England's western expansion, yet this is a key involvement that has been overlooked. Modern writers maintain that Catholic colonisers from Ireland could only have been involved in the colonial projects of other Catholic powers, and entire histories of early European colonisation now appear without mentioning Ireland at all.[10]

The binary categorisation of unfree labour into 'blacks' and 'whites' oversimplifies the importance of nationality, ethnicity and religion to English settlers in Barbados. For example, English servants normally had indentures: contracts that theoretically limited their term of labour with some legal rights of redress for unfair treatment. Prisoners and convict labour had fewer rights. In 1654 Scottish prisoners, shipped to Barbados in large numbers by Cromwell from the early 1650s, were granted the same rights as their English servants by the Barbados Assembly following Scotland's incorporation into the Commonwealth.[11] The Irish, however, as a conquered nation, were left out of this arrangement, just when transports of Irish prisoners and captives peaked. Assuming that all white labourers in the English Caribbean were indentured assumes that all were English, or later Scottish, and had access to formal institutions for redress. The Irish had no such access. In 1658, a Jesuit priest in Lisbon commented on a ship containing Irish captives he had seen, 'loaded with slaves bound for Barbados' and blown into harbour by a storm.[12] A Jesuit priest in Lisbon knew what a slave was. This document is in the collection of official state papers of John Thurloe, secretary to the English Council of State, yet current literature confidently states that European governments never contemplated Europeans as enslaved people.[13] Conflating 'white' and Irish, which is effectively conflating English and Irish, misses the central point of the status of the native Irish under the Commonwealth and Cromwellian Protectorate. The Irish, by a series of Acts and orders from August 1652 until May 1658, were collectively guilty of multiple crimes and misdemeanours that were punishable by indefinite transportation to Barbados, to work for subsistence as the property of English planters. There are no mentions in the surviving literature of indentures, nor have any ever been produced indicating that the people transported from Ireland during the 1650s could ever expect to be freed. From a practical perspective, it should also be considered whether the slave-owners and planters at the purchasing end of the slave trade had any intention of ever releasing their captive Irish labour. The mass forced transports from Ireland to Barbados were unique to the time of the Cromwellian Protectorate: just a few years, which is not enough time to draw firm conclusions as to what the long-term fate of these people might have been. During this period, the day-to-day lives of enslaved Africans and forced Irish labour appears to be similar, and only in death was it possible to separate enslaved Africans from white Irish servants.[14] As Christians, the Irish had to be buried according to Christian custom.

Ireland had a central role in the development of European colonies in the Americas during the first half of the seventeenth century. Its location made it a key provisioning stop for early expeditions from northern Europe to North America and the Caribbean.[15] Ireland also provided labour and capital for colonial expansion. As Europe's colonies expanded and began to produce agricultural commodities to exchange for European manufactured goods, well-populated and convenient Ireland also became an important market for incoming colonial produce. A unique combination of wealthy Catholic Old English and Protestant New English merchant houses enabled Irish ports to trade with vessels from most European states on a more or less equal basis. In 1610, for example, the port of Cork welcomed merchant vessels from France, Spain, Middelburg and London, in addition to supplying the Virginia Company of London's colonising expeditions to Jamestown.[16] By the 1630s, merchant houses from Ireland had become significant colonisers in their own right, especially on Caribbean islands patented to the James Hay, First Earl of Carlisle, by King Charles I, but this phase of colonial development came to an abrupt end with the outbreak of the Irish rebellion in October 1641.[17] Ireland's role as a commercial centre and colonising nation was irreversibly transformed by the expulsion of Irish merchants from major ports during the Commonwealth and Protectorate Governments of the 1650s. Since then, the narrative of colonial development in the Caribbean has been constructed using the orthodoxy of an English or British Atlantic world, and the role of Ireland in its early development has been more or less forgotten.[18]

With Ireland's role as a promoter of early colonial schemes excised from the broader narrative, the attention of historians has focused instead on the experience of the Irish as a source of labour. Irish labour was commonplace in all of England's colonies in the early seventeenth century, and there is also strong evidence of a sustained Irish presence in Dutch, Spanish and Portuguese colonial possessions.[19] Emphasising Irish labour while removing capital to the shadows has created an impression that the Irish were European victims of English colonial ambition and only occasional partners in the western expansion.

In fact, English colonial projectors relied heavily on resources from Ireland to realise their early ambitions. In 1618, King James I granted a patent to a consortium led by Lord Robert Rich, the future Earl of Warwick, to trade for gold and other goods on the Guinea coast and Bight of Benin.[20] A second patent was granted by Charles I in 1631 to a separate company, led by Oliver Clobery, Sir Nicholas Crispe and Humphrey Slany, to trade on the Gold Coast.[21]

Neither company's charter mentions enslaved people, and no English company was officially licensed to enter the slave trade fully until a reformed Royal Africa Company was chartered in 1663.[22] Instead, English merchants were preoccupied with finding gold, taking a particular interest in the River Gambia, and they sent regular expeditions hundreds of miles up-river, beginning in 1619. They built a small trading post they called James Island, about 30 km up-river from the Atlantic coast.[23] Another merchant, John Wood, who appears to have operated independently, established a trading post at Tumba on the coast of Sierra Leone, trading iron and alcohol for camwood, a timber that contains a dye used in cloth manufacture.[24] Although the coast of West Africa was theoretically a Portuguese trading area, it was successfully infiltrated at multiple locations by both English and Dutch trading operations by the 1630s.

The second Guinea Company established a highly valuable trade for gold, bartering iron sourced from the smelting operation of Richard Boyle, the First Earl of Cork, at Bandon.[25] This iron, cast into flat bars, was manufactured specifically for the African market. Bar iron became the standard currency in Senegambia during the early decades of the seventeenth century. Together with other manufactured goods, cheap Irish cloth, and especially iron, transformed the fortunes of local rulers within reach of the Europeans.[26] The impact of Boyle's iron could also be felt far into the African interior. Compared to English or Dutch iron, Irish iron was cheap, because of the plentiful supply of timber for smelting.[27] The competitiveness of Irish iron distorted the trade routes of the African interior, which had existed for centuries, drawing Senegambian gold away from interior markets such as Timbouktou and towards the coast. Coinciding with, and perhaps because of, these economic developments, the middle region of the Gambia became a conflict zone. A strong feudal state from the gold-producing upper region, the Malinke, began the process of conquering a weaker state in the middle, the Tenda, which was more a collection of cooperative clans rather than a centralised polity. The Malinke brought gold from Bambuk, around the upper tributaries of the River Senegal, and enslaved people from the Dyalonke in the uplands, to trade with the Europeans. The Tenda were eventually removed from their homelands.[28]

The English Caribbean developed in tandem with these early incursions into West Africa. These colonial projects also involved the Earls of Warwick and Cork, and a third peer, James Hay, the Earl of Carlisle. A patent covering the entire Caribbean was obtained by the Earl of Carlisle from Charles I in 1625, ignoring existing Spanish claims to the region in the same way that Portuguese claims to West Africa were disregarded. Carlisle contracted a merchant, Maurice Thompson, to help him develop St Kitts, at the northern end of the Antilles.[29] Maurice Thompson also worked for the Earl of Warwick and was already involved in establishing Warwick's colony in Bermuda. The St Kitts venture was financed from Munster by a consortium of merchants associated with the Earl of Cork, who obtained leases from Carlisle. One of these lessees, Phane Beecher Jr, left Bandon for St Kitts in 1627 to establish this Munster plantation.[30] Another Munster planter, Anthony Briskett of Dungarvan, arrived the following year to manage the colony.[31]

The Earl of Warwick revived his original Guinea patent from 1618, and contracted Thompson to charter three ships at Southampton, purchase sixty enslaved people in West Africa and transport them to St Kitts.[32] These people were intended to replace a large population of native Irish servants who had been forcibly transplanted from Wexford by Sir Arthur Chichester to make way for incoming English settlers in the 1620s.[33] It made commercial sense for the new investors to replace the Irish labourers, whose indentures had expired, with enslaved Africans. The Irish servants were moved first to the neighbouring island of Nevis, and to Montserrat after Nevis was attacked by a Spanish fleet in 1628.[34] Copying the model established by the Portuguese on São Tomé in the Gulf of Guinea, the Munster-financed colony of St Kitts – an island that was impossible to escape from and too small to hide on – became the first colony to depend on enslaved African labour in the English Atlantic world. Montserrat, with similar topography, continued to be dominated by Irish indentured labour. In its earliest and crudest form, therefore, what became the triangular slave trade of the English Atlantic world originated with New English associates of Richard Boyle in Co. Cork. Boyle's access to gold greatly helped the rapid expansion of his landed estates, while Caribbean tobacco swelled the profits of his local customs farm.[35] English merchants from London, however, were in overall control of the development of the colonies. Sir Thomas Warner was appointed Governor of the Leeward Islands by Carlisle in 1629, and his expedition was financed from the English capital by Maurice Thompson.[36]

The system of enslavement was also adopted on Barbados from its earliest settlement by English colonisers. The first, in 1626, bought thirty-two Amerindian and two African enslaved people from Portuguese dealers on the South American mainland shortly after their arrival, and brought them back to Barbados to do their farm work.³⁷ The island developed slowly as an agricultural colony until 1640, producing mainly cotton, tobacco, indigo and some sugar, but economic progress was far slower than on the smaller islands to the north. Generally, there was no shortage of colonists from England or Ireland prepared to try their luck in the new lands, although becoming an early coloniser was not without considerable risk to life during the initial phase of land clearances. One way the planter colonists devised to transfer some of the risk of their new enterprises to their workers was the widespread introduction of the 'indenture', borrowed from the urban apprenticeship system, although no training in new skills was on offer. The worker contracted to labour without wages for the planter for a defined period, normally four years; to repay their passage to the colony; and for their subsistence during their term of service. At the end of the term, they expected to receive their freedom and either a small parcel of land or a cash payment. During the early colonial period, while new land was continually being claimed and made available for clearing, not only was this system of indentured labour cheaper than acquiring enslaved people, but productivity was higher, as the servant was incentivised with the possibility of independence. While there were some attempts to introduce enslaved people into the labour system, the European indentured servant remained the mainstay of labour on Barbados throughout the 1630s.³⁸

Several events conspired at around the same time to upset this quiet and unremarkable progress. Early in 1639, James Hay, Second Earl of Carlisle, inherited the proprietorship of Barbados from his father and decided arbitrarily to increase the rents paid to him by the planters. A widespread revolt broke out on the island that only ended when a new Governor, Henry Huncks, was appointed, and Anthony Briskett was brought in from St Kitts to restore order. A petition was sent back to England on 24 March 1639, confirming obedience to the King and Carlisle and reportedly signed by 10,000 inhabitants.³⁹ 500 settlers, most likely Irish, decided to leave the crowded island and try their luck in Spanish Florida.⁴⁰ As workers left, in late 1640 the senior planters bribed Huncks to ban any further migration, while a more profitable crop needed to be introduced to pay the higher rent. Sugar was an obvious solution, but was highly labour-intensive and required a constant influx of new immigrants. With the eruption of widespread rebellion in Ireland on 23 October 1641, the supply of Irish labour slowed to a trickle, and the outbreak of civil war in England the following year brought an effective halt to all immigration. The economic survival of the island would require labour from another source.

Until 1641, a significant cohort of Old English merchants came to Barbados from the southern ports of Ireland with grander aspirations than the native Irish labourers. The most prominent of these was Stephen Rice, who hailed from a merchant family spread between Dingle and Limerick.[41] Rice consolidated a large estate, buying land from the English planters as well as small tracts from freed Irish servants.[42] Other planters from Limerick, David and Thomas Bourke, owned smaller lots and joined forces with two further planters, Thomas Cohan and Morgan O'Carry, to assemble another large Old English estate.[43] Waterford's Old English merchants were led by William Blake and Richard Fitzgerald, and there is evidence in the recopied deed books at the Barbados Department of Archives of small Old English plantations throughout the island.[44] Although the Catholic Church was suppressed on the island, their religious needs were met by a small community of friars at St Christopher's Parish.[45] The Old English planter families from Ireland had been trading with mercantile families in English ports for centuries, and ports such as Plymouth and Exeter provided many of the additional settlers. This peaceful co-existence ended abruptly in the aftermath of the Irish rebellion of October 1641, perhaps because they were no longer trusted by their English neighbours, but also because the home ports of the Old English planters in Ireland had become disrupted and, in some cases, destroyed. Ports seized by the rebels in Ireland quickly became bases for piratical attacks against English colonial shipping, further antagonising Protestant English settlers on Barbados against their Catholic neighbours.[46] Many Catholic planters sold up and moved to other areas in the Caribbean, or tried their luck elsewhere in the region.[47]

The outbreak of civil war in England in 1642 exacerbated the difficulties faced by both communities of Barbados planters, with English planters divided along royalist and parliamentarian lines, and Old English planters from Ireland firmly in the royalist camp. Necessity, however, drove intensified sugar cultivation and production to dominate the island's economy completely during the 1640s. Barbados became, quite quickly, entirely dependent on African slave labour, as this was the only source available. The direct slave trade, from Africa to Barbados, was supplied mainly by Dutch merchants who purchased captives in the slave markets of Accra and Lagos. The remaining labour was sourced in nearby slave markets such as Curaçao. By the end of the decade, Barbados had become a slave economy with a single crop – sugar – which also served as its currency. After the execution of Charles I in 1649, Barbados decided to support the exiled King, Charles II. A parliamentarian peer, Francis Willoughby, bought Carlisle's patent, defected, and set himself up as Governor of Barbados with the King's blessing. His son, Thomas, sailed immediately for the African coast in search of a cargo of enslaved people. What Willoughby's governorship meant, in effect, was that the staunchest parliamentarians, including many of the leading planters, either had their estates seized or were evicted from the island altogether. Parliament's response was to ban all English trade with

Barbados for the time being, but this meant that all of the sugar was sold to Dutch merchants, who eagerly seized the opportunity.

During the English civil wars, the royalist cohort from the old Guinea Company remained active in the African slave trade by working with the Portuguese. To contain their losses to Dutch privateers, in 1649 the Portuguese Government established the Portuguese Brazil Company in Lisbon.[48] Portuguese naval power was stretched to its limit protecting the East Indies trade and was unable to spare resources for the Atlantic, despite Brazil's remaining the largest market for enslaved African people. The Brazil Company decided to charter naval vessels from former royalist supporters of Charles I, keen to disrupt the parliamentarian merchants' dominance of trade with the English colonies.[49] A successful strategy of convoying immediately removed the Dutch naval threat, although a stand-off ensued between the two English fleets, royalist and parliamentarian, at Lisbon in March 1650.[50] It took over a year of legal wrangling before all of the ships were finally released and English involvement in the Portuguese slave trade resumed on a smaller scale.

Parliament's next move was to send naval forces to wrest control of the colonies from royalist sympathisers. The Caribbean fleet was commanded by George Ayscue, who had also commanded the invasion fleet for Cromwell's conquest of Ireland. Taking advantage of the opportunity presented by the parliamentary navy undertaking the subjugation of the colonies, the English parliamentary merchants decided it was time to organise the slave trade on a large scale and tried to coordinate a major private slaving expedition with the fleet sent to Barbados. The English Navigation Act of 1651 restricted the colonies to trade with English vessels, leaving the colonial slave trade ready for exploitation. In September 1651 Maurice Thompson and John Wood, both of whom had enjoyed a very lucrative civil war, joined forces and sent a ship, the *Friendship*, to the Gambia to purchase fifteen enslaved people and bring them to London.[51] It was an unusual and expensive mission, but the enslaved were to impress potential investors for a wider project. Thompson and Wood were awarded the Guinea Company patent by Cromwell the previous April, but appear to have had trouble raising support for a substantial venture until the Navigation Act was passed. The *Friendship* was soon replaced by a larger vessel, the *Supply*, and a frigate owned by Samuel Vassall and Robert Llewellin, the *John*, to purchase a full cargo of enslaved people and bring them to Barbados.[52] Vassall was a parliamentarian MP for London whose brother, William, resided in both Barbados and New England. The new partners intended a regular supply run between the Gambia and Barbados, built a fortified settlement in the middle of the River Gambia and contracted to deliver a further 200 enslaved people in 1652.[53] This expedition, however, soon ran into difficulties, as in the absence of any meaningful engagement in the region by the Guinea Company, a party of Courland merchants pre-empted the return of the English to Gambia and built their own fortifications.[54] To make matters worse for the English parliamentarian slaving expedition, an English royalist fleet under the command of Prince Rupert of the Rhine, nephew of Charles I, arrived soon after them. Initially, the Guinea Company ships attempted to hide up-river and wait out Rupert's blockade, but the crews became sick and began to die in large numbers. One ship was abandoned and the other two were forced to escape at night without their cargoes.

Barbados had not yet fully become a slave economy. English labour began to arrive voluntarily on the island during the 1650s, as the civil wars drew to a close and shrinking armies left a surplus of young men. There are even isolated cases of Irish migrants arriving at Bridgetown and voluntarily going into service with English masters. The most unusual case is that of a contingent of Irish prisoners of war, smuggled by their Irish commander to Barbados to serve in the plantation of a kinsman. Just before Barbados declared for the King-in-exile, Charles II, James Barry, an Old English kinsman of the Earl of Barrymore, who had doggedly kept his plantation going since 1641, was imprisoned on the instructions of James Drax, a parliamentarian military commander. Barry's servants were tortured to provide admissions of some type of impropriety. The Barrys were among the earliest investors in the development of Barbados, and creditors of the Earl of Carlisle. Prevented through lack of labour from developing his plantation while the sugar boom was gaining momentum in the early 1650s, in July 1652 Colonel William Barry oversaw the despatch of 238 Catholic soldiers from Great Island in Cork to Barbados. These soldiers were intended for Spain, but Barry had arranged an obscure legal instrument, 'special justice', to change these arrangements, and bribed Colonel Robert Phair, the Governor of Cork, with £138 to turn a blind eye.[55]

There is no documentary evidence of a sustained official policy to transport soldiers to the colonies. During the formal period of war, from the start of Cromwell's campaign in August 1649 until the surrender of Galway in June 1652, most garrisons surrendered under 'articles of war'. These surrenders were normally scrupulously adhered to by Cromwell and his subcommanders, making the instances when the normal rules of war were disregarded, for example at Drogheda and Wexford, all the more notorious.[56] Depending on the terms of these surrenders, soldiers could leave their besieged towns, partially armed and sometimes with full regimental colours, but had mainly promised to leave Ireland. During the early 1650s, the usual destination of soldiers was Spain, but from the middle of the decade soldiers were exiled to France, as hostilities broke out between England and Spain. The sale of soldiers to Spain and France was, of itself, a big business bringing in thousands of pounds in licensing fees to a financially beleaguered English Government in Ireland. It was a much larger business than the people-trafficking trade to the Caribbean at the same time. Cromwell's sole instruction regarding the transport of any Irish other than the garrison at Drogheda was issued to General George Fleetwood in January 1652. This was a recommendation that some 'merchants of Bristol' should be allowed to ship 400 Irish Tories and vagrants to the Caribbean.[57]

Cromwell's warrant was one of two immediate responses to the merchants' failure in the Gambia, the other being that James Drax began to send his own slaving expeditions directly from Barbados to the Guinea coast, although he could only afford to send one or two ships at a time. The Guinea Company, meanwhile, had promised to deliver 200 unfree labourers to Barbados in 1652. There may have been a contract with penalties for non-delivery, for on 7 October 1652, a London merchant, Robert Lewellin, purchased part of Cromwell's Bristol warrant and converted it into a licence to transport 300 male Irish prisoners to Barbados.[58] Lewellin was also involved in the Gambia expedition with Thompson, Wood and Vassall, as a part owner of the ships. Irish captives became, therefore, a direct alternative to enslaved African people. A further crisis struck the Barbados planter community in the summer of 1654 when the Dutch were driven from their South American strongholds by the Portuguese, ending their participation in the slave trade to Barbados for the time being. For the Barbados planters, with demand for sugar continuing to rise, the demise of the Dutch could not have come at a worse time. Desperate for labour, English planters had never paid much attention to the strictures of the Navigation Act, and relied on Dutch slave markets in the Caribbean for their labour. With the Dutch driven out, the planters once again turned to Ireland, the source of labour that had served them well when the Guinea Company had failed them in 1652.

Thus was Ireland drawn into the slave trade, caused in the first instance by the Gambia failure and then by the fall of Dutch Brazil. A combination of Cromwell's initiative and the presence of many Irish labourers on Barbados already made Ireland an obvious place to look.

Cromwell's vague instruction, which included petty vagrants as well as irregular soldiers, gave the impression that these were rules that could be stretched – something the Barbados planters had some experience at. They were not, however, experienced traffickers of people. In May 1653, a slave ship, the *Negro*, arrived in Dublin and purchased a cargo of prisoners from the jail. The ship moved on, calling at Kinsale and then Cork until it was full. The captain, Thomas Lockier, was often drunk, and the ship got lost, calling first at St Kitts and then at Montserrat, where the Irish captives were sold.[59] This amateur approach was of no help to the planters of Barbados, so steps were taken to license the trade formally through authorities in Ireland.

In May 1655, Robert Molesworth, a Dublin merchant whose brother was the treasurer of the Barbados Council, applied for and obtained a licence to ship 1,000 people convicted of common vagrancy to Barbados.[60] A second licence was awarded to Humberston Hurst to ship vagrants from Kinsale, and a third to John Moglane for Waterford.[61] On 9 August, Roger Boyle, Lord Broghill, secured a licence to ship a further 300 prisoners to Antigua. On 25 October, Lewellin received an expanded licence and was awarded permission to transport hundreds more men and women. The transports were organised through the ports of Dublin, Wexford, Cork and Kinsale. The trade was managed by Molesworth in Dublin, Thomas Smith in Waterford, Hurst in Kinsale, Thomas Sadlier in Wexford and William Hawkins in Cork.[62] Sadlier, Parliament's Military Governor of Wexford, had relatives in Barbados, and a London-based cousin who acted as a solicitor for English investors in the Caribbean.[63] Hawkins was both the brother-in-law of Maurice Thompson and High Sheriff of Cork precinct.[64] The involvement of Sadlier and Hawkins, and the return of Lewellin's vessels to Ireland, demonstrate that the large-scale transports, those of 1655–6, were an extension of the slave trade, organised by the Guinea Company merchants who were temporarily shut out of West Africa by hostile forces.

The forced transportation of people was organised throughout Ireland. William Rowe, an army supplier, handled the transports from Ulster.[65] Rowe was a close business partner of Martin Noel, one of Cromwell's leading financiers, whose brother lived in Barbados and was a member of the Assembly.[66] On 26 October 1655, the dragnet was widened beyond those convicted of a common criminal offence to encompass all who had failed to transplant themselves to Connacht. These people were not even paid for, but an extra ten provided with every hundred for the shipper to dispose of as they wished. In addition, the authorities in Dublin received licence fees, and the sheriffs and jailers hefty bribes to take part in what was the most profitable aspect of colonial trade, the supply of unfree labour. Business was so good that when faced with empty prisons, on 29 July 1656, the English Parliament's council in Dublin issued a warrant to William Hawkins that allowed him to arrest and deport any person suspected of not transplanting to Connacht.[67] It was no longer necessary for an Irish person to be convicted of failing to transplant; it sufficed merely to be suspected of such an offence. Unlike the previous orders, there was no upper limit put on the number of people who could be seized. This order meant that any Irish person could be snatched from the side of the road and thrown onto a ship, which is precisely what happened. A disorganised manhunt ensued as gangs of men roamed the country in search of Irish civilians who were induced or forced onto ships, taken to Barbados and sold at the quayside. The manhunts were stopped in March 1657, not because too many Irish had been taken, but because the overenthusiastic hunters had committed the great crime of kidnapping some English people as well.[68] The transports subsided, but continued in small volumes until the fall of the Protectorate.[69]

This episode is the heart of the Irish enslavement debate, in that there was no real difference between what had occurred in the Irish countryside and what was taking place in African regions close to the European trading outposts. People were captured based on their ethnicity, transported on foot of their guilt for the most minor of crimes, and often for no crime at all. They left Ireland on the assumption that they were the property of the merchants who were paying for their transport, without indentures, and were expected to be unfree for an undetermined period. For many, this was a life sentence, and a tragically short one. However, the transportation of the Irish to Barbados during this period cannot be considered an extension of the trade in enslaved Africans, as it was an alternative to it. There was no suggestion of a permanent and systemic exploitation of Irish people, the unwilling subjects of the English Commonwealth. Instead, there was an ad hoc exploitation of people that proved to be both short-lived and an embarrassment to the recipients of these Irish people in Barbados.

Ejected by parliamentary forces in 1652, Francis Willoughby's reappointment as Governor of Barbados in the wake of the Restoration of Charles II in 1660 coincided with the entrenchment of the English Caribbean colonies as plantation societies built on African enslavement. Thomas Windsor, the Governor of Jamaica, was told to expect a delivery of 300 enslaved people from Africa in 1662 by the Royal Africa Company alone.[70] Jamaica at that time had a European population of just 2,200 soldiers and navy personnel, and a similar number of planters and their families.[71] This was despite the forced transportation of thousands of servants from other Caribbean islands. The development of Jamaica, seized from Spain by Cromwell in 1655 and considerably larger than Barbados, was hampered by a shortage of unfree labour. Barbados had no such labour shortage, with an estimated population of 53,000 in 1660, divided equally between white settlers and servants, and African enslaved people. As was the case at St Kitts in 1627, the large Irish presence on Barbados quickly became a barrier to its rapid development as a slave economy. This was a more pressing consideration than the sudden willingness to right the wrongs suffered by these Irish captives under the Cromwellian Protectorate, namely 'those who were forced there by their suffering for and service in his Majesty's cause'.[72] As the Irish were subjects of Charles II and could no longer be kept in bondage, the choices were to set them free to roam the island in search of work, compel their masters to pay them or eject them from the island. A deal was therefore concocted to get the Irish off Barbados. Any Irish person agreeing to move to the much larger and underpopulated Jamaica would receive 30 acres if they could prove they had served for a minimum of two years. Their intra-island shipper would also receive 30 acres to defray the charge of supporting them to prevent a new indenture from being created. An Irish person who wished to escape English rule altogether had the option of 50 acres 'for the encouragement of any such as may plant on any desolate Indian island'.[73] The small cohort of Irish transportees of 1656–7, or the few that had survived, became the first, and last, contingent transported to Barbados against their will to be compensated for their suffering.

From this point, Barbados became a slave economy entirely dependent on unfree African labour and without too many troublesome Irish.[74] Indeed, it was the very absence of the Irish that encouraged many planters to sell or abandon their estates in Ireland under the Restoration land settlements and try their luck in Barbados instead.[75] England's share of the slave trade expanded dramatically, led by the newly constituted Royal Company of merchants trading into Africa and resurrected trading posts in the Gambia and Ghana. In expectation of an enormous influx of enslaved people from Africa, legislation to police the trade was passed by the Barbados Assembly on 27 September 1660.[76] England's slave trade became institutionalised.

The allure of gold ostensibly drew the Royal Africa Company back to the Gambia. An undated journal written before 1660 came to the company's attention that claimed a mythical '10,000 lbs of gold' could be retrieved from the upper reaches of the river.[77] Encountering few people, but attacked by baboons and suffering the sinking of one of their boats by an angry hippopotamus, the anonymous writer of this journal reported 'glittering sands' in an upper tributary of the Gambia that yielded twelve grains of gold from each pound of sand.[78] What was most probably an unsuccessful prospector's tall tale was apparently taken seriously by Crisp, Noel and the rest of the Africa merchants. Five vessels were borrowed from the King's navy that arrived in the Gambia at James Island, newly renamed Charles Island, in March 1660.[79] One vessel, the *Kinsale*, was sent up-river on the quest for gold while the remainder reoccupied the fort and organised the slave trade in that region.

The Africa merchants, with Charles II as their company's governor, maintained a cloak of secrecy about their real purpose. The quest for gold was entirely speculative, while the slave trade was real and widespread. The English company avoided dealing in enslaved people directly, but brought in factors from loosely associated merchants to complete the transactions at arm's length. It seems that the optics of owning enslaved people was acceptable in English America, but dealing in enslaved people by the royal family was not. By the 1670s a network of forts and small settlements was established along the river, and some gold was found, but the gold was completely eclipsed by the vast scale and profits of the slave trade. The Africa merchants' coyness as to the true nature of its business was not finally set aside until a renewed charter was issued by Charles II in 1674, which stated both the promise of gold mines and English plantations but also set out that the trade in enslaved people was the central goal of the company.[80] The Royal Africa Company that emerged was transformed into the global powerhouse of the transatlantic slave trade, and many of the new shareholders were descended from the original merchants who had brought the Caribbean plantations to this point. Although indentured European labour persisted on a small scale, Barbados and the remainder of England's Caribbean dominions became plantation societies built on African enslavement.

Once in Barbados, and despite having no other rights guaranteed by the colonial legal system, as Christians the Irish had to be buried according to Christian custom. Burial records only survive for two parishes in Barbados, but these show an eightfold increase in Irish deaths from 1652 to 1654, a level that was then sustained while the transports were at their height.[81] Half of the arrivals usually died within one year, hence the constant need for replacements. The burial records are also the only official records on Barbados that support the corresponding contemporary accounts from Ireland of large numbers of departures. Certainly hundreds, and perhaps thousands, of Irish people were sent to Barbados in the 1650s, divided from African unfree co-workers by being termed servants, but without the rights of servants. Unfree African labourers were never called servants, but conversely, and until the 1660s, were also rarely referred to as enslaved people in the official records. This two-faced approach was ingrained in English colonial administrations in Ireland and the Caribbean throughout the 1650s, avoiding committing to paper what was, in fact, taking place. Private records reveal a more accurate picture of contemporary attitudes towards labour in the plantations. When plantations were sold, they were sold with their inventory of unfree labour, as this represented much of the value of the estate. The enslavers prized their cattle the most and gave them childlike names: Daisy and so on. 'Negroes', as the enslaved were invariably referred to, though only occasionally as enslaved people, were sometimes given childish invented names, frequently derived from *Arabian Nights* and other tales from exotic parts, but normally only numbers are given in the deeds. Irish labourers were referred to by their first names, real or invented: 'Daniell the Irishman' or 'Little Nell'.[82] For the Irish, there is rarely any mention of a time left to serve, but this was important information, as it determined the value of the estate. If the time of service was unlimited, the servant was worth a lot more. The full names of English servants were normally given, together with the time left to serve.[83] Irish servants to Irish masters, however, tended to have their full names and terms listed, but to most English enslavers, captive Irish and enslaved Africans were clearly different, subtly non-equivalent classes of property, equal to farm animals but unequal to English servants. It is a differential only evident in deeds to property. This role for the Irish was peculiar to Barbados in the mid-to-late 1650s and there is no evidence of it anywhere else in the English Atlantic. This faint difference in the property status of Irish and African should neither cause it to be erased from the general narrative nor elevate it into a more important episode than it was. Crucially, the Irish at the time, and many others, believed they were being enslaved. Belief does not require overwhelming evidence, and the burden of proof diminishes further over time as great injustices are amplified in folk memory. It is a duty of the historian to uncover the evidence and interpret it as best they can, with empathy. The brief episode of mass forced Irish transportation, 1652–7, was a product both of its time and of the changes in Caribbean agriculture brought about by the sugar boom. It remains one of many of Cromwell's deeply unpleasant legacies in Ireland.

Notes

1 For Cromwell's campaign in Ireland see Micheál Ó Siochrú, *God's Executioner: Oliver Cromwell and the Conquest of Ireland* (London: Faber and Faber, 2008); for Ayscue's Barbados campaign see David Brown, *Empire and Enterprise: Money, Power and the Adventurers for Irish Land* (Manchester, Manchester University Press, 2020), pp. 126–30.
2 New research into this topic has been enabled by the *Commonwealth Records Project*, investigated by Professor Micheál Ó Siochrú at Trinity College Dublin, which has reassembled from transcripts the Irish State Papers from the 1650s that were originally known as the 'Commonwealth Records' at the Public Record Office of Ireland and destroyed in 1922. The principal Irish primary sources for this chapter are drawn from National Library of Ireland (NLI), MSS 11959–61; British Library (BL), Add. MSS 821–3 and Egerton MSS 1761–2; Library of the Honorable Society of King's Inns, Prendergast Papers (Prendergast), Vols 1–14; and the Jennings Collection at the Irish Military Archives (IMA), AL/CMG/1/14/1–11. Research at the Barbados Department of Archives (BDA) was supported by a Charlemont fellowship from the Royal Irish Academy (RIA), where the principal series consulted were RB3 (Deeds), RB6 (Wills) and RB12 (Burials). A fellowship to the Huntington Library in San Marino, California (HM) enabled an examination of the early records of the Royal Africa Company, and research was also undertaken at The National Archives in Kew, United Kingdom (TNA) using the series of State Papers, Colonial Papers and Admiralty Court Records.
3 For recent scholarship on Barbados's progression to independence see Rafael Cox-Alomar, 'An Anglo-Barbadian dialogue: The negotiations leading to Barbados' independence, 1965–66', *Commonwealth Journal of International Affairs* 93 (2004), 671–90.

4 Aubrey Gwynn, 'Early Irish emigration to the West Indies (1612–1643)', *Studies: An Irish Quarterly Review* 18:71 (September 1929), 377–93; 'Early Irish emigration to the West Indies: Part II', *Studies: An Irish Quarterly Review* 18:72 (December 1929), 648–63; 'Indentured servants and negro slaves in Barbados (1642–1650)', *Studies: An Irish Quarterly Review* 19:74 (June 1930), 279–94; 'Cromwell's policy of transportation', *Studies: An Irish Quarterly Review* 19:76 (December 1930), 607–23; 'Cromwell's policy of transportation: Part II', *Studies: An Irish Quarterly Review* 20:78 (June 1931), 291–305; 'The first Irish priests in the New World', *Studies: An Irish Quarterly Review* 21:82 (June 1932), 213–28; 'Documents relating to the Irish in the West Indies', *Analecta hibernica* 4 (October 1932), 139–286; 'An Irish settlement on the Amazon (1612–1629)', *Proceedings of the Royal Irish Academy* 41 (1932–4), 1–54.
5 Richard Ligon, *A True and Exact History of the Island of Barbados* (London, 1647).
6 Sir Hilary McD. Beckles, 'Sugar and white servitude: An analysis of indentured labour during the sugar revolution of Barbados, 1643–55', *Journal of the Barbados Museum and Historical Society* 36 (1981), 236–46; *White Servitude and Black Slavery in Barbados, 1627–1715* (Knoxville: University of Tennessee Press, 1989); and *A History of Barbados: From Amerindian Settlement to Caribbean Single Market* (Cambridge: Cambridge University Press, 1990); among many other publications on this topic and the general history of Barbados.
7 Sir Hilary McD. Beckles, A "riotous and unruly lot": Irish indentured servants and freemen in the English West Indies, 1644–1713', *William and Mary Quarterly* 47 (1990), 503–22 (p. 508).
8 Jerome Handler and Matthew Reilly, 'Contesting "white slavery" in the Caribbean: Enslaved Africans and European indentured servants in seventeenth-century Barbados', *Journal of the Barbados Museum and Historical Society* 63 (2017), 156–87.
9 Aidan Clarke, *The Old English in Ireland 1625–42* (London: MacGibbon and Kee, 1966), p. 27.
10 Kristen Block and Jenny Shaw, 'Subjects without an empire: The Irish in the early modern Caribbean', *Past and Present* 210:1 (February 2011), 33–60 (p. 36); Karen Ordahl Kupperman, *The Atlantic in World History* (Oxford: Oxford University Press, 2012).
11 TNA, CO 30/2, p. 8., 'An Act Establishing the Court of Common Pleas within the Isles declaring alsoe the method and mannor of proceeding both to judgement and execution which are to be observed in the said court', n.d. (Commonwealth period).
12 Thomas Birch, ed., *A Collection of the State Papers of John Thurloe*, Vol. VI (London: HMSO, 1752); Oxford, Bodleian Library, Carte MS 44, fo. 2r.
13 Handler and Reilly, 'Contesting "white slavery"', p. 177.
14 BDA, RB 12/1–2, recopied burial registers for Christchurch and St Michael's Parishes.

15 John C. Appleby, ed., *Calendar of Material Relating to Ireland from the High Court of Admiralty Examinations 1536–1641* (Dublin: IMC, 1992), *passim*.
16 RIA, MS EI 23, Inquisitions for Cork, Vol. V, pp. 210–33; James Morin, ed., *Calendar of the Patent and Close Rolls of Ireland, Chancery, Charles I, I to VIII* (London: HMC, 1863), p. 553.
17 H. T. Barlow, ed., *Colonising Expeditions to the West Indies and Guiana 1623–67* (London: Routledge, 1925), p. 31.
18 See, for example, Alison Games, 'Atlantic history: Definitions, challenges, and opportunities', *American Historical Review* 111:3 (June 2006), 741–57; Carla Pestana, *The English Atlantic in an Age of Revolution, 1640–1661* (Cambridge, MA: Harvard University Press, 2004).
19 Ralph Davis, *The Rise of the English Shipping Industries in the Seventeenth and Eighteenth Centuries* (Newton Abbot: Liverpool University Press, 1962), p. 198; Gwynn, 'Early Irish emigration (1612–1643)', 'Early Irish emigration: Part II'.
20 William Robert Scott, *The Constitution and Finance of English, Scottish and Irish Joint Stock Companies to 1720*, Vol. II (Cambridge: Cambridge University Press, 1910), p. 19.
21 J. M. Gray, *A History of the Gambia* (Cambridge: Cambridge University Press, 1966), p. 23.
22 TNA, T 70/75, Minutes of the Royal Africa Company, fo. 7r.
23 Now Kunta Kinteh.
24 Walter Rodney, *A History of the Upper Guinea Coast 1545–1800* (Oxford: Oxford University Press, 1970), p. 165.
25 Alexander Balloch Grosart, *The Lismore Papers of Richard Boyle, First and 'Great' Earl of Cork* (London: private printing, 1886), p. 318.
26 Toby Green, *A Fistful of Shells: West Africa from the Rise of the Slave Trade to the Age of Revolution* (Chicago: University of Chicago Press, 2019), pp. 89–91.
27 H. F. Kearney, 'Richard Boyle, ironmaster: A footnote to Irish economic history', *Journal of the Royal Society of Antiquaries of Ireland* 83:2 (1953), 156–62.
28 Walter Rodney, 'The Guinea coast', in Richard Gray, ed., *The Cambridge History of Africa*, Vol. IV (Cambridge: Cambridge University Press, 1975), pp. 223–325 (pp. 227–30).
29 Brown, *Empire and Enterprise*, pp. 28–31.
30 Barlow, *Colonising Expeditions*, pp. 4–5.
31 Robert Brenner, *Merchants and Revolution: Commercial Change, Political Conflict, and London's Overseas Traders, 1550–1653* (Princeton: Princeton University Press, 1993), p. 129.
32 *Ibid.*, p. 127.
33 Aubrey Gwynn, 'Documents relating to the Irish in the West Indies', p. 159.
34 Brenner, *Merchants and Revolution*, p. 185.
35 Morin, *Calendar*, p. 541.
36 Carl Bridenbaugh and Roberta Bridenbaugh, *The Antilles and the Spanish Main* (Oxford: Oxford University Press, 1972), p. 130.

37 Trinity College Dublin, MS 736, 'Papers relating to the Barbadoes and the Caribbean Islands', fos 80–4.
38 For population summaries see Russell R. Menard, *Sweet Negotiations: Sugar, Slavery and Plantation Agriculture in Early Barbados* (Charlottesville: University of Virginia Press, 2006), pp. 23–6.
39 BDA, RB 3/1, fo. 3, Council Minutes of Barbados, March 1639.
40 BDA RB 3/1, fo. 20.
41 David Brown and Micheál Ó Siochrú, 'The Cromwellian urban surveys, 1653–1659', *Archivium hibernicum* 69 (2016), 37–150 (pp. 95–6); BDA, RB 6/8/357, RB 6/13/398.
42 BDA, RB 3/1/419.
43 BDA, RB 3/1/928.
44 See, for example, BDA, RB 6/11, pp. 453 (O'Haire), 560 (Fynne), 561 (O'Shea), 565 (O'Gary); RB6/13, p. 282 (Swillivan).
45 BDA, RB 6/11, p. 560.
46 BDA, RB 6/15, p. 142.
47 See Block and Shaw, 'Subjects without an empire', pp. 38–40, for Captain James Hackett's perambulations. He returned to Barbados with his large entourage and died there in 1657; see BDA, RB 6/13, p. 214.
48 David Grant Smith, 'Old Christian merchants and the foundation of the Brazil Company, 1649', *Hispanic American Historical Review* 54:2 (May 1974), 233–59.
49 The English merchants in the Portuguese venture were led by William Cockaine, who was also the Governor of the English East India Company, and included Sir Oliver St John.
50 Leonor Friere Costa, 'Merchant groups in the 17th-century Brazilian sugar trade: Reappraising old topics with new research insights', *Journal of Portuguese History* 2:1 (Summer 2004), 1–11.
51 Elizabeth Donnan, *Documents Illustrative of the Slave Trade to America*, Vol. I (Washington, DC: Carnegie Institute of Washington, 1930), p. 126, the Guinea Company to James Pope, 17 September 1651.
52 *Ibid.*, p. 129, the Guinea Company to Bartholomew Howard. The corresponding merchant in Barbados was Francis Soame, a kinsman of John Wood.
53 *Ibid.*, p. 131, the Guinea Company to James Pope, 9 December 1651.
54 The Courlanders also intended to enter the slave trade; their Gambian outpost was meant to provide enslaved people for a projected colony on Tobago. See Karin Jekabson-Lemanis, 'Balts in the Caribbean: The Duchy of Courland's attempts to colonize Tobago Island, 1638 to 1654', *Caribbean Quarterly* 46:2 (June 2000), 25–44.
55 IMA, AL/CMG/1/14/2, p. 22, petition of William Molesworth.
56 The slaughter at both towns left very few prisoners to ship; only thirty survivors were ultimately shipped from Drogheda. See Gwynn, 'Cromwell's policy of transportation: Part II', p. 300.
57 Maynooth University, O'Rehehan MS 2, p. 510.

58 W. Noel Sainsbury, *Calendar of State Papers Colonial, America and the West Indies* (London: HMC, 1860), p. 387, 20 August 1652. The burst of activity occurred one week after Willloughby's return to London and coincided with a wave of vessels departing to the colonies in the wake of their rendition.
59 TNA, HCA 13/71, fos 598–624.
60 IMA, AL/CMG/1/14/2, p. 20.
61 IMA, AL/CMG/1/14/10, pp. 6, 11.
62 IMA, AL/CMG/1/14/10, p. 14.
63 BDA, RB 3/1, p. 853; 3/2, p. 653; 3/2, p. 502. In this last entry, Francis Sadlier was helping to resolve a dispute between Sir John Ireton and Robert Tichborne in London over sugar owed in Barbados. The planter communities and Cromwellian armies were always closely intertwined.
64 Hawkins was the secretary of Parliament's Committee for Irish Affairs throughout the 1640s and very well known in London. He came to Ireland with Cromwell as a commissary. See Brown, *Empire and Enterprise*, pp. 75–6, 127, 148, 155–8.
65 IMA, AL/CMG/1/14/2, p. 12; TNA, SP 18/34, fo. 3, Parliamentary Commissioners to Scottish and Irish Committee at Westminster.
66 TNA, SP 18/37, fo. 360, 20 June 1653, petition to Committee for the Posts.
67 IMA, AL/CMG/1/14/3, p. 44.
68 IMA, AL/CMG/1/14/4, p. 14.
69 IMA, AL/CMG/1/14/6, p. 23. Bonds for transporting prisoners from Galway were sold by Sir Charles Coote as late as May 1659.
70 HM, MS 57346, p. 29.
71 HM, MS 57346, p. 84, survey of Jamaica.
72 HM, MS 57346, p. 89, instructions to Willoughby.
73 HM, MS 57346, pp. 1, 21, granting of lands to Christian servants.
74 Ernst van den Boogart, 'The trade between Western Africa and the Atlantic World, 1600–1690: Estimates of trends in composition and value', *Journal of African History* 33:3 (1992), 369–85. For comparative figures see p. 370.
75 HM, MS 57346, p. 19.
76 TNA, CO30/2, Acts of Barbados, pp. 16–22, 'An act for the better ordering and governing of negroes'.
77 HM, Stowe Nugent, ST 9, 'Coppy of a Journall up the River Gambia found amongst Dr Hooks papers', p. 1.
78 HM, ST 9, p. 6.
79 HM, ST 9, pp. 11–19. The expedition was under the command of John Vermyden and William Cushin.
80 HM, ST 9, p. 37.
81 BDA, RB12/1–2, recopied burial registers for Christchurch and St Michael's Parishes.
82 BDA 3/1, p. 14, George Bulkeley's servants.
83 See BDA 3/1, pp. 638, 670, 689, 699, 711, 721, 738 and 791 for examples of these classifications of property.

4

Trade, plunder and Irishmen in early English Jamaica

Nuala Zahedieh

Jamaica was seized by the English in 1655. It was a consolation prize, captured after a massive expeditionary force designed to conquer the Spanish Indies met humiliating defeat in the larger and richer island of Hispaniola.[1] Yet, despite the initial disappointment, it was soon apparent that Jamaica had great value on account of its location in the heart of the Spanish Indies, better placed for trade or plunder than England's earlier settlements in the eastern Caribbean. Both an emporium and a plantation, by the early eighteenth century Jamaica was lauded as England's most valuable colony, and it was fitted into a national narrative in which a series of strikes against the Roman-Iberian Babylon – Spain – and its garrisoned treasure house in America allowed an elect nation to construct an expanding domain that considered itself to be, in David Armitage's words, 'Protestant, commercial, maritime and free'.[2] Roman Catholic Irishmen are more or less excluded from this story and, insofar as they do appear, it is mainly as ill-documented indentured servants. However, the received scholarly picture has not been unchallenged, and recent work has highlighted how England's imperial expansion was not shaped by its Protestant subjects alone.[3] In the case of Jamaica, a confessional pluralism allowed Roman Catholic Irishmen to take advantage of a range of opportunities, and reinforces arguments for reimagining the Catholic Atlantic.

Chronology and geography combined to place Jamaica on a different development path from that pursued in England's first Caribbean colonies, and this affected the Irish story. Early West Indian settlements were largely peopled by white indentured servants, and they drew heavily on Irish resources.[4] However, after the introduction of sugar into Barbados in the 1640s had demonstrated the heady profits that could be earned in tropical agriculture, there was a surging demand for labour; a rise in servant prices; and a shift to the use of enslaved Africans, who were available at lower cost.[5] By the time the English established civil government in Jamaica in 1662, Barbados had created a blueprint for slave society that was immediately adopted in the new colony, with an enthusiastic expansion of the enslaved population. No firm figures are available but it seems that in the next decade of settlement the island imported no more than 1,000–2,000 indentured servants, whereas it imported between 15,000 and 20,000 Africans. By 1673, the black population outnumbered the white, by the 1690s the ratio was 6 to 1, and by the 1720s it was 10 to 1.[6] Indentured servants were much less important in developing Jamaica than they had been in the earlier stages of English settlement – accounting for around a quarter of white immigrants – and, furthermore, only a small proportion were of Irish origin: Trevor Burnard suggests that Irish migrants accounted for only 1.4 per cent of indentured servants introduced into Jamaica between 1683 and 1696, and 2.3 per cent between 1719 and 1759.[7] There is evidence that soon after the conquest of Jamaica the authorities sought to secure cargoes of Irish servants, but there is no hard information about whether, when, or where they were unloaded. No doubt there were some Irish servants aboard the provision ships that supplied Irish pork, beef, butter and cheese from Jamaica's early years of settlement, but it was certainly not a massive trade.[8]

However, the absence of Irish indentured servants did not mean an absence of Irish migration, which, as observed by Louis Cullen, had a broader social base than is often supposed. The islands acted as a magnet for gentry (especially younger sons) and middling sorts who wished to try their luck and venture their capital overseas: a well-established strategy that underpinned the creation of extended commercial networks and helped to protect the patrimony and status of better-off families, including many of the Roman Catholic religion.[9] Whereas this group had experienced some hostility in the early English colonies in the eastern Caribbean, they were given a cautious welcome in Jamaica.

The English captors of Jamaica were quick to see that the island's geographical location made it well placed for trade across mercantilist boundaries, above all with the rich Spanish empire: located in its bowels, within easy sailing distance of the principal ports and straddling the major trade routes.[10] Although there was some decline in the early seventeenth century, Peru and Mexico continued to produce a vast treasure: between 1660 and 1700, annual silver output averaged £2.5 million, or two or three times as much as America's total sugar production.[11] Spanish America had a population of between 6 and 8 million in 1700 (twenty times as big as that of British America), including a number of large cities. Strong regional economies provided a market for enslaved people and capital goods, while a growing number of high-spending consumers demanded food, drink and a range of manufactures that, despite prohibitions, could be supplied from English Jamaica.[12] As George Montagu Dunk, Earl of Halifax, remarked, far better for Great Britian that the American mines should be in Spanish hands so that 'whilst the British manufacturers stayed at home, to mind and improve their manufactures they had so many slaves working abroad for them in the mines'.[13] Jamaica was also a good base for trade with the expanding French settlement in nearby western Hispaniola, which was moving from being a pirate base to become the largest sugar producer in the eighteenth-century Caribbean and provided a growing market for Irish provisions (pork, beef, butter and cheese) and other goods.[14]

Hopes of establishing a profitable inter-imperial trade at Jamaica made it important to attract settlers with the capital and commercial expertise that would make it work: merchants, mariners, professionals, and craftsmen with the appropriate skills and trade networks. Interested observers promoted an open-door policy in imitation of the Dutch example, which had highlighted religious pluralism's links with profit and power.[15] As William Petty argued, no monarch tasked with filling up so great a share of the unpeopled earth as English America could ground his policies on 'those gibberish denominations and uncertain phrases ... papist, protestant, fanatick'.[16] Liberty of religion would avoid a damaging drain of English labour; would syphon off dangerous or disaffected citizens and put them to useful labour; and, above all, would attract foreigners with valuable social and financial capital, including Irishmen.

From first settlement, Jamaica welcomed immigrants of all religions, and the policy endured beyond the fall of James II and the retreat from toleration at home, creating a cosmopolitanism and confessional pluralism that aroused surprise and comment. In describing the island in 1688, John Taylor noted that there was a strong Irish community and that 'they allow of a free toleration of all sects and religions'. In Port Royal, 'we find a Protestant church governed according to the doctrines of the Church of England, also a Presbyterian meeting house, a Roman chapel, a Quaker meeting house, and a Jews' synagogue all which sects live quietly and peaceably one with another faithfully serving together in arms for the defence of the island'.[17]

Although we do not have firm figures, it is clear that, by the end of the seventeenth century, the Irish population certainly numbered several hundred, and it was well represented at every level of society.[18] Most Catholic Irish were shadowy figures as, although all those owning property over £10 could vote in elections, the enforcement of the oaths of supremacy and allegiance excluded them from office-holding and also caused them to avoid the courts. Nonetheless, they appear in miscellaneous records such as diaries, letters, Assembly petitions, and probate inventories.[19] Some came to plant, such as Redmond McGragh, from a Jacobite family, who patented over 1,000 acres in the 1680s.[20] More came in search of commercial opportunities, such as the merchant John Stapleton, who also arrived in the 1680s and was from a family with well dispersed trading networks in Europe and the Caribbean, including a brother who was Governor of the Leeward

Islands.²¹ Inventories show that many artisans and tradesmen – such as Michael Farrell, a millwright; John Casey, a tavern keeper; Jane Fitzgerald, a garment trader; Michael Hanigan, a tailor; and Conn Connelly, a bricklayer and builder – were able to develop extensive trade and credit networks.²² Protestant Irishmen were more visible and included the Governor Lord Inchiquin (1690); numerous Councillors and members of the Assembly; and senior legal officials.²³ However, many were suspected of Catholic sympathies, especially those who were recent converts, and many did in fact have strong links with their Catholic countrymen, as seen in the case of Smith Kelly, who assisted several Catholics in fleeing the island.²⁴

Although successive Jamaican Governors did all they could to encourage commerce with Spanish America. its Crown continued to attempt to exclude all foreigners from its markets other than a licensed slave trade, or *asiento*.²⁵ Many Jamaican traders responded by resorting to plunder. Privateering required little start-up capital and it was easy to recruit crews from the pool of restless men roaming in the Caribbean, including a number of Irishmen. As a result, privateering dominated the island's economy during its early years in English hands, and employed around 1,500 men in 1664. Plunder offered quick rewards and helped the islanders to accumulate the funds necessary to develop the agricultural hinterland, but by the 1670s it faced diminishing returns as the privateers stripped the coastal regions of easy prizes and provoked the Spaniards into raising their defence capabilities.²⁶ They began building up the strength of their guarda-costas, often recruiting from the same pool as the Port Royal privateers, and proving especially attractive to Irishmen who had no love of the English and changed sides, such as Philip Fitzgerald, 'a runnagade Irish rogue', who went into the service of the Governor of Cuba after the Treaty of Madrid in 1670.²⁷

Plunder was not a strategy for sustained growth in Jamaica, and peaceful commerce promised far better returns over the long term, but while Protestant Englishmen were not allowed to access Spanish ports, or settle agents in Spanish territory except in very specific circumstances, it was difficult to obtain good commercial information or establish strong trading links.²⁸ Inter-imperial trade was, of course, subject to all the perils faced in any market: supply might not match demand; consumer preferences could change; goods might decay or perish. However, the greatest risk was opportunism among captains, supercargoes and customers, which was exacerbated in contraband trade by the lack of formal enforcement mechanisms.²⁹ Smugglers needed, of necessity, to minimise incriminating paper trails; transactions often rested on little more than a verbal agreement, and participants had little recourse to law even on their own side of the national border: a report of 1725 claimed that 'on their return [supercargoes] ordered the persons concerned their proportions without giving them any account of sales'.[30] Merchants did what they could to reduce risks by hiring experienced agents, trading with repeat customers, and following well-established routines and rituals to promote 'uneasy trust', but faced problems at every turn.[31]

In these conditions, small, tight-knit groups such as the Catholic Irish, or Sephardic Jews, with networks of kin and countrymen across mercantilist borders, were at an advantage in building bridges between empires: an advantage that was soon apparent in English Jamaica. At the Restoration, England had high hopes of using the newly chartered African Company to access Spanish markets for enslaved people and also provide cover for other illicit commerce. In 1662, merchant members secured a contract from the holders of the Spanish slave *asiento*, Domingo Grillo and Ambrosio Lomelin, to supply 2,400 Africans a year from bases in the Caribbean, including Jamaica.[32] By 1664, the first cargo of Africans for the *asiento* was ready for collection by Grillo's agent, Santiago Daza Villalobe, a Mexican merchant who owned his own ship and was experienced in interloping. After Villalobe and Gyles Lydcott, the supercargo, had collected the Africans at Jamaica, they returned to Vera Cruz, where they applied for necessary assistance (including victualling themselves and those they enslaved) to Morfa, or Murphy, a resident Irishman.[33] The transactions at Vera Cruz went wrong, resulting in a court case involving Martin Noell (who fronted the contract on behalf of the African Company) in Seville, and highlighting how, although the Irish did face suspicion in Spanish America, their religion allowed them to settle and tap into Spanish patronage networks to act as intermediaries in a lucrative trade, giving them valuable leverage in a Catholic enclave in the emerging English Atlantic economy.

The English slave trade was heavily disrupted by the Dutch war of the 1660s but regained strength in the 1670s. A new African Company was chartered in 1672, shortly after the 1670 Treaty of Madrid promised peace and friendship in the Indies and renewed hopes of breaking into Spanish American markets.[34] As competing Dutch networks were damaged by war with France, the *asientistas* settled a Spanish agent in Jamaica: James Castillo, who maintained a 'Romish chapel' in Port Royal with an Irish priest, John Baptist Dempsey.[35] The chapel was open to Irish Catholics and doubtless helped them create a sense of community, which seems to have incorporated some of their Protestant countrymen, such as the island's Provost Marshall, Smith Kelly.[36] Kelly was involved in the *asiento* business and helped Castillo escape the island in 1688 after he and Dempsey became embroiled in a dispute with the Governor, Albemarle, over the consecration of a second Catholic chapel by Father Thomas Churchill on the orders of James II.[37] The *asiento* business was a prominent cause of factional strife and suffered disruption in the period surrounding the Glorious Revolution, but it recovered under the governorship of the Irishman Lord Inchiquin, and William Beeston, and continued with minor interruptions until France gained the contract in 1702.[38] During this period, another Irishman, Manuel Menasseh Gilligan, played a shadowy role in Spanish American trade that was nonetheless sufficiently important to qualify him as the English representative in the negotiations in Madrid in 1713, which culminated in the granting of the *asiento* to the British Crown.[39] In 1715, when Arthur Moore, Director of the South Sea Company, was alleged to have framed a scheme for large-scale private trade (£20,000) out of Jamaica, he was in combination with a Jew, John da Costa, and an Irishman, Mr Dowdall.[40]

Although their contribution cannot be quantified in any systematic way, there is abundant anecdotal evidence that Jamaica's Irish community played a major role in trade with the Catholic Atlantic. James Houston, a Scottish surgeon who spent many years in the Indies (including at the South Sea Company's factories at Portobello and Jamaica), drew a picture of a strong, close-knit community, including 'professed and concealed papists'. Kinship ties and investment in the outsider group's social capital helped to secure high levels of economic cooperation among its members, which gave them an edge in illegal trade. However, it could be difficult for others to secure a share of the benefits, as he found to his cost. He described a 'cheat' worked on him by two Irishmen, Captain Fennell and John Curtin, in a trading venture to Vera Cruz, and found it difficult to recover his losses, despite a slow and expensive chancery case in which he claimed the jurymen were almost all Irishmen.[41] He noted that 'I always observed the Irishmen hunted in packs and divided the spoil; and whenever they miscarried, they all contributed towards the loss. They were deep-mouthed hounds! I had the misfortune to encounter with a pack of them, and they hunted me 'til I was almost worried several times. But I escaped from them at last by a long chancery suit.'[42]

Houston was among many who commented on the strong presence of Irishmen in the island and claimed that they were for the most part Roman Catholics in disguise: 'And it is a known truth that there are no enemies so inveterate against the English nation as the Irish Roman Catholics'. In 1719, the former chief justice, Thomas Bernard, complained that the Attorney General, Edmund Kelly – one of five Irish brothers who had come to Jamaica in the 1710s – had opposed a revenue bill with 'all imaginable bitterness, saying upon that occasion that King James had been forced to abdicate for his crimes; it is not at all surprising, a person of his religion should think the introducing of popery a trivial fault'.[43] In a later attack on Kelly, Vernon used arguments that painted Kelly as an Irishman with Catholic sympathies who continued to have Jacobite loyalties and could not be trusted, despite having a brother serving in the Church of England: he represented attitudes that only served to strengthen Irish group identity.[44]

English (and Scottish) mistrust of the Irish had long roots and was not entirely misplaced. During the ill-fated Western Design, as Kirsten Block and Jenny Shaw pointed out, Irish troops on both sides contributed significantly to English failures. After landing in Hispaniola, an 'old Irish man' led English troops into an ambush, and Don Juan Morfa, or Murphy, an Irishman, was in command of the Spanish troops who defended Santo Domingo.[45] Irish runaways from the English army offered intelligence and translation services to the Spaniards in exchange for sanctuary, and played on their religious identity to help persuade officials of their genuine loyalty.

Mistrust of the Irish was especially strong in the 1690s, as they were suspected of assisting the French enemy in planning an attack from their strong base in nearby Hispaniola: an attack that materialised in 1694. In July, Beeston noted that 'two days since four or five armed Irish with us contrived to run away to them [the French] but the plot was betrayed by one of them, and the ring leader tried by court martial and executed'.[46] Stapleton and another Irishman, Lynch, with trading links with the French, were suspected of providing them with information, and Beeston issued a warrant for their arrest on the grounds that they had refused to take oaths of allegiance and supremacy.[47] The two men sought protection from the protestant Irishman Smith Kelly, who harboured them at his plantation for six months. He managed to get them off the island under pretence of shipping indigo to Curaçao.[48] Stapleton, in fact, sailed for Saint-Domingue, where he purchased a plantation on the north coast and was later joined by his wife, Helen, and children. After a few years the family moved to live in the Irish community in Nantes, but when Stapleton died in 1701, he remained in possession of a plantation in Saint-Domingue and a Montserrat plot.[49] The war was a period of rising hostility and increasing difficulty for the Irish, reflected in a very strongly worded anti-Catholic message in the Assembly in response to a Jacobite assassination plot in England.[50]

However, the most notorious example of Irish infidelity was the case of Philip Fitzgerald, a privateer and logwood cutter operating out of Jamaica, who changed allegiance after the Treaty of Madrid, and went into the service of the Governor of Cuba.[51] In 1673, he was sent out of Havana and took eight or ten vessels in the Bay of Campeche, as well as seizing a number of ships trading from Jamaica.[52] Fitzgerald's activities caused serious diplomatic waves, as his victims launched claims for reparations for the 'barbarous cruelties and murders' he had committed. Edmund Cook, master of the *Virgin* of London, a pink bound for London with a cargo valued at £5,000, described how he was taken off Havana in May 1673. After fourteen days he and his crew were put into the *Virgin*'s long boat with a fortnight's provisions and left to return to Jamaica – a journey that took them two months and three days, during which one of the company died of starvation.⁵³ Fitzgerald's 'Irish' cruelties were connected to broader narratives of papist atrocities with stories of Spanish inhumanity and intransigence: Cook claimed to have sought victuals from the Governor of Trinidad in South Cuba, but met rejection with the command to go 'like a dog and a thief'.⁵⁴ Mathew Fox, master of the *Humility* of London, also lost his ship on the way home from Jamaica and claimed 'barbarous usage' at Fitzgerald's hands. The guarda-costa justified his behaviour as retaliation for the 'way that his countrymen were ill-used by the English 24 years ago', so that 'he should never be satisfied with English blood, but could drink it as freely as water when he was adry'.⁵⁵ According to Fox, the Spaniards in Havana claimed to have taken seventy-five ships of Jamaica, New England, Virginia and Old England since the peace of 1670.⁵⁶

Cases mounted, and the Lords of Trade and Plantations responded to the 'outrages' by ordering that a proclamation be issued recalling His Majesty's subjects from service of any foreign prince between the tropics in America, with promise of pardon 'if they render themselves within a convenient time'. Cooke travelled to Madrid in search of reparations, with support from William Godolphin, the English representative at court, but had no success and sought licence to take restitutive action. By 1675, the Lords of Trade issued a proclamation for 'bringing in the head of Fitzgerald the pirate'.⁵⁷

The historiography of the British Caribbean has traditionally concentrated on sugar and slavery, but recent work has broadened the focus to reveal a more complex picture. Jamaica's was a dual economy, in which plunder and contraband trade were as important as agricultural production into the mid-eighteenth century and beyond.⁵⁸ Furthermore, although the emerging Atlantic empire may have been, as Armitage claimed, 'commercial, maritime and free', it was certainly not exclusively protestant. Of necessity, the early English Atlantic needed to engage with the Catholic empires and, although Fitzgerald's career reveals the difficulties of commanding Irish loyalty, the Irish, with their well-established diasporic links in the Catholic world, did provide the English with a valuable tool in securing economic cooperation across the imperial and confessional divide. In so doing they were able to carve out a profitable niche for themselves in what was, ultimately, an increasingly secular and pragmatic world.

Notes

1 Carla Gardina Pestana, *The English Conquest of Jamaica: Cromwell's Bid for Empire* (Cambridge, MA: Harvard University Press, 2017).
2 K. O. Kupperman, 'Errand to the Indies: Puritan colonization from Providence Island through the Western Design', *William and Mary Quarterly* 45 (1988),

70–99; David Armitage, *Ideological Origins of the British Empire* (Cambridge: Cambridge University Press, 2000), pp. 61–3, 173 (quotation).

3 Kristen Block and Jenny Shaw, 'Subjects without an empire: The Irish in the early modern Caribbean', *Past and Present* 210:1 (February 2011), 33–60; Gabriel Glickman, 'Catholic interests and the politics of English overseas expansion 1660–1689', *Journal of British Studies* 55 (2016), 680–708.

4 Hilary McD. Beckles, ' "A riotous and unruly lot": Irish indentured servants and freemen in the English West Indies, 1644–1713', *William and Mary Quarterly* 47 (1990), 503–22; L. M. Cullen, 'The Irish diaspora in the seventeenth and eighteenth centuries', in Nicholas Canny, ed., *Europeans on the Move: Studies on European Migration, 1500–1800* (Oxford: Oxford University Press, 1994), pp. 113–49; Jenny Shaw, *Everyday Life in the Early English Caribbean* (Athens: University of Georgia Press, 2013); Natalie A. Zacek, *Settler Society in the English Leeward Islands, 1670–1776* (Cambridge: Cambridge University Press, 2010).

5 Hilary McD. Beckles and Andrew Downes, 'The economics of transition to the black labour system in Barbados', *Journal of Interdisciplinary History* 18 (1987), 225–47; D. W. Galenson, *White Servitude in Colonial America: An Economic Analysis* (Cambridge: Cambridge University Press, 1981), pp. 117–40.

6 When the first census was taken in 1662, the white population was 3,653; by the time of the next census, in 1673, the white population had doubled to 7,768. Despite steady migration in the 1670s and 1680s the population remained at the same level in 1693 after the destruction of an earthquake, disease and war. It reached 8,238 by 1730. Trevor Burnard, 'European migration to Jamaica, 1655–1780', *William and Mary Quarterly* 53:4 (October 1996), 769–96 (pp. 772–3).

7 Although evidence is fragmentary, Burnard suggests that European migration to seventeenth-century English Jamaica was dominated by free labour. Servants accounted for about 25 per cent of immigrants between 1671 and 1675, and similar figures are obtained for other periods with documentation; *ibid.*, p. 782.

8 Robert C. Nash, 'Irish Atlantic trade in the seventeenth and eighteenth centuries', *William and Mary Quarterly* 42:3 (July 1985), 329–56.

9 Cullen, 'The Irish diaspora', pp. 126–7. On eighteenth-century Irish networks in the Caribbean see Orla Power, 'Friend, foe or family? Catholic creoles, French Huguenots, Scottish dissenters: Aspects of the Irish diaspora at St Croix, Danish West Indies, *c.* 1760', in Niall Whelehan, ed., *Transnational Perspectives on Modern Irish History* (Abingdon: Routledge, 2015), pp. 30–44.

10 Nuala Zahedieh, 'Trade, plunder, and economic development in early English Jamaica, 1655–89', *Economic History Review* 39:2 (May 1986), 205–22.

11 Estimates of bullion produced are tabled in Stanley J. Stein and Barbara H. Stein, *Silver, Trade and War: Spain and America in the Making of Early Modern Europe* (Baltimore: Johns Hopkins University Press, 2000), p. 24. Estimates of sugar production are provided by Noel Deerr, *The History of Sugar*, 2 vols (London: Chapman and Hall, 1949–50); the British colonies accounted for 40–50 per cent of sugar output at the end of the seventeenth century.

12 Nuala Zahedieh, 'The merchants of Port Royal, Jamaica, and the Spanish contraband trade, 1655–1692', *William and Mary Quarterly* 43:4 (October 1986), 570–93.
13 James Houston, *Dr Houston's Memoirs of His Own Life Time* (London: Blackstaff, 1747), p. 275.
14 Nash, 'Irish Atlantic trade', pp. 341–4.
15 Josiah Child provided reasons for the Netherlanders' advance in trade: 'their toleration of different opinions in matters of religion: by reason whereof many industrious people of other countries, that dissent from the established government of their own churches, resort to them with their families and estates and after a few years co-habitation with them, become of the same common interest'; Josiah Child, *A Discourse Concerning Trade etc.* (London: A. Sowle, 1693), p. 7. Charles Davenant, *The Political and Economical Works of That Celebrated Writer Charles Davenant*, ed. Charles Whitworth, 5 vols (London: printed for R. Horsfield, 1771), Vol. II, discourse iii, pp. 2–8, 416.
16 As quoted by Glickman, 'Catholic interests', p. 704.
17 David Buisseret, ed., *Jamaica in 1687: The Taylor Manuscript at the National Library of Jamaica* (Kingston: University of West Indies Press, 2008), p. 240.
18 Using names in the St Andrew's militia lists, Burnard reckoned that the Irish accounted for 4 per cent of the white population, but he noted that 'sources may under-represent the Irish in the population' and it is probably a conservative estimate. Burnard, 'European migration', pp. 784–5.
19 Karst de Jong, 'The Irish in Jamaica during the long eighteenth century (1698–1836)', Ph.D. thesis (Queen's University Belfast, 2017), pp. 63–8.
20 *Ibid.*
21 Stapleton was from a well-established family originally from Co. Tipperary who fled Ireland in the Cromwellian wars, settling in both France and Spain and retaining connections there as well as links with the Caribbean. After the Restoration, William Stapleton became Governor of the Leeward Islands. John Stapleton seems to have settled in Jamaica in the 1680s and is recorded in 1687 as a signatory to the petition of support for Father Thomas Churchill (see n. 38). He is otherwise elusive and difficult to trace through records. There is no record of his owning property in Jamaica but the fact that he later settled in Saint-Domingue and purchased property shows that he had financial resources. It seems he was a merchant who regularly did business with the French; De Jong, 'The Irish in Jamaica', p. 62.
22 National Archives of Jamaica, Spanish Town, Inv. 1B/II/3/12, fo. 107; 1B/II/3/16, fo. 172.
23 Apart from the two Governors, John Bourden – born in Coleraine, and an early arrival who served as an assembly and Council member – briefly served as President after the earthquake of 1692; Frank Cundall, *The Governors of Jamaica in the Seventeenth Century* (London: West India Committee, 1936). In contrast to Scots, Protestant Irishmen could practise English law, and with a shortage of trained lawyers in Jamaica they began to fill these positions. Examples include William Broderick, from a Protestant family in Co. Cork,

who arrived in Jamaica in 1693, was elected to the Assembly in 1695, and was soon after raised to the Council, then Attorney General, and Judge of Admiralty in 1697; Totterdell, elected to the Assembly for Port Royal and Speaker in 1706; Edmund Kelly from Galway (one of five brothers who all arrived in the 1710s), who was appointed Attorney General in 1714 and Speaker of the Assembly in 1719; and Andrew Arcedeckne, who arrived sometime after 1714 and was a member of the Assembly alongside a brother. De Jong, 'The Irish in Jamaica', pp. 74–94.

24 'Petition of merchants and traders concerned in Jamaica', 20 April 1693, in J. W. Fortescue, ed., *Calendar of State Papers Colonial, America and West Indies*, Vol. XIV, *1693–1696* (London: HMSO, 1903), no. 285; Beeston to Committee of Trade, 24 August 1695, The National Archives, Kew (TNA), CO138/8, fo. 56; F. J. Osborne, 'James Castillo, asiento agent', *Jamaican Historical Review* 8 (1971), 9–18.

25 Clarence H. Haring, *Trade and Navigation between Spain and the Indies in the Time of the Habsburgs* (Cambridge, MA: Harvard University Press, 1918); John Stevens, *The Spanish Rule of Trade to the West Indies* (London, 1702); Geoffrey J. Walker, *Spanish Politics and Imperial Trade, 1700–1789* (London: Indiana University Press, 1979); John Cary, *An Essay on the State of England in Relation to Its Trade* (Bristol: W. Bonny, 1695), pp. 114–15.

26 Nuala Zahedieh, '"A frugal prudential and hopeful trade": Privateering in Jamaica, 1655–89', *Journal of Imperial and Commonwealth History* 18:2 (1990), 145–68; Zahedieh, 'Trade, plunder, and economic development', pp. 215–16.

27 Thomas Lynch to Benjamin Worsley, 8 July 1673, in W. Noel Sainsbury, ed., *Calendar of State Papers Colonial, America and West Indies*, Vol. VII, *1669–1774* (London: HMSO, 1889), no. 1115. See below, p. 000.

28 'The 'coast trade', outside the main ports, was firmly established by 1670 and became concentrated at fixed points, such as Monkey's Key in the Samballoes, a few miles outside Portobello; the Brew, which served Cartagena; and the South Keys of Cuba. 'Notes on illicit trade carried on by sloops from Jamaica with the Spanish', n.d., National Library of Jamaica, MS 1049; Nathaniel Uring, *A History of the Voyages and Travels of Capt. Nathaniel Uring* (London: printed by W. Wilkins for J. Peele, 1726), pp. 164–6. For a detailed description of Monkey Island see Thomas Erskines to Hans Sloane, n.d., British Library (BL), Sloane MS 4047, fo. 170.

29 Nuala Zahedieh, 'Defying mercantilism: Illicit trade, trust, and the Jamaican Sephardim, 1660–1730', *Historical Journal* 61:1 (2018), 77–102.

30 *Journals of the Assembly of Jamaica: 1664–1826*, 14 vols (Jamaica: [n.p.], 1811–29), Vol. II, p. 483.

31 Lauren Benton, *A Search for Sovereignty: Law and Geography in European Empires, 1400–1900* (Cambridge: Cambridge University Press, 2010).

32 K. G. Davies, *The Royal African Company* (New York: Longmans, Green, 1957); 'Approval of contract made with Srs Domingo Grillo and Ambrosio Lomelin', Minutes of General Court of African Company, 20 June 1664, TNA, T70/75, fos 11–12.

33 Information provided by Alejandro Garcia Monton, October 2016.
34 Both governments maintained strict prohibitions on commercial exchange, but the treaty did permit ships of either nation to enter the other's ports to wood and water when in distress, which was a long-established vehicle for covert trade. F. G. Davenport, ed., *European Treaties Bearing on the History of the United States and Its Dependencies*, 4 vols, Vol. II (Washington, DC: Carnegie Institution of Washington, 1929), pp. 187–96; A. P. Thornton, *West India Policy under the Restoration* (Oxford: Oxford University Press, 1956), pp. 67–123.
35 Sir Joseph Williamson to Lord Vaughan, 12 May 1677, TNA, CO1/138/2, fo. 150; Osborne, 'James Castillo, asiento agent'.
36 Smith Kelly was an early arrival; he was Deputy Provost Marshall in the 1670s, and promoted in 1686. He owned a 200 acre plantation in St Thomas-in-the-East. The wider Catholic community is glimpsed in a petition to the Duke of Albemarle in 1687 signed by John Jones, Francis Thomas, Redmond McRaugh, William Linwood, Bryan M'Grah, James Wate, John Stapleton, George Pigot, Edward Anthill, Richard Morton, Wm Worley, James Lispenasse and others; anon., 'An address of the Catholics in Jamaica to the Duke of Albemarle', in *Interesting Tracts relating to the Island of Jamaica, from its conquest, down to the year 1702* (Spanish Town, 1800), pp. 214–15.
37 Father Churchill petitioned the Governor to construct a new Roman Catholic church in Spanish Town. Castillo objected and claimed he had jurisdiction on the island. The Governor ruled in favour of Churchill. Castillo was found guilty of perjury, and together with Dempsey he fled to Cuba and subsequently to England with the assistance of Smith Kelly; 'The case of Smith Kelly', May 1688, in J. W. Fortescue, ed., *Calendar of State Papers Colonial, America and West Indies*, Vol. XII, *1685–1688* (London: HMSO, 1899), no. 1754. Castillo returned to the island in 1693 to recover his possessions and became a naturalised citizen. Osborne, 'James Castillo, asiento agent'.
38 Nuala Zahedieh, 'Regulation, rent-seeking and the Glorious Revolution in the British Atlantic economy', *Economic History Review* 63:4 (November 2010), 865–90; William Beeston to Lords of Trade and Plantations, 18 November 1694, in Fortescue, *Calendar of State Papers Colonial*, Vol. XIV, no. 1517.
39 Nuala Zahedieh, 'Monopoly and free trade: Changes in the organization of the British slave trade, 1660–1720', *Proceedings of the Instituto Internazionale di Storia Economica* 44 (2014), 651–62.
40 BL, Add. MS 25562 fos 17–18.
41 Houston, *Memoirs*, pp. 218–20, 280, 310–11.
42 *Ibid.*, pp. 279–80.
43 Thomas Bernard to John Chetwynd, February 1720, in Cecil Headlam, ed., *Calendar of State Papers Colonial, America and West Indies*, Vol. XXXI, *1719–1720* (London: HMSO, 1933), no. 548.
44 Extract of letter from Capt. Vernon to Mr Burchett, 7 November 1720, in Headlam, *Calendar of State Papers Colonial*, Vol. XXXI, no. 527.

45 Morfa defected from the privateer stronghold at Tortuga in the mid-1630s and allied himself with Spanish forces who attacked the island in 1634. He cultivated a close personal relationship with the Governor of Hispaniola and distinguished himself as a naval officer throughout the Caribbean. Military acumen and familiarity with Hispaniola's northern waters qualified him to lead the Spanish offensive against the French in Tortuga in 1652. Block and Shaw, 'Subjects without an empire', pp. 44–6.

46 Beeston to Lords of Trade and Plantations, 7 July 1694, in Fortescue, *Calendar of State Papers Colonial*, Vol. XIV, no. 1131.

47 Beeston to the Duke of Shrewsbury, 18 August 1694, in Fortescue, *Calendar of State Papers Colonial*, Vol. XIV, no. 1236.

48 De Jong, 'The Irish in Jamaica', pp. 61–3.

49 Will of Jean Stapleton, 1698, as noted in Guy Saupin, 'Les réseaux commerciaux des Irlandais de Nantes sous le règne de Louis XIV', in David Dickson, Jan Parmentier and Jane Ohlmeyer, eds, *Irish and Scottish Mercantile Networks in Europe and Overseas in the Seventeenth and Eighteenth Centuries* (Ghent: Academia Press, 2007), pp. 136–40.

50 De Jong, 'The Irish in Jamaica', p. 37; *Journals of the Assembly of Jamaica*, Vol. II, pp. 158, 169.

51 In 1673, Fitzgerald sailed from Havana to the Yucatan coast, where he took six ships carrying logwood. Testimonies of the capture and accounts of the prizes value the English ships and their goods at between 50,000 and 60,000 pesos, which, minus costs and food, left the total profits of the voyage at 40,000 pesos. After deductions for the King's 'royal fifth' and the outfitters, Fitzgerald himself earned just over 30,000 pesos on the voyage. Archivo General de Indias, Seville, Spain, 'Autos de Don Felipe Geraldino', Havana, 4 April 1673, Indif. 1600, no. 28.

52 Lynch to Worsley, 8 July 1673, Minutes of the Committee of Trade and Plantations, 30 September 1675, in W. Noel Sainsbury, ed., *Calendar of State Papers Colonial, America and West Indies*, Vol. IX, 1675–1676 (London: HMSO, 1893), no. 1115.

53 'Petition of Thomas Jarvis, William How, Robert Higgins, Richard Ashall, Edmond Cooke, Matthew Fox and divers others trading into the Western plantations to the King in Council', 27 February 1674, in Sainsbury, *Calendar of State Papers Colonial*, Vol. IX, no. 1226.

54 *Ibid.*

55 *Ibid.*

56 *Ibid.*

57 Minutes of the Committee of Trade and Plantations, 30 September 1675, in Sainsbury, *Calendar of State Papers Colonial*, Vol. IX, no. 687.

58 Zahedieh, 'Trade, plunder, and economic development'.

5

Doing business in the wartime Caribbean: John Byrn, Irish merchant of Kingston, Jamaica (September–October 1756)

Thomas M. Truxes

At seven o'clock on the morning of 1 December 1756, the French privateer *La Machaut* crossed paths with an Irish trading vessel, the *Europa* of Dublin, on its voyage from Kingston, Jamaica, to Holyhead and Dublin. The *Europa* carried a typical Jamaican cargo of sugar, rum, cotton, coffee, logwood, pimiento and mahogany plank. 'Flying French colours', *La Machaut* fired a warning shot, 'hoisted out her boat', took possession of the Irish ship and placed a prize crew aboard. Three weeks later, the *Europa* – now in French hands – was making its way to Brest when it fell in with a powerful British privateer, the thirty-two-gun *Defiance* of London, and its crew of 250. Out-gunned and out-manned, the Frenchmen surrendered without incident, after which the *Europa* was 'carried by the English into the port of Penzance in County of Cornwall'.[1]

A well-stocked mailbag was among the items stowed in the cabin of the *Europa*'s Irish captain, James Cook. Much of what it contained related to commercial life in Kingston and the management of the island's great sugar estates, but a large share was the correspondence of ordinary men and women in Jamaica to family and friends throughout the British Isles. Buried deep in that mailbag were four letters from an obscure Irish merchant – John Byrn of Dublin – to his associates in Dublin and London. The chapter that follows exploits this tiny collection of documents, together with miscellaneous correspondence in the *Europa* collection, to shed light upon the operations of a fledgling Irish trading enterprise in the early phase of the Seven Years War in Kingston.[2]

Kingston in the autumn of 1756

Kingston was 'the most trading, and only very considerable town in the island', wrote a British visitor (Figure 5.1). 'It is large and very well

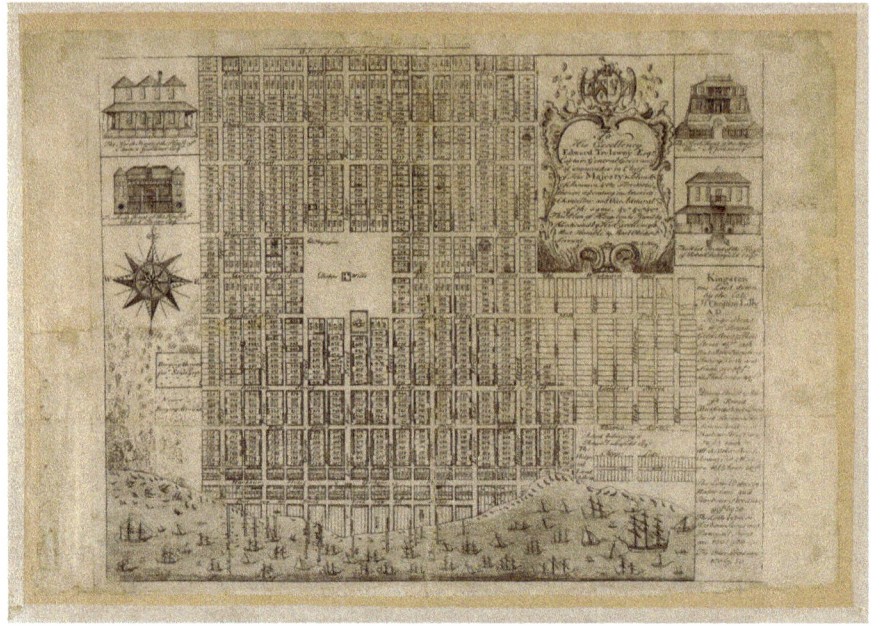

Figure 5.1 Michael Hay, map of Kingston, 1745, Library of Congress, Geography and Map Division, G4964.K5G46. 1745.H3.

inhabited', he said, 'the streets spacious, and regularly laid out, cutting one another at right angles'.[3] At mid-century, Kingston had a population of perhaps 10,000, and was on its way to becoming the third largest city in British America after Philadelphia and New York.[4] Roughly two-thirds of the population was composed of free and enslaved blacks, and, unlike other British West Indian cities, women played a prominent role in urban life. But Kingston's *raison d'être* was commerce. The city was the 'residence of the most considerable merchants, whose ships load and unload there, which makes it a place of vast trade', wrote Malachy Postlethwayt, a contemporary authority on commercial life, 'and there are never less than two or three hundred vessels in the bay before it'.[5]

The lion's share of Jamaican sugar, the island's largest export, went aboard vessels departing Kingston. This trade was mostly in the hands of commission merchants serving principals in London, the centre of British commercial life. The trade of Kingston 'depends wholly on the planting interest', wrote a mid-1750s resident, 'there being scarcely any thing imported there at this time, but what is immediately for their use'.[6] Vast quantities of foodstuffs and manufactured goods from Great Britain and Ireland poured into the shops that lined the city's thoroughfares. 'The islanders wear, eat, and drink, scares any thing', observed Postlethwayt, 'but what comes from [the British Isles and North America], except Madeira wine'.[7]

Not all commerce conformed to the legal requirements of the British commercial system. Kingston was the focus of a thriving contraband trade with the Spanish Main. It was, at its heart, the exchange of British manufactures and enslaved Africans for Spanish silver. 'Notwithstanding all the care that the courts of England and Spain have hitherto taken, to prevent a clandestine trade being carried on from Jamaica to the Spanish Main, they have not been able to suppress it', wrote Postlethwayt. Although reforms undertaken in Spain following the end of the War of the Austrian Succession (1748), together with the more frequent movement of ships between Cádiz and Spanish ports in America, reduced the scale of contraband trade, it accelerated once again with the opening of the Seven Years War. In 1756, merchants in Kingston were eager to serve this lucrative market. 'The Spaniards are as fond of it as the English', said Postlethwayt, 'though they run no less hazard in buying the merchandise, than the English do in selling it to them'.[8]

Kingston was the largest slave-trading venue in British America, and until 1758 Jamaica's sole port of entry for enslaved African men, women and children.[9] In the mid-1750s, roughly 11,150 captives arrived annually. The enslaved population had surged from about 88,000 in the mid-1740s and would reach about 140,000 by the late 1760s.[10] But in the autumn of 1756, uncertainty bred by war was dampening trade in African captives. 'The sale of the slaves is slow but keep at a good price', wrote a mariner arriving from the West Africa.[11] In the autumn of 1756, even the weather dampened sales. 'We have not sold near so many as we expected', said one merchant, 'owing, as an addition to the other causes, to the excessive rains which we have had for these three weeks past'.[12] But the main stimulant was demand for enslaved labour on the Spanish Main, a point emphasised by a large Kingston dealer:

> There is at present a demand for one thousand Bite and Angola negroes for the Spaniards, their agents here give £34 per head for assorted cargoes, and pay for them in silver at 7/6 per oz. generally at the return of the vessel that carries them over, but for the country there's little or no demand for negroes of any denomination, our planters having been for three years last past so amply supplied that they ask from twelve months to two years credit to take them off our hands, and more especially since the declaration of the French War, they are shy of purchasing at any rate.[13]

War brought scattered benefits to Kingston. Great Britain's unprecedented military spending spread cash around the island, putting money in the hands of contractors serving the fleet, labourers shoring up defences, and ordinary soldiers and sailors frequenting Kingston's taverns and brothels. The rising number of captured French merchantmen condemned in Kingston's Court of Vice Admiralty led to the availability of ships and cargoes at fire-sale prices. French prize vessels were especially appealing to merchants desperate to get goods off the island. Many of these ships were in a sorry state, however. 'The prizes taken before the declaration of war are condemned and they're selling this week', one merchant told his correspondent in Cork. 'They are much eaten with the worm', he said, 'but vessels being much wanted here, they go at a great price'.[14] Bidding for prizes created tensions between Kingston merchants and naval officers stationed at Port Royal. 'It is said the captains of the men-of-war intended to being large purchasers.'[15]

Even in peacetime, uncertain harvests, volatile markets, excessive mortality in the free and enslaved workforce, and devastating hurricanes were ordinary features of life on Jamaica. War brought additional anxieties. Although fighting in British America had been under way since the summer of 1755, the war was only beginning to affect Jamaica in a serious way. And the news from Europe and North America was ominous. 'We are credibly informed that Portmahon is taken', wrote the Irish merchant John Byrn (the subject of this chapter) in September 1756.[16] Loss of Britain's great naval base on Minorca in the Mediterranean would be a blow to national pride that had serious strategic implications. A few days later, the *Jamaica Courant* confirmed Byrn's fears, expressing the consternation felt throughout the empire and laying blame squarely on the British naval officer who had failed to protect the island. 'It is publicly said', the *Courant* reported, 'that Admiral Byng is to be put under arrest, and closely confined as soon as he arrives in any port in Great Britain'.[17] War news from America was equally bad. 'Our last advices from North America which came a few days ago inform us we are very unsuccessful', wrote John Thomson, an Irish merchant in Kingston.[18]

Most worrisome was the immediate threat to Jamaica by French forces gathering on Saint-Domingue, roughly 350 miles from Kingston. 'We are at a present in a very disagreeable situation', wrote John and Alexander Harvie in early October. 'The French have a squadron at Hispaniola greatly superior to ours here and this the ministry have known for sometime, yet they have not sent in any reinforcements.' But all was not lost, they added with a sneer. 'We are greatly obliged to the French for we do not as yet hear that they have so much as taken one of our vessels, though they have had it in their power to intercept our whole trade.'[19] The distress was widely shared. 'We greatly want more ships of war here', wrote John Byrn, and '[I] am surprised the government neglect so valuable an island as this of Jamaica'.[20]

John Byrn, Irish merchant of Kingston

There was a small Irish presence in Kingston's merchant community, unlike Bridgetown, Barbados, and elsewhere in the eastern Caribbean. In the middle years of the century, the most prominent Irish house on Jamaica was the partnership of Edmund & Dominick Duany, town agents for several large plantations. The Duanys, and similar enterprises, managed all phases of their clients' commerce with the larger world, from the marketing of sugar and other goods to the purchase of household and plantation supplies. Among the other Irish enterprises in Kingston at mid-century were those of Charles Inman, William Stewart and John Curtin. Although their firms functioned primarily as commission houses, they sometimes landed goods from Ireland on their own account.[21]

John Byrn, a recent arrival in the mid-1750s, was well connected with trading houses in Dublin and London. Although experienced in the intricacies of Atlantic commerce, Byrn did not rank among the leading merchants of Kingston. He appears, rather, to have fitted into the upper-middle tier of traders exporting plantation produce and importing articles suitable for Jamaica's planter and professional classes. It is likely that Byrn's business was situated near the city's waterfront, where he appears to have operated a retail shop attached to his dwelling and store rooms. If not among the city's great merchants on Port Royal Street, immediately adjacent to the Kingston wharves, he would have been close by, perhaps on Harbour Street (next back from Port Royal Street) or one of the adjoining cross-streets, such as Orange Street or Lower King Street (see Figure 5.1).[22]

Byrn was a commission merchant, the most common type of overseas trader in British America. As such, he represented clients on both sides of the Atlantic, transacting business 'for European merchants and others that supplied this market with different sorts of commodities at their own risk, as well as for different planters for whom they may be occasionally concerned', wrote Patrick Browne in his 1756 description of Jamaican commerce. Factors earned, he added, 'a regular commission on the sale and purchase of every thing that passes through their hands'.[23]

Byrn's exports of sugar, cotton, ginger and other island produce, as well as his imports of Irish provisions and assorted dry goods, were largely supported by capital in the British Isles. His own resources were stretched thin by office and warehouse expenses, the wages of employees, costs associated with loading and unloading ships, cartage fees, customs duties, and harbour and wharfage fees.[24] In addition to business conducted for others, he carried on a modest trade on his own account and appears to have held a half-share in a vessel, the *James and John*, trading between Kingston and Dublin. 'These people', wrote Browne, 'are generally industrious, and seldom fail making considerable fortunes when well befriended, or furnished with money'.[25]

In Dublin, John Byrn's principal correspondent, and occasional partner, was Alderman James Dunn (the recipient of two letters in the *Europa* collection). Dunn was a Presbyterian merchant-politician whose success in a parliamentary by-election in 1756 challenged the Anglican elite's domination of Irish political life.²⁶ From his counting house on Lower Ormond Quay, Dunn shipped a variety of salted provisions, articles that found a ready market in Jamaica where there was a preference for Irish beef and butter over their North American rivals. And through his connections in London's thriving Irish merchant community – in the vicinity of the London Guildhall – Dunn shipped tea and luxury dry goods. Byrn's correspondents in London included James Digges La Touche – another prominent Dubliner – and the London–Belfast partnership of George & James Portis, a firm anchored in the linen-producing region of the North of Ireland.²⁷ There were letters to LaTouche and the Portises in the *Europa* mailbag.

In the autumn of 1756, Byrn appears to have been in Kingston only a few months. 'Next Year will (please God) convince thee of the advantage accruing from this Trade', he told Dunn on the eve of the *Europa*'s departure for the British Isles.²⁸ But Kingston was taking its toll on Byrn. His health was fragile, and he missed his wife. Afflicted with asthma, she remained behind in Dublin, while he struggled with self-imposed bachelorhood. 'I am quite at a loss without her', he wrote. Byrn missed the stability of domestic life. 'I don't like public houses', he complained, 'yet can't avoid going to them'. Lonely and isolated, Byrn was disdainful of his fellow Kingston merchants. 'I refer thee to the body of merchants residing here', he told Dunn, 'and am confident that neither negligence nor inactivity, prodigality nor foppery, gaming nor excesses, as I've seen many involved in, are to be laid in any measure to my charge'.²⁹ Byrn's scorn for his fellow merchants – and their excesses – may have created social barriers to his advancement into the upper ranks of Kingston's trading community.³⁰

The scope of Byrn's trade

John Byrn's exports were the product of a powerful agricultural engine wholly dependent on an enslaved African workforce. In the mid-1750s, Jamaica annually shipped roughly 450,000 cwt (hundredweight) of sugar to ports in England and Wales. That level rose to better than 950,000 cwt by the outbreak of the American Revolution. Of the 75,000 cwt of British West Indian sugar re-exported from Great Britain to Ireland in 1756, about 30,000 cwt was Jamaican, an amount that exceeded 80,000 cwt by 1775. Sugar exports were driven by rising consumer demand in the British Isles, a protected home market in which West Indian produce was becoming, for many, a feature of daily life.³¹

Most Jamaican sugar entered the British market on consignment (with planters retaining ownership until their goods were sold). The largest planters preferred the consignment trade, largely in the hands of full-service London commission houses, many of them powerful firms with privileged access to financial and marketing resources. Charging a commission of typically 2½ per cent, they managed all aspects of the importation, warehousing and sale of their clients' sugar, rum, cotton, dyestuffs and other goods. Situated at the heart of British commercial life, these London houses could time the sale of their clients' produce to great advantage. For their correspondents in the British Caribbean, London commission houses supplied everything from household furnishings to the equipment required in sugar processing, fine wine and speciality foodstuffs suitable for the planter's table.[32]

In the autumn of 1756, John Byrn was eager to participate in this activity, if only as an intermediary between more modest planters and firms in London seeking a share in the lucrative consignment trade. 'I may with some friends here next crop procure thee a consignment [of sugar]', he told LaTouche, a fellow Dubliner doing business in London. 'If that will answer, more in course may follow'.[33] Most of Byrn's export trade, however, was as a commission merchant on behalf of principals in the British Isles who imported sugar, rum, cotton, ginger, pimiento, mahogany and other plantation articles on their own account.

Although Byrn typically bore a small share of the risk, he sometimes played a larger role. In the summer of 1756, for example, a vessel in which he owned a share departed Kingston 'for Holyhead and Dublin with a full lading of choice sugars, some mahogany, and a little logwood [a valuable dyewood re-exported from the Bay of Campeche]'. 'Our snow's sugars must go greatly to profit', he told LaTouche, his occasional Irish partner.[34] Gathering such a cargo strained Byrn's resources, and he was wary about accumulating debt. In a letter to Dunn, Byrn remarked on 'thy not having me purchase more goods than I can either pay for, or receive in payment'.[35] The retail shop in Kingston offered a practical means of raising cash.

Nearly all store advertising in surviving newspapers of Kingston, Montego Bay and St Jago in the middle decades of the century featured Irish linens, and many advertisements offered Irish provisions.[36] One of Byrn's competitors in Kingston, Gerard Nash, a man 'well situated with a store', urged his Bristol correspondent to make haste sending Irish goods: candles, tallow and 'Irish soap', together with beef, butter and '100 barrels herrings if they can be got so good as the last', adding 'they are much in demand'.[37] John Crow, another Kingston merchant, pressed his London correspondent 'for 50 barrels of full bound new beef to which add 50 firkins of best *Rose* or *Flower de Luce* butter, and 20 firkins tallow, which I desire may be sent by the first vessel that touches at Cork from London'.[38]

As with these men, Irish provisions were a mainstay of John Byrn's trade. But in September and October 1756, he was beginning to feel the pinch of reduced supplies brought on by French privateers disrupting trade in and out of the Caribbean. 'Good butter I am quite out of', he told Dunn, 'having only eighteen firkins of the old butter ... and 10 of them are engaged'. 'I shall want more cargo beef and pork', he wrote, and 'my moiety of the herrings on hand is but 38 barrels'.[39] Added to this was Byrn's annoyance over a recent shipment of Irish kosher beef. 'The Jew-beef is excepted to', he complained, 'as not properly sealed and made up ... [I] have only sold two barrels of it.' Byrn was trying to connect with Kingston's wealthy Jewish merchant community, and his frustration is palpable: 'I wrote that care should be taken both as to certificate, sealing, &c., had it been so, it would have sold at 60 shillings per cask the very day it was landed.'[40]

His other imports included fabrics (from common linens to delicate India silk), ready-to-wear apparel, tea, and miscellaneous light manufactures such as quills and pens. Irish linens – which, he reported, 'afford a good profit' – were transshipped through London, where they benefited from an export bounty.[41] In Kingston, Byrn served a wealthy and discriminating clientele. 'Damasks of the East Indies are used here for furniture', he wrote, 'but the good English silks, satins (white, blue and some green), Paduasoys [rich corded or embossed silk fabrics] ... never want a sale with us.' In addition to fabrics, Byrn dealt in men's and women's shoes, 'ladies ruffles',[42] satin petticoats, men's shirts, and 'thread and cotton hose for men, women, and children, course and fine'.[43] He likewise catered to discriminating Jamaican tea drinkers. 'The best Hyson [teas] are such as answer at this market', he wrote. 'A superfine Singlo might pass well, but Hyson much better.'[44] 'If all well laid in, [they] will certainly answer.'[45]

Managing the business

John Byrn was beset by the challenges of managing a business in Kingston. His was pretty much a one-man show, and there was much to do. He was responsible for purchasing the produce he exported; ordering, and later distributing, incoming cargoes; managing a retail shop; negotiating bills of exchange; securing space aboard outbound ships; overseeing the packing and loading of goods; arranging marine insurance; maintaining ledgers and other accounts; collecting debts; supervising employees, including clerks, day-labourers and a variety of enslaved workers; and staying abreast of his commercial correspondence. Success likewise required that he remain attuned to market conditions, sensitive to customer preferences and alert to quirks in the supply chain, and that he manage risk in all its disguises.

Byrn's focus was on satisfying customers. 'I would not send for more goods', he told Dunn, 'where my constituents seem not pleased, or, as it were, diffident'. His caution is exemplified in his comments on what sells – and what does not. 'I've sold several pieces of thy India silk to a large profit', he told Dunn, 'however the good rich English silks are greatly preferred to them, and a man can vend three pieces of English for one of India silk here'. Byrn was particular with regard to shoes. 'The women's feet here are very small in general', he said, 'therefore the shoes should be made suitable'. He liked 'the silk shoes which were neatly made and purchased reasonable', but those of callimanco, a worsted wool fabric finished with a glazed surface, were 'clumsy and large, and many of them sharped toed'.[46]

Too often, goods from Europe arrived in dreadful condition, and Byrn was driven to distraction by the ineptness of packers in London and Dublin. Part of the blame was owing to harsh conditions at sea. But some of the damage, perhaps most, was the result of incompetence and indifference. 'Thou never saw cheese in such order', he complained regarding goods sent from Ireland, 'nay none but Negroes would taste them and no wonder'. 'As they were packed', he added, 'they could not escape damage'. Aboard the same ship, 'all the tea-chests have been so damaged that not one of them is salable'. And one cask of the hams, he reported, 'is almost to an ham eaten by the rats, yet I could not stop one penny of the freight, as such accidents the master is not answerable for'.[47]

The capacity of planters to pay for imports hinged on getting their produce to market in a timely fashion. War added to the difficulty of turning sugar into credit balances in Dublin and London upon which Byrn could draw. Planters were slow to pay for their purchases, however. 'Several planters and dealers owe largely for goods', Byrn told Dunn in September, 'which was not in their power to discharge this season, as several have given sugar only on account, few in full, and many not one penny'. Byrn counselled patience. 'This can't be avoided in this island, for otherwise we should not have any trade.' He understood that a planter could use the courts to his benefit and create interminable delays. 'Leniency and forbearance often in this place get a man his money sooner than rigorous means.'[48]

Byrn, loath himself to accumulate debt, covered his expenses with funds generated in his retail shop and bills of exchange drawn against his Irish and British correspondents. Bills of exchange were the life-blood of long-distance trade. A bill was analogous to a modern-day cheque, except that the funds were drawn against money in private hands rather than in a commercial bank. They were the ubiquitous financial instruments of the early modern Atlantic economy and, according to John Mair, an eighteenth-century authority, 'foreign trade could not long subsist without them'.[49]

Implicit in the bills mentioned in Byrn's letters is his preference for sterling bills drawn against trading houses in London, as opposed to bills drawn in Ireland and payable in Irish currency. In the examples here, Byrn is drawing on James Dunn's sterling balance in the hands of James Digges La Touche. 'I wrote the 22^d July per the Countess of Effingham, Captain Crowly, advising my three drafts on the account [of] James Dunn Esqr £100, £150, £220 sterling at 70 days sight', he told LaTouche. The number of days after 'sight' refers to a bill's usance: that is, the number of days after the delivery of a bill before payment was required. At seventy days, Byrn's three bills had exceptionally long usances (possibly owing to strained wartime conditions), thirty or forty days being more typical. These bills were written in favour of persons to whom Byrn wished to transfer funds. 'The first and second in favour of Nicholas Brook Esqr. [and] the third William Patrick Browne Esq., to which I doubt not honour has been paid.'[50]

Managing risk was another of Byrn's preoccupations. And he employed a variety of strategies to mitigate risk. For example, he urged correspondents in the British Isles to avoid shipping large consignments in a single vessel, recommending instead that goods be sent in modest-size batches and that these be staggered. 'I am surprised thou'd send so many herrings in one bottom', he told Dunn. 'They were enough to glut the market, 250, or 300 barrels at a time are full sufficient.' If they were shipped 'by sundry vessels from Cork or Dublin, butter, pork and beef also; then they would be good and fresh, and people would much more readily purchase'.[51] On the return voyage home, 'Shipping sugars, &c. on different bottoms to London might answer well, especially in time of war', Byrn suggested to a London correspondent, 'as some probably may escape when others are taken'.[52]

The most immediate challenges Byrn faced in the autumn of 1756 arose from war. 'Goods [of] almost every kind never were scarcer here than at this instant', wrote a competitor.[53] Because of the growing number of seizures by French privateers, fewer British and Irish trading vessels ventured across the Atlantic. Fewer ships made it increasingly difficult for merchants and planters to get their sugar, rum, cotton and other produce off the island and into the hands of consumers. 'For want of shipping [the planters] are under great difficulties of transmitting their produce to your market', another Jamaican trader told his London correspondent, 'by which means bills of exchange are scarce to be had and very little current money in the country'.[54] And with fewer vessels arriving from abroad, it was difficult for merchants to keep their shelves filled and meet the needs of customers. The consequences were entirely predictable: severe shortages and sharply rising prices. 'I wish you would make me up two dozen shirts', wrote an Irish officer of the Marines to his sister in Co. Kerry. 'A shirt that I could buy in Ireland for eight shillings', he said, 'would cost thirthy [sic] shillings here'.[55]

There was little Byrn could do to control prices and guarantee the safety of cargoes. He relied heavily on the character and competence of the ship captains who carried his goods across the Atlantic. One such man was James Cooke, master of the snow *Europa* of Dublin. 'He is (in my opinion) a worthy, honest, careful man, in whom confidence may well be placed.'[56] Always prudent, however, John Byrn insured his cargoes.[57] But insurance premiums were rising fast, eating away the profitability of trade, and Byrn's competitors were beginning to self-insure. 'Would advise you to ensure with or without convoy if the premium be moderate, that is, if at 10 guineas or under', one Kingston merchant told his correspondent in Bristol in September. Otherwise, he said, '[I] would rather run the risk than give more.'[58] Nine months later, other Kingston merchants were capping premiums at 'twenty guineas per cent at the most'.[59]

'This damned wicked French war as it 'tis [sic] carried on will be the ruin of many, both planters and merchants', wrote a Kingston trader eight months after the departure of the *Europa* in October 1756.[60] Whether it was the ruin of John Byrn we may never know. But there are tantalising clues. In the mid- and late 1760s, for example, a Philadelphia 'John Byrn' operated a store on Second Street offering goods similar to those in the shop in Kingston, including 'a great assortment of hosiery, and many other things, too tedious to insert'.[61] This Byrn appeared for the last time in Philadelphia newspapers in April 1770.[62] A year later, a 'John Byrne' began a decade-long stint as a sugar baker and distiller in Dublin. Beginning in 1771, his name appeared in *Wilson's Dublin Directory*, and in 1780 it was included in a petition of Dublin sugar refiners, the year his will was recorded in the Irish Registry of Wills.[63] These men may or may not be our 'John Byrn, merchant of Kingston'. But the middle decades of the eighteenth century saw a pattern of enterprising Irishmen setting up as commission traders in British America and later returning to Ireland with capital to invest. The most successful were, like the flaxseed merchants of New York and Philadelphia, well connected in Irish ports and the Irish merchant community in London.[64]

Notes

1 Interrogations of Jean Elis, French mariner, and Anthony McClaren, British mariner, 25 and 26 January 1757, TNA, HCA32/189 (*Europa*); TNA, HCA26/5/54 (privateer *Defiance*).
2 Attestation of Andrew Mitchelson, midshipman aboard privateer *Defiance*, 22 February 1757, TNA, HCA32/189 (*Europa*).
3 'Journal of an Officer's [Lord Adam Gordon's] Travels in America and the West Indies, 1764–1765', in Newton D. Mereness, ed., *Travels in the American Colonies* (New York: Macmillan, 1916), pp. 369–87 (p. 377).
4 Trevor Burnard, ' "The Grand Mart of the Island": The economic function of Kingston, Jamaica, in the mid-eighteenth century', in Kathleen E. A. Monteith and Glen Richards, eds, *Jamaica in Slavery and Freedom: History, Heritage and Culture* (Kingston: University of the West Indies Press, 2002), pp. 225–41 (p. 225); Trevor Burnard and Emma Hart, 'Kingston, Jamaica, and Charleston,

South Carolina: A new look at comparative urbanization in plantation colonial British America', *Journal of Urban History* 39:2 (2012), 214–34 (p. 217).
5 Malachy Postlethwayt, *The Universal Dictionary of Trade and Commerce*, 2 vols (London, 1775), n.p.
6 Patrick Browne, *The Civil and Natural History of Jamaica* (London, 1756), p. 10.
7 Postlethwayt, *The Universal Dictionary*.
8 Adrian Finucane, *The Temptations of Trade: Britain, Spain, and the Struggle for Empire* (Philadelphia: University of Pennsylvania Press, 2016), pp. 151–3; Postlethwayt, *Universal Dictionary*.
9 Burnard and Hart, 'Kingston, Jamaica, and Charleston, South Carolina', p. 221.
10 Richard B. Sheridan, *Sugar and Slavery: An Economic History of the British West Indies, 1623–1775* (Baltimore: Johns Hopkins University Press, 1974), p. 504; Jack P. Greene, *Settler Jamaica in the 1750s: A Social Portrait* (Charlottesville: University of Virginia Press, 2016), p. 36.
11 William Miller, Kingston, to James Phelps, Bristol, 9 October 1756, TNA, HCA 32/189.
12 John and Alexander Harvie, Kingston, to James Laroche, Bristol, 3 October 1756, TNA, HCA 30/259.
13 Hibberts & Millan, Kingston, to Benjamin Titley, London, 1 October 1756, TNA, HCA 32/189.
14 Gerard Nash, Kingston, to Stephen Denroach, Cork, 8 October 1756, TNA, HCA 30/259.
15 Harvie and Harvie to Laroche, 3 October 1756, TNA, HCA 30/259.
16 John Byrn, Kingston, to Alderman James Dunn, Dublin, 21 September 1756, TNA, HCA 30/259.
17 *Jamaica Courant, and Weekly Advertiser*, 28 September 1756.
18 John Thomson, Kingston, to Mrs Jane Thomson, Bigg Strand Street, Near Jervis Street, Dublin, 10 October 1756, TNA, HCA 32/189.
19 Harvie and Harvie to Laroche, 3 October 1756, TNA, HCA 30/259.
20 Byrn to James Digges La Touche, London, 23 September 1756, TNA, HCA 30/259. For the state of defences against a French attack in the vicinity of Kingston see Richard Pares, *War and Trade in the West Indies, 1739–1763* (Oxford: Clarendon Press, 1936), 246–8.
21 Correspondence of Edmund & Dominick Duany (1740–53), in S. D. Smith, ed., 'The Pares transcripts of the Lascelles and Maxwell letter books, 1739–1769', in *The Lascelles and Maxwell Letter Books (1739–1769)* (East Ardsley: Microform Academic Publishers, 2002); *Kingston Journal*, 24 October 1761 and 8 August 1767; account of Daniel Mussenden, Belfast, with William Stewart, Kingston, Jamaica, 19 June 1755, in Mussenden papers, Public Record Office of Northern Ireland (PRONI), D354/575; bill of lading, 19 June 1755, PRONI, D354/574; Kelly and Roche, Limerick, to John Curtin, Jamaica, 6 June 1745, in letter book, Limerick, 1744–8, National Library of Ireland, MS 827. For Richard Curtin & Co. of Cork (*c*. 1754) see TNA,

CO 142/16/45; and Thomas M. Truxes, *Irish-American Trade, 1660–1783* (Cambridge: Cambridge University Press, 1988), pp. 103–4.
22 For the location of Kingston merchants whose trade approximated that of John Byrn see the advertising of Thomas Gray, William Jamison, and John and Edward Foord in the *Jamaica Courant, and Weekly Advertiser*, 28 September 1756.
23 Browne, *The Civil and Natural History*, p. 23.
24 Thomas M. Truxes, ed., *Letterbook of Greg & Cunningham, 1756–57, Merchants of New York and Belfast, 1756–57* (London: British Academy, 2001), pp. 34–5.
25 Browne, *The Civil and Natural History*, p. 23.
26 *Dublin Directory* (1760), 14; David Dickson, *Dublin: The Making of a Capital City* (Cambridge, MA: Harvard University Press, 2014), p. 173.
27 Byrn to LaTouche, 23 September 1756, TNA, HCA 30/259; Byrn to George and James Portis, London, 23 September 1756, TNA, HCA 30/259; Thomas M. Truxes, 'London's Irish merchant community and North Atlantic commerce in the mid-eighteenth century', in David Dickson, Jan Parmentier and Jane Ohlmeyer, eds, *Irish and Scottish Mercantile Networks in Europe and Overseas in the Seventeenth and Eighteenth Centuries* (Ghent: Academia Press, 2007), pp. 271–309; TNA, HCA 26/12/5 (ship *True Briton*); John T. Gilbert, ed., *Calendar of Ancient Records of Dublin*, 19 vols (Dublin: Dollard, 1889–1944), Vol. IX, pp. 48, 90.
28 Byrn to Dunn, 10 October 1756, TNA, HCA 30/259.
29 Byrn to Dunn, 21 September 1756, TNA, HCA 30/259; Thomson to Thomson, 10 October 1756, TNA, HCA 32/189.
30 The author wishes to thank Professor Trevor Burnard of the University of Hull for his observations on this point, as well as for his generous comments on the text of this chapter.
31 Sheridan, *Sugar and Slavery*, pp. 488–9; Truxes, *Irish-American Trade*, p. 289.
32 S. D. Smith, *Slavery, Family, and Gentry Capitalism in the British Atlantic: The World of the Lascelles, 1648–1834* (Cambridge: Cambridge University Press, 2006), pp. 96, 196–8; Richard Pares, 'The London sugar market, 1740–1769', *Economic History Review* 9:2 (1956), 254–70 (255); Truxes, *Irish-American Trade*, pp. 91, 98, 160.
33 Byrn to LaTouche, 23 September 1756, TNA, HCA 30/259; Byrn to Portis, 23 September 1756, TNA, HCA 30/259.
34 Byrn to LaTouche, 23 September 1756, TNA, HCA 30/259.
35 Byrn to Dunn, 21 September 1756, TNA, HCA 30/259.
36 *Jamaica Courant*, 28 September 1756; *Jamaica Gazette*, 3 January 1765; *Kingston Journal*, 8 August 1767; and *Saint Iago Intelligencer*, 16 April 1768.
37 Nash to John Read, Bristol, 8 October 1756, TNA, HCA 32/189.
38 John Crow, Kingston, to Horlock & Wagstaffe, London, 2 October 1756, TNA, HCA 30/259.
39 Byrn to Dunn, 10 October 1756, TNA, HCA 30/259.
40 Byrn to Dunn, 21 September 1756, TNA, HCA 30/259.

41 Byrn to Portis, 23 September 1756, TNA, HCA 30/259; Truxes, *Irish-American Trade*, pp. 176–9.
42 Ruffles were a feature of male and female dress: 'A strip of lace or other material, gathered along one edge to make an ornamental frill, esp. for the wrist, breast, or neck of a garment'; *OED*, s.v. *ruffle*, n.1.
43 Byrn to Dunn, 10 October 1756, TNA, HCA 30/259.
44 Byrn to LaTouche, 23 September 1756, TNA, HCA 30/259.
45 Byrn to Portis, 23 September 1756, TNA, HCA 30/259.
46 Byrn to Dunn, 21 September 1756, TNA, HCA 30/259.
47 Byrn to Dunn, 21 September 1756, TNA, HCA 30/259.
48 Byrn to Dunn, 21 September 1756, TNA, HCA 30/259.
49 John Mair, *Book-keeping Moderniz'd, or Merchant-accounts by Double Entry, According to the Italian Form* (London, 1793), p. 351; Richard Rolt, *A New Dictionary of Trade and Commerce* (London, 1756), n.p.
50 Byrn to LaTouche, 23 September 1756, TNA, HCA 30/259.
51 Byrn to Dunn, 21 September 1756, TNA, HCA 30/259.
52 Byrn to LaTouche, 23 September 1756, TNA, HCA 30/259.
53 Thomas Gray, Kingston, to R. Rust, Norfolk, 12 October 1756, TNA, HCA 30/259.
54 Hibberts & Millan to Titley, 1 October 1756, TNA, HCA 32/189.
55 Edward O'Neal (Lieutenant of Marines onboard HMS *Dreadnought* at Jamaica), to Miss Jean O'Neal, at Lohercannon near Tralee, Kerry, Ireland, 4 October 1756, TNA, HCA 30/259.
56 Byrn to Dunn, 10 October 1756, TNA, HCA 30/259.
57 Byrn to LaTouche, 23 September 1756, TNA, HCA 30/259.
58 Mark Elliott, Kingston, to Robert Scott, Bristol, 27 September 1756, TNA, HCA 32/189.
59 Robert Stanton, Kingston, to Henry Bright, Bristol, 24 June 1757, in Kenneth Morgan, ed., *The Bright–Meyler Papers: A Bristol–West India Connection, 1732–1837* (London: British Academy, 2007), p. 329.
60 Stanton to Bright, 24 June 1757, in *ibid*.
61 *Pennsylvania Gazette*, 5 November 1767.
62 *Pennsylvania Journal*, 19 April 1770.
63 *Wilson's Dublin Directory for the Year 1771* (Dublin, 1771), p. 19; *Wilson's Dublin Directory for the Year 1774* (Dublin, 1774), p. 21; *Wilson's Dublin Directory for the Year 1776* (Dublin, 1776), p. 25; *Wilson's Dublin Directory for the Year 1778* (Dublin, 1778), p. 24; *Wilson's Dublin Directory for the Year 1779* (Dublin, 1779), p. 24; *Wilson's Dublin Directory for the Year 1780* (Dublin, 1780), p. 24; petition from the sugar refiners of the city of Dublin, 1780, Foster/Masserene papers, PRONI, MIC 500/42, D562/8416A.
64 Truxes, *Irish–American Trade*, pp. 193–211.

Part II

Consolidating territories

6

Ireland and British colonial slave-ownership, 1763–1833

Nicholas Draper

The first phase of the *Legacies of British Slave-Ownership* (*LBS*) project, based on the records of the Slave Compensation Commission of the 1830s, contrasted the relative levels of absentee slave-ownership in Ireland at the end of slavery with those in Scotland and England, and suggested some structural constraints that help explain the comparatively low level of such Irish slave-ownership.[1] In the second phase, *LBS* has been seeking to build a history of slave-ownership in the British colonies between *c.* 1763 and the termination of the British colonial slave system through the compensation process. In parallel with our own work, which has included slave-owners of Ireland alongside the other three nations, there has, over the past five years, been a significant increase in scholarly research both in Ireland and abroad on Ireland's entanglement in slavery: the conference that gave rise to this volume testifies to the range and depth of such new work.[2] These recent efforts, by *LBS* and by scholars who are far more grounded in the history of Ireland than are we, have both provided rich detail on the paths to ownership of those in possession of 'property in people' in the 1830s, and identified a new cadre of slave-owners in Britain and Ireland active in the period before Emancipation. At the same time, the generosity of other scholars and of family and local historians has enabled us to flesh out many of our previously skeletal accounts of Irish slave-owners in the original *LBS* research based on the slave-compensation papers.[3]

This chapter draws on the second-phase *LBS* material and on the related expansions of the first-phase material to highlight new findings for Irish slave-owners and to develop the analysis of the 'backwash' of slave-ownership in Ireland. The new evidence does not, in our view, overturn the major perspectives from the first phase, either for Britain or for Ireland. For Victorian Britain we argued that slave-ownership was constitutive, and our recent work cements our understanding of the central role slave-ownership also played in late-eighteenth-century England and Scotland. For Ireland (as for Wales), we argued that absentee ownership was proportionally lower than in Scotland or England. Again, the new evidence confirms this: in the new dataset, the number of slave-owners connected with Ireland has risen in proportion to the increase in the universe of slave-owners overall.

Neither in the first phase nor now does *LBS* claim that our work allows us to assess the importance either of slavery to Ireland or of Ireland to slavery. Our research continues to focus on the slave-owners and other individuals (creditors, mortgagees, annuitants) with financial claims on the enslaved people as 'property'. It does not consider the systemic effects of Ireland's role in the slave economy as a whole: the importance of late-eighteenth-century Cork as the leading provisioning centre for the British Caribbean, for example, or the role of demand from slave colonies in the development of the Irish linen industry. However, in combination the original and the more recent *LBS* work has now identified hundreds of connections between Ireland and slave-ownership. We do not argue that this slave-ownership was constitutive for Ireland (partly because the weight of these connections was less than in England or Scotland and partly because we do not have the grounding in Irish history to make such an argument) but the accumulation of individual cases represents a myriad of local impacts, the aggregate significance of which can only be evaluated by other historians more equipped than us to define the extent of, and limits to, Ireland's debt to slavery. The more limited aims of this chapter are thus to present and contextualise the new *LBS* data as an enhanced resource, and to sketch preliminary findings and suggest future lines of enquiry in several areas, some particular to Ireland and others relevant to all four nations.

The second phase of the *Legacies of British Slave-Ownership* project

The first phase of *LBS* provided a synchronic picture of slave-ownership across the British colonies at the end of slavery. The second phase asked how this final structure of ownership had emerged, and aimed to provide a diachronic account of ownership of estates or other units of enslaved people, identifying slave-owners and their families who had ceased to be slave-owners by the 1830s, either because they or their heirs had sold out or because they had lost their slave property through financial failure.[4] Our periodisation for the second-phase work was set by the seizure of the Neutral and Ceded Islands in 1763 (Grenada, St Vincent, Dominica and Tobago) as the start point, and by the Abolition Act of 1833 as the end point, a period including of course the important additions to Britain's Caribbean slave empire of British Guiana, Trinidad and St Lucia in the early 1800s. These second- and third-wave colonies of 1763 and of the Napoleonic Wars have generally received less attention in the context of Ireland's involvement than have the first-wave colonies of Barbados, Montserrat or Jamaica.

The sources for *LBS*'s first phase were bounded: we drew on the compensation records to provide a snapshot of slave-ownership at the time of Emancipation. Those records existed in usable form because of Daniel O'Connell's insistence on accounting for the £20 million paid in compensation to the slave-owners. For the second phase there has been no such single archive nor bounded universe of slave-owners. For all colonies we have transcribed the ownership information in the Slave Registers, which take us back systematically only as far as 1813 for Trinidad, and 1817–20 for the other British colonies. For Jamaica, we have now comprehensively incorporated the ownership information from the Accounts Produce (which record all those estates owned by absentees and by 'dependent' slave-owners such as minors) back to the 1760s. But for most colonies, before the 1810s the sources explode and fragment, and we have only a discontinuous history of many estates.[5]

From these disparate sources, we now have over 400 individuals connected with Ireland among the slave-owners. Almost 200 are currently associated with addresses traced in Ireland; the others left money to relatives in Ireland or at some point lived there at addresses currently unknown to *LBS*. These 200 known Irish absentees represent 3–4 per cent of the total of British and Irish absentee owners identified to date, while Scotland represents 15–20 per cent (and Wales a much lower fraction than either).[6] The proportion of the whole represented by Irish slave-owners has thus remained roughly constant between *LBS*'s two phases.

The new dataset also includes considerably expanded information on the Irish diaspora, both in the Caribbean and Britain. We have added dozens of slave-owners of Irish origin resident in the Caribbean, whether from established families such as the Hon. John Black of Trinidad (d. 1836), the son of a Mayor of Belfast, or of almost wilfully obscure background, such as John Collins, for whom conflicting accounts exist of his roots in Ireland – variously given as Derry or Ramelton or birth at sea to Irish parents – to ownership of Southampton Pen in Jamaica on his death in around 1820. While we knew from the compensation records of Hamilton Brown, a large-scale attorney and slave-owner in his own right in Jamaica, and founder of Browns Town in St Ann, now we know he was from Co. Antrim (indeed one of his estates was named Antrim) and the work of others shows that he imported hundreds of Irish labourers between 1835 and 1840 to settle in St Ann and replace the formerly enslaved workforce there.[7] The new dataset also includes entries tracing the shift from the Caribbean into English gentry society of Irish slave-owners such as the family of Michael Keane of St Vincent and Barbados. In his will, made in 1796 and proved in 1799, Keane ordered the sale of his two estates (and the enslaved people attached to them) after specifically bequeathing four enslaved people, including a cooper named Shelaly, to his son and heir, Hugh Perry Keane, who later married into the Payne family of Bedfordshire – English slave-owning baronets – and who himself left behind an 'outside' family on St Kitts.

The additional *LBS* material reflects two categories: new information on slave-owners who were already recorded (a deepening of our knowledge), and the recording of 'new' slave-owners and of others closely connected to the slave economy who did not appear in the compensation records (a broadening of our dataset).[8]

In the first category for Ireland, we now know more, for example, about the firm of Joseph Wilson & Sons, which we previously recorded as the Dublin firm used by the Compensation Commissioners to distribute information about the compensation process to slave-owners and mortgagees in Ireland, and which had extensive slave-holdings in Trinidad. We can now see the firm's links to the Bank of Ireland, in which Joseph Wilson was a stockholder and of which his son Thomas was the Governor between 1838 and 1840.[9] Again, we had previously noted the presence of the Digges La Touche banking family in the compensation records: now we can see its ownership did not flow from the banking business but through inheritance from a family member who had gone to Jamaica and married into a slave-owning family. In the second category for Ireland, of new slave-owners in the dataset, in 2013 we had picked out the Tuite, Farrell, Hussey, Ryan and Staunton families cited by Nini Rodgers as slave-owners not appearing by the time of slave compensation. Now we have traced members of all of these families in earlier records.[10] It is important to stress that 'new' slave-owners comprise not only those who represent new research discoveries by *LBS*, but also those (such as the families cited by Nini Rodgers) who are simply new to *LBS*. For example, Edmund Burke's trusteeship of the Jamaican slave-owner James Ridge, who died in around 1784 leaving annuities of £50 p.a. to his mother of Loughrea and £150 p.a. to his nephew of Dublin, was traced by *LBS* in the will of James Ridge, which specified that the trustees should buy enslaved people for the estate, no more than eight a year or thirty in total: but Peter Marshall had independently identified this connection from Burke's correspondence, and highlighted it in his recent book on Burke.[11]

If we step back from the empirical work and the mass of individual cases to consider this universe from the vantage point of our work on England and (to a lesser extent) on Scotland, there are five themes that we would draw out for Ireland: the issue of 'visibility' or the remembering and forgetting of slave-ownership; the phenomenon of double absenteeism; the recurrence of linkages to Irish nationalism among slave-owners; the evidence for 'decline' among Ireland's slave-owners; and the legacies of slave-ownership, those impacts on the fabric of metropolitan life, whether in Ireland or made by colonial slave-owners of Irish origin in mainland Britain.

The visibility of slave-ownership

The question of the visibility and representation of slavery is common to all four nations of the United Kingdom, but its context and articulations are different in each case. Ireland has the historic dual experience of a colonised and colonising society, which is shared – to an extent that might be contested – by Scotland and Wales, but it also has the additional and perhaps most urgent challenge of the myth of 'white slavery' that is addressed in Natalie A. Zacek's chapter. But the ordinary elisions of slavery constitute failures to remember that cumulatively represent an act of forgetting in Ireland as in the other three nations.

For example, the catalogue of the Caldwell Collection of the Royal Irish Academy published in December 2011 is a very valuable 700-page piece-by-piece description of an important archive of family correspondence and papers, ranging over three centuries (1659–1872).[12] A search within it for the words 'slave' and the derivative 'slavery' generates eleven hits: seven of these are in the context of abolition, one in 1792 and six after 1833; three are metaphorical usages of 'slavery' for religious or political oppression; and one is an incidental reference to enslaved people in Honduras. But colonial slavery permeated the family's history and – unseen – permeates the collection. The Trans-Atlantic Slave Trade Database has fifteen voyages between 1759 and 1767 for Charles Caldwell as co-owner in Liverpool, and nine in partnership with the great slave-trading Heywood family into which Charles Caldwell of Dublin (1707–76) had married, and there are numerous items in the collection of correspondence between Dublin and Liverpool.[13] One of Charles Caldwell of Dublin's sons, William, went to Kingston, Jamaica, as a merchant, and died there in around 1819, leaving several natural children and instructing his executors to sell five named enslaved people. Another son and a nephew of Charles Caldwell of Dublin are shown in the family tree in the Caldwell catalogue as having married sisters of Sir William Abdy, 7th bart: Revd George Caldwell, who married Harriet Abdy, and his cousin Charles Andrew Caldwell, son of Admiral Benjamin Caldwell, who married Charlotte Ann Abdy. The mother-in-law of the two men, Lady Mary Abdy, was the sister of the large-scale slave-owner James Gordon. When James Gordon committed suicide in 1822, he made his nephew by marriage, Revd George Caldwell, one of his trustees, and left slave property in three estates on Antigua and St Vincent in trust with contingent remainder to George Caldwell's wife, among others. George Caldwell is in the compensation records in this capacity. None of this appears in the Caldwell catalogue except in the form of incidental references: to William Caldwell visiting America from Kingston, Jamaica, in 1806; to a 'sugar plantation' in Antigua; to a deed of settlement of 1830; and (three times) to the Antigua estates after Emancipation.

One of the great treasures of the National Museum of Ireland is the Fonthill Vase, the first piece of Chinese porcelain known to have arrived in Europe, recently celebrated by Edmund de Waal. Its provenance is well known, and it bears the name of the Wiltshire estate of William Beckford, the English aesthete and collector. But Fonthill was also an estate in St Ann, Jamaica, owned by Beckford along with the enslaved people attached to it. Beckford's wealth was the tail-end of his family's slave-derived fortune from over a century of engagement in slave-ownership. Nowhere in de Waal's discussion or in the National Museum of Ireland's catalogue is this apparent.[14]

In Britain, *LBS* approached the *Oxford Dictionary of National Biography* (*ODNB*) after we had established that in the online edition of the *ODNB*, launched in 2004, the search for 'slave-owner' generated only some twenty hits, mostly American slave-owners or people of colour (including Olaudah Equiano). Hundreds of slave-owners or their families in fact had entries, but they appeared under such euphemisms as 'Jamaica proprietor', 'landowner in the West Indies' or 'West India merchant'. In collaboration with the *ODNB*, we have since added an update of some thirty new entries of slave-owners as such, to begin to represent that class of Britons as a meaningful strand in British history, and we have begun to work on amendments to existing entries to make transparent the slave-ownership of the subjects.

In contrast to the *ODNB*, which inherited many entries from the original nineteenth-century *Dictionary of National Biography*, the *Dictionary of Irish Biography* (*DIB*) is an entirely modern resource. *Legacies of British Slave-Ownership* has looked briefly at the latter's coverage of slave-owners. As with the *ODNB*, there are two dimensions: the inclusion or otherwise of slave-owners, and the presentation of slave-ownerships in those entries that do exist.

Very few of the slave-owners in the *LBS* database appear in the *DIB*. It is not for us to debate the criteria for inclusion there, but among the entries recently added to the *ODNB* was Charles McGarel, a slave-owner in British Guiana who was important in the formation of the Hogg dynasty in British politics (two twentieth-century Lord Chancellors, the Viscounts Hailsham, carried his name). But McGarel also had a major impact on Larne, where his philanthropic legacies still suffuse the town. He is not reflected in the *DIB* or in the *Dictionary of Ulster Biography*.

The *DIB* entry for the O'Connor family of Dublin explicitly gives their mixture of transatlantic mercantile activity and ownership of estates and enslaved people – 'They dealt in wool, cotton, sugar, rum, wine, spirits etc.' – while Valentine O'Connor was 'owner of two-thirds of a sugar estate, Mount William, and its slaves, buildings etc.' on St Vincent. The entry's conclusion, however, appears to occlude the imperial context and the connections to slavery in the business itself: 'the O'Connors were a classic

Irish catholic [sic] merchant family of the late eighteenth and early nineteenth centuries, owing their business success and social position as much to advantageous marriages that brought them catholic merchant and gentry connexions, in Ireland and abroad, as to prudent management'.[15]

Cultural institutions – universities, galleries, museums, compendia of national histories such as the *DIB* – face multiple pressures in addressing the national past, in all four nations. Slavery, and within that slave-ownership, is only one piece of those pasts. But it is a piece: and the *LBS* material is one resource that can contribute to the basic fact-finding that an increasing number of institutions of the Atlantic world are undertaking as a foundation for their re-examination of their own pasts, as well as those of their respective nations.

Double absenteeism

When James Hewitt Massy Dawson, MP for Clonmel from 1820 to 1830, applied unsuccessfully for a baronetcy between 1823 and 1825, he was at pains to rebut the charge that he was an absentee landlord in Ireland:

> I have been told I am considered an absentee which is a bar to my prospects ... in reply to which I wish briefly to inform you that being in Parliament I am obliged to have a house in London, but I assure you I spend nearly six months of every year in Ireland and I have ... never missed attending both assizes in my county town ... besides which I keep in my own hands a considerable part of my own property consisting of large woods, and employ many hands of the labouring classes.[16]

Massy Dawson did not experience his Caribbean – as opposed to his Irish – absentee ownership as an obstacle to preferment, but absentee landlordism was explicitly problematised from the mid-eighteenth century for both the British Caribbean and Ireland. Double absenteeism, the simultaneous absence of the same owner, thus appears more particular to Ireland among the Four Nations, although the phenomenon has resonance too for Scotland and Wales – and arguably for parts of rural England. Recent work by *LBS* indicates that the extent and significance of such double absenteeism appear greater than originally suggested in phase 1, with many more cases now identified.

For example, in the will of John Sayers Esq. of Totnes, who had been a merchant in Dublin and subsequently in London, made in February 1807 and proved in 1808, he confirmed his settlement of an annuity of £500 p.a. on his wife, Margaret, payable out of his land at Wicklow. He left in trust £5,000 Irish currency, the fortune he had promised on the marriage of his sister Margaret to Richard Wogan Talbot (who was MP for Co. Dublin between 1807 and 1830), and a further £1,700 sterling, in both cases the income to be paid to his wife for her life and then to the Talbots' children. He also left her three houses at Malahide for life. He left his real estate and 'slaves, negroes and other stock' in Demerara, and his real estate in Ireland (other than the three houses at Malahide) in trust to be sold, the the proceeds being divided among his legatees in proportion to their monetary legacies.[17] Jeffrey French, MP for Milborne Port in 1740s, came from a family with large estates in western Ireland, resettled in England, and through his marriage came to own Lloyds estate in the Parish of St John in Jamaica: he ordered the sale of his freehold property in Co. Roscommon to repay his debts, and left his estate with its enslaved people, and his leasehold property, also in Co. Roscommon, to separate nephews.[18] Again, Jeremiah Milles was the son of the Dean of Exeter, also named Jeremiah Milles, the nephew and heir of Thomas Milles, the Bishop of Waterford and Lismore. Jeremiah Milles the son married Rose Gardiner, who brought into their marriage slave property in Jamaica as well as an estate and house at Pishiobury in Hertfordshire. The younger Jeremiah Milles bequeathed his leasehold house in Harley Street, the Pishiobury estate, and land in Ireland to his wife for life, and then to his heirs, who turned out to be his daughter, also named Rose. Revd George Caldwell of the Caldwell Collection was a further example of a recipient of slave compensation who was also an Irish absentee landlord. In his will, proved in 1848, he left his son William Browne Caldwell his house at 5 Sandford Place, Cheltenham (which in a codicil he said he had since sold), as well as land in Ireland (at Davidstown in Co. Meath and Harolds Cross in Co. Dublin). He left a further estate in Ireland, Adams Town in Co. Kilkenny, to his sister Henrietta Caldwell. His son William Browne Caldwell left £190,201 0s 4d on his death in Cheltenham in 1893.

Connections of Irish nationalists/nationalism with slave-ownership

The third dimension highlighted by *LBS*'s recent work, and one that is specific to Ireland, is that of the connections of slave-owners in the *LBS* universe to various forms of Irish nationalist politics. We cannot reliably make sense of these individually, or of their significance (if any) in total, or conclude whether they simply reflect the permeation of slave-ownership into tiers of middle- and upper-middle-class Irish society from which parts of nationalist leadership were drawn. All we can do is to record them.

The *DIB* reflects the activity of the O'Connor family in the Catholic Convention. Malachy O'Connor, with his wife, Lydia, the widow of the slave-owner Bryan Blake on St Vincent, had a daughter named Honoria who married John Sweetman (1805–56): their son was John Sweetman (1844–1936), the MP and President of Sinn Féin between 1909 and 1912.[19] Robert Bushe of Trinidad was the son of Gervase Parker Bushe and Mary Grattan, and nephew of the 'acknowledged champion of enlightened Ireland'. Arthur John Moore, the Nationalist MP for Clonmel from 1874 to 1885, was the son of the Liverpool and Barbados merchant Charles Moore. A more elaborate chain of connection is tied to Thomas Neilson (1789–1866), a slave-owner in Trinidad, apparently resident there at the time of compensation and given variously in secondary material as Dr or MD. He was the son of William Neilson of Strabane, Co. Tyrone, and appears to have returned to Ireland in the 1850s (his sister Rosina had died aged twenty-two in Trinidad in 1825). Neilson's or Bel Air or Stephenson's, one of the five Islands of Port of Spain, was granted to Thomas Neilson and used as a holding area for Indian immigrants (i.e. quarantined indentured labourers) after Emancipation. He died at Mountjoy Square Dublin aged seventy-seven in 1866. His will, of which the primary beneficiary was Eliza Darracott, either his niece or second cousin, was contested in the suit of *Underwood v Darracott*, in which the plaintiff was Thomas Neilson Underwood and the defendant Eliza Darracott or her heirs. Thomas Neilson Underwood (d. 1876) was a Presbyterian lawyer and nationalist from Strabane, and co-founder of the National Brotherhood of St Patrick in 1861; he was described as the nephew of Thomas Neilson MD. Although press coverage at the time suggested he was named after the brother of Samuel Neilson, the United Irishman and editor of the *Northern Star*, it seems clear that he was named after his slave-owning uncle.[20]

We recognise that the records also reflect the presence of slave-owners among the English or British in authority in Ireland at this time. Henry Goulburn, the Chief Secretary for Ireland from 1821 to 1827, was a major slave-owner, son of the Jamaican 'planter' Munbee Goulburn. Stapleton Cotton, named after his mother's family of St Kitts and Nevis slave-owners, was commander-in-chief of the army in Ireland from 1822 to1825. Anthony Hart, the Lord Chancellor from 1827 to 1830, was a slave-owner in St Kitts. Frederick Beckford Long, the grandson of Edward Long, the historian of Jamaica, was the Inspector General of Prisons in Ireland, and died of smallpox reportedly caught visiting a prison. Lucy Annesley and Sophia Annesley, daughters of Major Richard Annesley, were co-owners of the Diamond estate in Trinidad in 1828. Lucy Annesley married Revd Thomas Alfred Lyons, appointed chaplain to the Lord Lieutenant of Ireland (the Earl of Mulgrave) in 1836 (their son was the medieval historian Ponsonby Annesley Lyons).

The 'Decline' thesis

As we have moved from a synchronic analysis of the compensation records to a diachronic study of 1763 to 1833, so we have begun to amass evidence among Britain and Ireland's slave-owners that allows us to explore the 'decline' thesis for the slave economy. Both for British and Irish slave-owners, this supports the case for highly uneven fortunes across the Caribbean, even in the period from 1807 to 1833, which is agreed by both Eric Williams and his critics to have been a period of unambiguous decline.[21] In Jamaica, decline is clear. Fitzherbert Richards of Marlborough Buildings, Bath, who died around 1811, had been an absentee in Ireland at the time of William Hickey's visit to Jamaica in 1755–76, when Hickey recorded that 'two hundred men of the unhappy men belonging to Mr. Fitzherbert Richards' had 'destroyed themselves' by dirt-eating 'to the enormous loss of £6,000'. Richards's will embodies considerable confidence about the financial future of the slave economy, or at least of his own piece of it. He left his Jamaican estates (and enslaved people) in trust to support annuities totalling £1,350 p.a. to female relatives, including £400 p.a. to his niece, the Irish peeress Frances, Lady Viscountess Allen. He also left lump-sum bequests of £13,000 to three of the same annuitants, £10,000 to the younger children of Viscountess Allen to discharge her marriage settlement and £6,000 to discharge the portions of Nicholas Coddington. The estate themselves he left to his great-nephews, including Espine Batty and Fitzherbert Batty, the sons of Philip Batty of Castletown Delvin, Co. Westmeath. Twenty years later, Espine Batty wrote to Lord Goderich from Dublin in January 1832 appealing for lower sugar duties, and explaining that although he contributed £4,000 p.a. (in duties) 'I cannot get out of the estate £100 a year to live on.' Again, we can also see failures among merchant firms in Ireland exposed to the older slave colonies in the crisis of the sugar economy in 1830–1: Robert Hyndman & Son of Dublin, for example, tied to the slave economy of Antigua, were made bankrupt in 1831.[22] At the same time, Irishmen featured among the slave-owners making fortunes in the new slave colonies, above all in Demerara, Essequibo and Berbice (later British Guiana) in the last decades of slavery. Tully Higgins, Charles McGarel and David Hall were all Irishmen propelled by fortunes in British Guiana into the ranks of the richest individuals in Britain: each resettled in London.

Legacies

'Legacies' of slave-ownership included both literal and metaphorical legacies. Part of the backwash of slave-ownership was the bequest of monetary legacies to relatives and friends in Ireland, sometimes of amounts of money that (if paid) must have been material to the recipients and possibly to the local economies. The will of Henry Cuniffe of Kiltolla (Kiltullagh), Co. Galway (the founder of the town of Martha Brae in Jamaica) was subject to sustained litigation, but one of his Jamaica estates (together with the enslaved people on it) was reportedly sold in around 1805 for £30,000, of which £26,375 8s was remitted to one of his trustees and contingent heirs, Henry Concanon of Carrownacregg. Cuniffe had already settled £10,000 on his daughter Mary Jane on her marriage to Captain Charles Bingham. The apparent impact of such infusions of liquidity can only be properly analysed at the local level.

Legacies of British Slave-Ownership has organised its own findings on impacts in Britain and Ireland into six 'legacy' strands: Commercial, Physical, Cultural and Philanthropic, Imperial, Political, and Historical. Because of our lack of background in Irish (and indeed Scottish) history, we have tended to date to tread lightly on these legacy strands for Ireland, but now we are beginning to block them out. Under these six headings there are dozens of cases, individually exemplifying local impacts in Ireland and perhaps in aggregate coming to represent something else.

Commercial legacies

The debates over the significance of British colonial slavery in the Industrial Revolution – fought to exhaustion by the early 2000s – are reopening in light of the renewed attention in the USA to capitalism and slavery. The *LBS* project has concluded that slave-owners *did* invest in dozens of early industrial projects in Britain, but that the less direct but pervasive effects of slave-owners and their creditors in Britain's financial and commercial revolution – in new financial institutions, in infrastructure, in agrarian capitalism – were probably more important than direct investment.

In this context, Ireland certainly provides cases of both industrial and mineral investment by slave-owners, and of connections to commercial and financial institutions. Waddell Cunningham's diverse business interest included chemical and textile manufacturing around Belfast.[23] Earlier, Alexander Stewart of Acton Co., Armagh, who had inherited his mother's family's Fort Stewart estate in Jamaica through his father, undertook the development of coal mining and shipping at Ballintoy:

> In 1757, he petitioned the Irish House of Commons for aid in assisting to open coal mines at Ballintoy, stating that he had 'discovered a large body of coals in his lands there, great quantities of which had been exported to Dublin and other parts of the kingdom, that he had 'expended £500 in an attempt to construct a quay at Ballintoy, but was not able to proceed with the work

unless aided by Parliament; that such structure, when completed, would be of great advantage to the kingdom in general, and to the North of Ireland in particular, the same being the only harbour of safety between Larne and the Lough of Deny'.

He was granted £2,000. In 1759, Stewart petitioned successfully again, stating that he had expended £1,734 on the works, and asking for £1,234 to complete the quay. Stewart was soon afterwards obliged to sell his entire property in Ballintoy, for which he received £20,000 from Cupples of Belfast.[24] In terms of connections to financial institutions, we know Valentine O'Connor had been a subscriber on foundation of the Bank of Ireland in 1783, and that the London merchant and slave-owner Edmund Francis Green was among the early directors of Daniel O'Connell's National Bank of Ireland (founded 1835). We have not, however, performed the same work for these financial institutions of Ireland that we have done for the Bank of England, whose Governors were disproportionately drawn from London West India merchants in the early nineteenth century.

Each such commercial legacy – indeed each legacy of any kind – requires scrupulous analysis to establish what claims can and cannot be made for the contribution of slave-ownership to a specific firm or institution. The capital accumulated from slave-owning in British Guiana by Hugh McCalmont of Abbeylands, Co. Antrim, enabled him to put up £50,000 to fund his sons in the formation of McCalmont Brothers, an important City of London merchant bank in the mid-nineteenth century. The connection is direct and documented: McCalmont Brothers was indisputably a legacy of slave-ownership. As noted above, by contrast, for the Digges La Touche family, slave-ownership arose outside their banking business. A more complex case is presented by the Dublin firm of solicitors and town agents Pearts, which has an unbroken history under family leadership since its foundation in 1883, fifty years after the end of slavery, and bears the name of John Redmund Peart, who succeeded his father-in-law, Richard McNamara, in the firm. John Redmund Peart was descended from John Peart, an English slave-owner in Jamaica from the East Midlands who died at Cheltenham in 1847.[25] John Redmund Peart's grandfather, John Hobbs Peart, was born in Jamaica and had moved to Ireland from India in the 1850s. How much, if anything, does Pearts owe to slavery? The evidence tells us that John Hobbs Peart was effectively excluded from his father John Peart's will, under which he received only six books and six paintings (it is not known whether he had received *in vivo* gifts): the property in Jamaica passed to John Hobbs Peart's older brother Frederick. John Hobbs Peart was however the heir of his mother, Elizabeth, who died of Dundrum Castle Dublin in 1854. Her will in turn noted that she had not been paid all the £2000 left to her by her husband, whose estate could not support all his legacies.[26]

In assessing the overall significance of these commercial legacies, *LBS* previously noted the paucity in Ireland of mercantile and banking creditors of slave-owners relative to England and Scotland, which were characterised by the presence among slave-owners and mortgagees of dozens of London, Liverpool, Bristol and Glasgow merchants and bankers in dense networks that had substantial weight within their respective commercial communities. These 'West Indian merchants', the consignees of the slave-owners' sugar and often the final guarantors of the bill system, were at the heart of the slave economy. Their underdevelopment in Ireland, *LBS* has concluded, in large part reflected the lack of direct movement in the eighteenth century of sugar to Dublin or Belfast: instead, sugar mainly moved from the Caribbean to English or Scottish ports and only then to Irish commercial centres, originally reflecting the regulatory impediments under the Navigation Acts and then the cumulative comparative advantage for mainland merchants in capital, credit and expertise. This is not to deny the significance of diasporic networks of merchants and planters of Irish origin linking the Caribbean and Britain. Stephen Lynch of Ashtead, Surrey, for example, mandated in his will made in 1769 that the sugar from his estates in Antigua be consigned to Robert Skerret and John Lynch of London: all three men were of Irish origin, but the centres of credit for Irish slave-owners remained outside Ireland even if they comprised merchant compatriots. By the early nineteenth century, when the direct movement of sugar is evidenced by such figures as the Dublin–Trinidad merchant John Adair or the role of Robert Hyndman & Co. as consignees, the powerful role of the sugar economy as a catalyst for firing the development the financial revolution had been largely eclipsed by the onset of industrialisation and proto-industrialisation.

Physical legacies

Legacies of slave-owners permeate the built environment in mainland Britain, with especially significant clusters centred on Bristol, Liverpool and Glasgow. Such legacies span urban development, infrastructure and country houses, the latter the *locus classicus* of imperial backwash: one in ten of Capability Brown and Humphrey Repton's projects in England were executed for slave-owners or their families. Ireland's experience was of course shaped for many years by the sectarian nature of landownership, deterring successful Catholic slave-owners from any thought of return to Ireland. The relatively low number of slave-owners returning to Ireland led to a built environment less indebted to slave-ownership in Ireland than on mainland Britain.[27] There are clearly nevertheless noteworthy counter-examples in Ireland, each representing 'local', but often profound, impact.

The presence of Charles McGarel's several physical legacies at Larne has already been noted above. Other clusters include Co. Mayo, where John Denis Browne, First Marquess of Sligo, the son of the Second Earl of Altamont and the slave-heiress Elizabeth Kelly, reshaped Westport (both the town and the house) and built Louisburgh, and where Finola O'Kane has highlighted the example of John Kelly:

> having made their fortune, the Kelly family returned to Ireland, purchasing the Newtown estate in County Galway in 1802, together with its relatively modest eighteenth-century country house … In the desire to oversee and supervise the courtyard, and the work completed in it, views of the northern parkland were blocked from the principal rooms of the house, and in a design that was far from Palladian or Brownian ideal, echoes of the Caribbean plantation were transplanted into County Galway.[28]

(John Kelly left, among other legacies, £4,000 in trust, to be laid out on land 'and that only' in Ireland, Scotland or the counties of York or Middlesex, for the benefit of his natural child Mary Kelly by Sarah Edwards Innis (or Innes), a free woman of colour of St Thomas-in-the-East.) Elsewhere, the Hall-Dare family, whose paternal side had made its money from slavery in British Guiana, hired Sir Charles Lanyon to build Newtonbarry House, Co. Wexford, between 1863 and 1869.[29] William Drummond Delap was reported to be building a new house at Monasterboice, Co. Louth, in 1837, and went on to build the Drummond Tower in around 1858. Physical legacies might not always be extant: Monellan Castle in Co. Donegal, built by other members of the Delap family in the late eighteenth century, was demolished in the mid-twentieth century.

Cultural and philanthropic legacies

Money from owning, and from financing the ownership of, enslaved people flowed into the British mainland in the eighteenth and early nineteenth centuries, coinciding with both the urban renaissance (and its attendant commitment to new and existing philanthropic institutions) and the early stages of bourgeois collecting, much of the latter at the expense of European aristocracies undone by revolutionary upheaval. The fruits of this money suffuse many modern cultural and philanthropic institutions in Britain, either through earlier patronage and funding from slavery-derived wealth or through the provenance of individual pieces. Diasporic Irish slave-owners participated in this process of accumulation, and in so doing contributed to the formation of an asserted 'British' heritage for works of art originating abroad: the Arcedeckne family held, for more than a century, a pair of paintings of the Grand Canal in Venice by Francesco Guardi, bought and possibly commissioned by Chaloner Arcedeckne in 1768–9, both of which were subject to temporary export bans by the British Government in efforts to 'save them for the nation' in the 2010s after they were put up for sale by the Guinness family.[30] There is a portrait of Capt. James Massy-Dawson (the slave-owning son of the MP James Hewitt Massy-Dawson and Elizabeth Dennis) in the Royal Collection.

For Ireland itself, *LBS*'s work has also thrown up such legacies (including the National Museum of Ireland's Fonthill Vase, noted above). The Irish peer Clotworthy Upton, later First Baron Templetown, who speculated in slave property on a large scale in Grenada and Dominica in the early waves of British control of the islands after 1763 with a group of financiers around Lauchlin Macleane, appears in the provenance of works such as Carlo Dolci's *Madona*, of which Francesco Bartolozzi's print is now in the British Museum.[31] Robert Home's portrait of Waddell Cunningham hangs in the Ulster Museum. The philanthropic footprint of the Dublin merchant and slave mortgagee Thomas Wilson, Governor of the Bank of Ireland, trustee of the Royal Exchange and director of the National Assurance Company of Ireland, included his governorship of Sir Patrick Dun's hospital and membership of the Ouzel Galley Society, the locus of business collegiality and arbitration, and the origin of the Dublin Chamber of Commerce, and of the Royal Dublin Society.[32] Gordon Augustus Thomson was the principal donor of ethnographic objects to the Ulster Museum. Robert Simms the younger, a mortgagee of slave property in Antigua, was manager of the Royal Belfast Academical Institution.

The recording of such legacies for Ireland, however, has been as an incidental outgrowth of our work on slave-owners. We have not undertaken any systematic work on the funding and holdings of Ireland's modern cultural and philanthropic institutions: only the commitment of the institutions themselves can underwrite comprehensive work on their respective debts to slavery, to which the *LBS* work could contribute.

Imperial legacies

The *LBS* project has posited a shift of human and financial capital away from the Caribbean as slavery came to an end, with slave-owning families redirecting their sons (and some daughters) into the white settler colonies of Australia, New Zealand, Canada and the Cape, carrying ideas, attitudes and techniques into the wider empire. In this context, Ireland occupies an ambiguous position, as both the transmitter and receiver of such legacies. Dr Andrew Clarke exemplifies the first of these. Formerly of Trinidad, which he left in 1818 he appears in his will, made in 1835, as of Belmont near Lifford, Co. Donegal.³³ He left monetary legacies of nearly £20,000. His son, Lt-Col. Andrew Clarke (1793–1847), became Governor of Western Australia, and his grandson was the Australian public servant and military engineer Sir Andrew Clarke (1824–1902). Another grandson, Marcus Andrew Hislop Clarke (1846–81), was an Australian journalist and novelist. All the latter three men have entries in the *Australian Dictionary of Biography*. Again, John Scott Bushe, described as 'an English creole', the son of Robert Bushe (mentioned above) and great-nephew of Henry Grattan, acted as Colonial Secretary in Trinidad between 1861 and 1887, while John Scott Bushe's son Sir Henry Grattan Bushe was also a colonial Governor.

At the same time, Ireland was the object as well as subject of such transformations. A number of English officials and administrators in Ireland who were slave-owners themselves or came from slave-owning families were mentioned earlier. To them can be added, notably, Sir Charles Edward Trevelyan of the Great Famine, whose mother, Harriet, née Neave, was the daughter of a London merchant and slave-owner, and whose paternal grandmother, Louisa, née Simond, was also an heiress of 'slave-property': several members of the family including Harriet were recipients of compensation for hundreds of enslaved people in Grenada.

Political legacies

Legacies of British Slave-Ownership has attempted to track the access to metropolitan political power that was an important objective of British colonial slave-owners through our tracking of individuals participating both in national and local politics. In the mid-eighteenth century the 'West India interest' in the House of Commons was estimated at 50–60 MPs.³⁴ These members included MPs for English seats who were members of the Irish diaspora, such as Jeffrey French (Milborne Port, 1741–7, and briefly for Tavistock, 1754) and Chaloner Arcedeckne (Wallingford, 1780–4). In this period, the Irish Parliament did not perform analogous imperial functions, and was not therefore strategically as vital for slave-owners as the Westminster Parliament, although there were slave-owning members such as Peter Browne-Kelly (Mayo, 1761–8) in the Irish Parliament. In the combined Westminster Parliaments between the 1810s and early 1830s, some 60–80 MPs were either slave-owners themselves, members of slave-owning families or otherwise closely aligned with slave-ownership. These included: Irish members for Irish constituencies such as the previously mentioned James Hewitt Massy Dawson (Clonmel, 1820–30, and briefly Co. Limerick, 1830), Thomas Fitzgerald (Co. Louth, 1833–4), and Andrew Henry Lynch and Lachlan Maclachlan (both for Galway, the former 1833–41 and the latter briefly in 1833); and English or Scottish members for Irish constituencies, such as Samuel Boddington and James Evan Baillie (for Tralee in 1807 and 1813–18 respectively), Lt-Gen. John Michel (Belfast, 1816–18), John Bent (Sligo, 1818–20) and Sir Thomas Gladstone (Portarlington, 1832–4). Alongside these slave-owners and their representatives, of course, sat groups of Irish MPs around Daniel O'Connell, collectively focused until 1829 on Catholic Emancipation, but then following an abolitionist political leader into the struggles of the early 1830s over slavery.

The tail of political legacies continued beyond abolition, when the battlegrounds switched away from slavery. The London merchant John Irving sat for Antrim between 1837 and 1841; the MP for the same constituency from 1874, James Chaine (1841–85), was the son of Maria West Chaine, née Whittle (1815–94), in turn the daughter of Grace Mary Whittle (d. 1819) and as such a beneficiary with her siblings in a trust fund that included Peter's Rock and Mount Charles in St Andrew, Jamaica. Charles Moore, the diasporic Barbados–Liverpool merchant cited above as the father of the Nationalist MP Arthur John Moore, himself sat for Tipperary from 1865 to 1869. Sir John Young, MP for Cavan from 1831 to 1855, rather extraordinarily owned enslaved people in Surinam at the time of compensated slave emancipation by the Dutch in 1863, a long time after it had been made illegal for British subjects to buy or sell people. In local office, Henry Barry Coddington, the heir to 'slave property' in Jamaica from his great-uncle Fitzherbert Richards, was High Sheriff of Co. Meath in 1843.

Historical legacies

The final legacy strand explored by *LBS* comprises the cultural work done by slave-owners, their families and their connections in representing slavery – or their specific slave-ownership – as benevolent, and the enslaved people as inherently inferior, both prior to Emancipation and subsequently in (re)writing the history of slavery and abolition in the Victorian era. The earlier effort, led by Edward Long but supported by many other slave-owners, helped constitute 'race' as a category; the later effort, led by Carlyle and Frederick Marryat, reconstituted the slave-owners as the victims of slavery through their expropriation upon Emancipation, refashioned the withdrawal of British protection from the Caribbean sugar economy as the refusal of the enslaved people to work for wages, and consolidated notions of racial difference.[35]

We fully recognise that the tasks of imagining and then reimaging slavery were dwarfed by other concerns of literature and culture in Ireland in the eighteenth and nineteenth centuries. We also recognise that the most pressing problematic 'historical legacy' for historians of Ireland in the context of transatlantic slavery is the myth of 'white slaves'. But there are nevertheless noteworthy instances of Irish slave-owners contributing to both phases of the process of (re)writing the history of slavery and abolition.

The arguments made before Emancipation by the diasporic baronet Sir Henry William Martin (who inherited slave property in Antigua from his double-absentee father, and whose mother was both daughter and widow by her first marriage of Irish landowners near Cork, where Sir Henry William Martin was born) are neatly expressed in the full title of his work *A counter appeal*, which summarises the major anti-abolitionist rhetorical strategies of many other advocates of continued slavery.[36]

An 1868 commemoration of James Digges La Touche (who died in 1827) by William Urwick equally demonstrates a concern to minimise in retrospect the violence of slavery and ultimately to obscure slavery itself by overlaying it with abolition, in a chapter setting out La Touche's inheritance of what he himself called his 'transatlantic property' and his subsequent correspondence with the Revd J. M. Trew in Jamaica:[37]

> The First of August 1834 was kept as a day of jubilee throughout the British realm because from that day inclusive all slaves in places under the British crown were free … [Previously] Slavery was held as right, and necessary, and good, and useful, and benevolent, and even Scriptural and Christian … Nor, again, let us now, living when freedom is law on both sides of the Atlantic, too hastily and harshly judge as alike willfully guilty, all who held property worked by slave labour at a time gone by, when it had the sanction of law and when numbers of well-minded people gave their consent, if not their countenance, to it. Holding such property might afford the owners access for Christian purposes to *their* slaves, who else would have been, like others, fated to be unblessed … We may be sure that pity for the slave and abhorrence of slavery were as truly in the heart of … Mr. J. D. La T. himself.

Conclusion

The *LBS* dataset provides a tool for other historians, including historians of Ireland, who know what to apply it to, and what questions relevant to their own spheres it can help explore. There are projects now under way in Australia, Canada and the Indian Ocean drawing on the database to explore aspects of the development of the white settler colonies and of the plantation economy in south and east Asia. Behind all those projects, and for Ireland in this chapter and in other chapters in this volume, lies the issue of significance: the 'so what?'. There are challenges of both methodology and of evidence in framing how we can determine the importance (or otherwise) of slavery to European nations and to Europe as a whole. Ultimately, if we are in any way to try to settle the debts to slavery, we have to measure those debts, not as a reductive single figure or ratio but as a series of figures or ratios, varying widely across firms, families, institutions and countries, based on empirical evidence. We hope that *LBS*'s work can be useful in this context, including to historians of Ireland and of Ireland and empire. In turn, we can benefit further from the knowledge that such historians possess.

Notes

1 Nicholas Draper, 'Research note: "Dependent on precarious subsistences": Ireland's slave-owners at the time of Emancipation', *Britain and the World* 6 (2013), 220–42.
2 Nini Rodgers's pioneering work has been followed by recent research concerned not only with slave-ownership – the focus of *LBS* – but with the movement of people and ideas; the flow of tropical commodities; and the financing and supply of provisions, including: Karst de Jong, 'The Irish in Jamaica during the long eighteenth century (1698–1836)', Ph.D. thesis (Queen's University Belfast, 2017); Jennifer A. McLaren, 'Irish lives in the British Caribbean: Engaging with empire in the revolutionary era', Ph.D. thesis (Macquarie University, 2018); Jonathan Jeffrey Wright, ed., *An Ulster Slave-Owner in the Revolutionary Atlantic: The Life and Letters of John Black* (Dublin: Four Courts Press, 2019); and Fionnghuala Sweeney, 'Common ground: Positioning Ireland within studies of slavery, anti-slavery and empire', *Slavery and Abolition* 37:3 (2016), 505–20. Nini Rodgers, 'Ireland, slavery, anti-slavery, post-slavery and empire: An historiographical survey', *Slavery and Abolition* 37:3 (2016), 489–504.
3 This chapter uses the terms 'slave-owner', 'slave-owners' and 'slave-ownership' to denote those who claimed property in people. In doing so, it follows the convention adopted by the *LBS* project, which was concerned to redescribe as 'slave-owners' British and Irish individuals (and collectively their class) who resisted that label at the time, preferring to identify themselves and be identified as 'West India proprietors', 'Jamaica landowners', 'planters' and other such euphemisms.
4 In its phase 2 work, *LBS* aimed to provide a comprehensive account of all ownership of fifteen or more enslaved people in a single unit, a scale that captures smaller estates (in Trinidad for example) and more elaborate artisanal enterprises in colonial towns and ports, but omits many smaller-scale urban slave-owners and the enslaved people owned by them. We currently have some 12,000 estates and other units in the Caribbean, against 6,000 in phase 1.
5 Other decisions have also constrained the results. Our reliance on Prerogative Court of Canterbury records to provide access to thousands of relevant wills has biased our work away from Ireland, Scotland, Wales and northwest England, and towards the southeast of England.

6 Chris Evans, *Slave Wales: The Welsh and Atlantic Slavery 1660–1850* (Cardiff: University of Wales Press, 2010), argues that Wales's connections were in manufacturing rather than in slave-ownership.
7 Hamilton Brown is reportedly an ancestor of United States Vice-President Kamala Harris; Donald J. Harris, 'Reflections of a Jamaican father', *Jamaica Global Online*, updated 14 January 2019, www.jamaicaglobalonline.com/kamala-harris-jamaican-heritage/ (accessed 31 August 2022).
8 The number of Irish absentee slave-owners has nearly doubled in phase 2; that of Britain and Ireland combined has increased to 5,300 from *c.* 3,000. There are also now a further 1,500 or so slave-owners characterised as 'transatlantic' who appear to have moved between metropole and colony.
9 The entries for all individuals cited in this chapter can be found at the website of the Centre for the Study of the Legacies of British Slavery, www.ucl.ac.uk/lbs (accessed 8 August 2022), which includes a search function for surnames and first names. Unless otherwise noted, biographical information is derived from this database.
10 The new entry for Sir George Leonard Staunton (www.ucl.ac.uk/lbs/person/view/2146643829 (accessed 16 August 2022)) epitomises the help provided to *LBS* by more than 1,000 correspondents, in this case Professor Henrietta Harrison of Pembroke College, Oxford.
11 P. J. Marshall, *Edmund Burke and the British Empire in the West Indies: Wealth, Power, and Slavery* (Oxford: Oxford University Press, 2019), p. 230; *LBS* also found a Richard Burke as an early buyer of land in Tobago, although Peter Marshall is sceptical of the suggestion that this was Edmund Burke's brother, whose land transactions in St Vincent were previously known.
12 Royal Irish Academy, catalogue of the Caldwell Collection, www.ria.ie/sites/default/files/caldwell-collection-catalogue-sp-list-a040.pdf (accessed 18 March 2020).
13 Trans-Atlantic Slave Trade Database, www.slavevoyages.org/voyage/database (accessed 17 August 2022). The partner in the slave trade was probably Charles Caldwell (1737–1814), son of Charles Caldwell of Dublin (1707–72). Charles Caldwell Jr is known to have moved to Liverpool in around 1757.
14 Edmund de Waal, *The White Road: A Pilgrimage of Sorts* (London: Chatto & Windus, 2015), pp. 15–16.
15 C. J. Woods, 'O'Connor, Valentine', *DIB*, www.dib.ie/biography/oconnor-valentine-a6619 (accessed 17 August 2022).
16 *The History of Parliament: British Political, Social and Local History*, https://www.historyofparliamentonline.org/volume/1820-1832/member/massy-james-1779-1834 (accessed 31 August 2022).
17 'Will of John Sayers [formerly of the City of London but now] of Totness, [*sic*] Devon', proved 6 September 1808, The National Archives, Kew (TNA), PROB 11/1485/48. His Wicklow land appears to have been in the barony of Arklow; National Library of Ireland (NLI), Wicklow papers, MS 38, 571/20 and 21, www.nli.ie/pdfs/mss%20lists/wicklow%20papers.pdf (accessed 16 August 2022).

18 *The History of Parliament*, www.historyofparliamentonline.org/volume/ 1715-1754/member/french-jeffrey-1701-54 (accessed 16 August 2022).
19 NLI, Sweetman papers, www.nli.ie/pdfs/mss%20lists/156_SweetmanPapers.pdf (accessed 31 August 2022).
20 *Ulster Examiner*, 14 October 1876.
21 Eric Williams, *Capitalism and Slavery* (Chapel Hill: University of North Carolina Press, 1944); Seymour Drescher, *Econocide: British Slavery in the Era of Abolition* (Pittsburgh: University of Pittsburgh, 1977).
22 *Parliamentary Papers* (1833), 'Bankruptcies and Bankrupts Ireland', Vol. XXXI (293).
23 Thomas M. Truxes, 'Cunningham, Waddell (1729–1797)', *Oxford Dictionary of National Biography* (Oxford University Press, 2004), online edn (January 2008), www.oxforddnb.com/view/article/57700 (accessed 12 January 2016).
24 George Hill, 'The Stewarts of Ballintoy: With notices of other families of the district in the seventeenth century. The Stewarts of Ballintoy', *Ulster Journal of Archaeology*, Second Series, 7:1 (1901), 9–17.
25 www.peartssolicitors.ie/about-us/ (accessed 26 March 2020).
26 Will of Elizabeth Peart of Dundrum Castle, proved 5 December 1854, TNA, PROB 11/2202/55.
27 This is consistent with the broader analysis of imperial backwash in Stephanie Barczewski, *Country Houses and the British Empire, 1700–1930* (Manchester: Manchester University Press, 2014), pp. 247–69, which shows seven landed estates in Ireland among 347 such estates in Britain and Ireland purchased by colonial merchants, ten of 231 purchased by Indian nabobs, and six of 212 purchased by 'West Indian planters'.
28 Finola O'Kane, 'Moving landscapes to Saint-Domingue, Jamaica, and Ireland: Plantations, national identity, and the colonial picturesque', in Stephen Bending and Jennifer Milam, eds, *Huntington Library Quarterly* 84:3 (Autumn 2021), p. 583.
29 'Newtownbarry House, CARHILL, Bunclody originally Newtownbarry, WEXFORD', National Inventory of Architectural Heritage, www.buildingsofireland.ie/buildings-search/building/15602001/newtownbarry-house-carrhill-bunclody-originally-newtownbarry-county-wexford (accessed 31 March 2020). There is ambiguity as to whether Lanyon's client was Robert Westley Hall-Dare (1817–66) or his son of the same name (1840–76).
30 'RCEWA [Reviewing Committee on the Export of Works of Art] – *The Rialto Bridge with the Palazzo dei Camerlenghi*, Francesco Guardi: Statement of the Expert Adviser to the Secretary of State that the painting meets Waverley criteria two and three', www.artscouncil.org.uk/sites/default/files/EA%20statement_Guardi_0.pdf (accessed 2 April 2020).
31 See website of the British Museum, www.britishmuseum.org/research/collection_online/collection_object_details.aspx?objectId=3172880&partId=1 (accessed 31 March 2020).

32 Royal Dublin Society, Past Members, http://entrants.rds.ie/pastmembers/index.php?r=2943 (accessed 31 August 2022).
33 Andrew Clarke has yet to be associated by *LBS* with specific slave property in Trinidad (beyond a role for the Sevilla estate as guardian to a minor, John Clarke, tentatively associated with him), although in 1806 he identified himself as a 'proprietor', and biographies of his family refer to 'a large estate' there.
34 Williams, *Capitalism and Slavery*, p. 97.
35 Catherine Hall, 'Reconfiguring race: The stories the slave-owners told', in Catherine Hall, Nicholas Draper, Keith McClelland, Katie Donington and Rachel Lang, *Legacies of British Slave-Ownership: Colonial Slavery and the Formation of Victorian Britain* (Cambridge: Cambridge University Press, 2014), pp. 163–202.
36 H. W. Martin, *A counter appeal, in answer to 'An appeal' by William Wilberforce: designed to prove that the emancipation of the Negroes in the West Indies, by a legislative enactment without the consent of the planters, would be a flagrant breach of national honour, hostile to the principles of religion, justice, and humanity, and highly injurious to the planter and to the slave.* (London: printed for C. & J. Rivington and sold by Lloyd, 1823).
37 William Urwick, D.D., *Biographic Sketches of the late James Digges La Touche, Esq., Banker, Dublin, Honorary Secretary to the Sunday School Society for Ireland, during Seventeen Years from its commencement* (Dublin, 1868), pp. 167–83.

7

Soldiers, settlers, slavers: Irish lives on the Spanish borderlands of North America and the Caribbean in the revolutionary 1790s*

José Brownrigg-Gleeson

Night was drawing in on the banks of the Tensaw River, close to the Spanish outpost of Mobile in present-day Alabama, when an enslaved woman sounded the alarm: Luis, a fugitive from slavery imprisoned in the town's fort, had managed to escape and return to his enslaver's plantation, armed with a rifle and two knives, one on each side.[1] Alerted by the cries for help of the unnamed woman, four white men rushed to the kitchen to capture Luis and Enrique, another *cimarrón* ('maroon') later found hiding in the bushes nearby. Two of those white men – John Donovan, the plantation's overseer, and Daniel Lyons – were born in Ireland. Luis's enslaver, Cornelius McCurtin, although away on business on that evening in March 1789, was also Irish (Figure 7.1).

The judicial process brought against the maroons by one of the white men injured during the affray permits a broader, if still partial, reconstruction of the narrative of these events. Spanish court records show that Luis had already fled McCurtin's *habitación* at an earlier date, on being informed by a fellow enslaved person that 'he had heard his master [McCurtin] say that he wanted to hurt him [Luis]'.[2] The depositions also reveal that the enslaved woman who had alerted the men to the maroon's intrusion was in fact his partner, and that Luis had come to take her with him, seemingly against her will. Yet, as Martín Lienhard has rightly highlighted, the proceedings are also surrounded by thunderous silences and intentional omissions. Not only did the judge not request the testimony of the white women who were also on the plantation that evening; the enslaved woman who was first to alert the Irish overseer and his companions to the presence of the maroons was not questioned either, and her name is never mentioned in the reports.[3]

While the case against Luis and Enrique illustrates the challenges and limitations inherent in researching the lives and voices of the enslaved – and particularly of enslaved women[4] – it also showcases the relative abundance

Figure 7.1 *Dn. Cornelio McCurtin, y marca de su caballo*, 1796. Ministerio de Cultura y Deporte, Archivo General de Indias (Seville), MP-Estampas, 32.

of sources that enable a multifaceted approach to Irish interactions with slavery in the Americas at the end of the eighteenth century. In particular, this chapter places the focus on historical materials in Spanish, which, as acknowledged by Fionnghuala Sweeney, remain 'methodologically marginal' in the scholarship concerning Ireland, slavery and anti-slavery.[5] The census that the commandant of Mobile sent to his superiors in Spain only a few days after Luis and Enrique's capture, for instance, recorded the Irish planter as having a total of eleven enslaved people on this tract of land, which was devoted primarily to the cultivation of corn and chickpeas.[6] McCurtin's life in North America, from his arrival prior to the American Revolution and throughout his more than two decades as a loyal Spanish subject, generated a substantial paper trail. At one time an officer in the Pensacola militia, McCurtin had significant property in cattle, land and enslaved people, and was surrounded by an extensive network of Irish friends and collaborators whose livelihoods were strongly dependent on the fluctuations in inter-imperial relations and the wider geopolitics of the Gulf Coast and the Caribbean.

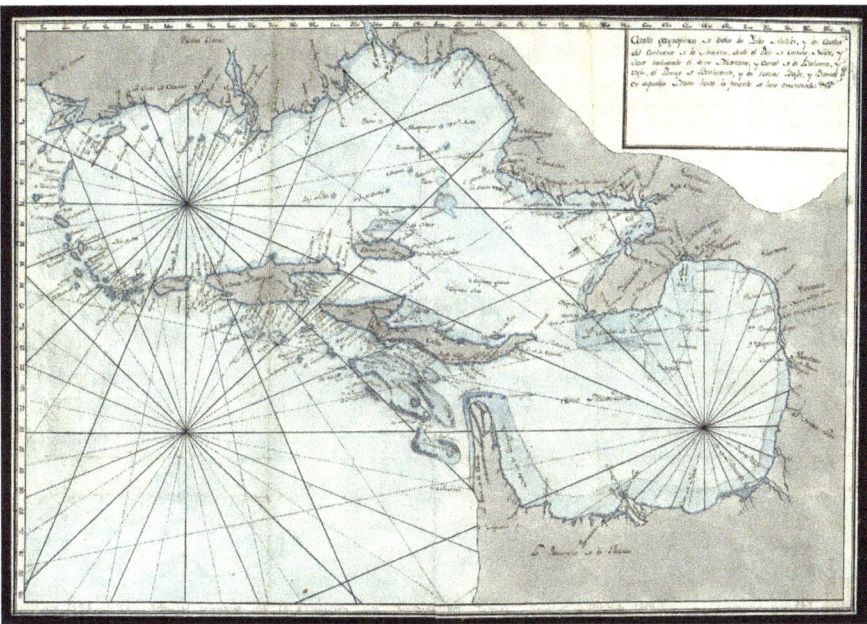

Figure 7.2 *Carta geográfica de todas las islas Antiles y las costas del continente de la América, desde el río Orinoco, Norte y Oeste, incluyendo el Seno Mexicano, y canal de la Bahama Viejo, el Pasaje de Barlovento, y las sondas, bajos y bancos que en aquellos mares hasta al presente se han encontrado*, ca. 1788. Ministerio de Cultura y Deporte, Archivo Histórico Nacional (Madrid), Estado, MPD. 769.

With notable exceptions, however, scholars studying the connections among Irish communities in the Atlantic, the extension of slavery, and the participation in and resistance to empire have tended to neglect the late-eighteenth-century Hispanic world (Figure 7.2).⁷ Although the need to continue 'the de-centring of national, and by implication, imperial narratives' has been acknowledged, the inherently polycentric, transimperial and multilingual dimension of the Irish experience of the Caribbean and its borderlands is yet to be fully revealed.⁸

This chapter showcases some of the 'uncomfortable and complex evidence' of Irish trading and ownership of enslaved people in Louisiana, Florida and the Greater Caribbean in the 1790s.⁹ It contends that Cornelius McCurtin was no exception: the Irish on these disputed zones were at times protagonists as much in the exercise and control of colonial violence as they might have been in limiting and preventing it on other occasions. The chapter first charts this Irish presence in Spanish North America and the greater Caribbean during the pivotal years that followed the Seven Years War and the geopolitical realignments after the American Revolution. Then it analyses the transformation in attitudes and circumstances that the Irish in these parts of the Spanish empire faced after the outbreak of the revolution in Saint-Domingue and during the turbulent times that ensued. In doing so, it proposes a reframing of the history of Ireland, the Irish and the Age of Revolutions that fully incorporates the Hispanic context into our scope.

The 'Irish hour' in Spanish America

The Irish presence in colonial Spanish America reached previously unknown heights during the second half of the eighteenth century.[10] Through a combination of factors – sometimes circumstantial, generally interdependent – multiple Irish communities in the Atlantic coalesced in the Hispanic New World during these decades. An early sense of the intensity of this presence can be found, for instance, in Havana, in the immediate aftermath of the evacuation of the British troops that had taken the town in 1762. At this point Alexander O'Reilly, the high-flying Meath-born officer whom the Spanish Crown had entrusted with introducing military and economic reforms on the island, needed to warm the Havana elite to the proposed changes. His mission was significantly facilitated by the mediation of Irish Jesuit Thomas Butler, who also introduced him to Oliver Pollock, a fellow countryman of standing in the foreign merchant community.[11]

Whether in the service of the Crown, as members of the clergy or operating as traders, the exponential involvement of the Irish in Spanish America was multifaceted indeed. There were individuals such as Cornelius Coppinger, who emerged at a crucial time in the extension of the slave trade in the Spanish Caribbean. In 1764, this native of Cork who had settled in Havana during the British occupation became the beneficiary of one of the first contracts to introduce enslaved people into Cuba that the Spanish treasury handed out to private individuals. Coppinger's position as an *asentista* ('merchant financier') was reinforced a year later, when Coppinger, Wilmont and Fogo were awarded another contract to introduce 7,000 enslaved people and 14,000 barrels of flour.[12] In addition to Cuba, where suppliers of forced labour introduced over 40,000 unfree person between 1762 and 1789 alone, Irish merchants redoubled their efforts to enter the slave trade in other areas of the Spanish empire.[13] Such was the case of Michael Kearney – an associate of Coppinger in the Spanish town of Alicante – and brothers José and Juan Bouligny, who, setting their sights on Louisiana, sought the Crown's authorisation to begin to introduce 2,000 enslaved people per year into that province in 1776.[14] This was a profitable business, involving also plenty of second-generation members of Hiberno-Spanish merchant networks with transimperial ramifications, such as Joaquín Power, the factor of the

Compañía de Asiento de Negros in Puerto Rico between 1770 and 1778, or Eduardo Barry, the Trinidad-born agent of the Liverpool house of Baker and Dawson in Port of Spain, awarded a contract in 1784 to introduce 4,000 captive workers into that jurisdiction.[15]

The growing importation of enslaved people reflected profound reformist shifts in the policy of the Spanish monarchy concerning its dominions in North America and the Caribbean. This was compounded by the acknowledgement that in certain parts of the empire, such as in Louisiana, 'the countryside ... cannot be advanced without [enslaved] blacks'.[16] A temporary decision to move beyond monopolistic arrangements by allowing *habaneros* to procure enslaved people from any viable source – which was later extended to other ports – marked the introduction of the principle of free trade into the Spanish slave market in 1789.[17] Coupled with these measures had come, of course, a progressive commercial liberalisation. Two of the main legislative milestones signalling reform were the 1778 Free Trade decree, which opened up new routes between Louisiana, Cuba and the Yucatán Peninsula, and the royal order that followed in 1782, thanks to which Spanish subjects were permitted to trade directly with French possessions.

These transformations had powerful effects. For one thing, they significantly dynamised the flow of foodstuffs, goods and stolen labour linking the francophone and anglophone Caribbean to the Spanish possessions. In 1787, for instance, more than half of the enslaved people re-exported from Kingston were sent to the mouth of the Mississippi.[18] They also made the Spanish dominions much more attractive to Anglo-American settlers. In 1776, the island of Trinidad, where Spain took resolute action to facilitate the establishment of foreigners, became the forerunner in the implementation of new immigration policies. When, soon after, a group of Irish Catholics from the Danish enclave of St Croix presented a plan to settle there, it received the swift blessing of Spanish authorities. By 1783, over 900 free foreigners had moved to that island, bringing with them almost 3,000 enslaved people, and the generous land grants provided by the *Cédula de Población* issued that year became the blueprint for similar measures in Spain's North American borderlands.[19]

Although Spain and Britain had shared a porous boundary in North America from the redrawing of the imperial map after the Seven Years War, it was at the conclusion of the American Revolutionary War, with the restoration of Spanish sovereignty to the East and West Florida provinces, that the Irish presence skyrocketed. Cornelius McCurtin was amongst those who chose to take an oath of allegiance on St Patrick's Day, 1780, and remained in the Spanish dominions; over the next few decades thousands of British loyalist refugees and new Anglo-American settlers flocked to these lands.[20]

There were entrepreneurs who came directly from Ireland, such as Daniel Clark Jr, who, after linking up with his uncle in New Orleans in 1786, attained notoriety as a slave trader connecting Louisiana to the wider commercial circuits of the United States and the Caribbean. Others proposed instead colonisation schemes to bring 'discontented' Irish Catholic families. In June 1788, Peter Bryan Bruin joined his Roscommon-born father in Natchez with a wife, three children and twenty enslaved people. In all, the group of Catholic settlers travelling from Virginia totalled around 100 people.[21] Royal officials received numerous other proposals to bring Irish settlers into the Spanish provinces during these years. Several were accepted, but the majority, deemed to represent excessive cost for the royal treasury, were unceremoniously rejected.[22]

The granting of permission for supervised settlement was accompanied by a decision that prompted the arrival of another distinct group of Irishmen on these borderlands. Faced with the vexing choice of either expelling or attempting to integrate the non-Spanish-speaking white population, the Crown approved the dispatch of Irish priests, presumed capable of communicating with the francophone and anglophone communities and thus able to try to attract them to Spanish faith and customs. Extracted initially from the Irish College in Salamanca, the first four priests arrived in New Orleans, via Havana, in August 1787; by the end of the century, at least another sixteen made their way to these contested boundaries.[23] Here they often came into contact with the remnants of the Hibernia Regiment, a distinctively Irish unit in the service of Spain that had been transferred in full to Havana in 1780 to fight British troops during the American Revolution. A selected few of the regiment's officers became salient protagonists in their own right, as for almost three decades between 1781 and 1811 one of the two Spanish Floridas was always under the command of a native of Ireland from this unit.[24]

Spanish policy was not without its contradictions. There was certainly an inherent degree of risk in recurring to 'people used to changing address as swiftly as they change clothes' in trying to improve stability and security on the borderlands of empire, prompting the Governor of Louisiana to suggest later that Anglo-Americans wishing to settle in the province should only be allowed to do so if possessing quantifiable means (i.e. at least ten enslaved people).[25] It was, in any case, an era of paradoxes: one that prefigured the birth of an Angloworld – 'Anglo' understood in 'its broadest usage as shorthand for Anglophone or English-speaking' – precisely when the Spanish territorial footprint in the Americas was at its peak.[26]

Fears of revolution/revolutions of fear

News of the French Revolution and of the slave insurrection in Saint-Domingue in August 1791 sent shockwaves through Spanish America.[27]

Official prospects envisioning a booming industry, expanding profits and growing returns quickly gave way to a generalised sense of fear, anxiety and commotion, a dramatic alteration to the context that had elicited Irish men and women to put down roots in the Hispanic Caribbean, Louisiana and the Floridas.

It was a change of atmosphere that David Fitzgerald, an emigrant from Cork who had moved with his wife and three children from New York to Trinidad around 1788, was to feel first-hand. Unable to procure the enslaved people and tools necessary to establish a profitable plantation in the Spanish West Indies, the family resolved to try their luck in Louisiana. By August 1789 they were in New Orleans, where without any apparent difficulty Fitzgerald obtained authorisation to sell three enslaved women (one black and two mulattas).[28] A year later, however, the Irish settler had been arrested for fraud: the more than forty enslaved people consigned to him in the *Sally* were confiscated, and Fitzgerald was sentenced to five years' imprisonment in North Africa. At the heart of the issue lay more than a simple contravention of a recent decree prohibiting the arrival of Indians, blacks or mulattos from the non-Spanish West Indies. What seemingly had put authorities on alert was to learn that on its voyage from Trinidad, the *Sally* had called at the French island of Martinique.[29]

A drunken duel between two men onboard a ship reaching New Orleans from Jamaica around the same time offers another valuable window into Irish transimperial mobility in the Caribbean. On reaching Louisiana, Michael O'Hagan (sometimes 'O'Haran') denounced fellow Irishman Maurice Nowlan for the injuries that he had allegedly sustained aboard the *Catalina* while trying to prevent Nowlan – a retired officer in half-pay of the British North Carolina Highlanders – from killing the frigate's captain.[30] The dispute had taken place at sea, somewhere between Martinique and Dominica, and although mention of the cargo was carefully omitted by all parties and witnesses, it is plausible that the ship had also been carrying captives: in September 1788, the same frigate had arrived at the mouth of the Mississippi transporting 200 enslaved people after calling at Dominica.[31]

Links to France and its colonies were already tainted with a degree of suspicion, but it was the conflagration in Saint-Domingue in the summer of 1791 that turned the Spanish possessions in the Caribbean and the Gulf basin into a powder keg. With thousands of refugees arriving from the French West Indies – as many as 10,000 would settle in Louisiana between 1792 and 1808 – Governor Carondelet began to see the ghosts of insurrection everywhere.[32] The geographic situation of the province implied that danger could come not just from the revolution-ridden Caribbean, but also from the opportunists, adventurers and interlopers exerting pressure on the colony's northern boundaries.[33]

In these circumstances, tightening the protection of Spanish North America without putting its economic survival at risk was close to impossible. Orders to interrupt all trade between Louisiana and the United States from September 1793, for example, also met with Carondelet's disapproval: in his view, the measure could well lead to the definitive 'insurrection and loss of this province, as its inhabitants do not have any other outlets for their indigo and tobacco'.[34] This interruption was a hurried reaction to anxious reports from Spanish agents in Philadelphia concerning the activities of Edmond Genêt, the French minister who had just arrived in the United States. Intent on revolutionising Spanish Florida with a militia of volunteers, Citizen Genêt in fact was to appeal directly to 'the generous and intrepid natives of Ireland' in the United States supporting revolutionary France in its war against Britain and its Spanish allies.[35]

A royal order issued in 1792 to facilitate the expulsion of foreigners who refused to swear allegiance to the Spanish King had done little to abate Carondelet's fears.[36] 'We are surrounded by traitors. They are among the main inhabitants, the populace, the troops, and even within the secular clergy', the Governor of Louisiana was to tell his brother-in-law and superior in Havana.[37] Colonial administrators tended to centre their vigilance on the black component of the population – 'one must always be suspicious of the men of colour, free and enslaved … more than of the whites' – but for good measure, some Irish individuals took advantage of this phase of paranoia in crescendo to affirm their loyalty to Spain and contribute to the tranquillity of that part of the empire.[38]

Amongst those esteemed to be most loyal to the Crown were the members of the clergy. The Irish priests in Louisiana and Florida were not without their personal faults: the intemperance of Charles Burke and Constantine McCaffrey (a Carmelite from Mullingar who had arrived by way of Salamanca in 1791) was legendary and indeed disturbing.[39] Generally, though, the Irish priests were reliable and thus capable of providing important surveillance services to the monarchy.

Some, such as Father James Maxwell, had actually arrived on the borderlands bearing staunch anti-republican credentials. Educated at the Irish College in Nantes, Maxwell had served for six years as a chaplain in the French army, from which he was expelled after refusing to take the civic oath required by the National Assembly's Civil Constitution of the Clergy. On suggestion of his cousin – an Irish officer in the Spanish navy – Maxwell had moved to Madrid and learned of the need for polyglot priests in Louisiana, making his way there in the company of his fellow countryman John Brady in May 1795.[40] Ministering in the largely francophone Parish of St Genevieve in Upper Louisiana (present-day Missouri), Maxwell offered a set of assurances that contrasted with the growing suspicion with which Spanish officials regarded some of his French colleagues.

Not long after the slave conspiracy in Pointe Coupée in April 1795, factionalism in Natchitoches, Louisiana's westernmost gateway to Texas, put Father Jean Delvaux on a direct collision course with Spanish authorities. Adopting much of the French revolutionary vocabulary – including calling the opposing party that of the 'aristocrats' – Delvaux rapidly antagonised the anglophone community.[41] Writing to a friend, Irish-born Thomas O'Reilly confessed that '[a] few of us English and Irish have offered our service to keep peace by patrolling'.[42]

Other Irish settlers assisted Spanish authorities in different capacities. In October 1795, the Governor of Puerto Rico reported that a coin with a potentially 'seditious' inscription had fallen into his hands. Two translators of French and English were swiftly brought in to offer their interpretations of the markings. It fell to James O'Daly, a native of Co. Galway who had arrived in Puerto Rico in 1776, to convince the nervous officers of the Crown that the legend (resembling the spelling of 'EIGHT' and thus probably a denominational countermark) had no apparent dangerous meaning in English.[43]

Multilingual competence situated a handful of the Irish in particularly relevant environments, where they were exposed to some of the main revolutionary concepts of the era. For instance, when in February 1794 authorities in New Orleans accused free mulatto militia officer Pierre Bailly of 'having burst into tirades against the Spanish government and being a manifest follower of the maxims of the French rebels', one of the court interpreters at the trial was Daniel Mortimer, an Irish Catholic enslaver.[44] Fifteen years later, another Irish enslaver and translator would publish the proceedings of the case against Pierre Benonime Dormenon, the Pointe Coupée parish judge brought to justice for supposedly having participated in the Haitian Revolution around 1793.[45]

The value of loyalty

In the Americas, the Age of Revolutions signified also an age of importation of an enslaved labour force. The Irish in Spanish North America and the Caribbean lived with and around enslaved people; in certain spaces, such as Trinidad and Louisiana, they were determined contributors in the extension of the plantation economy. Holding people in slavery was common practice, for instance, amongst the Irish priests in Florida and Louisiana, as exemplified by the busy transactions of Francis Lennan at the end of the century: in little over two years, he bought and resold Perina, a thirty-two-year-old black woman; purchased Elías, a mulatto boy of around ten years of age; and also paid for Mentee and Alexander, an African mother and son.[46]

Even in the turbulent revolutionary context of the early 1800s, there were men and women of Irish origin attempting to move and augment their enslaved property. In May 1802, Limerick-born Matthew Howard Hill appeared before a Spanish judge in New Orleans to declare that he had landed with wife and children to establish his residence there. There was, however, one caveat: it was almost impossible to find suitable bondspersons, and being 'mortified to see his family without domestic service and exposed to many other jobs of similar nature', he hoped to be allowed to import four *bozales* ('African slaves') whom he still owned in Havana. Although the private introduction of enslaved people into Louisiana had once again been outlawed, Hill was given permission to do so after becoming a Spanish subject, and on the basis of a 1788 dispensation that enabled the introduction of any form of property if beneficial to the agriculture and population of the country.[47]

The fluidity that connected the multi-imperial environments of the Caribbean and North America could sometimes benefit Irish enslavers. Patrick Uriel, a native of the village of Emper in Westmeath who had established himself in Puerto Rico around 1789 to work in the sugar and rum business, managed to preserve ownership of the people he held in slavery even after Spanish authorities ordered the expulsion of all foreigners from the island in 1797. When in 1800 he came to settle in Louisiana after a short time in New York, Uriel – who had also claimed people as property in St Thomas – still had a house and two enslaved people in St Croix.[48] Others, by contrast, reached Spanish America by accident. Following the sinking of the ship carrying them from St Croix to Curaçao, Irish enslaver Richard Bateman Lloyd, his wife Anna Elizabeth Kock and their four-year-old son landed in Puerto Cabello, on the coast of Venezuela, in November 1799 (Figure 7.3). There they found dozens of enslaved people who had absconded from their estates: Bateman and Kock rapidly presented a list of sixty names to Spanish authorities, noting nonetheless that 'there are other fugitive slaves of ours to upwards of one hundred more in said Puerto Cabello and Coro'.[49]

The unfree labour force represented a major portion of the wealth accumulated by these enslavers. When John Fitzpatrick, an Irish trader in Louisiana, passed away in 1791, the assessors appraised his estate at 6,200 pesos, over 40 per cent of which corresponded to the estimated value of his eleven enslaved people, which at 2,590 pesos surpassed the total value of his land (2,000 pesos).[50] On his death in 1788, Patrick Macnamara had more than thirty enslaved people on his plantation near New Orleans: a far from negligible increase on the seven captive workers that he had brought into his marriage. As per his will, his mother in Ireland received around 1,000 pesos and a chest full of indigo.[51]

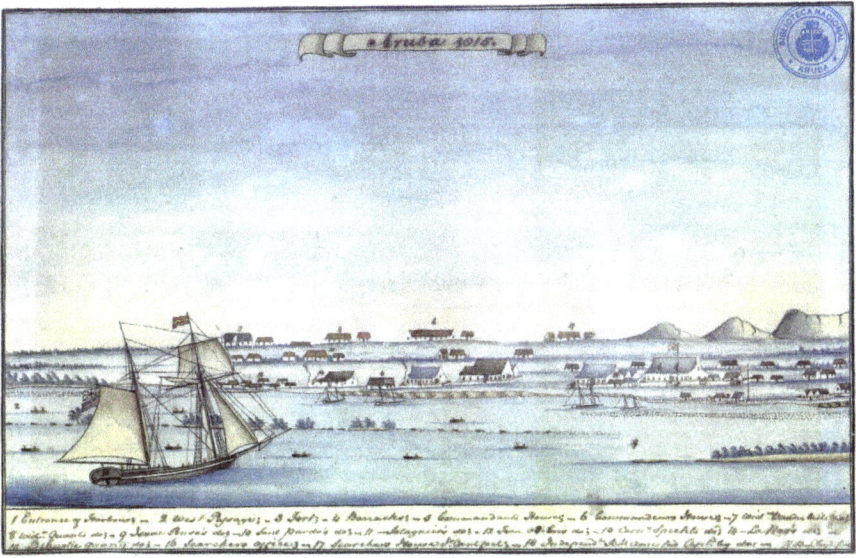

Figure 7.3 Richard Bateman Lloyd, *Aruba 1815*, watercolour depicting view of Oranjestad and Paardenbaai harbour, 42 cm × 29.5 cm. Coleccion Arubiana-Caribiana, Biblioteca Nacional Aruba. The image can be viewed at https://archive.org/details/BNA-DIG-LLOYD-1815 (accessed 9 September 2022).

An Irish age of revolutions on the borderlands?

The individuals and communities analysed in this chapter speak to a dimension of the Irish Age of Revolutions largely defined by instances of loyalty and subject to the preservation of the imperial status quo. This is not to say, however, that the Irish included in this survey were left untouched by the languages of revolution then riding the waves of oral communication.[52] It does not take much to imagine that John 'Quieco', a twenty-one-year-old Irishman who had been in Saint-Domingue in 1793, might have later shared his experience with family and friends in Louisiana.[53] The multilingual and occasionally diglossic environment of these communities just adds another level of complexity and intrigue.

In certain instances, the Irish in the Spanish Caribbean and its borderlands were even able to see the revolutionaries with their own eyes. In 1796, for example, members of the auxiliary troops of Jean Christophe were sent to Campeche, in Yucatán, where Governor Arturo O'Neill and the provincial junta of Mérida ordered the founding of a separate town for them.[54] Georges Biassou, the self-styled leader of the counter-revolution in Saint-Domingue, died in Spanish East Florida in 1801, and was given a military funeral presided over by Dublin-born Governor Enrique White.[55]

Kevin Whelan has written that 'looking at the 1790s as a whole, a republican triangle linked America, France, and Ireland'.[56] This chapter suggests that the triangle needs to be converted into a broader polyhedron that actively incorporates the Spanish-speaking world. Only then will the not-so-hidden Irelands of George Fleming's 'Hibernia', John Addison's 'Carrick Fergus' and Thomas Travers's 'San Patricio' come to the fore.[57]

Notes

* This chapter has been made possible by an Irish Research Council Postdoctoral Fellowship at the Moore Institute for the Humanities and Social Studies, National University of Ireland, Galway. I am very grateful to staff at the Archivo General de Indias in Seville and the Archivo Histórico Nacional in Madrid, and to Peter Scholing at the Biblioteca Nacional Aruba in Oranjestad, for granting permission to reproduce images in this chapter.
1. Archivo General de Indias, Seville, Spain (AGI), Cuba, leg. 172-A, fos 229–45.
2. AGI, Cuba, leg. 172-A, fo. 240r. All translations are the author's unless otherwise noted. Unknown to Luis and McCurtin, a new 'Instruction on the education, treatment and employment of slaves' seeking to improve the protection of the enslaved from their enslavers was being drafted in Madrid at the time. See Bianca Premo, 'As if she were my own: Love and law in the slave society of eighteenth-century Peru', in Daina Ramey Berry and Leslie M. Harris, eds, *Sexuality and Slavery: Reclaiming Intimate Histories in the Americas* (Athens: University of Georgia Press, 2018), pp. 71–87 (p. 74).
3. Martín Lienhard, *Disidentes, rebeldes, insurgentes. Resistencia indígena y negra en América Latina: Ensayos de historia testimonial* (Madrid: Iberoamericana-Vervuert, 2008), p. 79.
4. For a recent work making important use of court records to recover the historical voices of the enslaved see Sophie White, *Voices of the Enslaved: Love, Labor, and Longing in French Louisiana* (Chapel Hill: University of North Carolina Press, 2019). See also Jessica Marie Johnson, *Wicked Flesh: Black Women, Intimacy, and Freedom in the Atlantic World* (Philadelphia: Pennsylvania University Press, 2020); Vicent Sanz Rozalén and Michael Zeuske, eds, 'Microhistoria de esclavas y esclavos', special issue of *Millars: Espai i història* 42 (2017); and Marisa J. Fuentes, *Dispossessed Lives: Enslaved Women, Violence, and the Archive* (Philadelphia: Pennsylvania University Press, 2016).
5. Fionnghuala Sweeney, 'Common ground: Positioning Ireland within studies of slavery, anti-slavery and empire', *Slavery and Abolition* 37:3 (2016), 505–20 (p. 513).
6. AGI, Cuba, leg. 202, Vicente Folch, *padrón* ('census') of the Mobile district for 1788 (Mobile, 15 March 1789), cited in Jack D. L. Holmes, 'Alabama's forgotten settlers: Notes on the Spanish Mobile district, 1780–1813', *Alabama Historical Quarterly* 33:2 (1971), 87–97 (p. 96).
7. In addition to the work of several of the contributions to this volume, see for example Jorge Luis Chinea, ' "Spain is the merciful heavenly body whose

influence favors the Irish." Jaime O'Daly y Blake: enlightened foreign immigrant, administrator and planter in late Bourbon-era Puerto Rico, 1776–1806', *Tiempos modernos* 25:2 (2012), 1–33.
 8 Lee M. Jenkins and Melanie Otto, 'Introduction: "The Ocean in Us". Irish–Caribbean connections', *Caribbean Quarterly* 64:3–4 (2018), 377–91 (p. 379).
 9 Ciaran O'Neill, 'Not So Innocent', *Dublin Review of Books* 124 (January 2020), www.drb.ie/essays/not-so-innocent (accessed 18 August 2022).
10 For a broader discussion of the 'Irish hour' see Óscar Recio Morales, *Ireland and the Spanish Empire, 1600–1825* (Dublin: Four Courts Press, 2010), pp. 235–95.
11 Allan J. Kuethe, 'The development of the Cuban military as a sociopolitical elite, 1763–83', *Hispanic American Historical Review* 61:4 (1981), 695–704; Light T. Cummins, *To the Vast and Beautiful Land: Anglo Migration into Spanish Louisiana and Texas, 1760s–1820s* (College Station: Texas A&M University Press, 2019), p. 36. Butler purchased almost 400 forced labourers during the occupation; Elena Schneider, *The Occupation of Havana: War, Trade, and Slavery in the Atlantic World* (Chapel Hill: University of North Carolina Press, 2018), pp. 203–5.
12 Nikolaus Böttcher, 'Trade, war and empire: British merchants in Cuba, 1762–1796', in Nikolaus Böttcher and Bernd Hausberger, eds, *Dinero y negocios en la historia de América Latina = Geld und Geschäft in der Geschichte Lateinamerikas* (Madrid: Iberoamericana-Vervuert, 2000), pp. 169–98.
13 Pablo Tornero Tinajero, *Crecimiento económico y transformaciones sociales: Esclavos, hacendados y comerciantes en la Cuba colonial* (Madrid: Centro de Publicaciones del Ministerio del Trabajo y Seguridad Social, 1996), pp. 64–5.
14 AGI, Santo Domingo, leg. 2586, petition of José Bouligny, Juan Bouligny and Miguel Kearney (Alicante, 12 March 1776), cited in José A. Armillas Vicente, 'La Luisiana española y las Antillas francesas (1763-1785)', in Carmen Corona, Ivana Frasquet and Carmen María Fernández, eds, *Legitimidad, soberanías, representación: Independencias y naciones en Iberoamérica* (Castelló: Universitat Jaume I, 2009), pp. 40–58 (p. 54).
15 Bibiano Torres Ramírez, *La Compañía gaditana de negros* (Seville: Escuela de Estudios Hispanoamericanos, 1973), p. 121; José Luis Belmonte Postigo, 'Notas sobre el tráfico de esclavos en Santiago de Cuba', *Memorias: Revista digital de historia y arqueología desde el Caribe* 8 (2007), 1–18. Barry and his Irish associate John Black apparently defrauded the Liverpool firm of the funds from this contract; see Jonathan Jeffrey Wright, *An Ulster Slave-Owner in the Revolutionary Atlantic: The Life and Letters of John Black* (Dublin: Four Courts Press, 2019), p. 28.
16 AGI, Cuba, leg. 593, Martín Navarro to José de Gálvez (New Orleans, 20 July 1781).
17 Sherry Johnson, 'The rise and fall of Creole participation in the Cuban slave trade, 1789–1796', *Cuban Studies* 30 (2000), 52–75. The decree gave foreigners two years from the date of announcement to introduce enslaved people without taxation. In St Augustine, Florida, it was not read until 6 June

1793; see Jane Landers, 'Slavery in the Spanish Caribbean and the failure of abolition', *Review (Fernand Braudel Center)* 31:3 (2008), 343–71.
18 Jean-Pierre Le Glaunec, 'Slave migrations in Spanish and Early American Louisiana: New sources and new estimates', *Louisiana History: The Journal of the Louisiana Historical Association* 46:2 (2005), 185–209.
19 AGI, Caracas, leg. 443. Cited in Nikolaus Böttcher, 'Neptune's Trident: Trinidad, 1776–1840. From colonial backyard to Crown colony', *Jahrbuch für Geschichte Lateinamerikas* 44:1 (2007), 157–85 (p. 163); Rosario Sevilla Soler, *Inmigración y cambio socio-económico en Trinidad (1783–1797)* (Seville: Escuela de Estudios Hispanoamericanos–CSIC, 1988), p. 29. On Trinidad's 1783 *Cédula* see Kit Candlin, *The Last Caribbean Frontier, 1795–1815* (Basingstoke: Palgrave Macmillan, 2012), pp. 56–7.
20 AGI, Cuba, leg. 200, 'Serment de fidélité prêté par provision par les habitants anglais de la Mobile, le 17 mars 1780'.
21 Archivo General de Simancas, Valladolid, Spain (AGS), Secretaría del Despacho de Guerra, leg. 6919, exp. 3, memorial of Peter Bryan Bruin to the King (New Orleans, June 1796). See also David Narrett, *Adventurism and Empire: The Struggle for Mastery in the Louisiana–Florida Borderlands, 1762–1803* (Chapel Hill: University of North Carolina Press, 2015), p. 155; and William S. Coker, 'The Bruins and the formulation of Spanish immigration policy in the Old Southwest', in John Francis McDermott, ed., *The Spanish in the Mississippi Valley, 1762–1804* (Urbana: University of Illinois Press, 1974), pp. 61–71.
22 See Biblioteca Nacional de España, Madrid, Spain (BNE), MSS/19509, fos 161–3, report by Juan Nepumoceno Quesada on the proposal of Michael O'Reilly and Thomas Travers to introduce Irish families into Florida (St Augustine, 5 May 1791).
23 Gilbert E. Din, 'The Irish mission to West Florida', *Louisiana History: The Journal of the Louisiana Historical Association* 12:4 (1971), 315–34. See also University of Notre Dame Archives, South Bend, Indiana (UNDA), Archdiocese of New Orleans (LA) Collection, Cabinet IV, shelf 4, box K, 'Instrucción a la cual deberán arreglarse los vicarios, párrocos y demás eclesiásticos que ejerzan la *cura animarum* en las Provincias de la Luisiana y Florida Oriental y Occidental …' (San Lorenzo del Escorial, 30 November 1792).
24 The Governors were: Arturo O'Neill (West Florida, 1781–92), Carlos Howard (West Florida, 1792–3), Enrique White (West Florida, 1793–5; and East Florida, 1796–1811).
25 Archivo Histórico Nacional, Madrid, Spain (AHN), Estado, leg. 3898, Carondelet to Conde de Floridablanca (New Orleans, 25 February 1792).
26 James Belich situates the birth of the Angloworld in 1783: *Replenishing the Earth: The Settler Revolution and the Rise of the Anglo-World, 1783–1939* (Oxford: Oxford University Press, 2009), p. 49.
27 The scholarship on these aspects is vast. See, for example, Michael Zeuske, 'The French Revolution in Spanish America', in Alan Forrest and Matthias Middell, eds, *The Routledge Companion to the French Revolution in World History* (Abingdon: Routledge, 2015), pp. 77–96; Ada Ferrer, *Freedom's Mirror: Cuba and Haiti in the Age of Revolution* (New York: Cambridge University Press,

2014); Jane Landers, *Atlantic Creoles in the Age of Revolutions* (Cambridge, MA: Harvard University Press, 2010); and David B. Gaspar and David P. Geggus, eds, *A Turbulent Time: The French Revolution and the Greater Caribbean* (Bloomington: Indiana University Press, 1997).

28 AGI, Estado, leg. 66, n. 7, José María Chacón to Conde de Floridablanca (Trinidad, 2 March 1792); Spanish Judicial Records, Record Group 2, Louisiana State Museum Historical Center, New Orleans, USA (SJR), 'Información producida por Dn. David Fitzgerald para que se le autorice para la venta de varios esclavos' (New Orleans, August 1789).

29 AHN, Estado, leg. 3898, exp. 5, 'Sentencia contra David Fitzgerald y Francisco Driscoll' (New Orleans, 25 September 1790).

30 SJR, 'Criminales contra Mauricio Nowlan sobre la herida que dio a Miguel O'Hagan' (New Orleans, 11 November 1790).

31 Jean Pierre Le Glaunec, 'Slave migrations and slave control in Spanish and Early American New Orleans', in Peter J. Kastor and François Weil, eds, *Empires of the Imagination: Transatlantic Histories of the Louisiana Purchase* (Charlottesville: University of Virginia Press, 2009), pp. 204–38 (p. 208). In 1791, Nowlan himself requested permission to introduce slaves; see AGI, Cuba, leg. 177-B.

32 Julius Scott, *The Common Wind: Afro-American Currents in the Age of the Haitian Revolution* (London: Verso, 2018), p. 183; Jorge Victoria Ojeda, *Tendencias monárquicas en la revolución haitiana: El negro Juan Francisco Petecou bajo las banderas francesa y española* (Quintana Roo: Siglo XXI, 2005), p. 26.

33 See José Shane Brownrigg-Gleeson, 'Turbulent and intriguing spirits: Irish traders and agents on Spain's North American borderlands, 1763–1803', in Óscar Recio Morales, ed., *Redes de nación y espacios de poder: La comunidad irlandesa en España y la América española, 1600–1825* (Valencia: Albatros, 2012), pp. 311–26.

34 AHN, Estado, leg. 3898, exp. 4, no. 1, Carondelet to Duque de Alcudia (New Orleans, 27 March 1794).

35 David Wilson, *United Irishmen, United States: Immigrant Radicals in the Early Republic* (Ithaca, NY: Cornell University Press, 1998), p. 40.

36 Juan Andreo García, 'La Revolución Francesa y América: La Capitanía General de Venezuela 1790–1796. Notas para la comprensión de un rechazo', in Carmen M. Cremades Griñán and Antonio Díaz Bautista, eds, *Poder ilustrado y revolución* (Murcia: Universidad de Murcia, 1991), pp. 143–71 (p. 150).

37 AGS, Secretaría del Despacho de Guerra, leg. 6929, exp. 8, Carondelet to Las Casas (New Orleans, 3 May 1795). The sentiment was seconded by the Secretary of State, who voiced his concerns about a province 'surrounded by restless and bellicose neighbours addicted to revolutionary principles'; AHN, Estado, leg. 3898, exp. 1, Duque de Alcudia to Diego Gardoqui (Madrid, 1 January 1795).

38 AGS, Secretaría del Despacho de Guerra, leg. 6929, exp. 8, Las Casas to Carondelet (Havana, 12 June 1795). On Spanish 'paranoia' in relation to the arrival of free black persons see Kimberly S. Hanger, *Bounded Lives, Bounded*

Places: Free Black Society in Colonial New Orleans, 1769–1803 (Durham, NC: Duke University Press, 1997), p. 152.

39 See UNDA, Archdiocese of New Orleans (LA) Collection, Cabinet V, shelf 2, box F, 'Proceedings against Father Carlos Burk' (New Orleans, 20 November 1799); and UNDA, Archdiocese of New Orleans (LA) Collection, Cabinet V, shelf 1, box A, 'Testimony in the proceedings against Father Constantine McCaffrey' (St Augustine, 1795–7). By the end of the decade both had abandoned the province, much to the relief of local authorities.

40 AGI, Santo Domingo, leg. 2589, fo. 150, memorial of James Maxwell (Madrid, 1 November 1792).

41 Gilbert C. Din, 'Father Jean Delvaux and the Natchitoches Revolt of 1795', *Louisiana History: The Journal of the Louisiana Historical Association* 40:1 (1999), 5–33.

42 AGI, Cuba, leg. 178-B, Thomas O'Reilly to 'Dear Friend' (Natchitoches, 5 July 1795), cited in Din, 'Father Jean Delvaux', p. 12. On the contemptuous use of the word 'aristocrats' amongst Delvaux's followers, see BNE, MSS/19509, fo. 245, Luis Peñalver, Bishop of Louisiana, to Eugenio Llaguno (New Orleans, 1 February 1797).

43 AGI, Estado, leg. 10, n. 3, Governor of Puerto Rico to Príncipe de la Paz (Puerto Rico, 14 October 1795). Similar concerns had been raised in Caracas in November 1793: AGI, Estado, leg. 58, n. 4 (2a), report of the Junta de Caracas to the Council of the Indies (Caracas, 2 November 1793).

44 AGI, Estado, 14, n. 60, proceedings against Pierre Bailly (New Orleans, 11 February 1794). Mortimer held at least seven people in slavery according to Kristin L. Condotta, 'Foreign imports: Irish immigrants and material networks in early New Orleans, 1780–1820', Ph.D. thesis (Tulane University, 2014), p. 304.

45 Henry Paul Nugent, *Observations of the Trial of Peter Dormenon, Esquire, Judge of the Parish Court of Point Coupee* (New Orleans: published for the Author, 1809).

46 See Archives of the Spanish Government of West Florida, 18 volumes deposited in the Record Room of the Nineteenth Judicial District Court, Baton Rouge, National Archives and Records Administration microfilm T1116 (WFP), Vol. IV, pp. 39–40, 208–9, 332; and Vol. V, p. 38.

47 SJR, 'Juramento de fidelidad de Dn. Mateo Howard Hill' (New Orleans, 6 May 1802).

48 SJR, 'Información de utilidad del irlandés Dn. Patricio Uriel' (New Orleans, 13 July 1801).

49 AGI, Estado, leg. 62, n. 20, doc. 4, 'List of fugitive slaves in Porto Cabello and Coro the property of Richard Bateman Lloyd and Anna Elizabeth Kock' (Puerto Cabello, 12 December 1799). Interestingly, most of the fugitives named were women, despite maroons from the Danish West Indies being predominantly male; Neville A. T. Hall, *Slave Society in the Danish West Indies: St. Thomas, St. John, and St. Croix*, ed. B. W. Higman (Baltimore: Johns Hopkins University Press, 1992), p. 125.

50 WFP, Vol. II, pp. 454–60; inventory of the estate of John Fitzpatrick (4–11 May 1791). See also Margaret Fisher Dalrymple, ed., *The Merchant of Manchac: The Letterbooks of John Fitzpatrick, 1768–1790* (Baton Rouge: Louisiana State University Press, 1978).
51 SJR, 'Testamento de Dn. Patricio de Macnamara: Inventario y estimación de sus bienes' (New Orleans, 21 January 1788).
52 Cristina Soriano, *Tides of Revolution: Information, Insurgencies, and the Crisis of Colonial Rule in Venezuela* (Albuquerque: University of New Mexico Press, 2018). In the case of Ireland, by contrast, it has been stated that the printed word was 'the chief medium through which radical ideas were popularised'; Jim Smyth, *The Men of No Property: Irish Radicals and Popular Politics in the Late Eighteenth Century* (New York: St Martin's Press, 1998), p. 162.
53 This was revealed during Quieco's declaration as a witness in an alleged case of bigamy; UNDA, Archdiocese of New Orleans (LA) Collection, Cabinet IV, shelf 5, box B, declaration of Juan Quieco (New Orleans, 14 September 1795).
54 See AGI, Estado, leg. 35, n. 13, Arturo O'Neill to Príncipe de la Paz (Mérida de Yucatán, 22 April 1796). See also Jorge Victoria Ojeda, 'Tras los sueños de libertad: Las tropas de Jean François al fin de la guerra en Santo Domingo', in Salvador Broseta, Carmen Corona, Manuel Chust *et al.*, eds, *Las ciudades y la guerra, 1750–1898* (Castelló: Universitat Jaume I, 2002), pp. 509–24.
55 Landers, *Atlantic Creoles*, p. 93.
56 Kevin Whelan, 'The Green Atlantic: Radical reciprocities between Ireland and America in the long eighteenth century', in Kathleen Wilson, ed., *A New Imperial History: Culture, Identity and Modernity in Britain and the Empire, 1660–1840* (Cambridge: Cambridge University Press, 2004), pp. 216–38 (p. 237).
57 See Daniel L. Schafer, ' "A class of people neither freemen nor slaves": From Spanish to American race relations in Florida, 1821–1861', *Journal of Social History* 26:3 (1993), 587–609 (p. 595); Spanish Land Grants, State Archives of Florida, Tallahassee, USA, S991, box 1, folder 4, 'Addison, John', www.floridamemory.com/items/show/233338?id=6 (accessed 18 August 2022); Spanish Land Grants, State Archives of Florida, S990, box 32, folder 8, 'Travers, Thomas', www.floridamemory.com/items/show/232945?id=7 (accessed 18 August 2022).

8

Searching for sovereignties: The formation of the penal laws and slave codes in Ireland and the British Caribbean, *c.* 1680–*c.* 1720*

Aaron Graham

Among the many points of comparison between Ireland and the Caribbean during the eighteenth century was the importance of codes of law for social repression. In Ireland the penal codes excluded Irish Catholics from political, social and economic power, and attempted to crush the Roman Catholic hierarchy. In the Caribbean, and in British America generally, most colonies had collections of laws that regulated the position of enslaved people, subordinating them to the planter class. Each have been analysed in depth, and British slave codes have been compared both with each other and with those of other empires, such as the French *Code noir* and the Spanish *Siete de partidas*, but the slave codes and penal laws have not been compared and contrasted as examples of codes of law within the wider British Atlantic. A useful framework for doing so is Lauren Benton's suggestion that early modern European empires were engaged in a 'search for sovereignty' during this period.[1] Power was not exercised in the uniform, cohesive and unmediated fashion it was beginning to acquire back in Europe, but continued to be uneven, incoherent and marked by a number of intermediaries. These actors made use of the rule of law to advance their own agendas. Comparing the formation of the penal laws and slave codes in Ireland and the Caribbean from 1680 to 1720 demonstrates this process in action. In both cases, English – or British – sovereignty was exercised largely by local colonial intermediaries for their own ends. As bodies of law, these codes for social repression developed in a piecemeal fashion and were marked in some cases by tensions between colonial and imperial authorities that exposed the highly uneven nature of imperial power throughout the British Atlantic in the early modern period.

Context

'Even in the most paradigmatic cases', argues Benton, 'an empire's spaces were politically fragmented; legally differentiated; and encased in irregular, porous and sometimes undefined borders'.[2] In physical or geographical terms, this meant that imperial authority was not enforced evenly over homogeneous and clearly delineated boundaries, but was 'stringy', characterised by corridors and enclaves or exclaves of power.[3] In terms of political sovereignty, imperial power was exercised not always directly but through layers of intermediary authorities, and was stronger in some areas than others, depending on circumstances; 'a fluid legal politics surrounding subjecthood and authority', Benton notes, 'produced further variations within and across corridors and enclaves'.[4] Her analysis challenges work, primarily in legal scholarship, political science and international relations, that takes the sovereign state after the Peace of Westphalia in 1648, and its uniform exercise of political power within its own territory, as the basic unit of analysis. The state emerges instead as a complex and heterogeneous bundle of jurisdictions and powers, in which law was less a rigid code for imposing uniform imperial norms on subject territories, and more 'an important epistemological framework for the organisation and evaluation of evidence of all kinds'.[5] Law, in other words, was a flexible framework of processes and procedures that accommodated itself to some extent to local conditions. Benton notes how some particularly anomalous spaces, such as rivers, islands and mountains, generated rich traditions of legal heterogeneity, as laws were amended to accommodate the political variations and anomalies arising from the failure to project power fully into these areas, and the need to work through quasi-sovereign intermediaries.[6]

Although Benton noted the applicability of this interpretation for the analysis of piracy in the Caribbean of the late seventeenth and early eighteenth century, which formed its own anomalous legal space, so far it has chiefly been applied to analyse the end of slavery and the search for sovereignty in the British Caribbean during the early nineteenth century.[7] Benton and Lisa Ford have detected a 'rage for order' in the British empire between 1800 and 1850 that sought to impose a higher degree of legal and political uniformity on an increasingly unwieldy collection of colonial territories.[8] Islands such as Trinidad were testbeds or sandboxes for experiments in ameliorating the conditions of slaves, which were then wheeled out more widely in other islands, with increasing degrees of success. The enforcement of the ban on slave-trading provided an opportunity to systematise maritime laws while also extending British naval and imperial power.[9] This is implicitly contrasted with the diverse and uneven pattern of slave codes in the pre-1800 British Caribbean, but the full implications of this approach for reassessing the rich scholarship on the origins of the slave codes have yet to be explored. Recent studies of French and Danish slave codes have suggested that this can be a fruitful approach, but still focus mainly on the questions arising from earlier comparative studies of colonial slave laws about the relative severity of their provisions and the opportunities that they offered for agency.[10] The position of Ireland in general, and the penal laws in particular, has also yet to be studied through this particular framework, though there is now a growing amount of work on the penal laws in their colonial context in Quebec and Grenada after 1763 and their overlap with the relaxation of the laws in Ireland after 1778.[11]

Comparing the origins of slave codes and penal laws instead through the lens of the search for sovereignty, as examples of social repression distinguished by place and race but united by their common basis in law, therefore brings together not just two colonial spaces but also several historiographical preoccupations that have rarely been analysed together. The slave codes and penal laws existed within a broader British imperial political and legal system – the 'transatlantic constitution' described by Sarah Mary Bilder, Daniel Hulsebosch and others – and demonstrate that laws of social repression were unevenly created and enforced, because that legal system was itself engaged in a search for sovereignties against both foreign powers and its own colonial authorities.[12] An important strand in recent work has identified the many anomalous legal spaces created within the British empire even from quite an early stage. Transitory communities in regions of unclear sovereignty, such as the seasonal fishing encampments in Newfoundland and the logging settlements in Central America, still technically under Spanish sovereignty, created unclear layers of jurisdiction, while governors in late-seventeenth-century Jamaica manipulated their powers of martial law to suspend the civil constitution and delineate uneven areas in legal time rather than in legal space.[13] Chartered colonies such as Rhode Island, by contrast, had additional insulation from royal power, since charters often limited the Crown's rights and jurisdiction and forced imperial officials to govern through intermediaries.[14] Ireland and most colonies also had their own legislatures, which were able to exercise varying degrees of autonomy, introducing further layers of power, while the imperial institutions charged with imposing administrative and legal uniformity, including the Board of Trade and the Privy Council, exercised their oversight unevenly and unpredictably. Under these conditions it is not a surprise that law in general, and the slave codes and penal laws in particular, were uneven.

Enactment

An older historiography tended to treat the slave codes and penal laws as cohesive and coherent bodies of law, expressing the intentions of British imperial rulers and their local counterparts, the 'New English' Protestant elite in Ireland and the white British planter class in Jamaica and the Caribbean.[15]

Landmark legislation, such as the Barbados slave code of 1661, seemed to be uniform bodies of law that could be extracted from their immediate context and compared with other bodies of law, such as the *Siete de partidas* of the Spanish Americas or the *Code noir* of the French Caribbean, to judge their attitudes towards freedom, slavery and race. In the first systematic comparison of former Caribbean slave codes in 1947, for example, Frank Tannenbaum contrasted the severity of the British slave codes with those of Spain, which offered easier paths to freedom, though even Tannenbaum conceded that 'the slave systems in Latin and Anglo-Saxon America were not institutions differing absolutely one from another. Differences there were, and important ones, but they were differences of degree rather than kind.'[16] Subsequent work has expanded this remark, noting the composite nature even of the French and Spanish codes, as well as the presence of municipal and local regulations that moderated or accentuated their effects.[17] Yet even so, these codes lay on a continuum. The *Siete de partidas* and *Code noir* were comprehensive imperial codes drawn up in a tradition of civil law that accepted and accommodated such codes. By contrast, both the penal laws and the British slave codes were assembled primarily at the colonial level, by local elites rather than an imperial one, who piled numerous smaller laws on top of each other in response to circumstances. They exemplified both the layered nature of British imperial authority overseas and the unevenness of its sovereignty.

The penal laws in Ireland, for instance, were the product of a long process of social, political and legal development stretching back at least to the sixteenth century.[18] The core elements of the eighteenth-century laws were enacted in the first flush of victory after the defeat of Jacobite forces at Limerick in 1691, and established the outlines of the system, especially the banning of Catholics from public and political office, the further confiscation of land, and the dismantling of the clerical hierarchy, but refinements continued for several decades afterwards. For instance, one of the keystones of the laws was the attempt systematically to dispossess the Catholic Irish of the land they had left by banning purchase, limiting leases and enforcing partible inheritance in order to break up the remaining Catholic estates and make it easier for Protestants to purchase land. However, this was only passed in 1704, as 'An act to prevent the further growth of popery'.[19] Furthermore, these Acts were passed by the Irish Parliament, dominated by Protestants and asserting its right to legislate for Ireland.[20] Although the British Government still exercised a high degree of authority through its power to amend and disallow Irish legislation under Poynings' Law of 1494, and the role of the Lord Lieutenant as a representative of the British ministry, its role was therefore primarily reactive rather than proactive. Sean Connolly has argued as a result that 'in its confused chronology and absence of any clear set of priorities ... any suggestion of a coherent code is misleading', and that the penal laws as a whole were 'less the implementation of coherent policy than a by-product of new constitutional assumptions and of a new set of political relationships'.[21]

Much the same was true of the British Caribbean. A growing body of work has now excavated the process by which the slave code emerged, largely in Barbados, which passed 'An act for the better ordering and governing of negroes' in 1661.[22] Though this was a single code, more closely resembling the Spanish and French slave codes than the mass of separate laws found in Ireland, it was still less comprehensive than these, and was complemented by a greater range of supplementary legislation. It also developed alongside a parallel code for the regulation of indentured servants, many of them Irish men and women transported there since the 1650s, and the status of Barbados as the leading island of the British Caribbean meant that it was adopted by other colonies as a model for their own codes, such as Jamaica in 1664 and South Carolina in 1696. However, other colonies, such as Virginia and Maryland, developed their own codes, and even in Jamaica and South Carolina the planters adopted their own supplemental provisions, which all reflected similar principles but were in practice subtly different and divergent in their provisions and effects.[23] As in Ireland, the process was also gradual and accumulative, with important elements still being passed in the early eighteenth century to eliminate ambiguities or refine particular elements in response to new circumstances. Here, too, although the British imperial State played a role in the passage of these laws, by approving them and refusing to strike them down, and through the influence of the Governors and councils of the individual colonies, the slave codes were essentially the creation of the legislatures of the individual islands, and the leading planters and merchants. Their control of colonial law-making allowed them to take the initiative in legislating for an area in which the Crown was unprepared, uninterested and unwilling to be involved. Elsa Goveia argued that slavery and colonial legislation were thus two sides of the same coin, 'the two great institutional systems' of the British Caribbean, and that 'the slave laws were essentially a product of their interrelationship'.[24]

This process can be seen, for instance, in the pattern of Jamaican slave laws in the late seventeenth and early eighteenth centuries. The Barbadian slave code of 1661 was reproduced virtually wholesale in 1664 as 'An act for the better ordering and governing of negro slaves', which removed some of the limited protections built into the former.[25] However, Jamaica was for much of this period in a state of legal and political ambiguity. Because the island had been conquered rather than occupied, it was uncertain whether it had received English laws in the same way as Barbados and other islands, and thus whether colonists there had the same protections as their counterparts elsewhere. The 1670s and 1680s were marked by repeated contests between Governors and colonists over this point, peaking between 1679 and 1681, when the English Government attempted to impose a version of Poynings' Law upon the island that would have reduced the powers of the Assembly to the acceptance or vetoing of bills drawn up beforehand in England.[26] Multiple versions of the code were therefore passed, some at the instigation of the Assembly to assert their own powers of legislation, and others at the instigation of the Privy Council in England.[27] The latter conceded defeat in 1681 and allowed the laws passed by the Assembly, except the slave code, which imposed only a fine on whites killing enslaved people: 'the king will not confirm this clause', the Privy Council told the Governor, 'which seems to encourage the wilful shedding of blood, [and] some better provision must be found than a fine to deter men from such acts of cruelty'.[28] This led to another version in 1683, and a final version in 1696, as 'An act for the better ordering of slaves', which remained in place until 1781. However, it was hedged around by several further Acts, such as one passed in 1717 for punishing crimes committed by enslaved people, one in 1719 for banning the enticing or 'inveigling' of enslaved people, and one in 1730 for better regulation of both free and enslaved non-whites.

The penal laws in Ireland and the slave codes of the British Caribbean were therefore both products of the 'layered' sovereignty found in the British Atlantic in this period, whereby power was exercised not just by the British Government and its military and naval instruments, but also by colonial or provincial governments with independent sources of authority, finance and military power. As Jack Greene, Peter Marshall and others have shown with reference to British America, and Sean Connolly and others with reference to British Ireland, this relationship was uneven and volatile even in the late seventeenth and early eighteenth century, and the British Government could rarely take the cooperation of colonial and provincial elites for granted.[29] In Ireland, while the British and Irish Protestant elites were largely agreed after 1691 about the need to limit the economic, social and political power of the Catholic Irish in order to root out Jacobite support, they frequently differed over how this was to be achieved. The stubborn insistence of the Irish Parliament after 1692 in ignoring the provisions of the Treaty of Limerick signed by William III in 1691, which had guaranteed Irish Catholics certain privileges in return for their surrender, was merely one example, and a particularly egregious one that threatened the British alliance with various Catholic powers against Louis XIV in the 1690s.[30] As Ivar McGrath and Patrick Walsh have shown, the support offered by the Irish Parliament for the British war effort, by raising funds to maintain a large standing army, was undertaken largely to serve their own interests and to deter a Jacobite resurgence.[31] In the Caribbean, imperial authority was similarly uneven, and dependent upon the cooperation of local elites. Measures against piracy, for instance, were frequently ineffective, not only because pirates often had the support and protection of local interests who controlled the colonial state, but also because imperial Governors were aware that these pirates might be used in wartime to defend the islands and thereby help to fulfil one of the overriding aims of British strategic and imperial policy.[32]

Castration in the slave codes and penal laws

As a case-study to demonstrate how this process operated in practice, this section looks at several instances of one the most extreme and obnoxious measures that was incorporated into the slave codes and penal laws: that of castration. This was a form of punishment entirely unknown in English common law, though other forms of mutilation and physical punishment of course had an established history.[33] It was therefore not imposed by the British imperial state upon the colonists, but innovated by them and incorporated into colonial laws. Its presence reflected the fears and paranoia of colonial interest groups, particularly surrounding sex, rape, race and the 'bestial' character of black men, though Diane Somerville has argued that it was the result of a pragmatic desire in prerevolutionary slave codes to deter rapes and other crimes while avoiding the need to compensate owners for executing enslaved people.[34] It was also a product of a particular moment; acts prescribing castration for various crimes, including but not limited to the rape of white women, were passed in Pennsylvania in 1700, Antigua in 1702, Bermuda and New Jersey in 1704, Virginia in 1705, and South Carolina in 1712, the timing suggesting a process of piecemeal legislative imitation as the news spread.[35] The Antiguan and Bermudan acts, for instance, prescribed that any enslaved person striking a white person should be whipped, and that if that white person was hurt, wounded or disfigured, the perpetrator should have their nose slit, or be castrated, or executed, at the discretion of the court.[36] While planters still had the right to punish enslaved people as they saw fit, including by castration or other forms of mutilation, these acts elevated this from the private to the public sphere and made castration a matter of public policy in those colonies.

Consequently, the role played by the British imperial State was largely to attempt to restrain such excessively cruel punishments, when such instances were brought to their attention. The Board of Trade and the Privy Council had no way of knowing what planters did to enslaved people and took little effort to find out, but when these punishments were incorporated into colonial law they were brought into its purview by the practice of legislative review. Remote from the sexual hysteria and paranoia of colonists in the

British Atlantic, the Board of Trade and its counsel were less impressed by the need for the laws or their morality. The report on the Pennsylvania law in October 1704, for instance, argued that it was 'not fit to be confirmed, for that castration is part of the punishment ... which I think unreasonable, especially in the case of a [?married] man, besides that is a punishment never inflicted by any law [in] Her Majesty's dominions, and no care is taken for healing the [?castrated] person'.[37] A few months later the Bermudan law landed on their desks, including the similar punishment of castration for rape, and the Board warned the Governor that 'we do not think it fit that part of the law be executed, there being no doubt but that by your next you will hear it is repealed'.[38] This duly followed, the Board writing the very next day that the law had been repealed on account of these clauses, 'all and every of which are disapproved [of] as inhumane and contrary to all Christian laws ... and you are to take care hereafter not to pass acts of this nature, which are so unfit to be approved of, since the passing thereof does very much reflect on your prudence'.[39]

To clarify, this is not to suggest either that the British Government was motivated by humanitarianism towards enslaved peoples in this period, or that it was sufficiently powerful to impose its views upon the colonies and their slave codes. As Heather Kopelson notes, the letter to the Governor in Bermuda condemned castration but concurred that 'it is necessary that that generation of people should be kept under due obedience and correction ... [by] whipping and imprisoning them', and by other punishments appropriate for their crime, 'provided the same do not extend to the loss of limb or member'.[40] Oversight of colonial legislation was also patchy, with castration remaining on the books in Virginia beyond the end of British rule.[41] Moreover, sometimes the impetus for reform came not from the Board of Trade but from imperial officials on the spot. For example, in 1724 the Governor of Antigua obtained an Act 'to prevent the inhumane murdering, maiming and castrating of slaves by cruel and barbarous persons (as has been too much practised)', which laid down a series of fines for offenders.[42] Though not repealing the 1702 Act, it did at least prevent extra-judicial punishment, but the Governor reported at the same time that he had 'used my utmost endeavours to make the murdering a slave punishable by death, but could not get it passed in such a manner, nor in any other than as it is now ... [but] I take it as it is to be a great point gained, there being no law before this that laid any penalty on offenders for the crimes mentioned'.[43] There were therefore limits to the ability of imperial officials at home or on the spot to restrain planters from even their most egregious efforts, but the point is that occasionally this was possible, and the slave laws evolved through this ongoing process of negotiation.

Indeed, in Ireland, dynamic fact was deliberately exploited by politicians for their own particular ends. Among the most notorious episodes of the penal laws was the bill against regular clergy, unregistered priests and other Catholic clerics drawn up in 1719 in the wake of a failed Jacobite uprising in Scotland earlier that year.[44] The original bill required that outlawed clergy found in Ireland to be branded on the cheek. After the bill passed both houses of the Irish Parliament it moved to the Irish Privy Council, where the punishment was altered to castration, on the pretext that where branding had been used in the past, 'the rapparees in their robberies made it a common practice to brand innocent persons with that mark in order to destroy the distinction it was intended for'. As a result, the Privy Council felt that 'nothing less than a very severe punishment would be effectual to prevent the frequent arrival of priests here'. The cruellest and most brutal elements of the penal law therefore arose in Ireland itself, and proved an embarrassment to the British Government. The clause received widespread public attention, and considerably complicated ongoing diplomatic efforts while the King was in Hanover attempting to settle Europe in the wake of the Baltic Crisis.[45] As James Stanhope, the secretary of state, noted, the clause was both 'ridiculous' and inconvenient, '[because] it would be a handle to the Elector Palatine to continue his persecution of the Protestants in his dominions, against which proceedings His Majesty, together with several Protestant powers, are now representing'.[46] The clause was therefore excised.

As Connolly and others have pointed out, the clause was added not by opponents of the bill in Parliament in order to sabotage it, but in the Irish Privy Council by the Lord Lieutenant and by many of the leading figures in the Irish establishment, who should have been aware that the British Government would reject it.[47] Thus, he notes, the 'most probable explanation is that members of the Irish executive, knowing that ... [the bill] was not going to get past the English council, were determined to make sure that the recriminations that would inevitably follow would be directed at London' rather than themselves, and 'to reinforce the point that it was not they who were to be blamed for any failure to take more effective action against priests'. The clause was an elaborate double bluff that *depended* on the fragmented nature of the penal laws and British authority in Ireland, allowing the Irish establishment to posture and bolster its credentials in the wake of a Jacobite rebellion while relying on the bill's being rejected out of hand by an exasperated British ministry. Part of the context here was not only the failed Jacobite invasion but also the ongoing clash within the Irish political establishment between British and Irish interests in general, and British and Irish clergymen in particular, over policies towards Catholics on the one hand and Protestant nonconformists on the other.[48] Like many lay members of the Irish Parliament, bishops of the Church of Ireland from England tended to take a hard line against Catholics and nonconformists, while Irish bishops favoured a more moderate approach. McNally notes that many of the latter initially supported the bill with the castration clause but then opposed it when it returned from the British Privy Council with the clause excised, suggesting not only that 'the conflict between British and Irish interests … encouraged some Irish peers and bishops to oppose a piece of legislation which had the support of the English bishops', but also that they saw it as an opportunity to embarrass a British ministry asserting its political power.[49]

Conclusion

Examining the penal laws and slave codes as bodies of law for social repression that were assembled in Britain's colonial possessions in the late seventeenth and the early eighteenth century therefore reveals a number of suggestive parallels. In both cases British imperial authority or sovereignty proved uneven in practice, leaving British officials unable to head off the incorporation of distasteful or embarrassing elements into colonial laws, which nevertheless made sense to colonial interests. This search for sovereignty meant that the British imperial Government lacked the ability and capacity to develop, let alone enforce, a uniform body of laws resembling the French *Code noir*. The slave codes and penal laws instead developed by the gradual accumulation of laws, practices and precedents, including further elements such as case law and custom not considered here, which meant that the experience of these laws by subaltern peoples varied across space and time, as well as other aspects such as gender, race, status and circumstance. Within the common framework of politics, law and power provided by the British 'transatlantic constitution', colonial elites in Ireland and the Caribbean proceeded in parallel in a search – or even in practice a contest – for sovereignty, over themselves and subaltern peoples.

Notes

[*] I am grateful to Trevor Burnard, Lisa Ford, David Hayton, Patrick Walsh and the participants in the conference at University College Dublin in December 2017 on *Ireland, the British Empire and the Caribbean: Comparative Perspectives* for their comments and advice on various aspects of this work. The chapter expands on themes raised in a forthcoming article, 'The penal laws and the slave codes in Ireland and the West Indies, *c.* 1660–1840': A comparative historiographical survey', *Jamaican Historical Review*, and I would like to thank the *Jamaican Historical Review* for permission to elaborate on those themes here.

1 Lauren A. Benton, *A Search for Sovereignty: Law and Geography in European Empires, 1400–1900* (Cambridge: Cambridge University Press, 2014).
2 *Ibid.*, p. 2.
3 For sovereignty as 'stringy' see *ibid.*, pp. 2, 161.
4 *Ibid.*, p. 3.
5 *Ibid.*, pp. 26–7.
6 *Ibid.*, pp. 40–103, 161–278.
7 See below, n. 29. For an earlier study in the same vein see Eliga H. Gould, 'Zones of law, zones of violence: The legal geography of the British Atlantic, circa 1772', *William and Mary Quarterly* 60 (2003), 471–510.
8 Lauren A. Benton and Lisa Ford, *Rage for Order: The British Empire and the Origins of International Law, 1800–1850* (Cambridge, MA: Harvard University Press, 2016).
9 Lauren Benton, 'Abolition and imperial law, 1790–1820', *Journal of Imperial and Commonwealth History* 39 (2011), 355–74; Lauren Benton and Lisa Ford, 'Island depotism: Trinidad, the British imperial constitution and global legal order', *Journal of Imperial and Commonwealth History* 46 (2018), 21–46.
10 Laurie M. Wood, 'Across oceans and revolutions: Law and slavery in French Saint-Domingue and beyond', *Law & Social Inquiry* 39 (2014), 758–82; Gunvor Simonsen, 'Sovereignty, mastery and law in the Danish West Indies, 1672–1733', *Itinerario* 43 (2019), 283–304.
11 See in particular Karen Stanbridge, 'Quebec and the Irish Catholic Relief Act of 1778: An institutional approach', *Journal of Historical Sociology* 16 (2003), 375–404; Karen Stanbridge, *Toleration and state institutions: British policy toward Catholics in eighteenth-century Ireland and Quebec* (Lanham, MD: Lexington, 2003); and Jacqueline Hill, 'Religious toleration and the relaxation of the penal laws: An imperial perspective, 1763–1780', *Archivium hibernicum* 44 (1989), 98–109. For the penal laws in Quebec and Grenada see Hannah Weiss Muller, *Subjects and Sovereign: Bonds of Belonging in the Eighteenth-Century British Empire* (Oxford: Oxford University Press, 2017), pp. 121–65; and Aaron Willis, 'The standing of new subjects: Grenada and the Protestant constitution after the Treaty of Paris (1763)', *Journal of Imperial and Commonwealth History* 42 (2014), 1–21.
12 Mary Sarah Bilder, *The Transatlantic Constitution: Colonial Legal Culture and Empire* (Cambridge, MA: Harvard University Press, 2008); Daniel Hulsebosch, *Constituting Empire: New York and the Transformation of Constitutionalism in the Atlantic World, 1664–1830* (Chapel Hill: University of North Carolina Press, 2005). For examples of particular laws within this system see Paul D. Halliday, *Habeas corpus: From England to Empire* (Cambridge, MA: Harvard University Press, 2012); and John M. Collins, *Martial Law and English Laws, c. 1500–c. 1700* (Cambridge: Cambridge University Press, 2020).
13 O. Nigel Bolland, *The Formation of a Colonial Society: Belize, from Conquest to Crown Colony* (Baltimore, MD: Johns Hopkins University Press, 1977); Jerry Bannister, *The Rule of the Admirals: Law, Custom and Naval Government in Newfoundland, 1699–1832* (Toronto: University of Toronto Press, 2003). For martial law see Collins, *Martial Law and English Laws*, pp. 207–47.

14 Bilder, *The Transatlantic Constitution*.
15 For an overview of the history and historiography of the slave codes in the Americas see Sally E. Hadden, 'The fragmented laws of slavery in the colonial and revolutionary eras', in Michael Grossberg and Christopher L. Tomlins, eds, *The Cambridge History of Law in America* (Cambridge: Cambridge University Press, 2008), pp. 253–87.
16 Frank Tannenbaum, *Slave and Citizen: The Negro in the Americas* (New York: Alfred Knopf, 1947), p. 116.
17 For an overview see Hadden, 'The fragmented laws'. For an example of such a study see Malick W. Ghachem, *The Old Regime and the Haitian Revolution* (Cambridge: Cambridge University Press, 2012).
18 This section is based on S. J. Connolly, *Divided Kingdom: Ireland, 1630–1800* (Oxford: Oxford University Press, 2008), pp. 197–207, 249–59, 262–7; S. J. Connolly, *Religion, Law, and Power: The Making of Protestant Ireland, 1660–1760* (Oxford: Oxford University Press, 1992); James Kelly, 'Sustaining a confessional state: The Irish Parliament and Catholicism', in David Hayton, James Kelly and John Bergin, eds, *The Eighteenth-Century Composite State: Representative Institutions in Ireland and Europe, 1689–1800* (London: Palgrave Macmillan, 2010), pp. 44–77; Robert Burns, 'The Irish Popery Laws: A study of eighteenth-century legislation and behaviour', *Review of Politics* 24 (1962), 485–508; and the articles in John Bergin, Eoin Magennis, Lesa Ní Mhunghaile and Patrick Walsh, eds, *New Perspectives on the Penal Laws* (Dublin: Eighteenth Century Ireland Society, 2011).
19 Connolly, *Divided Kingdom*, pp. 202–3; J. G. Simms, 'The making of a penal law (2 Anne, c. 6), 1703–4', in David Hayton and Gerard O'Brien, eds, *War and Politics in Ireland, 1649–1730* (London: Hambledon Press, 1986), pp. 263–76.
20 Connolly, *Divided Kingdom*, pp. 191–240; James Kelly, *Poynings' Law and the Making of Law in Ireland, 1660–1800* (Dublin: Four Courts Press, 2007).
21 Connolly, *Divided Kingdom*, p. 199.
22 Elsa V. Goveia, 'The West Indian slave laws of the eighteenth century', *Revista de ciencias sociales* 4 (1960), 75–105; David Barry Gaspar, 'With a rod of iron: Barbados slave laws as a model for Jamaica, South Carolina and Antigua, 1661–1697', in Darlene Clark Hine and Jacqueline Mcleod, eds, *Crossing Boundaries: Comparative History of Black Poeple in Diaspora* (Bloomington: Indiana University Press, 1999), pp. 343–66; Edward Bartlett Rugemer, 'The development of mastery and race in the comprehensive slave codes of the Greater Caribbean during the seventeenth century', *William and Mary Quarterly* 70 (2013), 429–58.
23 Hadden, 'The fragmented laws', pp. 259–74.
24 Elsa V. Goveia, *Slave Society in the British Leeward Islands at the End of the Eighteenth Century* (New Haven: Yale University Press, 1965), p. 152.
25 Rugemer, 'The development of mastery'; Gaspar, 'With a rod of iron'; David Barry Gaspar, ' "Rigid and inclement": Origins of the Jamaica slave laws of the seventeenth century', in Bruce H. Mann and Christopher L. Tomlins, eds, *The Many Legalities of Early America* (Chapel Hill: University of North Carolina Press, 2001), pp. 78–96.

26 Agnes M. Whitson, *The Constitutional Development of Jamaica, 1660 to 1729* (Manchester: Manchester University Press, 1929), pp. 70–127; Robert M. Bliss, *Revolution and Empire: English Politics and the American Colonies in the Seventeenth Century* (Manchester: Manchester University Press, 1990), pp. 161–218; Richard S. Dunn, 'Imperial pressures on Massachusetts and Jamaica, 1675–1700', in A. G. Olson and R. M. Brown, eds, *Anglo-American Political Relations* (New Brunswick, NJ: Rutgers University Press, 1970), pp. 52–75.

27 Gaspar, 'Rigid and inclement'. For the bills and Acts see the first volume of *Journal of the Honourable House of Assembly of Jamaica*, 14 vols (Spanish Town, 1808–26). For the legislative context see Aaron Graham, 'Jamaican legislation and the transatlantic constitution, 1664–1839', *Historical Journal* 61 (2018), 327–55 (pp. 341, 349–51).

28 Andrew Fede, *Homicide Justified: The Legality of Killing Slaves in the United States and the Atlantic World* (Athens: Georgia University Press, 2017), pp. 47–8.

29 Jack P. Greene, *Negotiated Authorities: Essays in Colonial, Political and Constitutional History* (Charlottesville: University of Virginia Press, 1994); P. J. Marshall, *The Making and Unmaking of Empires: Britain, India, and America c. 1750–1783* (Oxford: Oxford University Press, 2005); Connolly, *Divided Kingdom*.

30 Connolly, *Divided Kingdom*, pp. 201, 203; Kelly, 'Sustaining a confessional state', pp. 49–50.

31 Patrick Walsh, 'The fiscal state in Ireland, 1691–1769', *Historical Journal* 56 (2013), 629–56; Charles Ivar McGrath, *Ireland and Empire, 1692–1770* (London: Pickering & Chatto, 2012).

32 Mark G. Hanna, *Pirate Nests and the Rise of the British Empire, 1570–1740* (Chapel Hill: University of North Carolina Press for the Omohundro Institute of Early American History and Culture, 2015); Benton, *A Search for Sovereignty*, pp. 104–60.

33 Winthrop D. Jordan, *White over Black: American Attitudes toward the Negro, 1550–1812* (Chapel Hill: University of North Carolina Press for the Omohundro Institute of Early American History and Culture, 1969), p. 155; Kirsten Fischer, *Suspect Relations: Sex, Race, and Resistance in Colonial North Carolina* (Ithaca, NJ: Cornell University Press, 2002), p. 248n. For wider forms of mutilation as punishment in the British Caribbean, including post-mortem, see Diana Paton, 'Punishment, crime, and the bodies of slaves in eighteenth-century Jamaica', *Journal of Social History* 34 (2001), 936–45; Dawn P. Harris, *Punishing the Black Body: Marking Social and Racial Structures in Barbados and Jamaica* (Athens: University of Georgia Press, 2017), pp. 15–29; and Vincent Brown, *The Reaper's Garden: Death and Power in the World of Atlantic Slavery* (Cambridge, MA: Harvard University Press, 2008), pp. 131–44.

34 Heather Miyano Kopelson, *Faithful Bodies: Performing Religion and Race in the Puritan Atlantic* (New York: New York University Press, 2014), pp. 249–69; Jordan, *White over Black*, pp. 137–78, esp. pp. 154–63; Karen A. Getman, 'Sexual control in the slaveholding South: The implementation and

maintenance of a racial caste system', *Harvard Women's Law Journal* 7 (1984), 115–52; Fischer, *Suspect Relations*, pp. 131–90. By contrast see Diane Miller Somerville, 'Rape, race, and castration in slave law in the colonial and early South', in Catherine Clinton and Michele Gillespie, eds, *The Devil's Lane: Sex and Race in the Early South* (Oxford: Oxford University Press, 1997), pp. 74–83. For the costs of compensation see David Barry Gaspar, ' "To bring their offending slaves to justice": Compensation and slave resistance in Antigua, 1669–1763', *Caribbean Quarterly* 30 (1984), 45–59.

35 Fischer, *Suspect Relations*, p. 248n.
36 *The Laws of the Island of Antigua … with, prefixed to each volume, analytical tables of the titles of the acts; and, at the end of the whole, a copious digested index*, 4 vols (London, 1805), Vol. I, pp. 159–60, 162 (no. 130, 'An act for the better government of slaves and free negroes'). The Bermudan Act is listed in *Acts of Assembly [of Bermuda] from 1690 to 1713–14* (London: printed by John Baskett, 1719), p. 68 ('An act to prevent the insolency of Negroes and other slaves'). For the content of the Act see Kopelson, *Faithful Bodies*, pp. 254–7.
37 W. Noel Sainsbury *et al.*, *Calendar of State Papers Colonial: America and West Indies*, 46 vols (London, 1860–1994) (*CSPC*), Vol. XXII, pp. 276–81; Kopelson, *Faithful Bodies*, p. 256.
38 *CSPC*, Vol. XXII, pp. 506–7, 254–7.
39 *Ibid.*, Vol. XXII, p. 509.
40 Kopelson, *Faithful Bodies*, p. 257; *CSPC*, Vol. XXII, p. 509.
41 Somerville, 'Rape, race', p. 78; Getman, 'Sexual control', p. 134n.
42 *CSPC*, Vol. XXXIV, pp. 56–9.
43 *Ibid.*
44 Connolly, *Religion, Law*, pp. 281–4; Kelly, 'Sustaining a confessional state', p. 58.
45 Andrew C. Thompson, *Britain, Hanover and the Protestant Interest, 1688–1756* (Woodbridge: Boydell and Brewer, 2006), pp. 61–96. For the wider diplomatic situation see Brendan Simms, *Three Victories and a Defeat: The Rise and Fall of the First British Empire, 1714–1783* (London: Allen Lane, 2007), pp. 88, 107–55.
46 Thompson, *Britain, Hanover*, pp. 15, 78; and The National Archives, Kew, SP 43/2, fo. 165v, Stanhope to Delafaye, 28 September 1719.
47 Connolly, *Religion, Law*, pp. 281–2.
48 Connolly, *Divided Kingdom*, pp. 208–40, 259–62, 267–79; Patrick McNally, *Parties, Patriots and Undertakers: Parliamentary Politics in Early Hanoverian Ireland* (Dublin: Four Courts Press, 1997); David Hayton, *Ruling Ireland, 1685–1742: Politics, Politicians and Parties* (Woodbridge: Boydell and Brewer, 2004).
49 McNally, *Parties, Patriots and Undertakers*, p. 161.

9

Comparing imperial design strategies: The Franco-Irish plantations of Saint-Domingue

Finola O'Kane

> Finally, if this really deplorable fate (its absolute loss) were what threatens Saint-Domingue, it would still be necessary for the History of Nations to bring together a chapter in the great book of experience to show what was, in its brief existence, a Colony whose nature, splendour and destruction made it the pre-eminent example of this kind in the annals of the world.[1]

And what of Saint-Domingue? While it might be acceptable to omit Saint-Domingue from a British history of the Caribbean, to do so from an Irish one is not. If the plantation complex was the essential building block of imperial and colonial space,[2] it reached its full maturity in Saint-Domingue, where French advances in engineering, map-making, landscape design and colonial governance made it the 'world's richest colony' for most of the eighteenth century.[3] The most striking instance of how the French empire's 'value far outweighed its limited geographic size',[4] by 1791, the year of the Haitian revolution, 'Saint-Domingue was the most lucrative colony in the world, with sugar exports outstripping those of all the British Caribbean islands combined.'[5] Jamaica, 'metropolis of the West Indies' for the British empire,[6] was 'only half the size of Saint-Domingue in terms of land mass and population'.[7] James McClellan, pre-eminent American historian of eighteenth-century Saint-Domingue, argues that 'although Indian and East Indian trade was important to the expanding world economy at the end of the eighteenth century', the Caribbean colonies 'and especially Saint-Domingue', whose exports doubled those of Jamaica in 1788, 'became the prizes'.[8] McClellan's legitimate concerns at the 'historical invisibility' of San Domingue,[9] particularly among those claiming to write of the 'Atlantic world', run through his introduction to the 2010 edition of his ground-breaking 1992 work *Colonialism and Science: Saint Domingue in the Old Regime*, where he singles out the 1987 publication *Colonial Identity in the Atlantic World, 1500–1800* for its 'complete omission of the French West Indian experience' despite its explicit claim to be 'a cross-cultural investigation'.[10] This oversight arguably continues today, despite Saint-Domingue's 'forging of a distinct colonial identity' and its remarkable 'transmogrification into Haiti' as the second independent and first black republic of the same Atlantic world.[11]

Researching Saint-Domingue is challenging, not least because of Haiti's current poverty and general state of upheaval. However, some aspects are easier to research than in the British Caribbean because of essential differences in imperial colonial governance structures. Saint-Domingue was governed as another French *département*, with most decisions made in Paris and then transmitted on paper to the Caribbean. Jamaica, in contrast, had a degree of self-government in its Jamaican Assembly, founded in 1664 and composed of elected white property-owners, led by a 'Speaker', in a manner similar to Ireland's eighteenth-century Dublin Government. Although the Assembly was subject to the courts and laws of Great Britain, it did enjoy some measure of independent rule, and this also, in the long term, ensured that many historic documents and maps remained in Jamaica. Saint-Domingue, in contrast, 'had no such legislative body where patriotic colonists could voice their discontent', and legislation was enacted by 'the colony's governor-general and often from the Naval Ministry at Versailles'.[12] Its 'virtually complete official government records' are preserved in France, and thanks to recent digitisation, the maps, in particular, are available at high resolution from anywhere in the world.[13] This contrasts with the resources and accessibility of the Jamaican archives, which are not digitised, and although it is possible to order documents from the online catalogues with sufficient patience and some ingenuity, they are frustratingly incomplete. Surprisingly, given the devastation wreaked by politics, war and hurricanes on the island itself, 'as much information is available about old Saint-Domingue as about any other comparable region of the world in the eighteenth century', making its general invisibility in the anglophone historiography somewhat embarrassing.[14] Another key hurdle remains for the anglophone world: only one-seventh of Louis-Elie Moreau de Saint-Mery's encyclopedic two-volume *Description topographique, physique, civile, politique et historique de la partie française de l'isle de Saint-Domingue* (1797–8)[15] has ever been translated fully into English, and that only in 1985.[16] The ambition of Moreau de Saint-Méry's work – to provide an in-depth description and assessment of every quarter of the island – is without parallel in the English Caribbean. The remainder of this chapter is concerned to reveal the potential of Moreau's volumes, when cross-referenced with Saint-Domingue's digitised cadastral maps and some other significant visitors' accounts, in exposing the environmental, landscape and architectural history of Saint-Domingue. Enabling a comparative analysis of the French and English Caribbean, and particularly the French and English plantation, the method also reveals how and why the landscape design of Saint-Domingue became the runaway design model for the eighteenth-century Caribbean.

Survey methods, and their importance for compiling an accurate map record of an island's changing environment, also differed among empires. British imperial power remained substantially unthreatened by nineteenth-century events, and its state records remain intact in its principal archives. The private archives of its landed families, unlike the vast majority of Saint-Domingue's, may be found in each family's principal seat, or in the county archive where the history of a family's transatlantic interests may be assembled from their private estate maps, pictures, drawings and accounts. But Great Britain's state map records are limited, particularly because of the continued use of compass-and-chain survey methods in its Caribbean islands, not being fully displaced until the 1840s in Jamaica.[17] In contrast, the French State and its surveyors and engineers employed the most avant-garde surveying techniques across their distant Caribbean colonies. Triangulation, where a survey is checked using long diagonal measurements and connected into a larger triangular network of long, benchmarked regional measurements, was not fully rolled out across the British isles until the nineteenth-century Ordnance Survey.[18] In contrast, triangulated survey methods were clearly employed in 1780 to make a detailed plan of the valley of the Rivière du Haut du Cap, which lay close to Cap Français, Saint-Domingue's administrative capital (Figure 9.1). Such detailed plantation surveys led to large-scale regional maps of Saint-Domingue from 1740 onwards (Figure 9.2). Produced for the ministry of the marine by the *ingénieurs du roi*, they reveal the owners, positions, areas, borders, building layouts, infrastructure and water engineering of many of the plantations.

Because the State taxed land, France had legal requirements for registering land area, use and ownership that did not exist for the British isles. Although the British parliamentary enclosure maps of the eighteenth century are somewhat similar in scale and detail to French eighteenth-century cadastral maps they only map the area to be enclosed – not the entire countryside. 'In continental European countries one of the main motives for a centrally organized mapped cadaster', as Roger Kain and Elizabeth Baignant have explained, was 'the desire to improve the efficiency with which land taxes were levied', and in many parts 'a mapped cadaster proved a vital weapon for the monarch in his battle to increase taxation'. In contrast, although the English 'propertied classes and central government also clashed over land taxation, when they reached a consensus, it was one in which it was in no one's interest to compile a mapped cadaster',[19] because 'a surveyed cadaster would necessarily have been in the hands of professional surveyors under the control of central government and would have removed control of the tax from the local landowners and as such was unthinkable'.[20] Large ancestral aristocratic estates,

Comparing imperial design strategies 159

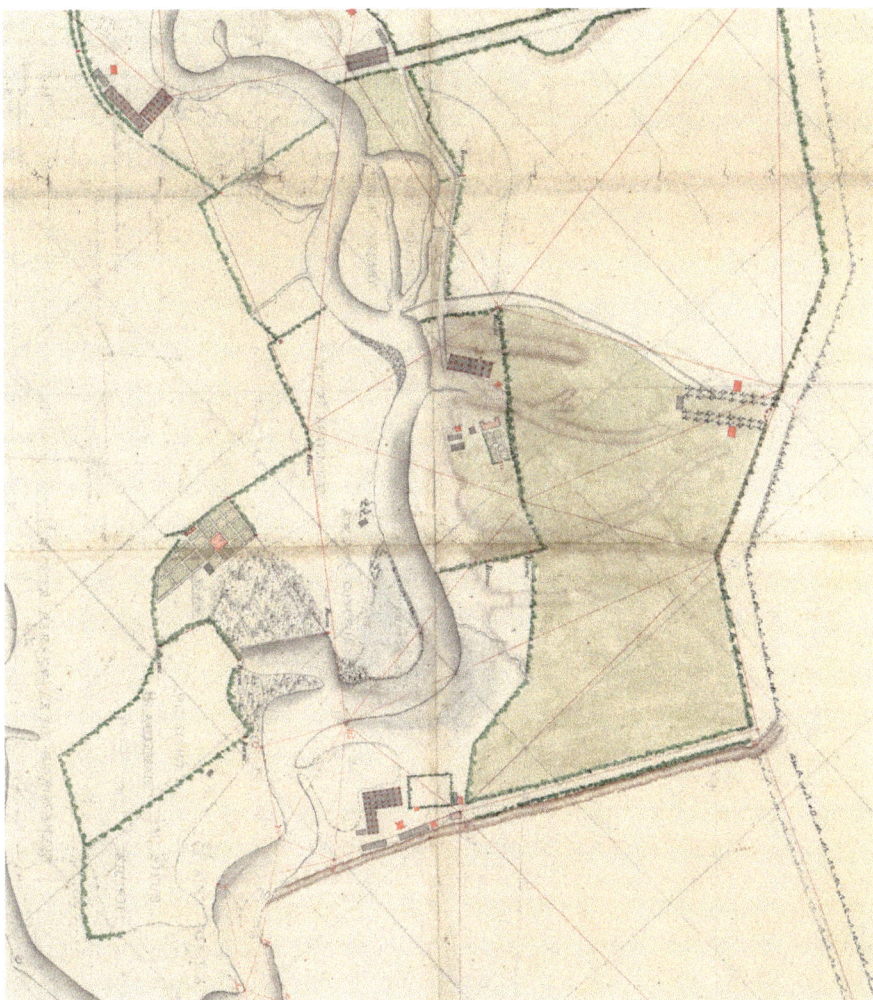

Figure 9.1 Detail of the Laborde plantation, Haut du Cap, Saint-Domingue. The Franco-Irish Walsh plantation was located immediately above the area drawn. *Plan de différentes possessions à St. Domingue [sur la Rivière du Haut du Cap, près de la ville du Cap-Français], concernant Ferrary, Beaujouan, Sicard, etc.*, 1780, Bibliothèque nationale de France.

where the property had been received directly from the Crown, often in the medieval period or earlier, were not required to register the size, exact location or boundaries of their property. This still makes it very difficult to identify property-owners in the United Kingdom – and also in Ireland, where the property laws were not substantially changed by the advent of the

Figure 9.2 *Plan de la ville du Cap et de ses environs depuis Limonade jusques et compris la baye de l'Acul pour servir à faire voir les ouvrages projetés pour sa déffense/dressé par ordre de Monsieur de Bellecombe, ... gouverneur général de St. Domingue*, 1760, Bibliothèque nationale de France.

Free State in 1922, or the Republic in 1949.[21] The absence of consistent and entire cadastral mapping across the British empire continues to hamper landscape design analysis at a large or intermediate scale, particularly before the nineteenth-century Ordnance Survey. The Irish Down Survey maps (1655–9), although very helpful for many purposes, are designed to 'record the boundaries of forfeited townlands and contain an inventory of land as cultivable, bog, mountain, or wood' for the purposes of property transfer rather than property development.[22] In this they differ profoundly from the state cadastral maps of Saint-Domingue. That island's wealth derived in part from the French State's ability to survey, draw and design an integrated plantation system, and not the jigsaw of separately surveyed pieces of land that made up Jamaica's state map record until the 1840s.

The French eighteenth-century cadastral maps of its Caribbean islands repay detailed analysis. The original set-out geometry of the French Crown's land grants to the *arpenteurs du roi* remained intact but was slowly subdivided over time. In the plains this geometry was slowly altered by the construction of roads, defence infrastructure and irrigation schemes. The map record exhibits far greater coverage at a large scale, and this was partly a legacy of the different approaches to infrastructure in both empires. The French State was implicitly bound up with the improvement of Saint-Domingue, and improvement projects were not necessarily instigated by the planters but by the State itself, often from Paris. France's more accurate and detailed survey

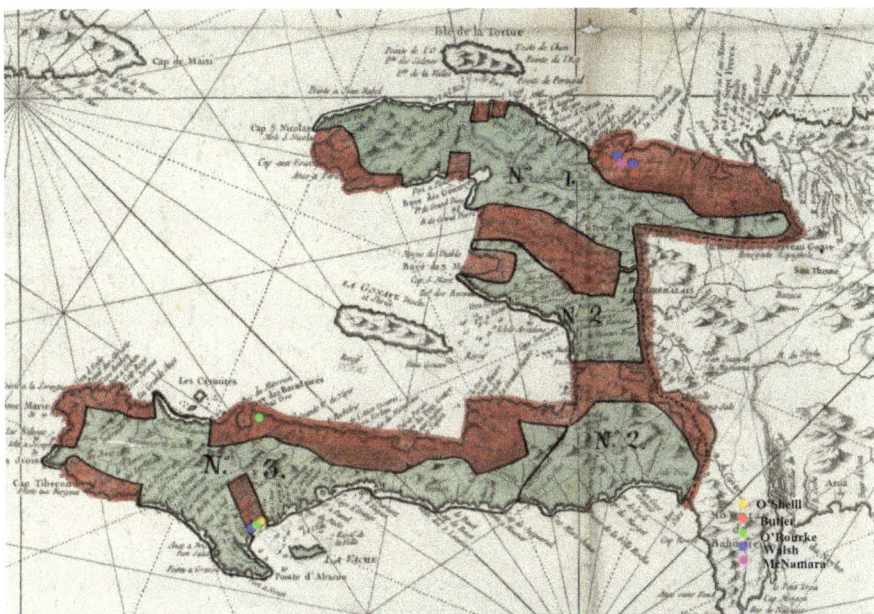

Figure 9.3 The Franco-Irish plantations discussed in this chapter, marked on Godino de Villaire and Jean-Baptiste Philibert, *Carte indiquant les parties levées de l'Ile de Saint-Domingue et celles qui ne le sont pas, 3 février 1789*, engraved nautical chart printed on paper, attached to M. Duchilleau's letter of 4 August 1789, Archives nationales d'outre-mer, France, FR ANOM 15DFC0218A.

methods facilitated and coordinated Saint-Domingue's many infrastructural projects because it made them automatically easier to organise, design and depict in plan. Successful irrigation works arguably cannot be planned and executed if they are not designed and drawn at such a scale. The mentality that stems from such large-scale landscape survey, analysis and design is perhaps most easily appreciated in an engineer's map indicating the elevated and non-elevated parts of Saint-Domingue (Figure 9.3). With the irrigation works concentrated and orchestrated on the flat plains of the river valleys that are coloured in red on the map, Saint-Domingue's plantations benefited directly from the French State's oversight and control of various group irrigation projects.

Saint-Domingue became a laboratory for French colonial landscape planning and, most especially, irrigation. A 'central element of Saint-Domingue's transformation after 1730', France itself had very few irrigation projects that predated 1789, with most of them constrained or terminated by 'litigation caused by competing or overlapping jurisdictions or property rights'. Trevor Burnard and John Garrigus conclude that 'in both

Saint-Domingue and France after 1760 the royal state eventually worked to promote irrigation schemes, but before 1760 irrigation works were private projects, involving dozens or even hundreds of planters'.[23] Yet a map such as that produced for the region around the town of Léogane shows how large infrastructural projects were unlikely ever to be purely 'private projects' because their impact is too great not to involve the entire interlocking geographical network of water (blue), roads (red) and canals (yellow) (Figure 9.4). Coordinating the design of the three networks and their many complex intersections, the map's numbers indicated what volume of water could be tapped by each private plantation from the yellow canals. It also stated carefully how the design had been 'enacted' by a group of gentlemen holding a variety of roles as public officials.[24] Involving the complicated asset of water, such systems had to run across public and private lands, and without some coordinating oversight they were unlikely to prove successful. The complexity of 'overlapping jurisdictions or property rights' was arguably greatly reduced on a Caribbean island when compared with the homelands of Europe. This positioned the Caribbean at the forefront of innovation in the design of such engineered landscape systems, greatly facilitated by the overlapping public and private identities of the gentlemen involved.

This chapter explores aspects of the design of the Saint-Domingue plantation using the Franco-Irish Walsh, Butler and O'Sheil/Sheill plantations as

Figure 9.4 *Plan de la plaine de Léogane indiquant la distribution des eaux de la Grande Rivière dans cette plaine. 15 février 1735, Orientation fleurdelysée. Echelle de 1*, Archives nationales d'outre-mer, France, FR ANOM 15DFC0685C.

examples. The sources employed are the map libraries of the Bibliothèque nationale de France and the Archives d'outre-mer, and the principal late-eighteenth-century travel descriptions of Saint-Domingue – those of Moreau de Saint-Méry; Alexandre-Stanislas, Baron von Wimpffen; and Pierre François Xavier de Charlevoix.[25] The two great map archives of the Bibliothèque nationale de France (588 maps and plans of Saint-Domingue) and the Archives nationales d'outre mer (583 maps and plans of Saint-Domingue), many of them digitised in the last few years, present an extraordinary resource for studying the design of the French island and its many habitations/plantations. The process reveals the scale, ambition and success of the Franco-Irish plantations of Saint-Domingue and suggests the power and impact of the planters who owned them. While many French historians, notably Jacques de Cauna, have published case-studies of specific families, their economic history and their plantations, little has been written of their patterns of landscape design, improvement and taste.[26] Recent architectural publications such as Gauvin Alexander Bailey's *Architecture and Urbanism in the French Atlantic Empire: State, Church, and Society, 1604–1830* do not explore the landscape design of the Caribbean's essential building block – the plantation/habitation – concentrating on town plans, fortifications, discrete public buildings and town gardens across all the French colonies, including those of Africa and North America.[27] Bailey admits that without a sustained study of French plantation houses, such as that produced by Louis P. Nelson for Jamaica,[28] it remains difficult to assess French plantation architecture, and its traditions of landscape design.[29] Saint-Domingue also appears to have had a hierarchy of plantation great houses, a hierarchy that was absent from the other French island colonies of Guadaloupe and Martinique.[30] This means that in the realms of architectural and landscape history we know surprisingly little of Saint-Domingue's plantations or other designed landscapes, particularly in the anglophone world. Detailed studies of some Franco-Irish plantations have been carried out by French historians, but these have not generally employed the map sources.[31] If other aspects of researching Saint-Domingue remain challenging, particularly site surveys, maps can initiate the analysis of colonial spatial paradigms. With Saint-Domingue's family archives often dispersed or compromised by the French and Haitian Revolutions, the maps can partially compensate for some of those absences.

The Franco-Irish plantations of the Walsh, Butler and O'Sheil/Sheill families of Saint-Domingue

> The landscape of Saint-Domingue spreads its taste of the great and the straight line, and while in force it offers the spectacle of ordered beauty.[32]

The Cromwellian wars of the 1640s led many Irish royalist Jacobites to emigrate to the French ports of Saint-Mâlo, Nantes and Bordeaux, among them the families of Walsh, O'Sheil/Sheill, Butler, Stapleton, O'Gorman, Bodkin-Fitzgerald, MacNemara and O'Rourke. There they became involved in mercantile activity, including the triangular trade, with Antoine Walsh notably becoming one of the leading French slave-traders. Philip Boucher, an American historian of the French Caribbean, writes of how a typical French Antillean town before the 1660s was composed primarily of 'Catholic Irish, Dutch Calvinists from Europe or those fleeing Brazil, [and] Portuguese Jews',[33] while a recent publication of the Haiti-based historian the Revd Jean Vanes Nicolas indicates that the Irish are still credited with substantial historical involvement in modern Haiti.[34] Although not among the original *arpenteurs du roi*, Irish names and families were soon involved in living, working and benefiting from the plantation system in Saint-Domingue (Figure 9.5).[35]

Figure 9.5 Location of Walsh, Butler and MacNemara plantations underlined on René Philipeau, *Plan de la plaine du Cap François en l'Isle St. Domingue* (Paris, 1786), Library of Congress, G4944.C3G46 1786.P5.

Another wave of emigrants followed the defeat of the Catholic James II by the Protestant William of Orange at the Battle of the Boyne in 1691, when a ship of Walsh's was sent to take the deposed King to Europe in its aftermath. Hugh Thomas found Irish Catholic émigrés to be 'among the foremost merchants' in 'the two nerve centers of the French slave trade in the eighteenth century – Saint-Domingue and Nantes', with Antoine Walsh one its 'most powerful figures'.[36] His marriage to Marie O'Sheil/Sheill, the daughter of the 'major slave trader' Luke O'Sheil/Sheill, 'united two of the most prominent Franco-Irish families.[37] The other major alliance was that made between the Butler, d'Héricourt and Bodkin-Fitzgerald families, producing a dynasty that stretched from the north and south coasts of Saint-Domingue to Nantes and La Rochelle.[38] The Butler family were among the earliest to gain a footing on the island with their recorded purchase of a plantation in 1715.[39]

The plain of Limonade on the northern coast of Saint-Domingue lay in the hinterland of Cap Français, Saint-Domingue's largest town and administrative capital. The cadastral maps of 1760 and 1786 show multiple plantations, drained by the Rivers Fossé, Haut-du-Cap and Mapou and the Grande Rivière, in the hands of the Walsh, Butler and MacNemara families. As David Geggus has shown from his analysis of more than 750 Saint-Domingue plantation inventories, 'generally speaking, sugar cultivation developed in the north in the first third of the eighteenth century, in the west in the middle third, and in the south only in the last third of the century'. This meant 'that most northern sugar estates were thus decades older than those in the south', with a financial value lying on average between those of the western and southern plains. Because the northern plains had a higher rainfall they required less irrigation, and 'water-driven mills were more common'. Changing hands or becoming subdivided over time, the northern plantations were 'generally less than 600 acres in area ... if anything, not medium-sized but small', and this was 'a sign of their greater age and development'.[40]

Moreau de Saint-Méry's references to the Walsh and Butler plantations on the River Fossé reveal much about their design and operation. Moreau credits the 'îlet de Limonade' – the area of ground between the Grande Rivière and the Fossé, as potentially 'the most fertile ground in the whole colony'.[41] The Franco-Irish families of Walsh and Butler were central to the development of these two river valleys, where the powerful waters of the Grande Rivière had the potential to power 'almost all the mills of the parish'.[42] The potential derived from a level difference of eight feet between the Grand Riviere and Fossé rivers, making the land between them particularly well-suited for water-powered mills.[43] The route of the River Fossé was easier to engineer because it was slower and less violent, and featured three raised dams – one shared among the Butler, de Berghes and l'Escarmotier plantations; one owned outright by the Walsh plantation; and one belonging to the Montholon plantation, which was maintained by the Walsh family (suggesting control of it) to keep the river bed from hollowing out by slowing the flow of water. Negotiations relating to water were constant, such as when the Walsh family, who had built a cofferdam and a mill on the Fossé, agreed to lose 2 feet in their fall of water (which powered their mill) for the benefit of the adjacent plantation of la Chapelle, which was located further downstream.[44]

If the plantations upstream had to protect their lands against flooding from the mountain streams, those at the river's mouth had to guard against high tides and salt-water ingress. Yet the owners of the delta plantations benefited from the ongoing sediment deposits carried downstream by the river. Constructing levées to retain the sediment and prevent it from being swept out to sea, they could slowly enlarge their plantation's land area.[45] The Government would fund the construction of such levées, particularly when the bed of the river was silting up, and surveyor Deville ordered the construction of a 500-foot-long levée on the Walsh plantation to prevent water from the canal that served the Walshes' watermill from discharging into the Fossé during flood periods.[46] The extent and ambition of these levées on both sides of the Fossé and in both the Walsh and Monthalon plantations are visible in a detail of René Philipeau's 1786 map of the Cap Français plain (Figure 9.6). The many diversions of the river into canals and irrigation channels on both banks and in two plantations suggest the complex interplay of mutually beneficial water systems. The large rectangular embankment on the Montholon side indicates a holding reservoir for the floodwaters. The scale of such building and engineering works is revealed in Philippe Becoulet's photographs of the Butler Bois de Lance plantations from 2000 (Figures 9.7 and 9.8).

The Walsh and Butler families owned another cluster of Franco-Irish plantations located upstream of the town of Cap Français. There, the Butler family's intermarriage with the d'Héricourt and Bréda families facilitated a concentration of landed interests focused on successful plantation design.[47] The Walsh family's large plantation lay immediately upstream of the town of Cap Français, and this indicates an early foundation. The defence and trading advantages of lying close to town were gradually diminished by the higher water pressure and volume enjoyed by plantations located further upstream, which led to greater productivity and income levels over time. In a detail of the Walsh plantation taken from a 1760 cadastral map of the Limonade plain the grey oblong structures arranged in long lines most probably indicate the enslaved workers' houses (Figure 9.9). The four pink buildings placed in a square of trees suggest white overseers' housing,

Figure 9.6 Detail showing the Walsh and Butler plantations on the River Fossé and the Grande Rivière from René Philipeau, *Plan de la plaine du Cap François en l'Isle St. Domingue* (Paris, 1786), Library of Congress, G4944.C3G46 1786.P5.

while the pink structure set within a walled enclosure was most probably the Walshes' *grand case*, or great house. It was probably the principal Walsh holding because of its adjacency to Cap Français, but as the family were predominantly absent their need for a stately and imposing residence was not high. As one of the French empire's 'real towns – some of them quite large by colonial standards, particularly in the later eighteenth century in places like Cap-François', the colony's plantation structure and purpose meant that 'true power rested with the seigneurs and plantation owners along the

Figure 9.7 Philippe Becoulet, photograph of an underground water-holding chamber on the Butler Bois de Lance plantation, *c.* 2000.

Figure 9.8 Philippe Becoulet, photograph of a collapsing brick-and-masonry wall structure on the modern-day course of the River Fossé on the Butler Bois de Lance plantation, *c.* 2000.

Figure 9.9 Detail showing the Walsh plantation, from *Plan de la ville du Cap et de ses environs depuis Limonade jusques et compris la baye de l'Acul pour servir à faire voir les ouvrages projetés pour sa déffense/dressé par ordre de Monsieur de Bellecombe, ... gouverneur général de St. Domingue*, Bibliothèque nationale de France, 1760.

rivers and coasts', and (as in the American south) 'there was no equivalent to the village, the most common form of "collective domicile" in France'.[48]

The plan detail also reveals how plantation building and defence infrastructure often proceeded in tandem. Yellow oblongs indicate military camp structures, while on the map's legend, 'R' indicates works at the head of the bridge, 'Q' a bridge with a lock to form a defensive flood barrier upstream and 'P' defensive works constructed as a retreat position behind a larger defensive structure.[49] The bridge over the Rivière du Haut-du-Cap was an important defensive position for the town and the Walsh's works were repurposed in the aftermath of the revolutionary period of 1791–1803. Figure 9.10 shows a beautifully drawn and coloured plan and

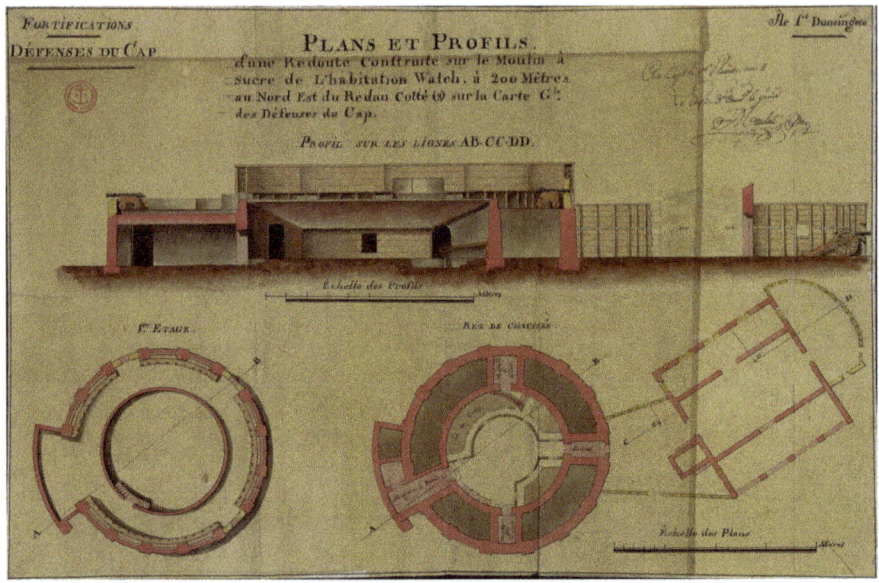

Figure 9.10 Walsh Sugar mill. Moulut, *Plans et profils d'une redoute construite sur le moulin à sucre de l'habitation Walch à 200 mètres au nord est du redan cotté 8 sur la carte générale des défense du Cap. Echelle de 10 mètres des profils et de 20 mètres pour les plans, 1er pluviose an 11 (1er février 1803)*, Archives d'outre-mer, France, FR ANOM 15DFC0411bisB.

section-drawing of the Walsh sugar mill's conversion into a military redoubt in 1803. Probably the circular structure shown in pink on Figure 9.9, its site position suggests that a dual-purpose defensive/productive character may have been intended from the outset. Unlike the Walsh and Butler plantations on the River Fossé this mill does not appear to have been water-powered, despite its adjacency to the river.

Another cluster of Franco-Irish plantations was located in the plain of Les Cayes (with a town of the same name) in the southern part of the colony (Figures 9.3 and 9.11). Moreau de Saint-Méry assessed the extensive Laborde plantations as the plain's largest and most successful, with 1,400 enslaved workers producing 1,200 *milliers* of white sugar. In the western part of the plain the greatest plantations were those of the Franco-Irish Walsh family, with 700 enslaved workers producing 700 *milliers* of Les Cayes's 'most beautiful sugar of all'.[50] Situated on the Rivière de Lacul, their holdings were probably strategically acquired: one at the highest point of the river, where the greatest volume of water was to be obtained, and the other at its mouth, where it bordered the extensive O'Rourke plantations,

Figure 9.11 Detail showing the Walsh and O'Rourke plantations, from René Philipeau, *Plan de la plaine du fond de l'Isle de vache de l'Isle St Domingue avec les divers cannaux d'arrosage*, Bibliothèque nationale de France, c. 1787[?].

creating an lengthy Irish waterfront (Figure 9.11).⁵¹ Producing such sugar on the drier southern plains demanded extensive irrigation, and Moreau de Saint-Méry described how the Les Cayes plain had been drained, irrigated and sometimes reclaimed with particular input from Jean-Joseph Verret, a New Orleans-born hydraulic engineer.⁵² Arriving in Saint-Domingue in 1772, Verret had quickly acquired a reputation for water-mill design, and in 1783, following a period of residence in France, he was appointed Saint-Domingue's *ingénieur-hydraulicien du roi*.⁵³ Work began on the plain's eastern system on 19 December 1786, and when it was complete it irrigated sixteen plantations on the east bank and five plantations on the west, creating 1,800 *carreaux* of productive agricultural land. Straddling the river before it entered the town of Les Cayes lay the O'Sheil/Sheill plantation, which benefited from the town's extensive urban design and improvement schemes. The second Walsh plantation and the O'Rourke plantation on the River Muscadin were among those Moreau listed as having benefited.⁵⁴ Of the fourteen plantations that make up the coastline of the Les Cayes plain between the Rivière de Lacul to the west and the Rivière de l'Islet to the east, the three largest had Irish names and occupied together over one-third of the coastline (Figure 9.11). Such substantial Franco-Irish presence along the major coastlines and along the power-generating and most fertile rivers indicates the level of such families' power and influence in Saint-Domingue.

Three out of four white French people who settled in the colonies returned to France,⁵⁵ but for families who were émigrés twice over – from Ireland to France and then from France to Saint-Domingue – home itself was blurred and indistinct, lending the different lenses of absenteeism and residency a further complexity. The legacies of French slave-ownership also have two revolutions to contend with – the French revolutionary period of 1789–99 and the Haitian revolutionary period of 1791–1804. In the aftermath of the French Revolution some Franco-Irish planters emigrated from the French Atlantic ports to the Caribbean,⁵⁶ only to find themselves forced to join further migrations of planters, freemen and enslaved workers to Louisiana and the states of the American south and other Caribbean islands, or reverse migrations back to France and in some rare instances back home to Ireland.⁵⁷ French troops sent to quell the Haitian Revolution included two Irish brigades among which 'some of the Irish officers had relations amongst the planter society and the local government'.⁵⁸

If the Caribbean Irish were often, in Kit Candlin's words, men and women who 'did not fit (or would not fit) into any one empire',⁵⁹ then the Franco-Irish planters of Saint-Domingue had more empires than most to contend with. The western half of a bisected island (ceded by Spain to France in the 1697 Treaty of Rysbrack), Saint-Domingue is the only major Caribbean island with a land border between two empires.⁶⁰ The existence of such a border inspired travellers to compare both empires, with Baron von Wimpffen finding the Spanish part 'infinitely more extensive, more fertile, and more abundantly supplied with water than the French; but, on the other hand' with 'too little industry to be found in it, and too many monks'.⁶¹ Travelling along the northern coast of the island and from the Spanish half to the French, 'the frequency of habitations which we saw along the coast, sufficiently announced that we had passed from the Spanish to the French part'.⁶²

The mobile, changing world of the Caribbean – where anyone, at any moment, might be obliged to jump ship, to another port, island or empire, acquiring new identities en route – was not new for Irish families, who had grown adept at such shape-shifting behaviour in seventeenth-century Europe. Such families have left a documentary record that is strewn across the homelands and public and private archives of the French, Danish and Spanish empires and is yet to be uncovered for the Portuguese and Dutch.⁶³ The legacies of Irish slave-ownership must be sought across and between such empires because this not just an Irish/British imperial story – it is also a wider European one. If, as Mary Dewhurst suggests, 'it is important to consider the rot that colonialism produced within the metropole as well' as in its colonies, then the legacy of Saint-Domingue in Ireland and Europe, as much as that of Ireland and Europe in Saint-Domingue, must also be sought in the future.⁶⁴

Notes

1 Louis-Elie Moreau de Saint-Méry (1750–1819), *Description topographique, physique, civile, politique et historique de la partie française de l'isle Saint-Domingue …*, 2 vols, 2nd edn (Paris: L. Guérin, 1875 [1797–8]), Vol. I, p. xix: 'Et enfin si ce sort réelement déplorable (de sa perte absoluë) était celui qui menace Saint-Domingue, il serait nécessaire encore à l'Histoire des Nations de réunir un chapitre au grand livre de l'expérience, pour montrer ce qu'à été, dans sa courte existence, une Colonie qui sa nature, sa splendeur et sa destruction rendreait le premier exemple de ce genre dans les annales du monde.'
2 Philip D. Curtin, *The Rise and Fall of the Plantation Complex* (Cambridge: Cambridge University Press, 1998).
3 James E. McClellan III, *Colonialism and Science: Saint Domingue in the Old Regime* (Chicago: University of Chicago Press, 2010), p. 18.
4 Robert Louis Stein, *The French Sugar Business in the Eighteenth Century* (Baton Rouge: Louisiana State University Press, 1988), p. x.
5 Mary Dewhurst Lewis, 'Legacies of French slave-ownership, or the long decolonization of Saint-Domingue', *History Workshop Journal* 83:1 (2017), 151–75 (p. 152).

6 Jonathan Wright, *An Ulster Slave-Owner in the Revolutionary Atlantic: The Life and Letters of John Black* (Dublin: Four Courts Press, 2019), p. 146.
7 McClellan, *Colonialism and Science*, pp. 12–13.
8 Ibid., p. 18.
9 Ibid.
10 Nicholas Canny and Anthony Pagden, *Colonial Identity in the Atlantic World, 1500–1800* (Princeton: Princeton University Press, 1989).
11 McClellan, *Colonialism and Science*, pp. 18–19.
12 Trevor Burnard and John Garrigus, *The Plantation Machine: Atlantic Capitalism in French Saint-Domingue and British Jamaica* (Pennsylvania: University of Pennsylvania Press, 2016), p. 17.
13 McClellan, *Colonialism and Science*, p. 20.
14 Ibid.
15 The volume dealing with the Spanish Hispaniola – Moreau de Saint-Méry, *Description topographique* – was translated into English by William Cobbett and published in 1798 as *A topographical and political description of the Spanish part of Saint-Domingo ... by M. L. E. Moreau de Saint-Méry*, 2 vols (Philadelphia, 1798). The first *abridged* English translation of the work was published in 1985, and at time of writing was hard to obtain: Médéric-Louis-Elie Moreau de Saint-Méry, *A Civilization that Perished: The Last Years of White Colonial Rule in Haiti ...*, trans. abridged and ed. Ivor D. Spencer (Lanham, MD: University Press of America, 1985).
16 Carolyn Fick, review of Moreau de Saint-Méry, *A Civilization that Perished*, trans. Spencer, *Hispanic American Historical Review* 66:4 (1986), 788–9.
17 B. W. Higman, *Jamaica Surveyed: Plantation Maps and Plans of the Eighteenth and Nineteenth Centuries* (Kingston: University of West Indies Press, 2001), p. 56.
18 J. H. Andrews, *A Paper Landscape: The Ordnance Survey in Nineteenth-Century Ireland* (Dublin: Four Courts Press, 2002), pp. 9–10.
19 Roger J. P. Kain and Elizabeth Baignet, *The Cadastral Map in the Service of the State* (Chicago: University of Chicago Press, 1992), p. 257.
20 Ibid., pp. 258–9.
21 Pierre Clergeot, 'The origins of the French general cadastre', FIG (International Federation of Surveyors) Working Week 2003, Paris, France, 13–17 April 2003, www.fig.net/resources/proceedings/fig_proceedings/fig_2003/PS_1/PS1_2_Clergeot.pdf (accessed 14 May 2020); and Richard Grover, 'Why the United Kingdom does not have a cadastre – and does it matter?', FIG Commission, Annual Meeting 2008, Open Symposium on Environment and Land Administration,Verona, Italy, 11–12 September 2008, www.fig.net/resources/proceedings/2008/verona_am_2008_comm7/papers/12_sept/7_2_grover.pdf (accessed 14 May 2020).
22 Kain and Baignet, *The Cadastral Map*, p. 336.
23 Burnard and Garrigus, *The Plantation Machine*, p. 35.
24 Archives nationales d'outre-mer, *Plan de la plaine de Léogane indiquant la distribution des eaux de la Grande Rivière dans cette plaine. 15 février 1735, Orientation fleurdelysée. Echelle de 1*, lieue Cote, FR ANOM 15DFC0685C.

25 Pierre François Xavier de Charlevoix, *Histoire de l'Isle Espagnole ou de S. Domingue*, 2 vols (Paris: Hippolyte Louis Guérin, 1731); Moreau de Saint-Méry, *Description topographique*; and Alexandre-Stanislas, Baron von Wimpffen, *A voyage to Saint Domingo, in the years 1788, 1789, and 1790* (London, 1797).
26 See in particular Gabriel Debien, *Les esclaves aux Antilles Françaises (XVIIe–XVIIIe siècles)* (Basse-Terre: Société d'Histoire de la Guadeloupe; Fort-de-France: Société d'Histoire de la Martinique, 1974); Jacques de Cauna and Cécile Révauger, *La Société des plantations esclavagistes: Caribes francophone, anglophone, hispanophone. Regards croisés* (Paris: Les Indes savantes, 2013); and Jean-Louis Donnadieu, *Un grand seigneur et ses esclaves: Le comte de Noé entre Antilles et Gascogne, 1728–1816* (Toulouse: Presses universitaires du Midi, 2009). See also Stein, *The French Sugar Business*; David Geggus, 'Slave society in the sugar plantation zones of Saint Domingue and the revolution of 1791–93', *Slavery and Abolition* 20:2 (1999), 31–46; and Carolyn Fick, *The Making of Haiti: The Saint Domingue Revolution from Below* (Knoxville: University of Tennessee Press, 1989).
27 Gauvin Alexander Bailey, *Architecture and Urbanism in the French Atlantic Empire: State, Church, and Society, 1604–1830* (Toronto: McGill-Queen's University Press, 2018).
28 Louis Nelson, *Architecture and Empire in Jamaica* (New Haven: Yale University Press, 2016).
29 Bailey, *Architecture and Urbanism*, p. 15.
30 Danielle Bégot, 'Maison de maître et gran'cases aux Antilles françaises (XIIe–XIXe siècles)', in Maurice Burac and Danielle Bégot, eds, *L'habitation/plantation: Héritages et mutations, Caraïbe-Amérique* (Paris: Karthala, 2011), p. 18: 'Un point, cependant semble acquis a cette époque, et sans doute depuis longtemps: l'opposition entre Saint-Domingue et les deux Petites Antilles, Guadaloupe et Martinique. L'article pionnier de G. Debien sur "Les grands'cases des plantations a Saint Domingue" parle indistinctement de maison principale, de case à demeurer, ou de grand'case, en s'appuyant cependent plus sur ce dernier vocable, sans toutefois en donner la raison.'
31 Natacha Bonnet has researched the MacNemara plantation in depth in her chapter 'L'organisation du travail servile sur la sucrerie domingoise au XVIIIe siècle', in Philippe Hrodej, ed., *L'esclave et les plantations de l'établissement de la servitude à son abolition* (Rennes: Presses universitaires, 2019), https://books.openedition.org/pur/97625?lang=en (accessed 20 August 2022). She draws from the following: Archives départementales de la Vienne: série J, dépôt 65/60, 'Inventaire de la plantation MacNemara, 12 juin 1786'.
32 Charlevoix, *Histoire de l'Isle Espagnole*, Vol. II, p. 491.
33 Bailey, *Architecture and Urbanism*, p. 36n10; Philip P. Boucher, *France and the American Tropics to 1700: Tropics of Discontent?* (Baltimore: Johns Hopkins University Press, 2008), p. 132.
34 Jean Vanes Nicolas, *What Happened to Haiti and What to Do about It* (Pittsburgh: Dorrance, 2020), pp. 30–3.

35 Marie-Antoinette Menier, 'Archives du Ministère de la France d'Outre-Mer: Saint-Domingue (abornements, domaines, recensements des biens domaniaux et urbains)', *Revue d'histoire des colonies* 44:155 (1957), 223–50.
36 Hugh Thomas, *The Slave Trade: The Story of the Atlantic Slave Trade, 1470–1870* (London: Weidenfeld & Nicolson, 2015), pp. 251–2.
37 Ibid.
38 Donnadieu, *Un grand seigneur*, pp. 47–8.
39 'Index Moreau de Saint-Méry Lettres N–O', www.ghcaraibe.org/livres/ouvdiv/stmery/stmery-N.html (accessed 20 August 2022):

> BUTLER (Robert). Fils de Jean B. Irlandais réfugié à la Rochelle en 1665, propriétaire à Saint-Domingue dès 1715. Il avait épousé en Irlande Jeanne Bodkins, fille de Patrice B. Gouverneur de Galway. Il avait une sucrerie au Bois de Lance près du Cap. Son frère Richard passa aussi à Saint-Domingue et épousa Marie-Louise Soulfour de Noville dont il eut deux enfants: Jean-Baptiste né en 1717 qui épousa Suzanne Bonfils puis Julie du Trousset d'Héricourt dont la mère était une Bréda, il mourut en 1755; et Pierre Antoine né en 1719 qui épousa Elisabeth de Bodkins-Fitzgérald, sa cousine, en 1740. Jean-Baptiste eut un fils Jean Pantaléon, né en 1743, qui fut capitaine de dragons (1784), Jean Pantaléon eut un fils Charles qui fut propriétaire de la sucrerie Leroux des Iles à Limonade. Les Bodkins étaient aussi propriétaire à Aquin.

40 Geggus, 'Slave society', p. 34.
41 Moreau de Saint-Méry, *Description topographique*, Vol. I, pp. 200–1: 'L'îlet de Limonade, dans lequel se trouve conséquemment une partie du terrain de quelques habitations du canton du Bois de Lance, que le *f*ossé partage, a peut-être le terrain "le plus fertile de la Colonie"; c'est cependant celui qu'on a laissé si long-temps en proie aux débordemens & du Fossé & de la Grande rivière.'
42 Ibid.: 'A ce sujet d'étonnement, s'en joint un second, c'est que tandis que la Grande rivière pourrait procurer des moulins à presque toutes les sucreries de la paroisse, & que les eaux du Fossé grossies de la vide de l'habitation Bullet en font mouvoir sept, il n'y en ait qu'un à la rive Occidentale de la Grande rivière, sur l'habitation Fournier de Bellevue.'
43 Ibid., Vol. I, p. 195: 'Et l'on en a une preuve à Limonade, dans la rivière du Fossé, dont le lit est plus élevé que celui de la Grande-Rivière. Cette différence, qu'on évalue à huit pieds, n'a cependant toujours existé; d'anciennes observations disent même que le Fossé était plus bas. Ce changement s'expliquerait par la nature du fond du lit du Fossé, placé entre les mornets de Limonade, et à leur pied. Il a moins d'eau, moins de vitesse et par conséquent moins de pente que la Grande-Rivière. Son lit est coupé par trois bâtardeaux élevés, savoir: celui commun aux trois habitations Butler, de Berghes et l'Escarmotier, celui de l'habitation Walsh et celui de l'habitation Montholon, que l'habitation Walsh entretient pour empêcher que le fond du lit ne se creuse.'
44 Ibid., Vol. I, p. 201: 'L'habitation d'Offemont, devenue l'habitation Walsh, fit aussi un batardeau sur le Fossé & un moulin, & l'habitation la Chapelle, aujourd'hui Montholon, en fit un au-dessous. Comme cette dernière avait peu de chûte, l'habitation Walsh a, par arrangement, consenti à en perdre deux

Comparing imperial design strategies 177

pieds, qu'elle lui a transmis, & la première a renoncé à une servitude qu'elle avait achetée sur l'habitation Walsh pour ses canaux.'
45 *Ibid.*, Vol. I, pp. 189–90: 'Des levées placées sur le bord de la mer ont garanti le terrain des invasions de l'Océan, et ont retenu les rapports que les eaux de la rivière déposent, après avoir été introduites avec beaucoup d'intelligence sur les terrains dessalines, pendant la durée des crues.'
46 *Ibid.*, Vol. I, p. 191: 'D'après une visite faite par l'arpenteur Deville, le 28 Janvier, 1764, une ordonnance du 3 avril prescrivit une levée de 500 pas de long, l'habitation Walsh, pour empêcher l'épanchement des eaux du canal de son moulin dans le Fossé, lors des crues, avec une pelle à bascule sur ce canal; un travail pour donné au Fossé, à la passe Walsh, un lit droit de 20 pieds de large sur autant de profondeur avec des levées; un autre travail pour ouvrir une portion de lit redressé au Fossé avec des levées.'
47 See Donnadieu, *Un grand seigneur*. The Haitian Revolutionary leader Toussaint l'Ouverture was born on one of the Bréda plantations.
48 Bailey, *Architecture and Urbanism*, p. 36
49 From the key to *Plan de la ville du Cap et de ses environs depuis Limonade jusques et compris la baye de l'Acul pour servir à faire voir les ouvrages projetés pour sa déffense/dressé par ordre de Monsieur de Bellecombe, … gouverneur général de St. Domingue*, Bibliothèque nationale de France, 1760 (of which Figure 9.9 is a detail). R: 'ouvrage a la tête du pont'; Q: 'pont avec écluse pour former l'inondation au haut du Cap'; P: 'retranchement en troisième ligne'.
50 Moreau de Saint-Méry, *Description topographique*, Vol. II, p. 686: 'Les habitations les plus considérables de la plaine des Cayes sont, dans la partie Orientale, les sucreries La Borde qui ont 1,400 nègres & qui donnent 1,200 milliers de sucre blanc. Dans l'ouest, ce sont les deux sucreries Walsh qui ont 700 nègres, & qui donnent plus de 700 milliers de sucre blanc & le plus beau de la plaine des Cayes.'
51 For the O'Rourke presence in Saint-Domingue see Orla Power, 'Stateless and destitute: The O'Rourke family of Saint-Domingue, Nantes and Wexford, 1788–1805', in Daniel Sanjiv Roberts and Jonathan Wright, eds, *Ireland's Imperial Connections, 1775–1947* (Cham: Palgrave Macmillan, 2019), pp. 233–49.
52 Moreau de Saint-Méry, *Description topographique*, Vol. II, p. 680.
53 *Ibid.*
54 *Ibid.*, Vol. II, pp. 680–1: 'Le travail fut commencé le 19 Decembre 1786, & il est terminé. Cette distribution procure de l'eau a 21 intéressé, dont 16 sur la rive Orientale & 5 sur la rive Occidentale, & pour 1,800 carreaux de terre … La seconde sucrerie Walsh en a un par Quitee-la-la … Les trois sucreries, Orourke, Marraud, & Leyritz & Marraud, ont chacune un moulin par la petite rivière du Muscadin.'
55 Bailey, *Architecture and Urbanism*, p. 36.
56 Philipp J. C. Elliot-Wright, 'The officers of the Irish Brigade and the British Army 1789–98', Ph.D. thesis (University of Leeds, 1997), http://etheses.whiterose.ac.uk/21155/1/731701.pdf (accessed 20 April 2020): 'The cousin of Count Walsh-Serrant, Anthony John Baptist Walsh, the titular Earl Walsh, had

emigrated with his family at the revolution to his estates in the colony and his eldest son, John Baptist Paul Oliver Walsh, was killed on 6 August 1792 in one of the massacres of whites in the colony. His father meanwhile fled to Kingston, Jamaica' (p. 109).

57 Power, 'Stateless and destitute', pp. 233–49.
58 F. W. Van Brock, 'Irish regiments in the French Service: Commands given in English', *Irish Sword* 15 (1983), 202–6, cited in Elliot-Wright, 'The officers of the Irish Brigade', p. 109n57; Marquis de Ruvigny, *The Jacobite Peerage* (Edinburgh: T. C. and E. C. Jack, 1904), pp. 331–2.
59 Kit Candlin, *The Last Caribbean Frontier, 1795–1815* (Basingstoke: Palgrave Macmillan, 2012), p. xxi.
60 Maria Cristina Fumagalli, 'Landscaping Hispaniola: Moreau de Saint-Méry's border politics', *New West Indian Guide = Nieuwe West-Indische Gids* 85:3–4 (2011), 169–90.
61 Alexandre-Stanislas, *A voyage to Saint Domingo*, p. 34.
62 *Ibid.*, p. 38.
63 See Orla Power, 'Irish planters, Atlantic merchants: The development of St. Croix, Danish West Indies, 1750 to 1766', Ph.D. thesis (National University of Ireland, Galway, 2011). For the Dutch Compensation Records of 1863, with no Irish names that I could find, see www.nationaalarchief.nl/onderzoeken/index (accessed 21 August 2022).
64 Dewhurst Lewis, 'Legacies of French slave-ownership', p. 166: 'In exchange for formal French recognition of its independence in 1825, Haiti agreed (with French warships outside its harbours) to pay an indemnity of 150 million francs to the former planters who had lost property as a result of the revolution.' Dewhurst Lewis explains how this indemnity, although far less in monetary terms than the British compensation of 1836, was insidious in the length of period over which indemnity and secours payments were made, allowing the former colonists and their dependants to develop victim identities and to mythologise their families' environments and experiences in Saint-Domingue.

10

Sir Eyre Coote and the governorship of Jamaica, 1805–1808

David A. Fleming

Of all the colonial administrations in the Caribbean, the governorship of Jamaica was the most prestigious. The office generally went to well-connected politicians and military men, the latter being preferred in time of war. For several it was a staging post on the way to other, better preferment in the United Kingdom. As one historian put it, those who sought the governorship felt that 'an efficient period as administrator could win further promotion at home providing the climate and tropical diseases did not finish them off, or at least incapacitate them first'.[1] Of the forty-one Governors of Jamaica appointed between 1661 and 1801 only two were Irishman: William, Second Earl of Inchiquin, and John Bourden, a Coleraine-born Jamaican planter, both holding the post in the 1690s, the latter in an acting capacity.[2] By contrast, six Scotsmen held the position in the same period. The nineteenth century saw a higher proportion of Irishmen filling the office. In that period four of the thirty-one Governors were Irish, namely Sir John Keane (1827–8); Somerset Lowry-Corry, Second Earl Belmore (1828–32); Howe Peter Browne, Second Marquess of Sligo (1834–6); and Sir Eyre Coote.

The decision, in 1805, to appoint Eyre Coote Governor of Jamaica was not surprising, given his reputation within the British military. Born in 1759, the son of a Limerick clergyman, he was early identified for the army, where his uncle and namesake had become a military hero by blazing a trail in India. The uncle took young Eyre under his wing, ensuring rapid promotion. When the general died in 1783, Eyre inherited his British estate and a desire to imitate his uncle's military prowess. He served in the American revolutionary war, and on his return was stationed in Britain and Ireland. His first encounter with the West Indies came in 1794 during an unsuccessful attack on the French colony of Saint Lucia. As the war with France intensified, he campaigned in the Netherlands. In 1796 Coote participated in a second West Indian campaign, and in the same year was promoted to brigadier-general on the Irish establishment. On his return from the West Indies in 1796, he was sent to Ireland and stationed at Bandon in Cork. He was the commanding officer there when the French attempted a landing at

Bantry, and although the weather scuppered the attempt, Coote was among the officers who were credited with preventing the attack. As a result, his reputation rose. On 1 January 1798 he was promoted to major-general and given command at Dover, where a French invasion of England was expected. He later served in the Netherlands and in Egypt, where he besieged and took Alexandria. For this singular achievement he was invested, in May 1802, as a knight of the Bath. Eager for more glory, he pleaded to be given some significant command, preferably in India, where he believed his destiny lay. But in 1805, William Pitt's Government, fearing that a combined French and Spanish naval force was about to invade Jamaica and other British Caribbean possessions, sent him back to the West Indies.[3] The choice of Coote as Governor, therefore, was predicated on his military talents rather than any other consideration.[4]

Although appointed Governor in May 1805, Coote had to wait in Cork while intelligence was gathered about the exact intentions of the French and Spanish fleet.[5] It was only on 28 October that he embarked for the Caribbean with his new wife, a large retinue of servants and attendants, and four regiments. Beset by a violent storm and enemy privateers, it took fifty-eight days before he arrived in Jamaica on 21 January 1806.[6] But within a month of his arrival, Coote's mission to deal a blow to French designs became redundant, when Admiral John Duckworth scored a significant victory over the enemy fleet off Saint-Domingue. This eliminated the threat to Jamaica and the rest of the Caribbean, leaving Coote without his hoped-for military engagement and in an office he was no longer eager to fill.[7]

As in Ireland, Governors were required to balance the expectations of the imperial Government with the concerns of the local political elite, which in Jamaica's case consisted of about 1,500 men, many of whom owned large sugar plantations worked by enslaved people.[8] Of these, a much smaller planter elite dominated the colony's forty-three-member house of Assembly, the legislative body that, with the Governor and his council of twelve, was required to make laws. The planters had become increasingly assertive in the eighteenth century and, though loyal, were nevertheless eager to defend their dominant position. In 1774, Edward Long, a planter and the author of a history of Jamaica, observed that 'the people of this island are fond of opposition to their governors, that they are ever discontented and factious', but went on to explain that in doing so planters only wished to uphold their constitutional rights as Britons and oppose the imposition of unjust 'innovations'.[9] Long went on to excoriate the type of vain and conceited Governor that 'on being elevated to a vice royalty, will pervert what little understanding they possess; and, when joined to a corrupt heart, and a selfish, servile turn of mind ... must necessarily be prompted to exercise every species of wanton caprice, and oppressive and arbitrary measures;

descending at the same time, to the lowest practices of venality and dishonour'. Conversely, he admired and respected a Governor who possessed 'a generous heart, a liberal and comprehensive mind, a suavity of manners, and virtuous principles'.[10] Notwithstanding this attempt to justify planter opposition on the grounds of liberty, virtue and public conduct, Long's narrative was a defence of planter interests against any imperial encroachments.[11]

Clashes between the Governor and the Jamaican Assembly in the 1720s and 1760s reinforced notions of liberty and colonial self-awareness, but did not result in the type of demands witnessed in the thirteen American colonies in the 1770s. Although that crisis heightened existing notions of liberty and representation, Jamaican planters remained loyal, and confident of their place within the empire.[12] Yet from the 1780s, the relationship between planters and the imperial Government began to deteriorate. Emerging calls for the abolition of the transatlantic slave trade highlighted the horrendous treatment of enslaved people which seemed to underpin the vast profits made by their owners. For planters, such notions were a betrayal of their position within the imperial system, where they had been treated as favoured subjects, essential for the enrichment of the empire. They increasingly viewed taxation as oppressive, unwilling to acknowledge the Government's argument that it was necessary for their defence. The shock of American independence resulted in a changed attitude in London towards its remaining colonies. From 1783, the imperial Government refrained from interfering in the internal affairs of colonies, such as Jamaica, which in turn gave Assemblies greater latitude in matters of administration.[13] But there were limits, particularly when it came to trade and defence, and ultimately the question of slavery. Clashes therefore seemed likely, and Coote, like his predecessors, had to tread carefully.

Prior to leaving Cork, Coote received a letter from a former Jamaican Governor, Alexander Lindsay, Sixth Earl of Balcarres, with advice on how he might approach his governorship. He recommended that Coote maintain a good relationship with the Assembly, but more especially that he develop an intimacy with the island's principal men, particularly two of the largest and wealthiest, Simon Taylor and William Mitchell.[14] Balcarres described Taylor, the Assembly member for St Thomas-in-the-East, as a 'somewhat difficult' person, likely to upset Coote's plans out of 'prejudice' but ultimately a 'loyal man, sincere in the love of his country'. Balcarres warned Coote that he could 'carry no question in the house of Assembly against the weight of Simon Taylor'.[15] Like many planters, Taylor became increasingly disillusioned about his place in the empire and the transatlantic relationship between metropole and colony. As Christopher Petley has put it, Taylor began to view British policies as 'a species of tyranny that was skewing the established reciprocal relationship into one of exploitation'.[16]

Coote was in no doubt of the domestic challenges he would soon face. Writing to Lord Castlereagh, Secretary of State for War and the Colonies, Coote viewed his position as one that had 'to reconcile the jarring and partial interests of the colonists, with the true and substantial interests of Great Britain and Ireland'. He hoped, despite the 'local and petty prejudices which are so generally and so unfortunately found to prevail in colonial assemblies', that the interests of both Jamaica and Britain could be equally accommodated. His intended approach was distinctly militaristic in tone, and he believed that he would win over the Assembly with 'attention, conciliatory manners, well timed firmness and an endeavour to keep a just view of the proper system to be pursued'.[17] In his arsenal was the extensive patronage that came with the office, which provided him with an opportunity to cultivate members of the political elite. Coote, following Balcarres's advice, invited Simon Taylor to name any person of his acquaintance to become his aide-de-camp, an early signal of Coote's determination to gain his confidence and support.[18] The sixty-seven-year-old Taylor had vast experience of Governors and their stratagems, having honed his skills as a politician in the Assembly since 1763.[19] Taylor, as chairman of the Board of Works, was essential to Coote's plans for improving the defence of the island, and had been warned that Coote 'could not drive a nail in a barrack without their consent and approbation'.[20] It is not known if Taylor took up Coote's offer, but the intent was clear enough. However, the Governor's plans were soon frustrated and undermined, not by planters but by politicians in London, who had placed their favourites ahead of his recommendations. In May 1806, he requested that the ministry desist and appoint his nominees, the better to control the Assembly.[21]

Like many Governors who came before and after him, Coote felt that the imperial Government was both ignorant of his situation and largely unresponsive to his requests. He privately complained that the cabinet believed the Governor of Jamaica enjoyed 'a very amiable and attractive situation – a sumptuous palace, an extensive patronage and emoluments out of calculation are imagined to be at his disposal', but that the opposite was the case. He claimed the official residence, in Spanish Town, was in bad condition, with 'rain pouring into almost every room', while his salary and emoluments were far short of what might be expected to keep up the dignity of the office.[22] Worse, he felt that he had limited powers, except when martial law was declared.[23]

Coote's two-year stay in Jamaica was defined by the lingering threat of a French and Spanish attack and the consequences of the abolition of the slave trade when it came in 1807. Of these challenges, he was better equipped to deal with the defence of the colony. Within three months of his arrival, Coote embarked on a tour of the island's fortifications and barracks, and reviewed its militia of 7,373 men. He found the defences in a very poor state and the militia not fit for purpose, surmising that an enemy force would easily capture the island.[24] But the imperial Government was not prepared to invest in any large-scale defensive works, advising him to put what was there in the best possible condition.[25] In this he faced a number of obstacles. The barracks were maintained by a Board of Works, while another board, formed in 1792, maintained the fortifications. A separate board of Commissioners of Accounts supervised the provisioning of the army. These institutions gave the Assembly control over what might be a significant drain on the island's resources, and ultimately their pockets. But for Governors, this bureaucracy had created a 'dangerous ascendency in military arrangements'.[26] Coote believed that the 'confused mixture of opposite interests of separate boards, [and] committees of establishments' had produced an ineffective system, and wished to reform it by abolishing them and placing their responsibilities under military control.[27]

Initially the colony's chief men were inclined to support Coote's endeavours, perhaps out of fear of the threatened invasion or to give a new Governor some tacit encouragement.[28] Availing himself of this good will, and unwilling to wait until the Assembly met in the autumn, Coote, in June 1805, wrote to Simon Taylor who, as chairman of the Board of Works, could authorise immediate works.[29] Taylor may have encouraged Coote to proceed, but as the threat of invasion diminished, he increasingly withdrew his support. By July 1806 Coote's efforts to repair a barracks at Stony Hill in St Andrew Parish had come to nothing, owing to what he said was the 'vexatious' opposition of Taylor and his board.[30] As the opening of the Assembly approached, the Governor was pessimistic about the prospects of obtaining its financial support for the island's defences.[31]

Apart from his military concerns, Coote was also anxious about Jamaica's economic circumstances. By 1806 the colony's national debt stood at £300,000 (Jamaican currency), the consequence of enormous spending on the island's defences since the 1770s. A slump in the demand for Jamaican sugar in 1806 compounded the situation.[32] Merchants also blamed the complete suspension of commerce with the United States of America (USA) since 1805 as detrimental to their interests. Merchants from the USA had gained an increasing share of Caribbean commerce, especially in the provisioning trade.[33] They could supply provisions more regularly and faster than either their United Kingdom counterparts or the remaining British colonies in North America.[34] Conscious of the difficulties that the suspension caused, especially for the enslaved population, who relied on salted provisions, Coote issued a proclamation on 1 April 1806 to reopen ports temporarily to US merchants.[35] As a result, the new Governor earned some immediate popularity among planters and merchants. But this move may have been designed to make way for a more controversial trade policy which would curtail reliance on American provisions by placing a duty on imported salted fish, while making imports from the British Empire, especially Newfoundland, more attractive by offering a bounty on those goods.[36] These measures required the consent of the Assembly, which Coote set about gaining in the summer months leading up to the opening of the 1806 session. His initial efforts were not encouraging. Members of the Assembly, he reported, were suspicious of 'all acts or measures proposed by or connected with England'. Planters believed that imposing duties on American fish would in turn damage overall trade between the colony and the USA, which negated efforts to reopen general trade with the former colonies.[37]

Coote worked hard throughout the summer of 1806 to garner support for both his economic and his military proposals. Although Taylor and his supporters decided to maintain their opposition, others, such as the Scottish-born planter John Shand of Spanish Town, member for St John, offered assistance. On 11 November 1806, Shand presented a fishery bill to the Assembly providing for a bounty on British-American fish, which passed a first reading by the slimmest of majorities, thirteen voting in favour with eleven opposed.[38] Despite continued opposition, Coote's supporters successfully carried the bill three days later by a slightly better majority of twenty-one to fourteen. As a concession Coote had agreed that the bill would expire after a year.[39] This was an important personal victory, as Simon Taylor had vehemently opposed the measure. Coote was also partly successful in his efforts to reform how the island's defences were maintained. The Assembly abolished the Committee of Fortifications, its powers given to the Governor. Significantly, he obtained £7,500 for maintaining the existing regiments on the island, which was to be spent on bedding and hammocks.[40] These were all important successes for Coote, and might suggest an ability to persuade and cajole suspicious planters. Whatever personal talents he had must be set against the heightened military anxiety of war and a possible invasion. However, there was a limit to what the Assembly was willing to give. Coote's other reform, to wrest control of provisioning the army from the Assembly, was unanimously rejected.[41] Despite this setback, Coote felt satisfied that there was a 'liberal spirit pervading that body'.[42]

Then, unexpectedly, the Assembly encountered a problem of its own making, when in December 1806 members agreed to grant 3,000 guineas (£4,000) as a gift to Admiral John Duckworth for his victory over the French and Spanish fleet in the Caribbean earlier in the year. Such extravagant rewards were nothing new. The most exquisite was an elaborate memorial building in Spanish Town to Admiral George Rodney, who, like Duckworth, had scored a significant victory over the French in 1782. However, given the colony's financial problems, the white population, represented in their parish vestries, baulked at the idea, and began to instruct their members to oppose the measure. When this failed, several parishes, in the early months of 1807, petitioned Coote to exercise his prerogative powers to dissolve the Assembly.[43] This was an extraordinary appeal, and one that lost the Assembly some of its popular mandate. Although Coote did not dissolve the Assembly, it may have given him some additional leverage over it.

While Coote's commercial and military reforms divided planters and the Assembly, the proposed abolition of slavery united all against him and the imperial Government.[44] Since the 1770s, planters, and the Assembly's agents in London had formed an active and powerful lobby against abolition.[45] To a large extent, these efforts had been successful, as William Wilberforce's regular motions in the British House of Commons to abolish the trade had all been seen off. But changing attitudes and the weight of popular opinion in the United Kingdom began to shift in favour of abolition. When the matter was again raised in February 1807, under the new ministry of William, First Baron Grenville, things had changed, and in March a bill abolishing the transatlantic trade in enslaved people was enacted, to come into force on 1 January 1808. The ministry hoped that planters would see the beneficial effects of abolition, and encouraged Coote to reassure those who had 'a great interest at stake'.[46] There was little the planters could do to resist the measure. In Jamaica the news contributed to an already uneasy relationship between owners and enslaved people.

Tension had existed for some time prior to abolition. The successful slave revolt in the French colony of Saint-Domingue (now Haiti) in November 1791, which had seen the overthrow of the colonial regime and the abolition of slavery there, encouraged the Jamaican enslaved and freed blacks to consider their own position.[47] For the white Jamaican population, the twin fears of a slave uprising and the possibility that the French revolutionary regime might use the situation to destabilise the colony caused profound anxiety. Strict laws were enforced preventing communication between the Jamaican black population and 'foreigners of colour' in order to prevent the spread of radical ideas and interaction.[48] Fears were realised when, in 1795, freed black communities – known as maroons – in western Jamaica staged a revolt over colonial grievances, which resulted in large-scale violence and attacks over an eighteen-month period. Although the maroons surrendered in 1796, many enslaved people had escaped their plantations to join the revolt and remained at large, while swades of the western part of the island were decimated. Given the size of the enslaved population, which stood at about 325,000 compared to 30,000 white settlers, the planter elite remained ever cautious of insurrection. Consequently, proposals to recruit black men and those of mixed white and black heritage known as 'mulattos' into the army were vehemently opposed, based on fears around mutiny and the sight of armed black and mulatto men.[49] Even proposals, in 1802, to employ black artificers to build barracks in Jamaica were rejected by the Assembly for similar reasons.[50]

The relationship between enslaved people and their enslavers on some plantations deteriorated further in the lead up to Christmas 1806. At the beginning of December rioting broke out on several plantations in Surrey County, in the west of the island.[51] During the holiday period, rioting spread to plantations in the Parishes of Portland and St George in the same county. Coote believed that the origin of this 'dangerous spirit' had been inspired by the actions of enslaved people in Saint-Domingue, which had gained independence from France in 1803. Coote went on to explain that a 'great number of French negroes' had settled in one of the affected parishes, and that these 'creole' enslaved people (those born in captivity) had instigated the violence.[52] The days leading up to and including Christmas were a particularly animated time for enslaved people, who enthusiastically celebrated the holiday.[53] Eventually the revolt was quashed by the army and militia. Several were tried and sentenced to transportation, while two of the leaders were executed. Two more had been acquitted, though Coote later ordered them to be transported from the colony, believing them to be dangerous ringleaders.[54] Coote went further by ordering lists to be drawn up of all French or foreign enslaved people, with the intention of transporting them.[55] He also attempted to limit the commercial intercourse between Jamaica and Saint-Domingue, but this threatened mercantile interests and had to be abandoned.[56] In London, the Government wondered whether Catholic priests had encouraged the revolt. Coote replied that there were but two priests on the island, one a Spaniard who tended to his countrymen, the other a Frenchman who had been evacuated from Saint-Domingue in 1798, and who ministered to the resettled French population of whites and blacks. Coote believed that he was a man of 'loose morals and destitute of any principles, who as it suited his convenience, was either a violent republican or a determined Royalist'. Neither man, Coote contended, was responsible for the agitation.[57] Some in Britain feared that news of the insurrection, which arrived in March just as the abolition bill was proceeding through Parliament, would be used by opponents to stymie the measure. Efforts were made to downplay the incident, with reports stating that such tumults were normal and that those accused of rioting had been acquitted.[58]

For Coote, the consequences of abolishing the slave trade was more troubling for his administration, as it caused unrest in the Assembly.[59] It had placed a tax of £4 on every enslaved person brought to the colony to pay for the maintenance of 3,000 soldiers, a measure which members reviewed annually. By abolishing the trade in enslaved people therefore, the

Governor's ability to pay for the army was threatened. When news of the abolition arrived, many in the Assembly were unwilling to alter the method of taxation, as a means of demonstrating their opposition.[60] In October 1807, a report from an Assembly committee to enquire into the effects of abolition was presented 'after much delay and difference of opinion'. For several Assembly men the imperial Government had betrayed planters, and argued that the army should not be maintained. But there was a significant number of planters who feared the consequences of refusing to support the army. In an attempt to win over moderates, hardliners recommended that a reduced amount be paid. The ensuing debate was particularly animated, and resulted in insults traded between John Shand and James Stewart, the member for Trelawny, which resulted in a duel.[61] Shand, who had supported the Governor's administration in the previous session, remained steadfast behind Coote's efforts, and it was he who was credited with scuppering the resolution. In the end the Assembly agreed to maintain the existing provision for the army, which was viewed as a victory for Coote's administration.[62] As the Governor required little else from them, and was eager that members be on their plantations before the Christmas festivities to maintain order among the enslaved, Coote prorogued the session on 28 November.[63]

Throughout 1807, Coote prepared for trouble among the enslaved population. He again appealed to Britain for more soldiers to be sent, but these were ultimately diverted to occupy the Dutch colony of Curaçao.[64] As Christmas time approached, Coote sent instructions to militia colonels to search for arms in the towns and plantations and to assemble their men. Enslaved people were already elated by the anticipated abolition of the slave trade, though Coote remarked that 'few of them rightly understand' what it actually meant.[65] Some believed that the bill would result in the complete emancipation of enslaved people. Their disappointment did not immediately produce trouble. It would take another three decades before slavery in Jamaica and across the empire was eventually abolished.

Coote's personal views on slavery are not known. He certainly had no qualms about the Crown's purchase of enslaved people for the West Indian regiments in the regular army, even as the abolition bill passed through Parliament.[66] Several enslaved people attended him in the Governor's house in Spanish Town. One of them, named Sally, stood out for her 'exemplary conduct' as a nurse to Coote's family, and as a result, in November 1807, was emancipated by an Act of the Assembly, and granted an annual payment of £20.[67] Another, named Affleck, 'displayed much attachment' to the Governor, which, it seems was reciprocated, for on Coote's departure from the colony in 1808 he requested that Affleck be allowed to accompany him to England. This too required legislation, which was duly passed on 20 May 1809, a year after Coote, and presumably Affleck, had left Jamaica.[68] This suggests that, like many, Coote could be sympathetic and even endearing to enslaved people close to him, while being contemptuous of the generality, as his transportation of those acquitted of insurrection in 1807 indicates.

In June 1807 Coote wrote to Lord Castlereagh requesting that he be replaced, reminding him of an earlier communication where he had desired not to be isolated from England for any long period, and believing that three years was long enough. He pleaded that his private affairs at home required his attention and that his 'harassed and impaired health' had encouraged him to apply for relief.[69] He repeated this request in November, citing his continuing ill health and blaming the Jamaican climate, which was well known for afflicting white settlers.[70] In January 1808, he was informed that he would be replaced on 5 April by William Montagu, Fifth Duke of Manchester.[71] As his time to depart approached, he received the usual complimentary addresses from Jamaica's parishes and other bodies.[72] At home, in July a 'grand dinner' was hosted in London by a group of Jamaican planters and merchants to thank him for his service, while in October the gentlemen of Bath with Jamaican interests held another to acknowledge his administration's 'impartial and disinterested conduct'.[73] Among those present at this dinner was Richard Taylor, nephew of Simon, who reported back to Jamaica that he would personally call on Coote, knowing that he had given his uncle 'more satisfaction than any other governor'.[74] This suggests that, notwithstanding Coote's clashes with Taylor over barracks and spending, the Governor had continued to keep Taylor close and on good terms. Indeed, the various dinners held in London on his return were used to reinforce and sustain the ties that had been formed in the West Indies between Jamaican interests and important figures, such as Coote, who might again be useful in the future. However, these older, informal ways of politics were becoming increasingly ineffectual as British attitudes towards planters became ambivalent and ultimately hostile.

Coote had managed to navigate two difficult sessions successfully, achieving most of what he and the British ministry had wanted, while at the same time avoiding a crisis over abolition, which threatened to produce a conflict between diverging colonial and British interests. Although he had no reforming impulse as other West Indian Governors occasionally demonstrated,[75] he nevertheless succeeded in wresting some power away from the Assembly and its chief men, demonstrating that even the most powerful factions in a colonial legislature could be managed. These victories contributed to the centralising forces at work across the empire. Although Governors might only remain for short periods, the incremental reforms they proposed had the effect of gradually weakening colonial Assemblies, and in time resulted in a new, more direct system of governance from London.[76] Whether Coote's Irish background had any influence on the way he managed the truculent Jamaican Assembly is difficult to gauge. Although he had served as a Member of the Irish House of Commons and later the British Parliament between 1790 and 1806, he was largely absent from Dublin and London. As a result he had not prominently sided with any political faction in either, though he had privately voiced his opposition to the Act of Union.[77] All that mattered to him was to come away from Jamaica with imperial objectives obtained and with as little controversy as possible, which, notwithstanding a self-assertive Assembly and the abolition of the slave trade, he succeeded in doing.

Notes

1 A. P. Kup, 'Alexander Lindsay, 6th earl of Balcarres, lieutenant governor of Jamaica, 1794–1801', *Bulletin of the John Rylands Library* 57 (1975), 327–65.
2 Karst de Jong, 'The life of John Bourden', *Irish Migration Studies in Latin America* 8:1 (2012), 87–98.
3 *Exeter Flying Post*, 9 May 1805; Michigan, Clements Library, Eyre Coote papers (1775–1925), 8/9 (Camden to Eyre Coote, 13 May 1805); 10 (Frederick, Duke of York, to Coote, 13 May 1805); 11, 13, 15 (Edward Cooke to Coote, 14, 18 and 26 May 1805).
4 J. Holland Rose, 'British West India commerce as a factor in the Napoleonic War', *Cambridge Historical Journal* 3:1 (1929), 34–46.
5 Coote papers, 8/11, 15: Edward Cooke to Coote, 14 and 26 May 1805.
6 Coote papers, 1/1 (patent appointing Coote as Lieutenant-Governor of Jamaica, 12 May 1805); 8/10 (York to Coote, 13 May 1805); 23 (Camden to Coote, 4 and 8 July 1805); 25 (York to Coote, 5 July 1805); 28 (Robert Stewart, Viscount Castlereagh, to Coote, 20 July 1805); 29 (William Windham to George Nugent, 5 March 1806) (Coote papers, 1/1; 8/10, 23, 25, 28, 29, 30, 45); *Maryland Gazette*, 13 February 1806; *Freeman's Journal*, 22 March 1806.
7 Coote papers, 20/2, p. 1: Coote to York, 27 February 1806.
8 George Metcalf, *Royal Government and Political Conflict in Jamaica, 1729–1783* (London: Longmans for the Royal Commonwealth Society, 1965).
9 Edward Long, *The History of Jamaica; or, General Survey of the Ancient and Modern State of that Island*, 3 vols (London, 1774), Vol. i, pp. 39–40.
10 *Ibid.*, p. 42.
11 For more see Christer Petley, *Slaveholders in Jamaica: Colonial Society and Culture during the Era of Abolition* (London: Pickering and Chatto, 2009).
12 Aaron Graham, 'The principle of representation in Jamaica and the British Atlantic in the age of revolutions, 1768–1807', *Parliaments, Estates and Representation* 40:1 (2020), 1–20.
13 P. J. Marshall, *Remaking the British Atlantic: The United States and the British Empire after American Independence* (Oxford: Oxford University Press, 2012), p. 316.

14 For Taylor see Christer Petley, *White Fury: A Jamaican Slaveholder and the Age of Revolution* (Oxford: Oxford University Press, 2018).
15 Coote papers, 8/12: Alexander Lindsay, Sixth Earl of Balcarres, to Coote, 15 May 1805. For Taylor see Petley, *White Fury*.
16 Petley, *White Fury*, p. 126.
17 Coote papers, 20/1, p. 3: Coote to Castlereagh, 21 January 1806.
18 Coote papers, 20/2, p. 4: Coote to Simon Taylor, 20 March 1806.
19 Petley, *White Fury*, p. 98.
20 Coote papers, 8/12: Balcarres to Coote, 15 May 1805.
21 Coote papers, 20/1, p. 17: Coote to Windham, 29 May 1806; *Finn's Leinster Journal*, 17 December 1806.
22 Coote papers, 20/1, pp. 1–3: Coote to Cooke, 13 February, 12 March 1806.
23 Coote papers, 20/2, p. 3: Coote to Earl of Chatham, 12 March 1806.
24 Coote papers, 20/1, pp. 11, 13–14, 49–50 (Coote to Windham, 21 April and 18 May 1806, 15 April 1807); 28/11 (notebook containing Coote's observations on the defence of Jamaica, 1807–8).
25 Coote papers, 20/1, pp. 31–2, 49–50: Coote to Windham, 3 October 1806, 15 April 1807.
26 Coote papers, 20/1, pp. 7–10: Coote to Castlereagh, 22 and 23 March 1806.
27 Coote papers, 8/27 (Camden to Coote, 6 July 1805); 20/2, p. 3 (Coote to Governor Charles Cameron, 5 March 1806); 20/1, pp. 8–10 (Coote to Castlereagh, 23 March 1806); 20/2, pp. 1–2 (Coote to Chatham, 12 March 1806); 20/3, pp. 8–10 (Coote to Cooke, 29 March 1806).
28 Coote papers, 20/1, pp. 13–14: Coote to Windham, 18 May 1806.
29 Coote papers, 20/2, pp. 19–20: Coote to Taylor, 15 June 1806.
30 Coote papers, 20/1, p. 21: Coote to Windham, 3 July 1806.
31 Coote papers 20/1, pp. 29–30: Coote to Windham, 1 September 1806.
32 Aaron Graham, 'The colonial sinews of imperial power: The political economy of Jamaican taxation, 1768–1838', *Journal of Imperial and Commonwealth History* 45:2 (2017), 188–209 (p. 199).
33 Coote papers, 8/45: Windham to Nugent, 5 March 1806.
34 Coote papers, 20/2, p. 14 (Coote to Anthony Murray, 27 May 1806); 20/1, p. 30 (Coote to Windham, 3 October 1806).
35 Coote papers, 20/1, p. 28: Coote to Windham, 28 August 1806.
36 Coote papers, 8/53 (Windham to Nugent, 2 April 1806); 9/25 (certificate of William Pitcairn, Custom House, Port Antonio, Jamaica, 8 September 1806); 10/1 (Windham to Coote, 8 January 1807); 10/41, 53 (Castlereagh to Coote, 7 May and 20 June 1807).
37 Coote papers, 20/1, pp. 17–20 (Coote to Windham, 30 May and 8 June 1806).
38 *Journals of the Assembly of Jamaica: 1664–1826*, 14 vols (Jamaica: Alexander Aikman, 1811–29), xi, p. 453.
39 *Ibid.*, xi, pp. 456, 469, 473.
40 Coote papers, 20/1, pp. 34–5, 40–1, 49–50: Coote to Windham, 10 November 1806, 9 January and 15 April 1807.

41 Coote papers, 9/20 (George Howell to Lieutenant-Colonel Thomas Walsh, 29 August 1806); 20/1, pp. 34–5, 36 (Coote to Windham, 10 and 15 November 1806).
42 Coote papers, 20/1, pp. 40–1: Coote to Windham, 9 January 1807.
43 Coote papers, 10/32 (Castlereagh to Coote, 4 April 1807); 20/1, p. 48 (Coote to Castlereagh, 7 April 1807). For more on this episode see Graham, 'The principle of representation in Jamaica', pp. 14–19.
44 Coote papers, 11/27: Castlereagh to Coote, 2 October 1807.
45 *The report from a committee of the House of Assembly of Jamaica, appointed in a session, which began on the 23rd of October, 1804, to inquire into the proceedings of the imperial parliament of Great Britain and Ireland, relative to the slave trade* (Kingston, 1805); Christer Petley, 'Slaveholders and revolution: The Jamaican planter class, British imperial politics, and the ending of the slave trade, 1775–1807', *Slavery and Abolition* 39:1 (2018), 53–79.
46 Coote papers, 10/25: Windham to Coote, 9 March 1807.
47 *Sun*, 27 October 1801; *Morning Post*, 16 February 1802; *Lancaster Gazette*, 27 February 1802; *Chester Courant*, 31 January 1804.
48 *Morning Post*, 31 December 1802; *Cumberland Pacquet*, 5 June 1804.
49 *Hampshire Chronicle*, 12 May 1800; *Exeter Flying Post*, 15 May 1800; *Sun*, 21 June 1802; *Newcastle Courant*, 5 February 1803.
50 *Sun*, 27 August 1802.
51 Coote papers, 20/2, p. 49: Coote to Dacres, 12 December 1806.
52 Coote papers, 20/1, pp. 40–1: Coote to Windham, 9 January 1807.
53 Maria Nugent, *Lady Nugent's Journal of Her Residence in Jamaica from 1801 to 1805*, ed. Philip Wright (Kingston: University of West Indies Press, 2002), p. 218.
54 Coote papers, 20/1, pp. 45–8: Coote to Windham, 20 February, 2 and 10 March 1807. Coote's actions later required an Act of the Jamaican Assembly to indemnify him and others involved: 48 Geo. III, c. 3: *Act to indemnify his honour the lieutenant-governor for having ordered four slaves of a dangerous description to be transported from this island, and all other persons concerned in carrying the said orders into execution* (1807).
55 Coote papers, 20/1, p. 46: Coote to Windham, 2 March 1807.
56 Coote papers, 20/1, pp. 53–4: Coote to Castlereagh, 2 June 1807.
57 Coote to Castlereagh, 2 June 1807.
58 *Cumberland Pacquet, and Ware's Whitehaven Advertiser*, 31 March 1807; *Morning Advertiser*, 4 April 1807.
59 See The National Archives, Kew, Colonial Office papers, CO 137–119: Coote's letters to Castlereagh, June–October 1807.
60 Coote papers, 20/1, p. 56: Coote to Castlereagh, 14 June 1807.
61 Coote papers, 20/1, pp. 66–7: Coote to Castlereagh, 29 October 1807.
62 Coote to Castlereagh, 29 October 1807.
63 Coote papers, 20/1, p. 71: Coote to Castlereagh, 4 December 1807.
64 Coote papers, 20/1, p. 57: Coote to Castlereagh, 21 June 1807.

65 Coote papers, 20/1, p. 71: Coote to Castlereagh, 4 December 1807.
66 Coote papers, 20/1, pp. 15–16, 18, 38, 42: Coote to Windham, 18 May, 3 June and 9 December 1806, 12 January 1807.
67 48 Geo. III, c. 27 (Jamaica): *Act for emancipating a slave named Sally, belonging to the public, in reward of faithful services* (1807).
68 49 Geo. III, c. 30 (Jamaica): *Act to permit a slave, named Affleck, belonging to the public to remove to England, and to emancipate the said slave* (1809); *Public Ledger and Daily Advertiser*, 9 June 1808.
69 Coote papers, 20/1, p. 55: Coote to Castlereagh, 3 June 1807.
70 Coote papers, 11/38: York to Coote, 5 November 1807.
71 Coote papers, 12/14 (Castlereagh to Coote, 19 January 1808); 20/1, p. 78 (Coote to Castlereagh, 5 April 1808).
72 Examples include: Coote papers 11/57 (address from the Custos, freeholders and inhabitants of the Parish of Westmoreland to Coote, 15 December 1807); 58 (address of the freeholders and inhabitants of the Parish of St Catherine to Coote, *c*. 16 December 1807); 62 (address of the freeholders and inhabitants of the Parish of St Thomas to Coote, *c*. 18 December 1807); 63 (address from the Registrar, Masters and solicitors of the High Court of Chancery of Jamaica to Coote, *c*. 19 December 1807); 66 (address of the clergy of Jamaica, Spanish town, to Coote, 22 December 1807. These were printed by John Lunan as *Addresses presented by the Honourable the Council, the Assembly ... to ... Sir Eyre Coote ... on his expected departure from that island ...* (St Jago de La Vega, 1808).
73 *Morning Post*, 7 July and 13 October 1808.
74 Institute of Commonwealth Studies, ICS 120/6/A/78: Simon Richard Brissett Taylor to Simon Taylor, 6 July 1808.
75 D. J. Murray, *The West Indies and the Development of Colonial Government, 1801–1834* (Oxford: Clarendon Press, 1965), pp. 33–9.
76 *Ibid.*, pp. 166–229.
77 For his views on the Irish Act of Union see David Fleming, 'The correspondence of Sir Eyre Coote with his brother, Charles Henry Coote, and others on the Irish Act of Union, 1799–1800', *Analecta hibernica* 40 (2007), 189–228.

11

In search of excess: Lambert Blair and his appetites

Ciaran O'Neill

In 1834, when the dust began to settle on the compensation claims of British enslavers, it was an Irish man with Scottish connections who sat at the top of the pile: Sir James Blair, MP (Figure 11.1). His compensation was paid out on the strength of the plantation estates of his uncle, Lambert Blair,

Figure 11.1 James Leakey, *Portrait of Mr James Blair (1789–1841)*, oil on ivory. Image Courtesy of Bonhams.

formerly of Newry, Co. Down, who had died in 1815, bestowing control of his vast estates in Berbice and Demerara-Essequibo on his nephew and grand-nephew, James Blair and John McCamon. McCamon died without issue four years later in 1819, and so it was that Sir James ended up with a colonial bounty that went to the Stopford-Green family at his death in 1841.[1] A particularly noxious individual, Sir James purchased the rotten borough of Saltash in 1818 with the apparent sole objective of defending enslavement and, by proxy, his own commercial interests.

Blair only spoke twice in Parliament in a sixteen-year career, both times clumsily, and both times in favour of retaining the slave trade. His votes were as predictable as his silence was typical. They were either cast against all concessions to his Catholic fellow countrymen, or firmly in favour of protection for his fellow planters. You can see something of his political ideology in a parliamentary response to Dr Lushington in March 1823 following the slave revolt in Demerara, where Blair had some of his possessions.

> Ministers should throw more decision into their measures, and let us know how far they mean to go. I conceive that unless a line be drawn and unless we are told where concession is to stop, the negroes will never enjoy quiet, nor the planters that undisturbed possession of their property, to which they are by law entitled.

As bad an egg as he was, James Blair was not considered by his peers to have been the worst of the Guyanese enslavers, but his story is reasonably well known, and it need not delay us.[2]

In this chapter I am much more interested in the story of Lambert Blair, the driving force of a colonial enterprise that had its origins in the Newry hinterland, an apparently unlikely town to have had such well-developed imperial links, albeit a town with one of the earliest summit-level canals (1742), and a modern ship canal built in 1769. It was one of several Irish ports through which tobacco, coffee and other imperial luxuries might be imported in the second half of the eighteenth century, and it is very likely that the economic effect that this transatlantic trade had on Newry provided encouragement for young Lambert. At any rate, he left it in his teenage years for a life of adventure and excess in the West Indies.[3]

Lambert Blair rose from relatively humble origins to control vast amounts of human and economic capital in the British empire, acting as a teenage agent and trader, and then in his adult years controlling a large share of sugar and cotton plantations in Berbice, across an area that would later become British Guiana. He was the perfect example of a West Indies trader, an archipelago full of what Sir James Marriot once called 'renegadoes of all nations'.[4] Thus far we can fit what we know about Lambert into a paragraph, and only Nini Rodgers has really noticed him at all within Irish historiography.⁵ David Alston has mentioned him in his work on Scottish planters, and he appears fleetingly in some scattered histories of St Eustatius and Berbice, as well as in some Dutch sources.⁶ The research produced by the *Legacies of British Slave-Ownership* project at University College London has now added some flesh to the bones, as well as a partial translation of his near-unreadable will, but his appearance on the historical record to date has been fitful, episodic, fleeting. This chapter aims to restore further flesh to Lambert's apparently ample frame, and to try to piece together his imperial career.

Lambert is sketched in anecdote in a well-known travel journal by Dr George Pinckard from 1796, published in 1806. In Pinckard's three-volume work we are given an image of a generous, even gluttonous, planter. He is variously described as a 'rich planter', 'opulent', with an enviable mansion and the wherewithal to dispense his generous bounty. Note how Pinckard gestures to the sensual in his first account of him, and how the language luxuriates in the excesses of empire:

> We have lately made a party from the fort, and spent two most pleasant days – one at the governor's – the other with Mr. Blair, a rich planter, residing at a short distance down the coast on the opposite shore of the river ... Mr. Blair is one of the most opulent planters in these colonies, and, not disliking the good things of life himself, he has assembled them at his place of residence in sufficient supply to enable him to treat his friends with the most sumptuous liberality. He is generous and social, and the riches of his table are dispensed with all the bounty of his nature. Instead of a plain cottage just rising from the wild woods of an infant settlement, we might have fancied ourselves feasting in one of the hospitable mansions of old England, nay, in some chartered hall, even, of voluptuous London itself.

Later, in the same passage, we will see a snapshot of the enslaved people on the plantation, and the coded deference of the plantation that so impresses this Scottish visitor. '[W]e were rowed across the mouth of the river by eight of the finest slaves of the estate, who pulled us on with surprising speed', Pickard noted; 'we had a pleasant ride about a mile and a half through fields of cotton and of plantains; the negroes running at the horses sides, according to the custom of the country, as fast as we chose to ride'.⁷ Christer Petley has recently argued for the importance of food and ritual in the British Caribbean as things that bound the planter class together and helped to maintain their hegemony as a white minority in charge of large numbers of enslaved people. By the time Lambert Blair was tabling his opulent feast, there was an entrenched opinion of Caribbean planters as gluttons, people who were given to excess. As Petler argues, travellers 'reported on the sumptuous meals and excessive drinking of the planter class'. Abolitionists associated these features of local society with the 'corrupting influences of slavery'.[8] This very act of excessive consumption somehow came to stand for the illegitimacy of planters' lives and fortunes. They were, in the memorable words of Maria Skinner Nugent, wife of the (Irish) Governor of Jamaica, 'men who ate like cormorants and drank like porpoises'.[9] Metropolitan elites began to define themselves against this image, ushering in an orthodoxy 'at home' that emphasised more cosmopolitan and benign virtues.[10] We will return to Pinckard's account, as I want to dwell a little more on the bounty of Lambert's nature, and the meaning of his many appetites.

Concentrating on one single Irish enslaver in Berbice may seem rather narrow, but I hope to use him as a way to problematise the scholarship on the Irish in empire, a growing field that has really blossomed since the mid-1990s. Since then we have seen the extraordinary growth in work on the Irish in India, a widespread recalibration of Irish migration and diaspora studies to include the imperial elements of the great migration from Ireland.[11] Only very recently has Irish history begun to query the empire 'at home' in the Catherine Hall sense of the term, and the field has yet to begin the work of thinking about indigenous receptions and reactions to Irish colonisers as Zoë Laidlaw and Alan Lester have recently advocated.[12] The inspiring work of those scholars engaging with the Irish Slaves meme on social media has generally tried to make the distinction between indentured labour and chattel slavery clearer to the general public, and that work is essential, but we can arguably come at these misconceptions by looking at the plantocracy as well. Arguably the best way to combat this misinformation would be to focus on the figure of the Irish planter or enslaver, and to increase the visibility of this type of figure in Irish historiography.

All of which has led me to Lambert Blair, his appetites, his estates and the bounty of his nature. What goods, people and ideas flowed through this Presbyterian planter with such apparently unremarkable origins in provincial Ulster? What can I learn from accounts of him, and by him, or from the layout of his table in Berbice to the inventory of his merchant ships?

Little is known of the personal life of Lambert Blair. He was born around 1767 in Newry to a merchant, James Blair (1710–70), and his wife Elizabeth (?) Jane Bolton (1722–96).[13] He married quite late, in 1809 and at around 42 years of age, at Clifton in Lancashire.[14] His wife was Jane Letitia Stopford, eldest daughter of Lieutenant-General Edward Stopford and Letitia Blacker, and thus a granddaughter of James Stopford, First Earl of Courtown, by his second son. She outlived her husband spectacularly, passing away in April 1871, some 56 years after him. Lambert had set aside £2,000 a year for her out of the colonial estates in his will, along with a £33,333 6s 3d lump sum to his executors.[15] The census of 1871 records her age at 85, which seems to indicate she was born in 1786, making her about 23 years old at marriage.

She died at Marylebone, where she lived with her younger sister, Elizabeth, who was also a widow. Elizabeth had married Lambert's nephew, James Blair (our beloved member for the rotten borough of Saltash) in December 1815, but she had also outlived him by a considerable span, her death occurring in 1884, some 43 years after his.

Lambert Blair seems to have spent his early merchant years in the company of his elder brother James, about whom a little more is known. James Blair operated out of a range of locations in the archipelago, including St Eustatius, St Thomas, Grenada, St Kitts and Dominica. His trade was triangular, taking advantage of postrevolution shortages in the United States of key commodities such as coffee and tea, and shipping large quantities of mackerel, linen or anything else that could be sold in the West Indies in order to obtain them.[16] His networks included several London merchants, as well as Philadelphia-based Irish traders such as Stewart and Nesbitt, and he seems to have been sending quantities of flax back to his family business in Ireland, often via New Orleans.[17] In 1780 he was sending bills of exchange to the President of the Continental Congress, Samuel Huntingdon.[18] Quite when Lambert split with his older brother is difficult to discern, but it certainly seems to have happened at some point in the mid-1780s, and probably marked the end of his apprenticeship or training. At any rate, the two remained in a loose business partnership into the early 1890s, helping each other and profiting from one another's expanding networks. James died in Dominica in early 1797.[19] A younger brother, John, seems to have run the domestic portion of the Blair brothers' trade from Co. Down and London.

The letters of Elizabeth and Ann Blair held at the Public Record Office of Northern Irleand (PRONI) indicate that the family home acted as a conduit of money and information from wherever James was based, and the family had extensive links to Liverpool and London as far back as the early 1770s. James and Lambert's mother, Elizabeth, in between lengthy sermons extolling the virtues of religious observance to her eldest boy, was wont to pepper her correspondence with references to news in trade and commerce. To Elizabeth, and her daughter Anne, they were 'Jemmey' and 'Lamby'. Elizabeth worked hard to source items for James by request, and also kept him abreast of any major developments that might affect trade or circulation of news, such as the imposition in 1774 of the 'Stamp Act', which Elizabeth notes caused much excitement in Ireland but no equivalent resistance to that of the 'brave Americans'.[20] Lambert enters into the slipstream of this family business in his teenage years, and it seems obvious that much of that was made easier by the work of his elder brothers and sisters, as well as his mother.

As Nicholas Draper and others have noted, it was typical for Irish planters to convert their plantation gains into solid assets close to London, and in the city itself. This was the route taken by Lambert late in life. While in

England he could be found at his country pile at Courtland, near Exmouth in Devonshire, or else at a fashionable London address in Gloucester Place.[21] Courtland was his address at death, and was sold immediately afterwards. He is buried at the parish church in Twickenham, where his memorial on the east wall of the north aisle states, somewhat boringly, that 'in a vault near this spot are deposited the remains of Lambert Blair Esq, of Berbice and Courtland, Devon, who, after a lingering illness which he supported with exemplary Fortitude and Resignation, departed this life on the 25th of January 1815. Aged 48 years'.[22]

This puts his birth date at about 1867, something of an issue later in this chapter. There is one surviving miniature painting of Lambert (Figure 11.2), believed to be by James Leakey, who was also responsible for the much better portrait of Sir James seen earlier, and may have been commissioned to produce this image of him at about the same time. The business account of Lambert Blair & Co. for 1795–9 details the extent of trade in coffee, cotton and enslaved people during the peak years of his estates in Berbice and Suriname.[23] This account book is now missing, so just about the only record we have for the business at its peak is a number photographs from PRONI covering the previous years of 1790–4, taken by my colleague Jonathan Wright. The book is an account of Dr William Stevenson with the brothers, detailing services from the two-day hire of a 'negro sailor' to purchase bushels of corn. William Stevenson was almost certainly the nephew of Cornelius Stevenson, a planter at St Eustatius, and the source of much of the Blair fortune, since it seems that they acted as agents to this plantation for much of the 1780s. It is on that island that Lambert Blair first appears in the Caribbean, as it were, although it is not at all clear how on earth he came to be there.[24]

Long before the era of excess, in 1781, Blair found himself witness to a controversial event at the tiny island of Saint Eustatius. He saw seventeen ships of the line off the coast of this tiny 21 km² Dutch colony in the Leeward Islands, where he had been resident for the previous two years, despite being no more than fourteen or fifteen years old, according to the dates I gave previously. The English fleet, under the command of Sir George Rodney, took possession of the unarmed island on 3 February 1781 and then proceeded to terrorise the Dutch inhabitants with a series of thirty-eight proclamations, claiming all of their goods on behalf of the Crown, and then confiscating them to the tune of about £3 million, according to Rodney. The confiscation, and Rodney's decision to remain in 'Statia', became an imperial scandal of major proportions, and his reputation was only saved by his later victory at the Battle of the Saintes off Dominica in 1782. At St Eustatius on 24 March 1781, Lambert's warehouse, was, according to Blair, broken open 'by order & in the presence of Capt Young & Mr Forster,

Figure 11.2 James Leakey (attributed), miniature portrait of Lambert Blair, head and shoulders, with short, powdered hair, wearing a black coat and white cravat, oval. Courtesy of Bearnes, Hampton & Littlewood.

the principal agents'. They alleged his property 'belonged to People in America as a Consequence of which they intended to proceed immediately to the Sale of the Whole'. He also alleged rough treatment by Rodney's men, that the French traders were allowed to smuggle their wares to Guadeloupe, and that the captives under Rodney's command were commanded to dig up private gardens and even tombs in their quest for money that might be confiscated.[25] He was careful to add that the same treatment was meted out to the most 'respectable merchants', who were 'torn from their families and sent on board the King's Ships on pretense that their having traded and corresponded with the Enemies of Great Britain was an Act of Treason'.[26]

A speech in Parliament from Edmund Burke (using much of the detail supplied by Lambert) raised awareness of the debacle, and indeed the success was a short-lived one. The island was soon back in the hands of the Dutch via a brief interlude under French rule. Lambert and James Blair were just two of the pirate traders Rodney robbed, but the contents of their claim to Parliament for compensation is where we can find the extent of the portfolio managed by this teenage trader.

Lambert Blair was the twenty-seventh claimant to submit paperwork to the Admiralty Dutch Prize Court on 5 November 1782. His claim began with an exultation or a cry for help, 'In the name of God Amen!', and proceeded to outline in no particular order exactly what had been taken from him in the Rodney raid. The first item listed was a trunk containing twelve dozen pairsof women's French 'heels and shoes', and indeed the majority of goods in the first section of the claim were of this type: handkerchiefs, men's shoes, thread of various types, Irish linen sheets, medicine, ivory-handled knives, gloves, stays and so on. Blair's warehouse was a mixture between a fine clothes merchant, a draper's and a haberdashery. There were also the makings of a grocer's inventory. Lambert was trading butter, tallow for candles, beef, mutton, cider, book-cases, muskets, ninety-two jugs of gin and 300 lb of tobacco. Lambert Blair would sell a customer just about anything from his warehouse in Statia; it was a sort of pirate version of Harrods of London. His inventory totalled, he estimated, about £4,195, some of which belonged to other parties.[27] Among the notes in the claim are several affidavits from Lambert, lots of duplicate accounting and some letters of support. One of those letters was sent by Stratford Canning (1747–87), an Irish-born (the family was at Garvagh, Derry, from about 1618) and London-based merchant, and father of future diplomat the First Viscount Canning, also named Stratford.[28] He suffered a loss of about £819.[29] It also reveals some of the chains of supply to St Eustatia. The Irish linen, for example, was routed through London, and Thomas Oliver, aboard the 'good ship Blake' to St Kitts, where Robert Crawford would then convey it to St Eustatia and to the Blair brothers.[30] Other London-based merchants mentioned in the file are people such as Hugh Johnstone and Robert Kennedy, who had lost about £590 because of the raid and subsequent auction.

In the end Blair seems not to have been compensated for his possessions; indeed, only nine of the claimants were, despite the very public intervention of Edmund Burke on behalf of the claimants in Parliament.[31] St Eustatius was famous as a pirating and smuggling hub, or, as Rodney put it, a 'nest of villains' that 'deserved scourging', so it may have been with a grimace that any claim was paid by the Crown.[32] The island had long been a thorn in the side of those seeking to regularise trade in the region, and a particular threat to British interests there, since it had helped to supply the Americans during the War of Independence. It first rose to prominence as a slave depot in the early eighteenth century, then sugar defined the mid-eighteenth century. It had been dubbed the 'Golden Rock' in the 1770s, having become a major tea- and tobacco-trading hub servicing North America. In fact, the Tea Act of 1773, which led to the Boston Tea Party and thus, in no small measure, to the American Revolution, was prompted by the fact that Statia, along with Curaçao, had become the largest (illegal) supplier of tea to the American colonies since 1770. Not content with helping to spark the revolution, Statian merchants (allegedly) profited handsomely when the conflict arose, providing a tariff-free trading hub for gunpowder and other war materials all through the war.[33] Rodney's attack of 1781, then, was not an accidental one. The British would have seen the Dutch-facilitated free trade on the Golden Rock as one of several reasons it lost the First British Empire.[34] The scandalous arrest of many Irish New York merchants in 1762 for trading with the French was an early harbinger of the same retributive system of punishment for trade with the enemy that now beleaguered Lambert Blair in St Eustatius.[35]

St Eustatius was a free-trade utopia where money could be made quickly (Figures 11.3 and 11.4). By the time the teenage Lambert Blair was resident, the Lower Town of this small island teemed with up to 600 warehouses along a one-mile stretch of beach, all competing for trade in contraband.[36] A Scottish traveller remembered vividly the competitive prices and the stink of tobacco smoke blown in her face.[37] It was on this beach that Lambert Blair probably made his first fortune. He retained a base there, at least until 1789–90, when Samuel Shaw travelled through the area and anchored at Statia. Shaw, the first American Consul at Canton, references the house of James and Lambert Blair at Statia, but in his hierarchy of the significant inhabitants of the island they came after several other houses that were all more respectable. Shaw and his companions dined with Henry Jennings, the principal merchant of the island, and had excellent things to say about the reputable nature of his trade and that of the House of Hardtman and Clarkson, as well as a Mr Haffey.[38] Jennings and several of the others mentioned were in fact originally Bermuda-based and, in the case of Jennings, descended from one of the most notorious pirates in the region during Queen Anne's reign. Shaw is likely to have been sympathetic to this odd crew because the island had proved so important to American trade in a time of recent intense crisis.[39]

Lambert and James Blair next turn up on the neighbouring island of St Christopher (St Kitts), where they were scalping a 12 per cent commission on all profits from reselling goods and enslaved people. They were in

Figure 11.3 P. F. Martin, map of St Eustatia, 1781, showing the warehouses on the lower beach at the bottom centre.

Figure 11.4 *The Late Auction at St Eustatia* (London: E. Hedges, 11 June 1781).

business with agencies such as Copland & Hodgson, and the Liverpool-based Backhouse & Co., and were therefore involved in the triangular trade among Dutch, British and Spanish interests, and particularly in the Jamaican and Cuban slave trade.[40]

Cornelius Stevenson seems to have left for St Croix, his estates breaking up some time after that, and he is most often noted as a merchant of New York by the 1790s.[41] His connections with the Dutch power in the region must have remained consistently strong, however. By 1792 Stevenson was being spoken of as a potential consul. By this point in the early 1790s, Lambert, now in his early twenties, could be found ferrying enslaved people to Berbice, his new centre of operations, and in a schooner named after Governor Pierre Godin, the Dutch official in charge of St Eustatius.[42] By the mid-to-late 1790s his brother James had died, having resided for some time in Dominica and Grenada, at least according to notices in the press.[43] From this point onwards Lambert seems to have traded on his own name. Douglas Hamilton notes a debt of more than £27,000 owed by Lambert Blair & Co. after the disastrous collapse in sugar prices in the region around 1794, which at least shows the scale of his operation, but other than this it is difficult to discern how Blair managed to accrue such a colossal fortune.[44] It is clear that much of his career was spent working between the English and the Dutch imperial interests, but that his fortune was made on the back of inter-island trade in humans as well as other commodities. At no point, however, does he seem to have involved himself in direct sourcing of enslaved people from Africa. Quite how he came to possess so many of them, then, remains something of a mystery, but it is possible that it resulted from a combination of good timing, as well as a sort of amoral liminality enjoyed by Irish traders operating at the interface of various empires.

The Berbice River ran from New Amsterdam through present-day Eastern Guyana and into what was often referred to as Suriname. Since the mid-eighteenth century the Dutch had controlled the three main colonies that ran from the coast into the hinterland via three large rivers, and these were Berbice, Essequibo-Demerara and Suriname. The Berbice colony fell into the hands of the British in 1796 but was restored in 1802 at the Treaty of Amiens, only to be lost to the British again in 1804. In the early nineteenth century the population was, according to the *Edinburgh Encyclopaedia* at any rate, about 43,500 in all, with 1,000 free non-whites; 2,500 whites; and the rest classified as negro, and thus enslaved.[45] The territory was sandwiched between Suriname, Demerara, and opening out into the Caribbean at New Amsterdam.

It would seem that Blair had recovered sufficiently from his indebtedness in 1794 to be able to take advantage of a late-eighteenth-century fire sale of lots along the Berbice River. A total of eighty grants were made by the Dutch Suriname Government between 1795 and 1799, and Lambert Blair received at least twenty of these, a quarter of the entire colony.[46] This grant was given despite an uncertainty as to who might be governing the colony of Berbice, and thus Blair appears to have gained possession at just the right moment. There was a delay in the arrival of Ralph Abercromby, the commander-in-chief of the naval forces in the area. Abercromby didn't get to Berbice until 1799, at which point Suriname came under British control, and that meant that Lambert Blair, as a British subject, was able to take advantage of the change of ownership.[47] In 1802 he expanded his holdings with the purchase of Le Rossignol, near the coast at New Amsterdam, and another 1,000 acres near Devil's Creek, bringing his total holdings to more than 20,000 acres of plantation land producing a mix of cotton and sugar.[48]

James Rodway, author of an 1893 history of Berbice, notes that Lambert Blair had taken up cotton plantations along the coast and was an 'inveterate enemy of Governor Abraham Van Batenburg' at the time of transfer into British hands. The Governor had survived the transfer of powers from the Dutch to the English in 1796, simply staying on under the new regime. An extended version of this enmity came to the notice of the Crown in 1806, when a memorial signed by George Baillie and Lambert Blair made its way to the Government, censuring the Governor in the most emphatic terms in a thirty-two-page diatribe.[49] It accused him of misappropriation of enslaved people, funds and property, as well as the issuance of proclamations. Van Batenburg maintained that he had no idea what lay at the root of Baillie's grievances, but he had some choice things to say about Lambert Blair:

> The zeal of Mr Blair for the general good had never yet been proved on any occasion, but the contrary was often complained of, and the steps he had now taken proceeded from a cowardly wish to avenge himself ... They all knew him; there were amongst them those who had experienced the sordidness of his interested disposition, and nobody would deny that when that man was actuated by motives of interest, the meanness of his character was fully displayed, while his pompous pride was likewise conspicuous when he exhibited his ridiculous vanity. Both had been wounded and hurt by him, and now Blair had avenged himself in a manner congenial to his feelings.[50]

Berbice had been rather slowly colonised since Walter Raleigh had first searched the region for the mythical El Dorado in the 1590s. The Dutch came at about the same time and remained the dominant presence through the seventeenth and eighteenth centuries, albeit with occasional interference from their French and British rivals. The Berbice River was, and remains, just one of several thousand rivers and creeks that created a 900-mile stretch of coastline between the Orinoco and Amazon Rivers. As Randy Browne notes, the 'brackish water was shallow, and a seemingly endless series of shoals, sandbars, and mudflats shifted faster than cartographers could update their maps'.[51] Part of the Greater Caribbean economy and society through trade and communication, the river is analogous to the Colombian coastline and several regions of the Mexican Gulf, in that its economy really answered outwards into the Atlantic world.[52] The harbour at the mouth of the river near New Amsterdam was considered too much of a risk for most transatlantic carriers: few enslavers or traders ever landed directly at Berbice, preferring nearby Demerara. This meant that the bulk of their goods and enslaved people were sourced from secondary markets of the type that reselling traders such as the Blair brothers specialised in. This particular problem restricted growth in the region until the British became more involved there in the 1790s. The three main colonies of the Guianas at Suriname, Berbice and Demerara-Essequibo all experienced a boom in this period and were, for a brief period, the most profitable plantations in the Greater Caribbean, before the rise of Cuba.[53] As the Dutch, French and British empires all readjusted, it was another of those periodical and cyclical moments where the liminality of Irish imperialists worked to their advantage. Their ability to work the lines among those empires, in much the same way that the New York Irish merchants had in the 1760s, was useful to all. Indeed, there is a notable rise of Irish presence in Suriname, Demerara and Berbice in these decades. This boom time, fuelled by slaves and human capital, is the context for Lambert Blair's excess.

Around the time that Blair was consolidating his wealth, Dr George Pinckard found himself scribbling his three-volume *Notes on the West Indies*, first published in 1806 but based on his experiences in the region around 1796. In and around this time we know from Colonial Office correspondence that the Blair brothers had in excess of 20,000 acres at Berbice, having bought the Rosignol plantation at the mouth of the river later in 1802, and having added two East Coast plantations near Devil's creek, both of about 1,000 acres or so at plantations 40 and 41; these must have been their original holdings, and the site that Pinckard visited, called Utile and Paisable.[54] It is difficult to estimate the value of Blair's human property in the 1790s, but on the nearby island of Carricou the going rate in 1784 was about £33 each. African males, depending on their place of origin, cost from £40 to £50 as field workers; their women counterparts sold between £30 and £40. If an African labourer was between twelve and eighteen, in six years they would be as valuable as a Creole, who sold for about £60 if male, and £10 less if female. By the 1790s the average price had risen to about £40.[55]

When Pinckard sat at Blair's table, then, he was being served by the enslaved people of a self-made late-plantocracy magnate and probable former pirate from Newry. The feast, as described by Pinckard, sounds extraordinary by the standards of any place and time, but is exceptional when one considers how remote the plantation, how inhospitable the climate, and how anachronistic the dishes were to both:

> It was a birth-day festival, and perhaps a more choice and sumptuous repast could not have been found, even in the proud city of London. The dinner table exhibited a happy combination of English taste, and Irish hospitality. It was served in the style of Europe, and displayed a profusion of the best and richest viands, without any of the more common dishes of the country, such as Moscovy duck, Guinea-fowl, kid, and the like. Amidst a crowded variety of other covers we had a large green turtle, with a great variety of the best European vegetables, and, to crown the feast, a complete course of sweets, consisting of no less than four-and twenty dishes. The fruits were endemic, and such as London with all its riches cannot produce. The drinking part of the feast was such as I have described to you before. At no other house in the colony are such entertainments given.[56]

The drinking was no less excessive.

> The cook was quite proficient, and did every justice to the feast, the whole dinner being well dressed, and as well served. We had afterwards pines, shaddocks, melons, water-lemons, and multitudes of other fruits. Nor were the fluids of the banquet less amply administered. Hock, Claret, Madeira, and Port wines were in liberal use. We had also Seltzer and Spa waters, likewise bottled small beer, ale, and porter, with brandy, rum, Hollands, noyeau, and other liqueurs – all in supply sufficient for a lord mayor's feast.[57]

The extent to which the entire estate simply served this need for opulence and excess can be gleaned from another of Pinckard's letters – this one marvelling at the systemic abilities of the plantation to serve the needs of the host and his guests:

> After our good eating and drinking we took a walk about the plantation, and found every corner of it equally plenteous as the table and the cellar. Such a store of living stock, both large and small, I had not seen upon any estate since my arrival in the Western world. Here were large herds of cows, oxen, sheep, and goats; droves of hogs, horses, and mules; flocks of geese, turkies, ducks, Guinea fowls, and chickens. A more gratifying assemblage of domestic plenty could scarcely be found in any country. Among the stock I should not omit to mention a pen of living turtles kept in readiness for the table:– whole droves of crabs were also running about near the door;– and the neighbouring sea is, at all times made tributary to the board. Several hundreds of negroes employed at work, or moving from place to place, improved the variety of the scene; while they added essentially to the value of the home – for, like the cattle, these are always included in calculating the stock of the estate. Together with the multitude of domestic productions at this all-supplying abode were likewise some of the more rare and curious specimens – such as the small lion, –monkey – and the large powys, or wild turkey of the woods; also the trumpeter, the flycatcher, and several other uncommon birds. Our walk was highly gratifying, and offered much to excite, as well as to interest our contemplations.[58]

Blair's opulence earned him great praise from his guest, who was apparently unperturbed by the gauche displays of the nouveau riche plantocracy. Lambert Blair's will also displayed appetites that ranged beyond his table. Although it is almost unreadable, we can see that he left £250 to a 'mulatto' man named James Lambert Blair who was in Berbice at the time and 'well-known' to his executors, and that he also left money to 'a mustee lad' James Blair, who was bred a ship carpenter in Lancaster but now resided in Berbice.[59] He manumitted his black servant David Maxwell, then living with him in England, and left him £100 and an annuity of £20 a year. He left £200 to a god-daughter whose name he could not recollect, the daughter of Kenneth Francis Mackenzie.[60] There is much to unpick here, but overall the impression is of a complex life with many questions arising from the way it was lived.

What can we learn from the excesses and tyrannies of a life such as Lambert Blair's? In this short piece we have encountered him in a series of disconnected episodes and have thus seen glimpses of a life observed mostly only through second-hand sources. Our subject is seen through the wide, drunk, eyes of George Pinckard, or the official testimony of a teenage Lambert Blair relating his memory of the Rodney affair of 1781: a series of letters from Newry during the childhood of 'Lamby' Blair. The recent work of Jonathan Wright and Mark Quintinalla has provided Irish historians with fuller reflections on Irish enslavers and traders than this fragmentary snapshot can allow. Their work draws out the presence of Irish people dotted among a diverse and dehumanising supply chain in the Caribbean economy in the late eighteenth century.[61] Blair gives us something else – a brief glimpse of excess consumption, of greed and avarice; an Irishman living large on human misery and converting all that economic and social capital to assets and cash that would later circulate through the generations at home, in London and in Ulster. Blair is a challenge to Irish historians, an unwanted reclamation project. A person we must admit to.

Notes

1. John McCamon was the only son of Lambert's sister, Anne Blair, and Moses McCamon, and therefore a nephew of Lambert's. He is named as a nephew in his will.
2. Lowell J. Ragatz, *The Fall of the Planter Class in the British Caribbean 1763–1833: A Study in Social and Economic History* (New York: Octagon Books, 1977), p. 52; further biographical detail from R. Thorne, 'Blair, Sir James (?1788–1841)', in *The History of Parliament: The House of Commons 1790–1820* (London: Secker and Warburg, 1986), p. 216.

3 See 'Newry', in George Henry Basset, *County Down Guide and Directory* (Dublin: Sealy, Bryers and Walker, 1886), pp. 71–134; and Tony Canavan, *Frontier Town: An Illustrated History of Newry* (Belfast: Blackstaff Press, 1989).
4 Sir James Marriott and Sir George Hay, eds, *Decisions in the High Court of Admiralty: During the Time of Sir George Hay, and of Sir James Marriott, Late Judges of That Court* (London: R. Bickerstaff, 1801), p. 261.
5 Nini Rodgers, *Ireland, Slavery and Anti-Slavery: 1612–1865* (London: Palgrave Macmillan, 2007), p. 94.
6 Douglas Hamilton, *Scotland, the Caribbean and the Atlantic World, 1750–1820* (Manchester: Manchester University Press, 2005), p. 104.
7 George Pinckard, *Notes on the West Indies*, 3 vols (London: Longman, Hurst, Rees and Orme, 1806), Vol. II, Letter XXII, p. 361.
8 Crister Petley, 'Gluttony, excess, and the fall of the planter class in the British Caribbean', *Atlantic Studies* 9:1 (2012), 85–106 (p. 85).
9 Maria Nugent, *Lady Nugent's Journal: Jamaica One Hundred Years Ago: Reprinted from a Journal Kept by Maria, Lady Nugent, from 1801 to 1815, Issued for Private Circulation in 1839* (Kingston: Institute of Jamaica, 1939). Also quoted in Petley, 'Gluttony', p. 85.
10 See Vaughn Scribner, 'Cosmopolitan colonists: Gentlemen's pursuit of cosmopolitanism and hierarchy in British American taverns', *Atlantic Studies* 10:4 (2013), 467–96, for a discussion of this contrast.
11 For the present state of the field of modern Ireland and empire see Jill C. Bender, 'Ireland and Empire', in Richard Bourke and Ian McBride, eds, *The Princeton History of Modern Ireland* (Princeton: Princeton University Press, 2016), pp. 343–60; and Barry Crosbie, 'Ireland and the empire in the nineteenth century', in James M. Kelly, ed., *The Cambridge History of Ireland*, 4 vols (Cambridge: Cambridge University Press, 2017–18), Vol. III, *1730–1880*, pp. 617–36.
12 See in particular a useful summary of the literature in Zoë Laidlaw and Alan Lester, eds, *Indigenous Communities and Settler Colonialism: Land Holding, Loss and Survival in an Interconnected World* (Basingstoke: Palgrave Macmillan, 2015), pp. 1–23.
13 John Blair to James Blair 16 January 1796, Blair Papers, PRONI, D717/17. A birth date of 1767 is given for Lambert in several biographical sources, and is approximately confirmed on his memorial in Twickenham.
14 'Marriages', *Lancaster Gazette*, 12 August 1809, 3.
15 The National Archives, Kew (TNA), Bank of England Wills Extracts 1717–1845, no. 38864, Lambert Blair, Reg. 665, 1 March 1815.
16 A very small amount of his correspondence can be found digitised in the James Blair Collection 1781–1792, University of Chicago Library, www.lib.uchicago.edu/e/scrc/findingaids/view.php?eadid=ICU.SPCL.BLAIRJ (accessed 24 August 2022).
17 Joseph A. Goldenberg, 'The *William* and *Favorite*: The post-revolutionary voyages of two Philadelphia ships', *Pennsylvania Magazine of History and Biography* 98:3 (July 1974), 325–38, for more on Stewart and Nesbitt. For James Blair's New Orleans connections see Kristin Condotta Lee, 'Trading

18 James Blair to Samuel Huntingdon, Blair papers, Public Record Office of Northern Ireland (PRONI), D717/21.
19 Noted by the *Scots Magazine*, 6 February 1797.
20 Elizabeth Blair to James Blair, 1 April 1774, Blair papers, PRONI, D717/2. For some context on Irish docility in relation to new imperial measures see T. F. Moriarty, 'The Irish absentee tax controversy of 1773: A study in Anglo-Irish politics on the eve of the American Revolution', *Proceedings of the American Philosophical Society* 118:4 (1974), 370–408.
21 The Gloucester Place house is mentioned in a public letter from John McArthur around the time of A. Cochrane Johnstone's court martial for the Dominica mutiny; *Cobbett's Political Register* 10 (1806), 367–9.
22 Richard Stuteley Cobbett, *Memorials of Twickenham: Parochial and Topographical* (London: Smith, Elder, 1872), p. 91.
23 Researchers should note that this account book is at present mislaid in PRONI. Lambert Blair & Co., West Indies merchants, account book, 1795–9, PRONI, D1125.
24 Cornelius Stevenson figures in the correspondence of Benjamin Franklin during his time at St Eustatius. See for example Benjamin Franklin to Charles-Guillaume-Frédéric Dumas, 9 December 1775, www.founders.archives.gov/documents/Franklin/01-22-02-0172 (accessed 30 April 2020).
25 National Library of Ireland, Burke Papers, Reel 18, Book 7/9d. See also Gwenda Morgan and Peter Rushton, *Banishment in the Early Atlantic World: Convicts, Rebels and Slaves* (London: Bloomsbury, 2013), p. 222.
26 Burke Papers, Reel 18, Book 7/9d.
27 TNA, HCA 42/151, claim 27, James and Lambert Blair.
28 Canning was based at 10 Clements Lane, London, in the 1870s and had arrived in London around 1760. He had married Mehitabel Patrick, daughter of a Dublin merchant, against his father's wishes, and had to set up his business solo. Giles Hunt, *Duel: Castlereagh, Canning and Deadly Cabinet Rivalry* (London: I.B. Tauris, 2008), 15–16.
29 Stratford Canning was a first cousin of George Canning, future Prime Minister of the United Kingdom of Great Britain and Ireland. See Stanley Lane-Poole, *The life of Stratford Canning, Viscount Stratford de Redcliffe, from his memoirs and private and official papers*, 2 vols (London: Longman, Green, 1888), Vol. II, pp. 1–24.
30 TNA, invoice no.7, claim 27, James and Lambert Blair.
31 'To His Excellency the Governor of St. Eustatius', 'Summons' signed by G. B. Rodney and J. Vaughan, 3 February 1781, in George Brydges Rodney Mundy, ed., *The Life and Correspondence of the Late Admiral Lord Rodney*, 2 vols (London: John Murray, 1830), Vol. II, pp. 12–13. See also Morgan and Rushton, *Banishment in the Early Atlantic World*, pp. 216–20.
32 G. B. Rodney, quoted in Mundy, *Life and Correspondence of Lord Rodney*, Vol. II, p. 13.

33 Kenneth Breen, 'Sir George Rodney and St. Eustatius in the American War: A commercial and naval distraction, 1775–81', *Mariner's Mirror* 84:2 (1998), 193–203 (pp. 199–200).

34 Victor Enthoven, '"That abominable nest of pirates": St. Eustatius and the North Americans, 1680–1780', *Early American Studies: An Interdisciplinary Journal* 10:2 (2012), 239–301. For background on why St Eustatius and the Dutch more generally came to be seen as the secret enemy of British interests in the region see Mark Dragoni, 'Operating outside of empire: Trading citizenship in the Atlantic world, 1783–1815', Ph.D. thesis (Syracuse University, 2018), pp. 5–10.

35 This episode is covered brilliantly by Thomas Truxes, *Defying Empire: Trading with the Enemy in Colonial New York* (New Haven: Yale University Press, 2008).

36 Enthoven, 'That abominable nest of pirates'; Norman F. Barka, 'Citizens of St. Eustatius, 1781: A historical and archaeological study', in Robert L. Paquette and Stanley L. Engerman, eds, *The Lesser Antilles in the Age of European Expansion* (Gainesville: University Press of Florida, 1996), pp. 223–38.

37 Janet Schaw, *Journal of a Lady of Quality, Being the Narrative of a Journey from Scotland to the West Indies, North Carolina, and Portugal, in the Years 1774 to 1776*, ed. Evangeline Walker Andrews (New Haven: Yale University Press, 1939), pp. 135–6.

38 Samuel Shaw and Josiah Quincy, *The Journals of Major Samuel Shaw: The First American Consul at Canton. With a Life of the Author* (Boston, MA: W. M. Crosby and H. P. Nichols, 1847), pp. 327–8.

39 Andrew Jackson O'Shaughnessy, 'The other road to Yorktown: The St. Eustatius affair and the American Revolution', *Maryland Historical Magazine* 97:1 (2002), 33–59.

40 For Backhouse & Co. see Joseph E. Inikori, *Africans and the Industrial Revolution in England: A Study in International Trade and Economic Development* (Cambridge: Cambridge University Press, 2002), p. 419. For the Blair brothers' business connections see Henry B. Prieto Lovejoy, *Yorùbá Kingship in Colonial Cuba during the Age of Revolutions* (Chapel Hill: University of North Carolina Press, 2018), p. 45.

41 See, for example, an entry for Nicholas Cruger 370, 22 February 1800, in Berthold Fernow, *New York Calendar of Wills on File and Recorded in the Offices of the Clerk of the Court of Appeals, of the County Clerk at Albany, and of the Secretary of State, 1626–1836* (Baltimore: Genealogical Publishing Company, 1967 [1896]), p. 85.

42 See Han Jordaan and Victor Wilson, 'The eighteenth-century Danish, Dutch and Swedish free ports in the Northeastern Caribbean: Continuity and change', in Gert Oostindie and Jessica V. Roitman, eds, *Dutch Atlantic Connections, 1680–1800: Linking Empires, Bridging Borders* (Leiden: Brill, 2014), pp. 273–308 (p. 288).

43 Several notices give his death as either late 1796 or early 1797 at Dominica. *Scots Magazine*, 6 February 1797; *London Gazette*, 18 April 1798, 784.

44 Douglas Hamilton, *Scotland, the Caribbean and the Atlantic World, 1750–1820* (Manchester: Manchester University Press, 2010), pp. 103–4.
45 Sir David Brewster, ed., *Edinburgh Encyclopaedia*, 18 vols (Edinburgh: William Blackwood, 1808–30), Vol. III, pp. 461–3.
46 What became known as 'Blairmont' was composed of lots 17–20 and 37–8. It seems that, for a time, Blair became the richest planter in Berbice by some distance, and the largest enslaver.
47 This boundary dispute is covered comprehensively by Alvin O. Thompson, 'The Guyana–Suriname boundary dispute: An historical appraisal, *c.* 1683–1816', *Boletín de estudios latinoamericanos y del Caribe* 39 (1985), 63–84; and Alvin Thompson, 'Dutch society in Guyana in the eighteenth century', *Journal of Caribbean History* 20:2 (1985), 169–91.
48 See Rawle Farley, 'The shadow and the substance', *Caribbean Quarterly* 4:2 (December 1955), 132–53.
49 This is mentioned in James Rodway, *History of British Guiana, from the Year 1668 to the Present Time*, 3 vols (Georgetown: J. Thompson, 1891–4), Vol. II, *1782–1833*, pp. 269, 271; but is also covered in some detail by Henry Bolingbroke, *A Voyage to the Demerary* (London: R Phillips, 1809), pp. 60–3.
50 Rodway, *History of British Guiana*, Vol. II, p. 271.
51 Randy Browne, *Surviving Slavery in the British Caribbean* (Philadelphia: University of Pennsylvania Press, 2017), p. 13.
52 For a really good recent overview of this see Ernesto Bassi, *An Aqueous Territory: Sailor Geographies and New Granada's Transimperial Greater Caribbean World* (Durham, NC: Duke University Press, 2017).
53 Gert Oostindie, '"British capital, industry and perseverance" versus Dutch "Old School"? The Dutch Atlantic and the takeover of Berbice, Demerara and Essequibo, 1750–1815', *BMGN: Low Countries Historical Review* 127:4 (2012), 28–55. See also Seymour Drescher's classic, *Econocide: British Slavery in the Era of Abolition* (Chapel Hill: University of North Carolina Press, 1977).
54 TNA, CO 111/74, Von Batenburg to Camden, quoted in Farley, 'The Shadow and the Substance', p. 135.
55 Edwina Ashie-Nikoi, 'Beating the pen on the drum: A socio-cultural history of Carriacou, Grenada, 1750–1920', Ph.D. thesis (New York Universty, 2007), p. 53.
56 Pinckard, *Notes on the West Indies*, Vol. III, Letter IV.
57 *Ibid.*, Vol. II, Letter XXII.
58 *Ibid.*, Vol. II, Letter XXII.
59 For a history of the eighteenth-century term 'mustee' – which means one-eighth negro on an ethnicity scale – see Monique Deeann Asandra Kelly, 'Jamaican ethnic oneness: Race, colorism, and inequality', Ph.D. thesis (University of California Irvine, 2019); Arnold A. Sio, 'Race, colour, and miscegenation: The free coloured of Jamaica and Barbados', *Caribbean Studies* 16:1 (1976), 5–21; and B. W. Higman, *Slave Population and Economy in Jamaica, 1807–1834* (Cambridge: Cambridge University Press, 1976).

60 This is very probably the Kenneth Francis Mackenzie who owned the nearby estate of Lusignan at Berbice. His eldest daughter, by his wife Anne, is the likeliest of his eleven children to have been the beneficiary of Lambert's absent-minded generosity. Her name, for the record, was Isabella Jessy Mackenzie, later Baines, and she was born around July 1801.

61 Mark S. Quintanilla, ed., *An Irishman's Life on the Caribbean Island of St Vincent, 1787–90: The Letter Book of Attorney General Michael Keane* (Dublin: Four Courts Press, 2019). Jonathan Jeffrey Wright, ed., *An Ulster Slave-Owner in the Revolutionary Atlantic: The Life and Letters of John Black* (Dublin: Four Courts Press, 2019).

Part III

Comparative perspectives

12

Two islands, many forts: Ireland and Bermuda in 1624

Emily Mann

As crisis grew in 1624, the military engineer Nicholas Pynnar produced a report titled *The State of the Forts of Ireland* for the English King's representative there, Lord Deputy Henry Cary, First Viscount Falkland. The surviving large folio manuscript, bound in calf-skin covers, consists of fourteen elegantly delineated and carefully coloured drawings: four maps showing the havens of Waterford, Cork, Lough Neagh and Carlingford, and ten bird's-eye plans showing the forts of Duncannon, Waterford, Haulbowline, Cork, Kinsale, Limerick, Culmore, Galway, Banagher and Charlemont (see, for example, Figures 12.1, 12.2, 12.3).[1] Interspersed among the drawings are notes commenting on the condition of each fort.

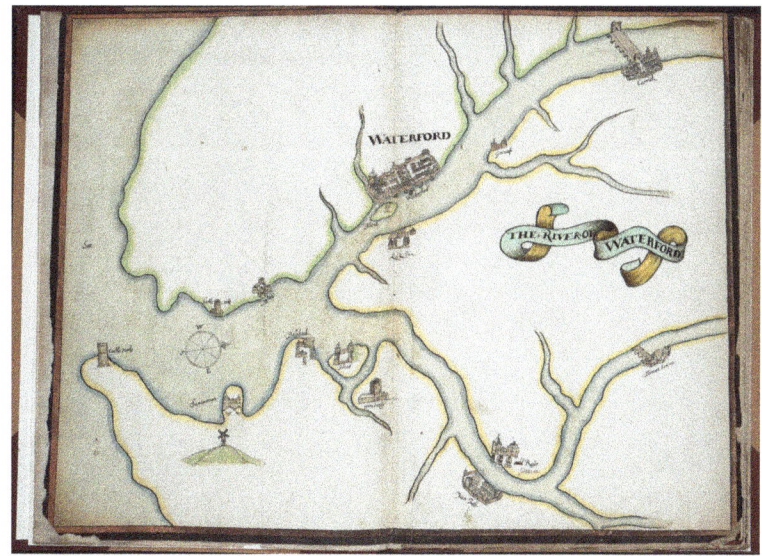

Figure 12.1 'The River of Waterford', in Nicholas Pynnar, *The State of the Fortes of Ireland as they weare in the yeare 1624*, British Library, Add. MS 24200, fos 2v–3r.

Figure 12.2 'The forte of Duncannon in ye harbor of Waterford', in Nicholas Pynnar, *The State of the Fortes of Ireland as they weare in the yeare 1624*, British Library, Add. MS 24200, fos 5v–6r.

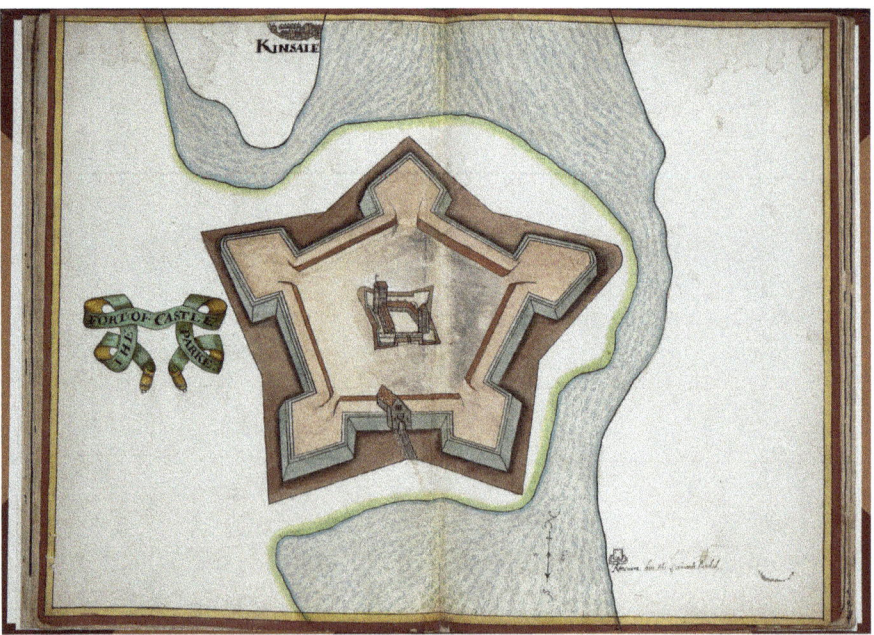

Figure 12.3 'The Fort of Castle Parke', in Nicholas Pynnar, *The State of the Fortes of Ireland as they weare in the yeare 1624*, British Library, Add. MS 24200, fos 20v–21r.

Captain Pynnar, who had been serving as director-general and overseer of fortifications and buildings in Ireland since 1618, concluded his report by expressing the hope that 'By this your Lordship may see the state of the forts as they were in times past when they were maintained and kept up, and how they are now at this present – all which I thought good to inform your Lordship, that some course may be taken for them as your Lordship in your wisdom shall think most fit.' In a letter included at the end of the volume, presumably also addressed to Falkland as Governor of Ireland and dated 5 May 1625, Pynnar reported on how he had, since receiving his Lordship's last letter, 'gone forward with the making of the new fort at Galway' as 'commanded by directions out of England', and how he would proceed directly to Cork with the aim of setting 'all things forward with as much expedition as I can'.

From the content as well as the presentation of the report, its leather binding embellished with the royal arms, we learn something of its significance and consequence. Pynnar's notes stress the disrepair and indefensibility of almost all of the forts featured, and his inserted letter from Galway (where the old fort was 'much decayed, for there is no parapet upon the walls') reveals that those who read the report did see fit to decide a course of action in response – though the engineer's urgent pleas for funds to continue the works under way indicate a degree of weakness in the administration, if not the construction. No other versions of Pynnar's report as presented here are known to survive, but its enduring value is suggested by its presence from the 1640s in the collections of the auditor-general and antiquarian of Ireland James Ware, whose manuscripts (acquired primarily for their bearing on Irish history) were purchased by Henry Hyde, Second Earl of Clarendon, when he was Lord Lieutenant of Ireland in 1686.[2] Clarendon deposited Ware's manuscripts in the public library that had been established in 1684 by the future Archbishop of Canterbury Thomas Tenison while rector of London's St Martin-in-the-Fields, and *The State of the Forts of Ireland* remained there until purchased by the British Library when the Tenison library was sold at auction in 1861.[3] Tenison's aim for the library, which contemporaries regarded as of national importance and was located just a short walk from the heart of government in Whitehall, had been to make accessible books and manuscripts 'which he regarded as most representative in English history'; two centuries later, as the British empire gathered force across the globe, the title page of Sotheby's catalogue for the sale of Tenison's 'highly valuable' manuscripts picked out Pynnar's depictions of forts in Ireland as among the items of 'great historical interest'.[4]

That Pynnar's report has since received little historical attention can be at least partly explained by its separation from related archival documents in Ireland and England, and its journey through successive (albeit prestigious) archival collections. Paul Kerrigan referred to the volume over a few pages in his survey of the development of artillery fortifications in Ireland from the fifteenth to the twentieth century, a study he prefaced with a quotation from John Hale that 'in the mainstream of architectural history fortifications are accorded but a fitful or embarrassed attention'.[5] Studies of architecture in Ireland covering the early seventeenth century have tended to centre on building types more typically favoured in the discipline of architectural history, and on localised areas of English colonisation. In essays focusing on the Ulster and Midland plantations, Rolf Loeber noted that comparative study is lacking between the architecture of these plantations and the rest of Ireland – and indeed beyond – and his own work on the period, as with Maurice Craig's, focused on castles and other elite domestic structures.[6] Eric Klingelhofer's work on English colonial fortifications in Ireland and further overseas is largely confined to the Tudor period, reaching only into the early years of James I's reign.[7] Whereas Craig, Loeber and Klingelhofer were led principally by standing remains and a growing body of archaeological evidence, researchers especially interested in early maps and plans of Ireland have shed most light on the surviving manuscripts produced by the surveyors Richard Bartlett, Francis Jobson, Josias Bodley (Pynnar's predecessor as director-general of fortifications) and Thomas Raven; Pynnar's maps and plans are rarely mentioned.[8] Similarly, historians trained on the written archive have found greater interest in Pynnar's 1619 text-only survey focused on the six counties of Armagh, Tyrone, Donegall, Cavan, Fermanagh and Londonderry, using it alongside other surveys – namely those of 1611 (by George Carew), 1613 (by Bodley) and 1622 (by a twenty-one-person commission including Thomas Phillips, who commissioned maps from Raven) – to assess progress, or not, through the first decade and a half of the Ulster plantation.[9] Thus Pynnar's 1624 report on the forts has fallen through disciplinary as well as archival gaps.

Pynnar's drawings and accompanying notes came to my own attention alongside other visual and verbal accounts of English colonial fortifications as part of comparison-based research of Ireland and the Greater Caribbean, including Bermuda as crucial to England's encroachments there – a retrieval that underlines how comparative strategies can help to excavate archives in freshly revealing ways.[10] After first establishing the immediate context of this overlooked manuscript and its importance as an English document or instrument of conquest that made Ireland visible and (in the colonial imagination at least) controllable and defensible, the rest of the chapter situates and studies it within the expanded spatial framework through which it was encountered.[11] Doing so reveals not simply the wider context of Pynnar's report, but the closely connected concerns and operations across landscapes lying thousands of miles apart, opening up these little-associated territories for comparative study. Responding to Audrey Horning's suggestions for the future direction of comparative analyses of Ireland and America, the comparative approach taken by this chapter moves beyond questions about the form, style, construction and even effectiveness of the fortifications discussed to consider the conditions and motivations for their representation and presentation on paper for viewers far removed from the lines on the ground.[12] More specifically, close attention to the documentary evidence illuminates an interconnectedness among colonies, in the vision and aims of contemporary authorities in the metropole, that can be inscrutable in the architectural and archaeological remains alone. The visual sources at the centre of this chapter expose the parallel construction in Ireland and Bermuda of militarised landscapes of subjugation and oppression that, in subsequent decades and centuries, were together crucial in shoring up English efforts to expand and maintain the empire, and to dominate the slave trade, in the Caribbean and beyond.

Ireland as 'inwork'

The arrival of Viscount Falkland as Lord Deputy in 1622 marked a turning point in Ireland's government. Through the figure of this English knight (albeit one with a Scottish title), who had served as comptroller of the royal household and member of the Privy Council as well as the Commons, the English court and Parliament asserted a new concern for and authority over Irish affairs.[13] Falkland was also a vigorous supporter of further confiscations and plantations as a means of securing Ireland under English rule and thereby achieving peace as well as profit – or so it was argued, despite the clear resistance of existing inhabitants of the territories targeted for expropriation.[14]

Falkland's governorship, including his personal ambition to establish plantations of his own in Co. Wicklow near the administrative centre of Dublin, was shaped by his belief that Irish lords were 'like nettles that sting being gently handled, but sting not being crushed'.[15] His chief engineer had helped crush Irish resistance during the Nine Years War (1594–1603), and was rewarded with land he had a hand in seizing. Falkland's fierce antipathy towards Catholicism was encouraged in Ireland when the attempted marriage settlement between Prince Charles and the Spanish infanta ended in failure in 1623, and a riled Charles, together with George Villiers, First Duke of Buckingham, stirred up support for war against Spain.[16] As part of Buckingham's expanding patronage empire in Ireland, Falkland wasted no time in resuming sectarian proclamations.[17] He ordered the 'Banishment of Jesuits and Priests &c' (whose confidence had been raised by the anticipated Catholic–Protestant alliance) and prohibited the import of 'warlike munition', such as gunpowder and firearms, in the same breath as cracking down further on the wearing of traditional Irish dress, which he observed had increased rather than abated: sheriffs and other officials were commanded to break long skeines (a type of knife), and to take off and cut to pieces 'before their faces' any 'mantles or trowses' worn in public.[18] Such legislative, cultural and physical attacks 'othered' the Irish in order to define and assert the superiority of English identity and so justify English rule in Ireland. It is in tandem with this suppression of the Irish, and against the background of the perceived threat of Spanish support and intervention (subsequent proclamations sought to halt the trade that had long flourished between the Irish and Iberian coasts), that we should read the report Pynnar produced on the forts for Falkland.[19]

Both engineer and Governor had already raised their concerns about the 'ruinous state' of Ireland's forts and castles. In 1621, Pynnar produced estimates for repairing multiple forts, and in September 1623 the Lord Deputy warned the Privy Council that, if they were not repaired, they were 'better to be razed' – rather that than offer any security for England's enemies.[20] Those enemies included Irish rebels as well as the Spanish, to whom they looked as potential allies. The strategic importance of Ireland from both English and Spanish perspectives is suggested by the chart made in Seville in 1520 by Juan Vespucio (Figure 12.4) which gives Ireland a

Figure 12.4 Chart by Juan Vespucio, 1520, Seville, Archivo General de Indias, MP-Europa_Africa, 125.

central position in the Atlantic world that was opening up in the geopolitics between the European powers – a perspective very often lost in more recent maps made for studies of early modern Anglo-Spanish relations, and in the arguments of many such studies too.[21] Vespucio imprinted on Ireland the English arms, and in English minds it stood as their 'back door', the ideal route and base for Spanish operations against them. In the words of an 'old prophesy' that Fynes Moryson, who served as secretary to Lord Deputy Mountjoy under Elizabeth I, suspected of encouraging the Irish rebellions of the Tudor Queen's reign: 'He that will England winne, Must with Ireland first begin.'[22] Elizabeth's Lord Deputy at the time of the Spanish Armada in 1588, William Fitzwilliam, warned of the weak state of the forts in 1590, stressing the 'danger of leaving the country unguarded, while the King of Spain makes such great preparations'.[23] The Spanish landing and occupation at Kinsale in 1601 proved the threat, despite being thwarted.[24] By the 1620s, the fear that Spain (or even France) would seize any opportunity to move in and keep the 'back door' open as a 'bridle upon England' was deeply embedded in English conceptions of and strategies towards Ireland.[25] Thus preparations for war, as Aidan Clarke explained, 'necessarily included taking steps to ensure the effective defence of Ireland', which was of 'the utmost strategic importance'.[26]

The centrality of Ireland in the preparations, and indeed machinations for war, are signalled by the Subsidy Act passed in April 1624. The Act represented a deal by which Parliament granted King James funds for war preparations on the conditions that he terminate the treaties with Spain and that the money be spent only on four specified purposes: 'the defence of this your realm of England, the securing of your kingdom of Ireland, the assistance of your neighbours the States of the United Provinces and other your Majesty's friends and allies, and for the setting forth of your royal Navy'.[27] A Council of War was appointed as part of the Act to approve how much was spent on what. Not only were senior-most members of the council of ten distinguished by their service in Ireland (Viscount Grandison, the first named, and Lord Chichester having both held the post of Lord Deputy; Lord Carew being a former President of Munster who returned to report on Ireland's condition; and Sir Thomas Button still serving as Admiral of the Irish Coasts), but a revised commission issued just three months later added Henry Docwra, chief adviser on Irish military affairs during the Nine Years War, first Governor of Derry and more recently treasurer of war for Ireland.[28] The wording of this commission also gave greater emphasis to Ireland – 'Whereas we are now to take such ways and means as shall be most requisite for securing our realm of Ireland, with the rest of our dominions, and putting our Navy Royal in readiness' – an emphasis echoed in many contributions to the parliamentary debates.[29] In these debates, following the King's speech on the matter, Ireland was envisioned not as an 'outwork' (as were the Low Countries), but as one of three 'inworks', a principal defence of England's 'dominiums' alongside the navy and the English ports.

As parts of this 'inwork', the forts surveyed by Pynnar had a role in the exercise of English power over both land and sea that is conveyed by the scope and organisation of the report. The first seven drawings cover the principal ports and harbours along Ireland's south coast, working from east to west, in effect offering an extension into the Atlantic of England's southwest coast (for Francis Bacon, Ireland was 'the second island of the ocean Atlantic').[30] The map of 'The River of Waterford' (Figure 12.1) is oriented west to show the expanse of 'goodly' harbour and the walled city at the centre, surrounded by urban settlements and a network of defences including the already historic Castle Hooke (the lighthouse at the harbour's entrance); Castle Crooke; Passage Fort; and Duncannon Fort, which was begun on the site of an earlier castle around the time of the Armada and strengthened under Bodley between 1608 and 1611.[31] The two subsequent drawings zoom in first on Duncannon (Figure 12.2) – occupying a peninsular jutting into the estuary but drawn to appear almost as a barrier across it, which in defensive terms it in effect was – and then on the fort under construction at Waterford, as an extension to the city walls. Next comes the fort on Haulbowline Island in the haven of Cork, a strategic deep-water position protecting the city beyond, and a map of the full haven (oriented west, as with the Waterford map) including King John's Fort and Corkbeg Fort at the harbour mouth; these are followed by a plan of the fort at Cork (Elizabeth Fort), which was constructed on high ground outside the city walls under Carew as President of Munster in 1601. This fort was built in direct response to the Spanish invasion of that year, as was the impressive pentagonal fort of Castle Park at Kinsale – shown in the final drawing covering the south coast (Figure 12.3) – which was completed to designs by the engineer and writer on fortification Paul Ive (who also designed Haulbowline fort) in the first decade of the seventeenth century, and added to by Bodley.[32]

The southern coastline of Munster thus surveyed in the report was understood to be particularly valuable and vulnerable by both England and Spain. David Wolfe, the Irish papal legate whose 'Description of the Realm of Ireland, Its Maritime Ports and Cities' urged a Spanish invasion in 1574, identified Waterford as Ireland's wealthiest city and, alongside Cork, Kinsale and others, to be the 'most serviceable for ingress into the kingdom … because with a fair wind one can sail from Biscay to those ports in four days'.[33] Over centuries, this coastline had become well known to the crews of Spanish fishing and trading vessels, and military knowledge was enhanced through the landings in 1601.[34] English memory and fear of this event is inscribed on Pynnar's plan of the fort at Kinsale. The modern pentagonal fort, large in reality yet drawn out of all proportion to the nearby town to the north and Rincurran castle to the southeast, is explained by a handwritten note added to the latter: 'Here the Spaniards landed.' However, the forts faced attacks led from land as well as sea. Wolfe noted Waterford and Cork as Catholic strongholds, and a half-century later, in 1625, Falkland reminded the Privy Council of the 'not-to-be-forgotten violence' with which the citizens of Cork, on hearing news of Queen Elizabeth's death in 1603, destroyed the new fort that had been named for her and 'built to command them'.[35] Kinsale's fort, according to its Governor, Admiral Button, would resist the Irish but not a foreign enemy.[36]

The next three drawings in Pynnar's report take the viewer north: first to the well-towered and turreted castle of Limerick – the strongest city in Ireland, according to Wolfe, and loyal to the English crown; then to Culmore at the mouth of the River Foyle, where Docwra had erected a fort on landing there in 1600, seeing its importance for taking and keeping Derry downriver (being, according to Pynnar in his survey of 1619, 'the only key and strength of the river that goeth to the Derry'); and from there to Galway, where English officials believed the Spanish would seek to land, if not 'in some Port of Munster', and heard rumours of 'Popish fathers' speaking in the Irish language of 'taking that fort'.[37] It was from Galway, in 1625, that Pynnar wrote his letter updating Falkland on progress at the new fort, which was considered the 'most necessary' alongside those at Waterford and Cork.[38] These forts were expected to serve a dual function of controlling the cities and protecting their harbours.[39]

By water the report shifts inland, to Banagher on the Middle Shannon, a contested site located near the intersection of the provinces (as set by the English) of Connacht, Leinster and Munster, at a bend in the river that natural fording made passable. Described as lying on a 'chief highway into Connaught', a fort was begun here on confiscated land in 1621, and on completion was named for Falkland as the new Lord Deputy.[40] Pynnar showed it newly finished, with strong defences facing both the river and the town, which it stood between. The map that follows depicts Lough Neagh and its river systems, which became the centre of Irish resistance in the Nine Years War and, from then on, central to England's hold on territories in the north, being renamed Lough Chichester after the new Lord Deputy and landowner who had led indiscriminate attacks on the rebels. The map is oriented roughly east so that closest to the viewer lies Co. Tyrone, which Pynnar noted was the 'only breakneck of the war in those parts'. In Pynnar's rendering, the great freshwater lake's shoreline is studded with forts, castles and settlements, while two boats on the lough signal their vital service (as the accompanying note explains) in transporting victuals and men. The 'fort of Blackwater' in the southwest corner of the lough indicates the inflow of the Blackwater River where, further upstream, the fort of Charlemont was rebuilt on the site of an earlier campaign fort for Lord Caulfeild, who had long served the English in Ireland and was now Master of the Ordnance. Pynnar's plan of Charlemont shows a strikingly handsome 'house or castle' at the centre of the fort, which he notes was 'lately built' at Caulfeild's 'own cost and charge', and his depiction of the town outside the fort's walls (seemingly including a mixture of building styles suggestive of both colonisers and colonised) points to the rents that made such luxury possible.

Pynnar's drawings end by returning to the coast with a map of Carlingford Lough, oriented roughly south to emphasise the importance of Carlingford itself, supported by the other English garrison towns of Greencastle and Newry on the opposite bank of the lough to east and west. The strategic importance of the harbour had been highlighted during the Nine Years War, when it was feared that Spain might attempt to invade here as the key to the northeast.[41]

Between the focal points of the first and last maps of the survey – Waterford and Carlingford respectively – sits Dublin, the administrative centre of English rule in Ireland, where the castle was similarly surveyed for repairs by Pynnar, and Falkland oversaw aggrandising architectural renovations including 'a stately long Gallerie and many other places of conveniences for the chief Governour and his family'.[42] Dublin, and by extension the Privy Council and King in England, to whom the administration there reported, is the implied vantage point of Pynnar's survey of the forts, suggesting its part in a wider process of centralisation. While the western orientation of the drawings of Waterford and Cork havens echoes earlier maps of Ireland as 'seen' from the east – such as John Goghe's 1567 manuscript map *Hibernia*, and subsequent printed maps by Abraham Ortelius, Baptista Boazio and Willem Blaeu – the shifting orientation as the survey progresses, with the sheets themselves moving the viewer west then north, followed by the map of Lough Neagh looking east and that of Carlingford Lough south, gives the impression of a roving, if not all-seeing, eye.

What did the eye see? Most clearly, it could see into the past, but it was also encouraged to envision the future. Pynnar's drawings were designed to enable the viewer, as he wrote in the report, to 'see the state of the forts as they were in times past when they were maintained and kept up', and so to see how they might appear anew. His written notes resound with evidence – rotten platforms, palisades lost, ordnance lying on the ground, houses ready to fall down (all this just at Duncannon) – of what was needed to restore them to their former state. Judging by Pynnar's clear, clutter-free plans, their former state was strong and orderly, free of encumbrance or obstruction by any person or thing. But that, as with the platforms and palisades, looked starkly different on the ground. Those employed in the design and construction worked in fear of attack by local citizens – the 'danger of disorder' being such in Cork and Waterford that Falkland considered it the 'safest course' to state his intention to begin at Haulbowline Island and Duncannon (near Cork and Waterford respectively) until the arrival of sufficient additional soldiers 'to repress any resistance of the proceedings of the engineers' in the cities themselves.[43] Such soldiers as there were had long suffered lack of pay, sustenance and morale.[44] In August 1625, Pynnar reported that work was going well at Cork, but urged the forwarding of funds, as menacingly large sums of money were being bet on the forts never being finished.[45] By 1626, Pynnar's fellow director-general of fortifications, Thomas Rotherham, was suspected of having left the new fort at Galway because he feared 'he could not resist an attack there', where 'talk of a plantation' was causing 'more fear than the Spaniards'.[46]

While holding out a memory and promise of military strength (however abstracted or illusionary), Pynnar's survey of the forts and subsequent reports draw attention to very real weaknesses in English rule in Ireland, especially as crisis threatened. In doing so, they compounded the troubling findings of the 1622 commission of inquiry into the condition and administration of the plantations and beyond, just as, through Falkland's lord deputyship, they could also be seen as part of the response to its findings – namely that the English Lord Treasurer Lionel Cranfield, Earl of Middlesex, had reduced military expenditure to the extent that Ireland was in effect defenceless as war with Spain once again loomed.[47] It was in 1624 that Thomas Phillips, as one of the appointed commissioners for Londonderry, petitioned the King for the impeachment of the City of London companies for long neglecting their responsibility to build and oversee their plantations, and Grandison, Carew and Chichester were called on to consider his charges and the consequence that 'their towns and fortresses are rather baits to ill-affected persons than places of security'.[48]

Phillips's accusations of mismanagement echoed those of Nathaniel Butler against the Virginia Company presented to the Privy Council the year before: if action were not taken, Butler claimed, the plantation there would 'shortly get the name of a slaughter house and so justly become both odious to ourselves and contemptible to all the world'.[49] Butler had spent several months in Virginia following the uprising against the colonists by the Powhatan people in 1622, having sailed there from Bermuda where he had been Governor since 1619 (his patron being Nathaniel Rich, another of the commissioners for Ireland); from this position he was particularly scornful of the lack of fortifications he found there, which left the colony

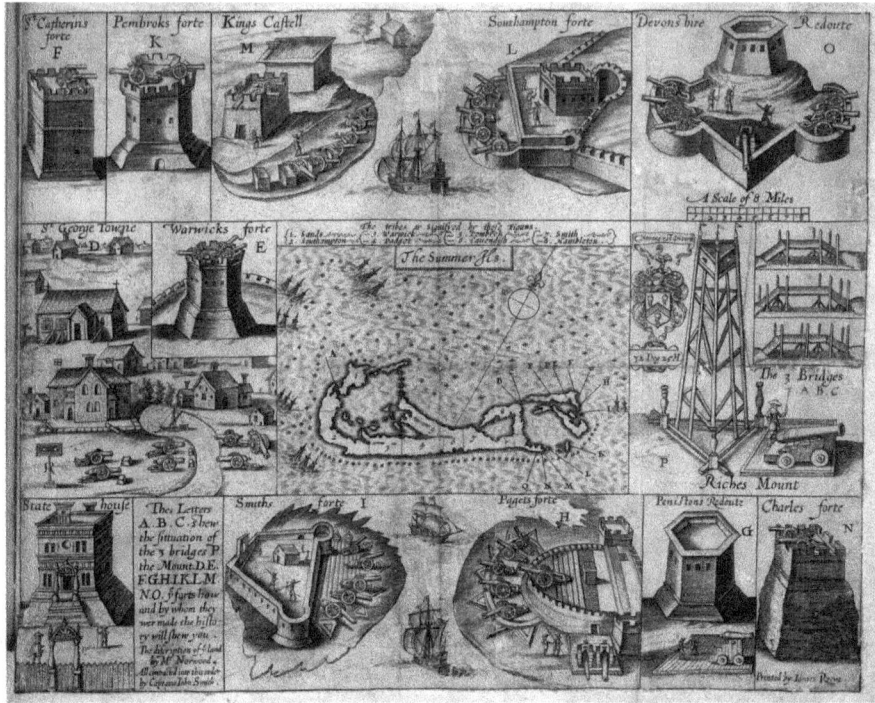

Figure 12.5 'A Mappe of the Somer Isles and Fortresses', in John Smith, *The Generall Historie of Virginia, New-England, and the Summer Isles* (London, 1624).

easy prey for a foreign enemy. As Horning has pointed out, 1622 – the year of the Ireland inquiry and of the Virginia 'massacre', as it became known – 'proved significant in the fortunes and legacies of each colonial project'.[50] I have argued elsewhere that the Virginia Company's failure to build an image of dominance in America as compared to Bermuda under Butler – a comparison Butler clearly made, at least in his own mind – helps to explain why the Virginia Company was dissolved in May 1624 while the Bermuda Company was allowed to carry on.[51] It is the image of Bermuda rushed into print the same year in John Smith's *Generall Historie of Virginia, New-England, and the Summer Isles* (which I previously compared to the reused earlier map of Virginia in the same volume) that, considered alongside Pynnar's contemporary survey, not simply widens the contextual frame, but offers a point of comparison that helps deepen our understanding of the functions of the fortifications, their representation and, more expansively, the specific significance of both islands as foundational (however unstable) in English colonial ambition and activity in the Atlantic world (Figure 12.5).[52]

Islands in the Virginian Sea

Captain Smith's printed image of Bermuda was designed to convey the strength and stability of the colony, which had been formally begun in 1612 following a providential shipwreck en route to Virginia in 1609. The map at the centre, drawn from a survey produced by Richard Norwood in 1616–17, shows the territory divided into eight 'tribes' (today known as parishes) named for the company's major investors. Working with compass and surveyor's chain, and probably starting from the shoreline and working inwards – as done in Chichester's plantations in Ireland, discussed in this volume's introduction – Norwood subdivided these large lots of land into thin strips, or 'shares', that bisected the narrow main island from coast to coast, at once maximising the settlers' access to water and enhancing security through the proximity of their houses.[53] The unnumbered slim stretch of land to the northwest, originally called Long Point, was soon renamed Ireland Island: the map of Bermuda produced in 1626 for John Speed's *Prospect of the Most Famous Parts of the World* (first published in 1627) – which constituted a historical as well as geographical project of mapping by including the Roman empire in addition to 'Great Brittaines empire' – inscribes this final fragment of a fully occupied archipelago as 'Ireland' (see Figure 12.6).[54] A further inscription

Figure 12.6 'A Mapp of the Sommer Ilands', engraved by Abraham Goos for George Humble, 1626, and published in John Speed, *Prospect of the Most Famous Parts of the World* (London, 1627).

in both Latin and English, located beneath the island at the centre of the map, recounts how 'About midsomer 1616, five persons departed from these Ilands in a Smal open boat of some 3 tunn and after 7 weeks arived al safe in Ireland, the like hath scarce bene hard of in any age.' Thus the map (a more detailed representation of Norwood's survey) made explicit the connections, both physical and psychological, between the two colonies. Echoing the geography and geopolitical relation of Ireland and Britain, Ireland Island eventually became Bermuda's principal defence.

Smith's image of Bermuda surrounds the measured and carved-up land with views of the fortifications, town and state house that had been built during the first decade of settlement, the views probably based on drawings produced by Butler while Governor. Castles and cannon point in all directions. Bermuda's forts included a series of low, thick limestone blockhouses and gun platforms (St Catherine's Fort, for example, and Peniston's Redoubt), as well as more complex designs with layered outworks (such as Southampton and Pagets forts) – a combination that was also found in the haven of Waterford in Ireland (see, in Figure 12.1, Castle Crooke and Duncannon Fort on the harbour's opposite banks). The defences in both places were constructed or updated with elements that reflect the growing influence of continental theories and practices on English military architecture, as translated and taught by Paul Ive: at Duncannon, over decades, outworks were added, including ramparts in the form of a *tenaille trace*, and earthworks were strengthened by walls of stone and lime mortar; at Southampton Fort in Bermuda, Butler oversaw the addition of ravelins, triangular bastions or outworks recommended by Ive for rapid defence.[55] In both cases, familiar coastal-defence types were adapted to new conditions, though the more considerable landward works in Ireland signal the perceived need for greater defence against internal threats on an island of a vastly different scale (over 32,000 square miles in total as opposed to Bermuda's 21 square miles).

However, forts were tools of defence and control not just in their designed form, but in the process of their construction and reconstruction. Faced with the threat of internal subversion, even 'an uncivil civil war', Bermuda's first Governor, Richard Moore, maintained civil order by keeping the settlers 'hard at work' building the forts and by presiding over their construction (in the view of the island's minister) like the pharaohs did the pyramids, thus 'oppressing his Christian brethren'.[56] The expedient use of large numbers of local labourers at Waterford and other forts probably served this additional purpose – as suggested by the order from England that the citizens of Cork, having razed Elizabeth Fort to the ground in 1603, should be made to rebuild it in recompense (and at their own expense).[57] Nonetheless, the tiny archipelago, with no pre-existing population and within a few years fully mapped and planted, was far easier to command as well as conceptualise, as Smith's image forcefully testifies. The very different prospects offered by the two islands are made clear (even if propagandised) in a London newsletter of 1611, which reported the decision to begin a colony in Bermuda, a place 'so opulent, fertile and pleasant that all men were willing to go thither', alongside rumours that the citizens of London were 'exceeding weary of their Irish plantation'.[58]

While both the image of Bermuda and the fortifications it represents are distinct from those of Pynnar's report, the arrangement of maps and views ('all contracted into this order by Captain John Smith', as noted in the print) is suggestive of a way in which Pynnar's drawings are likely to have been read. Smith drew on a form of map that was increasingly popular in the seventeenth century, the *carte à figures*, in which the central cartographic content is framed by a panelled border, typically decorated with full-length portraits and panoramas.[59] Malcolm Andrews associates this style of map-making, which offers much more than cartographical information, with the 'curiosity of an expansionist nation' wanting to know the distinctive features of foreign lands.[60] A 'Mr Griffin', serving on HMS *Tramontana* in 1601, employed such a format for his *A True Description of the North Part of Ireland* in around 1601 (Figure 12.7),

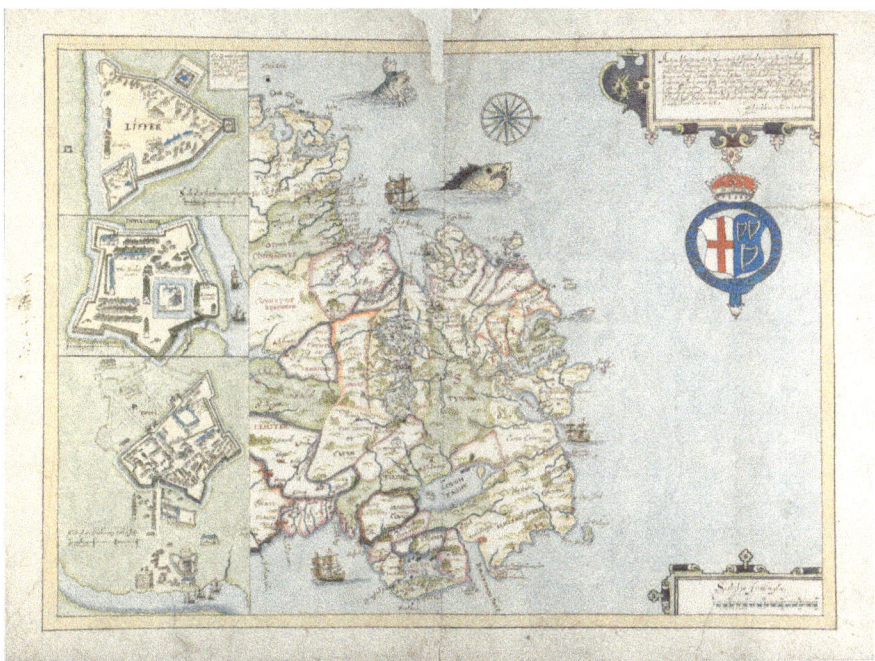

Figure 12.7 'Mr Griffin', *A True Description of the North Part of Ireland*, c. 1601, Trinity College Dublin, MS 1209/14. Reproduced courtesy of Trinity College Dublin.

which combines a map – reaching from Dundalk Haven in the northeast to Broad Haven in the northwest – with three inset bird's-eye plans of fortifications on the Foyle River at Lifford, Dunnalong and Derry.[61] This 'rare hybrid of information from land and sea', as J. H. Andrews described it, was to become an increasingly common mode of representation reflecting a way of experiencing territory, and directing a way of seeing it from a distance.[62] Smith's aim, by encircling the map of Bermuda with what appears to be a solid ring of forts (which were in fact concentrated around the most vulnerable coastline to the east), was to present an image of total control and conquest, emphasised in the words of the motto accompanying his coat of arms: *Vincere est vivere* (To conquer is to live). We see what had been known as the 'isle of devils' (in particular feared for its rocky reefs so dangerous to ships) tamed into an English stronghold.[63] Pynnar's survey is far more indeterminate, yet it performs a comparable kind of mapwork in the way it organises the images of dispersed structures and sites into one overall view that covers not one region or another, but plots out the whole of Ireland through the key infrastructure of English forts on land and English-patrolled waters in between. To borrow a phrase from the geographer Bernard Nietschmann, Pynnar provided a 'geographic montage of places that comprises a country'.[64] The map of that country may be missing on paper, but would be conjured in the mind by the encirclement of the drawings as bound.[65] And while individual forts may have needed urgent repairs, collectively they appear as a system evoking a comprehensive and coherent English presence – an entire island cognitively claimed, if not physically tamed.

Pynnar's decision to depict the forts in Ireland in their well-maintained state, using the accompanying notes to describe their current condition, points to the perceived power and effect of images – the reason why Phillips asked Raven to draw plans to help make his case against the City of London, and why Thomas Stafford, in his history of the wars in Ireland under Elizabeth, included maps and views 'for the better understanding of the story'.[66] Pynnar's drawings on their own build a hopeful picture designed to persuade decision-makers to fund and facilitate the repairs needed to restore them to the good order that they saw, just as Smith added his image of Bermuda to his *Historie* as evidence of the 'industry in fortifying' he wrote about in the text, aiming further to encourage new settlers and support for the company. Images could well deceive. That much is clear from Pynnar's notes, and from Butler's own account of Bermuda, in which he explained that his work at Southampton Fort was designed to make 'a very fair show out to sea' and warned that, without sufficient munitions, even the colony's best forts 'are little better than scare-crows'.[67] In both places, the importance of being *seen* to fortify was understood as crucial (Lord Deputy

Mountjoy, in 1602, proposed that 'if they [the Spanish] hear of our fortification works they may desist, and turn their malice another way'), and in both cases it was Spain that was felt to be watching.[68] In the same months that England prepared for an invasion of Ireland in 1624, Butler reported to Rich the discovery of a Spanish ship sent with a commission to make 'an attempt upon the Sommer Ilands [an English renaming of Bermuda] to cut our people's throats there'.[69] Images, including such stark verbal ones, were both a weapon and target in war and competition against Spain, from the English colonial maps that fell into Spanish hands in Seville to the painting of England's victory at Kinsale that Spanish ambassadors were accused of slashing in the corridors of Whitehall.[70] Smith's image was perhaps as much intended as a warning to Spain as it was as a lure to English viewers. Had Pynnar's drawings, or copies of them, been seen by Spanish eyes, they might have made a better impression of English defences in Ireland than did his words.

Despite their vastly different sizes, Ireland and Bermuda compare more closely in their strategic importance as islands whose contours were being made clear as part of England's expanding commercial and colonial world – an importance that explains the parallel concerns for their fortifications, and their representation, in 1624. In 1611, after reports of the English shipwreck on Bermuda spread, King Philip III claimed the archipelago for Spain; the islands fell among the territories granted to Spain in the Treaty of Tordesillas of 1494, but had been visited only occasionally by Spanish sailors (the early-sixteenth-century commander Juan de Bermúdez apparently giving the archipelago its name) and were left unoccupied. Hearing that the Virginia Company was preparing to send a ship equipped with 'whatever is necessary to erect a fort', intending to 'secure a better footing and continue more conveniently in their design', the Spanish authorities determined to act swiftly to halt English endeavours, which they considered a 'danger to their West Indies' (Norwood certainly saw Bermuda's value 'for the easy and commodious planting of other parts of this new world').[71] Soon after the English ships were dispatched to Bermuda in 1612, there was 'much talk about a Spanish Armada which is gathering; some say it is for Virginia, some for England, some for Ireland. The latter most probable'.[72] Spanish concern over the English settlement of Bermuda and English concern over the invasion of Ireland intersect in the two nations' rivalry for control of the seas between these islands – Spain saw Ireland as a potential 'bridle upon England', England saw Bermuda as a potential bridle on the Spanish empire – and England's tightening grip on both islands was crucial not just for the continued settlement of mainland America and the shapes that took, but for the increasing encroachments and consolidation of colonies in the Caribbean. When war with Spain was imminent in 1624, Butler proposed that Bermuda should be used as a base from which to attack the Spanish treasure fleets; that may not have been pursued (officially at least), but English possession of Bermuda, which served as a 'bridge' and 'nursery' to Virginia, encouraged the settlement of a series of islands in the Caribbean starting with St Kitts in that same year.[73] Ireland's role in provisioning those islands, the fleets on which they depended and their emerging slave societies – in which the hard physical labour of building fortifications became another means of subjugating the enslaved – would become even more key.[74]

The comparison opened up by the synchronous representation of English fortifications in Ireland and Bermuda emphasises the extent to which the militaristic colonisation of these divergent lands was primarily driven by wider designs on the seas. In the view of the Secretary of State William Cecil, Lord Burghley, in 1571, keeping a hold on Ireland was vital to further expansion because, should it fall instead into Spanish hands, Spain would be 'a more potent prince on the sea than England'.[75] Echoing English officials who subsequently spoke of the forts in Ireland as 'bridles' in the mouths of its citizens, Smith envisaged Bermuda as 'an excellent bit to rule a great horse'.[76] Ireland and Bermuda were vital in stitching and keeping a hold on the reins of an English imperial infrastructure, the built ruins of which maintain a hold on the landscapes and memories of both islands today.

Notes

1 British Library (BL), Add. MS 24200, Nicholas Pynnar, *The State of the Fortes of Ireland as they weare in the yeare 1624*. Apart from titles in footnotes and captions, I have in most cases modernised spellings throughout.

2 The complicated descent and present whereabouts of Ware's manuscripts are traced in William O'Sullivan, 'A finding list of Sir James Ware's manuscripts', *Proceedings of the Royal Irish Academy: Archaeology, Culture, History, Literature* 97C:2 (1997), 69–99. On Ware's political importance in Irish administration see Mark Empey, 'The diary of Sir James Ware, 1623–66', *Analecta hibernica* 45 (2014), 55–146. While there is no known copy of the report, the Hardiman Atlas at the library of Trinity College Dublin (TCD) contains similar plans, including two made by Pynnar while overseeing work at Waterford and Cork in 1626 (TCD, MSS 1209/50 and 1209/66); and the British Library holds equally similar plans of Duncannon, Limerick, Galway, Kinsale and Haulbowline (BL, Cotton MS Augustus I ii 31 and 33–6), suggested to be the work of Pynnar's predecessor, Josias Bodley, but possibly produced later. Paul M. Kerrigan, *Castles and Fortifications in Ireland, 1485–1945* (Cork: Collins Press, 1995), p. 81, took them to be Bodley's work, on which Pynnar based his own.

3 *Catalogue of a Highly Valuable Collection of Manuscripts, Formed by Archbishop Tenison during the Reigns of Kings Charles II, James II, William III, and Queen Anne, Comprising Very Early and Important Manuscripts on Vellum* (London: J. Davy and Sons, 1861), lot 76, p. 25. *The State of the Fortes of Ireland* was one of twelve manuscripts purchased by the British Library, mostly earlier and of a religious nature (BL, Add. MSS 24191–202).
4 On the establishment of the library see Edward Carpenter, *Thomas Tenison, Archbishop of Canterbury: His Life and Times* (London: SPCK, 1948), pp. 23–26 (p. 25). *Catalogue of a Highly Valuable Collection of Manuscripts*.
5 Kerrigan, *Castles and Fortifications in Ireland*, pp. 80–4; J. R. Hale, *Renaissance Fortification: Art or Engineering?* (London: Thames and Hudson, 1977). See also John Hartnett McEnery, *Fortress Ireland: The Story of the Irish Coastal Forts and the River Shannon Defence Line* (Bray: Wordwell, 2006), pp. 16–17.
6 Rolf Loeber, 'The early seventeenth-century Ulster and Midland plantations, part I: Pre-plantation architecture and building regulations', and 'The early seventeenth-century Ulster and Midland plantations, part II: The new architecture', in Olivia Horsfall Turner, ed., *'The Mirror of Great Britain': National Identity in Seventeenth-Century British Architecture* (Reading: Spire Books, 2012), pp. 73–99, 101–38. See also Rolf Loeber's posthumously published collection *Irish Houses and Castles, 1400–1740* (Dublin: Four Courts Press, 2019). Maurice Craig, *The Architecture of Ireland from the Earliest Times to 1880* (London: Batsford, 1989), pp. 111–36.
7 Eric Klingelhofer, 'Tudor overseas fortifications: A review and typology', in Eric Klingelhofer, ed., *First Forts: Essays on the Archaeology of Proto-Colonial Fortifications* (Leiden: Brill, 2010), pp. 65–83. Eric Klingelhofer, *Castles and Colonists: An Archaeology of Elizabethan Ireland* (Manchester: Manchester University Press, 2010), deals with fortifications principally in chapter 2, and otherwise discusses mainly domestic architecture, as does his chapter 'Colonial castles: The architecture of social control', in David S. Shields, ed., *Material Culture in Anglo-America: Regional Identity and Urbanity in the Tidewater, Lowcountry, and Caribbean* (Columbia: University of South Carolina Press, 2009), pp. 102–14.
8 William J. Smyth, in his monumental *Map-Making, Landscapes and Memory: A Geography of Colonial and Early Modern Ireland c. 1530–1750* (Cork: Cork University Press, 2006), includes Bartlett, Jobson, Bodley and Raven, but does not mention Pynnar. Nor do Pynnar's drawings seem to have interested J. H. Andrews in his extensive research on the mapping of Ireland. Annaleigh Margey's *Mapping Ireland c. 1550–1636: A Catalogue of Manuscript Maps of Ireland* is forthcoming from the Irish Manuscripts Commission; her previously published work on the subject has focused on the plantation maps of Ulster.
9 The copy of Pynnar's 1619 survey at Trinity College Dublin (MS 864) was first printed in Walter Harris, ed., *Hibernica; or, Some Antient Pieces Relating to Ireland* (Dublin: printed by Edward Bate, 1747), pp. 73–128; and subsequently in George Hill, *An Historical Account of the Plantation of Ulster at the Commencement of the Seventeenth Century* (Belfast: McCaw, Stevenson and Orr, 1877), pp. 449–590. Nicholas Canny, *Making Ireland British, 1580–1650*

(Oxford: Oxford University Press, 2001), only mentions Pynnar in relation to this survey: see pp. 207–8, 211. Canny uses the spelling 'Pynner'; alternative spellings found include 'Pynnor', 'Pinnar' and 'Pinner'.

10 The digitisation of selected drawings has separated word and image, as well as obscuring the volume as a whole.

11 The idea of a 'document of conquest' is borrowed from Smyth, *Map-Making, Landscapes and Memory*.

12 Audrey Horning, *Ireland in the Virginian Sea: Colonialism in the British Atlantic* (Chapel Hill: University of North Carolina Press, 2013), p. 357.

13 Canny, *Making Ireland British*, pp. 246–7.

14 *Ibid.*, pp. 260–4.

15 Oxford, Bodleian Library, Carte MS 30, Falkland to Buckingham, fos 211–12, cited in Canny, *Making Ireland British*, p. 261.

16 For a detailed study of the dramatic reversal in policy following the failure of the Spanish Match and its political context see Thomas Cogswell, *The Blessed Revolution: English Politics and the Coming of War, 1621–1624* (Cambridge: Cambridge University Press, 1989).

17 On Buckingham as 'grand bounty-master' in Ireland see Victor Treadwell, *Buckingham and Ireland 1616–1628: A Study in Anglo-Irish Politics* (Dublin: Four Courts Press, 1998).

18 See proclamations 247 and 252, in Robert Steele, ed., *Tudor and Stuart Proclamations 1485–1714*, 2 vols (Oxford: Clarendon Press, 1910), Vol. II, pp. 26–7.

19 See the proclamation 'forbidding the export of pipe staves' (no. 254) and that of January 1626 forbidding 'the subjects of the Realme of Ireland, to have any trade or commerce within any the Dominions of the King of Spaine, or the Arch-duchesse' (no. 269), in *ibid.*, Vol. II, pp. 27, 29.

20 Lord Deputy and Council to the Privy Council, 3 November 1621, in Charles W. Russell and John P. Prendergast, eds, *Calendar of the State Papers, Relating to Ireland, of the Reign of James I, 1615–1625* (London: Longman, 1880) (*CSPI, 1615–25*), pp. 339–40; Lord Deputy to the Privy Council, 5 September 1623: *CSPI, 1615–25*, p. 429.

21 Seville, Archivo General de Indias, MP-Europa_Africa, 125. In Cogswell, *Blessed Revolution*, for example, the single map showing 'Europe on the eve of the Thirty Years' War' (p. xiii) cuts off about halfway through Ireland and leaves it unnamed.

22 Fynes Moryson, *An Itinerary* (London: printed by John Beale, 1617), Part II, Book 1, Chapter 1, p. 3. The proverb was also cited in the 'Description of the Realm of Ireland' written by the Irish papal legate David Wolfe for the Spanish ambassador in Lisbon in March 1574, in which he urged 'that his Catholic Majesty should not let slip the opportunity of taking so good and beautiful a kingdom' and thus deal a blow to both English and Flemish heretics; J. M. Rigg, ed., *Calendar of State Papers Relating to English Affairs in the Vatican Archives, Vol. II, 1572–1578* (London: HMSO, 1926), www.british-history.ac.uk/cal-state-papers/vatican/vol2/pp148-169 (accessed 6 February 2021).

23 Lord Deputy to the Privy Council, 5 November 1590, in Hans Claude Hamilton, ed., *Calendar of State Papers, Ireland, 1588–1592* (London: HMSO, 1885), www.british-history.ac.uk/cal-state-papers/ireland/1588-92/pp370-372 (accessed 6 February 2021).

24 John J. Silke, *Kinsale: The Spanish Intervention in Ireland at the End of the Elizabethan Wars* (Liverpool: Liverpool University Press, 1970); Hiram Morgan, ed., *The Battle of Kinsale* (Bray: Wordwell, 2004); Ciaran O'Scea, 'The significance and legacy of Spanish intervention in West Munster during the Battle of Kinsale', in Thomas O'Connor and Mary Ann Lyons, eds, *Irish Migrants in Europe after Kinsale, 1602–1820* (Dublin: Four Courts Press, 2003), pp. 32–63.

25 'Memorandum on the Present State of Ireland', 11 November 1625, in Robert Pentland Mahaffy, ed., *Calendar of State Papers Relating to Ireland, in the Reign of Charles I, 1625–1632* (London: HMSO, 1900) (*CSPI, 1625–32*), pp. 46–7. In November 1624, reports reached England of a 'great and mightie' Spanish navy, 'far bigger than that of 1588 ... intended for Ireland'; see William Risam to the Earl of Northampton, 27 November 1624, forwarded to the Privy Council, 3 December 1624, in Mary Anne Everett Green, ed., *Calendar of State Papers Domestic: James I, 1623–25* (London: HMSO, 1859), www.british-history.ac.uk/cal-state-papers/domestic/jas1/1623-5 (accessed 20 March 2021) (*CSPD, 1623–25*).

26 Aidan Clarke, 'The army and politics in Ireland, 1625–30', *Studia hibernica* 4 (1964), 28–53 (p. 28). On the strategic significance of Ireland see also (for example) Pádraig Lenihan, ed., *Conquest and Resistance: War in Seventeenth-Century Ireland* (Leiden: Brill, 2001), especially pp. 25–52, 115–50, 151–76.

27 For the Act see J. R. Tanner, *Constitutional Documents of the Reign of James I* (Cambridge: Cambridge University Press, 1960), pp. 374–81; for analysis see Michael B. Young, 'Revisionism and the Council of War, 1624–1626', *Parliamentary History* 8:1 (1989), 1–27 (esp. pp. 2–6); also Cogswell, *Blessed Revolution*, pp. 135–262.

28 Tanner, *Constitutional Documents*, pp. 376–7, 380. The 'precedence' of Grandison as an Irish peer did not go undisputed by the English Lords Craven and Brooke; see Chamberlain to Carleton, 13 May 1624, in *CSPD, 1623–25*. The British Library's suggestion that the Cotton manuscript drawings of the forts were first held by Grandison supports the possibility that these five works were made at this time rather than earlier (by or under Bodley), or at least the possibility that they were presented to the Council of War, though it has not been possible at time of writing to investigate the provenance.

29 See, for example, the entries of 19 and 20 March 1624, in Philip Baker, ed., *Proceedings in Parliament 1624: The House of Commons, British History Online, 2015–18*, www.british-history.ac.uk/no-series/proceedings-1624-parl (accessed 3 February 2021). The increasing importance of Ireland in the work of the Privy Council is suggested by the accumulation of committees to which Irish affairs were delegated in the later years of James's reign; see E. I. Carlyle, 'Committees of council under the earlier Stuarts', *English Historical Review* 21:84 (1906), 673–85 (pp. 674–5).

30 Francis Bacon, speech to the House of Commons, 3 February 1621, in James Spedding, ed., *The Letters and the Life of Francis Bacon*, 7 vols (London: Longmans, Green, Reader and Dyer, 1861–74), Vol. VII, p. 175. In this way, the sea was more a pathway than a barrier: see Lenihan, ed., *Conquest and Resistance*, pp. 115, 175.
31 Moryson, *An Itinerary*, Part II, Book 2, Chapter 1, p. 119. Kerrigan, *Castles and Fortifications in Ireland*, pp. 41, 59–60.
32 Drawings of Paul Ive's designs for the forts of Haulbowline Island and Kinsale are included in the Hardiman Atlas, TCD, MSS 1209/52 and 1209/55. Kerrigan, *Castles and Fortifications in Ireland*, p. 61.
33 Wolfe, 'Description of the Realm' (see n. 22). Wolfe cited a speech made by Henry Sidney as Lord Deputy in 1569, in which he urged vigilance in all the seaports, especially on the southern coast.
34 Kerrigan, *Castles and Fortifications in Ireland*, p. 37. O'Scea, 'The significance and legacy of Spanish intervention'.
35 Lord Deputy of Ireland to the Privy Council, 10 March 1625, *CSPI, 1625–32*, p. 569. See also 'A Fort at Cork, Now Destroyed, Erected by Sir George Carew, Lord President of Munster', TCD, MS 1209/49.
36 Kerrigan, *Castles and Fortifications in Ireland*, p. 83.
37 'Captain Nicholas Pynnar's Survey of the Works and Plantations performed by the City of London in the City and County of Londonderry', 28 March 1619, *CSPI, 1615–25*, p. 379. Moryson, *An Itinerary*, Part II, Book 1, p. 34. Lord Deputy and Council to the Privy Council, 3 November 1621, *CSPI, 1615–25*, p. 339.
38 Copy of a letter from the Council of War to the Lord Deputy of Ireland 'touching the repair of the forts there', 22 June 1625, *CSPI, 1625–32*, p. 19.
39 Kerrigan, *Castles and Fortifications in Ireland*, p. 39.
40 Letter from Mathew De Renzi, a German planter, to the Lord Deputy and King of England, The National Archives, Kew (TNA), cited in Howley Hayes Architects, 'Historic Banagher, Co. Offaly: Conservation, interpretation and management plan' (April 2018), p. 8, www.offaly.ie/eng/Services/Heritage/Landscape-Streetscape/Banagher-Conservation-Plan-2018.pdf (accessed 25 August 2022). Kerrigan, *Castles and Fortifications in Ireland*, p. 81. On the confiscation see *CSPI, 1615–25*, p. 339.
41 Lord Deputy and Council to the English Privy Council, 28 April 1602, in Robert Pentland Mahaffy, ed., *Calendar of State Papers, Ireland, 1601–1603, with Addenda* (London: HMSO, 1912), www.british-history.ac.uk/cal-state-papers/ireland/1601-3 (accessed 31 December 2020) (*CSPI, 1601–1603*). On a scheme for building two fortifications in the north as the area of Ireland 'which lies most open to foreign invasion, and where the inhabitants are the most rebellious', see papers of 11 April 1624, *CSPI, 1615–25*, p. 479.
42 'Captain Pynnar's estimate of the charge for the repair of Dublin Castle', 5 April 1624, in *CSPI, 1615–25*, p. 479. Robert Ware (1678), cited in J. B. Maguire, 'Seventeenth-century plans of Dublin Castle', *Journal of the Royal Society of Antiquaries of Ireland* 104 (1974), 5–14 (p. 10). Although it is not

certain that Pynnar ordered his report in this way, the armorial binding of it in such a manner is what counts.
43 Lord Deputy of Ireland to the Privy Council, 10 March 1625, in *CSPI, 1615–25*, pp. 569–70.
44 See, for example, Lord Deputy and Council to the Privy Council, 13 October 1621, in *CSPI, 1615–25*, p. 337: 'speedy order for the payment of this poor army "to repair their tottered carcases, lean cheeks and broken hearts"'.
45 Extract from a letter from Captain Nicholas Pynnar (here spelled 'Pinner'), 25 August 1625, in *CSPI, 1625–32*, p. 33.
46 Copy of a letter of Justice Osbaldeston to the Earl of Clanricarde, touching the town and county of Galway, 1 February 1626, in *CSPI, 1625–32*, p. 89. Only a month before, Falkland had insisted that Rotherham knew 'the men in the town by long experience' and was 'very confident of their loyalty'; Lord Falkland to the Council, 26 January 1626, *CSPI, 1625–32*, p. 83.
47 Canny, *Making Ireland British*, pp. 245–7. Report of the 1622 commission, BL, Add. MS 4756. Victor Treadwell, *The Irish Commission of 1622: An Investigation of the Irish Administration 1615–22 and Its Consequences 1623–24* (Dublin: Irish Manuscripts Commission, 2006).
48 *CSPI, 1615–25*, pp. xxv, 514–15 (quotation p. 515); see also pp. 527–30.
49 Nathaniel Butler, 'The Unmasked face of our Colony in Virginia as it was in the Winter of the yeare 1622', TNA, PRO, SP 16/526/98, in Susan Myra Kingsbury, ed., *Records of the Virginia Company of London, 1622–24*, 4 vols (Washington: Government Printing Office, 1906), Vol. II, pp. 374–6 (quotation p. 76).
50 Horning, *Ireland in the Virginian Sea*, p. 276.
51 Emily Mann, 'To build and fortify: Defensive architecture in the early Atlantic colonies', in Daniel Maudlin and Bernard L. Herman, eds, *Building the British Atlantic World: Spaces, Places, and Material Culture, 1600–1850* (Chapel Hill: University of North Carolina Press, 2016), pp. 31–52.
52 John Smith, *The Generall Historie of Virginia, New-England, and the Summer Isles* (London: Michael Sparkes, 1624).
53 See Michael Jarvis, 'Bermuda's "Domesday Book": Richard Norwood's surveys and the development of the Somers Islands, 1616–63', *Post-Medieval Archaeology* 45:1 (2011), 54–73, esp. pp. 55–8.
54 John Speed, *A Prospect of the Most Famous Parts of the World* (London: printed by John Dawson for George Humble, 1627).
55 On Duncannon see Kerrigan, *Castles and Fortifications in Ireland*, pp. 41, 59–60. [Nathaniel Butler], *The Historye of the Bermudaes or Summer Islands*, ed. J. H. Lefroy (London: Hakluyt Society, 1882), p. 204. Lefroy attributed the 'Historye' (BL, MS Sloane 750) to John Smith, but comparison of the handwriting has since been used to confirm Nathaniel Butler's authorship; C. F. E. Hollis Hallett, *Butler's History of the Bermudas* (Bermuda: Bermuda Maritime Museum Press, 2007).
56 Smith, *The Generall Historie*, p. 178.

57 Kerrigan, *Castles and Fortifications in Ireland*, p. 41. See 'A Brief Declaration of Some Part of the Treasons, Offences and Misdemeanors Committed and Done by the Mayor, Recorder and Bailiff of the City of Cork Since They Had Notice of the Decease of Our Late Sovereign Lady Queen Elizabeth', 14 May 1603 (and surrounding reports), in Charles W. Russell and John P. Prendergast, eds, *Calendar of the State Papers, Ireland, 1603–1606* (London: Longman, 1872), www.british-history.ac.uk/cal-state-papers/ireland/1603-6 (accessed 31 December 2020). The recorder, in his testimony, remarked that 'the raising of the fort cost the Queen nothing, it being raised with the sweat of their brows'.

58 Newsletter dated 26 June 1611, printed in 'Advice for investors in Virginia, Bermuda, and Newfoundland, 1611', in David B. Quinn, *Explorers and Colonies: America, 1500–1625* (London: Hambledon Press, 1990), pp. 421–30 (pp. 429–30).

59 Jonathan Potter, *Country Life Book of Antique Maps* (London: Country Life, 1988), pp. 26, 166–7.

60 Malcolm Andrews, *Landscape in Western Art* (Oxford: Oxford University Press, 1999), pp. 82–3.

61 TCD, MS 1209/14.

62 J. H. Andrews, *Shapes of Ireland: Maps and Their Makers, 1564–1839* (Dublin: Geography Publications, 1997), p. 111 (the map is only partially illustrated on p. 108). The format was used by John Speed in *The Theatre of the Empire of Great Britaine* ([London?]: [n. p.], 1611/12) and *A Prospect of the Most Famous Parts of the World*.

63 Silvester Jourdain, *A Discovery of the Barmudas, Otherwise Called the Ile of Divels* (London: printed by John Windet, 1610). According to Jourdain (p. 9), 'no man was ever heard to make for the place, but against their wills'.

64 Bernard Nietschmann, 'Authentic, state and virtual geography in film', *Wide Angle* 15:4 (1993), 4–12 (pp. 6–7).

65 This mapwork is comparable to that of texts that 'traverse' and 'organise'; David J. Baker, 'Off the map: Charting uncertainty in renaissance Ireland', in Brendan Bradshaw, Andrew Hadfield and Willy Maley, eds, *Representing Ireland: Literature and the Origins of Conflict, 1534–1660* (Cambridge: Cambridge University Press, 1993), pp. 76–92 (p. 79).

66 [Thomas Stafford], *Pacata Hibernia: Ireland Appeased and Reduced. Or, An Historie of the Late Warres of Ireland*, 2nd edn (London: printed for A. M., 1633), quotation on title page. The illustrations include plans of Limerick Castle, Haulbowline Fort and Castle Park at Kinsale that are either copies of Pynnar's, or are based on the same earlier plans used as models by Pynnar (see pp. 108–9, 252–3, 353–4).

67 [Butler], *The Historye*, p. 279. Vernon A. Ives, ed., *The Rich Papers: Letters from Bermuda 1615–46* (Toronto: University of Toronto Press, 1984), p. 229.

68 Lord Deputy and Council to the English Privy Council, 28 April 1602, in *CSPI, 1601–1603*.

69 Nathaniel Butler to Nathaniel Rich, 22 February 1624, in Ives, *Rich Papers*, pp. 225–6.

70 See Seville, Archivo General de Simancas, MPD, 19, 163 and MPD, 04, 066. On the painting see Hiram Morgan, 'The affair of the pictures', *History Ireland* 24:3 (2016), www.historyireland.com/volume-24/the-affair-of-the-pictures (accessed 31 December 2020).
71 Letter from the English ambassador in Madrid, Lord Digby, to Lord Salisbury, 9 March 1612 (1613?), in Alexander Brown, *The Genesis of the United States*, 2 vols (Boston, MA: Houghton Mifflin, 1891), Vol. II, p. 539. Ives, *Rich Papers*, p. 380.
72 Giovanni Biondi to Carleton, 7 January 1613, in Mary Anne Everett Green, ed., *Calendar of State Papers Domestic: James I, 1611–18* (London: HMSO, 1858), www.british-history.ac.uk/cal-state-papers/domestic/jas1/1611-18 (accessed 31 December 2020).
73 William Crashaw, dedicatory epistle, in Silvester Jourdain, *Discovery: A Plaine Description of the Barmudas, now called Sommer Ilands* (London: W. Welby, 1613), sig. A3v. Neil Kennedy, 'William Crashaw's bridge: Bermuda and the origins of the English Atlantic, 1609–1624', in Nancy L. Rhoden, ed., *English Atlantics Revisited: Essays Honouring Professor Ian K. Steele* (Montreal: McGill-Queen's University Press, 2007), pp. 107–35.
74 On Ireland's role in provisioning see Raymond Gillespie, *Seventeenth-Century Ireland: Making Ireland Modern* (Dublin: Gill and Macmillan, 2006), Chapter 9, section on 'Economic restructuring'.
75 'Considerations for a League with France', 22 August 1571, in Allan James Crosby, ed., *Calendar of State Papers Foreign: Elizabeth, Vol. IX, 1569–1571* (London: HMSO, 1874), www.british-history.ac.uk/cal-state-papers/foreign/vol9/pp500-520 (accessed 31 December 2020).
76 Lord Deputy of Ireland to the Privy Council, 10 March 1625, in *CSPI, 1625–32*, p. 569. Smith quotation from the 1629 edition of *The Generall Historie*, cited in J. H. Lefroy, ed., *Memorials of the Bermudas*, 2 vols (Bermuda: Bermuda Historical Society and Bermuda National Trust, 1981 [1876–7]), Vol. I, p. 494.

13

Imperial barrack-building in eighteenth-century Ireland and Jamaica*

Charles Ivar McGrath

On 13 October 1703 the English Council of Trade and Plantations called before them the Jamaican Agents in London, in order to address the grievances of the soldiers stationed on the island. With the soldiers living in a climate and environment that resulted in high mortality rates from illness and disease, the key problem related to their quarters. By an Act of the Jamaican legislature, property-owners on the island could pay a weekly allowance to the soldiers instead of providing them with accommodation. The result was that many of the soldiers drank the money and then had nowhere to live, and were thereby even more likely to die of illness and disease. The agents agreed to write to the Jamaican House of Assembly members desiring that they make better provision for the soldiers. At the same time

> Their lordships then gave further directions for preparing a report upon the case and ... to propose that barracks be built for the officers and soldiers to lodge in, under the discipline established in Ireland, and to offer that Her Majesty would be pleased to direct the Lieutenant Governor to recommend to the Assembly to make further provision for the soldiery.[1]

The proposal of the English Council of Trade and Plantations was potentially problematic. In early modern England the building of permanent residential army barracks had long been associated with the idea of a permanent standing army, which in turn was associated with absolutism, tyranny, political corruption and Catholicism.[2] The alternative – and the normal practice in the seventeenth century – was to billet the soldiers among the general populace, but this too was contentious and was associated with martial law and arbitrary power.[3] The problem was exacerbated, especially during wartime, by the taking of 'free quarter', when the soldiers either refused or were unable to pay for their accommodation and subsistence.[4] Throughout the seventeenth century, from the 1628 Petition of Right onwards, billeting of the army was a regular focal point for discord between government and the wider populace. Increasing discontent eventually led to the assertion in

Westminster's 1689 Bill of Rights that soldiers should not be billeted among private subjects. Thereafter all English annual Mutiny Acts included a prohibition upon all such quartering.[5]

Throughout the eighteenth century, therefore, English taverns and inns bore the brunt of army quartering, at times to the ruin of such businesses.[6] Yet the alternative of building permanent residential barracks remained anathema to the English political community.[7] Even as government policy finally embraced the need for a country-wide network of barracks in the 1790s, political sentiment remained hostile.[8]

Ireland

As the October 1703 report from the English Council of Trade and Plantations had implied, the situation in Ireland was very different. The council's proposal 'that barracks be built for the officers and soldiers to lodge in, under the discipline established in Ireland' was in reference to the fact that in the 1690s the Irish Government had initiated an innovative and unique project for building a country-wide network of permanent residential army barracks. Only France, and to a lesser extent Spain, had as yet engaged with the concept of building military facilities of this type.[9] It was also evident from the comments of the English Council of Trade and Plantations that the benefit of that project for army discipline and governance had already been noted in London government circles.

The reason for this Irish barrack-building project was the fact that from the 1690s onwards Ireland began to maintain and pay for the single largest part of the British standing army in peacetime, and to serve as the first port of call for soldiers when the army was expanded in size whenever Britain went to war during the eighteenth century.[10]

But why was this so? The Williamite–Jacobite war in Ireland in 1689–91 had, for a time, threatened wholly to eradicate the political and economic power of the ruling Irish Protestant minority elite and replace it with a Jacobite Catholic hegemony.[11] Thereafter, during the years 1692–7, Ireland remained on a wartime footing, owing to the continuing war on the Continent, with usually somewhere between 12,000–15,000 soldiers stationed in the country.[12]

It is therefore not surprising that the restored Irish Protestant minority ruling elite were relatively comfortable with a substantially enlarged military presence in the country. There was no shortage of reasons: the recent history of three country-wide wars in less than 100 years; the deeply ingrained fear of the majority Catholic population; the Irish Jacobite army in exile fighting for James II and France; French and Jacobite privateer activity along the

Irish coasts; and a continuing internal security issue, with ex-Jacobite soldiers turning to outlaw activity in less populated parts of the country.[13] The same motivations, even with peace in Europe after 1697, ensured that the Irish Protestant political community continued to accept the ongoing maintenance of a large standing army in peacetime, paid for from the Irish treasury and from taxes voted by the Irish Parliament.[14]

As already seen, however, the same could not be said of England. Following the 1697 Treaty of Ryswick, a very successful anti-standing-army campaign in the Westminster Parliament culminated in the passage of the Disbanding Act of 1699, which settled the standing forces in England at 7,000 men and those in Ireland at 12,000. A number of much smaller units were to be stationed in the Channel Islands, the West Indies, Newfoundland and New York. Although Scotland was not mentioned, the evidence available suggests that the number of soldiers there was well below that of England and Ireland. Certainly by 1701–2 there were only around 3,000 soldiers north of the English border.[15] So it was that the single largest part of William's peacetime standing army was placed in Ireland. It was a decision that was to make Ireland a central part of the British empire throughout the eighteenth century.

Prior to the 1690s, quartering of the army in Ireland had for the most part been centred on inns and taverns, with the usual associated problems.[16] In 1692 the Irish Lord Lieutenant, Henry, Viscount Sydney, expressed how the problem genuinely affected all levels of society within the country, 'where there is so great a scarcity, where the inhabitants are so poor, and where there is not a public house in the kingdom able to give an officer credit for a week, and where, if [the army] are allowed to live upon free quarter, the country must be ruined'.[17] With a permanently enlarged military establishment from 1692 onwards, the increasing pressure of quartering on the general populace and the ever-increasing level of complaints in Parliament and elsewhere on the topic led to the relatively quick evolution of plans to alleviate the problem by building a country-wide network of residential barracks.[18] By so doing, from the 1690s onwards Ireland became the first testing ground for this new military innovation within the British empire.

Recognition of the need for building barracks was evident within government circles from 1691 onwards.[19] The first major undertaking in that regard was in Limerick city, where construction began in 1693–4 with funding raised from lands forfeited in the war. From the outset, there was a recognition that such permanent barrack complexes offered a greater chance of maintaining army discipline, given that 'the soldiers will be kept … continually under their officers' eye'.[20]

Although at a much later date an Irish government official suggested that initially several army officers and many 'country gentlemen' had been 'violently opposed' to the barrack-building project,[21] such opposition was not evident in 1697 when the Irish Parliament voted £25,000 for that purpose.[22] Only one MP, Wentworth Harman, objected, and he did so solely on the xenophobic grounds that the barracks would provide accommodation for five French Huguenot regiments that had served with William III throughout the Nine Years War.[23]

The voting of money in Parliament in 1697 was a recognition of the need for a dedicated source of public funds for sustaining the barrack-building project. The relevant legislation specified the core principles behind the project: the improvement of army discipline, and the alleviation of the burden of quartering. It also stated that the barracks should be built as quickly as possible in the most 'convenient and necessary parts' of the country.[24] It was soon evident that more money was needed, and in 1699 a further £33,000 was voted.[25] At the same time, it was resolved in the House of Commons that a subject could arrest, sue and prosecute an officer or soldier, and that legal officials in the execution of justice should be allowed to enter barracks free from obstruction, which suggested there was still some residual fear of a standing army at that time.[26] But in reality, apart from a few lone voices such as that of Jonathan Swift,[27] in the first half of the eighteenth century the issue of internal security for Irish Protestants, and the blanket comfort of a resident standing army, always trumped any latent desire to pursue a classical republican or 'real Whig' anti-standing-army ideology which championed the idea of a citizen militia instead.[28]

By the end of 1700, more than 100 barracks were either planned, built or under construction throughout Ireland. At the same time, Barrack Trustees, a Board of Management, and an initial cohort of barrack-masters had been appointed. In 1701 the official *Rules, Orders, Powers, and Directions, for the Good Government and Preservation of the Barracks* (Dublin, 1701) was published. It is of note that, almost a century later, the first set of *Rules* for the formalisation of England's belated engagement with a barrack network, published in 1795, drew heavily upon the 1701 Irish example.[29]

By 1714, when the German cartographer Herman Moll mapped the country, he was able to list 102 barracks in existence.[30] These included a lesser number of small redoubts in mountainous, sparsely populated areas for internal security purposes and a larger number of primarily residential barracks in villages, towns and cities for the housing and training of soldiers, described in 1715 as 'so many little military-colleges scattered up and down the country'.[31] Thereafter, the total number of barracks in existence at any given time tended to be around 100 or so, though the number in actual use could be significantly less. It was also the case that over time some barracks fell into disuse and decline while others were constructed elsewhere.[32] As a result, in total more than 250 separate barrack sites were utilised at some point in time through the eighteenth and into the early nineteenth century in Ireland, though never all at the same time.[33]

It was also the case that the building and ongoing maintenance of the barrack complexes had a significant economic impact through investment in localities: construction provided employment and circulation of money in the economy, and the presence of soldiers provided ongoing stimulus to trade and commerce and brought much-needed coinage into local circulation. The patronage associated with barrack-building also soon emerged, as it became apparent that having a barracks sited on your land was economically lucrative, whether in terms of rent from the Government or stimulus to the local economy. Barracks also sometimes served as a precursor to attempts at establishing settlements in sparsely populated areas, and preceded the granting of licences for fairs and other trappings of settlement and community, all of which brought economic development in their train.[34]

The voting of money by the Irish Parliament for the building of barracks constituted a core element of Ireland's evolving contribution to the British fiscal military State and empire in the eighteenth century. With the ongoing payment from the Irish treasury of the costs of maintaining all of the regiments stationed in Ireland and a number of those overseas, and the facilitation of the rotation of regiments in and out of Ireland to other parts of the empire, the Irish military establishment soaked up on average 82.5 per cent of the Irish Government's annual income in the six decades from 1699 to 1759, a pattern that continued thereafter in the century.[35]

The system can be seen at work in a couple of snapshots from different points in time. In the period from 1718 to 1728, a total of thirty regiments and one battalion were supported by the Irish treasury while stationed overseas.[36] Within these numbers were regiments that were rotated in and out of Gibraltar and Minorca, two key British strongholds in the Mediterranean. In 1719 seven regiments paid from Ireland were garrisoned at these two locations, while in 1727 there were six Irish Establishment regiments in Gibraltar.[37]

In the lead-up to and during the first years of the Seven Years War of 1756–63, the number of soldiers stationed in Irish barracks and those rotating in and out fluctuated even more dramatically. This regular movement of troops also meant that the official limit of 12,000 soldiers in Ireland was breached with regularity and led to the Irish Parliament's agreeing to a wartime increase in the size of the army in Ireland to 15,000 men. In an official report to the Irish Parliament in January 1760, it was noted that on only two occasions since March 1756 had there been fewer than 12,000 soldiers in the country. At most other times the number had been below 15,000, though on two occasions that temporary limit was also breached: in October 1756 and April 1757, when 17,372 and 16,242 soldiers respectively were in the country.[38] More significantly, these rapidly fluctuating numbers were part of significant troop movement in and out of the country. In a more focused period for March 1755 to May 1757, eighteen foot regiments and twenty-four additional companies were removed from the Irish Establishment and sent overseas, equating to 13,482 soldiers in total. At the same time a further four regiments stationed overseas were being paid from Ireland, amounting to 1,496 soldiers, while a further 12,986 soldiers continued to be stationed in Ireland. This meant that in a three-year period the Irish Establishment had accommodated 27,964 men and provided 14,978 of those for overseas imperial service.[39] Central to all of this troop movement was the country-wide network of barracks, which constituted a significant innovation both in terms of Irish public expenditure and of military practice in the wider empire.

Jamaica

Given the evident success of the Irish barrack-building project, the question remains as to how the 1703 proposal from the English Council of Trade and Plantations worked out in relation to Jamaica. It was clearly evident from the proposal that the issue of quartering was problematic elsewhere in the empire. In Jamaica itself during the Restoration period the non-payment of soldiers had meant that they were unable to pay for their subsistence from the inn-keepers and private householders with whom they were quartered, resulting in the civilian population being placed under an increased economic burden, while also creating bad blood between themselves and the soldiers.[40] Complaints also arose over quartering in the thirteen American colonies during the Restoration period, including in Massachusetts, Connecticut, New York, Virginia and South Carolina, as well as in Nova Scotia in Canada.[41] The response of the American colonial legislatures was to endeavour to provide legal protection against quartering on the grounds that as freeborn Englishmen they were entitled to the same rights as their fellow countrymen in England, especially against involuntary quartering as first defined in England's 1628 Petition of Right.[42] But without quarters, soldiers were more likely to die from disease and illness. In a particularly stark example, in the early eighteenth century the British Government received a petition from the Lieutenant-Governor of Bermuda regarding the problematic situation of the soldiers there, who had not received any bedding in fifteen years and had 'no quarters allowed them by the country'. By the time London responded a year later, all of the soldiers were apparently dead.[43]

With regard to Jamaica, from the time it first came into English possession in 1655 the armed forces on the island tended to be made up from an irregular militia of understandably unreliable indentured servants and enslaved Africans.[44] The stationing of regular army units on the island only occurred in exceptional circumstances such as wartime, when an invasion might be threatened. Yet it was also the case that Jamaica, considered to be the 'most boisterous and disorderly' of the empire's West Indian colonies, had been successfully defended by its irregular militia in 1694, when the French had attempted an invasion during the Nine Years War.[45]

The absence of a permanent regular army presence in Jamaica was a significant difference in comparison to Ireland. However, the outbreak of the War of the Spanish Succession in 1701–2 raised the threat of invasion once more for all of the English possessions in the West Indies.[46] As a result, and as an early example of how the Irish barrack system was beginning to facilitate troop rotation within the empire, during 1701–2 six regiments were dispatched from Ireland to the Caribbean, including two that were sent to Jamaica.[47] The commander of one of the regiments, Thomas Handasyde, was also the incoming Lieutenant-Governor of the island.[48]

As detailed at the outset of the chapter, within a year of their arrival these regular army soldiers had made a formal complaint to London about their deplorable living conditions.[49] Despite the apparent good intentions of the English Council of Trade and Plantations in its ensuing recommendation for building barracks in Jamaica, what unfolded thereafter was very different from the Irish experience. In February 1704 the council wrote to Handasyde, who had been promoted to the position of Governor, ordering him to recommend to the Jamaican legislature 'that absolute provision be made for the quarters of the two regiments now there; and not of money instead of quarters ... without which necessary and effectual provision Her Majesty will be obliged to recall those regiments from that island'.[50] However, there was soon evidence that such an approach would meet with resistance in the Jamaican legislature's House of Assembly. On 11 April Richard Thompson was appointed chairman of 'a committee of the Assembly to bring in a bill for the quartering of Her Majesty's forces'.[51] Thompson, however, quickly got himself excused from the position, and Hugh Totterdell, an Irish lawyer and regular thorn in the side of the Jamaican Government, was appointed in his place.[52] Totterdell in turn was said to have uttered

> scandalous and seditious words in the hearing of the said Richard and diverse others, to witt, 'I desire I may be likewise excused, for if anything should go amiss, I shall be rogu'd and rascall'd as before, and therefore desire the said Richard may not be excused, but continue chairman, that he may be rogu'd and rascall'd in his turne.'[53]

Totterdell was eventually expelled for his actions, but his words highlighted that quartering, and the emerging association with barrack-building, was not a popular proposition in Jamaica.[54]

In England, however, the focus remained on barrack-building. In September Secretary of State Robert Harley wrote to the Council of Trade and Plantations about the grievances of the soldiers in Jamaica, stating that 'If barraques can be built or certain quarters assigned, it will tend more to the security of the country, the ease of the inhabitants and the health of the soldier, and considering how far these poor men go, and venture their lives to defend a very unhealthful place.'[55] As a result, the council sent Harley an update on the matter, which was presented as part of a much more detailed report at the end of November to the Westminster House of Lords. The main argument with regard to Jamaica was that

> nothing can be better for the officer and soldier for Her Majesty's service and the security of the island, than the building of barracks in proper places where the regiments may be lodged under fitting regulations, as in Ireland, and in several garrisons of England, and wherein the officers may have due care of the health of their soldiers, by restraining them from many extravagancies they are subject to in open and distant quarters. We humbly offer that fresh provisions might be distributed to the officers and soldiers daily from the stores that may be brought from the northern plantations, either by undertakers, or officers to be appointed by Her Majesty for that purpose ... and we do not doubt but that the assembly of Jamaica might be induced readily to contribute a considerable sum towards the building of such barracks, if Her Majesty would be pleased to assist and enable them in carrying on of this work.[56]

However, at the very same time in Jamaica, Handasyde was being accused of arbitrary government by the Assembly – ostensibly, in his view, simply because he had pointed out the Queen's

> clemency and care, as well as the vast expense she is at, to preserve their lives and fortunes, and how far they ought to be concerned in preserving the lives of those Her Majesty had sent for their preservation, a great many whereof had already lost their lives for want of quarters, and daily more might be expected to follow.[57]

He was also 'mighty apprehensive of their unhuman proceedings to the two regiments here [at] the next Assembly'. With the existing Quartering Act due to expire on 1 August 1705, members of the Assembly were publicly declaring that 'they will allow 7s. 6d. per week to the private sentinels, and nothing at all to the officers, they saying they have no occasion for the officers, but for the soldiers to be their drivers and to people the country'.[58]

It was evident that Assembly members were looking to make life difficult for the Government. The existing Quartering Act allowed property owners to pay 10s. a week to officers and 5s. a week to private soldiers in lieu of quarters.[59] The threat, though, was that no provision at all would be allowed in the new Quartering Act, on the grounds that the regular army units were not needed on the island.

It was therefore not surprising that the problems persisted, despite the summoning once more of the Jamaica Agents in London in early 1705 to the council to be admonished for the failure of the Assembly to provide for the soldiers as ordered by the Queen.[60] Handasyde's growing frustration was evident when he wrote in February 1705 that 'I have nothing more to propose except that the inhabitants be obliged to quarter both the officers and soldiers, or to procure them quarters.' At that time he reported how 150 men from his regiment in Port Royal and Spanish Town were without quarters, and were having to sleep under platforms with 'the Heavens for the Canopee [sic]', while others were sleeping 'under a shade or an old house'.[61] Eventually, in November 1705, the Assembly passed a new Quartering Act, but again without provision for building barracks, and with 'such clauses tact [sic] to it as never were before heard of, that part relating to the soldiers being for only a year, and the other for ever, which excludes all foreigners serving either in civil employments or in the militia'. Handasyde therefore recommended to London that the Queen refuse the Royal Assent.[62]

The delays in communication between England and Jamaica were evident in that the Council for Trade and Plantations did not actually respond to Handasyde until April 1706, when they informed him that they agreed that the Quartering Act was 'not fit for Her Majesty's royal approbation'. Yet, once again, they pressed him 'to endeavour to make [the Assembly] ... sensible how much it is their interest to contribute towards the building of barracks for the lodging soldiers'.[63] However, despite Handasyde's efforts, the whole matter remained unresolved for the remainder of the War of the Spanish Succession.[64] And, once the war was over and the soldiers rotated elsewhere, there was even less chance of barracks being built.

The issue of barrack-building in Jamaica appears to have stagnated thereafter until the mid-1720s. As reported in a pamphlet published in London in 1726, entitled *The State of the Island of Jamaica*, in 1725 the Committee of Grievances in the Jamaica Assembly had highlighted the fact that the high mortality among soldiers stationed in Port Royal was owing to 'the want of proper lodgings'. As a result, the Assembly had resolved that 'convenient barracks be built' and that an address to that effect be presented to the Governor.[65] While this seemed reasonable, and a great advance on what had happened before, the then Governor, Henry Bentinck, First Duke of Portland, took umbrage with both the pamphlet and the Assembly, pointing out that in reality 'no provision had ever been before made by the Assembly for that purpose, nor none as yet, but an imaginary credit'.[66] The bottom line was that barracks could not be built without funds.

The pamphlet also hinted at the possible ideological reasons behind the Assembly's issues with the building of barracks. The author touched upon recent disquiet in Jamaica over suggestions that they were not entitled to a Habeas Corpus Act. Given that Magna Carta was deemed to have granted 'to the subject under English government' the rights against illegal imprisonment enshrined in later Habeas Corpus legislation, failure to recognise the extension of those rights and the requisite legislation to freeborn Englishmen in the colonies was seen as opening the way for arbitrary government. Certainly that was the view ascribed to the planters in Jamaica and the rest of the British West Indies, and was a viewpoint that would lead to the first great crisis of empire in the thirteen American colonies between the 1760s and 1770s. Crucially, as the 1726 pamphlet stated, 'is it not natural to fear, that their properties may by this means be wrested from them'.[67] There were clear echoes here of core elements of Harringtonian ideas of civic virtue, which favoured private property and an individual's right to bear arms as expressed through citizen militias rather than standing armies, which were deemed to be the tools of tyranny and absolutism.[68]

The fact that classical republican ideology of opposition to a standing army lay behind Assembly resistance to building barracks was more readily evident in October 1726. Writing to the Council of Trade and Plantations, the President of the Council of Jamaica, John Ayscough, pointed out that with regard to a bill for perpetuating existing laws, the only 'objection made to it' related to the two independent companies stationed on the island, 'which some say is intailing [sic] upon us a military force to perpetuity, whereas the people of England only provide for their forces there from year to year [in the annual Mutiny Act]'.[69]

As far back as the Restoration period problems over quartering soldiers in Jamaica had caused the question to be raised among the general populace as to whether the soldiers were there for 'their protection against a foreign foe or for their own suppression'.[70] Sir Alan Burns, in his *History of the British West Indies*, suggests that the negative attitude in Jamaica towards providing quarters for the regular army, which was also replicated on other islands in the West Indies and 'continued for many years ... can perhaps be explained by the deep-rooted objection in English minds at that period to a standing army'. In this regard, these colonial assemblies were looking to claim the same rights and privileges afforded to 'freeborn Englishmen'. But as Burns also pointed out, 'Jamaica was ... more in need of a regular garrison, even in times of peace, than any other colony, as a protection against the Maroons and possible slave revolts.'[71] It appears that the Jamaica Assembly, however begrudgingly, slowly began to recognise that fact in the later 1720s and early 1730s, as the activities of maroon rebels and escaped enslaved people became more daring, destructive and threatening.[72]

In the summer of 1731 two regiments were dispatched from Gibraltar to Jamaica to help counter a rebellion on the island. At that time, the Governor advised that the regiments 'bring tents with them'. Yet he had also seen fit to order the 'repairing [of] the old and building [of] new huts and barracks'.[73] By early 1732 barracks 'had been built by the several parishes at a great expense' on the borders of the most rebellious parts of the island. It was hoped that these would 'be kept in repair and guarded ... until the legislature fall upon some proper measures to do it'.[74] The following year the Assembly was finally convinced to engage directly with funding barrack-building on the island.[75] The first Acts for that purpose were passed in 1733–4, with further legislation in 1737–8.[76] With a small permanent garrison of eight companies stationed on the island from 1739 onwards, the necessity for barracks became even greater and spending thereon increased further, even if the barracks tended to be focused primarily on the frontier areas of the island.[77]

Following Tacky's Revolt in May 1760, considered to be 'the most serious slave rebellion ever seen' to that point in time, a more coordinated endeavour across the whole island began to develop, leading eventually to an island-wide and centrally controlled residential barrack system.[78] Such an outcome was best summed up by the Cornish-born and Grays Inn-educated Jamaican planter Edward Long, in his controversial *History of Jamaica* published in 1774: 'It must be granted that the maintenance of a standing army in a commercial colony is not the most eligible nor oeconomic plan ... and ought only to be admitted in a colony of that class when there is but little hope of settling and peopling it extensively', which circumstance he ascribed to Jamaica.[79]

Conclusion

The evidence suggests that the willingness to build barracks – and thereby maintain a standing army – was related in many ways to fears over internal security. In Ireland throughout the eighteenth century, even from the 1760s onwards when the *Freeman's Journal* and leading Irish Protestant patriots experimented for a time with anti-standing-army ideology, the majority of the Protestant ruling elite continued to see a standing army as the blanket of security that they had wrapped themselves in since the 1690s.[80] Similar motivations appear to have crept into Jamaican political decision-making from the 1730s onwards.[81] What this all suggests is that anti-standing-army ideology was in fact the luxury of a more secure polity, as in England or, indeed, in the thirteen American colonies after 1763. The American colonists' sense of greater internal and frontier security in the 1760s and 1770s ultimately led to a complete break away from the British empire.[82] But for those who felt less secure within their own polity, it was safer to remain within the empire and, eventually and however begrudgingly, to build barracks for housing a British standing army.

Notes

* I would like to thank Patrick Walsh for his insightful comments and advice on the chapter.
1 Cecil Headlam, ed., *Calendar of State Papers Colonial, America and West Indies*, Vol. XXI, *1702–1703* (London: HMSO, 1913) (*CSPCS 1703*), p. 722.
2 L. G. Schwoerer, '*No Standing Armies!*': *The Anti-Army Ideology in Seventeenth-Century England* (Baltimore: Johns Hopkins University Press, 1974), *passim*; John Childs, *Armies and Warfare in Europe 1648–1789* (New York: Holmes and Meier, 1982), pp. 185–6.
3 C. M. Clode, *The Military Forces of the Crown: Their Administration and Government*, 2 vols (London: John Murray, 1869), Vol. II, pp. 17, 19–20, 61; Barry Coward, *The Stuart Age: England 1603–1714*, 3rd edn (London: Longman, 2003), pp. 162–3, 312, 518.
4 John Childs, *The Army, James II, and the Glorious Revolution* (Manchester: Manchester University Press, 1980), pp. 86–8.
5 See Clode, *The Military Forces*, Vol. I, pp. 80–2, 229–37, 569–70; Schwoerer, '*No Standing Armies!*', pp. 56, 99–101, 137, 143; Childs, *The Army, James II, and the Glorious Revolution*, pp. 1–4, 85–91; and R. E. Scouller, *The Armies of Queen Anne* (Oxford: Clarendon Press, 1966), pp. 164–5.
6 Clode, *The Military Forces*, Vol. I, pp. 230–7, 569–77; John Brewer, *The Sinews of Power: War, Money and the English State* (London: Unwin Hyman, 1989), p. 49.
7 For example, see *The History and Proceedings of the House of Commons 1660–1743*, 14 vols (London, 1742–4), Vol. XII, pp. 148–9, 178. See also Clode, *The Military Forces*, Vol. I, p. 234; H. C. B. Rogers, *The British Army of the Eighteenth Century* (London: Allen and Unwin, 1977), p. 38; and Brewer, *The Sinews of Power*, p. 48.
8 See, for example, *Letters on the Impolicy of a Standing Army, in Time of Peace. And, On the unconstitutional and illegal Measure of Barracks …* (London, 1793); and *A Political and Military Rhapsody, on the Invasion and Defence of Great Britain and Ireland …*, 3rd edn (London, 1794). For English barrack-building in the 1790s see *The State of the Nation, with respect to its Public Funded Debt, Revenue, and Disbursement; Comprised in the Reports of the Select Committee on Finance (With the Appendices to each Report) Appointed by The House of Commons …*, 3 vols (London, 1799), Vol. III, pp. 1–29; and James Douet, *British Barracks 1600–1914: Their Architecture and Role in Society* (London: The Stationery Office, 1998), pp. 60, 67–94.
9 Douet, *British Barracks*, pp. 3–4, 17; Geoffrey Parker, *The Army of Flanders and the Spanish Road 1567–1659* (Cambridge: Cambridge University Press, 1972), pp. 166–7; Jeremy Black, *European Warfare 1660–1815* (London: University College London Press, 1994), p. 225.
10 For a more detailed discussion of the eighteenth-century Irish barrack-building project and the use of the Irish Military Establishment both within Ireland and throughout the empire see C. I. McGrath, *Ireland and Empire, 1692–1770* (London: Pickering and Chatto, 2012), pp. 69–166.

11 J. G. Simms, *Jacobite Ireland, 1685–91* (Dublin: Four Courts Press, 2000), *passim*.
12 McGrath, *Ireland and Empire*, pp. 121–3.
13 C. I. McGrath, 'Securing the Protestant interest: The origins and purpose of the Penal Laws of 1695', *Irish Historical Studies* 30 (1996–7), 25–32.
14 McGrath, *Ireland and Empire*, pp. 123–5.
15 William A. Shaw, ed., *Calendar of Treasury Books*, Vol. XVII, *1702* (London: HMSO, 1939), pp. ccx–ccxi; K. P. Ferguson, 'The Army in Ireland from the Restoration to the Act of Union', Ph.D. thesis (Trinity College Dublin, 1981), p. 54; S. H. F. Johnston, 'The Scots Army in the Reign of Anne', *Transactions of the Royal Historical Society*, 5th series, 3 (1953), 1–21 (pp. 12, 14). For consideration of the role of the army in Scotland, including the building of barracks, see Victoria Henshaw, 'A reassessment of the British army in Scotland, from the Union to the '45', *Northern Scotland* 2 (2011), 1–21.
16 See for example National Archives, Ireland, Wyche papers, 1/1/25, Lord Orrery to Lord Lieutenant Ormonde, 22 November 1678; David Hayton and Michael Page, eds, *Anglo-Irish Politics, 1680–1728: The Correspondence of the Brodrick Family of Surrey and County Cork*, Vol. I, *1680–1714* (Oxford: Wiley for the Parliamentary History Yearbook Trust, 2019), pp. 46, 47–8; Eoin Magennis, 'Select document: "The present state of Ireland", 1749', *Irish Historical Studies* 36 (2009), 581–97 (p. 592); and C. I. McGrath, 'Waging war: The Irish Military Establishment and the British Empire, 1688–1763', in William Mulligan and Brendan Simms, eds, *The Primacy of Foreign Policy in British History, 1660–2000* (Basingstoke: Palgrave, 2010), p. 105.
17 William John Hardy, ed., *Calendar of State Papers, Domestic: William and Mary, 1695; Addenda, 1689–1695* (London: HMSO, 1908) (*CSPD 1695 and Addenda*), p. 198.
18 See British Library (BL), Add. MS 21136, fo. 12; Harleian MSS 6274, fo. 116; 4892, fos 127–90. William John Hardy, ed., *Calendar of State Papers, Domestic: William and Mary, 1693* (London: HMSO, 1903) (*CSPD 1693*), p. 445; McGrath, *Ireland and Empire*, pp. 75–7.
19 See, for example, *CSPD 1693*, p. 115; Douet, *British Barracks*, p. 29.
20 *CSPD 1693*, pp. 227–8, 247; *CSPD 1695 and Addenda*, pp. 59, 146.
21 BL, Add. MS 61636, fo. 163, Eustace Budgell to Joseph Addison, 9 February 1715.
22 *The Statutes at Large passed in the Parliaments held in Ireland*, 21 vols (Dublin, 1765–1804) (*Stat. Ire.*), Vol. III, pp. 353–8.
23 McGrath, *Ireland and Empire*, pp. 78, 124–5.
24 *Stat. Ire.*, Vol. III, p. 353.
25 *Ibid.*, Vol. III, p. 471.
26 McGrath, *Ireland and Empire*, p. 79.
27 See C. I. McGrath, '"The grand question debated": Jonathan Swift, army barracks, parliament and money', *Eighteenth-Century Ireland* 31 (2016), 117–36.
28 For the evolution of classical republican ideology in eighteenth-century Ireland see Caroline Robbins, *The Eighteenth-Century Commonwealthman: Studies in*

the Transmission, Development, and Circumstance of English Liberal Thought from the Restoration of Charles II until the War with the Thirteen Colonies (New York: Atheneum, 1968), pp. 84–171; and Stephen Small, *Political Thought in Ireland 1776–1798: Republicanism, Patriotism, and Radicalism* (Oxford: Oxford University Press, 2002), pp. 22, 82–3, 93–7, 222.
29 See McGrath, *Ireland and Empire*, pp. 80–1.
30 Herman Moll, *A New Map of Ireland Divided into its Provinces, Counties and Baronies, wherein are distinguished the Bishopricks, Borroughs, Barracks, Bogs, Passes, Bridges, &c. with the Principal Roads, and the common Reputed Miles* (London, 1714).
31 BL, Add. MS 61636, fo. 163, Budgell to Addison, 9 February 1715.
32 For further discussion of these various matters see McGrath, *Ireland and Empire*, pp. 85–92.
33 For the number and locations of barracks throughout the eighteenth century see *Army Barracks of Eighteenth-Century Ireland*, https://barracks18c.ucd.ie/ (accessed 26 August 2022).
34 On these matters see McGrath, *Ireland and Empire*, pp. 89–90; 'Fourmile House', https://barracks18c.ucd.ie/fourmile-house/; 'Johnston's Fews', https://barracks18c.ucd.ie/johnstons-fews/; 'Blackbank', https://barracks18c.ucd.ie/blackbank/ (all accessed 26 August 2022).
35 McGrath, *Ireland and Empire*, pp. 169–70.
36 The National Archives, Kew (TNA), SP 63/390/234, 'An account of the regiments on the Irish Establishment that have been employed in England and abroad' (1728–9).
37 TNA, 63/389/117, 119, 121, anon. to the secretaries of the duke of Newcastle, 19 December 1727; Ferguson, 'The Army in Ireland', pp. 61, 99; David Murphy, *The Irish Brigades, 1685–2006: A Gazetteer of Irish Military Service, Past and Present* (Dublin: Four Courts Press, 2007), pp. 110, 129; McGrath, *Ireland and Empire*, p. 156.
38 *The Journals of the House of Commons of the Kingdom of Ireland*, 3rd edn, 21 vols (Dublin, 1796–1800) (*CJI*), Vol. VI, pp. 176, 179, and Appendix, pp. cclxxxviii–cclxxxix; McGrath, *Ireland and Empire*, pp. 133–5.
39 *CJI*, Vol. VI, Appendix, p. xxviii; McGrath, *Ireland and Empire*, p. 161.
40 S. S. Webb, *The Governors-General: The English Army and the Definition of the Empire, 1569–1681* (Williamsburg: Institute of Early American History and Culture, 1979), p. 280.
41 W. S. Fields and D. T. Hardy, 'The Third Amendment and the issue of the maintenance of standing armies: A legal history', *American Journal of Legal History* 35:4 (October 1991), 393–431 (p. 414); V. D. Anderson, 'New England in the seventeenth century', in Nicholas Canny, ed., *The Oxford History of the British Empire*, Vol. I, *The Origins of Empire* (Oxford: Oxford University Press, 1998), pp. 214–15; Webb, *The Governors-General*, pp. 384–5.
42 Fields and Hardy, 'The Third Amendment', pp. 411–14.
43 Webb, *The Governors-General*, p. 474.
44 Richard S. Dunn, *Sugar and Slaves: The Rise of the Planter Class in the English West Indies, 1624–1713* (London: Cape, 1973), p. 161.

45 *Ibid.*, pp. 149, 163.
46 For fears of invasion in Jamaica see Historical Manuscripts Commission (HMC), *House of Lords MSS, 1704–6*, n.s. (London: HMSO, 1966), pp. 100–2.
47 McGrath, *Ireland and Empire*, pp. 150–1.
48 Alan Burns, *History of the British West Indies*, 2nd edn (New York: Barnes and Noble, 1965), p. 430; Karst de Jong, 'The Irish in Jamaica in the long eighteenth century (1698–1836)', Ph.D. thesis (Queen's University Belfast, 2017), p. 85.
49 *CSPCS 1703*, p. 722.
50 Cecil Headlam, ed., *Calendar of State Papers Colonial, America and West Indies*, Vol. II, *1704–1705* (London: HMSO, 1916), p. 46 (*CSPCS 1704–5*).
51 *Ibid.*, p. 147.
52 For Totterdell, see De Jong, 'The Irish in Jamaica', pp. 82–9.
53 *CSPCS 1704–5*, p. 147.
54 *Ibid.*, pp. 171–2; De Jong, 'The Irish in Jamaica', p. 86.
55 *CSPCS 1704–5*, p. 248.
56 *Ibid.*, p. 276; HMC, *House of Lords MSS, 1704–6*, pp. 101–2.
57 *CSPCS 1704–5*, p. 340.
58 *Ibid.*, pp. 348–9.
59 HMC, *House of Lords MSS, 1704–6*, p. 102.
60 *CSPCS 1704–5*, p. 377.
61 *Ibid.*, pp. 393–4.
62 *Ibid.*, p. 700.
63 Cecil Headlam, ed., *Calendar of State Papers Colonial, America and West Indies*, Vol. XXIII, *1706–1708* (London: HMSO, 1916), p. 124.
64 Burns, *History of the British West Indies*, p. 430.
65 A. B. and James Knight, *The State of the Island of Jamaica* (London: printed for H. Whitridge, 1726), pp. 73, 76.
66 Cecil Headlam and Arthur Percival Newton, eds, *Calendar of State Papers Colonial, America and West Indies*, Vol. XXXV, *1726–1727* (London: HMSO, 1936) (*CSPCS 1726–7*), pp. 77–8.
67 A. B. and Knight, *The State of the Island of Jamaica*, pp. 35–6. See also J. P. Greene, 'Liberty and slavery: The transfer of British liberty to the West Indies, 1627–1865', in J. P. Greene, ed., *Exclusionary Empire: English Liberty Overseas, 1600–1900* (Cambridge: Cambridge University Press, 2010), pp. 56–7.
68 See in general J. G. A. Pocock, *The Machiavellian Moment: Florentine Political Thought and the Atlantic Republican Tradition* (Princeton: Princeton University Press, 2003), pp. 406, 410–13, 419–21, 428–9, 458.
69 *CSPCS 1726–7*, pp. 145–6.
70 Webb, *The Governors-General*, p. 280.
71 Burns, *History of the British West Indies*, pp. 430–1.
72 See for example *ibid.*, pp. 445–8; Aaron Graham, 'The colonial sinews of power: The political economy of Jamaican taxation, 1768–1838', *Journal of Imperial and Commonwealth History* 45:2 (2017), 188–209 (p. 190).
73 Cecil Headlam and Arthur Percival Newton, eds, *Calendar of State Papers Colonial, America and West Indies*, Vol. XXXVIII, *1731* (London: HMSO, 1938), p. 23.

74 Cecil Headlam and Arthur Percival Newton, eds, *Calendar of State Papers Colonial, America and West Indies*, Vol. XXXIX, *1732* (London: HMSO, 1939), pp. 8–9.
75 Cecil Headlam and Arthur Percival Newton, eds, *Calendar of State Papers Colonial, America and West Indies*, Vol. XL, *1733* (London: HMSO, 1939), pp. 140, 213, 216, 234–5, 273.
76 *An Abridgment of the Laws of Jamaica*, 2 vols (Jamaica: printed by Alexander Aikman, 1793), Vol. I, p. 20.
77 Graham, 'The colonial sinews of power', pp. 188–9, 192.
78 Trevor Burnard, *Jamaica in the Age of Revolution* (Philadelphia: University of Pennsylvania Press, 2020), pp. 8, 120–5; *An Abridgment*, Vol. I, pp. 20–1.
79 Quoted in Graham, 'The colonial sinews of power', p. 190.
80 See in general Small, *Political Thought*; Neal Garnham, *The Militia in Eighteenth-Century Ireland: In Defence of the Protestant Interest* (Woodbridge: Boydell Press, 2012), pp. 77–9, 82–3; Vincent Morley, *Irish Opinion and the American Revolution, 1760–1783* (Cambridge: Cambridge University Press, 2002), pp. 60–1, 72, 75–6; and M. J. Powell, 'The army in Ireland and the eighteenth-century press: Antimilitary sentiment in an Atlantic context', *Éire-Ireland* 50 (2015), 138–72.
81 Burnard, *Jamaica*, pp. 104–5, 120–5.
82 McGrath, *Ireland and Empire*, pp. 73–4. For detailed consideration of the role of barracks in relation to the American Revolution see J. G. McCurdy, *Quarters: The Accommodation of the British Army and the Coming of the American Revolution* (Ithaca, NY: Cornell University Press, 2019). For similarities in North American and Caribbean barrack-building designs see Philippe Oszuścik, 'Tropical similarities found in military barracks, hospitals and other structures in the West Indies and British Florida parishes', in Roger Leech and Pamela Leech, eds, *The Colonial Landscape of the British Caribbean* (Woodbridge: Boydell Press, 2021), pp. 15–37.

14

Architectures of empire in Jamaica: The Irish connection*

Louis P. Nelson

To find Colbeck Castle, a visitor has to have a keen sense of direction and just a bit of faith (Figure 14.1).[1] The road to the site is little more than a dirt path, fairly well removed from the paved roads and highways of Jamaica's south coast. Approaching the ruin, the visitor gets the clear sense that this is no ordinary British colonial house. Four corner towers, each rising a full three storeys, frame the large stone house, while elegant double arcades range from tower to tower on all four elevations. Visually striking circular windows on the ground floor of the south towers signal the south as the front elevation. Furthermore, the towered ruin stands in the midst of a huge square terrace positioned on a slight rise above the vast expanses of St Jago,

Figure 14.1 Colbeck Castle, St Catherine Parish, Jamaica, *c.* 1775, photo by the author.

Jamaica, an open plain of more than 50,000 acres of rich alluvial flatlands in St Catherine's Parish. For the American visitor used to visiting refined 'Georgian' plantation houses of early Virginia or South Carolina, or even the English visitor accustomed to elegant country houses, this building is something entirely different. Colbeck is certainly distinctive, yet it is not an aberration. This remarkable building opens a window into a largely unexplored realm: the forms and meanings of elite architecture of eighteenth-century Jamaica and their place in the shifting contours of the British empire.

Earlier work on Colbeck has suggested that its 'castellated' form might be part of the English practice of erecting Spenserian mock castles.[2] In English examples these castles are romantically ornamental and not martial: participants in the romance of chivalry, courtly combat, jousting and neo-medieval literature like *The Faerie Queene*.[3] An example is Lulworth Castle in Dorset, erected by Lord Howard Bindon in 1607 (Figure 14.2).[4] Lulworth was a 'little pile which he [Bindon] hopes to prove pretty'. The writer continues describing the house as in the form of 'a castle of the imagination', hardly a house built for defence.[5] The implications for castles in this mode are both in form and ornamentation, and in the arrangements of space. Tadhg O'Keeffe has effectively demonstrated Spenser's transformations of his own Kilcolman Castle in Munster, Ireland, where he actually wrote some portions of *The Faerie Queene*. Spenser expanded a fairly typical Anglo-Norman tower house to incorporate a more sophisticated suite of social

Figure 14.2 Lulworth Castle, Dorset, England, *c.* 1607, photo by the author.

spaces that accommodated more easily the practices of elite Elizabethan sociability.[6] But such a context of romantic indulgence in chivalry-dense literature seems, and in fact is, a world away from Colbeck Castle. Mock jousting and readings of Spenser are hard to imagine in eighteenth-century Jamaica.

There is an alternative context for the construction of postmedieval castles that could more comfortably extend to include these corner-towered buildings of early Jamaica. If new-built 'castles' provided a stage for the re-enactment of chivalric rituals as the prevailing interpretation supposes, they also recalled the elevated social status of the English nobility. Beginning with the dissolution of the monasteries under Henry VIII, England (and Ireland) witnessed a massive reorganisation of the landscape between the sixteenth and the eighteenth centuries.[7] Dana Arnold has very effectively argued that the eighteenth-century English elite depended on ownership of land and the construction of a country house to establish or preserve membership in England's privileged social circles.[8] The construction of country houses on these new estates secured the identity and the authority of the family and its patriarch in and over the landscape.[9]

By the eighteenth century, monumental houses with four corner towers had been associated with English authority in and over a landscape for centuries. An excellent late medieval example is the 1434–46 *donjon*, or central tower, of Tattershall Castle, in east Lincolnshire (Figure 14.3). Built by Ralph Cromwell, the Lord Treasurer to Henry VI, Tattershall Castle was outfitted with large, hardly defensible traceried windows, not as a fortification to withstand siege but as a symbol of his Lordly status.[10] In continuity with the late medieval tradition, many later country houses were also built with corner towers. Perhaps the most abundant evidence for this practice are the many houses of the late sixteenth and early seventeenth century designed by Robert Smythson (for example Hardwick Hall in Derbyshire, Figure 14.4). As Mark Girouard has suggested, these massive new houses were generally built not by England's well established families or those long associated with the aristocracy but by the wealthy gentry, most newly rich through the acquisition of former monastery lands, profit from law or success in commerce.[11] These newly wealthy families had a need to demonstrate their wealth, make clear their claim to substantial landholdings, and by extensions make claims to an elite – if gentry – social status.[12]

Archaeologist Matthew Johnson's discussion of the English castle in the fifteenth and sixteenth centuries offers a useful frame for understanding this penchant. He argues that the houses of the elite became more potently discursive in the late sixteenth century. In exactly the same season when the cultural systems that sustained the medieval castle were dissolving, the symbolic image of the castle was established. In this way, new 'castellated' houses, such as Wollaton, that gestured to the martial but were not actually

Figure 14.3 Tattershall Castle, Lincolnshire, England, 1434–46, photo by the author.

Figure 14.4 Hardwick Hall, Derbyshire, England, 1590–7, photo by the author.

defensible, were built to correspond to older castles, such as Tattershall, with the intent of being viewed as a continuous tradition, 'a conscious attempt to invoke values seen as being under threat'.[13] And his most powerful evidence to this end is the partial destruction, or 'slighting', of castles by Parliament after the Civil War. These buildings had been royalist strongholds of the aristocracy, and as material and symbolic evidence of their loss, castles – both defensible and indefensible – were slighted.[14]

But the tradition persisted, and the bold use of corner towers re-emerged after the Civil War. In the hands of eighteenth-century English architect John Vanbrugh, corner towers became explicitly connected with ennoblement. An excellent example is Blenheim Palace, with its four enormous corner towers: the great palace given to John Churchill, recently established as the Duke of Marlborough in thanks for his military successes in the War of Spanish Succession (Figure 14.5). Built for a man of less wealth than his peerage, the palace stands on the royal demesne of Woodstock, a huge tract of land that had been under royal governorship since Henry I. That the corner towers and crenellations on Vanbrugh's designs were associated in the architect's mind with ennoblement is made clear in a letter he wrote to a client, the Earl of Manchester, about the redesign of Kimbolton Castle: 'As to the outside I thought 'twas absolutely best to give it something of the castle air tho' at the same time to make it regular … I am sure this will make a very *noble* and masculine show and is of as warrantable a kind of building

Figure 14.5 John Vanbrugh, Blenheim Palace, Oxfordshire, England, 1705–24, photo by the author.

as any.'[15] As Michael W. Thompson has argued, this tradition was not just fashion; a 'castle air' was an ennobling practice that depended on a long tradition connecting the castle with the land to 'enhance the authority of a landowner', well into the eighteenth century.[16]

If the towered country house had symbolic associations with ennoblement in the heart of Britain, its associations with control of and authority over landholdings seems to have been particularly acute at the edges of empire. English architectural historian Michael W. Thompson has observed, not surprisingly, that the square tower as a visual form – usually in the form of well-defended tower houses – was most common in the British landscape in those regions where land had been most hotly contested, along the Scottish border (Figure 14.6).[17] As a result, he argues, the house with square corner towers was all the more responsible for asserting authority over contested, threatened or threatening landscapes. One of those landscapes, of course, was Ireland. The Munster plantation in southern Ireland, begun in the 1580s, was the first systematic attempt at English colonisation in Ireland.[18] In Munster, extensive Irish landholdings in the south – in the modern counties of Limerick, Cork, Kerry and Tipperary – were confiscated and resettled with English colonists called undertakers, largely from the southwest of England.[19] While the Irish set up a military resistance, the Battle of Kinsale established English authority over Munster through the seventeenth century. If the country house with four corner towers appears intermittently across Britain through the early modern period, there is a pronounced increase in the construction of this form in southern Ireland between the 1580s and 1620, decades immediately following the foundation of the Munster plantation and the widespread seizure of land by the English Protestants.

10 Map of tower-houses, fourteenth to seventeenth centuries, in Great Britain and Ireland, showing how they are largely confined to the latter, south Scotland and the Border area. (RCAHM, Wales)

Figure 14.6 Map locating tower houses in the British Isles, reproduced from Michael W. Thompson, *Decline of the Castle*, map, p. 22.

The earliest examples in this wave of construction were largely built by newly transplanted English settlers. The house at Rathfarnham was erected sometime just before the turn of the century by Adam Loftus the Elder (Figure 14.7).[20] Born and raised in Yorkshire, Loftus was both the

Architectures of empire in Jamaica 263

Figure 14.7 Rathfarnham Castle, Dublin, Ireland, *c.* 1585, photo by the author.

Protestant Archbishop of Dublin and the Lord Chancellor of Ireland, the highest judicial office in Ireland under Elizabeth I, from 1581 to his death in 1605. He built Rathfarnham Castle on lands confiscated from the Eustace family in 1583. Although much altered in the later eighteenth century, the essential form of the corner-towered house survives from the original construction of the building in the late sixteenth century. The house's corner towers are not square but are slightly canted to take the more defensible form of a bastion. The house originally exhibited crenellations along its parapet that were removed in the eighteenth century. These martial features were put to the test in 1600 when the house underwent assault from Irish attackers during the Nine Years War, another effort by Irish Catholics to unseat English Protestant rule. Southern Ireland offers numerous other examples of such buildings, including Portumna Castle (1609), Mountlong Castle (begun 1631) and Monkstown Castle (begun

Figure 14.8 Monkstown Castle, Co. Cork, Ireland *c.* 1636, photo by the author.

1636, Figure 14.8), all erected by new English or old English, not ancient Irish, patrons. Mountlong and Monkstown, both built by old English families, are far more martial in their design, reflecting the prevailing anxiety in the years after the 1628 passing of 'the Graces', commitments between old English families and the English Crown. By the 1630s it was increasingly clear that attempts by old English families to achieve land security were unlikely, generating growing anxiety realised in the defensive architecture of their houses. These two houses enlisted the towered form as evidence of their claim to ancient 'English' authority, and also as strongholds to defend old English claims to landholdings militarily.[21]

The claims to authority asserted by this house form are probably best evident in the construction of Kanturk in northern Co. Cork (Figure 14.9). Constructed with substantial corner towers with fairly large windows, quoining, and an elaborated classical doorframe, the house is highly refined. The lack of gun loops or even windows in the towers flanking the sides of the house undermines any interpretation of the house as primarily defensible. Its symbolic meaning is made clear in the fact that Kanturk is the only house of this type by a man of ancient Irish heritage. MacDonagh McCarthy enlisted the architectural language of colonial power, but to great frustration. Objections to the construction of such a house were so great among his English counterparts that he was forced to terminate construction before the house was completed.[22] The symbolic significance of this form was well understood by new and old English, and Irish alike.

Architectures of empire in Jamaica   265

Figure 14.9 Kanturk Castle, Co. Cork, Ireland, *c.* 1609, photo by the author.

If the house with four corner towers was commonly built by English settlers in Ireland in the seventeenth century, the same form was erected by English elites on Jamaica in the eighteenth century. An important example is Stokes Hall, erected in the late seventeenth century with a rectilinear core and four solid corner towers, each fitted out with loopholes – tall, thin slots originally intended for use with firearms – facing out over the edges of its hilltop site and along the flanks of the building, providing cover for the windows and doors. The house was probably built by Luke Stokes, an early property-owner in Jamaica. A mid-eighteenth-century account reports that the sites of this and other properties were all burnt in a French attack in 1693 and that Stokes Hall stood in ruins at the time of that writing.[23] When an eighteenth-century member of the Arcedeckne family (sometimes spelled 'Archdeacon' in Jamaica) removed to Jamaica to establish a plantation adjacent to Stokes Hall, he would have recognised the ruin as being not entirely unlike Monkstown, his Irish ancestral home.[24] Two others include Robert Turner's house in Kingston, and Philip Pinnock's spectacular great house near Half-Way Tree. But the most obvious example, of course, is Colbeck Castle. While the loopholes in Stokes Hall are tall thin openings, Colbeck's circular windows seem to recall round versions of the same form. Yet, the

Figure 14.10 Stewart's Castle ruins, Trelawney Parish, Jamaica, begun 1760s, photo by the author.

circular windows are far too large actually to protect the person firing from within the house. The windows also appear only on the three publicly visible elevations, suggesting that the circular examples are positioned for visual effect, not functionality. Such a desire to appear defensive, rather than being actually defensive, suggests that Colbeck's towers carried some symbolic burden to communicate English authority over a threatening and exotic land. Colbeck is clear evidence of an English penchant for the construction of houses with four corner towers, which carried with them the popular association of authority – even ennoblement – especially in a contested landscape. But Colbeck represents only one of two British colonial strategies.

Until fairly recently, the ruins of Stewart's Castle were almost completely lost in the bush of Jamaica's north coast (Figure 14.10). Less than a mile from the major east–west highway, the site of the early great house was known by locals but visited by almost no one else. Upon first blush, the site is a bewildering mass of roofless stone walls. But after some time a few distinguishing features come into view. Standing prominently in the complex are tall square towers, two embedded in the house complex and one freestanding. A very large yard enclosed by an 8-foot-high wall, with the footprints of other buildings within, dominates the far side of the house ruins. Loopholes cut through the masonry on all sides. What is now a sprawling ruin was once an imposing, if curious, plantation great house.[25]

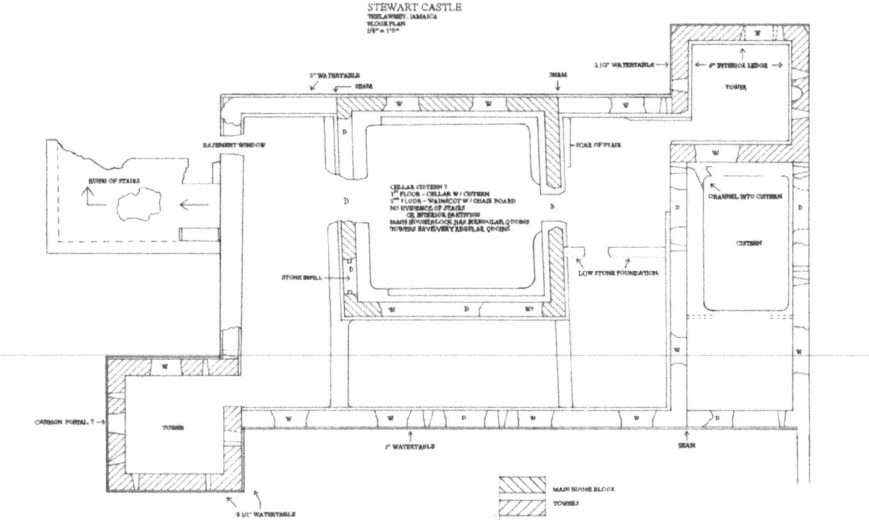

Figure 14.11 Plan of Stewart's Castle, drawn by students of Falmouth Field School, University of Virginia, 2008.

Stewart's Castle appears to have been constructed in two phases (Figure 14.11). Dominating the first phase was a large rubble limestone two-storey house with only one room per floor. This first phase included also two square towers, standing 12 feet distant from the main house, one to the northwest and the other to the southeast. That these towers were designed to provide military defence for the house is made explicit in the gun loops that open through almost every elevation, allowing both direct and enfilade fire. Archaeological evidence suggests that this phase of the house probably dates to the 1760s, soon after the plantation was patented by Scottish émigré James Stewart I in 1754.[26] The house was significantly expanded in the late eighteenth century by his son James Stewart II, who built a third freestanding tower fitted out with a cannon port, dug in a massive water cistern, and raised a huge courtyard wall of 8 feet in height complete with a total of thirty-six gun loops positioned every 10 feet along the length of the new wall.[27] Born in 1763, James Stewart II played a prominent role as a Lieutenant Colonel in the Maroon Wars of 1795. In these years, he undertook the massive expansion of his father's house into the footprint that remains on site today. As built by James Stewart I and expanded by his son, Stewart's Castle was a house site explicitly intent on military defence.

Like Colbeck Castle, Stewart's Castle has few peers in the American colonial context; it is a far cry from contemporary Georgian planters' houses in the Carolinas or Virginia. The few known fortified houses in the mainland colonies were erected in the frontier context of the seventeenth century. Lacking cousins on mainland America, the closest correspondents for Stewart's Castle are a collection of houses built in medieval and late medieval Scotland. Glenbuchat Castle, built in the late sixteenth century by Jacobite John Gordon, is a central-single-chamber but multistorey tower flanked at two corners by square towers, in plan very similar to Stewart's Castle on late-eighteenth-century Jamaica. Appearing as early as the twelfth century, Scottish tower houses were commonly constructed and occupied by middling gentry into the middle of the seventeenth century, especially in the Border regions, where the construction of tower houses peaked in the early seventeenth century.[28] While some are many storeys tall and boast complex plans, the majority of Scottish tower houses are actually fairly small in scale, often only a few storeys and only one room per floor.[29] The greatest concentration of these smaller tower houses date from the late sixteenth and early seventeenth century and are found in the Scottish Border counties.[30] Relative to their earlier counterparts, the majority have larger windows and thinner walls, since threats came not from invading siege armies but from lightly armed raiding parties. And the majority of tower houses originally boasted a walled courtyard, called a barmkin, even if few examples have survived. 'Z-plan' houses such as Glenbuchat were younger variants on smaller tower houses but included two towers positioned on opposite corners of the house. These towers were typically fitted out with gun loops protecting the elevations of the house.[31] Younger than the simple tower house, the Z-plan house became common in Scotland in the middle of the sixteenth century, and appeared most commonly in rural, contested territories.[32] Claypotts Castle, outside Dundee in Scotland, is another excellent surviving example. With a rectangular core flanked by rounded corner towers, this Z-plan castle has fairly small windows and cellar loopholes that are clearly intended for military protection (Figure 14.12). Stewart's Castle has far more in common with the architecture of Scotland than it does with that of Virginia, Pennsylvania or Massachusetts.

As with the British occupation of Ireland, the British occupation of Jamaica was from its inception marked by a sense of martial contest. Unlike any other British colonial holding in the region Jamaica was forcibly taken from another major European power – the Spanish. While the English were able to take the capital of Spanish Town easily, without a single casualty, control of the rest of the island took another five years of bitter guerrilla warfare with small bands of Spanish resistance fighters, familiar with the landscape, surprising English troops. As the Spanish eventually departed, they left behind abundant evidence of their previous occupation – houses,

Figure 14.12 Claypotts Castle, near Dundee, Scotland, 1569–88, photo by the author.

government buildings and churches – most of which the British colonials occupied and slowly adapted to their own uses.[33] But the threats were not all in the past. Jamaica's sugar plantations enslaved the largest population of Africans and a greater disproportion of blacks to whites than any other British colony by the early years of the eighteenth century.[34] Enslaved Africans were the majority population in Barbados by 1660, and in South Carolina by 1720.[35] While Virginian's owned a large number of enslaved Africans, their numbers were never greater than the colony's white occupants.[36] The disparity was by far the greatest on Jamaica where, by 1710, the island faced an eight-to-one black-to-white majority.[37] The number of Africans on the island more than doubled between 1700 and 1750, and increased again by a factor of five by the end of the century.[38] The Caribbean slave-based agricultural economy had distinct implications for the physical nature of the plantation landscape. The heat and humidity; the dense and lush vegetation; and the exotic flowers, animals and birds more closely approximated Africa than foggy England. One Englishman noted that the seemingly innumerable enslaved people in Jamaica were summoned to their labours not by European bells but 'by the sound of a Conche-shell'. He also noted that thatched huts on this tropical island made 'every Plantation look like a little African city'.[39] Writing in the 1740s, James Knight described the life of a planter on Jamaica as defined by 'great anxiety and trouble'. The large populations of slaves, he continued, generate 'great uneasiness and vexation'.[40] With good reason, Jamaica's planters were fearful of enslaved Africans.

The greatest decades of slave rebellion were those around the 1760s, right as towered houses become most prominent across Jamaica.[41] Tacky's Revolt in 1760 was followed by a horrific sequence of public executions.[42] Physical reminders of that punishment marked the landscape; severed heads left on poles, often for years, were only the most gruesome examples. Jamaica was a landscape shaped by ever-present violence.

But Jamaica was also a prized British possession in a region occupied by the French, the Spanish and rogue pirates. Settlements along the east coast of the island had been attacked by the French in 1694. Those same settlements remained ruinous until the middle of the eighteenth century, an episode that lived long in Jamaican memory.[43] James Knight noted in 1742 that many Jamaicans along the north coast were continuously 'under some apprehensions of being invaded by the French ... People are backward in settling there afterwards as it lay very much exposed to the Enemy, and is within 24 hours sail of the French settlements on Hispanola.'[44] Thomas Thistlewood's mid-century diary offers numerous accounts of raids or the fear of raids on Jamaican plantations by both French and Spanish marauders.[45] Edward Long noted in the 1770s that many of the planters in St Ann's had been attacked by Spanish privateers during the mid-century wars, 'in order to plunder the inhabitants of their Negroes'.[46] In the late eighteenth century, renewed hostilities between the English and the French and Spanish reawakened the fear of invasion.[47] War, or at least the fear of attack or invasion from enslaved people, maroons, or foreign enemies, was a persistent threat throughout the eighteenth century. Historian Trevor Burnard argues flatly: 'Jamaica was a society at war.'[48] That persistent martial character shaped the built environment in Jamaica, not just in the seventeenth century but throughout the period of slavery.

And in this way, colonial Jamaica echoes colonial Ireland. If the English house with four corner towers came to mark the landscape of English-colonised Munster, the defensive tower house of the Scots came to mark Scottish-colonised Ulster. Prior to the 1590s the Irish in the northern region of Ulster had most successfully resisted military and cultural incursion, and as a result had remained fiercely Gaelic. The beginnings of colonialism in the north, however, were made all the easier in 1607, when a confederation of Irish chiefs departed Ulster for Spain to gain an ally against the English. In their absence, the English Governor seized their lands. Resistance by Ireland's northern chiefs eventually led to the seizure of all land held by native Irish landowners, and the foundation of the Ulster plantation by James I in 1609. The subsequent colonisation process in Ulster was carefully orchestrated.

British undertakers in Ulster who received 2,000 acres were required to build a castle and a bawn. Those receiving 1,500 acres had to build a house and bawn: a walled, unroofed, fortified enclosure usually used for protecting cattle. Finally, those with only 100 acres were to build at least a bawn. As a result of an aggressive colonisation campaign during the first two decades of the seventeenth century, Northern Ireland was marked by the construction of plantation castles and houses by British settlers, the vast majority of whom were not English but Scottish.[49] Excellent examples survive among the collection of planters' houses erected at the dawn of the seventeenth century in Co. Fermanagh, a territory at the southwest edge of Ulster.[50] When colonising early-seventeenth-century Ireland, Scots brought with them the defensible tower houses of their own embattled landscape.

By the end of the seventeenth century, the English had invaded Jamaica and continued their campaign of claiming and dominating a landscape, only this time the dangerous 'savages' were the enslaved Africans and self-emancipated African maroons brought to Jamaica against their will. In this way, Ireland and Jamaica were part of a continuous colonising process, one that shaped these landscapes – both barbarous marchlands – in very particular ways.[51] Examples from Jamaica demonstrate that the English and the Scots employed different material strategies, that the power of defensive architecture is simultaneously real – actually martial – and symbolic – burdened with social message – and finally that the condition of being a marchland persisted in Jamaica through the eighteenth century.

While it is among the most extraordinary examples, Stewart's Castle is not atypical. The early house at Kew Park has a small, rectilinear core flanked by two tall square towers on opposite corners, in an arrangement much like that of the 1760s Stewart's Castle (Figure 14.13). Intact gun loops make clear that these towers were defensive in nature. The same is true of the diminutive and early house ruin called Edinburgh Castle in St Ann Parish, built soon after the arrival of its builder, Lewis Hutchison, in the 1760s (Figure 14.14 and 14.15).[52] Although they are rounded (rather than squared, as in most examples) the attached corner towers of Edinburgh Castle closely resemble the placement of the towers at Kew Park and Claypotts Castle in Scotland. These are Z-plan Scottish houses in the Jamaican landscape. Archaeological excavations of Auchindown Castle in Westmoreland reported on the site 'two imposing castellated towers' connected by a tall wall that probably defined an enclosed courtyard.[53] In another example, a freestanding tower, similar to that erected in the second phase of construction at Stewart's Castle, appears in an early-nineteenth-century print of Montpelier plantation in St James Parish.

This building type survives also in the documentary record. For example, the 1748 probate inventory of a plantation great house called Stewart's Fort

Figure 14.13 Kew Park, Westmoreland Parish, Jamaica, late eighteenth century, photo by the author.

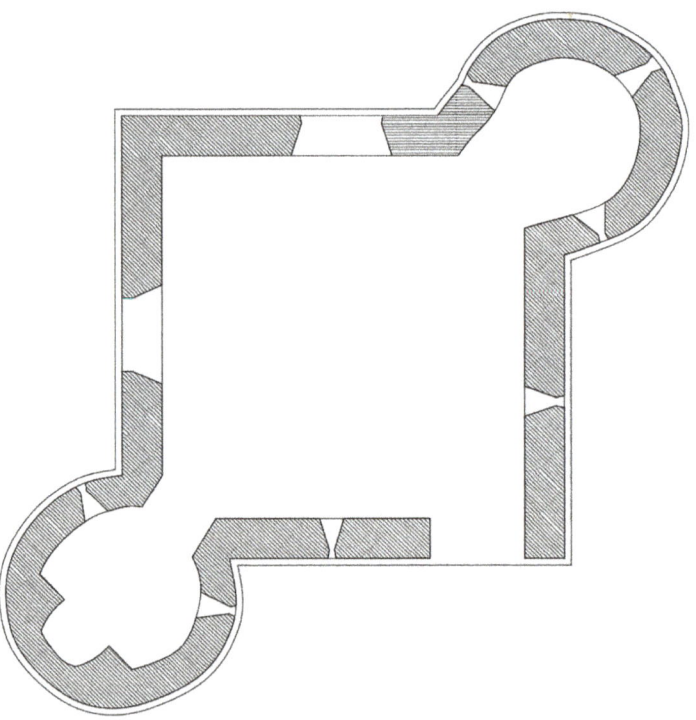

Figure 14.14 Plan of Edinburgh Castle, St Ann Parish, Jamaica, measured by the author, drawn by Jason Truesdale.

Figure 14.15 Edinburgh Castle, St Ann Parish, Jamaica, photo by the author.

in St George Parish indicates that the house boasted not only a great hall, a great room, a blue room and piazzas, but also three bastions: a stone bastion, Dr Stewart's bastion and the overseer's bastion. The first had a bedstead, chest of drawers and various table linens, but also two cutlasses and two blunderbusses. The overseer's bastion, too, was fitted out with a bedstead and table, but also two guns, two more blunderbusses and a 'Speaking Trumpet'. Dr Stewart's bastion was, not surprisingly, the finest, including a bedstead and fittings; a table with other furniture; fine specimens of silver; and, again, two blunderbusses and two pistols.[54] The bastions were the chambers most well fitted out with arms. These bastions, surely positioned at or near the corners of the main rooms of the house, were unquestionably intended for defence, and demonstrate that these substantial masonry bastions functioned as rooms in a house, all the while invoking the capacity for military defence. Like these examples, many late-eighteenth- and early-nineteenth-century houses erected in Jamaica's western and northern parishes were designed with defensive towers sometimes attached to the house on opposite corners or sometimes freestanding at some distance. Some also had enclosed yards or bawns defended by tall masonry walls fitted out with gun loops.

These smaller, clearly defensive houses of northern Jamaica have evident correspondence with the Scottish-settler-built houses of Northern Ireland.

Figure 14.16 Monea Castle, Co. Fermanagh, Ireland, *c.* 1616, photo by the author.

Examples survive among the collection of planter houses erected at the dawn of the seventeenth century in Co. Fermanagh. Begun by Scot Malcolm Hamilton in 1616, Monea is among the most impressive (Figure 14.16). The substantial two-and-a-half-storey masonry house is defined by two round towers that flank the end-wall entrance. The gun loops in the house walls and those of the end towers were reinforced by a 12-foot wall defining the 100-foot square courtyard or bawn, itself defended by rounded corner towers. Monea's defensible bawn is the Irish predecessor to that on Stewart's Castle on Jamaica over a century and a half later.

Not surprisingly, these west- and north-coast defensive great houses all appear to date from the mid-eighteenth to the early nineteenth century, built by planters who had recently emigrated from Scotland.[55] Scottish family- and place-names abound: Stewart, Ainslie, Sterling, Auchindown, Edinburgh and Hutchison. Historian Alan Karras has examined in detail the community he refers to as the Scottish sojourners to Jamaica.[56] He describes these men as second and third sons of middling and educated Scottish families who travelled to Jamaica with the specific intention of making a livable fortune and returning to Scotland. This was, however, a hope that few actually realised.[57] Karras notes that the emigration of Scottish sojourners to Jamaica began in earnest in the 1740s and escalated through the eighteenth century. As a result of the lateness of their arrival relative to their English counterparts, the majority of these Scottish planters purchased land in the frontier regions of the west and north coasts, principally Westmoreland, Hanover, St James, Trelawney and St Ann parishes. By the end of the eighteenth century, all of these parishes had a 25 per cent or more population of Scottish landowners.[58] As a result of this density, Karras argues, there emerged mutually reinforcing webs of relationships among Scottish professionals and planters. These worked as networks of support but also to reinforce kinship networks and to distinguish Scots on Jamaica from their English counterparts, at least through the second half of the eighteenth century.[59]

The houses erected in Jamaica by these Scottish sojourners are surprising. By the second half of the eighteenth century, the majority of middling educated Scottish families were building for themselves in Scotland single- or double-pile 'Georgian' houses with symmetrical front elevations and plans with central passages flanked by large, well-lit chambers.[60] In short, the houses of most middling Scots were not fundamentally differentiated from those of their English counterparts. The houses erected by a number of Scottish sojourners to Jamaica, however, drew upon older, more defensive architectural traditions long inscribed in the Scottish landscape, especially the tower house and the Z-plan house.

Jamaica's Scottish sojourners chose not to build for themselves genteel Georgian country houses with central passages and large glazed sash windows such as those most of these émigrés would have known in Scotland. In building towers houses and Z-plan houses, both of which were largely abandoned as forms for new buildings in Scotland by the mid- and late eighteenth century, they drew upon the memories of the defensive architecture of their homelands. If the main house erected at Stewart's Castle by John Stewart I was a tower house – a substantial house with a single room per floor – Stewart's Fort, Edinburgh Castle and Kew Park were all derivatives of the Scottish Z-plan house. In both cases, the choice to reject fashionable options in favour of defence was clear reflection of Scottish anxieties about personal safety in Jamaica's hostile environment. And the concentrated appearance of these houses in the 1760s is not at all a surprise; this was the same decade as the greatest number of Jamaica's slave rebellions. Hoping to reside but a while, these planters erected houses like those that had defended personal landholdings for centuries.

There are some extraordinary parallels between the plantation houses of early-seventeenth-century Ireland and mid-eighteenth-century Jamaica. Both are marked by two types of towered houses. Just as Munster in southern Ireland boasts a large number of English-built manor houses defined largely by four prominent corner towers, so too does that form prevail in the older more predominantly English parishes of Clarendon and St Dorothy on Jamaica. Built by both old and new English, the house with four corner towers was in Ireland sometimes a practical measure, but always a symbolic gesture of English claims to authority over the land. As a result of this history, the symbolic power of Jamaica's towered houses becomes all the clearer. Drawing from a centuries-long practice in the British Isles, newly wealthy planters in Jamaica used architecture to assert their authority over the landscape. The parallels between Jamaica and Ireland are evident not only in the architecture of English elites, but also in that of their Scottish counterparts. Just as Ulster in Northern Ireland exhibited a number of Scottish-derived tower houses, usually with appended or freestanding defensive flankers, often connected via a bawn wall, so, too, is this form evident in Jamaica, again built largely by Scots. Emigrating Scots were not unfamiliar with the militarisation of houses in a colonial context. The emigration of Scots to Jamaica in the eighteenth century was in many ways a repeat of an earlier emigration of Scots into Northern Ireland in the very early seventeenth century.

The architectural parallels between the two colonies suggest that alone among Britain's colonial territories, Ireland and Jamaica are the most typological of colonialism in Britain's early empire. Occupation of both islands by the British was a process hotly contested by 'others'. As a result, if Ireland was the contested frontier of the English empire in the sixteenth and seventeenth centuries, Jamaica appears to have matured on that same model by the early eighteenth century. In both cases, British occupation depended on the seizure of land, a process accompanied by forcible resistance from indigenes. In Ireland, that resistance took the form of armed rebellion through the late sixteenth and early seventeenth century. In Jamaica, resistance was first presented by the Spanish colonisers from whom Jamaica was seized, then the island's population of maroons, descendants of Africans enslaved by the Spanish who fled during the seizure of Jamaica by the English. The maroons offered periodic and violent resistance to English control of the island and remained a consistent threat until the English signed a peace treaty in 1739 recognising maroon nationhood and independence. As in Ireland, the towers on houses in Jamaica were sometimes actually defensive, as in the case of Stokes Hall, but were always intended as a symbolic claim to political authority and control of the land.

The reality of occupying a marchland had a profound impact on the *mentalité* of colonial residents. The British colonial presence in both Ireland and Jamaica was marked by a profound uncertainty, an unrelenting anxiety that found expression in their architecture. The houses built by Scottish and English planters demonstrate the coherence of a colonial marchland mentality and, furthermore, that planters, first in Ireland and then in Jamaica, were themselves agents of empire.

Notes

* An earlier version of this argument appears as Chapter 2, 'Castles of fear', in Louis P. Nelson, *Architecture and Empire in Jamaica* (New Haven: Yale University Press, 2016), pp. 36–64.
1 For a fuller examination of Colbeck Castle see Nelson, *Architecture and Empire*, pp. 152–7.
2 Eric Klingelhofer, 'Colonial castles: The architecture of social control', in David S. Shields, ed., *Material Culture in Anglo-America: Regional Identity and Urbanity in the Tidewater, Lowcountry, and Caribbean* (Columbia: University of South Carolina Press, 2009), pp. 74–102.
3 Mark Girouard, *Robert Smythson and the Elizabethan Country House* (London: Country Life, 1983), pp. 34–6, 206–30; Michael W. Thompson, *Decline of the Castle* (Cambridge: Cambridge University Press, 1987), Chapter 5; Colin Platt, *The Castle in Medieval England and Wales* (New York: Scribner and Sons, 1982), Chapters 7 and 8.
4 Mark Girouard described it as participating in the 'mysterious Spenserian world, neither Gothic nor classic'; see Girouard, *Robert Smythson*, p. 225.
5 Charles McKean, *The Scottish Chateau: The Country House of Renaissance Scotland* (Stroud: Sutton, 2001), p. 41.
6 Tadhg O'Keeffe, 'Kilcolman Castle, Co. Cork: A new interpretation of Edmund Spenser's residence in plantation Munster', *International Journal of Historical Archaeology* 21:1 (2017), 223–39.
7 Recognising the increasing significance of landholding as a sign of status, those whose wealth derived primarily from trade or business were especially motivated to purchase large tracts of land in the two centuries following the dissolution of the monasteries by Henry VIII. See James P. Cooper, 'Social distribution of land and men in England, 1436–1700', *Economic History Review* 20:3 (1967), 419–40; and Christopher Clay, 'Marriage, inheritance and the rise of large estates in England, 1660–1815', *Economic History Review* 21:3 (1968), 503–18. For work on this subject that foregrounds religious identity and includes Ireland see Alexandra Walsham, *The Reformation of the Landscape* (Oxford: Oxford University Press, 2012).
8 Dana Arnold, 'The country house: Form, function and meaning', in Dana Arnold, ed., *The Georgian Country House: Architecture, Landscape and Society* (Stroud: Sutton, 1998), pp. 1–19 (p. 18); Dana Arnold, 'Living off the land: Innovations in farm practices and farm design', in Arnold, *The Georgian Country House*, pp. 152–66. G. E. Mingay, 'The size of farms in the eighteenth century', *Economic History Review* 14:3 (1962), 469–88. See also H. A. Clemenson *English Country Houses and Landed Estates* (London: Croom Helm, 1982); and Edward P. Thompson, 'Patrician society, plebian culture', *Journal of Social History* 7:4 (1974), 382–405.
9 Malcolm Airs, in his study of Tudor and Jacobean country houses, notes the increasing power of the country house, newly erected on recently acquired

tracts of land, to fashion and communicate the identity of the patron and their family. Malcolm Airs, *The Tudor and Jacobean Country House* (Stroud: Sutton, 1995), Chapter 1.

10 Tracey Avery, *Tattershall Castle, Lincolnshire* ([n.p.]: National Trust, 1997), p. 5. See also Matthew Johnson, *Behind the Castle Gate: From Medieval to Rensaissance* (London: Routledge, 2002), p. 60.
11 Girouard, *Robert Smythson*, pp. 4–5.
12 Ibid., 83; David N. Durant, *The Smythson Circle: The Story of Six Great English Houses* (London: Peter Owen, 2011), p. 71.
13 Johnson, *Behind the Castle Gate*, p. 133.
14 Ibid., pp. 173–4.
15 Thompson, *Decline of the Castle*, p. 158 (emphasis mine).
16 Ibid.
17 Ibid., p. 22.
18 An excellent introduction to the theory and practice of colonisation in Munster can be found in Nicholas P. Canny, *Making Ireland British, 1580–1650* (Oxford: Oxford University Press, 2001), Chapter 3.
19 On the population of Munster with settlers from the southwest of England see Robert Dunlop, 'The plantation of Munster 1584–1589', *English Historical Review* 3:10 (1888), 250–69. See also Robert Dunlop, 'An unpublished survey of the plantation of Munster in 1622', *Journal of the Royal Society of Antiquaries of Ireland* 14:2 (1924), 128–46 (p. 143).
20 For more on Rathfarnham see Edward McParland, 'Rathfarnham Castle: A property of the Society of Jesus', *Country Life* (September 1982), 734. See also Tadhg O'Keeffe, *Irish Medieval Buildings, 1100–1600* (Dublin: Four Courts Press, 2015).
21 On 'the Graces', and confiscation of old English land, see Aidan Clarke, *The Old English in Ireland* (Dublin: Four Courts Press, 2000).
22 Maurice Craig, *Architecture of Ireland: From the Earliest Times to 1880* (London: Batsford Eason, 1982), p. 118.
23 James Knight, *Portions of a History of Jamaica to 1742*, British Library, Add. MS 12417, p. 77.
24 For more on the Archdeacon family in Jamaica see Barry W. Higman, *Plantation Jamaica, 1750–1850: Capital and Control in a Colonial Economy* (Kingston: University of West Indies Press, 2005), p. 147.
25 The best summary of the house site is found in Steven Panning, 'Exploring Stewart Castle estate', *Jamaican Historical Journal* 10:14 (1995), 172–9, 199–205. See also Jillian Galle, 'Stewart Castle main house: Background' (September 2007), Digital Archaeological Archive of Comparative Slavery (DAACS), www.daacs.org/sites/stewart-castle-main-house/#background (accessed 27 August 2022); and Lynsey Bates, 'Surveillance and production on Stewart Castle estate: A GIS-based analysis of models of plantation spatial organization', distinguished major's thesis (University of Virginia, 2007), p. 53.
26 Jillian Galle, 'Stewart Castle', in *Vernacular Architecture Forum Field Guide*, unpublished conference notes (2011); Jillian Galle, 'Stewart Castle main

house: Background' (September 2007), DAACS, www.daacs.org/sites/stewart-castle-main-house/#background (accessed 27 August 2022).
27 Jillian Galle, 'Stewart Castle main house: Chronology' (September 2007), DAACS, www.daacs.org/sites/stewart-castle-main-house/#chronology (accessed 27 August 2022).
28 John G. Dunbar, *The Historic Architecture of Scotland* (London: Batsford, 1966), pp. 36, 66; Kitty Cruft, John Dunbar and Richard Fawcett, *The Buildings of Scotland: Borders* (New Haven: Yale University Press, 2006), p. 45.
29 Dunbar, *The Historic Architecture of Scotland*, p. 44.
30 Cruft, Dunbar and Fawcett, *The Buildings of Scotland*, pp. 45–7.
31 Z-plan houses with towers at two corners were first identified as a type by David MacGibbon and Thomas Ross, *Castellated and Domestic Architecture of Scotland from the Twelfth to the Eighteenth Century*, 5 vols (Edinburgh: David Douglas, 1887). The Z-plan house also took on a non-defensive form among elites in the seventeenth century in the northeast of Scotland; see Miles Glendenning, Ranald MacInnes, and Aonghus MacKechnie, *A History of Scottish Architecture* (Edinburgh: Edinburgh University Press, 1996), pp. 46–9.
32 Dunbar, *The Historic Architecture of Scotland*, p. 42; Deborah Howard, *Scottish Architecture from the Reformation to the Restoration 1560–1660* (Edinburgh: Edinburgh University Press, 1995), pp. 51–3.
33 See James Robertson, 'Late seventeenth-century Spanish Town, Jamaica: Building an English city on Spanish foundations', *Early American Studies* 6:2 (2008), 346–90.
34 By the 1710s, blacks outnumbered whites on the island of Jamaica by eight to one. The number of Africans on the island more than doubled between 1700 and 1750 and increased by a factor of five by the end of the century. Trevor Burnard and Kenneth Morgan state decisively that 'Jamaica had the largest demand for enslaved people of any British colony in the Americas'; Trevor Burnard and Kenneth Morgan, 'The dynamics of the slave market and slave purchasing patterns in Jamaica, 1655–1788', *William and Mary Quarterly* 58:1 (2001): 205–28 (205). See also Richard S. Dunn, *Sugar and Slaves: The Rise of the Planter Class in the English West Indies 1624–1713* (Chapel Hill: University of North Carolina Press, 1972), pp. 164–5. On increasing absenteeism see Douglas Hall, 'Absentee-proprietorship in the British West Indies to about 1850', *Jamaican Historical Review* 4 (1964), 15–35.
35 Dunn, *Sugar and Slaves*, p. 226; Peter H. Wood, *Black Majority: Negroes in Colonial South Carolina from 1670 through the Stono Rebellion* (London: W. W. Norton, 1996), p. 131.
36 Isaac Rhys, *The Transformation of Virginia 1740–1790* (Chapel Hill: University of North Carolina Press, 2012), p. 12.
37 Dunn, *Sugar and Slaves*, pp. 164–5.
38 Burnard and Morgan, 'The dynamics of the slave market', pp. 205–6.
39 John Oldmixon, *The British Empire in America: Containing the History of the Discovery, Settlement, Progress and State of the British Colonies on the Continent and Islands of America*, 2 vols (London: Brotherton and Clarke,

1741), Vol. I, p. 120. The typical eighteenth-century slave quarter, earthfast, thatched and plastered inside, is described in detail in John Stewart, *An Account of Jamaica and Its Inhabitants* (London: Longman, Hurst, Rees and Orme, 1808), p. 231.

40 Knight, *Portions of a History of Jamaica*, p. 77.
41 Dunn, *Sugar and Slaves*, p. 256.
42 Michael Craton, *Testing the Chains: Resistance to Slavery in the British West Indies* (Ithaca, NY: Cornell University Press, 2009), pp. 125–39; see also Trevor Burnard, *Mastery, Tyranny, and Desire: Thomas Thistlewood and His Slaves in the Anglo-Jamaican World* (Chapel Hill: University of North Carolina Press, 2004), p. 10.
43 Knight, *Portions of a History of Jamaica*, p. 77.
44 *Ibid.*, p. 71.
45 Douglas Hall, *In Miserable Slavery: Thomas Thistlewood in Jamaica 1750–1786* (Warwick: Macmillan, 1989), pp. 124, 126, 239, 240, 253, 267, 269, 289.
46 Edward Long, *History of Jamaica*, 3 vols (London: T. Lowndes, 1774), Vol. II, p. 100.
47 *Ibid.*, Vol. II, pp. 171–2.
48 Burnard, *Mastery, Tyranny, and Desire*, p. 33.
49 On the history of seventeenth-century Ireland see Brendan Fitzpatrick, *Seventeenth-Century Ireland: The War of Religions* (Lanham, MD: Rowman and Littlefield, 1989); on the architecture of this period see Harold G. Leask, *Irish Castles and Castellated Houses* (Dundalk: Dundalgan Press, 1941), p. 137.
50 Edward Martyn Jope, 'Scottish influences in the North of Ireland: Castles with Scottish features, 1580–1640', *Ulster Journal of Archaeology* 15 (1951), 31–47. See also Edward Martyn Jope, 'Moyry, Charlemont, Castleraw, and Richhill', *Ulster Journal of Archaeology* 23 (1960), 97–123 (p. 111).
51 Bernard Bailyn, *Atlantic History* (Cambridge, MA: Harvard University Press, 2005), p. 67.
52 'Edinburgh Castle', in *Jamaica National Heritage Trust Report* (Kingston: Jamaica National Heritage Trust, 2005).
53 G. A. Aarons, 'Auchindown excavation 1983–84', unpublished report for the Centre for Archeological and Conservation Research, Port Royal, Jamaica.
54 Special thanks to Robert Barker for bringing this source to my attention.
55 For distribution, consider the presence of the same building types in Oman, some built by the Portuguese, but many built by the Omanis (special thanks to Dell Upton for making this observation). The connection between Scotland and Jamaica has been previously addressed, although with a very different trajectory, by Sophie Drinkall, 'The Jamaican plantation house: Scottish influence', *Architectural Heritage* 2:1 (1991), 56–68.
56 For a comparable assessment of the rise of Scottish merchants in the Chesapeake tobacco trade see Jacob M. Price, *Tobacco in Atlantic Trade* (Brookfield, VA: Variorum, 1995).

57 Alan Karras, *Sojourners in the Sun: Scottish Migrants in Jamaica and the Chesapeake, 1740–1800* (Ithaca, NY: Cornell University Press, 1992): for a profile of typical sojourners see pp. 4, 49–50. By contrast, poorer Scots, he notes, usually preferred to immigrate to the American mainland, which offered broader opportunities and required less start-up capital for success. On Scottish exportation to the colonies see T. M. Devine, *Scotland's Empire and the Shaping of the Americas* (Washington, DC: Smithsonian Books, 2004).
58 Karras, *Sojourners in the Sun*, pp. 122–9.
59 *Ibid.*, pp. 120, 139.
60 Glendenning, MacInnes and MacKechnie, *A History of Scottish Architecture*, Chapters 3 and 4; Dunbar, *The Historic Architecture of Scotland*, pp. 81–7.

15

Designed in parallel or in translation? The linked Jamaican and Irish landscapes of the Browne family, marquesses of Sligo

Finola O'Kane

Westport is one of Ireland's most admired eighteenth-century urban landscapes. Caught between Mayo's great conical mountain of Cruach Phádraig to the south and the wild Atlantic to the west it is also one of Ireland's most agreeable tourist destinations. Westport town's centrepiece is Westport House, a great eighteenth-century mansion designed by Richard Castle for the Browne family in c. 1730. It is surrounded by an important landscape garden that integrates the demesne's unusual sea prospect with a river that tumbles through the designed landscape from Westport's mall – a rare surviving example of the Georgian urban set piece that formally combined architecture and water. In Ireland a demesne is the land surrounding a great house that is managed and farmed by the owner directly and is not leased out to others. Bounded generally by a high wall of stone, a demesne is typically a designed landscape of considerable scale, with an attendant level of aesthetic and agricultural ambition. All contribute to making Westport one of the most elegant estate towns ever built in Ireland (Figure 15.1).

In the early eighteenth century Dennis Kelly and his four brothers emigrated from Galway to the Caribbean. There they prospered, so much so that by 1740 the brothers controlled some 20,000 acres across the entire island of Jamaica, ranging from the rich lowland plantation of Kelly's Walk, which lay close to town of Old Harbour, to the more upland plantation of Cocoa Walk (Figure 15.2).[1] Dennis Kelly inherited land from his brothers, and probably some also from his wife, Priscilla Halstead (b. c. 1700), whom he had married on 28 May 1725. She was the daughter of John Halstead (d. 1721, sometimes known as Col. Halstead) and Elizabeth Hyde (c. 1670–1734), both members of Jamaica's early planter families. Dennis Kelly reached the pinnacle of the island's plantocracy as Chief Justice of Jamaica in 1742 and then returned to Ireland, using some of the substantial profits of his Jamaican sugar plantations to acquire the Co. Galway estate of Lisduff. In 1752 his only daughter, the Jamaican-born heiress Elizabeth

Figure 15.1 James Arthur O'Connor, *View of Westport from the Northeast*, 1818, Victoria and Albert Museum.

Figure 15.2 Patrick Browne, *A new map of Jamaica; in which the several towns, forts, and settlements, are accurately laid down as well as ye situations & depts. of ye most noted harbours & anchoring places* (London, 1755), Library of Congress.

Kelly, married Peter Browne, Second Earl of Atlamont (1731?–80). He was the son and heir of John Browne (1709–76), First Earl of Altamont, whose mother, Mary Daly, as the daughter of Denis Daly (c. 1638–1721) of Carrownekelly, had united in marriage two major Irish-Jamaican families, whose web of members included the owners, lessors, agents or attorneys of many plantations and their hundreds of enslaved workers.[2] Both families also possessed substantial landed property in the poor and unimproved reaches of Galway and Mayo.[3]

In the early twentieth century Lord Arthur Howe Browne (1867–1951), the great-grandson of Elizabeth Kelly, and Eighth Marquess of Sligo from 1941, made an undated list of the Jamaican property that the family had inherited from Dennis Kelly via the dowry of his Jamaican-born daughter. Finding that their Jamaican estates 'stretched more or less North to South across the east centre of the island and includ[ed] land north of Oldharbour to Kingston road, [distancing] say 25 miles', he calculated that 'the most valuable plantations were Cocoa Walks, Kelly's, Gandy's, and Goffe's', and referred to the 'pictures of the first two' that were then at Westport, while he could not 'trace a house and place called Altamont'.[4] He was probably working from deeds and maps that were then in Westport House, and the vast extent of their Jamaican landed property is evident, although it is difficult to map it accurately or pinpoint the plantations on the relevant maps because of the speed with which they changed hands, and often names (Figure 15.3). Although they were not among the original families who took land grants from the Crown, the Kelly brothers were well positioned to profit from the peak advance in Jamaica's sugar frontier in the early eighteenth century.[5] Intermarrying with such leading island families as the Halsteads and the Fullers, they were among those who pushed into Jamaica's interior, developing the upper regions of St Thomas-in-the-Vale and St Andrew parishes. Early plantations generally took the name of their owners, and as these were often changed subsequently this makes them difficult to trace on the map record, particularly as maps of Jamaica's interior were not at all exact. Many of the newer names, such as 'Happy Valley' or 'Friendship' plantations, seem singularly inappropriate for sugar plantations. Some of the acres that Lord Arthur H. Browne itemised were probably never developed into the monocultural farmland characteristic of designed plantation landscapes but kept for the capital gains that rapidly increasing land values could generate for their owners. Itemising their acreage in one parish alone, Lord Arthur listed:

> In Parish of St. Thomas in the Vale, 200 acres bounding northerly on Negro River, south on Rio Pedro or New River, 240 acres in Rio Pedro Villiacoius bounded by Rio Pedro on three sides; 30 acres at Rio Pedro formerly in St. Catherine's Parish, now in St Thomas'; 240 acres in Rio Pedro bounding N. and NW on Rio Pedro and waste mountain; 200 acres bounding SW and

W on Sandy River walk to Lecunes?, 150 acres on New River, 500 acres near Hilliards Plantation; (and moiety of 46, 35, and 25 new-negro slaves thereon.[6]

Among these were included the 'various sugar or cocoa plantations from 6 to 230 acres in parish of St Thomas in the Vale near Golden River, Rio Pedron, Andrew Road, Rio de Diable, Rio de Arado, etc.', one of which was called 'Savage's Waterwork (conveyed by P. Savage)'. This appears on James Craskell's 1758 map of Jamaica, where it neighboured Fullers and Glengoff plantations, which may also have been controlled by the Kelly–Browne alliance: Fullers through Edmund Kelly's marriage, and Glengoff as the 'Goff's' of Browne's list (Figure 15.3).[7]

Figure 15.3 Detail of James Craskell, *Map of Middlesex*, Jamaica, 1756, showing some of the plantations known to have been owned or controlled by the Kelly family, Library of Congress.

The agricultural theorist Arthur Young included details of the improvements made by John Browne, First Earl of Altamont, to Westport town's urban development in his *Tour in Ireland 1776–1779*, describing his project for a fledgling linen trade and his general agricultural advances in improving the mountainous island and farming landscapes around Westport:

> In introducing the linen manufacture, his Lordship has made great exertions ... In order to establish it, he built good houses in the town of Westport, and let them upon very reasonable terms to weavers, gave them looms, and lent them money to buy yarn and in order to secure them from manufacturing goods, which they should not be readily able to sell, he constantly bought all they could not sell, which for some years was all they made; but by degrees, as the manufacture arose, buyers come in, so that he has for some time not bought any great quantity. The first year, 1772, he bought as much as cost him £200; the next year, 1773, £700; the next 1774, as much as £2,000; and in 1775, above £4,000 worth.[8]

Such initiatives required substantial initial investment. Although silent on the source of Browne's investment monies, and whether or not John Browne had control of the Jamaican estates that his daughter-in-law had brought into the family by marrying his son in 1752, Young does comment on the scale of the investment involved and its resultant impact on the rental income of the Westport estate.[9] For a family in receipt of a mere £700 per annum in the early eighteenth century,[10] and allowing for the fact that land rents 'had trebled in forty years',[11] Caribbean sugar plantations probably provided some of the funding required for the conspicuous improvements 'prosecut[ed]' with 'much spirit' in the 'various parts of husbandry'.[12]

The evidence suggests that many Irish gentlemen who profited from their Jamaican plantations in the early eighteenth century judged it wise to leave Jamaica once they had made their fortunes, and this has made the eighteenth-century history of plantation design and transfer difficult to reconstruct. As 'the fertility of cane land before modern fertilizers tended to decrease fairly rapidly over time',[13] Jamaican land was at its most valuable in the early half of the eighteenth century, and Dennis Kelly's exit strategy for Ireland, daughter and heiress in tow, neatly aligned with the Browne family's expansion and redevelopment of Westport town. Although no accounts for the eighteenth-century Browne estate are known to exist, the profits of these Jamaican plantations, inherited by Elizabeth Kelly, must have helped to fund the creation of the estate town of Westport, the 1770s expansion of Richard Castle's substantial 1730s house by James Ivory, and the attendant designed landscape. The profits of sugar appear therefore to have funded the improvement of one of the poorest regions of the British Isles, and also gave Ireland's most beautiful estate town a tangled legacy of enslavement and exploitation at its roots.

John Denis Browne (1756–1809), Third Earl of Altamont, was made Marquess of Sligo in 1800 as a reward for his strong support for the Act of Union. Such bribes and their accompanying substantial monetary compensation were awarded by the British Government to landlords who voted for the Union and who lost seats and political power in doing so. These large cash injections occasioned much rebuilding and improvement of Irish demesnes across the country, and many Irish architects benefited from the commissions. He was succeeded on his death in 1809 by his only son, Howe Peter Browne, Second Marquess of Sligo, and in 1815 the young Marquess wrote to his mother of how pleased he was with the 'good accounts his attorney William Caldwell' gave of his 'West India property'.[14] In contrast, he was not at all happy with the management of his Irish estates, where he had 'at last laid the axe to the root of the expenditure of' his 'fortune by clearing out the farmyard of every person who was in it'. 'Such roguery and robbery' as he had found in Westport 'could not be imagined by any person who had not witnessed it'.[15] A conflicted character, whose reputation was not helped by a criminal conviction and a jail sentence in 1812, the less-than-mature Howe Peter Browne acquired a mixed reputation as an improving landlord, and was widely and much too generously credited with having 'emancipated' Jamaica's enslaved workers.[16]

How the Browne family perceived and represented their transatlantic landscapes in this post-Union period in Ireland leading up to Emancipation in Jamaica is documented by the survival of a rare conjoined survey book (1817) and two series of landscape paintings commissioned within twelve years of one another – one of Connacht by James Arthur O'Connor, Ireland's premier landscape painter of the early nineteenth century (1824), and one of Jamaica by Isaac Mendes Belisario, arguably Jamaica's first and greatest landscape painter (1836). Family letters and some meagre accounts also survive for both landscapes. A small leather-bound book of some 10 in × 3 in contains the only extant survey of the Browne family's home of Westport House and demesne (Figure 15.4).[17] The survey book is not a typical estate survey, which would contain a key overall map. Made and signed by George W. Hildebrand, subsequently the family's agent, rather than by a commissioned professional surveyor, it is a sliced representation, with the estate diced out across forty-five pages, of varying orientation and descriptive detail. With some exceptions most of the drawings are at a standard scale of 24 perches to an inch. Difficult, if not impossible, to read as an entirety, the book jumps eccentrically from the woodland at Barrett's Hill to the Marquess's new racecourse and the turf yards near the river. Many of its small, jigsaw-like pieces, when cross-referenced with the landscape paintings, provide the only extant three-dimensional configuration of lost buildings and sites, such as the walled apertures of the Irish turf yard by the

Figure 15.4 Cover of George W. Hildebrand, *Marquess of Sligo*, survey book of Westport, Co. Mayo and Kelly's Pen plantation, Jamaica, 1817, private collection.

lakeside. The book's most elegant and detailed drawing is of the area north of the great house, where a filigree planting plan for shrubberies, flower gardens and walks complemented the broad eighteenth-century Brownian strokes of the wider landscape garden (Figure 15.5). When pieced together, the survey's trajectory moves sequentially from east to west, from the demesne's interface with the town towards the pier, the islands and the bogs of Ireland's western frontier (Figure 15.6). Replicating in miniature the Irish landscape's precarious nineteenth-century imbalance, the pretty flower gardens, shady tree-lined walks and elegant lakeside boating slips eventually trickle downstream and out into the dangerous waters of the wild Atlantic, where a commercial pier sometimes greeted Jamaican ships, and sodden bogs surrounded the Marquess's grass racecourse.

The parkland southeast of the house, with its Brownian clumps and carefully curved approach route, was not included in the survey. As the landscape's most ambitious aesthetic component its absence is noteworthy, in that it reveals that the survey's concern lay westward, where the hills and bogs were to be tamed, improved and brought into the demesne. Beneath the aesthetic veneer lay the constant economic logic of land improvement, complete with all its drainage, scrub clearance and land reclamation concerns. The final pages describe in detail the slow, staged process of improving the poor soil of a distant portion of the estate, its inclusion within the demesne left ambiguous by its position in both book and landscape. Compiled on one hand to measure accurately the land uses of its numbered areas, these also reveal that an earlier survey must have been used to compile it, as they do

Designed in parallel or in translation? 289

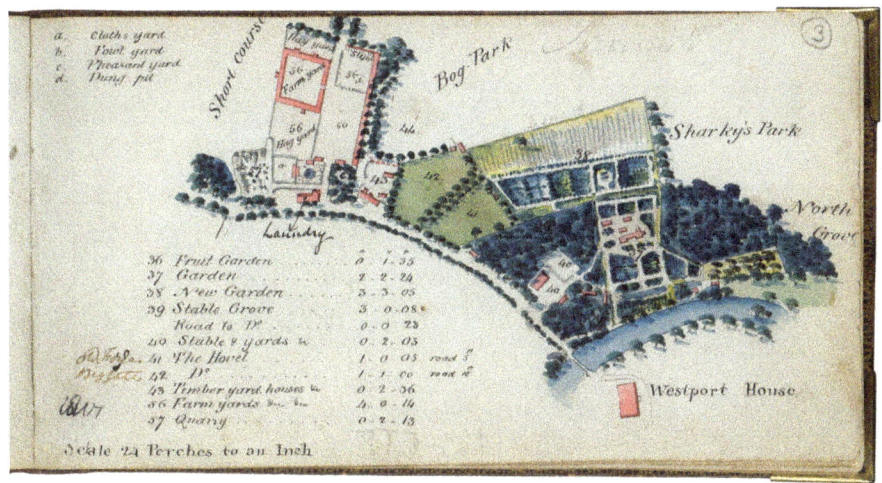

Figure 15.5 George W. Hildebrand, *Marquess of Sligo*, survey book of Westport, Co. Mayo and Kelly's Pen plantation, Jamaica, 1817, p. 3, private collection.

Figure 15.6 Amalgamated collage by Neil Crimmins of the forty-six Westport, Co. Mayo pages of the complete survey by George W. Hildebrand, *Marquess of Sligo*, survey book of Westport, Co. Mayo and Kelly's Pen plantation, Jamaica, 1817, pp. 1–46, private collection.

not run sequentially and some numbers are absent. The survey also describes a linguistic geography, its westward trajectory mapping the English replacement or translation of Irish place names, or 'dinnseanchas', as the inner 'paddock' leads to such jarring translations as 'Bauvin', 'Lenarievagh' and 'Gibeleen' (Figure 15.6).

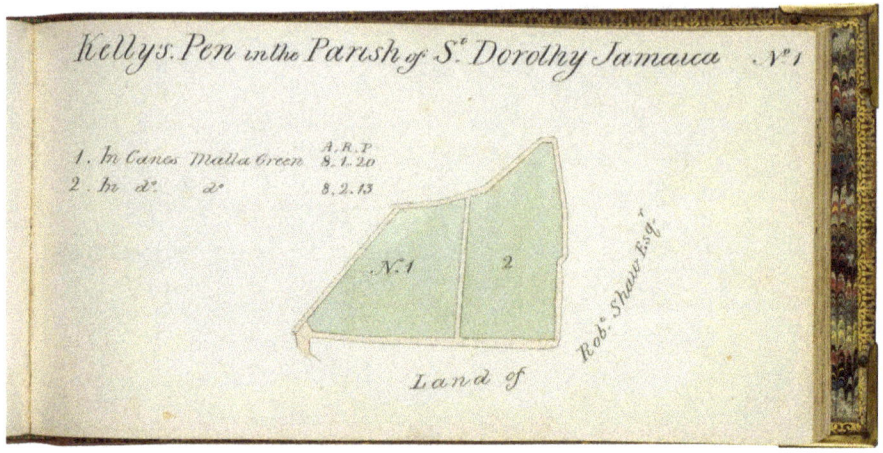

Figure 15.7 George W. Hildebrand, *Marquess of Sligo*, survey book of Westport, Co. Mayo and Kelly's Pen plantation, Jamaica, 1817, p. 1, private collection.

Most intriguing and unusual of all is the survey book's sudden leap from an Irish demesne to a Jamaican plantation, carefully identified on the inner leaf as 'Kelly's Pen in Parish of St Dorothy Jamaica. Survey made G. W. Hildebrand (Agent) October 1817'.[18] At page 46 the reader segues abruptly from a formal drawing of 'The Connected Gardens' of Westport House, with a pale-pastel walled garden, flower garden and fruitery, to 'Kelly's Pen in the Parish of St Dorothy Jamaica' (Figure 15.7), a sugar plantation complete with cane fields, slave houses and gardens, a great house, and a substantial sugar works (Figure 15.8). Parcelled out across ten pages, these can be rotated and manoeuvred into place to complete the Jamaican jigsaw (Figure 15.9). The survey book's 64 small pages of equal size lend both similarity and parity to two very different places located on the opposite sides of a great ocean, collapsing real geographical boundaries and distances as a consequence. By portioning two such disparate landscapes into many small and separate pieces, the process of their reamalgamation suggests the empire as a board game, divorced from any real spatial or human context.[19] This survey book reveals that these Jamaican and Irish properties were slowly visualised in the same way, piecemeal and field by field. Designed and drawn by the same hand and at the same time, this extraordinary survey book reveals that Jamaican landscape/architecture and Irish landscape/architecture at that moment were as one, bound together in one book, bound together in one history. Unlike most sources, this survey book acknowledges the give-and-take, borrow-and-benefit design process followed by the Browne family on both sides of the Atlantic. The lands' boundaries, avenues, ditches, grasses

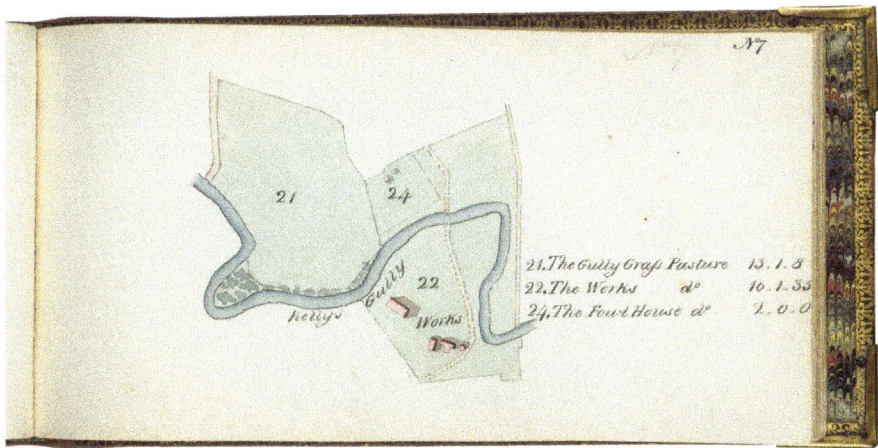

Figure 15.8 George W. Hildebrand, *Marquess of Sligo*, survey book of Westport, Co. Mayo and Kelly's Pen plantation, Jamaica, 1817, p. 7, private collection.

and trees are not represented as those of different countries – they follow the same familial traditions of measured survey, enclosure, improvement, planning and design. The colour palette of each separate piece of land is carefully modulated to reveal the land's use, and all partake in the same tonal language, running from a watery teal, through pink, to ochre and dun colours. Harmonising the Jamaican cane fields with the rich, green verdure of Westport's parkland, the wider reach and vocabulary of Westport's landscape condition stretched to yellows for the islands and the mountains and a salmon pink tone for the western bogs (Figures 15.6 and 15.9).

Estate portraiture acknowledged the symbiotic relationship of villa and landscape and experimented with their compositional balance. It usually took the form of a series of landscape paintings, typically commissioned by the owner of an estate. When a series was commissioned, the painter typically modified his received instructions to suit his own spatial hierarchy and choice of emphasis. Often commissioned during a time of family change or crisis, an estate portrait can suggest the estate's mentality at a precise moment in its history. The leading image of the great house is typically balanced by placing the building centrally and below the midpoint of the picture plane, at a scale that allows the overall image to retain a broad landscape border (Figure 15.1). Starting typically at the core and then spiralling outwards into the wider countryside, the centrifugal motion of a series of estate portraits oscillates between architecture and landscape, uncomfortable with precedence. Although deferential to the villa's central role, a long

292 Comparative perspectives

Figure 15.9 Amalgamated collage by Neil Crimmins of the ten Kelly's Pen, Jamaica pages of the complete survey by George W. Hildebrand, *Marquess of Sligo*, survey book of Westport, Co. Mayo and Kelly's Pen plantation, Jamaica, 1817, pp. 48–58, private collection.

series automatically creates a progressive imbalance by counterweighting core with edge. Estate surveys are also portraits, in that a plan may be drawn from a subjective viewpoint, with none of the objective orientation of such commissioned state cartography as that of the Ordnance Survey. Together the survey and the landscape paintings act as a record of the estate's perception of itself, its core great houses, satellite buildings, farms, industries, towns, neighbouring estates and connected roads, routes and vistas.

Howe Peter Browne, Second Marquess of Sligo, commissioned the Irish landscape painter James Arthur O'Connor to paint twenty views of the extended Browne family's Connacht estates in the years 1814–20.[20] O'Connor began on the eastern bank of the Shannon River before crossing over into the province of Connacht to paint four views of the town of Ballinrobe. He then moved on to Westport, via the lesser seat of Mount Browne, quartering the estate town into four views. The pre-eminent and largest Westport view was taken from the east, looking westward towards the house, the mountain of Cruach Pádraig and out into Clew Bay (Figure 15.1). It sought to reveal the context of the town, its great house and its western trading routes. Bleeding out into the surrounding countryside, the town is mostly one house deep with only a thin veneer of urbanism to coat an overwhelmingly agricultural reality. A long funnel of light, accentuated by planted curves of trees, leads from quay to town, broken by the house in silhouette. The western thrust of the composition was answered by a reverse pendant view that looked towards the house from the bonded warehouses of the estate port. In 1802 ships sailed to Jamaica from Westport's quays carrying a variety of brown Irish linen 'suitable for [enslaved] Negroes use',[21] while others landed puncheons of rum on these quays on the return voyage to Bristol with some of the estate's annual sugar crop. Mundane but financially significant farming insights also crossed the Atlantic, such as when the estate's Jamaican agent, Samuel Queensborough, wrote to inform the Marquess in 1803 that the continuing drought would 'shorten this year's Crop', as the sugar canes had 'acquired a greater degree of acidity from the dry Weather than usual' and would 'therefore require greater quantity of Alkali to correct it, which never fails to darken the Sugar'.[22] The Bristol sugar merchants Gibbs, Richards and Gibbs received the Sligo sugar, furnishing annual sugar accounts to the Marquess.[23]

Spiralling out into the wilder regions of unplanted Connacht, James O'Connor, together with his friend Francis Danby, was the first landscape painter to represent the wild west of Conamara, with its new roads, bare mountains, poor soils and thatched cottages, devising an aesthetic vocabulary of considerable influence (Figure 15.10). Dispossessed of people, these barren mountainous images and bare new roads counterbalance Westport's bustling, if commercially unconvincing, quaysides and ambitious, if threadbare, townscapes. Such 'extreme recesses of the western parts of Ireland' were opened up to view for the first time in the late eighteenth century and early nineteenth century, when 'the cutting of new roads westward' allowed O'Connor to end his series at 'the final reach of the colonial frontier in Ireland'.[24]

Figure 15.10 James Arthur O'Connor, *A View of Fin Lough and Delphi Lodge*, 1819, private collection.

Appointed Governor of Jamaica in 1833, Howe Peter Browne, the Second Marquess of Sligo, arrived in Jamaica soon to be 'much displeased' at his unruly estate manager's 'leaving [his] district in St. James ... without leave'. 'Having maturely considered' his 'private prospects' in Jamaica he wrote to George Hildebrand that 'the first thing' he wished to do was to 'get out here three individuals to locate on Kelly's', namely 'an expert Blacksmith, a Cooper and a Ploughman as sobriety is nearly as requisite a skill in their respective possessions'. He feared that his 'own country men' would therefore not 'suit' him, and wanted to get people 'from Scotland of religious and sober habits'.[25] Soon afterwards, on the 28 September 1835, the Marquess was awarded £2,304 15s 2d in compensation for the 119 enslaved people he owned at Kelly's and Cocoa Walk plantations in the Parish of St Dorothy, Jamaica.[26] As Governor, his appointment being connected to his identity as a significant Jamaican landowner, planter and enslaver, the Marquess was central to the whole Emancipation process, where his political naivety often worked against his prospects. When he made a political blunder, in part because of his unfamiliarity with the Jamaican plantocracy's habits and procedures, his father-in-law, the Earl of Clanricarde, tried to advise his inexperienced son-in-law from afar:

> The government position seems most decided that you must be supported and that you are quite right in all general questions, & in policy; but that in point of form or etiquette you were wrong in communicating with the assembly on a matter then under discussion ... The fact is that these assemblies are nuisances, & never of service to the colonies.[27]

Clanricarde advised him to 'choose' the 'time to talk of coming away whenever you can find a comparative calm, or a very successful moment; to avoid any possibility of misapprehension, or even misrepresentation, which to be sure will not be wanting, as to the causes of your coming away'. Clanricarde also made it his business to seek out alternative employment for his son-in-law, regretfully informing him of 'one situation' that had 'just been disposed of' and that he considered in 'every way preferable to Jamaica … the Governorship of Madras'.[28]

During this delicate year of 1836, the Second Marquess again commissioned a landscape series, but this time of his Jamaican properties. The Jamaican-Jewish artist Isaac Mendes Belisario (1795–1849)[29] painted six oils of the family plantations in Jamaica.[30] O'Connor had threaded Connacht together from its historic river frontier of the Shannon via the villa of Westport House and town to the wilder countryside of Conamara. Belisario did the same, beginning at the waterside plantation of Kelly's Pen before moving inland to the hillsides of Cocoa Walk. Unlike O'Connor, who used Westport's great house to orientate the viewer (Figure 15.1), Belisario employed the sugar works as a linchpin for his two paintings of Kelly's Walk (Figure 15.10 and 15.12). Only by cross-referencing the landscape paintings with the maps in the survey book can the buildings' relative positions be revealed and the overall early-nineteenth-century figure of Kelly's Pen plantation be reassembled (Figure 15.9). As at Westport, the sea view fixes the position of the architectural and landscape elements. Moving along the avenue from the main road to Old Harbour, an oblique view catches the three sugar mill buildings against the sea horizon (Figure 15.11, viewed from point A on Figure 15.9). The next positions the sugar works centrally at close range, while in the background commercial ships stray along the same horizon line into the Old Harbour (Figure 15.12, viewed from point B on Figure 15.9). The Cocoa Walk plantation lay inland from Kelly's Pen in the Jamaican hills. These areas developed later as sugar plantations and also contained the land allotted to enslaved people for growing their own food, enabling slave communities to have some modicum of a private life and to continue their own spatial and cultural traditions.[31] Belisario chose a low riverside approach road to the distant sugar works for his leading view of the Cocoa Walk plantation (Figure 15.13). Its corollary was the reversed viewpoint taken from the green enclosure of a private slave garden found high up on the less valuable, marginal land (Figure 15.14).[32] By carefully including Jamaica's own 'native' cottages and a woman carrying her own food while turned away from his glance, Belisario creates a questioning counterview to that of the sugar works (Figure 15.12). Such reversed vistas implicitly undermine any dominant viewpoint, and by extension any centralised hierarchical history, as their reciprocity invokes an oscillating and unstable point of view.

Figure 15.11 Isaac Mendes Belisario, *Kelly's Walk Plantation, the Great House*, Jamaica, *c.* 1836–42, National Gallery of Jamaica.

Figure 15.12 Isaac Mendes Belisario, *Kelly's Walk Plantation, the Sugar Works*, Jamaica, *c.* 1840, National Gallery of Jamaica.

Figure 15.13 Isaac Mendes Belisario, *View of Cocoa Walk Plantation*, Jamaica, *c.* 1840, National Gallery of Jamaica.

Figure 15.14 Isaac Mendes Belisario, *View of Cocoa Walks District*, Jamaica, *c.* 1840, National Gallery of Jamaica.

While both series document the design strategy of successful plantation – all still spins about the great house – the route and course of each respective series undermine the villa's central authority through the cumulative perceptual weight of many points of view and, eventually, the villa's absence from any. The envisaged trajectory of both landscapes is also markedly different. While O'Connor's paintings arguably helped to inform the future infrastructural design of both Mayo and Galway, the undercurrent of poverty at their edges and their foreshadowing of famine lends a terrible beauty to the central villa landscapes. In contrast, Belisario's Jamaican landscapes depict a happily declining transatlantic geography of influence and power, with the sugar works slowly displaced by the work habits and gardens of the emancipated. Jamaica is represented as a landscape emerging from the monoculture of sugar island slavery, while Connacht, in contrast, is represented as the last problematic frontier of Ireland's long amalgamation into the space of empire. Hanging together in Westport House, the family and their visitors could read the linked landscapes of both islands and the family's role in both islands' histories. Their position in the home villa drew a perceptual comparative geography between home and abroad, surrounding countryside and distant plantation, planter's viewpoint and native's viewpoint. In their structure, sequence and choice of viewpoint the paintings reveal the transnational design relationship between two very distant landscapes. Although the colonial picturesque typically postdates the British and Irish picturesque, Jamaica and Connacht become integrated into the picturesque view, tour and way of seeing at approximately the same time – in the early decades of the nineteenth century. Colonial Ireland, if substantially erased from the political mentality of the nineteenth century, continued to reveal itself in its peripheral spaces and their representations.

The rare honesty of a conjoined survey book, with no comparative example known to date on the neighbouring island, reflects a certain realism about depicting the landed estate as it really worked in both Ireland and Jamaica. Likewise, the double estate portrait series belies any perceptual distance between the home country and its colony – or perhaps Connacht, described by Willie Smyth as the 'final frontier' of the British spatial advance in Ireland, was also still sometimes perceived as a colony, even as late as 1834?[33] Did the Brownes really perceive a substantial difference between their two estates? The evidence suggests that they did not. A plantation is a precise acreage of land, a piece of real estate owned, managed and designed for the residence, enjoyment, representation, profit and manipulation of the family that owns it. The order of its design rationale may change, with enjoyment trumping profit when the family are resident, the reverse when they are not. But it is all ordered within the purview and control of one person (or by delegation to his or her agents), and if parts of it are separated by a great ocean this still does not divide the overarching whole. Did Ireland seem to be like Jamaica, or Jamaica like Ireland? For the Brownes, both Westport and Jamaica were valuable, constituent and interdependent parts of the one bulging property portfolio. Paintings, survey books and landscape designs reveal how such landscapes were designed in parallel and in translations that oscillated from Jamaica to Ireland and back again. As plantations and slavery became part and parcel of Europe's greedy property portfolio, so are they integral to the history of Europe's landscape design at home.

Notes

1 The total of 20,000 acres that Dennis Kelly had acquired by 1740 was computed by Lord Arthur H. Browne in the early twentieth century from the family papers then held in Westport House (he became a lord in 1903). The list is now included in National Library of Ireland (NLI), Westport estate papers, MS 41,058/7–8. Dennis Kelly's underreporting of his property, probably to evade tax, is suggested by 'A list of landowners in the Island of Jamaica', www.jamaicanfamilysearch.com/Members/1754lan3.htm (accessed 12 May 2005), where the Jamaican quit-rent books allocate Dennis Kelly a total of 4,002 acres in 1754.
2 See Martin J. Blake, 'Families of Daly of Galway with tabular pedigrees', *Journal of the County Galway Archaeological and Historical Society* 13:3–4 (1927), 140–51. See also Eoin Kinsella, 'Denis Daly (*c.* 1638–1721)', in *Dictionary of Irish Biography (DIB)*, www.dib.cambridge.org/articleId=a2372 (accessed 28 August 2022).
3 Karst de Jong, 'The Irish in Jamaica during the long eighteenth century (1698–1836)', Ph.D. thesis (Queens University Belfast, 2017), pp. 89–108.
4 NLI, Westport estate papers, MS 41,058/7–8, 'List of the Jamaican estates in Denis [sic] Kelly's possession in 1840 compiled by Lord Arthur H. Browne'.
5 Arthur L. Stinchcombe, *Sugar Island Slavery in the Age of the Enlightenment: The Political Economy of the Caribbean World* (Princeton: Princeton University Press, 1995), p. 95.
6 NLI, Westport estate papers, MS 41,058/7–8.
7 NLI, Westport estate papers, MS 41,058/7–8.
8 Arthur Young, *A Tour in Ireland, 1776–1779* (Shannon: Irish Academic Press, 1970), p. 256.
9 *Ibid.*, pp. 251–4; Young describes in detail the Earl's seven 'Experiments' in land improvement and the related increases in rent per acre, and then computes the clear profit of £480 on a square mile (640 acres) of such improvements after an initial outlay on the 'first improvement' of £3,406.00.
10 James Quinn, 'John Browne (1709–1776)', *DIB*, www.dib.ie/biography/browne-john-a1035 (accessed 12 May 2015).
11 Young, *A Tour in Ireland*, p. 259.
12 *Ibid.*, p. 255.

13 Stinchcombe, *Sugar Island Slavery*, p. 98.
14 NLI, Westport estate papers, MS 40,912/1 (14), power of attorney from Second Marquess to William Caldwell of Surrey and Jamaica, 19 April 1815.
15 Trinity College Dublin (TCD), MS 6403 (six folders containing 252 letters (1815–39) to and from Second Marquess of Sligo), folder 1, Marquess of Sligo's correspondence, 1–35, no. 8, c. 1815.
16 For a generally positive view of Howe Peter Browne see Anne Chambers, *The Great Leviathan: The Life of Howe Peter Browne, 2nd Marquess of Sligo 1788–1845* (Dublin: New Island, 2017).
17 George E. Hildebrand, *Marquess of Sligo*, survey book, 1817, private collection.
18 *Ibid*. The dating of the survey is complicated by a handwritten note on the page: 'From notes in 2nd Marquess's papers it would appear that the surveys were made in 1817, but this book appears to have been made later – It is referred to in 1827.' This indicates that the book's drawings were made in 1827 from survey measurements and notes taken in 1817.
19 Board games of the period also sought through route and itinerary to interpret the empire as an innocuous and educational children's game where learning a highly prescriptive and propagandist geography could be concealed by being simultaneously infantilised and trivialised. For examples see *Walker's Tour through Ireland: A New Geographical Pastime* (London: William Darton, 1812); and *Walker's Tour through England and Wales: A New Pastime* (London: W. and T. Darton, 1809).
20 John Hutchinson, *James Arthur O'Connor*, exhibition catalogue (Dublin: National Gallery of Ireland, 1985), p. 89.
21 NLI, Westport Estate papers, MS 40,911/1 (5), Samuel Queensborough to the Marquess of Sligo, Jamaica, 15 November 1802.
22 NLI, Westport Estate papers, MS 40,911/1 (6), Queensborough to the Marquess of Sligo, Jamaica, 11 January 1803.
23 NLI, Westport Estate papers, MS 40,911/1 (7), Gibbs, Richards and Gibbs to the Marquess of Sligo, Bristol, 17 May 1802.
24 See William Smyth, *Map-Making, Landscapes and Memory: A Geography of Colonial and Early Modern Ireland, c. 1530–1750* (Cork: Cork University Press, 2006), pp. 426–7.
25 National Library of Jamaica, MS 228, letterbooks of Howe Peter Browne, Second Marquess of Sligo, Vol. VI, Highgate, Jamaica, 18 July 1835, Second Marquess to George Hildebrand.
26 Centre for the Study of Legacies of British Slavery, www.ucl.ac.uk/lbs/person/view/20713, Howe Peter Browne, Marquess of Sligo (accessed 28 August 2022).
27 TCD, Marquess of Sligo MSS, MS 6403, fo. 6, no. 220/1, 27 March 1836, John de Burgh, Earl of Clanricarde to the Second Marquess of Sligo.
28 TCD, Marquess of Sligo MSS, MS 6403, fo. 6, no. 220/1.
29 See Tim Barringer, Gillian Forrester and Barbaro Martinez-Ruiz, eds, *Art and Emancipation in Jamaica: Isaac Mendes Belisario and His Worlds* (New Haven: Yale University Press, 2007); and Jackie Ranston, *Belisario, Sketches of Character: A Historical Biography of a Jamaican Artist* (Kingston: Mills Press, 2008).

30 These are all reproduced in Ranston, *Belisario*, together with some of the attendant watercolour studies.
31 For a discussion of the continuance of cultural and spatial traditions see Philip D. Morgan, *Slave Counterpoint: Black Culture in the Eighteenth-Century Chesapeake and Low Country* (Chapel Hill: University of North Carolina Press, 1998); and Dell Upton, 'White and black landscapes in eighteenth-century Virginia', *Places* 2:2 (1985), 59–72.
32 For discussion of the representation of plantation landscapes see Michael Vlach, *The Planter's Prospect: Privilege and Slavery in Plantation Art* (Chapel Hill: University of North Carolina Press, 2002); and Kay Dian Kriz, *Slavery, Sugar, and the Culture of Refinement: Picturing the British West Indies 1700–1840* (New Haven: Yale University Press, 2008).
33 Smyth, *Map-Making*, p. 427.

16

Formations and deformations of empire: Maria Edgeworth and the West Indies

Claire Connolly

When I began to research the writings of Maria Edgeworth in the 1980s, the question of her place within Irish literary history was a vexed one. Edgeworth was an Anglo-Irish writer whose family were beneficiaries of the Cromwellian plantation of Ireland. Some of her novels were set in Ireland, including the widely admired *Castle Rackrent* (1800), but she also wrote books that were far removed from the realities of pre-Famine Ireland: courtship fictions set in England, plots of British public life, tales addressed to children and young adults. Postcolonial and feminist criticism offered a way of integrating her work into our understanding of Irish literature while also revising and renewing some of its founding assumptions. Edgeworth is now more widely taught and read, and the richness and complexity of her writing are recognised. But there remains a need to investigate and understand the relationship of her writing to empire. While postcolonial criticism (in different modes) denounced her privilege or admired her inscription of hybridity,[1] it did not engage with her own writings on empire or offer any reckoning with her views on race. Feminist scholarship proved better prepared to investigate her writings on the West Indies, especially in relation to her novel *Belinda*, but such work has tended to conflate Ireland with Britain, or invoke Irish history in fairly loose ways.[2]

The present volume presents a welcome opportunity to consider Maria Edgeworth's views on the Caribbean and to develop our understanding of themes of race, slavery and empire in her writing. In this chapter, I trace the threads of scattered details, repeated images and occasional plot twists found in the fiction and letters in order to consider the scope and extent of Edgeworth's engagement with the West Indies throughout her career. In doing so, I take up Anne Mulhall's challenge to rethink invocations of politics within Irish studies under the sign of race.[3] A consideration of Maria Edgeworth's whiteness may feel like a return to an earlier critical dynamics that excluded her work on the basis of her colonial background and class privilege, but a closer investigation of her imperial investments is a necessary step as we open up Irish romanticism to the 'ineradicable antagonisms' of literature and empire.[4]

The Ireland of Edgeworth's day was closely bound into the Atlantic economy and played its part in the formation of an imperial Englishness within the crucible of Britain's second empire. For Maria Edgeworth, to write about the West Indies was to inscribe the global interconnections wrought via that empire, especially in relation to questions of work, education and domestic life. Edgeworth was also interested in the function of imaginative writing within the empire, including the profession of literature itself. She often used scenes and stories from the West Indies to question the utility of literature as it travels between times and places, part of a larger commitment to a culture of experiment. But the threat of violent revolution forms a kind of threshold in her thinking. Her ability to imagine slave societies was affected by her own planter history, as well as by a close encounter with the 1798 rebellion at home in Edgeworthstown.

If Edgeworth's writing produces many moments of conflict between what Clíona Ó Gallchoir calls 'the limits of strict probability' and 'her desire to produce stories of transformation', then these tensions are particularly acute in her representations of the West Indies.[5] The topic of slavery makes an uncomfortable home within the context of Edgeworth's broader intellectual interests, not least because Edgeworth does not set the ownership, sale and exchange of people apart from the trade in ideas, books and goods. In what follows I show how, in particular West Indian contexts, the kinds of violent improbabilities that help to form the particular texture of Edgeworth's realism often concern seeds and plants. Within the specific scenes that flow from Edgeworth's thinking about slavery in the context of improving debates about education and domesticity, she draws on 'the overlapping languages of botanical transplantation and plantation slavery' so that seeds, plants and gardens shape lines of imperial connections across her plots.[6] It might even be argued that, just as colonial bioprospecting carved out new contours of nature, so too the modes of exchange imagined within Edgeworth's improving narratives are not only formed but also deformed by their imperial horizon.

When Maria Edgeworth visited a ship that carried enslaved Africans berthed on the London docks in October 1792, she wrote home to her cousin Sophy Ruxton in Co. Meath with an account of 'the dreadfully small Hold in which the poor slaves are stowed together so that they cannot stir – Some of the slaves are sent every morning to scour the decks with brine & the ship, we were told, was daily fumigated with vinegar &c – But probably you know all this –.'[7] That final phrase is telling: Edgeworth assumes that Sophy Ruxton was aware of the horrific trade that saw African people transported across the Atlantic as chattel to the sugar islands of the Caribbean. But what did Edgeworth herself know of the Caribbean – and how did she react and respond? In the 1790s, she was just beginning a long and successful career as a writer, over the course of which she thought seriously about the ways in which society and economy of the British empire were shaped by and through the exploitation of Atlantic and Caribbean worlds. Like Jane Austen, she mentions slavery from time to time in her letters and fictions, and included short, passing references to plantation wealth as a backdrop to some of her novels and tales. Unlike Austen, however, Edgeworth wrote about slavery in relatively direct ways. She did not practise the kinds of narrative evasion that make the discussion of West Indian slavery in *Mansfield Park* (1814) so enigmatic, and went so far as to situate one of her tales on a Jamaican plantation: 'The Grateful Negro', written in March 1802 and published as one of Edgeworth's *Popular Tales* in 1804, gives us her most direct and troubling representation of the brutal slave society of Jamaica and is discussed below.

Although none of the Edgeworth family appears to have benefited directly from Jamaican wealth, her older brother Richard left home in 1779 and settled in South Carolina, founding a settlement named Sneedsborough (named after his stepmother) on the farthest reach of the Pee Dee River as it flowed south to Charleston. He became a farmer and returned only once, in 1792, meeting the family in London, receiving money from his father and visiting a slave ship together. Family correspondence from the period wonders whether Richard will spend his father's money on preparing 'land for a plantation either of rice or indian corn or for planting peach orchards for peach brandy'. Maria Edgeworth wrote to her aunt Margaret Ruxton wishing for 'a telescope that could reach to the Backwoods of America', but not mentioning the enslaved labour that underpinned plantation life.[8] Richard Edgeworth died in South Carolina in 1796 at the age of thirty-two. Susan Kroeg suggests, though, that the relatively small plantation that he owned (200 acres, more or less) 'probably would not have supported a significant slave labor force', and no enslaved people are mentioned in the will.[9]

It is rather easier to trace lines of connection between the Edgeworths and the abolitionists. The family was closely connected with liberal and radical circles in Britain and Ireland, for whom slavery was an urgent issue. Her friend and correspondent Anna Laetitia Barbauld published her 'Epistle to William Wilberforce, Esq. on the Rejection of the Bill for Abolishing the Slave Trade' in 1791. Other classics of anti-abolitionist writing included poems by Richard Lovell Edgeworth's friends Erasmus Darwin and Thomas Day, *The Botanic Garden* and *The Dying Negro* respectively. Edgeworth met Darwin in 1799 (he died in 1802), and later in Liverpool in 1813 she discussed Darwin with William Roscoe.[10] Edgeworth used an abolitionist quotation from *The Botanic Garden* in 'The Good Aunt', a story with a West Indian subplot, discussed below: 'Hear him, ye Senates! Hear this truth sublime, / "He, who allows oppression, shares the crime." '[11]

But such connections did not always mean an alignment of views: in the summer of 1799, when Barbauld and her husband called to visit the Edgeworths in Clifton, near Bristol, they brought their own 'East India sugar' to sweeten their tea, so that they 'might not share our wickedness in eating that made by the negro slave'.[12] So the Edgeworths did not necessarily share the views of their abolitionist friends. In another 1792 letter sent to Sophy Ruxton, Edgeworth asked her cousin if she had read 'the things that have been lately published about the Negroes', referring to 'a very small pamphlet of about ten pages, merely an account of the facts stated to the House of Commons'.[13] Based on Nini Rodgers's research into the Irish history of anti-slavery, it is possible to identify the pamphlet as the *Address to the People of Great Britain (respectfully offered to the People of Ireland) on the utility of refraining from the use of West Indian sugar and rum* (published in London in 1791 and Dublin in 1792).[14] The Quaker diarist Mary Leadbeater read this 'little book', and she asked her friend Molly Bewley to help get it reprinted in Dublin while other Quaker women helped to circulate it across the country via chapmen.[15] Edgeworth, then, was well aware of the power of public opinion in Britain and Ireland to shape public debate. But she was cautious in her assessment of abolitionist calls for ethical eating:

> 25,000 families in England have absolutely entirely left off eating West india sugar in any thing – from the hope that when there is no longer any demand for sugar the slaves will not be so cruelly treated to force them to rear the cane. Children in several schools have given up their taste for sweet things, which is surely very benevolent – Tho' whether it will at all conduce to the end proposed is perhaps wholly uncertain – and in the meantime we go on eating applepie sweetened with sugar instead of applepie sweetened with honey. At Mr Keir's, however, my father avers that he ate excellent custards sweetened with honey. Will it not be rather hard upon the poor bees in the end?[16]

The Edgeworths' sympathy stopped at the bees, and they did not change their shopping habits. But the trade in sugar and sweet things forms a backdrop to a short fiction by Edgeworth, 'The Good Aunt'. The story was written in March and April of 1797 and published just after *Belinda* (1801), a novel also occupied with the question of a West Indian fortune.

The 'good aunt' of Edgeworth's tale is Frances Howard, a woman who spent her youth in the West Indies and returns to England as the beneficiary of plantation wealth. Her nephew, Charles, has been in her care since a child, and the tale as a whole advocates for a broad and tolerant approach to education, seeking to hold in balance arguments between domestic and institutional education and a classical syllabus versus a modern one. Charles learns the value of reading choice selections from Shakespeare and Adam Smith's *Wealth of Nations* over and above rote learning; meanwhile his interest in natural history is fostered via curious cases drawn from across the imperial domain of natural history: the hummingbird, the tailor bird, the hermit crab and the Jamaican trap-door spider.[17]

'The Good Aunt' spells out the moral consequences of possessing a fortune by enslaving others: Mrs Howard 'did not particularly wish to be the proprietor of slaves; and from the time that she came to the management of her own affairs, she had been desirous to sell her West India property'.[18] Though Mrs Howard sells her estate and effects the manumission of her enslaved people, her goods and money are lost in a shipwreck, meaning that she has to undertake a new mode of life. Recognising the need for boys to engage in public education while also economising as she must, Mrs Howard arranges for Charles, now thirteen, to attend Westminster School as a day pupil while she buys a small house nearby. At the great public school, Charles Howard befriends a miserable Creole boy named Oliver, whose previous education has not prepared him for such practices as fagging and bullying, the former compared to being made into 'a negro-slave'.[19] Charles protects Oliver from Augustus Holloway, an older boy who is the son of Mrs Howard's attorney. Just before Mrs Howard's fortune was lost at sea, Augustus had been working on some trite lines in Latin celebrating the freeing of the people formerly enslaved on her estates, showing how Edgeworth connects her dislike of prejudice in favour of the ancient languages with a suspicion of glib abolitionist verse.

A further West Indian thread in the story concerns the appearance in London of a former enslaved woman named Cuba. Her appearance in the tale is the result of an accident: Augustus overturns a coach during a schoolboy escapade and a 'mulatto woman' is left behind 'in great pain', speaking only in broken English.[20] Augustus would abandon her there, but the postillion feels sorry for the 'poor copper-coloured soul' and helps her to find the house of an old gardener named Paul, the only address known to the woman. She ends up lodging next door to the home of Mrs Howard, who is in turn revealed to be her former owner. Because the new owner of Mrs Howard's West Indian property has not respected her rights to her provision ground, Cuba has travelled to London in search of Mrs Howard, bearing seeds and sweets from Jamaica as gifts for her former mistress.

The plot threads these lines of connection together via its commitment to Enlightenment science and the value of observation: when Charles Howard notices how cold and smoky the room is in which Cuba is housed by the kindly gardener, he turns to Benjamin Franklin's *Observations on Smoky Chimneys, Their Causes and Cure* (1793) and applies its remedies. In the newly bright and clean room, the sharp-eyed Oliver in turn notices a distinctive thimble made from old gold worn by Cuba as she sews. On discovering that the thimble originated in Jamaica as a gift from a former mistress, Oliver deduces a connection with his friend's good aunt. Cuba was one of the enslaved people whom Mrs Howard had 'set at liberty' and who, because the promise was broken to give over to her 'some little *provision ground*, upon the plantation', has travelled to England in search of Mrs Howard.[21]

Rather than end the story with this reunion, though, Edgeworth continues to build on her themes of observation, discrimination and empire, returning to the topic of literature via a debate in Mrs Howard's house about art and taste: from a discussion of Joseph Warton's 'Ode to Fancy', the company move 'to the never-ending debate upon original genius; including also the doctrine of hereditary temper and dispositions'.[22] Oliver meanwhile sits apart from the group, reading Bryan Edwards's *History, Civil and Commercial, of the British Colonies in the West Indies* while 'his left arm embraced a thick china jar, against which he leaned his head'.[23] He emits a 'groan' that disturbs the group, who find him so absorbed in Edwards's book that he fails to notice the danger of a candle wick about to burn out. A note directs readers to the particular scene that draws the boy's attention: Edwards's gruesome description of the horrific punishment and execution of the enslaved people who took part in Tacky's Revolt of 1760, an account that inspired Edgeworth's tale 'The Grateful Negro'. At the same moment, narrative attention falls on the china jar, which Oliver believes contains Jamaican sweetmeats sent by his father, and which he refuses to relinquish to the adults. A tussle ensues, and it emerges that the jar contains not sweets (as expected by all, including the boy) but rather 'pieces of crumpled paper' that testify to a school lottery in which both Charles and Oliver have refused to participate on principle.[24] The discovery of the lottery results in the summoning of a Jewish jeweller to the house; his ill-gotten treasure hoard includes a sewing needle that matches the Jamaican thimble and other items that had once been the property of Mrs Howard, and that were supposed to be lost at sea. As the consequences of this 'disquieting, mysterious scene' play out, Mrs Howard is reunited with her property and her fortune.[25] Charles Howard retains his 'love for literature', now supplemented with his aunt's fortune, while Oliver grows in understanding and 'affection' for his first friend.[26]

A strange detail in 'The Good Aunt' is that the young Creole boy, Oliver, cannot be seen to blush because of his skin colour. He is ridiculed and disgraced in public school but the effects of bullying don't show on his skin: 'his cheek burned with blushes ... but his dark complexion ... prevented those blushes from being noticed by his companions'.[27] A few of Edgeworth's early stories make reference to colour and skin complexion, starting with *Belinda*. In *Belinda*, the heroine chooses between two men, one an upright Englishman who has lost his way, and the other a West Indian

Creole planter named Mr Vincent, whose gambling habit proves an insurmountable obstacle to his prospects. Connected to Mr Vincent is his black servant Juba (after whom he has also named his dog), who, in the first edition of the novel, marries an English country girl named Lucy. In the novel, Lady Anne Percival playfully draws attention to Lucy's 'fear of poor Juba's black face' and is answered with reassurances: 'The girl reddened, smiled, and looked at her grandmother, who answered for her in an arch tone, "O, yes, my lady! We are not afraid of Juba's black face *now*; we are grown very great friends … our Lucy takes no offence at his black face now, my lady, I can assure you.'[28] This characteristically monitorial scene seems to educate readers away from racist assumptions about colour and yet leaves in place the image of the silent, blushing white woman. The novel further frames that image via an item of jewellery given by Juba to Lucy, a 'necklace of Angola pease' that she wears about her neck.[29] Edgeworth may have taken the image of the necklace from Jacques-Henri Bernardin de Saint-Pierre's primitivist romance *Paul et Virginie*, from which she drew other aspects of *Belinda*'s plot. Within the frame of the imagined possibilities of cross-racial romance within the first edition of her novel, this humble object stands in for the Afro-Caribbean entanglements wrought by the colonial trade in seeds, plants and people: connections that Edgeworth apprehends but whose contexts cannot be fully expressed within the genre of the courtship novel. Indeed, such was the burden of the West Indian material that Edgeworth removed the reference to inter-racial marriage in a revised edition published in 1810, reporting to Anna Laetitia Barbauld that 'My father says that gentlemen have horrors upon this subject, and would draw conclusions very unfavorable to a female writer who appeared to recommend such unions; as I do not understand the subject, I trust to his better judgement.'[30]

References to skin colour recur in the writings, often in seemingly slight ways. In 'Mademoiselle Panache' from *Moral Tales* (1801), the French governess cannot bear the sight of negroes and also fears the sight of a black horse, while in a tale from 1804, 'To-Morrow', a child starts for fear of a dark negro servant. In contrast to the reasonable position outlined by Lady Anne Percival, these tales contain echoes of Edmund Burke's account of the sublime as connected to the terrifying power of darkness and what he calls the 'effects of blackness'.[31] The example that Burke gives concerns a blind boy who regains sight: 'the first time the boy saw a black object, it gave him great uneasiness; and that some time after, upon accidentally seeing a negro woman, he was struck with great horror at the sight'.[32] In W. J. T. Mitchell's reading of Burke's text, the black woman represents the 'doubled figure of slavery, of both sexual and racial servitude' made to appear in 'the natural colors of power and sublimity'.[33] For Edgeworth, as perhaps for Burke, those natural colours are further shaded by a knowledge of violence in

Ireland. A letter to Edgeworth's aunt Mrs Ruxton about Defenderism in Longford in January 1796 suggests the connection:

> All that I crave for my own part is, that if I am to have my throat cut, it may not be by a man with his face blackened with charcoal. I shall look at every person that comes here very closely, to see if there be any marks of charcoal upon their visages. Old wrinkled offenders I should suppose would never be able to wash out the stains; but in others a *very* clean face will in my mind be a strong symptom of guilt, clean hands proof positive, and clean nails ought to hang a man.[34]

Even these interconnections among race, property and skin colour do not quite prepare us for 'The Grateful Negro', Edgeworth's most direct and troubling representation of the brutal slave colony of Jamaica, written in March 1802 and published as one of her *Popular Tales* in 1804. As with 'The Good Aunt', she draws on Bryan Edwards's *History, Civil and Commercial, of the British Colonies in the West Indies* and gives his name to one of her characters. The tale concerns two planters with neighbouring estates, Mr Jeffries and Mr Edwards, each of whom holds people in slavery. Where Mr Jeffries abuses his slaves, Mr Edwards is kind and trusting, allowing the enslaved people to keep the goods grown on their own provision grounds. The grateful slave of the title, Cæsar, along with his wife, is purchased by Mr Edwards when Mr Jeffries threatens to split them up and sell them separately. Cæsar's gratitude consists of informing on a rebellion planned by his fellow enslaved people, an event that is closely modelled on the Tacky Rebellion of 1760 as described by Edwards, but that may also borrow from Edgeworth's experience of the Battle of Ballinamuck in September 1798. In the end, the tale suggests, it is better to work on gradual improvements of the conditions in which enslaved people live rather than abolish the dreadful practice.

Critics within Irish studies have tended not to write about the tale, uncomfortable with Edgeworth's ameliorationist approach to slavery. Debate about 'The Grateful Negro' was sparked off by George Boulukos's 1999 essay 'Maria Edgeworth's "Grateful Negro" and the sentimental argument for slavery', which diagnoses the tale in terms of broader problems with 'sentimental humanitarianism'. Where Boulukos reads Edgeworth as an apologist for slavery, however, Susan Manly has made a case for the ways in which Edgeworth sought 'to stimulate her readers' powers of thought through the representation of conflict and debate'.[35] It is difficult, however, to deny Boulukos's case in relation to Edgeworth's advocacy of 'slave gratitude' and her 'reluctance to acknowledge' the 'contradiction between free labor principles and the practice of slavery'.[36] Within the context of Caribbean literary history, the tale is remembered as 'a narrative that showcases colonial anxieties surrounding the threat of – and the ability to contain – African-Caribbean insurrection'.[37]

Edgeworth's 'good' planter shares a name with Bryan Edwards, from whose *History* Edgeworth draws, in particular his account of the 1760 Tacky Rebellion and his discussion of Obeah, presented by him as a type of incendiary magic responsible for isolated delusions and now understood as 'a network of spiritual, religious, and cultural practices brought by enslaved Africans to, and creolized in, the anglophone Caribbean'.[38] From Edwards, Edgeworth also takes her focus on the reforming possibilities of so-called slave gardens or provision grounds, already seen in 'The Good Aunt' and inflected here by Edgeworth's ideas about fair treatment of tenant farmers in Ireland. 'The Good Aunt' had already made troubling use of images from Bryan Edwards's *History*, while the Edgeworths' *Essay on Irish Bulls* quotes Edwards on 'unfortunate negroes' who 'learn cowardice and cunning after they become slaves'.[39] More broadly, the argument seems to follow Adam Smith's sense of the 'law of slavery' as an 'unfortunate' aspect of progress, implicitly agreeing with him that economic outcomes improved when enslaved people were kindly used.[40]

Though 'The Grateful Negro' is located 'in the island of Jamaica', it yields little by way of topographical specificity.[41] Edgeworth's narrative affords neither a fully realised picturesque landscape nor a historical sense of a colonial settlement characterised by jails, courthouses and barracks. Instead, she depicts an island whose single and singular reality is a plantation life dedicated to the production of 'rum, sugar, and indigo'.[42] The rebellion begins on the plantation of the idle and profligate Mr Jeffries and spreads to the neighbouring estate of the well-meaning Mr Edwards, before being thwarted by the noble Cæsar, the 'grateful negro' of the title. It concludes with the downfall of Mr Jeffries, an event imagined in specifically economic terms: he loses £50,000 and is 'obliged to live in obscurity and indigence' as an absentee owner in England.[43] The shame of enforced absenteeism takes its charge from Irish politics, while the imagined horrors of Jamaican plantation life in turn lent force to Edgeworth's criticism of Irish estate management in her Irish novel of 1812, *The Absentee*, where a peasant character remarks of his landlord that 'He might as well be a West India planter, and we negroes, for any thing he knows to the contrary – has no more care, nor thought about us, than if we were in Jamaica, or the other world.'[44]

'The Grateful Negro' has a fable-like quality that it shares with *Murad the Unlucky*, an orientalist story in the same collection of *Popular Tales*, in which the stories are all aimed at ordinary middle-class readers. The simple style, though, comes under strain as Edgeworth incorporates details from political economy into the narrative. She describes how Mr Edwards treats his enslaved people with 'all possible humanity', fearing their 'sudden emancipation' and working instead towards 'amelioration' and a 'reasonable' form of plantation proprietorship.[45] In discussion with Mr Jeffries, Edwards admits that labour is needed to cater for the European appetite for 'rum, sugar, and indigo', but asks 'If we hired negroes for labourers, instead of purchasing them for slaves, do you think they would not work as well as they do now? Does any negro, under the fear of the overseer, work harder than a Birmingham journeyman, or a Newcastle collier; who toil for themselves and their families?'[46] Ashley Cohen discusses the political and geographic 'capaciousness' of Edgeworth's definition of slavery and understands the *Popular Tales* as imagining a 'global Jacobin crisis' that 'threw into relief the ease with which processes of exploitation, dispossession, and political and economic oppression subverted boundaries between the domestic and the imperial, free and unfree labor'.[47] Yet the naturalisation of enslavement within a global world of work is challenged not only by contrasting scenes from Mr Jeffries's estate (an enslaved person whipped in the boiling room, rebels that set fire to the cane in order to 'extirpate every white man, woman, and child') but also by the wider historical context that Edgeworth seeks to capture.[48]

Edgeworth's choice of a largely domestic setting for a tale that represents the brutal plunder colony of Jamaica results in some striking contrasts. The wife of Mr Jeffries, a 'languid fine lady', is depicted 'reclining on a couch' or 'extended on a sofa', fanned by enslaved people.[49] The image draws on abolitionist writing by Anna Laetitia Barbauld and William Cowper, in particular Barbauld's depiction of the idle planter's wife in her *Epistle to William Wilberforce*. Meanwhile, what Cohen calls Mr Edwards's 'Progressive labor management techniques'[50] are framed by the particularities of the plantation landscape: huts, the cottage and cultivated 'provision ground' of the enslaved Cæsar, Mr Jeffries' dining-room and drawing-room and the sofa on which his wife languishes; the sound of the conch shell calling the enslaved people to their labours; the sugar boiler over which they toil; the 'spreading palm-tree' under which Mr Edwards gathers his 'well clad' slaves for a holiday;[51] the woods in which the rebels hide; the burnt-out house of Jeffries's overseer, Mr Durant. This constellation of images form part of a larger cultural process by which 'the different, disruptive and dangerous landscape of Jamaica – a place of death, disease and disorder for all who found themselves there – is brought to order through the conventions of European landscape depiction'.[52] The 'holiday' scene on the estate is particularly noteworthy in this respect: 'the pleasing spectacle of this negro festival' is framed by trees, with enslaved people 'bringing baskets of avocado pears, grapes, and pine-apples, the produce of their own provision grounds'.[53] The mentions of these and other plants such as banana and tamarind in the tale (as with the earlier reference to Angola peas in *Belinda*) are reminders of 'Africa's botanical legacy in the Americas'.[54]

Scholars including Jill Casid and Vincent Brown have written about contradictions inherent in depictions of flourishing plant life within West Indian landscapes deadly to the enslaved populations.[55] Edgeworth pursues these links in her discussion of Obeah, which she describes in a long footnote that quotes from Edwards's *History*. In the tale, 'an old Koromantyn negress' named Esther uses 'poisonous herbs' to induce a coma in Cæsar's wife, Clara, threatening Cæsar that Clara will never recover life as long as he fails to support the rebellion.[56] Instead, he warns his master Mr Edwards of the danger, and suffers a knife attack from his friend, Hector. Both Cæsar and Clara regain life, and Mr Edwards's 'eloquence' and humanity see an end to the rebellion.[57]

References to the West Indies in Edgeworth's fiction thin out after the second series of *Tales of Fashionable Life* in 1812. In *Patronage* (1814) she turns her attention to the East India company, though when Godfrey Percy's ship is sent to the West Indies as a punishment (Mr Falconer hopefully predicts that Godfrey will die of plague), there is a passing reference to the fear of 'yellow fever' and the challenges of the climate: 'temperance and spice are the best preservative in that climate; so you need not fear for me, for you know I love pepper better than port'.[58]

A lasting and important line of connection between Edgeworth, the West Indies and the politics of slavery is found in her correspondence with Rachel Mordecai Lazarus. Their correspondence began in 1815, when Lazarus addressed an admiring letter to Edgeworth from her home in Virginia. She all but regarded the Edgeworth family as 'individual friends', such was her admiration of *Practical Education*, but wrote that her reading of the fiction was marred by the representation of Jewish characters as 'mean, avaricious and unprincipled'[59] (examples would include the 'extremely cunning, profoundly ignorant'[60] Jewish jeweller in 'The Good Aunt'). A long correspondence ensued, through which are threaded the topics of education, literature and family, with regular reports on births, marriages and deaths. Topics also include slavery, government, botany, prison reform, sea-bathing, lacemaking, cholera, British rule in India and steam trains. The letters span from 1815 to Lazarus's death in 1838, taking in such milestones as the Nat Turner Rebellion in 1831, the British Reform Act of 1832 and the 1833 abolition of slavery in the British sugar colonies.

Herself someone who held people as property (as well as a Jew who converted to Christianity shortly before her death), Lazarus lived in Wilmington, Virginia, a place that she described to Edgeworth as being 'situated thirty miles up the Cape Fear river, which is navigable to this town, its principal commerce with the West Indies, direct communication with Europe unfrequent'.[61] There is no reference to 'The Grateful Negro' or to any of Edgeworth's writing about the West Indies in the correspondence, but as in the fiction itself, discussions of literary taste often serve to draw in wider political contexts. The first mention of slavery came in 1824 when, in discussing 'an American novel which had then just appeared' (Catherine Maria Sedgwick's *Redwood*), Lazarus assured Edgeworth that:

> The condition of our slaves both in this and the sister states is far less miserable than that of the poorer classes of white people. They are comfortably maintained and with very few exceptions kindly treated. So long as the benefits of education are denied them, their state must be abject, and the necessity of retaining them is by all admitted to be an evil tho' at present an unavoidable one; but their usual cheerful demeanour argues well for the humanity of their masters.[62]

In 1825, Edgeworth turned from Lady Blessington's *Conversations with Byron* to 'the Greeks, the West Indian slaves, the Irish "poor slave"', the connections animated by 'the subject of *Catholic emancipation* which has occupied these countries and the English parliament for some months past'.[63]

Writing again about 'the unfortunate Irish' in 1831, Lazarus described their condition as the result of a British 'system' akin to slavery:

> The more I learn of the actual state of Ireland, the more am I inclined to wonder at the mistaken policy of a wise and enlightened government in pursuing a system so glaringly oppressive, and, I should say, injurious to their own interests. Much has been humanely urged in the British Parliament on the subject of Negro slavery; yet is the condition of the Irish poor incomparably worse than that of the slave, either here, or as far as I am informed, in the Islands? I do not mean to defend the Slave System, of which I feel and acknowledge all the evils; but where is the consistency of practising, without even a similar shadow of apology, a system which wants but the name to render it more than equally odious?[64]

Lazarus's account of the Nat Turner Rebellion is often quoted in histories of that conflict, and the event loomed large in her life. In August of 1831, enslaved spiritual leader Nat Turner led between fifty and sixty people to rebellion; fifty-five people were killed across eleven plantations in Virginia. The militia put the rebellion down quickly, but fear was widespread throughout the region afterwards. The letter that Lazarus wrote to Edgeworth about the events is missing but, in early October, she expressed her continuing fears of rebellion to her brother, even speculating that African-Americans might be repatriated from the southern states:

> To be necessarily surrounded by those in whom we cannot permit ourselves to feel confidence, to know that unremitted vigilance is our only safeguard, and that soon or late we or our descendants will become the certain victims of a band of lawless wretches who will deem murder and outrage just retribution is deplorable in the extreme. The United States government might possibly find a remedy by rendering some equivalent to slave owners and exporting the slaves in as large numbers as practicable to Africa.[65]

The rebellion broke apart the fiction of good or paternalist enslavement, the very prevalence of which was part of a result of the popularity of Edgeworth's often-reprinted tale 'The Grateful Negro': 'an ur text for the representation of blacks in nineteenth-century US children's fiction' according to Boulukos, 'and hence a shaping influence on white Antebellum citizens' concepts of race'.[66]

The letters from the early 1830s discuss and compare English mobs, Irish Repealers and the prospect of the abolition of slavery, with the two women often returning to their shared belief in education and the view that, as Edgeworth put it, the 'slaves must be prepared by education to be free and to provide for themselves before they can be set free without danger to others and destruction and misery to themselves and society'.[67] Lazarus meanwhile wondered 'what can be said of men who blindly, madly urge the slave to seek his freedom through a sea of blood, who promise to aid him in the commission of a crime, without even glancing at the too-certain consequences, and who, while pledging themselves to the cause of suffering humanity, would spread horror and devastation among their brethren and over one half of their mother land?'[68] In 1835, Edgeworth received a gift from the Scottish writer Mrs Carmichael of her pro-slavery book, *Domestic Manners and Social Condition of the White, Coloured and Negro Population of the West Indies*, a title that she subsequently recommended to Lazarus's attention for its discussion of 'Trinidad and St Vincent's specially'.[69] Edgeworth's copy of the book contains marginal notes in her own hand, sometimes noting curiosities of natural history (a type of toad called a 'crappaud', and 'parasol' or leaf-cutter ants) but also a correction to Carmichael's blithe account of the comforts enjoyed by restrained and humiliated slaves: 'Nonsense. They often have pillows when in stocks – but never mosquito nets – & all feel it a punishment.'[70]

A discussion of Harriet Martineau's *Society in America* (1837) led to a disagreement between the two women. Edgeworth admired the book greatly and was drawn by its discussion of republican government, democracy and slavery: 'I agree with Miss Martineau', she told Lazarus, 'in all she says on the question of Slaves and on the inconsistency of American liberty and slavery'. She went on: 'I know this is a dangerous, a tabooed subject.'[71] Edgeworth's distrust of 'the government by majority of numbers' and democracy itself comes through in the letter (which also touches on the proper care of a 'spotless anemone' that is to be sent from Virginia to Edgeworthstown via Liverpool),[72] and Lazarus's response reminded the Irish author that Martineau's 'republican or Democratick opinions' were not what 'I or any of my friends consider reasonable'.[73] On 'the slave question', Lazarus cannot disagree with the incomptability of slavery with liberty, but blames the iniquities of colonial history: 'it was English Colonies planted in America ... who entailed this curse upon our land'.[74] Edgeworth's final letter to her friend recognises the 'indignation' of this response but also insists on Martineau's 'courage',[75] as if to illustrate Marcus Wood's description of Martineau as 'a unique transatlantic cultural barometer' in the imagination of slavery.[76]

A distinct thread running through the Edgeworth–Lazarus correspondence is the women's shared interest in botany. The last paragraph of Edgeworth's final letter, sent in June 1838, moves from Martineau and slavery to family matters; friends; and, finally, natural history: 'Pray tell me what is meant by *Broomcorn* and whether it is a common crop in America ... Pray enclose in your next one seed of Broomcorn for Ireland in return.'[77] The letters give extensive evidence of regular seed and plant exchanges across the ocean between the two women. The carefully wrapped packages that they shared with extended families include Venus fly-trap seeds, pods of cotton, crocus and primrose bulbs, a humming bird's nest, 'the wings of a rice bird',[78] grasshopper legs, and alligator eggs. Seeds from the East Indies, sent to Ireland for Edgeworth's stepmother, in turn were sent on to Lazarus. Edgeworth even requested a live mocking bird, which died in transit. To facilitate these transatlantic packages, Edgeworth used the address of her publisher Hunter in London, along with other friends in office in Dublin. Botanical curiosities sent on by Lazarus went via Edgeworth to her friend Mr Mackay in the Botanical Gardens in Dublin and to Glasgow Botanical Gardens, as well as being shared out among friends and neighbours, while Lazarus obtained anemone specimens for Edgeworthstown from the Botanical Garden in New York.

These international public gardens were themselves part of an imperial history that has been discussed by Finola O'Kane. The Dublin Botanical Gardens were inspired by those in Kew, London. The Dublin Society purchased lands at Glasnevin in 1795 and, in May 1800, the public gardens opened as 'the largest publicly supported botanical garden in Europe and the largest in the British Empire apart from a seventy-acre garden near Kingston, Jamaica'.[79] Edgeworth's early writings often mention seeds and exotic plants, always connecting exotic plants to power and sometimes explicitly acknowledging the colonial dimensions of the traffic in seeds. In *Belinda* (1801), two fashionable ladies quarrel over who gets to show a 100-year-old aloe, just about to bloom, at their salon; meanwhile, the gardener who has raised this precious plant in his greenhouse (and who had planned to show it for a fee) is deprived of income. A rare geranium is at the centre of a similar plot of cross-class intrigue and deceit in Edgeworth's tale *Forester* from 1801.

The proximity of botany to slave rebellion and political conditions in Ireland and Britain is a striking aspect of Edgeworth and Lazarus's correspondence, not least because of its regular proximity to the topic of what is 'new', 'admirable' and *valuable* in the world of literature.[80] These relationships return our attention to the ways in which Edgeworth's fictions realise a recurring set of exchanges – of people, goods and plants – across the empire. Such interconnections have unpredictable effects in Edgeworth's narratives, as in the strange scene in 'The Good Aunt' discussed above, where adults tussle with a Creole child absorbed in the details of torture of enslaved people for possession of a jar that does not in the end contain the West Indian sweets for which he longs. The jagged details somehow fit the shape of this strange tale, with its exploration of the question of what makes a good education in the context of a domesticity made precarious by loss, accidents and the colonial circulation of people and property. And while the narrative of 'The Grateful Negro' seems to effect a harmonious arrangement of enslaved people, plants and landscape it can only do so via the effects of violent contrast, including the image of a plantation in flames.

The discussion presented here is intended to unlock Edgeworth's interest in the West Indies throughout her writing life and to shape further research. Not least of the surprises in Edgeworth's thinking about the West Indies are the strange lines of connection between gardening and 'the attempted conversion of human subjects into extractable, exchangeable, saleable, transplantable "objects"': testament to Edgeworth's grasp of what Jill Casid describes as the 'terrible alchemy' between plantation landscapes and the trade in people.[81] But where the 'narrative alchemy'[82] of Edgeworth's Irish tales can transform the materials of a painful past into the stuff of literary gold, her fictional treatments of the West Indies fail to find the philosopher's stone.

Notes

1. See Seamus Deane, *Strange Country* (Oxford: Clarendon Press, 1997); and Colin Graham, 'History, gender and the colonial moment: *Castle Rackrent*', *Irish Studies Review* 4:14 (1996), 21–4.
2. See for example Kathryn Kirkpatrick, '"Gentlemen have horrors upon this subject": West Indian suitors in Maria Edgeworth's *Belinda*', *Eighteenth-Century Fiction* 5:4 (1993), 331–48; and Susan C. Greenfield, '"Abroad and at home": Sexual ambiguity, miscegenation, and colonial boundaries in Edgeworth's *Belinda*', *PMLA* 112:2 (1997), 214–28.
3. Anne Mulhall, 'The ends of Irish studies? On whiteness, academia, and activism', *Irish University Review* 50:1 (2020), 94–111.
4. Manu Samriti Chander, *Brown Romantics: Poetry and Nationalism in the Global Nineteenth Century* (Lewisburg, PA: Bucknell University Press, 2017), p. 3.
5. Clíona Ó Gallchoir, 'Maria Edgeworth's revolutionary morality and the limits of realism', *Colby Quarterly* 36:2 (2000), 87–97 (p. 97).

6 Michelle Burnham, *Transoceanic America: Risk, Writing, and Revolution in the Global Pacific* (Oxford: Oxford University Press, 2019), p. 153.
7 Maria Edgeworth to Sophy Ruxton, October 1792, quoted in Susan Manly, 'Intertextuality, slavery and abolition in Maria Edgeworth's "The Good Aunt" and "The Grateful Negro"', *Essays in Romanticism* 20:1 (2013), 19–36 (p. 21).
8 Letters quoted in Rachel Hewitt, *A Revolution of Feeling: The Decade that Forged the Modern Mind* (London: Granta, 2017), p. 128.
9 Susan M. Kroeg, '"The transmigrated soul of some West Indian planter": Absenteeism, slavery, and the Irish national tale', in David T. Gleeson, ed., *The Irish in the Atlantic World* (Columbia: University of South Carolina Press, 2010), pp. 109–28.
10 The *Quarterly Review* picked out Roscoe as a target in its vicious review of Anna Laetitia Barbauld's *Eighteen Hundred and Eleven*, *Quarterly Review* 7 (1812), 309–13.
11 Erasmus Darwin, *The Botanic Garden. Part Two: Containing The Loves of the Plants*, 3rd edn (London, 1791), p. 127.
12 Augustus J. C. Hare, ed., *The Life and Letters of Maria Edgeworth*, 2 vols (Boston, MA: Houghton Mifflin, 1895), Vol. I, p. 69.
13 *Ibid.*, Vol. I, p. 23.
14 Nini Rodgers, 'Two Quakers and a Utilitarian: The reaction of three Irish women writers to the problem of slavery, 1798–1807', *Proceedings of the Royal Irish Academy* 100C:4 (2000): 137–57 (p. 153). Susan Manly speculates that the pamphlet 'might well have been the anonymously authored Short Sketch of the Evidence, for the Abolition of the Slave Trade', but the pamphlet discussed by Rodgers seems more likely. Manly, 'Intertextuality, slavery and abolition', p. 21.
15 Rodgers, 'Two Quakers and a Utilitarian', p. 144.
16 The text of the letter comes from Susan Manly, 'Intertextuality, slavery and abolition', pp. 20–1. Manly notes that other widely reproduced versions of the letter contain inaccuracies, usually drawn from the version transcribed by Augustus Hare. Manly's transcription omits the final two sentences, which I quote here from Hare, *Life and Letters*, Vol. I, p. 23.
17 Maria Edgeworth, 'The Good Aunt', in *Tales and Novels by Maria Edgeworth*, 18 vols (London, 1832–3), Vol. I, p. 223.
18 *Ibid.*, p. 228.
19 *Ibid.*, p. 245.
20 *Ibid.*, p. 259.
21 *Ibid.*, p. 297.
22 *Ibid.*, p. 310.
23 *Ibid.*, p. 311.
24 *Ibid.*, p. 313.
25 Manly, 'Intertextuality, slavery and abolition', p. 24.
26 Edgeworth, 'The Good Aunt', pp. 332–3.
27 *Ibid.*, p. 239.

28 Maria Edgeworth, *Belinda*, ed. Linda Bree (Oxford: Oxford University Press, 2020), p. 223.
29 *Ibid*.
30 Quoted in Kirkpatrick, 'Gentlemen have horrors', p. 342.
31 Edmund Burke, *A Philosophical Enquiry into the Origin of Our Ideas of the Sublime and the Beautiful*, ed. Adam Phillips (Oxford: Oxford University Press, 1990), p. 135.
32 *Ibid*., p. 131.
33 See Meg Armstrong, ' "The effects of blackness": Gender, race, and the sublime in aesthetic theories of Burke and Kant', *Journal of Aesthetics and Art Criticism* 54:3 (1996), 213–36.
34 Hare, *Life and Letters*, Vol. I, p. 44.
35 George E. Boulukos, 'Maria Edgeworth's "Grateful Negro" and the sentimental argument for slavery', *Eighteenth-Century Life* 23:1 (1999), 12–29; Manly, 'Intertextuality, slavery and abolition', p. 35.
36 Boulukos, 'Maria Edgeworth's "Grateful Negro" ', p. 19.
37 Janelle Rodriques, 'Obeah, religion, and nineteenth-century literature of the anglophone Caribbean', in Evelyn O'Callaghan and Tim Watson, eds, *Caribbean Literature in Transition, 1800–1920* (Cambridge: Cambridge University Press, 2021), pp. 198–212 (p. 202).
38 *Ibid*., p. 198.
39 Maria Edgeworth and Richard Lovell Edgeworth, *Essay on Irish Bulls*, in Vol. I of *The Novels and Selected Works of Maria Edgeworth*, ed. Jane Desmarais, Tim McLoughlin and Marilyn Butler (London: Pickering and Chatto, 1999), pp. 69–154 (p. 101).
40 Adam Smith, *An Inquiry into the Nature and Causes of the Wealth of Nations: A Selected Edition*, ed. Kathryn Sutherland (Oxford: Oxford University Press, 2008), p. 349; see Edwin Van De Haar, 'Adam Smith on empire and international relations', in Christopher J. Berry, Maria Pia Paganelli and Craig Smith, eds, *The Oxford Handbook of Adam Smith* (Oxford: Oxford University Press, 2013), pp. 417–39.
41 Maria Edgeworth, 'The Grateful Negro', in *Popular Tales*, 3 vols (London, 1804), Vol. III, pp. 191–240 (p. 193).
42 *Ibid*., p. 202.
43 *Ibid*., p. 239.
44 Maria Edgeworth and Richard Lovell Edgeworth, *The Absentee*, Vol. V of *The Novels and Selected Works of Maria Edgeworth*, ed. Heidi Van de Veire, Kim Walker and Marilyn Butler (London: Pickering and Chatto, 1999), p. 101.
45 Edgeworth, 'The Grateful Negro', p. 195.
46 *Ibid*., p. 202.
47 Ashley L. Cohen, 'Wage slavery, oriental despotism, and global labor management in Maria Edgeworth's *Popular Tales*', *The Eighteenth Century*, 55:2–3 (2014), 193–215 (p. 195).
48 Edgeworth, 'The Grateful Negro', p. 207.
49 *Ibid*., p. 228.
50 Cohen, 'Wage slavery', p. 196.

51 Edgeworth, 'The Grateful Negro', p. 255.
52 Miles Ogborn, 'Slavery, freedom and the Jamaican landscape', *Picturing Places*, British Library, www.bl.uk/picturing-places/articles/slavery-freedom-and-the-jamaican-landscape (accessed 19 February 2021).
53 Edgeworth, 'The Grateful Negro', p. 232.
54 Miles Ogborn, 'Discriminating evidence: Closeness and distance in natural and civil histories of the Caribbean', *Modern Intellectual History* 11:3 (2014), 631–53. See Judith A. Carney and Richard Nicholas Rosomoff, *In the Shadow of Slavery: Africa's Botanical Legacy in the Atlantic World* (Berkeley: University of California Press, 2009).
55 Vincent Brown, *The Reaper's Garden: Death and Power in the World of Atlantic Slavery* (Cambridge, MA: Harvard University Press, 2008); Jill H. Casid, *Sowing Empire: Landscape and Colonization* (Minneapolis: University of Minnesota Press, 2005).
56 Edgeworth, 'The Grateful Negro', pp. 216–17.
57 *Ibid.*, p. 239.
58 Maria Edgeworth, *Patronage*, 4 vols, 2nd edn (London, 1814), Vol. I, p. 260.
59 Edgar E. MacDonald, ed., *The Education of the Heart: The Correspondence of Rachel Mordecai Lazarus and Maria Edgeworth* (Chapel Hill: University of North Carolina Press, 1977), pp. 4, 6.
60 Edgeworth, 'The Good Aunt', p. 232.
61 MacDonald, *The Education of the Heart*, p. 132.
62 *Ibid.*, p. 69.
63 *Ibid.*, p. 80.
64 *Ibid.*, p. 111.
65 *Ibid.*, p. 212.
66 George Boulukos, *The Grateful Slave: The Emergence of Race in Eighteenth-Century British and American Culture* (Cambridge: Cambridge University Press, 2008), pp. 237–8. Boulukos describes Edgeworth as the key figure in the dissemination of '"the grateful slave" in nineteenth-century England and America'. He draws on Sarah N. Roth, 'The mind of a child: Images of African Americans in early juvenile fiction', *Journal of the Early Republic* 25:1 (2005), 79–109.
67 MacDonald, *The Education of the Heart*, p. 279.
68 *Ibid.*, p. 274.
69 *Ibid.*, p. 280.
70 Thanks to Karen Ievers of Mount Ievers, Co. Limerick, for sharing these pages with me.
71 MacDonald, *The Education of the Heart*, p. 298.
72 *Ibid.*, p. 299.
73 *Ibid.*, p. 302.
74 *Ibid.*, p. 305.
75 *Ibid.*, pp. 310–11.
76 Marcus Wood, *Slavery, Empathy, and Pornography* (Oxford: Oxford University Press, 2002), p. 256.
77 MacDonald, *The Education of the Heart*, p. 314.

78 *Ibid.*, p. 114.
79 Finola O'Kane, 'The Irish botanical garden: For Ireland or for Empire?', *Studies in the History of Gardens & Designed Landscapes* 25 (2008), 446–55.
80 MacDonald, *The Education of the Heart*, p. 199.
81 Jill H. Casid, 'Epilogue: Landscape in, around, and under the performative', *Women & Performance: A Journal of Feminist Theory* 21:1 (2011), 97–116.
82 Julia Anne Miller, 'Acts of union: Family violence and national courtship in Maria Edgeworth's *The Absentee* and Sydney Owenson's *The Wild Irish Girl*', in Kathryn Kirkpatrick, ed., *Border Crossings: Irish Women Writers and National Identities* (Tuscaloosa: University of Alabama Press, 2000), pp. 13–37 (p. 22).

17

How the Irish became black

Natalie A. Zacek

In a well-known scene from the 1991 film *The Commitments*, based on Roddy Doyle's 1987 novel of the same name, several members of the eponymous soul band express their doubts that a group of working-class teenagers from north Dublin will be able to play music written and performed by African-Americans. Their manager, Jimmy Rabbitte, responds by informing them that 'the Irish are the blacks of Europe. And Dubliners are the blacks of Ireland. And the Northside Dubliners are the blacks of Dublin.' Having reassured his friends of their ability to replicate the performance styles of black musicians such as James Brown, Rabbitte concludes his exhortation by citing one of Brown's most famous lyrics: 'So say it once. Say it loud. I'm black and I'm proud.'[1] In Doyle's novel, the dialogue in this scene is both cruder and more incisive. Rabbitte refers to himself, his friends, and their fellow inhabitants of North Dublin's Barrytown community not as 'blacks' but as 'niggers' within the context of Europe, Ireland and Dublin, and he claims that they are disadvantaged because 'the culchies [residents of the city's affluent suburbs] have fuckin' everythin''. When he posts an advertisement for additional musicians in a local magazine, he mandates that 'rednecks and southsiders need not apply'.[2]

This dialogue rings both true and false. It is plausible to argue that in the mid-to-late 1980s Ireland was indeed an economically marginal nation in comparison with much of western Europe; in 1986 its unemployment rate was 17 per cent, many of the jobless had been out of work for over six months and net emigration offset the birth rate.[3] Dublin, the capital and the largest city, had the country's highest unemployment rate; it was a declining industrial city with an undereducated labour force. While the north side of Dublin had been an aristocratic neighbourhood throughout the Georgian era, by the end of the nineteenth century most of its mansions had become dilapidated, overcrowded tenements, and when twentieth-century reformers agitated for improved accommodation for the city's poor, the latter were decanted into council housing in newly created northern exurbs such as the fictional Barrytown, communities of which Jimmy Rabbitte's despised 'southsiders' and 'culchies' were either disdainful or oblivious.[4]

While Rabbitte and his friends had reason to feel marginalised within their city, their country and the European Community, which Ireland had joined in 1973, his comparison of their challenges to those faced by past and present African-Americans is unlikely to have resonated among Irish people or those of Irish heritage in the United States.[5] In the 2016 census, only 1.3 per cent of the Republic's inhabitants identified themselves as 'black', and this percentage would have been lower in the years of economic depression prior to the rise of the 'Celtic Tiger' in the mid-1990s, which saw an influx of migrants, including some of African descent. At the time at which the members of the Commitments would have grown up, the best-known individual of black heritage in Ireland, with the possible exception of the mixed-race Manchester United football player Paul McGrath, was probably the musician Phil Lynott, the lead singer and songwriter of the successful rock band Thin Lizzy. Lynott's father was a man of colour from Guyana, but Lynott was raised in Dublin by his white mother's parents, attended a local Catholic school, and drew inspiration for his lyrics from Celtic folklore and Irish history, rather than from the cultures of the African diaspora – Thin Lizzy's first hit was a version of the well-known Irish folk song 'Whiskey in the Jar'.

But if Irish people of the 1980s are not likely to have felt much kinship with African-Americans, the same was true of Irish-Americans, despite their having considerably more experience of black people and black cultures. As the radical historian and self-identified 'race traitor' Noel Ignatiev argued in his seminal 1995 work *How the Irish Became White*, from the early nineteenth century onwards Irish migrants to the United States soon recognised that the nation's social hierarchy was based upon race much more than it was on class, ethnicity or religion, and that for them and their descendants to climb the ladder it was essential that they did all they could to distinguish themselves from people of colour.[6] Although Irish-Americans of the *Commitments* era were aware of their immigrant ancestors' struggles against poverty and religious and ethnic prejudice, they considered their historical experiences in the United States to be most comparable to those of other white ethnic groups, such as Poles and Italians, rather than to those of black Americans. Robert Kennedy's 1968 presidential campaign drew much of its support from African-Americans, but throughout the previous century and a half politicians who were Irish-American, or who hoped to appeal to Irish-American voters, ranged from apathetic to openly hostile towards black Americans and their concerns. In the late twentieth century, Americans of Irish descent might recall with anger the 'No Irish need apply' signs that had supposedly barred their ancestors from jobs and housing, but few would have interpreted this expression of ethnic prejudice as comparable to the complete racial segregation of public facilities in the southern states until the 1960s – as is shown by the bitter clashes between Irish-Americans and African-Americans over forced public school busing that convulsed the Boston area throughout the 1970s.[7]

If a generation ago neither the Irish nor Irish-Americans would have considered their historical experiences to have paralleled those of African slaves and their American descendants, and Jimmy Rabbitte's comments on page and screen evoked laughter for their hyperbolic nature rather than nods of approval at their accuracy, why, over the past two decades, has the figure of the 'Irish slave' become increasingly visible in culture and politics on both sides of the Atlantic? Why has it been deployed as a symbol, variously, of England's colonial tyranny over Ireland; of Anglo-Saxon Protestant Americans' prejudices against Irish Catholic immigrants; and, most significantly, of the allegedly non-racial nature of Atlantic plantation slavery – and thus of the moral bankruptcy of demands from African-Americans and Afro-Caribbeans for reparations, and of anti-racist movements such as Black Lives Matter? Where did this image of 'Irish slavery' come from? Why has it gained so much traction in such a short period of time? And what can historians do to combat the not merely inaccurate but dangerous idea that Irish men, women and children constituted 'the forgotten white slaves' of the New World?[8]

The foundational text of the myth of Irish enslavement in the Americas is a monograph titled *To Hell or Barbados: The Ethnic Cleansing of Ireland*, published in 2000 by the journalist Sean O'Callaghan. Viewing relations between England and Ireland in the seventeenth century through the prism of ethnic cleansing, a concept associated with the descent of the former Yugoslavia into genocidal warfare among its diverse ethnic and religious populations throughout the 1990s, O'Callaghan claimed that the political prisoners taken by Oliver Cromwell's forces during their conquest of Ireland in the 1650s, some of whom are recorded as having been exiled to England's fledgling West Indian colonies, 'were not sent as indentured servants, but were sold in perpetuity to the sugar planters of Barbados. They became the first white slaves in relatively modern times, slaves in the true sense of the word, owned body and soul by their masters.' O'Callaghan proceeds to make increasingly lurid, *Mandingo*-esque claims about the experiences these Irish exiles in Barbados allegedly endured: that Irish women were sold as sex slaves to English planters who operated 'stud farms' and forced them to mate with African men; that racially mixed plantation slave drivers stripped Irish women naked before 'satisf[ying] their lust by taking them from the rear', and that homosexual male English settlers purchased Irish boys with whom they fulfilled their sexual fantasies. Throughout *To Hell or Barbados*, O'Callaghan commits many of the methodological sins against which historians caution their students: when primary sources are not available to support a particular point, he bases his arguments on assumptions and assertions ('As there is no record of how the Irish on the slave ships were treated, we have to assume that they were treated exactly the same as African slaves'); he draws upon evidence from other periods and locations in West Indian history and applies it uncritically to mid-seventeenth-century Barbados; he seizes upon the most horrific examples of the abuses endured by enslaved Africans and asserts that all of these horrors were perpetually visited upon Irish servants; and he relies heavily on highly problematic secondary sources, chief among which is an article published in 1883 in a Guyanese newspaper by a British army officer whose principal qualification to tell the story of the Irish 'white slaves' of the seventeenth century was that he had previously been stationed in the West Indies.[9]

Not surprisingly, O'Callaghan's book has received harsh criticism from scholars of early modern Irish history, including Nini Rodgers, Liam Hogan and Donald Harman Akenson; the latter described it as 'an end-of-the-pier act that is just a shade short of being hate literature'.[10] But although O'Callaghan died just before *To Hell or Barbados* was published, and thus did not promote the book or defend its historical accuracy, it became a bestseller and remains in print today (indeed, it is usually available in the 'Irish History' section at Hodges Figgis, Dublin's oldest and most intellectually prestigious bookseller), continuing to reap enthusiastic reviews on sites such as Amazon and Goodreads, and even inspiring a song of the same name by the Irish folk musician Damien Dempsey. Dempsey's song, released in 2007, includes these lyrics:

> You sent me far cross the sea to be owned
> ...
> ... a whiplash licks my heels
> And my scorched skin bursts and peels
> Though my people were not made for these burning fields
> ...
> Good men like old Wilberforce, they came far too late
> Far too late to save us from the fate
> Of Hell or Barbados.[11]

Many readers found O'Callaghan's argument both fascinating and convincing, including Philip, who wrote on Goodreads in 2009 that 'every Irish man and woman needs to read this book to understand what really happened', and John King, who praised it in 2013 for 'show[ing] how complex and multi layered Irish history is'.[12] Google Books' listing of literally hundreds of works whose titles include the phrase 'hidden history' is evidence that many readers are attracted to the idea of learning about an aspect of the past that appears to have been, until recently, deliberately suppressed. And the historiography of the Cromwellian conquest of Ireland leaves no doubt as to the brutality with which the Lord Protector carried out his campaign, and the contempt that he and many English people of his era felt towards Irish Catholics. If 'Old Noll' loathed and feared the Irish so much that he permitted his soldiers to massacre both combatants and civilians, as they did at Drogheda and Wexford, it is not difficult to imagine that he might have ordered the survivors to be sold into chattel slavery in the English colonies. As Jerome Handler and Matthew Reilly have observed, O'Callaghan's depiction of the fate of Irish political prisoners who were sent to the Caribbean is replete with errors and exaggerations, but it dovetails neatly with 'the historical narrative that stresses Cromwell's brutal subjugation of Ireland'; with the far longer history of hostilities between England and Ireland; and with narratives of Irish victimisation at English hands, epitomised by the 'no blacks, no Irish, no dogs' signs that were allegedly all too common among London landlords and publicans in the 1950s.[13]

Prior to the publication of O'Callaghan's book, the experiences of Irishmen and women in the seventeenth-century English West Indian colonies had not received much attention from historians, at least in part because of the limited corpus of primary sources that describe them. The most substantive works on this subject were a pair of articles that appeared in quick succession in the *William and Mary Quarterly*, the leading journal of early American and Atlantic history: Riva Berleant-Schiller's 'Free labor and the economy in seventeenth-century Montserrat' and Hilary McD. Beckles's ' "A riotous and unruly lot": Irish indentured servants and freemen in the English West Indies, 1644–1713'. Whereas the former essay centred on the attempts of Montserrat's early Irish settlers to find their physical and economic niche within the island, the latter took a more radical perspective, arguing that Irish indentured servants in the West Indies were, echoing the title of one of Beckles's previous articles, 'Black men in white skins', forced into a state of 'proto-slavery'. According to Beckles, many of these men (and throughout the seventeenth century the great majority of the Irish inhabitants of these islands were male) lived and worked in conditions that were no better than those experienced by enslaved Africans. They faced the additional disadvantage that enslaved people were valuable objects of property, and might thus merit better treatment from their owners than short-term indentured servants did. Beckles asserted that, because these Irishmen appeared to have lost the privileges that West Indian society associated with whiteness – wealth, land ownership, political rights and personal liberty – they were in some instances willing to make common cause with the enslaved among whom they worked and lived, even on occasion joining with them in rebellion against their hated English enslavers.[14]

The reality that these men experienced was a bit more complicated. In my 2010 monograph *Settler Society in the English Leeward Islands, 1670–1776*,

I argued that the Irish inhabitants of the English West Indian colonies throughout the seventeenth and eighteenth centuries were not desperate and miserable 'black men in white skins' who suffered constant victimisation by a rapacious and prejudiced English plantocracy. Many of them were men, and occasionally women, drawn from the tenantry of the estates of wealthy Irish Catholics, most notably the 'Fourteen Tribes' of Galway, 'a great tangled cousinry' of long-established and cosmopolitan mercantile families from the west of Ireland who dispatched their younger sons and nephews to the West Indian colonies in order to expand their trading networks across the Atlantic. While these people of peasant stock were undoubtedly socially and economically subordinate to members of such 'Tribal' families as the Frenches, the Lynches and the Blakes, the latter did not despise them for their Irish ethnicity and their Catholic faith, which they shared, nor did they view them as comparable to enslaved Africans in either legal or racial terms. In many cases, these Irish servants were able to establish themselves in non-plantation employment at the end of their indentures, frequently as artisans or small independent cultivators. Rather than being viewed by the planters as a bestial rabble whose loyalty to white authority was always in doubt, they were valued as a population that could be mobilised in the defence of the islands against foreign invasion or slave rebellion, and being of Irish heritage and Catholic faith (as long as the latter was practised discreetly and in private) was not an insuperable obstacle to the acquisition of wealth, social status and even political office.[15] These conclusions are echoed in the most recent study of Irish experiences in the English West Indies, Jenny Shaw's *Everyday Life in the Early English Caribbean*, which explores in meticulous detail the challenging circumstances that many Irish men and women faced in these settlements, but also emphasises that, while pathways existed that they could follow to improve their situations, no such possibilities existed for African or Afro-Caribbean bondspeople, whom both law and custom designated as an inherently and permanently subordinated group.[16]

Despite the considerable popular, if not critical, success of O'Callaghan's book, the image of the Irish man or woman whose experience of servitude in the West Indies was indistinguishable from the enslavement of Africans therein was little known in the United States prior to the 2008 publication of Don Jordan and Michael Walsh's *White Cargo: The Forgotten History of Britain's White Slaves in America*. Although neither author was trained as a historian – Jordan is a film and television producer and Walsh a journalist and television presenter – the book was published by New York University's respected scholarly press. *White Cargo* takes a far broader perspective on the subject of 'white slavery' than *To Hell or Barbados*; Jordan and Walsh assert that English and Scots were also subjected to enslavement, and that this phenomenon existed in the New England and Chesapeake colonies as well as in the West Indies. But the authors devote most of their attention to the experiences of the Irish, and they assert that, in the course of the Cromwellian conquest, Ireland was subjected to 'ethnic and religious cleansing', and that the nation 'became a major source of slaves for the New World'.[17] Because Jordan and Walsh claim that whites were enslaved not only in England's Caribbean colonies but in those that would be incorporated into the United States, the figure of the Irish slave arrived in North America, and became incorporated into American popular historical discourse.

The idea that Irishmen and women had suffered enslavement at the hands of Protestant Anglo-Americans played neatly into the longstanding narrative of the centuries-long mistreatment both of Irish migrants and of their Irish-American descendants, a story familiar in well-known cultural texts from the Civil War-era folk tune 'Paddy's Lamentation' to recent films such as *Gangs of New York*. If it seems plausible to some Irish readers that Oliver Cromwell would have sentenced those who had fought against him to lifelong slavery in England's plantation colonies, it strikes some contemporary Irish-Americans as equally possible; they may not recall the atrocities of the 1650s as vividly as those who have grown up and been educated in Ireland, but they are deeply aware of the 'No Irish need apply' signs that were supposedly ubiquitous throughout the nineteenth-century United States, as well as of the cartoons of, amongst others, Thomas Nast, which depicted Irish people as ape-like beasts whose laziness, stupidity and alcoholism made them the least desirable of white immigrants.[18] Although *White Cargo* was dismissed by academic historians as an unreliable and misleading work because of its repeated conflation of slavery and indentured servitude, it has not only remained in print with New York University Press but was praised by the Nobel Prize-winning African-American novelist Toni Morrison, who used it as a source for her 2008 novel *A Mercy*, which depicts white, black and Native American characters enduring varying forms of servitude in seventeenth-century America. More significantly, *White Cargo*'s provocative subtitle and its striking cover image, of a pair of white hands bound with rope, have gone on to inspire an internet meme that posits as equivalent black chattel slavery and white indentured servitude in the Americas, an equation that has in recent years been eagerly embraced within the USA's burgeoning white nationalist movement.

It is crucial to emphasise that there is no evidence whatsoever that O'Callaghan, Jordan or Marsh were/are racists. While most scholars are highly dubious with regard to their methodologies and sources, they wrote their books with the goal of illuminating what they considered to be the 'hidden history' of the relationship between race and slavery in the Atlantic world. That these works are among the best known of the texts (the majority of which are far less well researched and historically objective than theirs) that have served as inspirations to racist activists is in no way their fault, nor was it their intention. Although *To Hell or Barbados* was published just twenty years ago, and *White Cargo* almost a decade later, the political and cultural contexts into which they emerged seem almost unreachably distant from today's often toxic social media world. Why, then, has their promulgation of the myth of Irish slavery been so influential in the formation of the contemporary white nationalist/'alt-right' movement within the United States?

According to the prolific and well-respected independent scholar Liam Hogan, the internet meme of the 'Irish slave' first appeared in 2013, when an article called 'The Irish slave trade – The forgotten "white" slaves', first published in 2008, went viral on Facebook, on which it has now been shared almost a million times. Illustrated with the cover image from *White Cargo*, though without its authors' endorsement, and first published on the website of Global Research, a Canadian non-profit group that proclaims on its homepage that 'in an era of media disinformation, our focus has essentially been to center on the "unspoken truth"', this short essay, written by John Martin, about whom no information is available, asserts that 'if anyone, black or white, believes that slavery was only an African experience, then they've got it completely wrong'.[19] But while historians may bridle at the inaccuracy of this claim, the fact is that popular history, whether that of the United States, of Ireland or of any other nation, has long been replete with misunderstandings, omissions, exaggerations and outright myths, tendencies accelerated by the rise of social media. Scholars of the history of Atlantic slavery may deplore mischaracterisations such as the equation of white indentured servitude and African chattel slavery, but why should such errors seem innately more problematic than the endless speculations engaged in by huge numbers of people regarding the 'truth' about who really assassinated President Kennedy, or whether German Second World War general Erwin Rommel was truly a Nazi?

Why? Because the meme of the Irish slave is currently being deployed not only as a symbol of an alleged historical atrocity, but as a weapon with which to undermine current initiatives to redress past and present racial injustices – against African-Americans, not the Irish. Circulated by far-right groups ranging from the Tea Party to the Sons of Confederate Veterans to the neo-Nazi Stormfront and White Aryan Resistance, the claim that white people (sometimes specifically described as 'Irish' – in 2015, 10 per cent of Americans claimed to be of Irish descent, the second largest ancestry group in the United States – and otherwise simply referred to as 'white') were enslaved just as were people of African heritage is frequently used in attempts to invalidate the claims of African-Americans that they have, since their earliest arrival in what would become the United States, been treated in a uniquely cruel and unequal manner, and that the source of this abuse was and remains racism on the part of white Americans.[20] Just as some white Americans' response to the Black Lives Matter movement has been the counter-claim that 'All Lives Matter', the myth of the Irish slave, arising as it does from centuries of conflicts over imperialism, nationality, religion and race, can be and is used to sabotage the assertions of black Americans that their sufferings have been both extreme and exceptional, and, more importantly, that they continue to have a devastating effect on black life chances, and are thus not just something for modern black Americans to 'get over'. If whites too endured slavery, the argument runs, why have they been able to become economically, politically and educationally successful in the United States, and, at least as importantly, why have they relinquished their resentments over their ancestors' sufferings? And, then, why are many African-Americans still embittered about their past, and why do they feel that they deserve reparations or other forms of redress from white America? As a white man from Mississippi stated in a 2015 article in the *Washington Post*, 'Even the Irish, we were slaves. At some point, you just have to get over it.' This claim was echoed the following year by the then Fox News host (and now partner of Donald Trump Jr) Kimberly Guilfoyle, herself of Irish descent, who asserted that 'the Irish got over it. They don't run around going "Irish Lives Matter."'[21] Thus, the trope of the alleged enslavement of white men and women, and of the Irish in particular, has been mobilised both to bolster a discourse of white victimhood and to deny the significance of the historical and contemporary abuse of African-Americans.

But if historians of the Anglo-Atlantic world do not believe that the Irish or other white migrants, despite the numerous disadvantages they may have suffered, were subjected to chattel slavery in the West Indies or North America, and if they do not expect African-Americans to 'get over' their own and their ancestors' experiences of racist abuse, especially in the face of the increase in verbal and physical violence against people of colour by white nationalist groups, by some police officers and by many contemporary politicians, how can they mobilise their historical expertise to dismantle this meme and strip it of its alarming power?

One way to do so is to advocate, not just as individuals but through national professional organisations, for academic historians to play a more significant role in the development of primary- and secondary-school history curricula. In the United Kingdom, many students, parents, teachers and academics deplore the fact that the current National Curriculum offers few opportunities to study either black British history or the history of British imperialism. This lacuna has been defended by former education secretary Michael Gove and other influential Conservative politicians with the argument that the goal of school-level history instruction is to teach children Britain's 'island story', a story that, Gove and his supporters claim, barely involved people of colour prior to the post-Second World War migration to Britain of imperial subjects from the Caribbean, Asia and Africa.[22] But the situation is far more problematic in the United States, in which it is much more difficult than in the United Kingdom to claim that slavery occurred 'somewhere else', or that people of African descent were until recently a very small segment of the national population. Yet most American schoolchildren are taught very little about the history of slavery and racial inequalities in their country. Sometimes this silence stems from educators' reluctance to criticise any aspect of the nation's past, especially that which involves slave-holding national heroes such as George Washington and Thomas Jefferson, or it may come from a sense, conscious or otherwise, that the American story was and is really the story of white people. It may be the result of benevolent intentions, to downplay uncomfortable aspects of history that might generate feelings of resentment or guilt among students of different races and ethnicities. In some cases, it has a financial aspect: school districts may be unable or unwilling to invest in more up-to-date history textbooks that bring racial issues to the fore, and textbook authors and publishers are aware that educational materials problematising the triumphalist narrative of American history are unlikely to be adopted in more conservative districts, and are thus financially unviable.

The study of the history of slavery and race is well developed within both British and American academia. The majority of university history departments in both countries offer undergraduate and master's-level modules on topics such as the Atlantic slave trade, the plantation system, the black American/British experience and the civil rights movement, and produce new Ph.D.s whose dissertations focus on these areas. It is difficult to imagine an academic conference in American history that would not include a significant number of papers or panels related to the African-American experience, and increasingly gatherings of historians of Britain include in their programmes scholarship on topics related to slavery, race and empire. A high percentage of US universities, including those in the South, sponsor programmes or institutes that centre on the study of race, and over the past two decades UK institutions have followed this path, establishing such facilities for research and public outreach as the Wilberforce Institute for the Study of Slavery and Emancipation at the University of Hull, and the Centre for the Study of International Slavery at the University of Liverpool. But despite the dogged efforts of professional organisations such as the American Historical Association and the Royal Historical Society to persuade educational decision-makers to expand primary- and secondary-school curricula, neither system has yet seen significant changes in the teaching of the history of slavery and race. But this is an area in which scholars must continue with their efforts, rather than disengaging from what may seem an unpromising struggle – the stakes are simply too high for us to withdraw.

Whether or not the fault lies primarily with the schools, the fact remains that many contemporary Britons and Americans have little understanding of the actual nature of slavery. Even those who may be willing to acknowledge white responsibility for past and present racial injustices are sometimes deeply unaware of the specific nature of this exploitation. For example, after the release in 2013 of black British filmmaker Steve McQueen's *Twelve Years a Slave*, some viewers were shocked to realise that it was far from uncommon for enslaved girls and women to experience sexual and physical violence from their owners. Many people tend to focus their indignation about the history of slavery on the various types of abuse that enslaved people endured: the ever-present threat of harsh physical punishment, an unending routine of gruelling and uncompensated physical labour, constant surveillance by owners and overseers, and a very low material standard of living. Of course, the majority of enslaved African-Americans endured these forms of abuse, but many 'free' labourers in both historical and contemporary contexts experienced or are experiencing labour conditions that are nearly as exploitative and immiserating as plantation slavery. British and American media report frequently not only on the terrible working and living conditions of Asian migrant workers in the United Arab Emirates but on their employers' seizure of their passports, and on the unsafe working condition founds in the warehouses of Amazon and SportsDirect.

But if we depict the horror of enslavement as having to labour in miserable conditions, we really miss the point, particularly in drawing parallels between slavery and indentured servitude in the seventeenth- and eighteenth-century Anglo-American world. Yes, many white servants, Irish or otherwise, found the experience of indentured labour extremely difficult. It was the combination of improved possibilities at home and growing awareness of the miseries of colonial indenture that resulted in a decline in the availability of white servants, and thus an increased dependence on enslaved people of African descent as a plantation labour force. But the fact remains that indentured servitude was neither racialised nor inheritable, and those who survived their years of service would regain their liberty and, with hard work and a measure of luck, might significantly improve their economic and social status. As W. E. B. DuBois stated in *Black Reconstruction*, 'no matter how degraded the [white] factory hand, he is not real estate'.[23] But in all but the most exceptional circumstances, an enslaved person would remain enslaved, and could not plan or even realistically hope for a better future for him/herself or for his/her children. This, more than anything, is the line that separates servitude from enslavement, and that gives the lie to the previously discussed attempts to transform the Irish servant into the white slave.

It may be comforting to attribute the frequent blurring of this line between servitude and slavery to either malice or ignorance on the part of contemporary white nationalists, but I urge scholars who are concerned about the political effects of this conflation to make every effort to correct the misuse, over centuries, of the term 'slavery'. Many idealistic reformers, whether in the American Revolution, in the campaign for women's suffrage or in turn-of-the century initiatives against forced prostitution, have described themselves or those for whom they claimed to speak as 'slaves' when, no matter how deep their sufferings may have been, this term was simply not applicable to their situations. We can see this same problematic conception of 'slavery' at work today in the activities of non-profit organisations such as Anti-Slavery International. These campaigners' dedication to raising awareness of and combating such evils as sex-trafficking, child marriage and bonded labour is entirely admirable, but collapsing these practices under the umbrella of 'slavery' amplifies the sufferings of the present by muting those of the past.[24] In the majority of situations to which these groups respond, the individuals who have been forced into various types of uncompensated or coerced labour, trafficked into sex work, or compelled to marry without their consent are not considered chattel in legal terms; they have not forfeited their human rights, and their servitude is not passed on to their children. If they run away from their captors, the latter cannot expect law enforcement officials to locate them and return them to servitude, and it is those captors who will face legal consequences for their actions. When confronted with horrific accounts of unfree labour that range from eastern European and African girls being trafficked to European cities to work in the sex industry to English teenagers from troubled backgrounds who have been groomed to join 'county lines' drug-dealing gangs, this distinction may seem semantic, but misconceptions regarding the nature of slavery, as opposed to other forms of forced labour and related abuses, have unfortunately contributed to the power of the image of 'Irish slavery', and thus have worked to minimise the sufferings of enslaved Africans and their descendants in the Americas.

The problems that can result from this linguistic slippage are encapsulated in a reader's letter published several years ago in the *Guardian* newspaper:

> I was moved to read Jen Wilson's letter about the fortune grabbed by the owners of Penrhyn Castle [a stately home in Wales] from the labour of slaves in their West Indies sugar plantations. When I visited this opulent pile, I was nauseated by the conspicuous consumption of its owners, particularly as I knew their wealth was built on the backs of Welsh slate miners and their families. Slate mines were dangerous places, the work was generally back-breaking, and the workers were not generously paid and were often forced to accept tokens (in lieu of money) that had to be spent at company stores. Anyone British should be ashamed by the exploitation, cruelty and racism of the empire, but it's good to remember that the working class here were enslaved too.[25]

This letter offers a very clear example of the misconceptions engendered by the equation of impoverished people enduring terrible work situations with those who are enslaved. The slate miners of Wales endured difficult and hazardous working conditions and were cruelly exploited by their employers, but they were not legally or physically compelled to remain in these jobs, although it is likely that many felt that they had few other options, owing to a lack of opportunity to gain the skills that would allow them to find better-paid and less onerous work. But the slate miners were not born into this form of labour, and their children were free to seek other types of employment. They were not physically distinct from those who managed and owned the mines, and although they could never match the legal and political advantages such people possessed, they were British subjects who were inherently endowed with basic political and legal rights. Perhaps most importantly, even the most rapacious employers had no power to separate the members of their workers' families, or forcibly to relocate them away from their homes.

In closing, it is incumbent upon all of us who are concerned about this slippage between servitude and slavery, and by its implications in the volatile current political situation, to teach our students well and carefully. Works such as those of O'Callaghan and Jordan and Walsh were produced in good faith; their misconceptions stem not from the authors' dishonesty or racism but from their inexcusably sloppy use of sources. For example, the only eyewitness account that depicts in any detail the experiences of Irish indentured servants in the seventeenth-century English West Indies, Richard Ligon's *A True & Exact History of the Island of Barbados* (1657), describes the 'cruelty' with which Ligon claims that some of the English planters treated their servants, but he contrasts these enslavers with those 'merciful' individuals on the island who 'treat their Servants well', and asserts that, in recent years, enslavers in general have become 'discreeter and better natur'd', and now provide their indentured labour force with a reasonable work regimen and decent living conditions.[26] Ligon's vivid narrative of his voyage to and residence in Barbados has been used by nearly every scholar who has studied the history of the West Indies in this period, but even otherwise meticulous historians have tended to emphasise the cruelty and ignore the mercy when writing about the treatment of servants in this context. Historians have no power to right the wrongs of past centuries, and are, alas, very limited in their ability to resolve current injustices, but if we can help our students to interpret whatever sources that previous eras have left for us, and to distinguish between reality and fantasy, fear and wishful thinking, we will have made our small contribution to dismantling a pernicious misconception that mobilises an inaccurate view of the past to undermine the possibilities for racial justice in the present.

Notes

1 *The Commitments*, dir. Alan Parker. The scene can be viewed on YouTube: 'Blacks of Europe', www.youtube.com/watch?v=_e9WDfg2idk (accessed 29 August 2022). The song from which Rabbitte quotes is 'Say it loud – I'm black and I'm proud', written by Brown and Alfred 'Pee Wee' Ellis in 1968 and released the following year on Brown's King Records album of the same name.
2 Roddy Doyle, *The Commitments* (London: Vintage, 2013 [1987]), pp. 13, 15. Barrytown, the setting of several of his novels, is a fictional working-class suburb of north Dublin, based upon Kilbarrack, where Doyle grew up; Eoghan Smith and Simon Workman, 'Suburbia in Irish literary and visual culture', in Eoghan Smith and Simon Workman, eds, *Imagining Irish Suburbia in Literature and Culture* (London: Palgrave Macmillan, 2018), pp. 77–95. See also Bryan Fanning, 'Racism in Ireland', in Bryan Fanning, *Racism and Social Change in the Republic of Ireland* (Manchester: Manchester University Press, 2018), pp. 8–29; Diane Negra, ed., *The Irish in Us: Irishness, Performativity, and Popular Culture* (Durham, NC: Duke University Press, 2006); and Bill Rolston, 'Are the Irish black?', *Race and Class* 41:1–2 (1999), 95–102.
3 Brendan M. Walsh, 'When unemployment disappears: Ireland in the 1990s', CESifo Working Paper 856, February 2003, www.ideas.repec.org/p/ces/ceswps/_856.html (accessed 4 April 2020), p. 1; Patrick Honohan, 'Fiscal adjustment in Ireland in the 1980s', *Economic and Social Review* 23:3 (1992), 258–314.
4 Veronica Crossa, Montserrat Pareja-Eastaway, Josep Miquel Pique and Didier Grimaldi, 'Reinventing the city: Barcelona, Birmingham and Dublin', in Sako Musterd and Alan Murie, eds, *Making Competitive Cities* (Oxford: Blackwell, 2010), pp. 67–92 (p. 73); Kostas Ergazakis, Kostas Metaxiotis and John Psarras, 'An emerging pattern of successful knowledge cities' main features', in Francisco Javier Carrillo, ed., *Knowledge Cities: Approaches, Experiences, and Perspectives* (Abingdon: Routledge, 2011), pp. 3–15 (p. 8); Mark Crinson, 'Georgianism and the tenements, Dublin 1908–1926', *Art History* 29:4 (September 2006), 625–59 (p. 630). See also Ellen Rowley, *Housing, Architecture and the Edge Condition: Dublin Is Building, 1935–1975* (Abingdon: Routledge, 2018).
5 It is worth noting that, in the later nineteenth and earlier twentieth centuries, some African-American activists and artists conceptualised their struggle for self-determination as parallel to that of Irish political and cultural resistance to English imperial rule; see Evelyn O'Callaghan, 'Black Irish, white Jamaican', *Caribbean Quarterly* 64:3–4 (2018), 392–408 (p. 395); and Kathleen Gough, *Kinship and Performance in the Black and Green Atlantic: Haptic Allegories* (New York: Routledge, 2013).
6 Noel Ignatiev, *How the Irish Became White* (New York: Routledge, 1995). See also Sinéad Moynihan, *'Other People's Diasporas': Negotiating Race in Contemporary Irish and Irish American Culture* (Syracuse, NY: Syracuse University Press, 2013), p. 6; and Peter D. O'Neill, *Famine Irish and the American Racial State* (New York: Routledge, 2017).

7 On the Boston busing controversy see Ronald P. Formisano, *Boston Against Busing: Race, Class, and Ethnicity in the 1960s and 1970s* (Chapel Hill: University of North Carolina Press, 2004).
8 John Martin, 'The Irish slave trade – the forgotten "white" slaves', Global Research, Centre for Research on Globalization, 14 April 2008, www.globalresearch.ca/the-irish-slave-trade-the-forgotten-white-slaves/31076 (accessed 5 April 2020).
9 Sean O'Callaghan, *To Hell or Barbados: The Ethnic Cleansing of Ireland* (Dingle: Brandon/Mount Eagle Publications, 2000), pp. 93, 119, 87.
10 Liam Hogan, 'Critique of Sean O'Callaghan's *To Hell or Barbados*', https://limerick1914.medium.com/critique-of-sean-ocallaghan-s-to-hell-or-barbados-aea31469d3a2 (accessed 2 September 2022); Nini Rodgers, *Ireland, Slavery and Anti-Slavery: 1612–1865* (Basingstoke: Palgrave Macmillan, 2007), 38; Donald Harman Akenson, *Ireland, Sweden, and the Great European Migration, 1815–1914* (Montreal: McGill-Queen's University Press, 2011), p. 130n62.
11 Damien Dempsey, 'To Hell or Barbados', *To Hell or Barbados* (Sony BMG, 2007). The song's lyrics are available at www.genius.com/Damien-dempsey-to-hell-or-barbados-lyrics (accessed 6 April 2020).
12 Goodreads, www.goodreads.com/book/show/1662002.To_Hell_or_Barbados (accessed 7 April 2020).
13 Jerome S. Handler and Matthew C. Reilly, 'Contesting "white slavery" in the Caribbean', *New West Indian Guide* 91:1–2 (2017), 30–55 (p. 47). Some scholars have cast doubt on the prevalence of both the 'No blacks, no Irish, no dogs' signs and the 'No Irish need apply' variant in nineteenth- and twentieth-century England and the United States. See Richard Jensen, '"No Irish need apply": A myth of victimization', *Journal of Social History* 36:2 (Winter 2002), 405–29; Donald MacRaild, '"No Irish need apply": The origins and persistence of a prejudice', *Labour History Review* 78:3 (2013), 269–99; and John Draper, 'No Irish, no blacks, no dogs, no proof', *Guardian*, 21 October 2015, www.theguardian.com/money/2015/oct/21/no-irish-no-blacks-no-dogs-no-proof (accessed 29 August 2022).
14 Riva Berleant-Schiller, 'Free labor and the economy in seventeenth-century Montserrat', *William and Mary Quarterly* 46 (1989), 539–64; Hilary McD. Beckles, '"A riotous and unruly lot": Irish indentured servants and freemen in the English West Indies, 1644–1713', *William and Mary Quarterly* 47 (1990), 503–22; Hilary McD. Beckles, '"Black men in white skins": The formation of a white proletariat in West Indian slave society', *Journal of Imperial and Commonwealth History* 15 (1986), 5–21. Beckles's work was the inspiration and the source of much of the historical background for the Irish writer Kate McCafferty's 2002 novel *Testimony of an Irish Slave Girl*, a text that has been described as 'a neo-slave narrative'; O'Callaghan, 'Black Irish, white Jamaican', p. 398.
15 Natalie A. Zacek, *Settler Society in the English Leeward Islands, 1670–1776* (Cambridge: Cambridge University Press, 2010), Chapter 2. The phrase 'a great tangled cousinry' is borrowed from Bernard Bailyn, 'Politics and social

structure in Virginia', in James M. Smith, ed., *Seventeenth-Century America* (Chapel Hill: University of North Carolina Press, 1959), pp. 90–115 (p. 111).

16 For example, an Irish indentured servant named Cornelius Bryan, who was punished numerous times for his insubordinate words and acts, as a free man acquired a small plantation and a dozen slaves; Jenny Shaw, *Everyday Life in the Early English Caribbean: Irish, Africans, and the Construction of Difference* (Athens: University of Georgia Press, 2013), pp. 144, 154. See also Rodgers, *Ireland, Slavery and Anti-Slavery, 1612–1865*.

17 Don Jordan and Michael Walsh, *White Cargo: The Forgotten History of Britain's White Slaves in America* (New York: New York University Press, 2008), p. 7.

18 On Nast and his ilk see L. Perry Curtis Jr, *Apes and Angels: The Irishman in Victorian Caricature*, rev. edn (Washington, DC: Smithsonian Institution Press, 1997 [1971]).

19 Martin, 'The Irish slave trade.'

20 Drew DeSilver, 'The fading of the green: Fewer Americans identify as Irish', *Fact Tank*, Pew Research Center, 17 March 2017, www.pewresearch.org/fact-tank/2017/03/17/the-fading-of-the-green/ (accessed 9 April 2020).

21 'In Mississippi, defenders of state's Confederate-themed flag dig in', *Washington Post*, 18 August 2015; Scott Eric Kaufman, 'Fox News' Kimberly Guilfoyle slams "Black Lives Matter"', *Salon*, 18 March 2016, www.salon.com/2016/03/18/fox_news_kimberly_guilfoyle_you_dont_hear_irish_people_shouting_irish_lives_matter_because_they_got_over_racism/ (accessed 9 April 2020). In fact, Amazon and other online vendors sell 'Irish Lives Matter' T-shirts; www.amazon.com/Irish-Lives-Matter-T-Shirt-Colors/dp/B07N5SJQ2H (accessed 9 April 2020).

22 Michael Gove, 'All children will learn our island story', speech on 5 October 2010, Conservative Party Speeches, www.conservative-speeches.sayit.mysociety.org/speech/601441 (accessed 10 April 2020). In this address, Gove claims that 'our [English] literature is the best in the world', and lists in support of this statement nine white writers (all except Jane Austen are male), the most recent of whom, Thomas Hardy, died in 1928. He promises to 'put British history at the heart of a revived national curriculum' in response to 'a trashing of our past' that 'denies children the opportunity to hear our island story'.

23 W. E. B. DuBois, *Black Reconstruction in America* (New Brunswick, NJ: Transaction Publishers, 2013 [1935]), p. 7.

24 The definition of 'modern slavery', as used by Anti-Slavery International, includes 'forced labour', 'debt bondage/bonded labour', 'forced and early marriage' and 'human trafficking'. See 'What is modern slavery?', www.antislavery.org/slavery-today/modern-slavery/ (accessed 10 April 2020).

25 Pippa Richardson, 'Penrhyns enslaved Welsh working class', *Guardian*, 27 November 2017. The letter to which Richardson was responding was published on 22 November 2017; www.theguardian.com/world/2017/nov/22/historians-working-towards-a-full-imperial-reckoning-for-britain) (accessed 29 August 2022).

26 Richard Ligon, *A True & Exact History of the Island of Barbados* (London: Humphrey Moseley, 1657), p. 94.

18

'Where are you actually from?': Racial issues in the Irish context

Sandrine Uwase Ndahiro

Contemporary Ireland is, by any metric, becoming a more multicultural and diverse nation. The increasing visibility of a multi-ethnic population has exposed the deep-rooted issues of race, identity and belonging. In 2016 more than 11 per cent (535,475) of people resident in Ireland were classified as non-Irish nationals by the Central Statistics Office, with a further 104,784 classed as dual Irish nationality.

In this chapter I wish to address the question of racial issues from the perspective of somebody who is Rwandan-Irish, and thus well placed to think about what these classifications mean in contemporary Ireland. One of the ironies of contemporary Ireland is that the history of colonisation on the island is often invoked to invalidate the stories of those who experience racism here. As the chapters that precede mine in this volume have shown, the roots of Ireland's relationship to colonialism and race are much more complex. In what follows, I try to make sense of both the changing landscape of racial issues in Ireland post-Black Lives Matter (BLM), and the various ways that history has been put to use in the debate.

Being Rwandan-Irish places me in a uniquely liminal position in Irish society. Living in this liminal space I constantly feel like am battling two versions of myself. Through the white gaze, I am made to feel like I cannot unapologetically exist with a dual identity. Instead, there is pressure to choose one over the other, all in the hopes of proving that I am Irish. Having a hybrid identity in contemporary Ireland becomes more complicated the more exposed I am to the Irish colonial past. Through my research I am constantly discovering how at various moments in time Irish migrants went through periods of being, or feeling, hybrid, as explained by Andrew Murphy, who posits that '[t]he Irish are curiously hybrid, approximating both to the colonial stereotype and, simultaneously, to the English themselves'.[1] In the past the Irish, too, went through a process of trying to define Irishness. The same process that I am currently going through. At the same time, this shared commonality makes it difficult for me to understand why there is such resistance to Irish people with a dual identity like me.

The resurgence of the global BLM movement in 2020 in response to the killing of George Floyd on 25 May 2020 in Minneapolis, Minnesota, provoked a national conversation on the issue of racism in Ireland. Racism is defined by Linda Alcoff as 'socially constructed, historically malleable, culturally contextual, and reproduced through learned perceptual practices'.[2] Although race is a social construct, racism is a lived reality for many ethnic minority groups, as we are living in a racially articulated society. The global effect of BLM instigated a debate in Ireland on what it means to be Irish and why the default of this identity is whiteness.

Racism is an issue that has always been a feature of life in Ireland. However, until the transformative period of 2020, it was an issue that was persistently overlooked and used as a scapegoat to further the tensions of 'Us' versus 'Them'. Lucy Michael argues that racism against people of African descent in Ireland 'is not a new phenomenon at all, but one which has failed to be recognized by the State and wider society, even as it has evolved from colonial times',[3] while journalist Ellen Coyne notes that 'a study by the European Fundamental Rights agency found instances of racism in Ireland were often above the European average'.[4] The report further noted that in Ireland, Black Irish people are twice as likely as White Irish people to experience discrimination when seeking work and three times as likely to experience discrimination in the workplace.[5] Over the past few years, the number of racist incidents in Ireland has increased. Data from Irish Network Against Racism (INAR) in 2020 noted a rise in racist incidents from 530 in 2019 to 700 in 2020. According to INAR '[t]he system recorded 159 criminal incidents, a record 51 racist assaults and a record 334 incidents of hate speech'.[6] These racist incidents occurred both online and offline, and affected minority groups, from people with African heritage to other minority groups such as those with Asian heritage.

Black Lives Matter has moved beyond a social movement that resonated solely with the black Irish community. It has increased the visibility of racial issues ingrained in every aspect of our society. For example, BLM brought to our attention the need to address racism in our education system. Brid Ni Chonaill points out that 'Ireland witnessed a voicing of experiences of racism, particularly from young Black people through social media channels, with education, including higher education.'[7] The voicing of such opinions was long overdue.

Moreover, BLM has uncovered the ways in which racism is deeply embedded within Irish society: an issue that has been misunderstood, overlooked and brushed aside. This political movement clarified how different communities experience racism. Coyne points out how this period was transformative, as '[i]t made some white Irish people critical or dismissive, uncomfortable at the perceived suggestion that Ireland and America were the same'.[8] Before BLM, when it came to talking about racial issues in Ireland, the experience of racism in America was often invoked: as if to say that racial issues only affected African-Americans rather than the lived realities of marginalised communities in Ireland.

Ireland was England's first colony, and the relationship evolved in extraordinarily complex ways from the twelfth century, through to the plantations of the sixteenth and seventeenth centuries. The presence of British colonial power in Ireland created a dichotomous relationship between 'Irishness' and 'whiteness'. David Cairns and Shaun Richards place an emphasis on 'the reality of the historic relationship of Ireland and England; a relationship of the colonised and the coloniser'.[9] This complex relationship had a longlasting effect on the construction of an imagined 'true' Irish identity, with overarching consequences for the construction of Irish global identity, and it remains a leading factor in present debates around race in Ireland.

First, the colonisation of Ireland placed the Irish in the category of the 'other', leading to internalised ideas of inferiority. This differed from other colonial experiences in settings such as the African continent, where the angle of inferiority was heavily focused on race and blackness, which were viewed as subhuman. Terry Eagleton has argued that the Irish experience of colonialism was defined by a potential usefulness: 'it was never of much interest to British imperialism whether the Irish were Irish or Eskimo, white, or black ... It is not their ethnic peculiarity but their territory and labor power that have entranced the British.'[10] Even though the Irish were white, colonisation placed them in a liminal space, with their territory, culture, language and history all targeted in the hope of civilising the uncivilised.

During the colonial period, the Irish were often openly considered racially inferior when compared to the rest of developed Europe. The Irish were placed in the category of subhuman where they were described as 'Blacks of Europe'.[11] Phenomenologist Sara Ahmed explores the colonial experience through a white gaze and states that '[c]olonialism makes the world white, which is of course a world ready for certain kinds of bodies, as a world that puts certain objects within their reach'.[12] Andrew Murphy's analysis of the racial identity that was projected onto the Irish highlights the discrepancy when '[t]he white skin of the Irish signifies a certain connection of racial kinship between the colonizer and the colonized'.[13] White skin acted as a common and distinctive trait between the Irish and the English, yet this proximity still saw a division of 'Us' versus 'Them'.[14]

Moreover, the concept of race appeared to be an oversimplified term used when describing the Irish visible presence in America and the United Kingdom. In the United Kingdom, the Irish were stereotyped and described as 'dirty Irish', and this was the accepted norm in the nineteenth century. Irish migrants in the United Kingdom 'were subjected to racialization, social disadvantage and discrimination'.[15] The role of the 'other' ensured that the Irish were hyperaware of their positionality and lack of power in their new host countries. Bronwen Walter points out that 'a key aspect of constructions of Irishness is the paradox by which the Irish are represented by dominant Western groups simultaneously as other'.[16] This 'otherisation' exposes the dichotomy of whiteness and what it entails. Through this otherisation, the Irish were viewed as inferior, and this inferiority complex was then projected onto their black counterparts.

Additionally, the Irish were described through the lens of animality: savage, uncivilised, premodern and barbaric individuals. Linda Alcoff points out how certain communities/ethnicities were biologically white but were nevertheless socially excluded from the privileges of being white. Alcoff highlights how 'Jews, Irish, Italians, and other southern Europeans were sometimes excluded from whiteness and at other times enjoyed a halfway status as almost white, but not quite.'[17] The Irish were stuck in this in-between space where they were trying to construct their identity while trying to understand what it means to be white in a society that had continuously 'otherised' them.

The racialisation of the Irish throughout history paved the way for a distinctive and internalised need for Irishness to be linked with whiteness. The racialisation process that took place in Ireland followed the general projection of western modernity and of whiteness to denote superiority, a distinctive feature of European colonialism. Throughout the period from the sixteenth to the early nineteenth century Irish people were interconnected with the transatlantic slave trade, and the Irish formed a significant minority in many urban American environments in the late nineteenth and early twentieth century. Peter O'Neill has insisted that 'race formed the single most important element in the construction of Americanness', and that this involved placing Irish migrants in inferior categories.[18] This shaped Irish understanding of not only their identity but the visible tension between whiteness and blackness. The proximity to blackness prompted the Irish to construct an identity that distanced them from the formerly enslaved through the process of becoming white. Rather than increasing empathy or identification with oppressed categories of people, the diaspora experience of the Irish in settler imperial contexts such as Australia and America did in fact increase differentiation in many instances: especially from people of colour.

After the revolutionary period of 1916–23 Irish nationalism paved a way for Irish people to resituate themselves in a global sense and to create a distinctive Irish identity: one that departed from the longlasting colonial link with the English. Seamus Deane touches on this distinctive feature when he observes how 'Irish nationalism is, in its foundational moments, a derivative of its British counterpart'. Through nationalism, Irish people were trying to answer 'What does it mean to be Irish?', and Irishness could now be understood through a disruption of the relationship between the coloniser and the colonised. As a result of this more confident nationalism, Irish people developed a strong sense of what it meant 'to be Irish'. This was prevalent in the distinctive Gaelic revival period of cultural production in literature, music and the creation of the Gaelic Athletic Association. Inevitably, as this new Irish identity was established it aligned itself with whiteness. Race and nationalism are linked together, as '[a]lmost all nationalist movements have been derided as provincial, actually or potentially racist, given to exclusivist and doctrinaire positions and rhetoric'.[19]

The Irish racial inferiority status led to a new sense of determination when constructing an Irish identity. The creation of Irish nationalism proved complex as an urgent need to move away from negative stereotypes associated with Irishness developed while searching for a new definition of what it meant to be Irish. A distinctive aspect of constructing this new image of Irishness relied on masculinity, and Aidan Beatty argues that '[c]rafting an image of strong and racially redeemed Irish men was a key part of this'.[20] Irish nationalism became linked with whiteness and the male privileges attached to it.[21]

Consequently, Caitríona Ní Laoire argues that the 'earlier process of Irish nation-building, in part a response to the racialization of the Irish, perpetuated a myth of the homogeneity of Irish society and produced exclusionary ideologies of social belonging in the development of the Irish state in the 20th century, linked to, for example, anti-Semitism and anti-Traveller racism'.[22] Through the journey taken by the Irish in becoming white, they ended up perpetuating the same exclusionary ideals that they too had once been subjected to. These exclusionary ideologies influence present conversations about race in Ireland. A national effort is needed to dismantle the outdated tradition of viewing Irishness as solely white. The presence of multiculturalism and the visibility of multi-ethnic communities in Ireland should serve as clear indicators of how Irish identity is dynamic and contingent.

Through the disguise of the philosophy of modernity and progress, those that reside outside the Global North have been fed a false notion: that the only way of availing a future is by escaping the Global South. The false sense of a European dream is evident in the harsh realities that await the new arrivals. Migrants arriving in European countries are often met with racism and xenophobia, and Ireland is no exception.

The normalisation of racism is a prominent issue across the globe, and in Europe in particular. Ní Laoire argues that '[t]he numbers of African migrants ... in Europe have risen dramatically over the last 10 to 15 years as a result of conflict, persecution and persistent poverty in African societies'.[23] Across Europe, fluidity of identity is complicated by the concept of race.

This shared European experience gives this book a new relevant urgency while centring the Irish context. By addressing racial issues in a global context and more specifically an Irish context, we can examine how European identities are intertwined through colonialism.

Benedict Anderson has connected rapid social change with a consequent rise in racism, and the Celtic Tiger (1994–2007) period proved to be such a transformative time in Ireland.[24] That moment of economic prosperity brought about a new Ireland that was diverse and multicultural. This caused a dramatic shift in Irish society as the old perceptions of Ireland were challenged, and this fundamentally changed the taxonomy of Irishness as the island became home to an influx of migrants from many cultures, whether as asylum seekers, refugees, international students, European Union migrants or returning Irish emigrants. This cultural, social and economic shift sometimes enabled racism.

In 2006 it was estimated that a total of 35,326 migrants of African descent had moved to Ireland. This number has significantly risen since then, as '[b]y 2011 just over 65,000 respondents defined their ethnicity as Black on the Census, and this number was similar in 2016'.[25] Many black/African migrants came to Ireland from Nigeria and South Africa in this period (Figure 18.1). The Traveller community in Ireland makes up for the largest ethnic minority population, at 0.7 per cent of the total. The size of the Black Irish community in Ireland is significantly less than in places such as the United Kingdom and France, which have a history of migration from various African countries. According to the 2011 census, Black

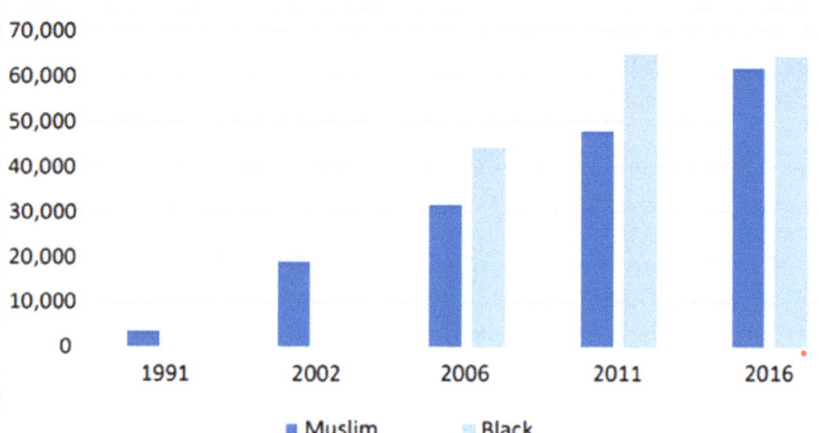

Figure 18.1 Presence of black population in Ireland between 2006 and 2016. Source: CSO Statbank Tables E7016, E7057, CO507, CO501 and B1201.

British people made up 3 per cent of the United Kingdom's population.[26] Recent figures from 2018 that assessed the continuous increase of migration into the UK identified the 'Irish-born population for the UK at ... 380,000 without the ethnicity of such Irish migrants'.[27] Meanwhile, in France, statistical representation of different ethnic groups is far more difficult to assess. Jean Beaman notes that 'France does not collect official statistics on race and ethnicity and does not have state-level racial and ethnic categories',[28] while Patrick Simon observes that statistics on ethnic groups expose 'the fear of a slippery slope by invoking apocalyptic forecasts of what will follow' such ethnic categorisation,[29] which is often seen as a conflict in the public sphere. The rising presence of African migrants paved the way for a rise in racism across Europe. In the Irish context, a kind of moral panic was induced by the fear of diluting Irishness by mixing with other ethnic groups. The rise in the African presence in Ireland constantly creates this sense of an 'Us' versus 'Them' mentality and reminds the 'other' that they do not belong to this new Ireland.

Being black in Ireland means being hyperaware that your skin colour is the reason your Irishness is being constantly denied. This awareness becomes overwhelming and frustrating. Having a dual identity is itself proof that being Irish is no longer something synonymous with whiteness. Members of the black and Irish community are all too familiar with the harsh reality of being black in Ireland. Joella Dhlamini, who is South African and Irish, recalls 'As a black Irish teenager in a country that's predominantly white, I also felt the pressure and the burden of not being accepted due to the constant encounters with discrimination and stereotyping',[30] while Nigerian and Irish Segun Junaid recalls the painful experiences of growing up black in Ireland as he remembers 'Drunk old men would attempt to kick down our front door in the early hours of the morning and telling [sic] us to "go back where we came from"'.[31] Once again, black skin is used as a way of being 'othered' and discriminated against. The message is clear: because you are black you do not belong in Ireland.

Steve Garner believes that '[w]hile Travellers are seen as competing for land, asylum seekers, the other scapegoats of the Celtic Tiger, are perceived as competitors for work, space, and social security'.[32] The 'other' must be feared because they are perceived to be diluting whiteness, which is a constituent element of Irishness. Through that fear, there is a refusal to see how those that are in the category of the 'other' could have acquired their Irish citizenship through naturalisation or birth.

Geraldine Meaney notes that '[n]ational identities are structured by the binary of them and us, and outsiders, natives and foreigners'.[33] This binary cannot resolve how those who come to Ireland with a foreign cultural identity might later call Ireland home and adopt a dual identity. Benedict

Anderson looks at the concept of nationalism through the lens of imagined communities, which is a concept that is applicable in any society in the Global North. He explains nationalism as 'imagined because the members of even the smallest nation will never know most of their fellow-members, meet them, or even hear of them, yet in the minds of each lives the image of their communion'.[34] Nationalism leaves newcomers, who have no history of the nation's struggles, out of this imaginary. Racism in the Irish context proves to be complex as it moves beyond the generic binary of race, black and white. In Ireland, 'racism is fuelled in part by dominant, historically informed, narrow conceptions of Irishness, which are themselves subservient to a neoliberal agenda'.[35]

Rahul Sambaraju and Anca Minescu's work highlights how 'racism takes place in less explicit and covert ways' that make it difficult to prove that an action is racist.[36] The most prominent example of this constant denial is the question 'Where are you actually from?' – the question I am most often asked in Ireland. It happens when someone first meets me and hears my Irish accent, and it is my black skin that confuses them, as the default of Irishness is whiteness. This question is often presented not out of simple curiosity but to put aside my dual identity and assume that my identity just equates to blackness.

Emma Dabiri's book *Don't Touch My Hair* (2019) touches on this hyperawareness of being an 'other' in Ireland through a particular focus on the distinctiveness of Afro hair, which acted as a physical marker of racial difference. Talking about finding her place in Ireland, Dabiri states that 'You are constantly under surveillance. You become achingly aware of your every gesture; your movements, your very posture are at all times under analysis.'[37] This constant surveillance becomes suffocating, as it's a constant feeling that you are living in a world that is anti-black. Being hyperaware of every movement is the only way that ensures a clear understanding of why the black body is perceived as something that must be feared in society. This hyperawareness is a subconscious effort to show that your black essence poses no threat.

Robbie McVeigh, when exploring the complexity of Irish racism, points out that it 'has been theorised out of existence by the disingenuous use of the racism = prejudice + power equation to argue that Irish people, like Black people, have no power to be racist'.[38] These conversations about Irishness and racism are visible on social media, as people are using these platforms to engage with this ongoing debate (Figure 18.2). Twitter's weaponisation of history denigrates the current realities that Irish people like me face in contemporary Ireland. My experience of racism is not something that should be brushed aside and dismissed because of Ireland's former experience of

Racial issues in the Irish context 345

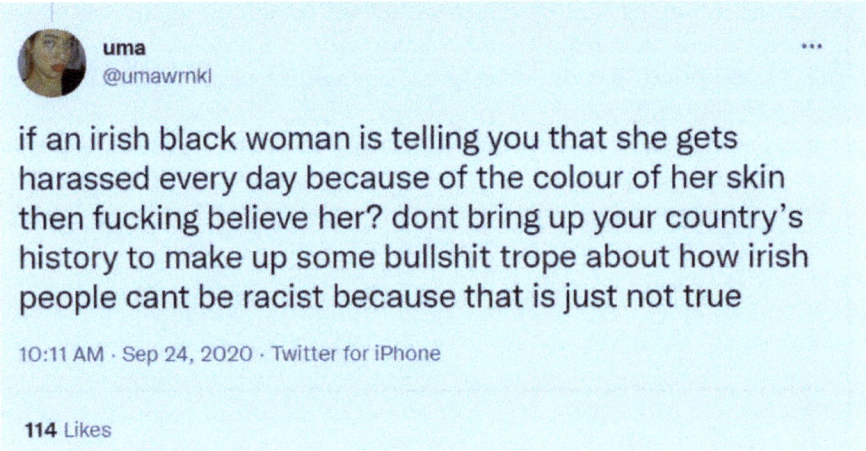

Figure 18.2 A Twitter handle arguing against the constant need to bring up Irish colonial history.

colonisation. Instead, questioning whiteness and its link to Irishness should be a point of mutual understanding. It is something that bonds us together in the complexities of history. Race questions in contemporary times should not be met with rejection and dismissal. As a nation, developing a shared history could prevent the 'New Irish' from having to spend decades constructing a new identity and the meaning of Irishness. A volume of essays such as this one can historicise and deepen our understanding of Irish involvement in enslavement and the slave economy across faith and class lines. Thus, it addresses the knowledge gap faced by black Irish people – like me – who face discrimination in an Ireland that has not yet reckoned with these legacies. I may not be of Caribbean descent, but Ireland's historical relationship with this other Atlantic archipelago has the power to affect the way I am perceived in both a positive and a negative sense. It is part of the same Irish story.

Being hyperaware of your blackness and what it entails is a common experience in the black Irish community. Predominantly white communities do not have to engage with this heightened self-awareness. Ahmed looks at this visible double standard in her work, arguing that 'white bodies do not have to face their whiteness; they are not orientated towards it'.[39] Understating the whiteness question creates clear tensions when it comes to talking about racism in Ireland. A small minority of white people will immediately become uncomfortable and defensive around the topic of race, as it can be the first time that they are made to think about the concept of white privilege. Their discomfort leads them to make dismissive claims such as

'I don't see colour' or 'The Irish were colonised', and such statements undermine the current lived realities of being an 'other' in Ireland.

The assumption that the issue of racism against people of African descent is a new phenomenon proves to be problematic. Often the Celtic Tiger period is seen as the first time that Ireland faced issues of race through the visible presence of African migrants. This is patently untrue. The presence of African migrants has been traced back to previous centuries in Ireland. One example is the visible presence of Africans in 1787, when African men were part of the British 29th Military. There were African merchants operating in Cork in the eighteenth century. Although it was difficult to give a clear estimate of the African population in Ireland in the eighteenth century, Theophilus Ejorh argues 'historical evidence suggests that during this time Dublin, second to London, was host to the largest black population in the whole of Europe'.[40] William Hart takes a step further, noting 'that there were significant numbers of black people living in Ireland in the eighteenth century is clear from the casual references to "blackamoors", "negro blacks", or simply "blacks", encountered in contemporary Irish newspapers, parish registers and other documentary sources'.[41]

Ireland is in a unique position to think about its relationship to race and coloniality more productively and in historical terms. Furthermore, it may pay dividends to think about these relationships in a more holistic way, so that the experience of people of African heritage in Ireland can be considered alongside the experiences of those of Afro-Caribbean descent rather than as simply a separate category altogether.

Moreover, individuals who are black and Irish, like me, are tasked with having to present our blackness in a way that proves that we do not dilute Irishness. The navigation of dual or hybrid identity is something that is learned from being hyperaware of our racially articulated society. Ní Laoire taps into how those with a dual identity must navigate the world as 'sometimes reproducing their blackness in ways that are culturally intelligible to their peers'.[42] Blackness through these interactions becomes diluted to fit in and showcase how we do not pose a threat. Through this act, an aspect of your blackness needs to be given up in order to fit in.

Spaces that were once perceived to be solely white should be questioned and dismantled in order to showcase a more accurate representation of contemporary Ireland. This is happening in other sectors, most notably in the performing arts. One example can be seen in the music industry, which is becoming more diverse. Earlier black performers are not documented to have spoken so outwardly against racism, an example being 1970s rock musician Philip Lynott, who is a celebrated figurehead in the music scene, as his 'towering presence in Irish music lore is emblematic of the fact that music in Ireland was always a healing, unifying force'.⁴³ The unifying force of music and its power to connect people took precedence, compared with current debates that see the music industry tainted by racism. Silence around the topic of racism and the music industry is changing. A new generation of black Irish artists are calling out racism and actively engaging with the question 'What does it mean to be Irish?'.

Black and Irish artists such as Zambian Irish rapper Denise Chaila and Nigerian Irish singer Tolü Makay are reshaping the Irish music scene while also openly talking about racism. They are facing racism as they are accused of taking up these spaces that are perceived to be solely white. Journalist Siobhan O'Connor conducted an interview with Tolü Makay in the wake of the BLM movement in Ireland, in which Makay poignantly explained: 'Black Lives Matter was traumatic. I think the one thing I got out of it was to love myself so vigorously, that any form of racism or anything that makes me feel different, it's that person's problem.'⁴⁴ The trauma that emerged out of this movement woke Irish society from its complacency regarding racism, and made it less possible for people to pass it off as an American issue.

Personally, the BLM movement in Ireland provided me with the opportunity to tackle the issue of racism through an artistic lens. Far too often I found that I was staying silent on the issue of race and identity, as I had been assigned the role of the 'other' from the moment I arrived in Ireland. In 2020 I found that a minority of Irish people were quick to identify racial issues in the USA but were incapable of understating how racism is also a prevalent issue in Ireland. The lack of empathy sparked a need for me to capture this significant moment and make sure that people whose lives are impacted by racism on a daily basis are central to these conversations. I first did this with the creation of the documentary *Unsilencing Black Voices* (2020) with co-director Catherine Osikoya. We wanted to highlight the lived realities of being black and Irish in contemporary Ireland. The documentary showed how racism exists and operates in Ireland, and that it needs to be addressed. Being Irish is no longer a fixed identity. It is fluid and ever changing.

Throughout this chapter I have highlighted the lived realities of minority communities who are subjected to racism in Ireland. Currently Ireland has no hate crime legislation to deal with specifically racist incidents. The Prohibition of Incitement to Hatred Act 1989 is intended for situations demonstrating 'hatred against a group of persons in the State or elsewhere on account of their race, colour, nationality, religion, ethnic or national origins, membership of the travelling community or sexual orientation'.⁴⁵ Bryan Fanning and Ronaldo Munck have argued that 'if racism is to be taken seriously, tangible definitions of racism within legal and policy processes capable of redressing specific acts of discrimination and specific institutional barriers are required'.[46] This declaration proves to be vital to the ongoing debate about whether racism exists in Ireland. Individuals subjected to racism are not taken seriously when they talk about their lived realities. Those who dispute the existence of racism in Ireland refuse to see how it is ingrained in Irish society. Racism is all around us in the form of access to housing, institutions, education, media, employment, health care. The list is endless.

Ireland is at a cultural crossroads where we are engaging in conversation about what it means to be Irish. Racism is a topic that needs to be given the same urgency as other social issues. Refusal to take racism seriously will lead us into another decade of ignoring the lived realities of those who are marginalised in our society. Racial institutions need to be dismantled, as Ahmed states: 'whiteness is what the institution is orientated around, so that even bodies that may not appear white still have to inhabit whiteness, if they are to get in'.[47] Institutions that perpetuate racist ideologies need to be challenged and dismantled. These spaces need to be accessible for all if we are to have a just and equitable future.

Although we are just at the beginning of this conversation, I am very hopeful about the exciting new projects that are centralising African presence in Ireland. The Colonial Legacies Project at Trinity College Dublin is an ongoing project on re-examining the oldest Irish university and its colonial past, and was partly inspired by BLM, as explained by then-Provost Dr Prendergast, who argues that 'we are conscious that we, as one of the world's oldest universities, have a particular responsibility to study our past, and to reflect the impact of Trinity as an institution on the lives of people, both positive and negative'.[48] This shows the power of BLM in sparking change and questions about the past, the present and what the future of Ireland ought to look like. Other timely projects include a project developed at Queen's University Belfast that aims to look at the history of African presence in Ireland.[49] These projects are building on the work of networks that were active in previous decades, such as the now-defunct African Studies Association of Ireland. Projects such as these may prove to be integral in explaining the future trajectory that we are now approaching. The re-emergence of BLM in 2020 highlighted the need for a national conversation about the issue of racism in Ireland. As a nation, we are confronted with the changing nature of Irishness, the need to understand how racism is ingrained in Irish society and that it is historically constructed. To move forward as a nation, we must admit that racism is real and visible in Ireland. Only then can we find tangible steps forward to a place where those who are subjected to racism feel that they belong, and are seen, heard and protected.

Notes

1 Andrew Murphy, *But the Irish Sea betwixt Us: Ireland, Colonialism, and Renaissance Literature* (Lexington: University Press of Kentucky, 2009), p. 15.
2 Linda Alcoff, *Visible Identities: Race, Gender, and the Self* (New York: Oxford University Press, 2006), p. 182.
3 Lucy Michael, *Afrophobia in Ireland: Racism against People of African Descent*, European Network Against Racism (ENAR) report (Dublin: ENAR, 2015), p. 4.
4 Ellen Coyne, 'Just because the gardaí are not kneeling on necks does not mean there's no racism in Ireland', *Irish Independent*, 6 June 2020.
5 Frances McGinnity, Raffaele Grotti, Sarah Groarke and Sarah Coughlan, *Ethnicity and Nationality in the Irish Labour Market* (Dublin: Economic and Social Research Institute, 2018); European Union Agency for Fundamental Rights, *Fundamental Rights Report 2019* (Luxembourg: Publications Office of the European Union, 2019).
6 European Website on Integration, https://ec.europa.eu/migrant-integration/library-document/ireland-reports-racist-incidents-2020_en (accessed 11 December 2021).
7 Brid Ni Chonaill, 'Black Lives Matter and higher education', *Sociological Observer: Black Lives Matter* 2:1 (2021), 49–56 (p. 52).
8 Coyne, 'Just because the gardaí'.
9 David Cairns and Shaun Richards, *Writing Ireland: Colonialism, Nationalism and Culture* (Manchester: Manchester University Press, 1988), p. 1.
10 Terry Eagleton, Frederick Jameson and Edward Said, *Nationalism, Colonialism, and Literature* (Minneapolis: University of Minnesota Press, 1990), p. 29.
11 Noel Ignatiev, *How the Irish Became White* (London: Routledge, 1996).
12 Sara Ahmed, 'A phenomenology of whiteness', *Feminist Theory* 8:2 (2007), 149–68 (p. 154).
13 Murphy, *But the Irish Sea betwixt Us*, p. 15.
14 Mary J. Hickman and Bronwen Walter, 'Deconstructing whiteness: Irish women in Britain', *Feminist Review* 50:1 (1995), 5–19.
15 Mary J, Hickman, Sarah Morgan, Bronwen Walter and Joseph Bradley, 'The limitations of whiteness and the boundaries of Englishness: Second-generation Irish identifications and positionings in multiethnic Britain', *Ethnicities* 5:2 (2005), 160–82 (p. 162).
16 Bronwen Walter, *Outsiders Inside: Whiteness, Place and Irish Women* (New York: Routledge, 2002), p. 22.
17 Linda Alcoff, *Visible Identities*, p. 208.
18 Peter D. O'Neill, *Famine Irish and the American Racial State* (New York: Routledge, 2017), p. 2.
19 Seamus Deane quoted in Eagleton, Jameson and Said, *Nationalism, Colonialism, and Literature*, pp. 7–8.
20 Aidan Beatty, 'Zionism and Irish nationalism: Ideology and identity on the borders of Europe', *Journal of Imperial and Commonwealth History* 45:2 (2017), 314–38 (p. 319).

21 Aidan Beatty, *Masculinity and Power in Irish Nationalism, 1884–1938* (London: Palgrave Macmillan, 2016).
22 Caitríona Ní Laoire, *Childhood and Migration in Europe Portraits of Mobility, Identity and Belonging in Contemporary Ireland* (Burlington, VT: Ashgate, 2010), p. 8.
23 *Ibid.*, p. 45.
24 Benedict Anderson, *Imagined Communities: Reflections on the Origin and Spread of Nationalism* (London: Verso, 2006), pp. 1–47.
25 Frances McGinnity, Matthew Creighton and Eamon Fahey, *Hidden versus Revealed Attitudes: A List Experiment on Support for Minorities in Ireland* (Luxembourg: Publications Office of the European Union, 2020), p. 3.
26 Office for National Statistics, 2011 census, www.ons.gov.uk/census/2011census (accessed 5 January 2022).
27 Ciara Kenny, 'Britain's shrinking, ageing Irish population', *Irish Times*, 9 March 2019.
28 Jean Beaman, 'Are French people white? Towards an understanding of whiteness in Republican France', *Identities* 26:5 (2019), 546–62 (p. 547).
29 Simon Patrick, 'The choice of ignorance: The debate on ethnic and racial statistics in France', *Social Statistics and Ethnic Diversity* 26:1 (2008), 7–31 (p. 15).
30 Tamilore Awonusi, '"Where are you really from?" Growing up black in Ireland', *Irish Times*, 4 July 2020.
31 Aoife Bannon, 'I take pride: Six Black and Irish people open up and share stories about life in Ireland', *Irish Sun*, 11 October 2020.
32 Steve Garner, 'Ireland: From racism without race to racism without racists', *Radical History Review* 104 (2009), 41–56 (p. 51).
33 Geraldine Meaney, *Gender, Ireland and Cultural Change: Race, Sex and Nation* (New York: Routledge, 2010), p. 6.
34 Anderson, *Imagined Communities*, p. 6.
35 James Carr and Amanda Haynes, 'A clash of racializations: The policing of "race" and of anti-Muslim racism in Ireland', *Critical Sociology* 41:1 (2015), 21–40 (p. 22).
36 Rahul Sambaraju and Anca Minescu, '"I have not witnessed it personally myself, but …": Epistemics in managing talk on racism against immigrants in Ireland', *European Journal of Social Psychology* 42:2 (2019), 398–412 (p. 399).
37 Emma Dabiri, *Don't Touch My Hair* (London: Penguin, 2019), p. 6.
38 Robbie McVeigh, 'The specificity of Irish racism', *Race & Class* 33:4 (1992), 31–45 (p. 31).
39 Ahmed, 'A phenomenology of whiteness', p. 156.
40 Theophilus Ejorh, 'The African diasporic community in contemporary Ireland: Intersections of ascriptive and circumstantial identities', *Ethnicities* 12:1 (2012), 67–85 (p. 76).
41 William A. Hart. 'Africans in eighteenth-century Ireland', *Irish Historical Studies* 33:129 (2002), 19–32 (p. 20).

42 Ní Laoire, *Childhood and Migration*, p. 40.
43 Niall Stokes, 'On Philip Lynott, music and racism in Ireland', *Hot Press*, 8 June 2020.
44 Siobhan O'Connor, 'Rising star Tolu [*sic*] Makay opens up about dealing with racism and Black Lives Matter movement', *Irish Mirror*, 1 February 2021.
45 Prohibition of Incitement to Hatred Act 1989, Electronic Irish Statute Book, www.irishstatutebook.ie/eli/1989/act/19/section/1/enacted/en/html#sec1 (accessed 10 December 2021).
46 Bryan Fanning and Ronaldo Munck, 'Migration, racism and integration: Beyond vision vs pragmatism?', *Translocations: Migration and Social Change* 2:1 (2007), 1–11 (p. 7).
47 Ahmed, 'A phenomenology of whiteness', p. 157.
48 Ronan McGreevy, 'Trinity to examine colonial legacy in reply to Black Lives Matter', *Irish Times*, 19 February 2021.
49 Africa and Africans @ QUB, https://blogs.qub.ac.uk/africa/category/africans-qub/ (accessed 23 November 2021).

Index

Note: Page numbers in *italics* denote figures. Page numbers followed by 'n' indicate a note. Literary works can be found under authors' names.

Abdy family
   Charlotte Ann 107
   Harriet 107
   Lady Mary 107
   Sir William 107
Abercromby, Ralph 204
Abolition Act (1833) 104
absentees/absenteeism 1, 2, 4, 103, 105, 122n.8, 172, 310
Accounts Produce 105
Accra 61
Adair, John 115
Addison, John 136
Address to the People of Great Britain ... (pamphlet) 305
Affleck 187–8
African-Americans 322–3, 334n.5
   enslavement and abuse 331
   fears of 313
   injustice against 328–9, 339
   physical and sexual abuse of 331
African Company 78
Age of Revolutions 128, 133, 135–6
Ahmed, Sara 339, 345, 348
Airs, Malcolm 277–8n.9
Akenson, Donald Harman 324
Albemarle, Christopher Monk, Second Duke of 78
Alcoff, Linda 338, 340
Allen, Lady Viscountess 112
Alston, David 195

ameliorists 33
American Historical Association 330
American Revolution 23, 25, 31, 92, 126–7, 129, 130, 201, 332
Anderson, Benedict 342, 343–4
Andrews, J. H. 230
Andrews, Malcolm 5, 229
Anglo-French war 21, 26
Anglo-Spanish relations 28, 221
Annesley family
   Lucy 111
   Richard 111
   Sophia 111
Anthill, Edward 85n.36
Antigua 23, 28–30, 33
   castration, 1702 Act 148, 149
   slave economy of 112
   transport of prisoners to 65
Antilles 54, 59
Anti-Slavery International 332, 336n.24
Arcedeckne family 29, 116–17, 265
   Andrew 84n.23
   Chaloner 117–18
Archives d'outre-mer map library 163
Armitage, David 74, 81
Arnold, Dana 258
Atkins, Jonathan 42
Austen, Jane 304
   Mansfield Park 304
Ayscough, John 249
Ayscue, George 54, 62

Bacon, Francis 222
Baignant, Elizabeth 158
Bailey, Gauvin Alexander 163
   Architecture and Urbanism in the French Atlantic Empire 163
Baillie, George 204
Baillie, James Evan 119
Bailly, Pierre 133, 140n.44
Baltic Crisis 150
Bambuk 58
Banagher 215, 223
Bank of England 114
Bank of Ireland 30, 106, 114, 117
Barbados 1, 8, 41, 48, 54, 66
   African enslavement in 54
   and African slave labour 61
   as an agricultural colony 60
   enslavement system in 59–60
   hurricane (1780) 21
   independence struggle 54
   Irish property-owners in 43
   Old English merchants in 60–1
   slave codes 145, 146
   slave economy 61, 63, 66–7, 68, 74–5
   and slave trade 64–5
Barbados Assembly 56, 67
Barbauld, Anna Laetitia 304, 305, 308, 311
   Epistle to William Wilberforce 304, 311
Barczewski, Stephanie 123n.27
Barrack Trustees 243
Barrell, John 5
Barringer, Tim 5
Barry, Eduardo 129, 137n.15
Barry, James 63
Barry, William 63
Bartlett, Richard 218
Bartolozzi, Francesco 117
Batty family
   Espine 112
   Fitzherbert 112
   Philip 112
Beaman, Jean 343
Beatty, Aidan 341
Beckford, William 108
Beckles, Sir Hilary McD. 7–8, 55, 325, 335n.14

"Riotous and unruly lot, A" 325
Becoulet, Philippe 166
Beecher, Phane, Jr, 59
beef trade 25–6, 92, 94
Beeston, William 79, 80
Belfast 23, 31–2, 33
Belisario, Isaac Mendes 1, 287, 295, 298
Bent, John 119
Bentinck, Henry 248
Benton, Lauren 142, 143
Berbice 112, 194, 195, 196, 198, 203, 204, 205
Berkeley, Bishop George 3–4
Berleant-Schiller, Riva 325
   'Free Labor and the economy in seventeenth-century Montserrat' 325
Bermuda 59, 219, 226, 227–32
   and Berkeley 4
   codes and laws 148, 149
Bernard, Thomas 79
Bewley, Molly 305
Biassou, Georges 135
Bibliothèque nationale de France map library 163
Bilder, Sarah Mary 144
Bill of Rights (1689) 241
bills of exchange 94, 95, 96, 197
Bindon, Howard 257
Black Atlantic 4–5
Black, John 105, 137n.15
Black Lives Matter (BLM) movement 337, 338–9, 347, 348
blackness 339, 340, 346
Blackwater River 224
Blaeu, Willem 224
Blair, Ann 197, 198
Blair, Elizabeth 197
Blair, James 193, 194, 200, 201, 203
Blair, Jane Letitia 196–7
Blair, Lambert 193–8, 200–1, 203–7, 211n.46
Blake family 43, 44–5, 48, 49
   Henry 43–5
   John 41–2, 43–5, 52n.32
   William 61
Blenheim Palace 260, *261*
Block, Kirsten 80

Board of Trade 144, 148–9
Boazio, Baptista 224
Boddington, Samuel 119
Bodley, Josias 218, 232n.2
Bolton, Elizabeth Jane 196, 197
Bonehill, John 5
Boucher, Philip 164
Bouligny, José and Juan 128
Boulukos, George 309, 314, 319n.66
  'Maria Edgeworth's "Grateful Negro"
    and the sentimental argument
    for slavery' 309
Bourden, John 83n.23, 179
Bourke, David and Thomas 61
Boyle, Richard (First Earl of Cork) 58, 59
Boyle, Roger (Lord Broghill) 65
Boyne, Battle of (1691) 165
Bradshaw, Richard 26
Brady, John 132
Brazil Company 62
Brett, Curtis 29
  St Jago Intelligencer 29
Bridgetown 22, 23, 45, 63
Brien, Dennis 46
Briskett, Anthony 59, 60
Bristol 22, 24, 26, 115
Britain 7
  elites 46
  institutionalised slave trade in 67
  involvement in Portuguese slave
    trade 62
  island story of 329–30
  perceptions on Irish 40–1
  Privy Council 144, 147, 148, 150, 151,
    219, 220, 223–5, 235n.29
  slave codes 142, 145
  tower houses in 262
British America 24, 75, 76, 88, 90,
  142, 147
British Atlantic 24, 57, 81, 142, 147, 149
British Caribbean 81, 93, 104, 109, 143,
  146–7, 156, 157, 180, 195
British Guiana 104, 108, 112, 114, 116,
  194, 211
Broderick, William 83–4n.23
Brown, Hamilton 105, 122n.7
Brown, Lancelot (Capability Brown) 115

Brown, Vincent 6, 312
Browne family
  Arthur Howe 284, 299n.1
  Henry 179
  Howe Peter (Second Marquess of
    Sligo) 287, 293, 294
  John Denis (First Marquess of Sligo)
    116, 287
  John (First Earl of Altamont) 284, 286
  Patrick 29, 91
    *Civil and Natural History of
     Jamaica, The* 29
  Peter 28, 284
  Randy 204
Browne-Kelly, Peter 118
Bryan, Cornelius 40, 41, 42, 45–6, 48, 49,
    336n.16
Bryan, Margaret 42, 45, 48
Burke, Charles 132
Burke, Edmund 32, 106, 200, 308
Burke, Richard 122n.11
Burnard, Trevor 75, 82n.7, 83n.18,
    161, 270
Burns, Alan 249
  History of the British West Indies 249
Bushe family
  Gervase Parker 111
  John Scott 118
  Robert 111, 118
  Sir Henry Grattan 118
Butler Bois de Lance plantations 166, *168*
Butler, Nathaniel 225, 226, 228, 230–2
Butler plantation 165, *167*
Butler, Thomas 128, 137n.11
butter, Irish 23–4, 25, 92, 93–4
Button, Thomas 221, 223
Byrn, John 87, 90–2
  business management 94–7
  scope of his trade 92–4
Byrne, Edward 30

cadastral mapping 158, 160, 165, 166
Cairns, David 339
Caldwell Collection of the Royal Irish
    Academy 107
Caldwell family
  Benjamin 107

Charles (1707–72) 107, 122n.13
Charles (1737–1814) 122n.13
George 107, 110
Henrietta 110
William 107, 110, 287, 300
Candlin, Kit 172
Canning, George 209n.29
Canning, Stratford (First Viscount Canning) 200, 209n.28
Canny, Nicholas
  Colonial Identity in the Atlantic World, 1500–1800 (with Pagden) 156
Cape Fear river 312
Cap Français 165, 166
Cardiff, Mathew 30
Carew, George 218, 221, 222, 225
Carlisle 59
Carondelet, Francisco Luis Héctor de 131, 132
Carricou island 205
carte à figures map-making 229–30
Casey, John 77
Casid, Jill 5, 312, 316
castellated houses 257, 258–9, 271
Castillo, James 78, 85n.37
castle air 260–1
Castle Crook 222, 228
Castle Park 222
Castle, Richard 282, 286
Castlereagh, Lord 182, 188
castration, in the slave codes and penal laws 148–51
Catalina 131
Catholic Church 61
Catholicism 2–3, 8, 26, 42, 43, 49, 56, 219, 223
  bill against Catholic clerics 150
  and Protestantism, conflict between 40–1, 74
  and slavery 34, 77, 78
Caulfeild, Lord 224
Cecil, William 232
Cédula de Población 129
Celtic Tiger period (1994–2007) 342, 346
Central Statistics Office (Ireland) 337
Chaila, Denise 347

Chaine, James 119
Chaine, Maria West 119
Charlemont 215, 224
Charles I, King 57, 59
Charles II, King 54, 61, 66, 67, 68
Charles, Prince 219
Chichester, Sir Arthur 3, 59, 221, 225
Child, Josiah 83n.15
Chonaill, Brid Ni 338
Christchurch Parish 43, 46
Christophe, Jean 135
Churchill, Father Thomas 78, 83n.21, 85n.37
Churchill, John 260
Church of England 47, 48, 79
Church of Ireland 150
Citizen Genêt 132
civil wars in England 61, 62, 63
Clancy family
  Cornelius 46
  Honor 46
  Katherine 46
  Wynefrid 46
Clark, Daniel, Jr 129–30
Clarke family
  Aidan 55, 221
  Andrew (1793–1847) 117–18, 124n.33
  Andrew (1824–1902) 118
  Marcus Andrew Hislop (1846–81) 118
  Thomas 43
Claypotts Castle 268, 269
Clerke, John Page 42
Clobery, Oliver 58
coast trade 84n.28
Cockron, Daniel 43
Cocoa Walk plantation 282, 284, 294, 295, 297
Coddington, Henry Barry 119
Coddington, Nicholas 112
Cogswell, Thomas 234n.16
Cohan, Thomas 61
Cohen, Ashley 311
Colbeck Castle 256, 256–7, 265–6
Collins, John 105
Collins, Patrick 48
colonial administrations, Irish within 41, 57

Colonial Legacies Project 348
Committee of Merchants 33
Commonwealth 56
Commonwealth Records Project 69n.2
compensation process 103
compensation records 105
composite trade 23
Connacht 65, 223, 287, 293, 295, 298
Connelly, Conn 77
Connolly, Sean 145–7, 150
Connor, Bryan 43
Conoghlan, Teague 43
consignment trade 92–3, 96
contraband trade 77, 81, 89, 201
Cook, Edmund 80, 81
Cook, James 87
Cooke, James 96–7
Coote, Eyre 179–82, 188–9, 191n.54
   attempts at slave trade abolition 185–8
   on Jamaica's economic circumstances 183–4
   and Jamaica's fortifications and barracks 182–3
Copley, Stephen 5
Coppinger, Cornelius 128
Cork 21, 24–5, 31, 57, 179, 180, 222, 223, 225, 228, 261
   and African slave trade 26
   degree of local agency in trade 26
   French beef in 25
   Irish beef exports 25–6
   slave trade abolition initiatives 33
Corkbeg Fort 222
Cork Gazette 33
corner towered buildings 258–66, 271, 276
Cosgrove, Denis 5
Costa, John da 79
Cotton, Stapleton 111
Courant 90
Courlanders 72n.54
Courtland 198
Cowper, William 311
Coyne, Ellen 338
Craig, Maurice 218

Cranfield, Lionel 225
Craskell, James 285
Crawford, Robert 200
Crispe, Sir Nicholas 58, 67
Cromwell, Oliver 41, 54, 56, 62, 63, 64, 66, 69, 323, 325, 327
Cromwell, Ralph 258
Cromwellian Protectorate 54, 55, 56, 57, 66
Crosthwaite, Leland 30
Crow, John 93
Cullen, Louis 75
Culmore 215, 223
Cunningham, Waddell 31–2, 113, 117
Curaçao 61, 201
Cureen, Susannah 46
Cureen, Teague 46, 48
Curtin, John 79, 91

Dabiri, Emma 344
   Don't Touch My Hair 344
Danby, Francis 293
Daniels, Stephen 5
Danish empire 9
Danish slave codes 143–4
Darcy, Patrick and Mathew 43
Darracott, Eliza 111
Darwin, Erasmus 304
   Botanic Garden, The 304
Daumier, Honoré 11–13
   Actualités 11
   Irlande et Jamaique - Patience! 11–12
Day, Thomas 304
   Dying Negro, The 304
Deane, Seamus 340
de Bermúdez, Juan 231
de Cauna, Jacques 163
'decline' thesis, for the slave economy 112
Defenderism 309
defensive towers 273–4
Defiance 87
Delap family 116
   William Drummond 116
Delvaux, Father Jean 133
Demerara-Essequibo 110, 112, 194, 205
Dempsey, Damien 324

Dempsey, John Baptist 78, 85n.37
Derry/Londonderry 3, 4, 218
de Waal, Edmund 108
Dewhurst, Mary 173
Dhlamini, Joella 343
Dictionary of Irish Biography 13n.3, 35n.6, 108, 299n.2
Dictionary of National Biography 108
Dictionary of Ulster Biography 108
Digges La Touche family 30, 93, 95–6, 106, 114
    James 92, 95, 120
    John James 30
Disbanding Act (1699) 242
Docwra, Henry 221, 223
Dolci, Carlo 117
Donovan, John 125
Dormenon, Pierre Benonime 133
double absenteeism 109–10
Doyle, Roddy 321
    Commitments, The 321-2
Draper, Nicholas 6, 197
Drax, James 63, 64
Driscol, Denis 33
Duany, Edmund and Dominick 91
Dublin 21, 22, 27, 65, 87, 91, 95, 224
    Botanical Gardens 315
    Hurricane Fund 30
    in mid-to-late 1980s 321
DuBois, W. E. B. 331
    Black Reconstruction 331
Duckworth, John 180, 184
Dun, Sir Patrick 117
Duncannon 215, 222, 224, 225, 228
Dunk, George Montagu (Earl of Halifax) 75–6
Dunn, Alderman James 91–5
Dutch empire 9
Dutch merchants 61, 62
Dutch slave markets 64
Dutch war, impact on English slave trade 78

Eagleton, Terry 339
Earl of Clanricarde 294–5
Edgeworth, Maria 302–3, 319n.66
    Absentee, The 310

Belinda 302, 305, 307–8, 311, 315
Castle Rackrent 302
correspondence with Lazarus 312–15
Essay on Irish Bulls 310
Forester 315
'Good Aunt, The' 304, 305–7, 310, 312, 316
'Grateful Negro, The' 304, 307, 309, 310, 314, 316
interest in botany 315–16
Moral Tales (with Opie and More) 308
Murad the Unlucky 310
Patronage 312
Popular Tales 304, 309, 310–11
Practical Education 312
on slavery 303–6, 309–11
Tales of Fashionable Life 312
Edgeworth, Richard Lovell 304
Edinburgh Castle 271, 272, 273, 275
Edinburgh Encyclopaedia 203
Edwards, Bryan 33, 309, 310, 312
    History, Civil and Commercial, of the British Colonies in the West Indies 309, 310, 312
Ejorh, Theophilus 346
elite 44
    British 46
    Catholic 45, 46, 49
    Havana 128
    planter 41, 180, 185
    Protestant 147
Elizabeth I 221
Elizabeth Fort 222, 228
emancipation 7, 13, 32, 34, 105, 107, 119–20, 187, 287, 310
Encumbered Estates Act 6
English attitudes, Irish embracement of 44–6
English Council of Trade and Plantations 240, 241, 245–9
Enrique 125–6
Equiano, Olaudah 32
    Narrative of the Life of Olaudah Equiano 32
estates 6, 291, 292–3
ethnic cleansing 323
ethnic prejudice 322–3

Europa 87, 92, 96–7
Exeter 61

Falkland, Lord 215, 217, 219–20, 223, 224, 225, 237n.46
Fanning, Bryan 347
Farrell family 106
   Michael 77
   Richard 28
Fennell, Captain 79
Fitzgerald, David 131
Fitzgerald, Jane 77
Fitzgerald, Philip 77, 80–1, 86n.51
Fitzgerald, Richard 61
Fitzgerald, Thomas 118
Fitzgerland, Morris 43
Fitzpatrick, John 134
Fitzpatrick, Sir Jeremiah 33
Fitzwilliam, William 221
Fleetwood, George 64
Fleming, George 136
Floyd, George 338
Fogo 128
Fonthill Vase 108, 117
Ford, Lisa 143
'Fort of Castle Parke, The' 216, 222
'forte of Duncannon in ye harbor of Waterford, The' 216, 222
'Fourteen Tribes' of Galway 43, 326
Fox, Mathew 81
France 63, 172, 241, 246, 343
   Code noir 142, 143–4, 145, 151
   dependence on Irish supplies 25
   plantations 6
   privateers 96
   prize vessels 90
   slave-ownership, legacies of 172, 178n.64
Franklin, Benjamin 306
   Observations on Smoky Chimneys, Their Causes and Cure 306
free labour 82n.7
Freeman's Journal 250
free quarter 240, 242
freestanding towers 271, 273
free trade 22, 31, 85, 129, 201

Free Trade decree 129, 137–8n.17, 144
French, Jeffrey 43, 110, 118
French Revolution 130
French, Robert 43, 44, 45
Friendship 62

Galway families 28, 223, 284, 298
Gambia 62, 67
Gangs of New York (film) 327
Gardiner, Rose 110
Garner, Steve 343
Garrigus, John 161
Garside, Peter 5
Geggus, David 165
Genêt, Edmond 132
Gilligan, Manuel Menasseh 79
Gilroy, Paul 5
Girouard, Mark 258, 277n.4
Gladstone, Sir Thomas 119
Glasgow 22, 32, 115, 315
Glenbuchat Castle 268
Glorious Revolution 78
Goderich, Lord 112
Godin, Pierre 203
Godolphin, William 81
Goghe, John 224
   Hibernia 30, 224
gold 58, 67
Gordon, James 107
Gordon, John 268
Goulburn, Henry 111
Goulburn, Munbee 111
Gove, Michael 329, 336n.22
Goveia, Elsa 146
'Graces, the' (1628) 264, 278n.21
Grande Rivière 165
Grandison, Viscount 221, 225, 235n.28
Grattan, Henry 118
Grattan, Mary 111
Great Hurricane 21, 23–4
Green Atlantic 4–5
Green, Edmund Francis 114
Greencastle 224
Greene, Jack 147
Greg, Thomas 31
Grenada 117, 144, 197, 203
Grillo, Domingo 78

Guardi, Francesco 116
Guilfoyle, Kimberly 329
Guinea Company 58, 62–3, 64, 65
Guinness family 117
Gwynn, Aubrey 8, 54–5

Haiti 185
Haitian Revolution 33, 133
Hale, John 218
Hall-Dare family 116
    Robert Westley (1817–66) 123n.29
    Robert Westley (1840–76) 123n.29
Hall, David 112
Hall, Hardwick 258, *260*
Halstead, Priscilla 282
Hamilton, Douglas 203
Hamilton, Scott Malcolm 274
Handasyde, Thomas 246, 247, 248
Handler, Jerome 55, 325
Hanigan, Michael 77
Harley, Robert 247
Harman, Wentworth 243
Harris, Kamala 122n.7
Hart, Anthony 111
Hart, William 346
Harvie, John and Alexander 90
Haulbowline Island 222, 225
Hawkins, William 65, 73n.64
Hay, James 57, 59, 60
Heaney, Seamus 8
Henry, Viscount Sydney 242
Henry VIII, King 258
Heywood family 107
Hiberno-French families 27
Hickey, William 112
Higgins, Tully 112
Higman, B. W. 6
Hildebrand, George W. 287, 290, 294–5
    Marquess of Sligo 287, 288–92
Hill, Matthew Howard 134
Hispaniola 74, 76, 80
Hodgson, Kate 27
Hogan, Liam 324, 328
Hogg dynasty 108
Home, Robert 117
Horning, Audrey 218, 226
Houston, James 79

Hulsebosch, Daniel 144
Humility 81
Huncks, Henry 60
Huntingdon, Samuel 197
Hurst, Humberston 65
Hussey family 106
Hutcheson, Francis 31–2
Hutchison, Lewis 271
Hyde, Henry 217

Ignatiev, Noel 322
    How the Irish Became White 322
immigration 41, 55, 60, 75, 76, 129, 323, 327
imperial barrack-building
    Irish 240–5
    and Jamaica 245–50
Inchiquin, Lord 77, 79
independence struggles 54
indigenous food production 26
Industrial Revolution 113
Inishowen 3, *3*
Inman, Charles 91
Innis (or Innes), Sarah Edwards 116
inter-imperial trade 77–8
'inwork,' Ireland as 219–26
Ireton, Sir John 73n.63
Irish-Americans 322–3
Irish-Caribbean identities 2
Irish Catholics 10, 41–2, 47–8, 55, 74, 77–9, 130, 142, 147, 325
    British perceptions 2
    and colonial hierarchy 40, 56
    elite status 45, 46, 49
    indentured servants 29, 75
    planters 61
    property-owners and enslavers 42–4
    traders 27, 30
Irish Down Survey maps (1655–9) 160
Irish enslavement 55, 323
    in America, myth of 323
    and Irish ethnicity in West Indian colonies 326
    meme of 328
    myth of 323, 328–9
    sex slavery claim of exiles in Barbados and 323–4

Irish famine (1845–9) 2
Irish nationalism 340–1
Irishness 337, 346
   Black Lives Matter and 338, 347, 348
   and blackness 346
   and black population in Ireland 342–3
   and moral panic 343
   and otherness 343, 344
   and whiteness 339, 340, 341, 344, 345
Irish Network Against Racism (INAR) 338
Irish Privy Council 150
Irish Rebellion 41, 61
Irish servants 59, 68
Irish slave-owners 42–4, 105
'Irish slave trade' (Martin) 328
iron trade 58
Irving, John 119
Ive, Paul 222, 228
Ivory, James 286

Jacobite rebellion 150
Jamaica 1, 8, 66, 74, 87
   architectures of empire in 256–76
   Christianity in 77
   Committee of Grievances 248
   and Cork 24
   dual economy 81
   English Jamaica 82n.7
   enslaved population in 89
   and French forces 90
   hurricane (1780) 21
   imperial barrack-building and 240, 245–50
   indentured servants in 29, 75
   Irish community and Catholic Atlantic 79
   and Irish infidelity 80–1
   and Irish landscapes compared 282–99
   and legislatures 144
   privateering in 77
   religious liberty in 76
   slave laws 146
   slave-ownership in 105
   and Spanish America 77
   sugar trade 92
   and trade opportunities 75–6

Jamaican Assembly 157, 180–9, 191n.54
James, Lispenasse 85n.36
James I, King 58, 221
James II, King 48, 76, 78
James and John 91
James Island (Charles Island) 58, 67
Jefferson, Thomas 330
Jennings, Henry 201
Jobson, Francis 218
John 62
Johnson, Matthew 258
Johnstone, Hugh 200
Jones, John 85n.36
Jordan, Don 326–7
   White Cargo: The Forgotten History of Britain's White Slaves in America (with Walsh) 326–7, 328
Joseph Wilson & Sons 106
Jourdain, Silvester 238n.63
Junaid, Segun 343

Kain, Roger 158
Kanturk Castle 264, 265
Karras, Alan 274–5, 281n.57
Keane, Hugh Perry 106
Keane, John 179
Keane, Michael 105–6
Kearney, Michael 128
Kelly family 28, 116
   Dennis 28, 43, 282, 286, 299n.1
   Edmund 79, 84n.23
   Elizabeth 28, 282, 284, 286
   John 116
   Mary 116
   Smith 77, 78, 80, 85n.36, 85n.37
   Walk plantation 282, 284, 294, 295, 296
Kennedy, Robert 200, 322
Kerrigan, Paul 217–18, 232n.2
Kerry 261
Kew Park 271, 272, 275
kidnapping, for unfree labour supply 65–6
Kilcolman Castle 257
Kimbolton Castle 260
King John's Fort 222

Kingston 15, 17, 23, 29–30, 83, 88–94,
    97–100, 107, 174, 178, 191,
    278, 280
  in the autumn of 1756 87–90
  French prize vessels 90
  map (1745) *88*
  raison d'être 88
  trade of 89
Kinsale 67, 222
Kinsale, Battle of 261
Klingelhofer, Eric 218
Knight, James 269–70
Kock, Anna Elizabeth 134
Kopelson, Heather 149
Kriz, Kay Dian 5
Kroeg, Susan 304

Laborde plantation *159*, 170
Lagos 61
Laidlaw, Zoë 196
Lambert Blair & Co. 198, 203
Lanyon, Sir Charles 116, 123n.29
Lazarus, Rachel Mordecai 312–13
Leadbeater, Mary 305
Leakey, James 198
Leeward Islands 43, 46–7, 59, 198
Legacies of Bristish Slave-Ownership
    (LBS) project 6–7, 10, 37, 103,
    104, 108, 109, 113, 118, 120–1,
    124, 195
  first phase of 105
  Irish nationalists/nationalism and
    slave-ownership 110–11
  second phase of 104–6
  slave-owners categories 106
Leinster 223
Lennan, Francis 133
Les Cayes plain 170, 172
Les Cayes town 172
Lester, Alan 196
Lewellin, Robert 64, 65
Lienhard, Martín 125
Ligon, Richard 55, 333
  History 55
  True & Exact History of the Island of
    Barbados, A 333
Limerick 27–8, 31, 61, 223, 242, 261

Limonade 165, 166
Lindsay, Alexander 181, 182
linens and cottons trade 31, 93, 94
Linwood, William 85n.36
Liverpool 22, 24, 107, 115, 197
Llewellin, Robert 62
Lloyd, Richard Bateman 134
Lockier, Thomas 64
Loeber, Rolf 218
Loftus, Adam (the Elder) 262–3
Lomelin, Ambrosio 78
London 21–2, 24, 26, 32, 47–8, 93, 95–6,
    186, 188–9, 229, 241, 325
London commission houses 92–3
Long, Edward 111, 119, 180–1, 250, 270
  History of Jamaica 250
Long, Frederick Beckford 111
Lords of Trade and Plantations 81
Lough, Carlingford 224
Lough Chichester 224
Lough Neagh 223, 224
Louisa, née Simond 118
Louisiana 1, 127–35, 172
Louis XIV, King 147
Lowry-Corry, Somerset 179
Luis 125–6
Lulworth Castle 257
Lydcott, Gyles 78
Lynch family 43, 80
  Andrew Henry 118
  John 115
  Stephen 115
Lynott, Philip 322, 346
Lyons, Daniel 125

Macartney, Earl 23
MacBready, Bryan 43
McCabe, Thomas 31
McCafferty, Kate 8
McCaffrey, Constantine 132
McCalmont Brothers 114
McCalmont, Hugh 114
McCamon, John 194, 207n.1
McCarthy, MacDonagh 264
McCurtin, Cornelius 125, 126, 127, 129
McClellan, James E., III,
  Colonialism and Science 156

Maccoline, Daniell 43
McDermott, Anthony 30
McDonnell, Randall 30
McGarel, Charles 108, 112, 116
McGarrity, Maria 8
McGragh, Redmond 76
McGrath, Ivar 147
MacGranah, Daniel 43
McGrath, Paul 322
Machaut, La 87
Mackenzie, Francis 207, 212n.60
Maclachlan, Lachlan 118
Macleane, Lauchlin 117
McNally, Patrick 151
Macnamara, Patrick 134
McNamara, Richard 114
McQueen, Steve 331
McRaugh, Redmond 85n.36
McVeigh, Robbie 344
Mair, John 95
Makay, Tolü 347
Malinke 58
Manly, Susan 309, 317n.14, 317n.16
Marriot, James 194
Marryat, Carlyle and Frederick 119
Marshall, Peter 106, 122n.11, 147
Martin, John 328
Martin, Peter 5
Martin, Samuel 33
Martin, Sir Henry William 120
   counter appeal, A 120
Martineau, Henry 314, 315
   Society in America 314
Martinique 21, 27
Marzagalli, Silvia 9
masonry bastions 273
Massy Dawson, James Hewitt 109, 117, 118
Maxwell, David 207
Maxwell, Father James 132–3
Mayo 28, 282, 284, 298
Meaney, Geraldine 343
M'Grah, Bryan 85n.36
Michael, Lucy 338
Michel, John 119
Milles family
   Jeremiah, Jr 110

Jeremiah, Sr 110
   Thomas 110
Minescu, Anca 344
mistrust of Irish 80–1
Mitchell, William 181
Mitchell, W. J. T. 308
mock castles, Spenserian 257
Moglane, John 65
Molesworth, Robert 65
Moll, Herman 243
Mollony, Dermon 42
Monea Castle 274
Monkstown Castle 264
Montagu, William 188
Montholon plantation 166
Montserrat 1, 8, 28, 43, 47–8, 59
Montserrat Act 47
Moore, Arthur John 79, 111, 119
Moore, Charles 111, 119
Moore, Richard 228
Moreau de Saint- Méry, Louis Elie 157, 165, 170, 172
   Description topographique 157
Morfa (or Murphy), Don Juan 78, 80, 86n.45
Morrison, Toni 327
   Mercy, A 327
Mortimer, Daniel 133
Morton, Richard 85n.36
Moryson, Fynes 221
Mountjoy, Lord Deputy 221, 231
Mountlong Castle 264
'Mr Griffin,' *A True Description of the North Part of Ireland* 229
Mulhall, Anne 302
Munck, Ronaldo 347
Munster 28, 59, 222, 223, 278nn.18–19
Murfee, Dennis 42
Murfee, Teague 42
Murphey, Bryan 43
Murphey, Dennis 46
Murphy, Andrew 337, 339
music, unifying force of 346–7
Mutiny Acts 241

Nagle, Nano 33
Nantes 26, 27

Nash, Gerard 93
Nast, Thomas 327
Natchitoches 133
National Bank of Ireland 114
National Curriculum (United
    Kingdom) 329
National Museum of Ireland 108
Nat Turner Rebellion (1831) 313–14
Navigation Acts 22, 31, 62, 64, 115
Ndahiro, Sandrine Uwase 347
Negro ship 64
Neilson family
    Samuel 111
    Thomas 111
    William 111
Nelson, Louis P. 163
Netherlanders, advance in trade 83n.15
Nevis 59, 111
New England 55, 57, 81
Newry 194, 196, 205, 207, 224
Nicolas, Jean Vanes 164
Nietschmann, Bernard 230
Ní Laoire, Caitríona 341, 346
Nine Years War (1594–1603) 219, 221,
    223, 224, 243, 246, 263
Noel, Martin 65, 67
Noell, Martin 78
Northern Star 33–4
Norwood, Richard 227, 231
Nowlan, Maurice 131
Nugent, Maria Skinner 196

O'Callaghan, Sean 8, 323–5
    To Hell or Barbados 323, 326, 328
O'Carry, Morgan 61
O'Connell, Daniel 34, 105, 114, 119
O'Connor family 30, 108–9, 110
    Honoria 111
    James Arthur 287, 293, 295
    Lydia 110
    Malachy 110
    Siobhan 347
    Valentine 108, 114
O'Daly, James 133
Ó Gallchoir, Clíona 303
O'Hagan, Michael 131
O'Kane, Finola 116

O'Keeffe, Tadhg 257
    Faerie Queene 257
Old English 55–6, 57, 60–1, 81
Oliver, Thomas 200
Oman 280n.55
O'Neill, Arturo 135
O'Neill, Peter 340
Ordnance Survey 158, 160
O'Reilly, Alexander 128
O'Reilly, Thomas 133
Orinoco River 204
O'Rourke plantations 170, *171*
Ortelius, Abraham 224
O'Sheil/Sheill, Marie 165
O'Sheil/Sheill plantation 172
Osikoya, Catherine 347
Ó Siochrú, Micheál 69n.2
othering 340, 343, 344, 346
*Oxford Dictionary of National
    Biography* 108

'Paddy's Lamentation' (song) 327
Pagden, Anthony
    *Colonial Identity in the Atlantic World,
    1500–1800* (with Canny) 156
Passage Fort 222
Peace of Westphalia 143
Peart family 114
    Elizabeth 114, 123
    John 114
    John Hobbs 114
    John Redmund 114
Pee Dee River 304
Pennsylvania law 149
people-trafficking trade 64
Perrie, John 28
Peter Bryan Bruin 130
Petition of Rights (1628) 240, 245
Petley, Christer 181, 195
Petty, William 76
Phair, Robert 63
Philipeau, René 166
Philip III, King 231
Phillips, Thomas 218, 225, 230
Pigot, George 85n.36
Pinckard, George 195, 205–7
    Notes on the West Indies 205

piracy 61, 143, 148
Pitt, William 180
plantation-owners and enslavers, Irish 41
plantocracy 29–30, 196, 205, 207, 282, 294, 326
Plymouth 61
Pointe Coupée 133
Pollock, Oliver 128
Portis, George and James 92
Port Royal 76
Portuguese, and slave trade 62
Postlethwayt, Malachy 88–9
Power, Joaquín 128
Power, Orla 9
Poynings' Law of 1494 145, 147
Prendergast, John 54, 348
Presentation Order 33
Preston, William 33
Prince Rupert of the Rhine 62
prisoners of war, Irish 63
privateering 28, 77, 87, 93, 96
Prohibition of Incitement to Hatred Act (1989) 347
property acquisition 42–4
Protestant churches 47–8, 76
Protestant elites 147
Protestant émigrés 28
Protestant Irishmen 77, 83n.23
Protestants and Catholics conflicts 40–1, 74
Public Record Office of Ireland, destruction of 55
Public Record Office of Northern Ireland 197, 198
Pynnar, Nicholas 215, 217, 218, 220, 223, 225

Quaker merchant families 32
Quartering Acts 247, 248
quartering, of army 241, 242–3, 245–9
Quebec 144
Queensborough, Samuel 293
Queen's University (Belfast) 348
Quieco, John 135, 141n.53
Quilley, Geoff 5
Quintinalla, Mark 207

racial hierarchies 45–6, 48–9
racism, normalization of 341
Raleigh, Walter 204
rape 148, 149
Rathfarnham Castle 262–3, *263*, 278n.20
Raven, Thomas 218, 230
Reilly, Matthew 55, 325
religions
  liberty 76
  threats 46–8
Repton, Humphrey 115
Restoration 54, 67, 78, 245
return cargoes 23
Rhode Island 144
Rice, George 44
Rice, Nicholas 44, 45
Rice, Stephen 60–1
Rich, Lord Robert (Earl of Warwick) 58
Rich, Nathaniel 225
Richards, Fitzherbert 112, 119
Richards, Shaun 339
Ridge, James 106
Riordans 26
River Fossé 165–6, *168*, 170
River Foyle 223, 230
River Mapou 165
River Muscadin 172
'River of Waterford, The' *215*, 222
Rivière de Lacul 170, 172
Rivière de l'Islet 172
Rivière du Haut du Cap 158, 165, 169
Robert Hyndman & Co. 115
Robert Hyndman & Son 112
Rodgers, Nini 7, 106, 121n.2, 194, 305, 317n.14, 324
Rodney, George 184, 198–201
Rodway, James 204
Roscoe, William 304
Rotherham, Thomas 225, 237n.46
Rowe, William 65
Royal Africa Company 58, 66, 67, 68, 69n.2
Royal Historical Society 330
Rules, Orders, Powers, and Directions, for the Good Government and Preservation of the Barracks 243

rum trade 23, 30, 31, 34, 89, 93, 108, 134, 209
Russell, Jacobin Thomas 33
Ruxton, Margaret 304, 309
Ruxton, Sophy 303, 305
Ryan family 106

Sadlier, Francis 65, 73n.63
Saint-Domingue 1, 25, 27, 128, 156–63
  cadastral mapping and 158, 160, 165, 166
  irrigation and 161–2
Saint Eustatius 198, 200–1, *202*, 210n.34
Saint-Pierre, Jacques-Henri 308
  Paul et Virginie 308
St Christopher's Parish 61
St Eustatius 1, 195, 197, 198, 200, 201, 203
St James's Parish 42
St Kitts 59, 66, 201–2, 232
St Michael's Parish 42
St Peter's Parish 42
St Philip's Parish 44
Sally 131
Sambaraju, Rahul 344
Sarah, John Page 42
Sayers, John 109–10, 122
Sayers, Margaret 109
Scottish prisoners 56
Scottish sojourners, to Jamaica 274–5, 281n.57
Scottish tower houses 268, 270, 271
Senegambia 58
Serraint, Château 27
servants 43, 49, 55, 68, 82n.7
  blacks 308
  English 56, 68–9
  forced transportation of 66
  indentured 2, 24, 29, 56, 60, 68, 74–5, 146, 246, 324, 325
  Irish 44, 57, 59, 61, 68, 74, 325, 331, 333
  women 44–5
servitude and enslavement
  linguistic slippage between 332–3
  separation of 331–2
Seven Years War 87, 89, 127, 129, 244–5

Shand, John 184, 187
Shannon River 293
Shaw, Jenny 80, 326
  Everyday Life in the Early English Caribbean 326
Shaw, Samuel 201
Sheils 26
Simms, Robert 117
Simon, Patrick 343
Skerret, Robert 115
Slany, Humphrey 58
slave codes and penal laws 151
  Barbadian codes 145, 146
  bill against Catholic clerics 150
  and Board of Trade 144, 148–9
  and British Privy Council 144, 147, 148, 150, 151
  castration in 148–51
  and Church of Ireland 150
  Danish slave codes 143–4
  enactment 144–8
  French *Code noir* 142, 143–4, 145, 151
  and Irish Privy Council 150
  Jamaican 144, 146
  Poynings' Law of 1494 145, 147
  and social repression 142, 144
  and sovereignties 143, 144, 151
  Spanish *Siete de partidas* 142, 145
  transatlantic constitution 144, 151
slave economy 115
  of Antigua 112
  of Barbados 61, 63, 66–7, 68, 74–5
  'decline' thesis for 112
slave-ownership 103–4
  commercial legacies 113–15
  cultural and philanthropic legacies 116–17
  cultural work by slave-owners 119
  'decline' thesis 112
  double-absenteeism 109–10
  historical legacies 119–20
  imperial legacies 117–18
  and Irish nationalist/nationalism 110–11
  legacies 112–20
  physical legacies 115–16

slave-ownership (*continued*)
  political legacies 118–19
  visibility of 106, 107–9
Slave Registers 105
slavery and slaves
  African 33, 54, 57, 66, 68, 134, 323
  African workforce 59, 92
  compensation 110
  demand on the Spanish Main 89
  financial compensation for historical enslavement 55
  modern slavery, definition of 336n.24
  opponents of 31–2
  and racial inequalities 320
  sex slavery 323–4
  spatial impact of 5
  transatlantic 119
  white 107
  women 45–6, 48
slave trade 64, 128
  abolition initiatives 33–4, 185–8
  African 26–7, 48, 61–2
  African slave trade 26–7
  ban on 143
  and Barbados 64–5
  British 62, 67
  direct 61
  and Dutch war 78
  impact of Dutch war 78
  licensed (*asiento*) 77, 78–9
  and Portuguese 62
  Spanish 128–9
  voyages 23
Smith, Adam 310
Smith, John 226, 227, 229–31, 232
  Generall Historie of Virginia, New-England, and the Summer Isles 226, 230
  'Mappe of the Somer Isles and Fortresses, A' 226
Smith, Thomas 65
Smyth, Willie 298
Smythson, Robert 258
Soame, Francis 72n.52
social repression, codes of law for 142, 144
Somerville, Diane 148

Southampton Fort 228, 230
sovereignties 143, 144, 151
Spain 63, 74, 89, 241
  asiento 77, 78–9
  and Bermuda 219, 221, 222, 224, 225, 231–2, 232
Spanish America 75, 78, 132
  Irish presence in 128–30
  and loyalty 133–4
  and revolutions 130–3
  Siete de partidas 142, 145
Spanish Florida 132
Spanish Indies 74
Spanish Main 89
Spanish monarchy, slave trade 128–9
Spanish Town 168, 182, 184, 187, 248
Speed, John 227
  Prospect of the Most Famous Parts of the World 227
Spenser 257–8
square tower 261, 266, 271
Stafford, Thomas 230
Stanhope, James 150
Stapleton, John 76, 80, 83n.21, 85n.36
Stapleton, Sir William 27, 41–2, 44, 46–8, 49, 83n.21
State of the Forts of Ireland, The 215, 217
State of the Island of Jamaica, The 248, 249
Statia 198, 200, 201
Staunton family 106
  George 23
Steele, Joshua 33
Stevenson, Cornelius 198, 203, 209n.24
Stevenson, William 198
Stewart, Alexander 113–14
Stewart, James, I 187, 267
Stewart, James, II 267
Stewart, William 91
Stewart's Castle 266, 266–8, 267, 271, 275
Stewart's Fort 271, 273, 275
Stokes Hall 265, 276
Subsidy Act (1624) 221
sugar boom 41, 54, 69
sugar trade 22, 61, 62, 76, 115
Supply 62

Suriname 203, 204, 205
Sweeney, Fionnghuala 126
Sweetman, John 111
Swift, Jonathan 243

Tacky's Revolt (1760) 250, 270, 307, 309, 310
Talbot, Richard Wogan 109
Tannenbaum, Frank 145
Tattershall Castle 258, 259, 260
Taylor, John 76
Taylor, Richard 188
Taylor, Simon 181–4
Tea Act (1773) 201
Tenda 58
Tenison, Thomas 217
Thistlewood, Thomas 270
Thomas, Francis 85n.36
Thomas, Hugh 165
Thompson, Maurice 59, 62, 64
Thompson, Michael W. 261
Thompson, Richard 246
Thomson, Gordon Augustus 117
Thomson, John 90
Thurloe, John 56
Tichborne, Robert 73n.63
Timbouktou 58
Tipperary 261
Tone, Wolfe 34
Totterdell, Hugh 84n.23, 246
transatlantic constitution 144, 151
transatlantic provisions trade 23
Trans-Atlantic Slave Trade Database 107
transatlantic triangle 13
Travers, Thomas 136
Treaty of Amiens (1802) 203
Treaty of Madrid (1670) 78, 85n.34
Treaty of Ryswick (1697) 242
Treaty of Tordesillas (1494) 231
Trevelyan, Charles Edward 118
Trevelyan, Harriet 118
Trew, Revd J. M. 120
triangulation 4, 7
Trinidad 1, 143
Tuite family 106
Tuite, Nicholas 28
Twelve Years a Slave (film) 331

Ulster 31, 56, 270–1, 276
Underwood, Thomas Neilson 111
Underwood v Darracott 111
unfree labour(ers) 55, 56, 64, 65, 66, 128, 134
  and African enslavement 54, 57, 66, 68
  and African slave trade 61–2
  blacks in 55, 56
  and British involvement in slave trade 62, 67
  burial records 68
  captive Irish labour 57
  and Dutch merchants 61, 62, 64
  and enslavement 55, 59
  exploitation of people 65–6
  forced transportation of 57, 65–6, 69, 128
  and kidnapping 65–6
  names of labourers 68–9
  people-trafficking trade 64
  transport of prisoners/convicts for 56, 65
United Irish activists 34
Unsilencing Black Voices (documentary) 347
Upton, Clotworthy 117
Upton, Dell 5
urban apprenticeship system, 60
Uriel, Patrick 134
Urwick, William 120
'Us' versus 'Them' mentality 338, 339, 343

Van Batenburg, Abraham 204
Vanbrugh, John 260
Vassall, Samuel 62, 64
Vassall, William 62
Vera Cruz 78, 79
Vernon, Captain 79
Verret, Jean-Joseph 172
Vespucio, Juan 220–1
Villalobe, Santiago Daza 78
Villiers, George 219
Virgin 80
Virginia 81
Virginia Company 57, 225–6, 231
Virginian Sea islands 227–32

Vlach, John Michael 5
von Wimpffen, Baron 173
voting of money, by Irish Parliament 243, 244

Walcott, Derek 8
Walsh, Antoine 26, 27, 164, 165
Walsh, Michael 326–7
  White Cargo: The Forgotten History of Britain's White Slaves in America (with Jordan) 326–7, 328
Walsh, Patrick 147
Walsh plantation 165, 166–7, *167*, *169*, 169–70, *171*
Walsh sugar mill 170
Walter, Bronwen 340
Ware, James 217, 232n.2
Warner, Sir Thomas 59
War of Spanish Succession (1701–2) 246, 248, 260
War of the Austrian Succession (1748) 89
Washington, George 330
Wate, James 85n.36
Waterford 61, 222, 223, 225, 228
West Africa 58, 65, 89
Westminster House of Lords 247
Westport 282, 286, 293, 299
Westport House 282, 284, 298
Whelan, Kevin 136
White, Enrique 135
white slaves 119

Whittle, Grace Mary 119
Wilberforce, William 185
William, First Baron Grenville 185
William III, King 147
William and Mary Quarterly 325
William, Second Earl of Inchiquin 179
Williamite–Jacobite war (1689–91) 241
Williams, Eric 112
Willoughby, Francis 61, 66, 73n.58
Willoughby, Thomas 61
Wilmont 128
Wilson, Joseph 106
Wilson, Thomas 106, 117
Windsor, Thomas 66
Wolfe, David 222, 223
  'Description of the Realm of Ireland, Its Maritime Ports and Cities' 222
Wood, John 58, 62, 64
Wood, Marcus 315
Worley, Wm 85n.36
Wright, Jonathan 198, 207

Young, Arthur 286, 299n.9
  Tour in Ireland 1776–1779 286
Young, Sir John 119

Zacek, Natalie A. 107
  Settler Society in the English Leeward Islands, 1670–1776 325–6
Z-plan houses 268, 271, 275, 279n.31

EU authorised representative for GPSR:
Easy Access System Europe, Mustamäe tee 50,
10621 Tallinn, Estonia
gpsr.requests@easproject.com